Changing World, Changeless Christ

CHANGING WORLD, CHANGELESS CHRIST

The American Lutheran Publicity Bureau, 1914-2014

† † †

RICHARD O. JOHNSON

ALPB Books
Delhi, NY

Cover Images Acknowledgements

Top row, left to right: Henry P. Eckhardt (image courtesy of Concordia Historical Institute, St. Louis, MO); Paul Lindemann (image courtesy of Concordia Historical Institute, St. Louis, MO); J. F. E. Nickelsburg (image courtesy of Dr. George Nickelsburg); Adolf F. Meyer (image courtesy of William and Marie Meyer); Fred H. Lindemann (image courtesy of Jim Lindemann); August F. Bobzin (ALPB Archives).
Center row, left to right: Theodore Wittrock (image courtesy of Concordia Historical Institute, St. Louis, MO); Glenn C. Stone (image courtesy of ELCA Archives); Richard E. Koenig (image courtesy of ELCA Archives); Richard John Neuhaus (image courtesy of ELCA Archives); Paul R. Hinlicky, image courtesy of ELCA Archives); Dorothy A. Zelenko (ALPB Archives).
Bottom row, left to right: Russell E. Saltzman (image courtesy of ELCA Archives); Donna Kathmann Roche (image courtesy of Mrs. Roche); Frederick J. Schumacher (image courtesy of Pr. Schumacher); John R. Hannah (image courtesy of Pr. Hannah); Sarah Hinlicky Wilson (image courtesy of Dr. Wilson); Paul Robert Sauer (image courtesy of Pr. Sauer).

The American Lutheran Publicity Bureau wishes to acknowledge with deep appreciation the work of John Hannah, Linda Shipman, Dorothy A. Zelenko and Jeff Zell for their expert assistance in proofreading.

Paul Robert Sauer
Executive Director, ALPB

ISBN 1-892921-36-7

American Lutheran Publicity Bureau
PO Box 327
Delhi, NY 13753

Changing World, Changeless Christ:
The American Lutheran Publicity Bureau, 1914-2014
(Delhi, NY: ALPB Books, 2018), xiv + 512 pp. [+16 image pages]

This book is dedicated to the memory of
those courageous editors of the ALPB's publications
who are now in the Church Triumphant:

Paul Lindemann

Adolf Meyer

John Tietjen

Glenn C. Stone

Richard Koenig

Richard John Neuhaus

Table of Contents

PREFACE

I've been reading the publications of the American Lutheran Publicity Bureau for one third of its 100 years. Back in 1983, I was a United Methodist pastor, struggling with my increasing discontent and seriously thinking about becoming a Lutheran. My father-in-law, the late Richard Solberg, gave me a gift subscription to the *Forum* package. "This is what you must read," he said, "if you want to understand the Lutheran church today." I quickly became one of those who say, "When *Forum Letter* arrives, I stop what I'm doing and read it immediately." In those days, Richard John Neuhaus was the editor. Reading his reflections on Lutheranism in *Forum Letter*, as well as the fascinating articles in *Lutheran Forum*, convinced me that I was making the right move, that I was, in fact, a Lutheran at heart. Here I found thoughtful writing on themes that were important to me: liturgical and sacramental theology, social concerns, ecumenism. When I was received into the American Lutheran Church in 1984, I was already a devoted and eager fan of the ALPB.

I could not then have imagined that eighteen years later I would be invited to be the associate editor of *Forum Letter*, and then, five years after that, to succeed Russ Saltzman as editor. Being asked to take on the task of writing the ALPB's centennial history was an even more surprising development and a great honor. As I began to work on the project, a basic question was this: "Just who is the ALPB?" I had wondered that back in the '80s; the name was peculiar enough, with a whiff of a long-past era. Who anymore, outside of the newspaper business, speaks of a "bureau"? And what did these periodicals have to do with "publicity"? Even after several years of editing *Forum Letter*, those questions were puzzling to me.

But the answers soon became clear, and they were fascinating. I thought I was reasonably well-versed in American Lutheran history—I had even taught that course a time or two as a seminary adjunct professor. I quickly discovered that I didn't know much about the Missouri Synod, the context in which the ALPB was founded. As it turned out, to write the history of the ALPB's first fifty years was essentially to write the history of the LCMS during that period. And then the ALPB's next fifty years was the story of an even wider swath of American Lutheranism during that time. In each case, of course, it was Lutheran history viewed through a specific lens. But then that is always true about writing history, and in this case I found the lens to be an exceedingly helpful and interesting one. It is history from a perspective not tied to any individual synodical loyalty, but to a vision of Lutheranism that was confessional, liturgical and ecumenical. It is a perspective and a vision that I share.

There were several challenges to be addressed. One was the almost complete lack of ALPB board minutes for several decades of its existence. Somehow the minutes from the first fifteen years or so have been preserved, but then there was nothing until the 1970s. I eventually found some ways to fill in the gaps. There were scattered copies of minutes during the missing decades in the personal papers of some board members deposited at Concordia Historical Institute; for a few years, brief summaries of board minutes were published in the *American Lutheran*. But for much of the period between 1920 and 1970, the primary source for the ALPB is what was published in the *American Lutheran* and, later, *Lutheran Forum*.

In many ways, the history of these publications *is* the history of the Bureau. While the editors have always been granted complete editorial freedom, the periodicals (and later, the books) have represented in general the perspective of the Bureau's board of directors. While occasionally board members have squirmed at some of what has been published in their name, they have never demanded that an editor retract what has been said—though occasionally a board member has resigned in unhappiness over something an editor has printed. The Bureau's ministry has been much more than the periodicals, of course, and I have tried to do justice to the full scope of that ministry—the tracts, the commemorative stamps and medals, the parochial programs for (among many other things) stewardship and evangelism, the billboards in Times Square, even the European tours. But it is the periodicals, and the way they have interpreted events in the Lutheran world for thousands of readers, that are the clearest and the most constant theme in this story.

There were things I originally hoped to do which proved impossible. I thought a comprehensive list of the ALPB's hundreds of tracts would be a helpful appendix, but it simply couldn't be done. No such list appears to have been kept, and the tracts themselves have been printed without dates and (usually) without authors' names. The most complete collection appears to be at Concordia Historical Institute. I also began to keep a list of all who have served as board members over the years, but the lack of board minutes for so many decades made that a futile effort. If such a list could have been compiled, it would have certainly numbered in the hundreds of clergy and laity.

A word about typography: I have chosen to maintain, as much as possible, the original typographical style, punctuation and spelling in all quotations from publications, correspondence and other documents. While this has resulted in some wild inconsistencies, I hope it gives the reader a better sense of the times and situations in which each document was written.

There are many people to thank for their encouragement and support of this project. I greatly appreciate the ALPB board's offering me the opportunity to take it on. I owe special thanks to John Hannah and Dorothy Zelenko, who read each chapter as it was finished and made valuable comments (particularly regarding the years through which they lived). Martin Conkling generously turned over the materials he had gathered when he was initially working on the project. Martin Christiansen was unceasingly helpful in the layout and design process.

I cannot speak too highly of the assistance given by the good folks at Concordia Historical Institute, whose aggressive dedication to preserving Lutheran history makes their collection invaluable. I anticipate that the ALPB archival material collected for this project will ultimately be deposited at CHI. The Archives of the ELCA also offered extremely helpful resources; in particular, Joel Thoreson always went the extra mile by finding and scanning anything I asked for. Some of the ALPB's own archives are currently located at the library of Gettysburg Theological Seminary, and the staff there was also helpful.

I spent many fruitful hours in the library of the Graduate Theological Union in Berkeley, which has a nearly complete file of ALPB periodicals, as well as other relevant publications. Visits to the library of Concordia Seminary in St. Louis were also useful; the library at Fuller Theological Seminary helped by lending copies of a few materials I could not find elsewhere.

Many individuals provided additional assistance. Dr. George Nickelsberg, great-nephew of long-time ALPB business manager Julius Nickelsberg, sent a wonderful packet of ALPB memorabilia. Alan Graebner allowed me access to some of the material from his dissertation which is still under seal at Concordia Historical Institute. Bill and Marie Meyer provided some valuable material from Bill's father, Adolf Meyer, that was not in the ALPB archives. Paul Hinlicky and Russell Saltzman spent time talking with me about their years with the Bureau, and Paul scanned and sent dozens of pages of personal correspondence and other documents related to his tenure. Hinlicky, Saltzman and Leonard Klein also read some chapters and made helpful corrections or comments. Many others too numerous to mention offered material or information of one kind or another.

Finally, my wonderful wife Lois endured without complaint what turned out to be a more extensive "retirement project" than anticipated (and a full file cabinet or more of materials, which often didn't quite stay in the file cabinet). I have thoroughly enjoyed it, and I confess that I bring it to completion with mixed feelings; Lois's feelings, on the other hand, are decidedly enthusiastic.

Richard O. Johnson
October 31, 2017

ABBREVIATIONS

ACP: Associated Church Press
AELC: Association of Evangelical Lutheran Churches
AL: *American Lutheran*
ALC: American Lutheran Church (used for both the body established in 1930 and the successor established in 1960)
ALPB: American Lutheran Publicity Bureau
CCM: *Called to Common Mission*
CHIQ: *Concordia Historical Institute Quarterly*
CN: *Christian News*
CNLC: Commission for a New Lutheran Church
ELCA: Evangelical Lutheran Church in America
ELCIC: Evangelical Lutheran Church in Canada
ELIM: Evangelical Lutherans in Mission
ELS: Evangelical Lutheran Synod
FL: *Forum Letter*
ILCW: Inter-Lutheran Commission on Worship
ILLL: International Lutheran Laymen's League
IRD: Institute on Religion and Democracy
LCA: Lutheran Church in America
LCMS: Lutheran Church—Missouri Synod (including previous official names)
LCUSA: Lutheran Council in the United States of America
LF: *Lutheran Forum*
LFA: Lutheran Film Associates
LLL: Lutheran Laymen's League
LSAA: Lutheran Student Association of America
LW: *Lutheran Witness*
LWF: Lutheran World Federation
LYO: Lutheran Youth Organization
NALC: North American Lutheran Church
NLC: National Lutheran Council
NYT: *New York Times*
STS: Society of the Holy Trinity (*Societas Trinitatis Sanctae*)
ULCA: United Lutheran Church in America
WELS: Wisconsin Evangelical Lutheran Synod

Chapter 1

FOUNDING THE BUREAU

Henry Eckhardt was frustrated. The pastor of Grace Lutheran Church in Jersey City, NJ, Eckhardt had recently finished his tenure as the first president of the English District of the *Deutsche Evangelische Lutherische Synode von Missouri, Ohio, und andern Staaten*. He had, in fact, been the president of the English Evangelical Lutheran Synod of Missouri and Other States who had guided the process leading to its formal affiliation with the still largely German Missouri Synod. Eckhardt had been born in Baltimore to a German immigrant couple; he was thoroughly Lutheran, but also thoroughly American. He was coming to realize that despite the Missouri Synod's willingness to bring his church body under its organizational wing, the Synod remained very much German in culture and ethos, and Americanization was going to be a long haul. After well over half a century in the United States, the Synod's congregations and schools were still overwhelmingly German-speaking.[1]

But in the metropolitan New York area, there were others who felt as Eckhardt did—pastors and lay people who understood that the future of their brand of confessional Lutheranism required a deliberate effort to engage the American culture. Certainly this would require a transition to English, but much more; what was needed was a way to introduce confessional Lutheranism to a country that largely dismissed it as a foreign faith. Pastor John Fritz later recalled:

The English-speaking people of our country ... read nothing of the Lutheran Church. ... I well remember that in those days a public school teacher, upon hearing that I was a Lutheran pastor, said, 'Tell me, what is the Lutheran Church?' ... Surely that public school teacher, although she was an intelligent and educated woman, knew nothing about our Lutheran Church; nor did many others.[2]

Laying the foundations
"Lutheran Forward Movement"

And so, on January 21, 1914, Pr. Eckhardt convened a group of like-minded Lutherans who gathered at Immanuel Lutheran Church at Lexington and 88th in Manhattan to organize the American Lutheran Publicity Bureau. The minutes of that meeting were signed by Pr. Otto H. Pannkoke, "secretary *pro tem*," but they do not reveal who else was present. Certainly Pr. William Schoenfeld, pastor of Immanuel, was there. Presumably all those elected to the executive committee (see below) were present as well. Eckhardt's obituary years later said there were fourteen in all, including both clergy and laity. A comment in the first issue of the *ALPB Bulletin* suggested that there were persons present from New York City, Jersey City, Philadelphia, Boston and Pittsburgh, and that others from as far away as Milwaukee had hoped to attend but were unable to do so.[3]

The proposal was "presented by a free conference of Pastors"—which is to say there was no official synodical authorization for this project. The initial plan was sketched out in broad strokes. It was to be what they called a "Lutheran Forward Movement." At least in retrospect, that could be understood in two ways. They intended to put their church "forward" before the wider public, but they also hoped to move their church "forward" into engagement with American culture. They would "present the doctrines and practices and history of the Lutheran Church," they said, but also "defend it against all enemies of the truth, such as Rome, false Protestants, etc."[4]

The Bureau was to be a membership organization, open to any church, society, club or individual affiliated with the Synodical Conference, with the proviso that "contributions from individuals ... be not less than $1.00."[5] They agreed that the Bureau would be governed by an executive board consisting of the officers and five additional members (three clergy and two laity). They proposed a constitution that outlined the organization's structure. A statement of purpose was appended to the minutes, apparently with the intention that those present would sign (though unfortunately the copy that has been preserved does not contain the signatures). The statement reveals both their intent and the seriousness with which they took their task:

We the undersigned, convened this 21st day of January, 1914, in Immanuel, New York City, being convinced of the great need of acquainting the American people with the teachings and principles of the Lutheran Church and bringing such teachings to bear in largest measure possible upon American life and being convinced that special organization will best meet this need, herewith combine and organize and subscribe to the following articles of organization.

They then proceeded to elect officers and board members: president, the Rev. H. P. Eckhardt; vice president, the Rev. Martin Walker; treasurer, Mr. F. C. Lang; and executive committee members, the Rev. John Volk (who was named chair of the committee), the Rev. Paul Lindemann, the Rev. John Fritz, Mr. Henry Ressmeyer, and Mr. Charles Schmidling.[6]

Organizing for ministry
"to further the interests of the Bureau"

This executive committee met a few days later; among other actions, they authorized the printing of 20,000 copies of a brochure outlining the Bureau's proposed work. This was designated as *"Bulletin* No. 1." Pr. Fritz was appointed permanent secretary. The executive committee met almost monthly for the next several months. At the next meeting, Fritz informed the committee he must resign, as he had just accepted a call to a congregation in St. Louis. Pr. Lindemann was appointed to succeed him as secretary; he would remain a key player in the Bureau for the next twenty-five years. Pr. C. Ferdinand Schumm was appointed to fill Fritz's place on the executive committee. The secretary was authorized to rent a typewriter—though that expense was saved when F. C. Lang presented the committee with the gift of an Underwood typewriter![7]

Those early months were taken up with publicizing the new organization and its mission. President Eckhardt gave promotional lectures at various congregations in New York and New Jersey. It was agreed "to have no collections at the lectures," but membership applications were distributed. In March, it was "resolved to send the secretary to Chicago to further the interests of the Bureau." A second series of lectures was scheduled in May, with Pr. Walker designated as the speaker. Another series sent Pr. Eckhardt to Baltimore, Philadelphia and Washington to promote the Bureau. Later that year additional lectures were scheduled for Detroit, Buffalo, Chicago, Ft. Wayne, Kingston NY, Albany, and Schenectady.[8]

The Bureau sent representatives to the Synod convention in Chicago that summer. At a luncheon meeting many of the 100 or so guests filled out membership applications, including two Concordia Seminary professors, George Mezger and Ludwig Fuerbringer. Lindemann would later recall "how encouraging we found the support of these two men who had been our instructors."[9]

Eagerness to publicize the Bureau led to a delicate situation in September 1914, when Pr. Pannkoke offered his services "for lectures in several western cities." Pannkoke had been present at the organizational meeting in January, but he was something of a loose cannon. He had already scheduled a tour on behalf of the Guardians of Liberty, an anti-Catholic group that had attracted many Lutherans to its membership. Pannkoke thought he could combine his Guardians of Liberty lecture tour with promotion of the Bureau—with the expectation that the Bureau might help defray the cost of the trip.

A lengthy discussion led to a very firm "thanks, but no thanks." The board was forthright in stating the reasons for its decision:

> First: The principles of the American Lutheran Publicity Bureau and those of the Guardians of Liberty have absolutely nothing in common.
>
> Secondly: There has been great confusion, especially in the Middle West ... in regard to these two organizations.
>
> Thirdly: Many of the western Lutherans, particularly among the clergymen, are very much opposed to the Guardians of Liberty.
>
> Fourthly: The Executive Committee does not think it wise to have a representative of the Guardians of liberty speak one night in the interest of that organization and the following night in the interest of the Publicity Bureau; and, furthermore, the Committee deems it inadvisable that a trip which is partly financed by the G. of L. should also receive financial support from the American Lutheran Publicity Bureau.

Perhaps in part because of this incident, Pannkoke's relationship with ALPB would prove to be problematic for the next several years.[10]

An official membership meeting "for permanent organization" was held at Trinity Lutheran Church in Brooklyn on October 14, 1914. President Eckhardt reported to the assembled group on what had been done over the past nine months. They approved a more detailed constitution, heard a financial report, and elected four officers and a somewhat larger executive committee—adding to the existing group Pastors Karl Kretzmann and Walter Koenig, and Messrs. H. J. Thunhorst and Gustav Zimmerman. The executive committee would thus consist of seven pastors and five laymen—all men, most of them living in the New York City area. This highlights two continuing realities for the ALPB: the strong leadership of laity, and a New York based ministry that intended to be national in scope. This latter intent was expressed in the constitution's authorization for district vice presidents who would "represent the interests of the Bureau in the various sections of the country." The convention also once again thanked Mr. Lang for his gift of the typewriter.[11]

The newly elected leaders met the very next evening. Pr. Eckhardt, whose vision and energy had been so important during the past months, had recently accepted a call to St. Andrew's Lutheran Church in Pittsburgh, but no one wanted him to give up his leadership of the ALPB. He would continue to serve as president; but recognizing that he couldn't attend meetings regularly, the executive committee appointed Pr. Karl Kretzmann to act as chair. This would establish a practice that lasted for the next several years: the Bureau would have a president of some prominence, but it would be governed by an executive committee in which the president did not take a regular part.[12]

The committee also "resolved to ask a number of the prominent men of the Lutheran Church, both of the laity and the clergy, to act as advisory directors." They developed a list of some two dozen whom they would invite—most of them from the Midwest, but also persons from North Carolina and California. At a subsequent meeting, the committee decided to change its terminology somewhat: these advisors would be given the title "vice president," while the previously approved "vice presidents" (a smaller group of pastors whose task was to promote the Bureau in each geographical area) would be dubbed "district presidents." Most of those invited agreed to serve; many who found it necessary to decline offered to recruit someone or suggested other names. It appeared that the Bureau's goals were finding strong affirmation among "prominent men of the Lutheran Church."[13]

This executive committee agreed that *Bulletin* No. 1 would be followed by a regular quarterly publication. They also appointed several other committees: a Tract Committee, a Press and Magazine Committee, a Lecture Committee, and a Committee for Libraries, Public Places and Universities. To these program committees were added more mundane administrative committees for finance and membership.[14]

Minutes of meetings during the next several months offer tantalizing glimpses of the issues and problems being dealt with by this new ministry. A local pastor submitted a manuscript of a book of his poetry with the request that ALPB publish it; they politely declined. An essay previously written by Theodore Graebner, Concordia Seminary professor and editor of the Synod's organ, *Lutheran Witness,* was given to ALPB for its use. They decided to publish it as a tract, but it "was resolved that the paragraph on war be omitted." That enigmatic comment has no further explanation, but it may have been related to two terse comments from the same meeting: "It was resolved that in the future all the tracts be sent to the editors of our Church papers for review" and "It was furthermore resolved that in [the] future all tracts be passed by the whole Executive Committee."[15]

Giving lectures
"all were won over"

The plan of action devised at the initial meeting in 1914 had four prongs. First, they would set up a "lecture lyceum," providing speakers who would promote the work of the ALPB in congregations and at various church meetings. These promotional lectures were presented in many cities from New York to St. Louis, often with good success. In February 1915, Pr. Schumm visited the pastors of the Baltimore Conference, and he was given a half-hour to present his case. "At first some of the Pastors did not seem favorably disposed towards the movement," he reported. "But, in the course of discussion, all were won over." During the first few years, the minutes of every meeting list several lectures given far and wide to pastoral conferences and local congregations.[16]

In the ALPB archives is a document entitled "Lecture Material for American Lutheran Publicity Bureau." It is undated, but it notes that correspondence should be sent to Pr. Lindemann in Jersey City; this means the document must have been written prior to 1920 when Lindemann moved to Minnesota, and probably closer to 1915. It appears to be a sample or prototype that board members might adapt for their own purposes, and it begins with a summary of the history of Lutheranism, emphasizing the reality of Lutheran unity. The Reformed tradition, the lecture material says, "lacking from the outset the real basis for Christian unity, became productive of many denominations and creeds." Not so with Lutherans:

> The Lutheran Church has not produced any sects nor creeds differing from the old standards that were raised up during the period of the Reformation. There are indeed different synods within the Lutheran Church, but some of these are united in doctrine and practise [sic] ... Others are not as loyal to Lutheran confessions as we would like to have them be, and there are movements on foot to bring about a closer union, but no Lutheran synod in this or any other country has drawn its own particular creed; wherever you find Lutherans, you will find the Confessions of the Lutheran Church, notably the Augsburg Confession and Luther's Catechism.

Already in its earliest days the Bureau emphasized the essential unity of Lutherans and the importance of fostering and supporting that unity.[17]

The lecture then expresses the concern that it is "our duty to let people know what we teach and believe." Many organizations within the Synod—hospitals, schools, orphanages, etc.—have their own associations to carry out their ministries; there should be "a similar organization, the purpose of which shall be to give wider publicity to sound Lutheran principles and offer to the general public at least an opportunity to inform themselves correctly from our own sources as to what we believe, teach and confess." The lecture concludes by outlining the organization and purpose of the ALPB, and inviting people to join the organization.[18]

Using the secular press

"Church advertising was almost an unknown art"

The second prong was the use of the secular press to publicize church activities. "Church advertising was almost an unknown art in our circles," Lindemann would recall:

> Church directories either did not list Lutheran churches at all, or listed locations from which the churches had moved years before. Pastors were listed who had been

dead ten years. ... Newspaper ads were a rarity. The Church appeared in print only when attacked. All in all the Lutheran Church was hiding its light under a bushel.

The Bureau quickly learned that newspapers were more willing to publish articles about Lutheran churches if Lutheran churches bought advertisements in the papers, so it began to encourage congregations to advertise, offering to teach them how to write advertising copy.[19]

The ALPB also took it upon itself to publicize Lutheran activities and events, particularly in the New York area. Press releases were sent to several papers concerning the 250th anniversary of St. Matthew's Lutheran Church, "the oldest Lutheran congregation in America." An "up-to-date list of our churches" was submitted to the *New York Staate Zeitung*, a major German language newspaper. Beyond New York, the ALPB encouraged district presidents to appoint press committees in advance of their district conventions so that articles about the sessions might appear in local newspapers.[20]

At the second annual meeting in 1915, several speakers argued that as the Reformation quadricentennial was approaching, use of the public press should be given top priority. The executive committee had proposed hiring someone to manage the affairs of the Bureau, and the quadricentennial made that seem even more urgent; the membership authorized the executive committee to proceed. The enthusiasm waned somewhat at the next meeting of the executive committee, when the financial realities were faced: "The matter was discussed from all sides," the minutes record, "but the difficulties in the way seemed to make the engagement of such a man at the present time almost an impossibility."[21]

They decided to consult further with several knowledgeable persons outside of the executive committee. It was finally agreed to attempt to raise $300 annually to hire a "press secretary" whose job would be primarily "of a local character"—in other words, he would deal with publicity matters in the New York City area. The group asked Pr. Karl Kretzmann (who was not present at the meeting) to serve in this capacity. Kretzmann, however, found it impossible to accept the appointment.[22]

In January 1916, Pr. Emil L. Schwankovsky agreed to take the position for one year at a monthly salary of $150. He promptly visited the religion editors of all the New York and Brooklyn newspapers and began to submit articles about topics ranging from Synod president Friedrich Pfotenhauer's trip to South America to activities of the Orphan Asylum Committee; several newspapers published the stories. Enthusiasm was somewhat less, however, among local pastors and congregations. Schwankovsky sent out some 40 letters seeking cooperation in the work of publicizing the church—especially hoping to find churches who would be willing to purchase advertisements in local papers; only two positive responses were received. Schwankovsky soon thereafter took a call in Michigan, and the position of local press secretary was left vacant.[23]

There was still concern that hiring a "national press secretary" to focus on the quadricentennial should be a priority. Prof. George A. Romoser at Concordia College in Bronxville, who had joined the board that year, agreed to take the position. There were some frustrations, however, in working with other agencies who were making plans for the quadricentennial, and Romoser resigned just two months after accepting the job. The executive committee decided not to replace him but to ask its own press committee to work on the quadricentennial "in conjunction as far as possible with the [Joint Committee on the Celebration of the Quadricentennial of the Reformation] in Philadelphia ... [and] the committee appointed by the Lutheran Society of New York."[24]

Despite these false starts, the idea of a paid staff person would not die. In September 1916, Julius F. E. Nickelsburg agreed to assume the role of local press secretary previously held by Pr. Schwankovsky. "Nicky," as he was known, had been in his family's dyeing and cleaning business, and he had experience in advertising. A downturn in business had led him into a second career as a newspaper man. These skills in advertising and journalism made him uniquely qualified for the job of press secretary, and he set at it enthusiastically. The following August, he agreed to come to work for the Bureau as "secretary" at a salary of $75 per month; in October, his title was changed to "business manager." He would be a mainstay of the ALPB for nearly forty years.[25]

Books in the library

"keep on asking until the book is gotten"

The third prong was a program to place Lutheran-oriented materials in public libraries. Someone discovered that the only biography of Luther in the New York Public Library was a condemnatory work by a Roman Catholic author, so the ALPB donated more positive accounts of the reformer's life. They suggested titles that Lutherans elsewhere might buy and present to their local library. One of their early actions was to place copies of *Theological Quarterly, Lutheran Witness,* and *Lehre und Wehre* in the reading room of Union Theological Seminary—not a place one might expect much return on the investment, one would think, but they had high ambitions. In 1915, Lutheran books or magazines were placed in 107 public libraries by the ALPB.[26]

The following year, libraries in another 125 cities were the recipients of Lutheran resources; in addition, the Bureau's Library Committee convinced Johns Hopkins University to purchase a complete set of the St. Louis edition of *Luther's Works.* The committee also promoted placing Lutheran literature in hotels and other public places.[27]

The founders of ALPB were convinced that simply getting Lutheran materials before the public would reap great benefits. They liked to tell an anecdote:

> Some years ago, a certain grocer wrapped up a pound of butter in a copy of the 'Lutheraner.' The buyer took his butter home, looked at the strange wrapper, read

it, and the result was the establishment of a Lutheran congregation in that locality. Who can imagine the results if the millions who go to our public libraries and reading rooms and know not the truth as to certain questions might have free access to our leading publications, and see what stand our Lutheran Church takes on these questions, what enlightenment that would give to many minds![28]

The aim was for faithful Lutherans to donate books to their local libraries, but other methods were sometimes suggested:

As to Lutheran books, a Christian layman declared ... 'Let Lutherans who go to the public libraries ask for some Lutheran book and let others ask for the same book, and keep on asking until the book is gotten. If the public libraries use our money for the purchase of all kinds of books, some of which are of a very doubtful value, why should they not also buy good Lutheran books?'

While this kind of guerrilla tactic wasn't a main thrust of ALPB, it does illustrate how important these publicists thought the library project was—and how innovative they could be in carrying it out.[29]

Tracts and booklets

"Interesting Facts Concerning the Lutheran Church"

The fourth prong—the most important in the long run—was the publication of tracts and booklets, aimed both at educating Lutherans about their faith and informing others about the Lutheran Church. The first two tracts were authorized in June 1914. One was to be written by Pr. H. B. Hemmeter, to be titled "Interesting Facts Concerning the Lutheran Church" (though this tract seems not to have ever been published); the other, by Pr. Karl Kretzmann, was ultimately released as the Bureau's very first tract, entitled "The Lutheran Church, a Short Historical Survey." A run of 5,000 of each was authorized.[30]

While the term "tract" sounds rather quaint today, this was essentially the mass medium of the day, the Facebook or Twitter. It was an innovative way to get your message out. What was the Lutheran church, anyway? There's a quick and easy to digest answer in this little pamphlet. Some of the early tracts carried names like "The Reformation and the Open Bible" and "The Bible Church." Others were more practical in nature: "Prayer," "Family Worship." Some were apologetic or controversial: "Christian Science Unchristian," "Why I Am a Lutheran and not a Seventh-Day Adventist." When America entered World War I, several tracts were aimed at soldiers and their families: "Going Over? Take the Captain Along," "Lutheranism and Americanism," "Lutherans and the War."

The tracts arose from various circumstances. Sometimes the executive committee would come upon a piece written by a pastor or professor and would think it worthy of wider distribution, such as the one by Theodore Graebner previously mentioned. That tract, "What the Lutheran Church Stands For," led to a serious misunderstanding when it turned out the essay was also being published by Concordia Publishing House. Graebner was embarrassed by this "peculiar situation." The publishing house editor claimed that he had been in communication with the ALPB about this, but "no letter has been received from him," and the executive committee sent a "night letter" (i.e., a telegram, sent at a cheaper nighttime rate for delivery the next morning) to CPH's board of directors to explain their side of the misunderstanding. The ruffled feathers were apparently smoothed, and the next issue of the *Bulletin* (which unfortunately is lost) clarified the reason for the dual publication. Graebner conscientiously returned the ten dollars he had been paid by the ALPB.[31]

Other tracts were suggested or submitted by ALPB supporters or others. The executive committee evaluated these ideas carefully; in one instance, for example, a proposal by Baltimore pastors for a tract on Luther was rejected because of its length and the probable expense.[32]

But most of the tracts came at the initiative of the Tract Committee based on what they believed might be useful to the church. A topic would be proposed and discussed, potential authors would be considered, and then the contact would be made. Authors were apparently offered a nominal fee for their work, though it is likely that many of them refused payment for their help in what they viewed as a significant ministry.

Over the first several years, the ALPB printed millions of copies of these tracts. The earlier decision to have them approved by authorities in St. Louis was sometimes a frustration. Paul Lindemann wrote a piece entitled "The Formation, Deformation and Reformation of the Church." The request came back that part of the tract be changed because "it was historically untenable." The executive committee made clear that they did not share that opinion, but they nonetheless asked Lindeman "to try to meet the wishes of the St. Louis Committee." Eventually the ALPB decided that, as an independent organization, they did not need to have their publications cleared by St. Louis.[33]

The Reformation quadricentennial

"this vexing question"

In the years leading up to 1917, Lutherans of all stripes made plans for a great celebration of the 400th anniversary of Luther's posting of the 95 Theses on October 31, 1517. This would prove to be of great significance in American Lutheran history, spurring unity efforts which led to the formation of the Norwegian Evangelical Lutheran Church in 1917 and the United Lutheran Church in America in 1918. The Missouri Synod, while eager to commemorate the event, was cautious about any joint activities with Lutherans with whom they were not in fellowship. As Theodore Graebner put it in an editorial in *Lutheran Witness*, "Where there is no unity, there can be no joint worship nor joint celebrations of the jubilee." The Synod thus established its own committee to foster the jubilee celebration.[34]

In New York, however, some Missouri Synod Lutherans had been involved with a pan-Lutheran group known as the Lutheran Society of New York, and this agency set up the New York Reformation Quadricentenary Committee. It chose LCMS pastor Otto Pannkoke as its director—the same Pannkoke whose relationship to ALPB had been somewhat strained after the executive committee refused his offer to promote the Bureau along with a lecture tour for the Guardians of Liberty. LCMS authorities looked on the New York committee unfavorably because of its inter-Lutheran nature. The difficulty some in St. Louis had in distinguishing between the two organizations of New York Lutherans complicated the Bureau's desire to promote the Reformation celebration.[35]

And, in fact, there was tension between the ALPB and the Lutheran Society of New York. Pannkoke's group was unwilling to coordinate their publicity plans with the ALPB, leading to some unfortunate duplication of efforts. The executive committee in February 1917 asked Mr. Nickelsburg to "get in touch with Pastor Pannkoke ... for a solution of this vexing question." The next month it was reported that the ALPB had received a letter from Pannkoke regarding cooperation, "but that Pastor Pannkoke gave little satisfaction." The executive committee decided "to drop the idea of cooperation in this particular with the Luther Society Committee." Continuing tension led to further correspondence; Mr. Ressmeyer was asked to speak personally with Pannkoke, but he reported that "it seems impossible to get together" on the matter.[36]

But the ALPB's inability to work with Pannkoke's committee did not prevent other cooperation with non-Missouri Lutherans. In the summer of 1916, Bureau president Eckhardt and treasurer F. C. Lang met with leaders of the Joint Lutheran Committee on the Celebration of the Quadricentennial of the Reformation in Philadelphia. This group, a cooperative endeavor of the General Synod, the General Council, and the United Synod of the South, would soon become the catalyst for the formation of the United Lutheran Church in America. For the next several months, the ALPB and the Joint Committee kept in close contact, with the Bureau promoting and distributing some of the materials produced by the Joint Committee. The general secretary of the Joint Committee, General Synod pastor Howard Gold, attended and addressed the ALPB's annual meeting in September 1917, commending the Bureau for its good work.

Despite the controversies, and despite having struck out in its efforts to hire a staff person to coordinate publicity for the Reformation quadricentennial, the Bureau played a significant role in the celebration. Through an agreement with the official Missouri Synod committee, the ALPB took on the task of producing English language tracts for the observance. Some thirteen tracts were published in this "Quadricentennial Reformation Series"; they were sold through Concordia Publishing House as well as the publishing houses of some other synods. The Bureau also published a book advising local parishes how to plan and publicize the event. It sold some 120,000 "Luther Stickers." It made available electrotype representations of Luther, suitable for reprinting in newspapers or other publicity. Outlines of suggested Reformation sermons were sent to every pastor in the Synodical Conference.[37]

The *American Lutheran*
"there seems to be a need"

The first executive committee meeting had authorized the printing of an eight-page piece outlining the purposes of the organization. It was to be designated "*Bulletin* No. 1" and would be the first issue of a publication which Paul Lindemann would later describe as "spasmodically issued."[38] Edited initially by Pr. Fritz, Lindemann took it over when Fritz moved to St. Louis. The evangelical intent of the ALPB was highlighted on the first page, which quoted Mark 16.15: "Go ye unto all the world and preach the GOSPEL to every creature." The *Bulletin* gave a brief account of the origins of the ALPB, recalling the coming of the Saxon immigrants who "at once began to teach the truth which was so dear to them also unto others." It argued that the current situation called for a recommitment to that goal:

> Who will deny that the visible Church of Christ in this our country today is in a sad, deplorable condition? Spiritual indifference, rationalism and materialism are found not only without but also within the church. Many no longer believe that 'all Scripture is given by inspiration of God.' The denial of this fundamental fact has opened the flood-gates of error and false teachings. The cardinal truth of justification, not by works of man, but by grace, for Christ's sake, through faith, is in many churches not clearly presented. A Christian life, acceptable to God, has largely been replaced by a 'go-as-you-please Christianity.'

But this "deplorable condition," the author went on, can be addressed by the Lutheran Church:

> Our Lutheran Church by the grace of God has the whole truth and proclaims it to the glory of God and the salvation of man. Our Lutheran Church is, though, practically unknown outside of our own circles. Our American people as such know not our church and its doctrines and work. This is another sad fact. This is largely due to the fact that we have been working among them in a language which they did not understand. We are now getting more and more into touch with our English-speaking fellow citizens. We have as yet, though, made but a good beginning in this direction. It must be our purpose and zeal to continue.

"Our opportunities are great," the writer concluded, "but equally great are our responsibilities."[39]

The *Bulletin* then outlined "some things we hope to do":

We hope, first of all, to arouse a much greater Lutheran consciousness among our own people. Some of us, we fear, do not appreciate our great blessings as the fathers did. We hope to be given the opportunity, in much larger measure than heretofore, to speak to people outside of our circles. ... We hope to make use of the public press [which is] the one source from which we get most of our news [and which] is largely moulding [*sic*] the thought of the people. ... We hope to spread more of our Lutheran literature among the people at large [and] to put our books and church papers into our public libraries. ... We hope, in short, to make our American people acquainted with our Lutheran Church. WILL YOU HELP?

And "of course, money is needed," so there were instructions as to where one might send a contribution for the work of the Bureau.[40]

The *ALPB Bulletin* was published twelve times over the next three years, though only a few issues have survived. Usually a four-page newsletter, the *Bulletin* offered brief articles on the importance of publicity, reports from the various ALPB committees, and news about what was being done around the country to further the goals of the Bureau. It also advertised ALPB tracts and solicited financial support. The ministry was now costing an average of $500 a month, the May 1917 issue reported, "in spite of the fact that the executives are giving their services free of charge." "The work has grown beyond our heads," the editor reported, "and the time is near when it must be placed into the hands of a salaried executive, who can devote all his time to it."[41]

The final issue of the *Bulletin* was published in October 1917, and it announced the ALPB's decision to inaugurate a monthly magazine devoted to the cause of "practical church work":

The annual convention passed the important resolution that the executive committee be authorized to publish a monthly magazine. The intention is not to merely add another to the already large number of periodicals, but there seems to be a need and a want for a paper dealing with the practical phases of church work, with emphasis on the dignified methods of publicity, an almost unexplored field in our circles. Publicity is becoming such an indispensable adjunct to the mission work of the day, particularly in cities, that a magazine, bringing practical articles on effective methods of church work, together with interesting news items from various centres [*sic*], seems to be able to justify its existence. ... Naturally this new paper will supplant our Bulletin.

The *Bulletin* assured readers that membership in the ALPB would include a subscription to the new magazine. The membership fee would remain $1.00 or more, but "on account of our increasing expenses we desire to emphasize that 'or more.'"[42]

There was hesitation about this project on the part of some board members, who wondered if a monthly magazine was financially feasible. It was the lay members of the board (particularly treasurer F. C. Lang) who finally pushed the issue by guaranteeing the funds to get started. And so, in January 1918, the first issue of the *American Lutheran* appeared. It would continue regular publication until 1966, when it would be succeeded by *Lutheran Forum*.

The Lutherans of the ALPB

"a few silly boys who want something to do"

Who were these Lutherans who had such a passion for the work of the ALPB? Alan Graebner, in his dissertation on the acculturation of the Missouri Synod, did a fascinating study of the men involved in the Bureau during its first fifteen years. He restricted himself to pastors, since it was more difficult to find detailed information about the laymen involved. His conclusion was that the clergy fell into two categories. The first group, older pastors, were members of the English District, mostly born and raised in the East, and they were strong advocates for English language work in the Synod. The other group was made up of younger pastors, generally also born and raised in the East and often the son or son-in-law of a pastor, often university trained, anxious to see the church grow and ready to try new methods that might broaden the appeal of the Missouri Synod. Both these groups were cut from a rather different cloth than the much more conservative Missourians who inhabited the Midwest.[43]

It is easier today to learn more about the laity involved as board members and officers in those early years. They tended to be a bit older than the pastors, and they were generally successful businessmen, very much convinced of the necessity of advertising. Henry Ressmeyer was a financial executive of a major New York retail clothing store. Charles Schmidling was in the insurance business. Frederick C. Lang, the Bureau's first treasurer, was a partner in the Tietjen & Lang Dry Dock Company in Hoboken, NY, and a director of the Hoboken Trust Company. Theodore Lamprecht, who would be elected president of the ALPB in 1920, was a wealthy and philanthropic dry goods merchant. Paul Overhage, another board member, owned the printing company which produced much of the ALPB's early material. Most were native-born, but even those who were immigrants had become highly acculturated. They were stalwarts in their local parishes—frequently charter members, often officers of the congregation. Many of them were also active in other Lutheran agencies. Lamprecht, for instance, was the founder and first president of the Lutheran Laymen's League, a president of the Bethlehem Orphans' Home, and a mainstay of the American Lutheran Board for Relief in Europe. Schmidling served on the board of the Wartburg Home of the Aged, and was active in the Lutheran Society and the Lutheran Hospital Association of Brooklyn. Ressmeyer was the first president of the Lutheran Educational Society and a leading force in establishing Concordia College, Bronxville.[44]

It must be said, however, that the enthusiasm of these pastors and laymen was not unanimous among Missouri Synod Lutherans; far from it. The very idea of publicity was an alien concept to many old-school Missourians. Lindemann would later recall that "in some circles there was vehement antagonism, in others tolerant contempt." One wag condemned the group for engaging in "*kirchliche Marktschreierei*"—roughly translated, "ecclesiastical ballyhoo" (an expression Lindemann admitted he thought was rather clever). One Missouri Synod elder dismissed the ALPB as "*Ein paar dumme Jungens wollen etwas anstelen*"—"a few silly boys who want something to do."[45]

But as it turned out, this whole endeavor could not have been more timely. That very year war broke out in Europe, and as the United States moved inexorably toward joining the allies, foreigners of all stripes—but especially Germans—became the target of one of the strongest waves of xenophobia ever to wash over these shores. Lutherans were particularly suspect because of their church's German roots. Rumors abounded that the Kaiser was secretly the Lutherans' pope and that parochial school children began each day by singing "*Deutschland uber alles*." And since they were teaching and worshiping in German, who knows what treason they might be spouting? Those were the suspicions being directed toward German Americans, especially Lutherans. Dragging the Missouri Synod into the mainstream of American life suddenly became a matter of survival.

Notes

1. For the sake of simplicity, I will generally use the terminology "Missouri Synod" or "LCMS" even though it is anachronistic until later in the twentieth century.

2. *AL* 10, no. 12 (Dec. 1927), 5.

3. "Rev. H. P. Eckhardt, Lutheran Leader," *NYT*, 13 May 1949; *ALPB Bulletin* No. 1 (Mar. 1914), 4. This note refers to the initial meeting as having been in February, but this is likely simply an error.

4. Minutes, ALPB Organizational Meeting, Jan. 21, 1914, ALPB Archives. Unless otherwise indicated, all minutes of ALPB meetings cited are in the ALPB Archives.

5. The Evangelical Lutheran Synodical Conference of North America, founded in 1872, was an association of Lutheran synods who had a conservative interpretation of the Lutheran confessions. In 1914, the constituent members included, in addition to the Missouri Synod, the Evangelical Lutheran Joint Synod of Wisconsin, Minnesota, Michigan and Other States (later known as the Wisconsin Evangelical Lutheran Synod), the German Evangelical Lutheran District Synod of Nebraska and Other States (soon to merge into the Wisconsin Synod), and the Slovak Evangelical Lutheran Church of the Augsburg Confession in the United States of America (Slovak Synod).

6. Minutes, ALPB Organizational Meeting, Jan. 21, 1914. The terminology for this governing group was a bit fluid. They spoke first of "executive board" but this soon morphed into "executive committee." There was early talk of a "board of directors" that would be composed of a broader representation, but that group apparently never actually materialized. By 1921, what had been called the "executive committee" would be consistently referred to as the "board of directors."

7. Minutes, ALPB Executive Committee, 19 Feb. 1914, 17 Mar. 1914.

8. Minutes, ALPB Executive Committee, 17 Mar. 1914, [Apr. 1914], 16 June 1914, 22 July 1914.

9. *AL* 10, no. 12 (Dec. 1927), 2.

10. Minutes, ALPB Executive Committee, 15 Sept. 1914.

11. Minutes of the American Lutheran Publicity Bureau for Permanent Organization, 14 Oct. 1914.

12. Minutes, ALPB Executive Committee, 15 Oct. 1914.

13. Minutes, ALPB Executive Committee, 15 Oct. 1914, 25 Oct. 1914.

14. Minutes, ALPB Executive Committee, 15 Oct. 1914.

15. Minutes, ALPB Executive Committee, 17 Nov. 1914.

16. Minutes, ALPB Executive Committee, 16 Feb. 1915.

17. "Lecture Material for American Lutheran Publicity Bureau," n.d., ALPB Archives.

18. Ibid.

19. *AL* 10, no. 12 (Dec. 1927), 2.

20. Minutes, ALPB Executive Committee, 15 Dec. 1914.

21. Minutes, ALPB Executive Committee, 16 Nov. 1915.

22. Minutes, Special Meeting of the Executive Committee, 30 Nov. 1915.

23. Minutes, ALPB Executive Committee, 15 Feb. 1916, 22 Mar. 1916.

24. Minutes, Special Meeting of the ALPB Executive Committee, 5 May 1916.

25. Minutes, ALPB Executive Committee, 16 October 1917; George Nickelsburg, unpublished biographical sketch of his great-uncle, Julius Fritz Ernst Nickelsburg, n.d.

26. Minutes, Executive Board, ALPB, 22 July 1914; *ALPB Bulletin*, No. 6 (Feb. 1916).

27. Minutes, ALPB Annual Meeting, 13 Oct. 1916.

28. "Lecture Material for American Lutheran Publicity Bureau."

29. Ibid.

30. Minutes, ALPB Executive Committee, 16 June 1914.

31. Minutes, ALPB Executive Committee, 16 Feb. 1915, 16 Mar. 1915.

32. Minutes, ALPB Executive Committee, 16 Feb. 1915.

33. Minutes, ALPB Executive Committee, 21 Nov. 1916. The largest collection of ALPB tracts available today is at Concordia Historical Institute in St. Louis (hereafter cited as CHI).

34. [Theodore Graebner], "Joint Reformation Celebrations," *LW* 36, no. 19 (25 Sept. 1917), 292, cited in Carl S. Meyer, "Some Aspects of the Observance of the Reformation Quadricentennial by America's Lutherans," *CHIQ* 41, no. 1 (Feb. 1968), 18. See also John C. Wohlrabe, Jr., "The 1917 Quadricentennial of the Reformation: American Lutheran Unity and Union Attempts," *CHIQ* 87:4 (Winter 2014), 12-34.

35. For Pannkoke's somewhat self-serving version of these events, see Otto Pannkoke, *A Great Church Finds Itself* (Quitman, GA: Private Printing, 1966), 44ff.

36. Minutes, ALPB Executive Committee, 20 Feb. 1917, 19 Mar. 1917, 17 Apr. 1917, 14 May 1917.

37. Minutes, ALPB Executive Committee, 12-14 July 1916.

38. *AL* 1, no. 1 (Jan. 1918), 1.

39. *ALPB Bulletin*, no. 1 (Mar. 1914), 6-7.

40. Ibid., 7-8.

41. *ALPB Bulletin*, no. 10 (May 1917), 1.

42. *ALPB Bulletin*, no. 12 (Oct. 1917), 3.

43. Alan N. Graebner, "The Acculturation of an Immigrant Lutheran Church: The Lutheran Church—Missouri Synod, 1917-1929" (PhD diss., Columbia University, 1965), 237-242.

44. On Lamprecht, see the tributes in *AL* 11, no. 6 (June 1928); on Ressmeyer, see obituary in *AL* 4, no. 10 (Oct. 1921), 7; on Schmidling, see obituary in *NYT*, 8 Jan. 1936; on Overhage, see obituary in the *NYT*, 6 Sept. 1941.

45. "Humble Beginnings," *AL* 10, no. 12 (Dec. 1927), 2.

Chapter 2

Trying Times

T|he ALPB's efforts couldn't have come at a more propitious time. The same year the
Bureau was organized, war broke out in Europe—a war that would come to be
known as "the Great War" (and eventually as "World War I"), finally, in 1917, drawing
even the United States into its deadly dance. German-Americans found themselves the
objects of a great outpouring of xenophobic hysteria. German immigrants had generally been regarded favorably by Americans, but in the heat of war, anything German
became immediately suspect. German American Lutherans, who thought of themselves
as loyal citizens of the United States, suddenly found themselves accused of treason.
The ALPB assisted the church in navigating these tumultuous waters during the war,
and it helped Lutherans adjust to new realities after the armistice.[1]

Targeting Lutherans
"What bond have these people with Americanism?"

For a number of reasons, Missouri Synod Lutherans were particularly targeted by this
xenophobia. Like many non-German Americans, Lutherans had generally favored
neutrality in the war in Europe; when war was declared in April 1917, Lutherans were

stunned into silence. For the most part they felt obligated to support the United States in this effort, but in the furor of war, their previous neutrality became evidence for some super-patriots that the Lutherans had favored Germany all along. Typical was the accusing question posed by Samuel Hopkins Adams in a popular magazine: "What bond have these people with Americanism?"[2]

An editorial in the *Lutheran Witness* in December 1917, in Alan Graebner's words, "had the impact of an anarchist's bomb." The editorial, written by Theodore Graebner, called for a complete reversal of course among Lutherans and an overt show of loyalty. Synod president Pfotenhauer strenuously disagreed, as did Concordia Seminary professor Franz Pieper; both were concerned that Graebner was dragging the church into an untenable relationship with the state. But as the months passed, even the conservative Synod leadership began to see the wisdom of supporting the war effort.

They began as well to accept the inevitability of the transition to English. Agitation for the use of English in church and school had been growing slowly for some years, but when the war began the Synod's work was still overwhelmingly in German. There was considerable regional variation; German was predominant in the Midwest, while English was gaining strength elsewhere. But the pressures of the war led to a rapid abandonment of German, and that in turn led to a more robust interaction between the Missouri Synod and American culture. It began to look as though the ALPB's original vision had been prescient indeed. Paul Lindemann claimed as much in a July 1918 editorial in the *American Lutheran*:

> The trying times through which certain portions of the church are passing emphasize the need of the policy of publicity which our Bureau advocated long before the war. Present conditions can only persuade us to pursue this policy with even greater vigor than before.

The ALPB was ready and eager to help the Synod accept this new reality.[3]

Practical church work

"the adaptation of our church work to modern methods"

The Missouri Synod was struggling with repercussions of the war when the first issue of the *American Lutheran* appeared in January 1918, but little reference was made to the conflict in its first months of publication. The magazine's stated purpose, after all, was much narrower in scope. Editor Paul Lindemann outlined its intent in his opening editorial:

> We have been led to believe that there is in our circles room for a periodical dealing primarily with the practical side of church work, with the enforced adaptation of our church work to modern methods, and offering a medium for the interchange of ideas and plans.

The editorial was followed immediately by an article entitled "Why Advertise?" by ALPB president Henry Eckhardt. He argued that Luther's posting of the 95 Theses was really an "act of publicity," and that Lutherans "ought to be in the very first line trenches in aggressive publicity work." Assisting in that task, he wrote, "is the aim of the American Lutheran Publicity Bureau and this new publication." Over the next months the magazine emphasized advertising: *why* the church should advertise, *what* it should advertise, and *how* it should advertise.[4]

Lindemann knew he was fighting the attitude of many in the Synod who saw advertising as undignified and unsuitable for the church, and he understood some of the reasons they felt that way. Some churches, he wrote, "have resorted to sensationalism, not only in their 'services,' but also in their advertising." That should not prevent Lutherans from using appropriate means, including advertising, "to get the disinterested outsider under the influence of the Word and give the Holy Spirit the opportunity to work upon his heart."[5]

Even in these early issues, however, there was an awareness of the wider concerns being faced by the Synod as it struggled with continuing anti-German prejudice. The second issue included an article by F. Pieper entitled "Is Lutheranism Limited Nationally?" He was responding to an article in the Episcopalian magazine the *Churchman* which argued that both Luther and the church bearing his name were so completely tied to German history and culture that they could not flourish outside of it. Pieper would have none of it; Lutheranism, he wrote is nothing more than the rediscovery of the central tenets of the gospel, and the Episcopalian writer's ignorance simply makes obvious "the importance of publicity work, the chief object of which shall be to let the world know what the Lutheran, in doctrine first, and then also in practice, stands for." It is unlikely that the author here was Prof. Franz Pieper, the synod's respected theologian, but the editor didn't take any pains to prevent a reader from making that assumption.[6]

While the emphasis in these early issues was on publicity, the *American Lutheran* soon began to broach other topics related to "practical church work." An early editorial advocated the development of children's choirs in the congregations. Another offered suggestions for reinvigorating "that evening service"—"the preacher's bugaboo, the organist's hour of self-sacrifice and the deacon's dread." Each issue carried news of interesting programs or projects carried out by various local churches, offering them as suggestions of things to be tried elsewhere.[7]

Lindemann stressed both the responsibilities and the partnership of pastors and laity in the work of the church. Pastors, he said, must "deliver the goods."

A half-baked, only partially thought out sermon, a stumbling, hardly intelligible ramble, which gives every evidence of insufficient preparation, is an act of infidelity toward God, a desecration of a sacred office, an affront to the congregation and a breach of faith with the stranger who by our advertising has been led to expect a worthy presentation of a lofty subject.

But the layperson must also be "on the job":

> First of all, you must be present. The stranger is not apt to give the 'goods' much consideration, if the members of the firm are not regular users of the 'goods' and seem to consider them lightly. Furthermore, the stranger whom you have attracted by your advertising will take note of your own attitude ... or, in other words, of the decorum or indecorum you observe in church. ... The layman's responsibility is not much less than that of the preacher.[8]

Ministry in time of war

"a real patriotic service"

The *American Lutheran* first overtly addressed the war in June 1918, with that month's issue devoted almost entirely to the subject. The lead editorial, "A Patriotic Service," lauded clergy who were serving as camp pastors, "ministering to the spiritual needs of our men in the service." These camp pastors were civilian clergy who agreed to serve on a volunteer basis during the war to help deal with a shortage of military chaplains. Lindemann noted that the Synodical Conference had some forty men serving in this capacity full time, adding that the National Lutheran Commission, representing most of the other Lutheran synods, had sixty-two camp pastors in the field. This, Lindemann wrote, is "a real patriotic service." It is "the Christian boy" who "makes the best soldier" because of his "well-developed sense of honor and duty." The camp pastors have a high calling: "Watching over their souls, while our country is conditioning their bodies, are we not rendering a splendid service to America's cause?"[9]

The next several issues would carry reports from the camp pastors in various army camps. The reports were printed under the title "Publicity in the Camps"; they were really rather publicity *about* the camps, as camp pastors related, sometimes in moving detail, the ministry they were performing among young Lutheran soldiers.

The question of camp pastors became a matter of controversy within the Synod, and while there was no reflection of the dispute in either the minutes of the ALPB's executive committee or the pages of the *American Lutheran*, key ALPB leaders were in the middle of it; the controversy most likely played a part in forming attitudes about the Bureau and its ministry. The Synod's triennial convention in June 1917 appointed a committee to deal with the question of providing spiritual care to Lutheran men in the military. For the sake of efficiency, this group was centered in Chicago. In an action that demonstrated how tone deaf some Missourians could be, the appointed group designated themselves *Evangelische Lutherische Missionsbehörde für Heer und Flotte* and recorded their minutes in German! It was quickly pointed out to them that this was not a wise strategy in the context of the current war hysteria; they changed the name to the Lutheran Church Board for Army and Navy and began to conduct their meetings in English.[10]

The controversy arose because the federal government wanted to streamline the process of coordinating the camp pastors. The expectation was that Protestant churches would relate to the government through the Federal Council of Churches or the YMCA. After some negotiation, the government agreed to treat Lutherans as a separate group—but as *one* separate group, not a plethora of different synods. There followed a battle within the Missouri Synod between those who were willing, in this emergency situation, to work together with the National Lutheran Commission for Soldier's and Sailor's Welfare (an agency formed for the purpose by most of the Lutheran groups outside the Synodical Conference) and those who found this an egregious instance of unionism. The latter group prevailed, and the Missouri Synod backed out of its initial plan to work with the National Lutheran Commission.

But this caused a counter protest by pastors, particularly in the East. Led by Paul Lindemann and several other ALPB members, this group organized itself as the Eastern Army and Navy Board. Their purpose, they said, would be to "take charge of chaplaincy work among our Lutheran boys in the camps along the Atlantic coast." They stated forthrightly that they would "cooperate in external matters with the National Lutheran Commission."[11]

The Easterners advocated an arrangement whereby Lutheran pastors of any synod could be certified to minister to Lutheran soldiers of any synod. "If I were a preacher of another synod and were assigned to a camp, I would consider it an affront [if it were implied that I] was in my Lutheranism entirely too unreliable to minister unto them. Such an arrangement would be the source of everlasting friction," Lindemann wrote to W. C. Kohn, chair of the Synod's Board for Army and Navy. The armistice a month later brought an end to the controversy, but Lindemann would long remember his frustrations at the unwillingness of his synod to cooperate with others; it would be a building block in a growing passion for Lutheran unity that would characterize the *American Lutheran* and the ALPB for decades to come.[12]

Meanwhile, however, the Bureau had directly addressed the war concerns in several other ways—particularly in the publication of tracts to be used both with the servicemen and on the home front. The American Library Association organized a "War Library Committee" to raise funds to establish libraries in the various military camps, and the ALPB's own Library Committee worked with them to suggest "Lutheran books" that should be included. In September 1917, the Tract Committee was directed to produce "a series of tracts to be used for war services." A decision was made that the authors' names should not be included on these tracts—apparently because those names were likely to be German-sounding. The tracts were mostly evangelical in nature, intended to shore up the faith of young soldiers. One of the first was entitled "Prayer." "While on the march," it advised, "while in the trenches, you may not be able to read your Bible, you may not be able to attend chapel services, but you can always pray." And a soldier *should* pray, not just "because God has commanded it" but "because of the temptations which beset his path"—and, of course, "because of the uncertainties of war."[13]

Others were written at the specific request of the Lutheran Church Board for Army and Navy, which asked for tracts addressing gambling, profanity, purity, and peace and refuge. The Bureau supplied them, but with much more engaging titles: "The Devil's Game" (by Prof. Romoser), "What Is Thy Name?" (by Pr. Schumm), "Her House Is the Way to Hell" (by Pr. Fritz), and "Under His Wings" (by Pr. Eckhardt).

Other tracts were intended for those at home. "Lutherans and the War" was originally a resolution approved by the Atlantic District, defending the patriotism of Lutherans against those accusing them of "spreading German propaganda" and "making their schools subservient to the cause of German autocracy and militarism." Lutherans "most emphatically repudiate such insinuations and accusations as coming either from ignorance or malice," it said. Lutherans "are among the most loyal citizens of our country."[14]

Navigating the war on occasion proved tricky, however. One of the early publications in the war tracts series was Theodore Graebner's essay, "War and Christianity." Essentially an exposition of Luther's just war theory, Graebner advised that a Lutheran should "give his own country the benefit of the doubt" but admitted it was "possible the aggressor may have a good cause." This raised concerns in the minds of American military officials; the tract was published in late 1917, but the May 1918 executive committe minutes report that its sale had been "discontinued at the request of the War Department." The remaining 3,500 copies "were taken from the office by a representative of the War Department on May 18th."[15]

Graebner wrote to Lindemann, asking what had happened. "We were compelled to take this tract off the market," he replied—and then offered the details.

> Some time ago, a Secret Service man came to our office at 234 East 62nd Street, which as you know is in the building occupied by the Lutheran Immigrant Society. He wanted to see the tract 'War and Christianity' and was supplied with every tract that we issue. Some time later he appeared again with orders that we discontinue the sale of 'War and Christianity.' I was not at the office at the time and when I heard of it was inclined to protest, since I did not see anything wrong with the tract. I therefore arranged an interview with the Secret Service man at which I inquired as to the matter. He told me that he had simply received orders from Washington that they preferred to have the tract withdrawn. I wanted to know why, and he told me that the tract said neither yes or no, and was not the kind of stuff which the government wanted our boys to read. ... There is, of course, no use in protesting against these things and so we had to tie up the bundle of tracts still in our possession ... and the Intelligence Officer called for them. This man, a certain Captain Squires, upon orders

from Washington made a complete investigation of our Publicity Bureau. Unfortunately, he came for the bundle of your tracts to our office when only Restin was at home, and Restin's wife had mislaid the package and Restin went around the house shouting, 'Lena, wo ist das Packet?' You can imagine that Captain Squires was very much impressed with the Publicity Bureau, and had a thousand and one suspicions. But when Brunn and I saw him at his office we soon satisfied him completely and we now have a clean bill of health.[16]

A less controversial publication was "War Time Hymns for Church and Home." Intended to be used at "patriotic services," the pamphlet contained eighteen hymns and "may be inserted in the church hymn books or used separately." Another by Pr. Kretzmann entitled "The Great Physician" was written in such a way that it could apply to any sick or hospitalized person, but its primary intent was for "our boys in the military and naval hospitals."[17]

Lutheran Publicity Week
"We must act before erroneous views become fixed"

As important as these wartime projects were, the ALPB's executive committee kept its eye on the main purpose of its ministry: publicity. In the Bureau's eyes, much of the struggle the church was having could be ascribed to the widespread ignorance about the true nature of the Lutheran Church. "There is grave danger," wrote Walter Koenig, "that many will believe the slanders on our church simply because they have not been acquainted with its teachings. ... We must act before erroneous views become fixed judgments." Editor Lindemann was even more outspoken:

> The name we have chosen for our magazine is not a misnomer. The 'American Lutheran' desires to further American Lutheranism. We are not going to indulge in lamentations because of the disappearance of the German language as a medium of worship in the Lutheran Church of America. We rather welcome the accelerated transition, and we hope to be helpful in solving the new problems with which many Lutheran congregations are so suddenly faced.[18]

In developing ALPB's publicity program, J. F. E. Nickelsburg played a key role. Many years later one of his early associates would recall that "Nicky always had ten or twelve ideas at every meeting. All but one or two would be just impossible. But there would always be a few that would work; some became huge successes." One of his early successes was a proposal for a "Lutheran Publicity Week."[19]

The idea, first discussed in March 1917, was originally tied to the quadricentennial celebration. Pastors and congregations would be urged to give a special push to advertise events related to that observance in October. The ALPB published an eight-page folder with suggestions and ideas for how to do this, and some 7,000 copies were mailed to all pastors in the Synodical Conference as well as the Norwegian Synod. Unfortunately, the war and the influenza epidemic dampened the 1917 plans, but the program still got a lot of attention; even the *Women's Wear* printed a notice about it. It was thought to be such a good idea that it was repeated the next year, and then became a regular part of the ALPB ministry.[20]

Other aspects of the Bureau's program were expanding rapidly as well. Subscriptions to the *American Lutheran*, which had begun at about 400 after the initial issue, had grown to 2,300 by May 1919. The Bureau was gaining a reputation as a place to get information. Nickelsburg delighted in reporting the wide variety of inquiries he received (he liked to refer to these as "queer queries"). "One pastor writes, 'The mortgage on my church will become due within two months. The mortgagee does not wish to renew. Can you tell me where we can borrow $6,000?'" Or "I am coming to New York. While looking for a place to live, can you suggest a hotel for me to stop at?" Another inquirer planned to buy a farm in a particular county: "Can you tell me if there is a Lutheran Church near there?"[21]

One reader sent the ALPB office a screw. The writer explained that "his lectern was shaky" because it was missing a screw. "He could not obtain another one of the same type, and asked whether we would be kind enough to see 'if the big New York stores did not have such a screw.'" Still another inquired "if you know a pastor who needs a housekeeper in California, one who is about 35 years old, not older. ... The climate here is very cold and changing. ... Send him my address so he could write to me if it is some one who would marry."[22]

There were also more mundane inquiries about how to produce a parish paper, how to conduct patriotic meetings, how to canvass for Sunday School students. Rather than seeing these inquiries as a nuisance, the Bureau took them as indicative of serious needs, and many of them led to articles in the *American Lutheran*.

Engaging with the culture

"a tremendous missionary opportunity"

Educating Americans about Lutheranism was one goal of the ALPB, but pushing the church into engagement with American life was the other, and Lindemann was ruthless in his insistence that some very basic things needed to change. The increasing legal restrictions against the use of German, he wrote, "are not unmixed blessings" but the mysterious ways of God. The forced transition to English "will open up to our church a splendid vista of tremendous missionary opportunity."

> [The church has] clung too long to the idea that the duty of the Lutheran Church on the field of home missions consisted in gathering in the stray Lutherans, particularly those of German extraction, and perpetuating among them, willy-nilly, the

worship of God in the language of their fathers. May God in His mercy not hold to our account the appalling losses and neglected opportunities which may be laid at the door of this shortsighted policy.

Two months later he pushed the envelope even further by stating "our firm conviction that catechetical instruction should be imparted only through the medium of English."[23]

Beyond the language question, however, Lindemann's implicit criticism of the Synod's home mission program drew a mild rebuke from Theodore Graebner, who insisted that there was still a need for work among German-speakers and that what the Synod needed was "not a transfer but a broadening out of missionary policy." Lindemann thanked him for the response, though he denied that "there is any radical difference between his views and those of the editor." This was the first salvo in a long battle by the *American Lutheran* for a more aggressive home missions policy—a campaign which would help to bring ALPB into a closer alliance with Graebner.[24]

Organizational issues
"Keep the night watchman in good humor"

In any organization, there are practical issues which have little to do with program or philosophy. An immediate problem for the ALPB was the location of its office. In the early years, the Bureau's office, such as it was, existed at Grace Lutheran Church, Jersey City, where Lindemann was pastor. With the hiring of J. F. E. Nickelsburg, followed not long after by a part-time stenographer, larger quarters were needed; in 1918, the Bureau opened an office at 234 East 62nd St. in Manhattan, occupying space offered by the Lutheran Immigration Society. It soon became clear that this was inadequate, and in April 1919, the office was moved to the Hartford Building on East 17th St., sharing a facility that Theodore Lamprecht, president of the Lutheran Laymen's League, had procured for that organization's use as well as his own. An enigmatic comment in the minutes directs that future meeting of the executive committee will be held in the new office "and that the business manager be authorized to keep the night watchman in good humor."[25]

A few years' experience led to some structural changes in the Bureau. In response to several inquiries, the executive committee discussed offering associate membership in the ALPB to persons not members of Synodical Conference congregations—though they would not have the privilege of voting. This was never formally incorporated into the ALPB constitution, but the discussion is another indicator that already the Bureau was thinking about inter-Lutheran cooperation. It was also agreed to add two additional vice presidents to the group of officers and to have a meeting of the entire membership on a triennial (rather than annual) basis. The 1917 membership meeting agreed that the ALPB should be incorporated (though that wasn't accomplished until 1927).[26]

Financial concerns were a continuing problem, particularly the cost of the *American Lutheran*. After eight months of publication, Paul Lindemann presented the executive committee with three possible scenarios: (1) reduce the quality of the paper on which the magazine was published; (2) discontinue publication entirely at the end of the year; or (3) raise more money to support the magazine at its present quality. The committee voted to continue the magazine in its present form, and they appointed a committee to address the financial difficulties.[27]

Of course, the magazine wasn't the only expense. Most of those working on behalf of the Bureau—editing, lecturing, publicizing in other ways—were volunteers who at most were reimbursed for expenses. But when staff are hired, they must be paid, and at a reasonable rate. In January 1919, Mr. Nickelsburg asked if the executive committee might "kindly consider the salary of the Business Manager?" He noted that "$100. per month averages about $23. per week. The ever-increasing cost of food, rent, clothing makes it really impossible to support a family at this figure." The matter was laid on the table until the next meeting, but wasn't brought up again until August. At that time Theodore Lamprecht, who had recently joined the board, made a plea for each member to be more active in soliciting support for the Bureau's operational costs, and he personally pledged to raise $500 for the coming year. "In view of this generous offer," the meeting minutes record, "it was resolved to increase Mr. Nickelsburg's salary $25 per month," retroactive to January.[28]

The Bureau also had to deal with continuing friction between itself and Otto Pannkoke. Pannkoke had established the "Lutheran Bureau," an intersynodical New York agency dedicated to gathering and disseminating news of interest to Lutherans. He would later admit that during that period, "I carried this load alone. In fact, I was the Lutheran Bureau." The confusion caused by the similar names (some of which seems to have been deliberately fostered by Pannkoke) led the ALPB to send a letter to all Synodical Conference pastors, emphasizing that the groups were not identical: "Permit us to inform you that these are two separate organizations with absolutely no connection. ... Since the literature of the Lutheran Bureau is being disseminated in our circles and appeals for funds have gone forth to our people we feel compelled to inform you of these facts." At the following meeting, Lindemann reported that "this letter had brought a complaint from Pastor O. Pannkoke," and the letter of complaint was read (and apparently ignored by the executive committee). The problem eventually took care of itself when the Lutheran Bureau was taken over by the newly organized National Lutheran Council and Pannkoke stepped away from the organization.[29]

In fairness to Pannkoke, it should be said that in later years he generally spoke very kindly of the ALPB and its leaders. He would describe Paul Lindemann as "my lifelong friend" and "an evangelical spirit who reacted more and more against the intellectual intolerance of Missouri." He would also contribute several articles to the *American Lutheran* in years to come.[30]

The issue here was not simply that the Lutheran Bureau was duplicating the efforts of the ALPB; as an inter-Lutheran organization, the Lutheran Bureau had come under strong attack from Synod authorities, and especially from *Lutheran Witness* editor Graebner. The ALPB leaders were no doubt concerned that confusion between the two agencies would pull the ALPB into that fracas and inhibit its ability to develop support within the Missouri Synod. The controversy did, however, have one salutary consequence. The treasurer of the Lutheran Bureau was Theodore Lamprecht, a wealthy New York businessman who had been active in many Lutheran causes and who was one of the founders and the first president of the Lutheran Laymen's League (LLL). Graebner, who at this stage in his career was something of a self-appointed guardian of Missouri Synod purity among the English-speaking segment of the Synod, put pressure on Lamprecht to disassociate himself from the Lutheran Bureau. At the same time, he published editorials in *Lutheran Witness* attacking the Lutheran Bureau and Pannkoke. Lamprecht wrote to Graebner in early 1919, lamenting that the editorials had been "breathing the desire to pillory and hurt rather than to correct and save a brother charged with error! But this is done, and the consequences must be accepted by every one affected."[31]

Among those consequences, Lamprecht went on to say, was the taking over of the Lutheran Bureau by the new National Lutheran Council (NLC). And given that the NLC was not endorsed by the Missouri Synod, Lamprecht, as a Missouri Synod layman, felt obliged to disassociate himself from the Lutheran Bureau. "Thus the result which you desired will be brought about as far as I am concerned," he told Graebner. The controversy would also bring about another consequence: "my quiet withdrawal as head of the Lutheran Laymen's League." Four months later Lamprecht accepted the invitation to join the executive committee of the ALPB; the next year he would be elected president and would become a primary financial supporter and spokesman for the Bureau until his death.[32]

Lamprecht's first association with ALPB had come even before he resigned from the Lutheran Bureau. The Lutheran Laymen's League had embarked on a campaign to establish an endowment fund to support pensions for LCMS pastors, and they hoped to raise three million dollars for this purpose. Since a carefully planned publicity campaign would be essential to the success of this endeavor, Lamprecht met with the executive committee in January 1919 to discuss the possibility of the ALPB taking over this task. They were not able to come to an agreement—perhaps because the ALPB believed the proposed cost of the campaign, $25,000, would be inadequate—and there is no further mention of the proposal in subsequent meetings. The LLL set up its own campaign committee, which Lamprecht personally chaired. The Bureau, however, lent support in other ways. The March issue of the *American Lutheran* was devoted to the pension campaign. "Any contribution to this fund," Lindemann wrote, "is not charity but the payment of an honest debt, and a payment which has been long deferred. ...

Not charity, but equity." Lamprecht requested the ALPB to mail 45,000 copies of the issue to laity in the Atlantic and English districts, paid for by the LLL. The executive committee also authorized Mr. Nickelsburg to give some limited assistance to the campaign committee in writing newspaper copy.[33]

Synodical control

"We are of divided opinion as to the advisability of such a step"

Perhaps because of the confusion and controversy about the Lutheran Bureau, or perhaps because of the negotiations with the Lutheran Laymen's League, there was some sentiment in 1919-20 for the ALPB to come under the direct control of the Missouri Synod. The discussion began in January 1919 when Theodore Graebner wrote to the executive committee, proposing that the ALPB "take steps to become an official synodical body with synodical recognition and sanction." Graebner, not uncharacteristically, also expressed his opinion publicly in a *Lutheran Witness* editorial complaining about the proliferation of agencies not directly under the supervision of the Synod.[34]

This editorial, the ALPB executive committee agreed, "had been almost unanimously construed as applying to the Publicity Bureau," and they communicated their objection to Graebner. The next month, however, ALPB president Henry Eckhardt, who was also serving as a vice president of the Synod, made the trip from Pittsburgh to attend the executive committee meeting. He "reported on a certain sentiment against the activities [of ALPB] in some circles of Synod on account of the fact that the Bureau is an organization working in the Synodical Conference without being a Synodical organization or having Synodical sanction." The matter was discussed at length over two days by Eckhardt, Lindemann, and Arthur Brunn, now chair of the executive committee, and they finally recommended that the board call a special meeting of the membership for October and ask them "to petition Synod ... to give Official endorsement to the American Lutheran Publicity Bureau and its aims." This was duly published in the April issue of the *American Lutheran,* with the comment that "already at the inception of the Bureau six years ago its founders expressed the desire for eventual Synodical endorsement ... when the time seemed right and the Bureau had proven its value." But for reasons not clear, the special meeting was never held.[35]

In April 1920, the executive committee received another letter from Pr. Eckhardt about the issue. Eckhardt had met with President Pfotenhauer and apparently was under some pressure to bring the Bureau into a formal relationship with the Synod. The executive committee was having second thoughts, however, and the matter was laid on the table for some months. At last Eckhardt directly asked that the executive committee "petition Synod to take over the work [of ALPB] and expand it." In Eckhardt's plan, the agency would then be run by a board elected by the Synod and call a secretary to be paid by the Synod. Alternatively, he suggested, perhaps the LLL could be asked to take over the ALPB's ministry.[36]

There was disagreement within the executive committee about this proposal, and after what was likely some heated discussion, it was agreed "that we do not come before the Synod at this time as we are of divided opinion as to the advisability of such a step." This seems to have ended, at least for the present, any discussion of the idea that the ALPB should come under the control of the Missouri Synod.[37]

There was further conversation, however, about the possibility of ALPB merging with the LLL. In the end, both groups decided this was not desirable. From the ALPB side, one issue was that LLL's membership was restricted to laymen, while the ALPB, though not without strong lay leaders, had been mostly directed by clergy. There also seemed to be some resistance in the LLL board to the *American Lutheran*'s commitment to "free discussion"; some felt this was not appropriate because the LLL saw itself as organically connected to the Synod. The two groups, however, pledged to find ways to work together, and that would indeed happen. The *American Lutheran*, for example, would give significant space to the programs and projects of LLL. The same would be true of the ALPB and the Walther League, the Synod's youth organization. Founded originally in 1893, the young people of the Walther League (as might be expected) were in sympathy with the ALPB's efforts to bring the Synod out of its German ghetto and into the mainstream of American life. As early as 1915, the League had endorsed the ALPB and its work; in return, the ALPB frequently publicized the League's programs and for several years managed the publicity for annual drives to raise money for the League's primary charity, the sanitorium at Wheat Ridge, CO. Beginning in 1918, ALPB would regularly be represented at Walther League conventions. The League called Pr. Walter A. Maier as its executive secretary in 1920, and Maier would become a frequent and popular speaker at ALPB events and a contributor to the *American Lutheran*.[38]

Notes

1. The persecution of German Americans during World War I has been frequently chronicled; see, for instance, Frederick C. Luebke, *Bonds of Loyalty: German Americans and World War I* (DeKalb, IL: Northern Illinois University Press, 1974).

2. Samuel Hopkins Adams, "Invaded America," *Everybody's Magazine* 38, no. 1 (Jan. 1918), 33.

3. "Editorial," *AL* 1, no. 7 (July 1918), 1.

4. "Editorial," *AL* 1, no. 1 (Jan. 1918), 1; H. E. Eckhardt, "Why Advertise?" *AL* 1, no. 1 (Jan. 1918), 3.

5. "What Should the Church Advertise?" *AL* 1, no. 2 (Feb. 1918), 1.

6. F. Pieper, "Is Lutheranism Limited Nationally?" *AL* 1, no. 2 (Feb. 1918), 5.

7. "Editorial: A Children's Choir," *AL* 1, no. 3 (Mar. 1918), 3; "Editorial: That Evening Service," *AL* 1, no. 4 (Apr. 1918), 1-2.

8. "Editorial: Delivering the Goods," *AL* 1, no. 5 (May 1918), 1-2.

9. "Editorial: A Patriotic Service," *AL* 1, no. 6 (June 1918), 1-2.

10. The best study of this incident is Alan Graebner, "World War I and Lutheran Union: Documents form the Army and Navy Board, 1917 and 1918," *CHIQ* 41, no. 2 (May 1968), 51-64.

11. Ibid., 57-58.

12. Paul Lindemann to W. C. Kohn, 4 Oct. 1918, Theodore Graebner Papers, Box 123, Folder 7, CHI (hereafter cited as Graebner Papers).

13. "Prayer," [ca. 1917]; Minutes, ALPB Executive Committee, 27 Sept. 1917, 16 Oct. 1917.

14. "Lutherans and the War," [ca. 1917].

15. Quoted in Ralph L. Moellering, *Modern War and the American Churches* (New York: The American Press, 1956), 35-36; Minutes, ALPB Executive Committee, 21 May 1918.

16. Paul Lindemann to Theodore Graebner, 18 June 1918, Graebner Papers, Box 122, Folder 6.

17. "Office Chat," *AL* 1 no. 8 (Aug. 1918), 11; Minutes, ALPB Executive Committee, 20 Aug. 1918.

18. Walter Koenig, "Paying Pays," *AL* 1, no. 6 (June 1918), 5; "Editorial: Publicity Needed," *AL*, 1, no. 7 (July 1918), 1-2.

19. Alan Graebner, "Meet 'Mr. Lutheran Publicity,'" *AL* 46, no. 7 (July 1964), 8.

20. "Office Chat," *AL* 1, no. 11 (Nov. 1918), 11.

21. J. F. E. Nickelsburg, "Nineteen Months of Office History," *AL* 2, no. 6 (June 1919), 7.

22. *AL* 7, no. 2 (Feb. 1925), 6; *AL* 3, no. 11 (Nov. 1920), 5.

23. "Editorial: A Blessing in Disguise," *AL* 1, no. 8 (Aug. 1918), 1; "Editorial: This Year's Catechism Class," *AL* 1, no. 10 (Oct. 1918), 2.

24. "Neglected Opportunities," *AL* 1, no. 10 (Oct. 1918), 10-11.

25. Minutes, ALPB Executive Committee, 8 April 1919.

26. Minutes, ALPB Executive Committee, 15 Jan. 1918; Minutes of Meeting of the American Lutheran Publicity Bureau, 27 Sep. 1917.

27. Minutes, ALPB Executive Committee, 20 Aug. 1918.

28. Minutes, ALPB Executive Committee, 7 Jan. 1919, 19 Aug. 1919.

29. Pannkoke, 65; Minutes, ALPB Executive Committee, 20 Aug. 1918.

30. Pannkoke, 58, 76.

31. Theodore Lamprecht to Theodore Graebner, 21 Feb. 1919. Graebner Papers, Box 66, Folder 4.

32. Ibid.; Minutes, ALPB Executive Committee, 17 June 1919.

33. "Editorial: Equity Not Charity," *AL* 2, no. 3 (Mar. 1919), 1; Minutes, ALPB Executive Committee, 18 February 1919.

34. Minutes, ALPB Executive Committee, 7 Jan. 1919; "Unity of Effort in the Church," *LW* 38, no. 2 (Jan. 21, 1919), 22.

35. Minutes, ALPB Executive Committee, 18 Feb. 1919; "Members, Attention!" *AL* 2, no. 4 (Apr. 1919), 9.

36. Minutes, ALPB Executive Committee, 17 June 1919; "Members, Attention!" *AL* 2, no. 4 (April 1919), 9; Minutes, ALPB Executive Committee, 19 April 1920.

37. Minutes, ALPB Executive Committee, 19 April 1920.

38. On the history of the Walther League, see Jon Pahl, *Hopes and Dreams of All: The International Walther League and Lutheran Youth in American Culture, 1893-1993* (Chicago: Wheat Ridge Ministries, 1993).

Chapter 3

The Roaring Twenties

A s the "roaring twenties" began, the ALPB had come to the end of its first generation. The only executive committee member who had served since the beginning, Paul Lindemann, announced in March 1920 that he had accepted a call to Bethlehem Lutheran Church in St. Paul, MN. In addition to editing the *American Lutheran*, Lindemann was the Bureau's executive secretary; with his departure, that position was now filled by his brother, Pr. Fred H. Lindemann. At the 1920 membership meeting, Theodore Lamprecht was elected to succeed Pr. Eckhardt as president. It was the Bureau's first major time of transition.

Changing priorities
"Office magazine, Sermonettes, Tracts, Helps and Hints"

Recognizing the need to increase membership and financial support, the ALPB leaders decided to hire a field secretary to do promotional work. Pastor Rudolph S. Ressmeyer agreed to take the position half time at a salary of $100/month. Ressmeyer worked hard for a few months, but he resigned in July 1921 when he accepted a call in Baltimore. His good results convinced the executive committee to replace him with a full-time field secretary. This proved to be more difficult than anticipated; several pastors declined the call. Finally, in 1923, the position (now renamed "executive secretary") was accepted by 26-year-old Pr. Arthur Herbert, a Brooklyn native and pastor of St. Mark's in Yonkers, NY. But Herbert worked only for several months and then returned to parish ministry, and he was not replaced.

With new leadership and a new situation, there was a shift in priorities. In early 1921, the executive committee made this explicit. The ALPB's work, they said, would be in the following order of importance: "Office Magazine [i.e., the *American Lutheran*], Sermonettes [i.e., brief devotional pieces in the public press], Tracts, Helps and Hints for practical church work, the placing of literature and public lectures." Remarkably, the top priority, the magazine, was something not even contemplated in 1914. As early as 1921, it was clear that the ALPB's publications were going to be the most significant aspect of its ministry.[1]

The *American Lutheran*

"nothing advertises so well as success"

When Paul Lindemann moved to St. Paul, he offered to resign as editor of the *American Lutheran*. The executive committee insisted that he continue; the magazine, they believed, could be edited from a distance, and they would find a way to make it work. They asked Pr. George Koenig to be managing editor, leaving Lindemann free to focus entirely on editorial responsibilities. This was a relief to many admirers of the magazine; Arthur Brunn reported from the 1920 Synod convention in Detroit that "there were many anxious inquiries ... whether or not [Lindemann] would continue to wield the pen. We were glad to be able to tell all of our many friends that Brother Lindemann even in distant St. Paul will continue to sit in the editorial sanctum."[2]

Lindemann now began to widen the range of articles in the magazine. In May 1920, he published a special "synodical number" aimed at delegates to the Detroit convention, and nearly 18,000 copies were distributed. In an editorial entitled "The Future of American Lutheranism," he noted that the magazine had surpassed 3,000 paid subscribers, and he described his vision of what he wanted the *American Lutheran* to be:

> We have not confined ourselves strictly to matters of Lutheran Church publicity, but have touched upon various phases of practical congregational work. After all, true church efficiency is a wonderful means of publicity. Nothing advertises so well as success.

The line between "practical work" and larger matters was not always easy to discern, however, and the *American Lutheran* began to take on some very significant issues.[3]

In June 1920, for example, Lindemann made the case for better financial support for pastors. "The bitter poverty in the preacher's homes," he wrote, "usually borne without complaint, is a reproach to the Church for which she will find it difficult to make excuses." In Lindemann's view, one of the biggest problems with such penury is the "intellectual starvation" of the pastor. "Let us wake up!" he demanded, and recognize that pastors need "intellectual food" and that "books and magazines cost money."[4]

Lindemann's understanding of "practical church work" thus went beyond simply offering advice about how to perform specific tasks; he had a much larger view of what must be done to address a new era. While the Lutheran Church is "conservative" in the sense that we are unwilling "to change our doctrinal position to suit the demands of an unbelieving age," he argued, it must not maintain an "ultra-conservatism of methods" that have "nothing in their favor except the sentimental prestige of age." So, for example, he urged major changes in congregational finance and advocated an understanding of stewardship that went beyond fundraising.[5]

The *American Lutheran* increasingly beat the drum for home missions. In September 1921, Lindemann published a "Home Missions Number" devoted primarily to that cause. The ALPB, he declared, "was organized for the purpose of lending a helpful hand in the cause of the Home Missions"—a framing of the Bureau's goals that was novel, yet not inaccurate. Lindemann was convinced the Synod was failing miserably in its responsibility, and he pulled no punches. Describing the work of district mission boards as "feeble," he insisted that major changes were necessary.[6]

The highlight of the issue was an article by Theodore Graebner entitled "Entering by the Open Door." Graebner, who just three years before had chastised Lindemann for his criticism of the Synod's German-oriented mission policy, now came down squarely on the other side:

> Let me tell you the story of a young missionary in a northern state. He told it thus: 'When I was called to F., the mission board told me to look up the Lutherans there, the German Lutherans, and minister to them. Well, I did this, and received much praise from the board. I realize now that I deserved censure. For what was the situation? Here was my flock of 240 souls. But the community numbered 2,000. And there was not another church or mission there. I had the entire field to myself! If I had started English services, I *might* have had the church packed every service. But my commission was to the Lutherans'—to Jerusalem and Judea, not to Samaria—'and I lost my opportunity. Now five sectarian churches have entered the field. And we have our little congregation.' ... The blame, of course, falls not on this worker, but on the board that restricted his work by assigning to him work in German, work among Lutherans only, and actually informing him that he had no work to do among the unchurched. What awful folly!

This was not a new concern for Graebner, though in the pages of the Synod's official *Lutheran Witness* he had constraints on what he could say. But the *American Lutheran* was not sponsored by the Synod, and in its pages Graebner could be more forthright in his criticism of aspects of the Synod's program.[7]

A year later, another issue focused on home missions, and again Graebner wrote the keynote article, "Wanted—A Missionary Policy." "We are not sailing," Graebner complained, "we are drifting." In the same issue, Lindemann took precisely the same stance: "Radical changes in our whole Home Mission policy are a necessity. Let us [not] ... dismiss the claims made with a shrug of the shoulders as the rantings of a disgruntled pessimist. Let us face the facts."[8]

But the magazine wasn't content simply to criticize; the same issue featured "A Plan for Unifying Our Home Mission Work," proposed by Frederick R. Webber. He sketched out a "Unification Plan" entailing centralized strategy and direction which he called "the only logical" option, and he urged that the Synod take it up at the next convention. Lindemann knew that this would be controversial; in the next issue he commented that "we are writing these lines before [the home mission issue] has reached the hands of our readers" and thus don't know how it has been received. But "we shall not be deeply disturbed by the voices of disapproval which are bound to come to our ears." That would be the attitude of Lindemann and the ALPB as they went forward: calling things as they saw them and not worrying too much about the expected opposition.[9]

The *American Lutheran* hit a bump in January 1923 when Paul Lindemann resigned as editor. The minutes do not indicate the reason, but the executive committee responded with two motions: the first asked Lindemann to continue as "Contributing Editor," the second resolved to "endeavor to procure a salaried man as Editor-in-Chief." There was no further recorded discussion of this matter (other than Lindemann's agreement the next month to serve as "Contributing Editor").[10]

But Lindemann did not give up the editorial responsibilities, and beginning with the May issue, the masthead listed him as editor-in-chief rather than simply editor. This suggests that Lindemann agreed to continue if the board would make some changes that relieved him of some of his responsibilities. The masthead listed Pr. George Koenig as associate editor, Pr. Arthur Herbert as managing editor, and Mr. Nickelsburg as business manager. With Herbert's departure, Koenig temporarily became managing editor once again, but was soon succeeded by Pr. Adolf "Ade" Meyer. Meyer had been ordained in 1923 and installed as pastor of St. Mark's Lutheran Church in Yonkers. Immediately after the ordination service, he had been cornered by George Schmidt, Atlantic District vice president, and essentially ordered to attend an ALPB board meeting the next evening. Meyer was promptly voted onto the board and began serving as a proofreader for the magazine. In July 1925, he was named associate editor, and then managing editor the following February. He would play a major role in the magazine for decades.[11]

In the tenth anniversary issue in 1927, the various responsibilities of the then three-person staff were outlined. Lindemann as editor-in-chief "furnishes only the editorials." Managing editor Meyer does "the rest of the work. ... He gets the contributed articles, plans the mechanical make-up of each issue, writes occasional articles himself, and does the proof reading," with business manager Nickelsburg handling the advertising, printing and other technical aspects. The trio met together for a few days once a year to plot out the next twelve issues. Several issues a year were typically devoted to some specific theme—the Walther League, evangelism, Lutheran music, church architecture, missions, home missions, stewardship, church organization.[12]

The *American Lutheran* quickly became the primary public voice of the ALPB, "must reading" for many in the Synod. Lindemann's forthright—often acerbic—commentary, coupled with a wide variety of articles, both practical and philosophical, proved a winning combination. Despite a reduction of the magazine's paper quality in 1919 (but "we do not intend to cheapen its contents") and a doubling of the subscription price (from fifty cents to a dollar a year) in 1920, the readership continued to grow. Subscriptions were reported to be 4,500 in 1925; by 1929, perhaps 30% of the pastors in the Missouri Synod were subscribers.[13]

The public press

"you are invited to hear God's traveling directions"

During the 1920s, the ALPB continued its efforts to publicize the Lutheran Church in the secular press. For a time, the Bureau published what it called "sermonettes" in "papers with large circulation." These were essentially paid advertisements which "carried brief statements of Lutheran doctrine and teaching." It was an expensive proposition, but the ads were thought to have reached over a million readers, and they elicited "many letters to the office asking for more Lutheran literature."[14]

The *American Lutheran* occasionally published groups of these sermonettes and invited local congregations to incorporate them into their own newspaper notices or advertisements. These were generally quite evangelistic in their tone. Here, for example, is a sermonette entitled "A Sense of Values," published in 1933:

> It is difficult to understand the reasoning process of a man who will pay the strictest attention to the needs of his body but will persistently neglect his soul. ... His temporal welfare is to him a matter of grave concern but his spiritual wellbeing troubles him not at all. But life is just a short span of time, and the most important question for any man to consider is: 'Where shall I spend my eternity?' We are travelers on a short journey. God has given us the traveling directions in His Word. We are just hopeless drifters unless we follow these directions. ... You are invited to hear God's traveling directions at —[the local congregation would place its information here].

It is impossible to know how widely these spiritual blurbs may have been used; this one, for instance, was placed in the *Salem [Ohio] News* by Emmanuel Lutheran Church in 1937—nearly four years after it had appeared in the *American Lutheran!*[15]

Given the success of the Reformation quadricentennial campaign, the Bureau took advantage of other "400th anniversaries" of Reformation events in the next several years. In 1921 John H. C. Fritz, dean of Concordia Seminary and one of the ALPB's founders, wrote an article commemorating the anniversary of the 1521 Diet of Worms—an event, Fritz argued somewhat hyperbolically, which "marks the end of the Middle ages and the beginning of the Modern Era in the history of the world." The ALPB distributed the article, and it was carried in many newspapers, large and small.[16]

Tracts

"our 'silent messengers'"

The tract program, such an important part of the Bureau's work in the beginning, had focused in 1917 on the Reformation quadricentennial; then, after the United States entered World War I, attention was diverted to the war tracts. In January 1919, the minutes lamented that "our tract business has almost come to a complete standstill because half our stock are Reformation and Wartime tracts." During 1918 only two tracts other than the war tracts had been issued. "We ought to publish at least one tract each month," the executive committee resolved.[17]

With that statement of intent, the publication of tracts picked up almost immediately. Nearly every month the Board approved one or more new tracts. Several of the best-selling older pieces were also reprinted—or, in some cases, new tracts on the same topic were commissioned. While the earlier tracts primarily offered information about Lutheranism, the post-war publications went in many different directions. There were tracts on parochial versus public education, and on creation versus evolution; there were others on doctrinal themes such as salvation and atonement. Several attempts were made to publish a tract on the frequency of Holy Communion, but it seemed a more difficult topic. A first draft was discussed at length, then sent back to the committee, then assigned to a different writer. It was eventually published under the title "This Do! How Often?"

But the tracts were not making money—indeed, they weren't even paying for themselves. In 1919, the Tract Committee asked permission to experiment with distributing a tract at no cost. The trial was a success, and soon all the tracts were offered without charge—but with an invitation to contribute to the "Free Tract Fund" (originally set up to provide tracts to mission pastors). At the end of 1920, the Tract Committee reported that the new policy had been a resounding success. "Contributions as well as requests for tracts poured in. The deficit was wiped out. Our shelves were emptied. New editions were printed and immediately paid for—something unheard of in the history of the bureau."[18]

The ministry blossomed even further with the promotion of "Tract Distribution Week" in 1920, a reconceptualization for that year of "Lutheran Publicity Week." The

Tract Committee reported that more than 400,000 tracts were shipped to congregations representing perhaps 15% of the Synod for use during this special campaign. Reports came from far and wide of how the tracts were utilized: tract racks were installed in congregations, tracts were mailed to prominent people in various communities and distributed door to door by enthusiastic Lutheran congregation members. "Many were the methods used to get out our 'silent messengers.'"[19]

Practical church work

"The Sunday School is an institution that has come to stay"

In the post-war period, the ALPB's understanding of "publicity" expanded even further. The ALPB assumed that effectiveness in just about any sphere of church life was really "publicity"; that was, after all, what attracted people to a congregation. Already in 1919 Lindemann published an article by Carl Romoser on "Church Decorum," the lack of which, Lindemann noted, "is a serious detriment to the growth of the Church." Romoser's article itself focused on behavior, both of pastor and congregation. "It adds not a whit to the dignity of the service," Romoser complained, "when the pastor approaches the altar swaggering leisurely, or strutting hastily about in nervous excitement." The pastor "is handling divine things and divine things demand a natural, calm and reverent attitude and conduct." He also had an opinion about church announcements:

> We let others debate the questions whether they belong in the service, before the service, after the service, after the sermon or before it. To us, however, there is no doubt about the fact that they are not to rival the sermon in their length nor to be a 'sandwich' interjected to offer passing relaxation and perhaps offer occasion for the pastor to indulge in careless speech, slang and witticism. Briefness and dignity in announcement are in keeping with church decorum.[20]

Parishioners also have some responsibility for "decorum." "[God] doesn't come late" to church, so neither should Christians. Furthermore, "useless conversation is unbecoming the house of worship." Romoser wondered if Protestantism "in its revulsion from the gross and superstitious formalism of the mediaeval ages, has not swung to the other extreme. The Church's danger to-day is not in superstition so much as in flippancy." Lindemann added his own comment about "the sin of irreverence."

> The stranger is not favorably impressed when he is compelled to wind his way carefully through gossiping groups or finds the service commencing ten or fifteen minutes later than the time advertised. ... True church efficiency presupposes proper church decorum.[21]

The *American Lutheran* also began to devote attention to the attractiveness of the worship space. It started with an article by Frederick Roth Webber on "The Floor Plan of a Lutheran Church." "A good church, architecturally speaking," he wrote, "is not the result of an accident. Neither is an ugly one." In the end, he went on, "an ugly church nearly always costs more ... than a beautiful one." He argued that "we invariably have built our churches much too wide and too short."[22]

Webber, pastor of Faith Lutheran Church in Cleveland, OH, would become a regular writer for the *American Lutheran*, perhaps the most frequent contributor over many years except for Paul Lindemann himself. He was recognized as an authority in the field of church architecture, and he was influential in moving many congregations away from the popular "Akron plan" of design to a more liturgically sophisticated English Gothic style. His many articles in the *American Lutheran* fueled the magazine's interest in matters liturgical. In October 1923, for example, there appeared a lengthy article on "Altar Vestments" by Luther D. Reed, professor at the ULCA's seminary in Philadelphia—signaling Lindemann's conviction that the Missouri Synod didn't have a lock on scholarship and ideas that would be useful for its congregations. The demand for copies of Reed's article was so great that it was reprinted in the magazine in 1928.[23]

The next year the magazine took up the theme of church music—a topic about which Lindemann confessed his own "abysmal ignorance," but he recognized that "church music as a means of attracting people to the church services has its legitimate place in a church's publicity program." He criticized "organ gymnasts who can 'emote' effectually to provide the atmosphere for some lurid melodrama" but are "out of place in a church service." The organist, he wrote, "must have a religious consciousness, a sense of fitness, a good portion of consecrated common sense." Choir directors and members must be similarly consecrated, though it has sometimes "required a good deal of Christian charity to condone the musical crimes committed by [volunteer] choirs in the name of the Lord." He suggested that "it is worth the minister's while to visit the choir occasionally" to impress on them "the humble spirit of Christian devotion."[24]

All in all, the *American Lutheran* advocated a worship service "in conformity with the dignity of the Church's message and never subversive of the Church's one fundamental purpose." To those clamoring for a "popularization" of Lutheran worship, Lindemann had a clear response:

> Yes, we can 'popularize' our Lutheran service in many cases, not by resorting to cheapness and the methods of the show-house, but by placing our Gospel gem into the most attractive setting possible, by emphasizing promptness, cleanliness, orderliness, joyousness, earnestness, and beauty.[25]

Webber also argued for maintaining and embracing the distinctiveness of Lutheran liturgy:

Why should a Lutheran congregation seek to add one more church that is just like all the others in order of service, style of dress and ways of doing things? Shoe stores may be needed where plenty of hardware stores already exist. ... We have a valuable hand-maid in our traditional liturgical forms and in our church music, and there is no good reason why its educational value ought not to be employed to the utmost to supplement our more important modes of instruction.

These were the roots of what would be a continuing and growing commitment in the ALPB's ministry to the centrality of the liturgy in the life of the Lutheran churches.[26]

The *American Lutheran* also came out strongly in support of the institution of Sunday schools. This was controversial among Missouri Synod Lutherans, many of whom saw Sunday schools as in competition with, and perhaps in opposition to, parochial day schools. Lindemann insisted the ALPB was firmly in support of parochial schools, but he argued that "the Sunday School is an institution that has come to stay. ... Since we have it we may as well make it as good as possible."[27]

The magazine gave "how-to advice" about many aspects of parish ministry—archives and libraries, improved stewardship methods, more effective annual congregational meetings. It stressed the importance of good parish newsletters. "Personally we are rather resentful," Lindemann snorted, "when parish papers come to our desk giving evidence that the editor has exercised nothing but the scissors and the paste-pot." They never offer anything original. "Such papers," he fumed, "deserve the judgment pronounced by a certain auditor at a concert who was asked, after a vocal solo had been rendered: 'What do you think of the singer's execution?' and answered: 'I am in favor of it.'"[28]

The *American Lutheran* suggested the use of a weekly bulletin "handed the worshipper each Sunday as he enters the church." Printing the order of service, Rudolph Ressmeyer argued, can "make it easy for the visitor to find his way through the service and [eliminate] the announcing of the hymns and location in the hymnal [of] the order of service." It can also be used for announcements, synodical information, daily Bible readings, and many other things that "the aggressive pastor" might determine. Pr. Ressmeyer invited readers to write to him if they'd like samples from his own church in Baltimore.[29]

Lutheran literature in libraries

"Let us do something"

The early ALPB program included placing Lutheran literature in public libraries and other public places, and a good deal was done for several years toward that goal. This was an endeavor whose success was difficult to evaluate, but the Bureau believed that progress, though slow, was being made. In 1920 the Library Committee surveyed public libraries in many cities, and while the findings "were in the main disappointing, they are more gratifying than a similar investigation would have been ten years ago." Still, there was much to be done. Lindemann underscored the continuing importance of the project:

> We bemoan and begroan the superior activity of Romanism, Christian Science and other destructive fallacies—and usually do nothing to offset it. Instead of joining in the full-voices, well-rehearsed chorus that ends all its songs of lament with the refrain: 'Something ought to be done,' let us rather organize our efforts under the slogan: 'Let us do something.'

The Library Committee also urged local congregations to establish their own parish libraries, and suggested books which ought to be included.[30]

Public lectures

"trouble arose over a camp-meeting speech"

The ALPB had sponsored public lectures to promote its ministry, but now the Bureau was well-established; furthermore, the board expected the new field secretary would take on much of the promotional work. So while ALPB representatives continued to speak on the Bureau's behalf, attention shifted to lectures that would introduce the Lutheran Church to a wider audience. One ambitious project, begun in 1921, was the sponsorship of what was called "Luther Day" at Asbury Park, a Methodist conference facility in Ocean City, NJ. Thousands of non-Lutherans would join thousands of Lutherans, coming by bus, train, boat or automobile, to enjoy a day in at the beach and then hear some prominent Lutheran speaker in the evening. The first event took place August 8, 1921, with Pr. George A. Romoser speaking on "Luther's Message to the Church of Today." This was followed in 1922 with Paul Lindemann asking, "What is the Matter with the World?" In 1923 Otto C. A. Boecler, pastor of St. Luke's Lutheran Church in Chicago, considered "The Religious Education of the Child."

A lecture, of course, has only limited appeal, and "Luther Day" offered much more. In 1922, a sand bust of Martin Luther was erected at Asbury Park to publicize Luther Day. The ALPB sponsored a contest for the best photograph of the sculpture; the winning photo appeared in the *New York Times* (as well as in the *American Lutheran*), and the sand sculpture remained through the rest of that summer. Music was also an important part of the day; in 1922 an organ recital was presented by Edward Rechlin, one of America's most acclaimed interpreters of Bach. He became a regular at Luther Day, often joined by other prominent musicians.[31]

These annual events were by all accounts wildly successful, and they attracted notice well beyond the Missouri Synod. The ULCA's magazine the *Lutheran*, for instance, reported that the 1922 Luther Day "proved to be in every respect an event worthy of the occasion and might well be repeated at some prominent seashore resort every summer. They usually present speakers and a program that do the Lutheran Church credit." Specially chartered steamers left New York City to carry folks to Ocean Grove.[32]

The event hit a snag in 1926 when a Brooklyn pastor and Bureau executive committee member, Hugo Burgdorf, spoke before some 8,000 attendees on the theme "The Lutheran Church and Modern Problems." Of course, when one begins to identify specific "problems," controversy is almost to be expected. Burgdorf's first concern was crime—hardly controversial on the face of it, but the pastor argued that an increasing crime rate was due in part to lax law enforcement and judges who are too political. He then took up religious education, criticizing those trying to force instruction in the Bible in the public schools. This, he said, "would be the most flagrant violation of our Constitution." Religious education must be left in the hands of the church. The third "modern problem" was disarmament—popular in postwar 1920s, but to the speaker "the height of folly."[33]

But Burgdorf really stirred up a hornet's nest when he took on prohibition. His opinion was summarized in the *New York Times*: "Prohibition has resulted in the worst drinking conditions in the history of the country, in increased lawlessness and in corruption, and in a flood of debauchery and licentiousness." In good Lutheran "two kingdoms" fashion, Burgdorf insisted that the churches have no business advocating either for or against prohibition because "it is a social and a political question, pure and simple. ... Any attempt on [the church's] part to interfere with legislative procedure must be construed as a violation of the divine prerogative of the State and expose the Church to criticism, ridicule, scorn and contempt."[34]

The Methodist owners of the conference ground, strong prohibitionists, were appalled by the speech, and they weren't the only ones. The Tri-State Conference of the Women's Christian Temperance Union denounced Burgdorf in no uncertain terms; they were astounded, they said, "that a minister of the Gospel should give such a speech before an audience made up of church people, a large percentage of them young people, and should make an attack against the principles of prohibition, peace and the Bible in the schools." The president of the Ocean Grove Camp Meeting Association decreed that Burgdorf would never again be allowed to speak at Ocean Grove. When contacted by the *New York Times*, Burgdorf "emphatically adhered to the views he expressed" at Ocean Grove, but "refused to comment further."[35]

The *American Lutheran* didn't say a word about the incident and the board minutes for 1926 are missing, but some diplomatic conversation between the Bureau and "proper officials" allowed the event to continue in 1929. The *New York Times* reported that this "was the first gathering of this nature in three years, since trouble arose over a camp-meeting speech opposing the Volstead law."[36]

Most years the keynote speaker was Walter A. Maier, a consistently popular draw for Lutherans and non-Lutherans alike. Maier began teaching at Concordia Seminary in 1922 and soon began a radio ministry which in 1930 became the popular "Lutheran Hour." He had spoken at Luther Day in 1925, before the incident with Burgdorf. After the hiatus, he was invited back and then was the keynoter at least five times over the next decade. Sometimes his addresses had a distinctly Lutheran cast, as in 1929 when he spoke about the quadricentennial of the publication of Luther's Small Catechism. Other years he took up a more controversial theme. In 1936, in a speech provocatively titled "Reformation or Revolution," he called for "a twentieth-century reformation that will restore God to His supremacy in the affairs of the American people and recognize His leadership in the direction of His Church and the shaping of our individual lives." He criticized judges who sanction divorce and pornography, educators who "[laugh] away at the Ten Commandments"; he blasted both Roman Catholics and the Federal Council of Churches. Maier's controversial speeches did not officially represent the ALPB, of course, and yet he was continually invited back.[37]

The ALPB continued to sponsor Luther Day until 1937, though there were apparently no events in 1934 and 1935—likely a result of the Great Depression. The event was revived in 1949 with Maier once again the keynoter, but that seems to have been the last Luther Day at Ocean Grove. There were also a handful of attempts to replicate the success of Luther Day in some other locations, though none proved as long lasting as the Ocean Grove event.

In addition to the Luther Day events, the Lecture Committee of ALPB had several other projects. They promoted the idea of "Noonday Lenten Services," joint programs by Lutheran churches in large cities that would be held in the business district for the convenience and benefit of working people. They encouraged congregations to sponsor joint summer vesper services "at a centrally located church" for the specific "purpose of attracting non-Lutherans." The Bureau arranged for "Lutheran displays" at events like the International Exposition in Philadelphia in 1926 and urged Lutherans to do something similar at city, county and state fairs. They sponsored and publicized a concert by the St. Olaf College Choir at the Metropolitan Opera House in 1921, joined in this endeavor by the Lutheran Bureau; there would be other St. Olaf concerts under ALPB auspices in the coming decades. The ALPB also sponsored for several years the organ concerts by Edward Rechlin in New York's Aeolian Hall and encouraged Lutherans elsewhere to do the same with local talent—an acknowledgement that "the Word" can be proclaimed in media other than words.[38]

Organizational changes and broadening interests
"without any concession to the Zeitgeist"

In the early ALPB structure, the executive committee had been the real governing body. There was in theory a larger board of directors consisting of the executive committee plus the several officers, most of whom did not live in the New York area and hence did not regularly attend meetings; the full board of directors met seldom, if ever. But in 1923, for no apparent reason, what had been called the executive committee now began to be called the board of directors. When the Bureau finally incorporated in 1927, the articles of incorporation listed a board of directors of 25 persons—though again this included several officers who lived at great distance from New York. It was a considerable expansion of the six-person executive committee plus two officers with which the Bureau had begun in 1914.

A set of bylaws approved by the board in 1929 give a glimpse of how the Bureau organized itself for ministry in this period. The bylaws specified that there be five vice presidents, four of them "from various parts of the country so that the Bureau be represented in all parts of the United States." The board was to meet monthly. There was to be a business manager appointed by the board; part of his responsibility was to "direct the office force" and "employ and discharge help as required." There were five standing committees, each of which was expected to "hold at least one meeting a month": Tract, Public Libraries and Public Places, Lecture, Radio, and Membership. A Service Department was given the task of "[sending out] to the pastors suggestions to aid them in a systematization of their time and work and to aid them in training co-laborers from among the laymen, also to offer helpful hints and suggestions ... regarding church life and work." Finally, there was to be a Reference Department that would gather data about "our own and other church bodies" which would then be offered "free to all who request it." It was an ambitious plan indeed![39]

The ALPB's interests were expanding far beyond what had been conceived a decade earlier. The Bureau promoted Lutheran higher education, urging the establishment of a Lutheran university. While the ALPB had no direct hand in the purchase of Valparaiso University by the Lutheran University Association, the *American Lutheran* took great pride in printing the "scoop," claiming for years afterward that an article in the August 1925 issue was the "first public announcement" of the purchase. The *American Lutheran* would continue to publicize "the Lutheran university," and longtime Valparaiso president O. P. Kretzmann would be a key player in the ALPB in years to come.

The Bureau also became interested in the new media of radio and film. As early as April 1923, an editorial in the *American Lutheran* called for a Lutheran radio station. KFUO was founded at Concordia Seminary the next year with the assistance of the St. Louis Lutheran Publicity Association, and the station was regularly promoted in the magazine.

By the 1920s, much of the early suspicion from old guard Missourians had abated—so much so that the Synod requested ALPB to handle the publicity for its 75th anniversary celebration in 1922. The Bureau happily agreed; one result was a special "synodical issue" of the *American Lutheran* sent to all pastors, dedicated to the history of the Synod (with the offer that additional copies might be ordered for local distribution) and including several pages of suggestions for how to promote the jubilee locally. These pages were also reprinted as a stand-alone publicity guide for congregations. A letter from J. F. E. Nickelsburg to President Warren G. Harding informing him of the anniversary elicited a congratulatory letter in return. Harding admitted that he hadn't known anything about the origins of the Missouri Synod, and he suggested that the story probably isn't "as generally known as it deserves to be" since from the immigration of the Saxon company "developed a great community which has contributed vastly to the material and spiritual development of our country." Harding's letter was printed in the *American Lutheran*; the Bureau then arranged for it to be noted by the Associated Press, and it was picked up by newspapers across the country. In a tacit gesture of appreciation for the work of the Bureau, Paul Lindemann was asked to contribute a chapter on "Publicity Work in the Missouri Synod" to the official jubilee history, *Ebenezer*; about a quarter of the chapter dealt specifically with the ALPB's ministry.[40]

In its report to the membership in 1925, the board of directors recalled the earlier attitude in the Synod as "one of if not open hostility at least of grave suspicion. The conduct even of some of the leaders years ago would have led one to think that the Bureau was endeavoring to disseminate typhoid fever germs." But now, they went on, that attitude has changed, and they were happy to cite a letter from Theodore Graebner: "The Bureau has won a place for itself in the heart and mind of our Synod. ... It has done this without any concession to the Zeitgeist and without yielding any Scriptural principle."[41]

Defending Lutheranism

"In its pulpits it wants God to speak"

And indeed, as the ALPB matured, the Bureau—and especially Lindemann—emphasized that promotion of modern methods does not mean it abandoning Lutheran doctrine. In the 1920s, some American denominations were being roiled by the Fundamentalist/Modernist controversy, and Lindemann was clear about where Lutheran sympathies ought to lie. In an article (deliberately not framed as an editorial) in March 1926, he discussed "The Lutheran Church and Pulpit Liberalism." He criticized liberals like Harry Emerson Fosdick, the Baptist/Presbyterian clergyman who would in 1930 become the first pastor of New York City's Riverside Church and the *bête noire* of conservative Protestants, in no uncertain terms:

> The battle is on ... between those who still adhere to the Word of God as the divinely inspired norm of faith and conduct and those who ... have given themselves up to pious moralizings and a self-made creed of doctrinal negatives and practical ethics to which every decent heathen can subscribe.

He thanked God that Lutheranism in America has "remained comparatively free from this disrupting movement" because it "professes a complete subservience to the Word of God." Lutherans stand for the truth, which is "not a matter of human speculation" but "the revelation of God." "The modern 'Liberal' would evolve [truth] out of his inner consciousness; and what a sorry mess he has made of it." But "Lutheranism will have none of it."

> It refuses to parley with unbelief. It claims that there can be no neutral ground, that there is no room for human opinion and interpretations where God has spoken. It dare not consent to compromise or silence. It rightfully demands of its preachers the proclamation of the Word of God in its truth and purity. In its pulpits it wants God to speak. May that standpoint never change.[42]

In the next issue, he took up the theme again. Sometimes, he wrote, "we are called bigots by people who take their religion very seriously." That accusation comes because "we do not fraternize with those of different faith" and because "we refuse to join in the campaign of sensationalism with which so many churches are seeking to voice their ebbing vitality." Furthermore, Lutherans "still dare to preach against popular sins." "As to methods and tool[s]," he insisted, "we may still learn. Different times and surroundings call for different methods." But Gospel principles do not change. "Times have changed. Man's heart does not change."[43]

And so Lindemann began rather gingerly to move from the strictly practical concerns that had characterized the *American Lutheran* to a defense of the theological principles that must inform those concerns. He was blazing a path that would continue to characterize the ALPB—a strong affirmation of confessional fidelity, a pointed critique of popular religious thought, and yet an insistent openness to "different methods" of proclaiming the Gospel truth.

Notes

1. Minutes, ALPB Executive Committee, February 21, 1921.
2. Arthur Brunn, "The A. L. P. B. and the Convention," *AL* 3, no. 7 (July 1920), 6.
3. "The Future of the American Lutheran," *AL* 3, No. 5 (May 1920), 1.
4. "Intellectual Starvation," *AL* 3, no. 6 (June 1920), 1.
5. "Conservatism," *AL* 3, no. 11 (Nov. 1920), 1-2.
6. "Our Great Task," *AL* 4, no. 9 (Sept. 1921), 1-2.
7. Th. Graebner, "Entering by the Open Door," *AL* 4, no. 9 (Sep. 1921), 4.
8. Th. Graebner, "Wanted—A Missionary Policy," *AL* 5, no. 10 (Oct. 1922), 11; "Facing the Facts," *AL* 5, no. 10 (Oct. 1922), 1.
9. F. R. Webber, "A Plan for Unifying Our Home Mission Work," *AL* 5, no. 10 (Oct. 1922), 13-14; "Editorial: The Home Missions Number," *AL* 5, no. 11 (Nov. 1922), 1.
10. Minutes, ALPB Executive Committee, 29 Jan. 1923.
11. Adolf Fred Meyer, "The Autobiography of Adolf Fred Meyer: Ministry in THE AMERICAN LUTHERAN and the AMERICAN LUTHERAN PUBLICITY BUREAU," n.d., 1.
12. "The Managing Editor," *AL* 9 no. 12 (Dec. 1927), 4.
13. "The Future," *AL* 2, no. 1 (Jan. 1919), 2; *AL*, 8, no. 2 (Feb. 1925), 6; Alan N. Graebner, "The Acculturation of an Immigration Lutheran Church," 228.

14. "Report of the Board of Directors," *AL* 8, no. 2 (Feb. 1925), 5.

15. "Sermonettes for the Newspaper," *AL* 14, no. 7 (July 1933), 12; *Salem News*, 24 April 1937, 5.

16. See, for example, the bi-weekly *Lincoln County News* in Lincolnton, NC, 14 Apr 1921.

17. Minutes, ALPB Executive Committee, 7 Jan.1919.

18. Ibid.

19. George C. Koenig, "Tract Distribution Week: A Report," *AL* 3, no. 12 (Dec. 1920), 3.

20. Carl A. Romoser, "Church Decorum," *AL* 2, no. 2 (Feb. 1919), 3-5; "Editorial: Church Decorum," *AL* 2, no. 2 (Feb. 1919), 2.

21. Ibid.

22. F. R. Webber, "The Floor Plan of a Lutheran Church," *AL* 5, no. 8 (Aug. 1922), 2.

23. Luther D. Reed, "Altar Vestments," *AL* 6, no. 10 (Oct. 1923), 12-13, concluded in no. 11 (Nov. 1923).

24. "Editorial," *AL* 7, no. 11 (Nov. 1924), 1-3.

25. "'Popularizing' the Service," *AL* 8, no. 3 (Mar. 1925), 3.

26. F. R. Webber, "the Educational Value of the Liturgy," *AL* 9, no. 2 (Mar. 1927), 6.

27. "Try to Get Our Viewpoint," *AL* 2, no. 10 (Oct. 1919).

28. "Parish Papers," *AL* 6, no. 4 (Apr. 1923), 2.

29. Rudolph S. Ressmeyer, "The Advantages of the Weekly Bulletin," *AL* 10, no. 4 (Apr. 1927), 14.

30. "A Neglected Opportunity," *AL* 3, no. 7 (July 1920), 1.

31. "The Second Luther Day at Ocean Grove," *AL* 5, no. 9 (Sept. 1922), 4.

32. Quoted in *Luther League Review* 36, no. 5 (Aug. 1923): 20.

33. "Prohibition Blamed for Corruption In Nation By Lutheran Minister At Meeting," *Indiana Gazette* (Indiana, PA), 22 July 22 1926.

34. "Promotion Blamed for Corruption in Nation by Lutheran Minister at Meeting," *Indiana Gazette* (Indiana, PA), 22 July 1926, 21.

35. "Ocean Grove to Bar Burgdorf as Wet," *NYT*, 22 July 1926.

36. Minutes, ALPB Board of Directors, 31 Mar. 1927, 13 April 1927; *NYT*, 21 Aug. 1929.

37. Walter A. Maier, *Reformation or Revolution: An address delivered at Ocean Grove N. J. on the Occasion of Luther Day August 1, 1936* (New York: The Lutheran Press, 1936), 4, 7-11.

38. "Report of the Board of Directors," *AL* 8, no. 2 (Feb. 1925), 5.

39. "Annual Meeting American Lutheran Publicity Bureau," *AL* 12, no. 12 (Dec. 1929), 21-22.

40. "The President's Letter," *AL* 5 (Apr. 1922), 3; Paul Lindemann, "Publicity Work in the Missouri Synod" in *Ebenezer: Reviews of the Work of the Missouri Synod during Three Quarters of a Century*, ed. W. H. T. Dau (St. Louis: Concordia Publishing House, 1922), 456-465.

41. "The Triennial Meeting: Report of the Board of Directors," *AL* 8, no. 2 (Feb. 1925), 4.

42. Paul Lindemann, "The Lutheran Church and Pulpit Liberalism," *AL* 9, no. 3 (Mar. 1926), 4.

43. Paul Lindemann, "The Lutheran Church a Liberal Church," *AL* 9, no. 4 (Apr. 1926), 8.

Chapter 4

DEPRESSION YEARS

The 1920s were an optimistic time in the United States, but it was not to last. The stock market crash of 1929 and the ensuing Great Depression affected every aspect of American life, and the churches were no exception. It took some time, however, before the full implications of the crisis were realized. At the membership meeting of the ALPB in January 1930, business manager Nickelsburg could report that "the outlook for this year looks bright." It would prove to be an inaccurate prediction, but at that moment things *did* look bright. Much had happened over the past few years that was very encouraging for the Bureau and its mission.[1]

Growing success
"the largest subscription order ever placed"
One great affirmation had come in 1926 when the Synod appointed a Press Committee to publicize that year's convention, and the committee promptly asked the ALPB to help them. When the convention authorized a permanent Press Committee to do

public relations for the Synod on an ongoing basis, it was a tacit acknowledgement that the Bureau's advocacy for more sophisticated publicity had been embraced. Even more striking was the list of initial appointees to that committee: J. F. E. Nickelsburg, Adolf Meyer, and George Koenig—all ALPB staff or board members.[2]

It was thus not surprising when one of the new Press Committee's first actions was to propose a National Lutheran Publicity Week in 1927—thereby turning a longstanding ALPB emphasis into an official denominational program. The *American Lutheran* warmly and enthusiastically commended the decision, with no trace of resentment that the ALPB's own idea had been co-opted; it "deserves our best efforts," the *American Lutheran* insisted. The program was repeated in 1928, but when the Press Committee reported its efforts were being "crippled because of the meager Synodical appropriation for carrying its work," the ALPB agreed to underwrite the expenses for that year. The week before Lent was generally designated National Lutheran Publicity Week in a bid to increase church attendance leading up to Easter. This would become a regular part of the Synod's program well into the 1950s, and the ALPB would support it each year by supplying congregational resources. For the 1928 observance, for example, the Bureau reprinted a million copies of some three dozen tracts and supplied them without charge to congregations requesting them. The emphasis was publicized annually in the *American Lutheran*.[3]

An exciting 1927 ALPB program was what the Bureau hoped would become an annual "American Lutheran European Tour," sponsored by the *American Lutheran* and led by ALPB personnel. The first tour took 225 travelers on the SS Luetzow, departing from New York on July 14, 1927. Paul Lindemann wrote extensive reports of the five-week journey which were published over the next several months in the magazine. A similar trip was sponsored the following year, and then a third in 1929—though there was some frustration that the ULCA's *Lutheran* magazine had refused to accept advertisements for the event. "It seems impossible to get these people to see the European Tour as an affair into which synodical lines ought not be drawn," huffed Nickelsburg, noting that there had been no problem advertising in the Ohio Synod's *Lutheran Standard*.[4]

The fact that the ALPB advertised these tours beyond the Missouri Synod was not insignificant. The itinerary included regular devotional services, at least one of which in 1927 was led by a superintendent of the United Lutheran/Reformed church in Germany. This elicited a stern rebuke from William Oesch, an LCMS pastor who had taken a call to serve the Evangelical Lutheran Free Church in Saxony after graduation from the St. Louis seminary. Oesch wrote to Lindemann, complaining that the services violated the Synod's teaching against unionism. He hoped "that future tours will be absolutely free of such obnoxious features." Oesch would become an increasingly strident critic of the *American Lutheran* and the ALPB over the next several years.[5]

But Oesch was an exception, and many others were finding the *American Lutheran* an important resource. To cap off the bright outlook at the end of the decade, an anonymous layman in New York, appreciative of a series of articles on stewardship in the *American Lutheran*, purchased a one-year gift subscription for every Missouri Synod pastor in the nation. The National Lutheran Council took note of the gift in a press release: "A total of 2,106 pastors will benefit by this gift. It is believed that this is the largest subscription order for a religious publication ever placed by one individual at one time." The *American Lutheran* welcomed its new readers warmly: "This magazine is your publication. We can make it better and better with your cooperation. Keep us informed of doings in your congregation, mail us your parish paper. ... Call upon us for our service which will be cheerfully given."[6]

A slogan

"A changeless Christ for a changing world"

A 1928 ALPB contest for a "Lutheran slogan" attracted attention far beyond the Missouri Synod. Advertised in the *American Lutheran* in January under the headline "WANTED: A SLOGAN," the only rule was that proposals had to be no more than twelve words. First prize was passage on the 1928 European Tour. The Bureau emphasized that this slogan would not belong to the Missouri Synod exclusively but was intended for use by all segments of the Lutheran Church; in fact, the committee of judges included the Rev. G. L. Kieffer of the National Lutheran Council, a ULCA pastor—yet another early hint of the ALPB's impatience with the Missouri Synod's isolation from other Lutherans.

The contest was given wide publicity, and some 2,500 entries were received—not all from Lutherans. Ironically, the winner was a Baptist woman from Florida, Mattie McLeod Matheson, whose suggestion was "A Changeless Christ for a Changing World." Mrs. Matheson did join the European tour that year, though Ade Meyer later recalled that she had been a little problematic; the devout Baptist wouldn't touch alcohol, and it was not always easy to find drinking water in Europe.[7]

The Associated Press disseminated a story about the contest and its winner. Not all reaction was positive; the story attracted the attention of Arthur Brisbane, editor of the *New York Post*. Brisbane wrote a syndicated column called "Today," read by millions of Americans (*Time* magazine said it was probably read more regularly than the weather and market reports). He noted the slogan, and then opined:

> Fortunately the changing world changes its ideas of Christ and His teachings. It no longer burns witches in His name, nor tortures those that choose to think as they please religiously. When Protestants in Switzerland burned Doctor Servetus alive, on a slow fire, mocking his appeals for a speedier death, they thought they were pleasing Christ. They were mistaken.

The *American Lutheran,* clearly delighted at the notice taken by the widely-read Brisbane, eagerly responded. In a signed editorial, Adolf Meyer pointed out that Luther had absolutely nothing to do with the death of Servetus, which was the responsibility of Calvin and his followers.

> Lutherans are proud to tell the world that they accept the changeless Christ as the only remedy for this changing world. The love which Christ showed to the thief upon the cross is unchanged for the spiritual thief today; the might of the changeless Christ which changed civilization for the better in the past, still exerts its incomparable influence today.

Meyer would later comment that "confronting nationally famous Columnists with the Truth was a healthy experience for me."[8]

More ominous was a sarcastic comment by the *Northwestern Lutheran,* magazine of the Wisconsin Synod. Editor John Brenner pointed out that the committee of judges included, in addition to Missourians, a pastor from the ULCA and "professional advertising men." He found the idea preposterous. "One begins to weary of the many different things," he wrote, "that are being inflicted on the church we love." After the winner was announced, Brenner noted again that the judges had included "Lutherans from bodies that do not fellowship with each other" and marveled that the winning entry was submitted by someone who was not a Lutheran at all. "But whether we wanted it or not," he sighed, "we now have our Lutheran slogan. Our only worry is that some enthusiastic Lutheran, feeling that there is still something lacking, will appeal to the public to suggest a synodical 'yell' for the various Lutheran bodies."[9]

Despite Brisbane's criticism and Brenner's sarcasm, the slogan was widely used in ALPB materials (and elsewhere) for years to come. In many other ways, too, the ALPB's reputation was growing. In 1930 Nickelsburg reported a letter from the new publicity agency of the Norwegian Lutheran Church of America: "Our work is not developed to the point of issuing material like yours. I ... shall be very glad if you will place me on the mailing list to receive sample copies." Another letter from the Publicity Committee of the Ministerium of Pennsylvania ordered a subscription to the *American Lutheran* "as part of the equipment of its office."[10]

Subscriptions to the *American Lutheran* were also increasing. In November 1929, the board was told that some 8,000 copies were now being printed each month, 7,398 of them being mailed to individual subscribers and another 146 in "bundle orders." In Lindemann's view, this success was due in part to the fact that the magazine had avoided being "led into fields which from the outset we promised to avoid" and had "[left] the dogmatic, the devotional, the polemic and other fields to the official organs of the Church."[11]

Other aspects of the ALPB program also continued to grow. The 1930 annual meeting was informed that the total distribution of tracts since the Bureau's founding had now reached the two million mark. A special tract was ready for printing that would commemorate the 400th anniversary of the presentation of the Augsburg Confession in 1530, and plans were in the works for a special issue of the magazine on that theme as well.[12]

The Augsburg Confession quadricentennial provoked a controversy which the ALPB leveraged into national publicity. A commemorative stamp was sent to President Hoover, eliciting a *pro forma* presidential response; it was framed as a letter to the *American Lutheran* and published in the magazine:

> I send cordial greetings to the Americans of Lutheran faith who are celebrating on October 31 the anniversary of the Protestant reformation and the 400th anniversary of the reading of the Augsburg confession, from which date so many of the changes in point of view from older conceptions both of religion and government. The effects of these historical events are reflected in our national life and institutions, in religion through the predominant numbers of adherents to Protestant faiths and in government through the principle of separation of Church and State. It is fitting that we should commemorate the persons and events from which mighty forces have sprung.[13]

American Roman Catholics were understandably miffed at the words of the Quaker Hoover, and an angry response came from the Rev. John J. Burke, secretary of the National Catholic Welfare Conference. The statement, he said, "clearly violates the spirit if not the letter of his oath of office" and is "an insult to many millions of American citizens." Furthermore, he fumed, "the statement is historically inaccurate. Luther was not a champion of the separation of church and state but a most arbitrary defender of state absolutism." The president should "respect the religious rights of all" and not congratulate "one particular religious body." Hoover made a predictably political response, agreeing that some of the phraseology of the letter was, in the words of the United Press, "unfortunate and inexpressive of his sentiments in at least one particular," and that the letter had been prepared by a secretary (but of course he "was prepared to accept full responsibility"). The controversy went on for several days, and each time a story appeared in the newspapers, the President's original letter was quoted. Thus the ALPB's soliciting of a *pro forma* congratulatory letter resulted in extensive coverage of Lutheranism in the secular press.[14]

Changing of the guard
"the stewardship of life"

Though the Bureau's ministry was generally going well, a crisis came in 1928. The April meeting of the board discussed a letter from ALPB president Theodore Lamprecht, who was at that time in Europe. Lamprecht urged the board to establish an endowment fund to help ensure future financial stability for the ALPB, a concern that had always been close to his heart. The board affirmed the wisdom of such a move, and set procedures in motion to make such a fund a reality.

But two weeks later came the shocking news that Lamprecht had died in France. He had not been in the best of health when he set sail from San Francisco a few months earlier for a trip to Asia. He became seriously ill en route and was hospitalized in Java for several weeks; doctors then recommended that he go to France to recuperate and seek further medical attention. He died in Cannes April 30, 1928.

His death was a serious blow to the ALPB. Lamprecht's importance to the organization was summarized by Paul Lindemann in the June issue of the *American Lutheran*, which was dedicated to the late president's memory and filled with tributes to his contribution to Lutheranism:

> We shall not be accused ... of overstating the case when we claim that through Lamprecht's death the Lutheran Church has been deprived of the valuable offices of one of its most useful and lovable constituents. ... There was probably not a single progressive synodical movement in which his influence was not felt. ... To meet Lamprecht and confer with him on the affairs of God's kingdom was an inspiration, not only to his fellow laymen, but to the pastors. Many a timid, hesitating and faltering spirit has been bolstered up by his unquenchable enthusiasm and his consecrated optimism. ... He believed in the objects of the Bureau and was willing to foster them also in a financial way. But valuable as Mr. Lamprecht's financial support was, we owe even more to his sage counsel, his sound judgment and his optimistic faith. We have had our periods of depression in our editorial capacity but they always proved short-lived under Lamprecht's inspiring encouragement. We shall cherish in grateful memory the smiling heartiness with which he more than once raised our drooping spirits. ... We have lost an inspiring leader and a precious friend.[15]

The board's immediate response was to name the new endowment fund in Lamprecht's honor—the Theodore Lamprecht Memorial Endowment Fund. The fund's purpose was succinctly outlined:

- The awakening and the constant reawakening of progressive church movements among Lutherans.
- The extending and the better equipping of Free Tract distribution.
- The expansion of the *American Lutheran*—a greater and better magazine.
- The printing of separate manuals treating practical problems of Church work, which at a later date may be assembled in book form.
- The realization of a National Program for Lutheran Publicity.
- The financing of other worthy purposes for which the American Lutheran Publicity Bureau was founded.

Unfortunately, efforts to raise the endowment shortly ran into the realities of the depression, and it never came to more than a few thousand dollars. Decades later, when memory of Lamprecht's contribution had faded, what remained was simply folded into the ALPB's general financial resources.[16]

At the board's meeting that June, Paul Lindemann was present. Perhaps as a result of his reflections on Lamprecht's life and contributions to the ALPB, he spoke movingly about what he himself saw as the heart of the work the ALPB was doing:

> It seems to me that the great job of the Bureau in the coming years will be the steady attempt to spread the principle of Christian stewardship together with its practical suggestions of methods. I am not referring only to the stewardship of money. I speak of the stewardship of life, the stewardship of our time, our mental and physical gifts, our very selves. After all, the various phases of the Bureau's work are but suggested avenues along which this stewardship may be exercised. ... It will be slow work. But in the end it will tell. Let us pray that we ourselves be animated by this principle and give ourselves in renewed consecration to our Saviour's cause.

Henry A. Dahlen, a New Jersey businessman who had served on the board for several years, was chosen to complete Lamprecht's term as president. This change in leadership came at a key moment in the ALPB's life. Despite the successes of the past few years, the Bureau was struggling financially. At that June meeting the board appointed a committee of three "to investigate the Bureau's finances thoroughly and present a possible solution."[17]

There was also another movement afoot to merge the ALPB with the Lutheran Laymen's League. The context of this renewed discussion was a reorganization of the LLL. The plan was to bring the League, which had been an independent agency, more closely under the wing of the Synod to assist in fundraising for various synodical causes; one stated purpose of the reorganized League was "Lutheran publicity."

But when Paul Lindemann and Fred Lindemann met with the LLL reorganization committee, they came away with concerns, which they immediately relayed to the ALPB board:

> It was suggested by the L. L. L. committee, that the L. L. L. take over the work of the A. L. P. B. This, of course, would mean that the A. L. P. B. be moved to St. Louis and lose its identity. In view of the embryonic status of the present L. L. L. movement, the members of the A. L. P. B. committee felt it unwise to enter into any agreement with the L. L. L. on the matter of an amalgamation at this time.

One does not have to read too much between the lines to sense a reluctance to give up the independence of the ALPB for what seemed to be little gain. The board agreed to hold the matter in abeyance, but it wasn't seriously discussed further (though the LLL continued to express interest as late as June 1930).[18]

Another matter that came up again late in the decade was the need to hire a full-time field secretary who could do promotional work for the Bureau—and, it was hoped, thereby address the continuing financial issues. The effort was no more successful than it had been at the beginning of the decade. Several conversations with potential candidates were held and at least one call was extended, but to no avail; as the economy continued its downward spiral, the idea was quietly shelved.

The economic crisis takes hold

"crippled for lack of funds"

Despite the optimism expressed at the 1930 annual meeting, things soon took a turn for the worse. One sign of trouble was a rapidly declining subscription list for the *American Lutheran.* The printing run reported in November 1929 as 8,000 was reduced to 7,000, and then to 6,000, and then, by September 1930, to 4,000. Paid-up subscriptions had dropped by September 1930 from the previous high of over 7,000 to just 2,891. There was some fluctuation through the rest of the year, but the subscription list would never again match the numbers shown at the end of 1929.[19]

The financial issues were inhibiting other aspects of the Bureau's program. In October 1930, the Tract Committee reported "its activities were crippled for lack of funds." That same month a desperate-sounding action was taken: "In view of the emergency existing in the finances, the board authorized the President to appoint an Emergency Deficit Committee to raise funds locally and wherever possible, to tide the Bureau over."[20]

Only very spotty minutes have survived from December 1930 until the mid-1940s, so it is difficult to trace the details of how the ALPB weathered the depression. Clearly things were looking bleak. In August 1932, the *American Lutheran* announced an "ALPB Emergency Fund." "These are troublous times," the notice began, "but they are also times of opportunity. ... Our Lord will take care of this work, but He will use human agencies, interested Christians, to do it." Twenty-five percent of the funds raised from this appeal were designated for the publication of tracts, another twenty-five percent for the general fund, while half would be used to repay the bank loan that was keeping the agency afloat.[21]

But things continued to deteriorate. The low point came in 1933 with the closure of the bank in which the Bureau had its funds. Legal action was taken which resulted in funds being released so that the Bureau could continue operations. Meanwhile, a letter was sent to subscribers and other supporters warning that "the prevailing economic conditions had placed both the Bureau and the magazine into a precarious state." The aid came in a response, Lindemann wrote, that was "one of the most astonishing and heartening experiences of our life."

The letters were warm and decided, and sometimes very vigorous and emphatic to the effect that our work must not be permitted to die. Many sought to impress upon us that it was indispensable and that ways and means must be found to keep it operating. Fortunately these many assurances of moral support and approbation were in most cases backed up by contributions of the wherewithal to keep us alive. Some of them were sent at personal sacrifices which touched us to the quick. It looks now as though we would be enabled to weather the storm.

But keeping the ministry afloat financially continued to be a challenge throughout the depression years.[22]

The work continues

"still asking the same old questions"

Despite these challenges, the ALPB kept at least the rudiments of its ministry moving along. Tracts continued to be published, although not in quite as great a number. In 1932, the Bureau vacated its office at 69 Fifth Ave—a move, the board admitted frankly, that "was chiefly for the sake of economy. ... There was no choice. Our rental savings will total $600 a year." The office was relocated to 1819 Broadway, where it would remain for the next twenty years.[23]

The 1920s had seen the establishment of a Radio Committee, and it soon had its fingers in several pots. The Bureau cheered and commended the establishment of station KFUO in St. Louis. They encouraged the development of "The Lutheran Hour," which became the platform for Walter A. Maier, frequent speaker at ALPB's "Luther Day" and occasional contributor to the *American Lutheran*. Funded by the Lutheran Laymen's League, the program made its debut October 2, 1930. At the ALPB board meeting later that month, there was a "lengthy discussion of the board's reaction to the Lutheran Hour." The minutes do not give any hint as to the nature of that reaction, but the result was a resolution that the board "recommend to the Lutheran Hour Radio Committee of the Lutheran Laymen's League, that Dr. Walter A. Maier be continued as the radio speaker." They also advised that a small choir be trained to provide regular music on the broadcast.[24]

The Radio Committee encouraged the use of radio in local communities, especially the broadcasting of church services. "The Lutheran Hour" did not eliminate the usefulness of such work, they pointed out, since "people will always be interested in programs of their own city or town" and it will "always be good publicity if the people get to hear a local pastor." Such broadcasts, the committee urged, can often be arranged at "practically no cost."[25]

The ALPB itself also ventured into national broadcasting. To celebrate the 450th anniversary of Luther's birth, the Bureau sponsored a nationwide airing on the Columbia Network of an address by Lindemann entitled "Martin Luther and Our Modern Age." He argued that "Luther is a distinctly modern figure. His principles are not only adaptable but absolutely necessary to a happy life today." Humanity is "still asking the same old questions" and hearing "the same old unsatisfying answers." We must, as Luther proclaimed, return to the Word of God. The address was subsequently printed in full in the *American Lutheran*.[26]

The *American Lutheran*
"Any and all ideas are welcome"

The *American Lutheran* did not miss an issue through the 1930s, and its importance as the public voice of the Bureau continued to grow. For the most part Lindemann stuck to his guns about focusing on "practical church work," but the emphasis began to change somewhat. Some of this was due to changing conditions. For instance, in 1932 he noted that the language question seemed to have faded away, for which "we have reason to be grateful." But other issues were still on the agenda, particularly the Synod's home mission policy. The *American Lutheran* continued to push for changes, noting that if the Synod had developed "a far-seeing mission policy to run parallel with the intensive drive for [seminary] students and buildings, the present discrepancy between ministerial candidates and the fields to place them might not be nearly so acute."[27]

During these years, the *American Lutheran* began running some regular features which it came to call "departments." The first was a book review section—generally rather brief comments about a wide variety of religious books. In 1931, the already prolific contributor F. R. Webber began a feature entitled "Fine Arts in the Service of the Church." Lindemann described its purpose:

> We are in the midst of a significant period of artistic restoration. The fine arts, most valuable hand-maids of religion, were ejected from the Church by Calvinism, Puritanism and Rationalism. Churches became ugly, bare, forbidding. ... Even those sects that substituted the crude emotional outlet of the tent-meeting and the sawdust-trail, are returning today to better forms of expression. ... Lutherans and Anglicans never gave up entirely the old traditions. They kept well ahead of the procession. Now that other church bodies are overtaking us, what shall we do? Shall we stand still? Shall we let others pass us? Or shall we continue to keep ahead of the movement?

Webber discussed many different aspects of liturgy beyond just the fine arts; he also regularly answered questions submitted by readers.[28]

Another feature was called the "Service Department," begun 1933. Lindemann solicited "progressive ideas" from church leaders about "church ushering, treasurer's records, how to run a financial campaign, the outdoor and indoor bulletin boards,

Sunday School methods, samples of attractive printing, etc., etc. ... Any and all ideas are welcome." Suggestions poured in, and the Service Department published them. The magazine offered numerous other articles on an equally wide variety of "practical church work." It gave instructions on how to use a mimeograph machine and how to conduct a Vacation Bible School. It suggested how a pastor could effectively plan an annual planning meeting with newly elected congregational officers and committee chairs.[29]

Another *American Lutheran* department, begun in 1934, was "Lutheran News from All Over." It contained just what the name suggests: brief news items about the entire Lutheran communion—all the American Lutheran church bodies, as well as Lutheran churches in Europe and elsewhere. The ALPB was showing once again that its interest and concern went beyond the Missouri Synod.

Still another department was called "Bible Book of the Month Club." Each month a different Biblical book was featured, and a brief introduction, with some study questions and ideas, was offered. Club "members" were encouraged to spend 15 minutes each day reading portions of the book featured that month. The program began in 1935 and continued, usually monthly, until 1937, when Lindemann announced that the author (unidentified, but he was apparently Adolf Meyer) needed to discontinue the series "due to the pressure of other church work." Later, however, the series was completed and reprinted as a resource for congregational Bible classes.[30]

One of the most significant additions to the *American Lutheran* was Otto A. Geiseman's column "While It Is Day." Geiseman was pastor of Grace Lutheran Church in River Forest, IL; he was something of a "rising star" in the Synod, at 43 already a popular preacher and lecturer. His column began to run in November 1936 and would continue until his death in 1962. He was introduced to readers as one who "brings to his new task not only the background of broad erudition and sound scholarliness, but the practical experience of a successful pastorate." The column consisted of personal pastoral reflections on a wide range of issues—parochial, denominational, and social. Geiseman would be a key contributor to the *American Lutheran*, not just as a regular columnist but eventually as an influential member of the editorial board.[31]

Bigotry and prejudice

"the arrogant faces of rampant Jewry"

A darker aspect of the *American Lutheran* is troubling to later generations: an occasionally recurring anti-Catholic bigotry and a casual anti-Semitism. Neither prejudice was uncommon among American Protestants in that era; this does not excuse them, of course, and we can wish that ALPB leaders had been more enlightened, but they must be viewed in context and with the realization that attitudes would change dramatically over the coming decades.

The anti-Catholic bias showed itself in 1928 when Al Smith, the Roman Catholic governor of New York, was the Democratic presidential nominee. In the September issue, Lindemann suggested that Reformation Day was an opportunity for preachers to reaffirm the "Reformation principles as they apply to separation of Church and State." This election year, he argued, "the political situation ... presents a menace to the institutions on which the enjoyment of our precious liberties is predicated." Lutherans have always avoided political entanglements and have never made religion a test of political eligibility. Nonetheless, we have "the right and duty to inform our people of the facts ... in order that they may not be hoodwinked into a state of security over against a danger which is decidedly real."

> The mere mention of the possibility of a Roman Catholic as president of the United States has aroused the Lutherans all over the country. Today Rome has reached one of its long sought goals. It well behooves us to emphasize before our people those cardinal principles which came forth as a fruit of the Reformation. ... The statement need have no political flavor. It may be made dispassionately and objectively. But it ought to be made. ... To our mind a sound presentation of the subject 'Lutheranism and Americanism' at this year's Reformation Festival will be very timely. 'Eternal vigilance is the price of liberty.'

It would be overstating the case to say that this kind of bigotry was rampant in the pages of the *American Lutheran* or in other ALPB publications, and yet neither was it an isolated incident. Some of Walter A. Maier's Luther Day addresses, speeches which were sponsored by ALPB and sometimes printed and circulated after the event, contained anti-Catholic rhetoric. This attitude—again, not uncommon among Protestants of the era—would begin to fade with the presidential candidacy of John F. Kennedy in 1960; it finally vanished entirely in the wake of Vatican II.[32]

The anti-Semitism in the *American Lutheran* was more casual; it appeared in comments made by editor Lindemann when reporting on his annual visits to the New York offices of the Bureau. In 1930 he concluded his report by admitting that, while he enjoyed visiting the office, "the rather intimate physical contact with the human element that seems to turn New York into a modernized Jerusalem is not so pleasant." The next year he was even more blatant:

> Once every year the editor leaves his field of toil in beautiful Minnesota for his annual visit to the headquarters of the *American Lutheran* in the great and only New York, fortifying himself against the ordeal of metropolitan rush crowds with their ruthless haste, brutal assertiveness and variegated smells. ... Predominant in the seething multitude are, of course, the descendants of Abraham, eager and arrogant, engrossed in their chase after the elusive dollar. Judging by the female representatives of Israel the paint and cosmetic industry is not sharing in the prevalent business depression.

Lindemann expressed palpable relief when the ALPB headquarters was moved. In the new location, things were more amenable to the Minnesotan:

> Gone are the colorful surroundings of Fourteenth Street, the venders and peddlers and panhandlers, the lame, the halt and the blind, the unwashed representation of two score nations, the wild-eyed communists of Union Square, the arrogant faces of rampant Jewry.

It's hard to know how much of this was Lindemann's personal prejudice and how much reflected attitudes within the ALPB; it does not seem to have infected other materials or other articles in the magazine.[33]

Tension with Synod

"a movement of this kind must be polemical"

The *American Lutheran* had first taken on the liberal theology of Harry Emerson Fosdick in 1926, with Lindemann's editorial "The Lutheran Church and Pulpit Liberalism." As time went on, "modernism" became the most common term for the liberal theology movement, influenced by Shailer Mathews' 1926 defense, *The Faith of Modernism.* Mathews was dean of the University of Chicago Divinity School, and he may have attracted the attention of Lutherans when he described "Modernists" over against "Confessionalists." At any rate, many Lutherans were increasingly disturbed by the apparent success of the movement; they were realizing that, despite Lindemann's 1926 confidence that Lutherans had "remained comparatively free" from liberal theology, it was now becoming a serious threat because of its pervasive presence in the culture and particularly in the public media. Lindemann sounded the alarm:

> The modernistic tendencies in religion are a distinct menace to every local congregation and to its individual members. ... The contact with it on the part of our Lutheran people is simply unavoidable. As the intellectual standard among the clientele of our congregation[s] goes up, these points of contact are bound to increase. Modernism, under Satanic direction, has the faculty of employing every possible modern means of bringing its faith-destroying teachings to the attention of the people. The radio sends forth the philosophic conclusions of modernistic preachers into millions of conservative Christian homes. ... The Federal Council of Churches of Christ in America uses every possible publicity means to advertise its vaporings under the guise of religion. Even the secular magazines of our land are carrying almost regularly articles of a religious or semi-religious nature, and almost in every case the religious views presented are distinctly modernistic in character. ...

Modernism is, Lindemann wrote, "a present, local menace, affecting the lives of our people and the very life of our church."[34]

And so it was that in the October 1931 issue, the *American Lutheran* announced a new campaign:

> The Synodical Press Committee, using the machinery of the American Lutheran Publicity Bureau, proposes that our Lutheran Church fight the menace of modernism, not

by a merely defensive and protective attitude, but by an aggressive policy of vigorously proclaiming the saving gospel of Christ. ... In an aggressive campaign, which will last over a period of years, and which, we hope, will become the very life and habit of the Church, the Synodical Press committee proposes to contest modernism's claims upon the souls of men with the conquering weapon of the Word of God. ... The current season is no time for a dilly-dallying church. If ever, the Church must now mean business.[35]

The Press Committee, however, was hard to distinguish from the ALPB. At this time it was chaired by Fred Lindemann (who also chaired the ALPB's board of directors); the other members were J. F. E. Nickelsburg and the Rev. Erwin Kurth, pastor of the Church of Our Saviour in Brooklyn and an ALPB board member.

The announcement caused a stir in St. Louis. It was not that the Missouri Synod hierarchy supported modernism; far from it. But the Press Committee/ALPB had violated the Synod's protocols. They had acted on their own, without prior consultation with Synod officials (particularly the St. Louis faculty). They had overstepped their authority in calling for such a campaign; it should have been the Committee on Missionary Expansion that took up such a task. That group had begun an evangelism campaign entitled "The Call of the Hour," which had been favorably noted by Lindemann earlier that year. But there was concern in St. Louis that the initiative by the Press Committee/ALPB would interfere with or otherwise complicate the official evangelism campaign. Furthermore, there was no little unhappiness that the Press Committee had apparently enlisted the *American Lutheran* to serve as its vehicle, rather than one of the official publications of the Synod. To make matters worse, Paul Lindemann's editorials announcing the campaign had quoted some prominent Protestants about the dangers of modernism—but no Lutherans. The St. Louis faculty disliked a statement in Lindemann's editorial that the campaign should have "not so much in view the berating and denunciation and exposure of modernism's untenable claims, but rather an aggressive, persistent proclamation of the antidote of truth."[36]

Theodore Graebner wrote to Adolf Meyer expressing his concern over this whole situation, and there followed exchanges of letters between Graebner, Fred Lindemann, Paul Lindemann, and Lawrence "Lorry" Meyer, public relations director for the Synod. Fred Lindemann tried to put out the fire. The Press Committee, he said, had in fact contacted Pr. Streufert, chair of the "Call of the Hour" campaign, but had received no response. While admitting that the Press Committee had perhaps technically overstepped its bounds, he insisted that their intentions were good; their primary aim, he insisted, was to get material into the secular press opposing modernism—an endeavor that more clearly fell into their area of expertise.[37]

Lindemann defended the use of the *American Lutheran* as their vehicle, arguing that the topic needed more space than would be available in *Lutheran Witness*. He also defended the caution about possible "berating and denunciation":

When the project was first discussed fear was expressed that our pastors would spend all efforts on contradicting the claims of Modernism and the usual preaching of the Gospel would be neglected. There is of course the danger that one become too offensive, but a movement of this kind must be polemical. But we have tried to obviate both extremes, to prevent polemics at the expense of the Gospel preaching and the preaching of generalities and the hammering away at certain abstractions by insisting that we need not become UNDULY polemical. We must of course never become 'unduly' in anything.

Paul Lindemann, in a letter to Graebner (with a copy to Lorry Meyer), made the same point:

We proceeded from the supposition that the best Reformation Day sermon is one which does not drag the pope by the hair all over the premises, but which presents in an inoffensive way the glorious truths which Luther again uncovered to the world. Naturally, we are in favor of a vigorous attack against modernism.[38]

Lorry Meyer responded to Fred Lindemann with a conciliatory letter. "Let's admit that your committee perpetrated a 'boner' in not taking the Committee on Missionary Expansion into its confidence," he wrote. But they had no hard feelings, even after this "inauspicious start," and even though "as far as I am able to judge your 'movement' is not meeting with the unanimous approval of the clergy." The best solution at this point, he suggested, would be for the two committees to meet and attempt to "bring about a harmonious collaboration which would benefit the plans of both committees."[39]

It doesn't appear that such a meeting ever took place. The Press Committee did confer a few days later with President Pfotenhauer, who happened to be in New York, and Fred Lindemann reported to Lorry Meyer that "we were able to clear up a number of things." But he confessed that he was "at a loss just what to propose as a method of cooperation with your committee." He cited the distance between New York and St. Louis, as well as the time and money it would take for a joint meeting, as an impediment. He also insisted that the ALPB's mail was running strongly in favor of the campaign against modernism, though he acknowledged "there is a class which resents every suggestion which would imply work. But they dare not give that as a reason, so must look for another excuse."[40]

The controversy was something of a tempest in a teapot, and in fact, other than an occasional comment about modernism over the next few years, there wasn't much of a campaign after the initial blast. But the resentment over the incident set Lorry Meyer, an increasingly influential voice in St. Louis, on a path of suspicion toward the ALPB and the *American Lutheran*. While he would remain cordial in his personal dealings with ALPB personnel, he would work behind the scenes to oppose what he viewed as the Bureau's attempts to undermine the Synod's administration.

Notes

1. Report of the Business Manager, Annual Meeting of the American Lutheran Publicity Bureau, 13 Jan. 1930.
2. *LW* 45, no. 12 (15 June 1926), 203.
3. "The National Lutheran Publicity Week," *AL* 10, no. 1 (Jan. 1927), 1; Minutes, ALPB Board of Directors, 19 Sept. 1927.
4. Report of the Business Manager, ALPB Board of Directors, 16 Jan. 1928.
5. Oesch's letter to Lindemann does not seem to have survived; the quote is from a document apparently written by Oesch some time later. It is not clear whether here he is quoting from the letter itself, or simply reiterating his criticism. Office of the President, Behnken Administration, Box 4, Folder 38, Concordia Historical Institute (hereafter cited as Behnken Papers).
6. "A Word of Welcome," *AL* 12, no. 1 (Jan. 1929), 5.
7. Adolf Meyer, interview by Alan Graebner, transcript of tape recording, 28 Oct. 1962, in the possession of Dr. Graebner.
8. *Evening News* (Harrisburg, PA), 20 Apr. 1928, 21; A[dolf] F. M[eyer], "A Changeless Christ for a Changing World," *AL* 11, no. 5 (May 1928), 5; Meyer, "Autobiography," 11.
9. "A Slogan," *Northwestern Lutheran* 15, no. 9 (29 Apr. 1928), 131; "Our Slogan," *Northwestern Lutheran* 15, no. 13 (24 June 1928), 199.
10. Report of the Business Manager, ALPB Board of Directors, 13 Jan. 1930, ALPB Archives.
11. "The Future," *AL* 11, no. 1 (Jan. 1928), 1; Minutes, ALPB Board of Directors, 18 Nov. 1929.
12. Minutes, ALPB Annual Meeting, 13 Jan. 1930.
13. *AL* 13, no. 10 (Oct. 1930), 1.
14. *Pittsburgh Press*, 14 Oct. 1930, 5.
15. "A Great Loss," *AL* 11, no. 6 (June 1928), 4.
16. "Theodore Lamprecht Memorial Endowment Fund," n.d., ALPB Archives.
17. "A Duty Accepted," *AL* 11, no. 7 (July 1928), 5; Minutes, ALPB Board of Directors, 24 June 1928.
18. Minutes, ALPB Board of Directors, 18 Mar. 1929, 16 June 1930.
19. Minutes, ALPB Board of Directors, 15 Sept. 1930.
20. Minutes, ALPB board of Directors, 20 Oct. 1930.
21. "A.L.P.B. Emergency Fund," *AL* 15, no 8 (Aug. 1932), 10.
22. Meyer, "Autobiography," 14; "Weathering the Storm," *AL* 16, no. 11 (Nov. 1933), 4.
23. A. F. Bobzin, "The ALPB Moves On," *AL* 15, no. 10 (Oct. 1932), 9.
24. Minutes, ALPB Board of Directors, 20 Oct. 1930.
25. "The A.L.P.B. Radio Committee Report," *AL* 13, no. 10 (Oct. 1930), 10.
26. "Coast to Coast Broadcast," *AL*, 16, no. 12 (Dec. 1933), 6-8.
27. "Good-by Language Question?" *AL* 15, no. 7 (July 1932), 5; "Will It Come at Last?" *AL* 15, no. 6 (June 1932), 5-6.
28. *AL* 14, no. 8 (Aug. 1931), 17.
29. "Service Department," *AL* 16, no. 1 (Jan. 1933), 17.
30. "Shall We Continue the 'Bible Book of the Month' Club?" *AL* 21, no. 2 (Feb. 1938), 21; Meyer, "Autobiography," 15.
31. "Introducing O. A. Geiseman," *AL* 19, no. 10 (Oct. 1936), 3.
32. "The Reformation Festival This Year," *AL* 11, no. 9 (Sept. 1928), 5.
33. "Summer Experiences," *AL* 16, no. 9 (Sept. 1933), 6.
34. "The Greatest Menace to the Church," *AL* 14, no. 10 (Oct. 1931), 5-6.
35. Ibid., 6.
36. Ibid., 8.
37. Fred Lindemann to Lorry Meyer, 27 Oct. 1931, Lorry B. Meyer Papers, Box 42, Folder 3, Concordia Historical Institute (hereafter cited as Meyer Papers).
38. Paul Lindemann to Theodore Graebner, 29 Oct. 1931, Graebner Papers, Box 67, Folder 3.
39. Lorry Meyer to Fred Lindemann, 3 Nov. 1931, Meyer Papers, Box 42, Folder 3.
40. Fred Lindemann to Lorry Meyer, 12 Nov. 1931, Meyer Papers, Box 42, Folder 3.

Chapter 5

FACING TOMORROW

A s the economic depression deepened, the Missouri Synod, like most American institutions, was experiencing serious difficulty. The 1932 convention learned that the Synod was some $856,000 in debt. The Synod's board of directors took several actions to deal with the crisis. Salaries of synodical officials were cut by twenty-five percent, and a special synod-wide self-denial offering was authorized. The crisis fueled a sense that significant changes were required. For the ALPB, it confirmed a longstanding conviction that their church was dragging its feet in addressing the realities of the contemporary world.

"Today and tomorrow"
"I do not desire to be muzzled"
In 1934, in consultation with several colleagues, Paul Lindemann drafted a "Plan for the American Lutheran Covering the Issues from October, 1934, to May or June, 1935," which he submitted to the ALPB board for their information (and which clearly stated

"Not for Publication"). "There can be no doubt," he began, "that our Church is not measuring up to the needs of the day." Four years of depression have left the church "in a desperate condition, [yet] no corrective measures have been proposed except those of salary cutting and curtailment of work." The church "seems to be marking time, hoping for the return of conditions which never will return," with no clear understanding of "the defects from which we are suffering." Lindemann despaired of any "official action regarding constructive changes" and insisted that the only solution was "pressure from below." But the first need was "an intelligent survey of the whole modern situation," and he wanted the *American Lutheran* take up that cause.[1]

Lindemann proposed adding an 8-page supplement to the magazine for the next eight months, with articles on specific topics written by various authors. He hoped the board might find the funds to send the magazine to all pastors in the Synod for the stated period and make bulk quantities available to congregations for study by the laity. He also suggested that the magazine "agitate and inaugurate summer schools and retreats for pastors" over the next year, hoping to generate an "aroused interest and consecrated helpfulness" from the clergy. These retreats would be centered in worship and silent reflection; the program would focus on stewardship and the pastor's role as an "ambassador of Christ."[2]

Lindemann intended to begin by discussing the changes in society the church must address. He believed the focus of Lutheran work must shift away from its ethnic and rural preoccupation and address the "steady urban trend" and the "rapid industrialization" of the age. The church must understand that "our people are surrounded by countless diversions" such as "the auto, the movies, the radio, the repeal of prohibition," all of which "have given strong impetus to the increase of worldliness." The time available for leisure is increasing, and "the devil is bidding for this time. ... The [questioning] spirit is abroad in the land." And, of course, the economic crisis forces the church to address a vanishing middle class and rising unemployment.[3]

The editor then sketched out how the church should respond. Not surprisingly, the first strategy should be a radically revised home mission policy—one providing for more centralization of planning and funding and paying more attention to urban areas. He anticipated that this would result in the amalgamation of small rural parishes for the sake of efficiency. This reduction in parishes would require fewer clergy, so the educational program of the Synod should be revised "with an emphasis on quality rather than on quantity." This should be accompanied by "more stress on the training of lay leaders." But changes needed to impact congregations, as well as the Synod. There should be "a cultivation of the spirit of worship" and "stimulation of prayer life" on the local level. Congregations should be "laying claim to part of the leisure time" by developing their educational programs and by emphasizing their "missionary duty towards the community."[4]

We have no record of the discussion within the ALPB board of Lindemann's proposal; they apparently approved its general thrust, since the special series in the *American Lutheran* was published (though it did not begin until January 1935, three months later than Lindemann had proposed). But in St. Louis the proposed plan caused a firestorm. Somehow the "not for publication" document fell into the hands of Lorry Meyer. Already suspicious of the magazine's motives, he took it as a frontal attack on the administration of President Pfotenhauer (who, not insignificantly, was Meyer's uncle).

Meyer immediately contacted Geiseman, E. J. Friedrich, and perhaps others associated with the *American Lutheran* (though not Lindemann, at least not initially), trying to get a better handle on just what was happening. He and Geiseman agreed that a meeting between the ALPB group and synodical officials would be useful. They proposed bringing together Lindemann, Geiseman, Arthur Brunn, Rudolph Ressmeyer, and O. P. Kretzmann on the one side, and Concordia Seminary president L. E. Fuer-bringer, first vice president John W. Behnken, second vice president F. J. Lankenau, Synod board of directors member Paul Schulz, and perhaps President Pfotenhauer on the other (Meyer thought Pfotenhauer wouldn't attend, yet should be invited).

On October 8, Meyer wrote to Paul Schulz. He had met with Geiseman, he said, and discovered that "the whole thing has become very serious."

> I do believe that a meeting with this group is not only advisable but imperative unless we want to sit idly by and see something done which, I am sure, will cause untold, if not irreparable harm. There are developments in the case which even you, who have taken a very negative position, haven't even dreamed of. There is much more to it than merely high churchism. In fact, high churchism is not an issue but something much more dangerous than that, I fear.[5]

Geiseman and Friedrich both independently reported these developments to Lindemann, who was honestly perplexed—and disturbed—by the reactions in St. Louis:

> I am very sorry that Lorry is putting his finger into this pie. The way he is trying to shape the thing is putting us in the light of starting an opposition party. ... I hate to have our movement construed in this way. Lorry also told Prof. Friedrich that he and others were construing our movement as a direct attack against the president of Synod and an effort to make his re-election impossible. I don't see how the movement can be so construed. Personally I am endeavoring to put certain ideas across which will lead to definite and constructive action and am not in the least interested in aiming any shafts of attack at personalities. ... [The] kind of meeting that Lorry suggests looks as though the officials of Synod had to be summoned in order to quell a revolution.[6]

If such a meeting were to take place, Lindemann went on, he would be "unalterably opposed to having Schultz [*sic*] ... in the group." But he didn't see the point of a meeting. What would be the purpose? Is it "to try to persuade us to withdraw our plans? Is it to make us keep silent? You may be absolutely sure that the synodical officials will not come over to our side, and the only purpose ... could be to squelch any possible aggressive steps that we might take." "I have no personal axe to grind," he insisted, "and I haven't the slightest vestige of personal ambition, but I do not desire to be muzzled."[7]

Geiseman thought that Lindemann was overreacting. "Your pessimism," he wrote to his friend, "half frightens me to death." He thought Lorry Meyer might in fact be sympathetic, and he had sensed that several members of the board of directors were "fed up" with Pfotenhauer's unwillingness to take action. "I believe that Behnken, Lankenau and others are more our spiritual kin than their official position would indicate," he suggested, and such a meeting could only have good results—if for no other reason than that it would necessarily publicize the proposed *American Lutheran* series.[8]

Subsequent events suggest that Geiseman was too optimistic in thinking that Meyer, Lankenau and Behnken were sympathetic. In any case, Lindemann was not convinced. He wrote a long letter to Meyer, explaining that he had heard from Geiseman and Friedrich that Meyer had seen the plan and reacted badly. Lindemann tried to reassure him:

> This plan must inadvertently have gotten into your hands, although there was no element of secrecy attached to it. From the information which I have received from both Friedrich and Geiseman it looks as though you had an altogether warped idea of the situation.
>
> Your attitude seems to indicate that a fire has broken out in Synod and that the synodical fire department will have to be summoned to put out the blaze. You also seem to be under the impression that our campaign of education is a personal attack directed against officials of Synod. I don't see how you could possibly put such a construction on the plan as outlined. ...
>
> We have started no revolution. We have no political axes to grind. We are not in the least interested in personalities, and you ought to know by this time that I haven't in the slightest measure any official ambitions.
>
> What the American Lutheran wants to do is to analyze the present day situation and to present the changing conditions under which the Church of today is compelled to work. ... There will be no direct criticism of official procedure. There will be no stepping on official corns. But God knows that we need to wake up to the fact that we are living in a changing world and that the methods of bygone ages need to be abolished.

Lindemann reaffirmed his loyalty to the Synod; but "if anybody is afraid of a cold-blooded analysis, it is just too bad."[9]

Meyer sent a copy of Lindemann's letter to Schulz, who responded angrily that "any meeting with people who take this attitude is utterly hopeless. Until now, we might have said that their action was reprehensible, but Lindemann's ... letter makes it contemptible." Schulz's opinion was that President Pfotenhauer should address "these gentlemen" directly—and that Friedrich, "who is directly employed by Synod, should peremptorily be told to keep his hands out of this affair."[10]

A few days later Meyer responded to Lindemann's letter, protesting (disingenuously, it would be fair to say) that Lindemann had "greatly exaggerated" Meyer's concerns. "Naturally," he wrote, "I was interested in your plan, but I am not too much exercised over it" (compare his comment to Schulz about the potential for "irreparable harm"!). He reproved Lindemann for not having raised his concerns with synodical officials before planning a broadside in the *American Lutheran*. He accused Lindemann of having "thoroughly misinterpreted, and unjustly so, my interest in the movement." He had hoped the proposed meeting would be productive, but if Lindemann was opposed to it, he would drop the matter. Meyer sent a copy of the letter to Geiseman—and, apparently, a blind copy at least to Schulz.[11]

Geiseman responded to Meyer that both he and Kretzmann still thought a meeting would be helpful and that they would be in touch with Lindemann, who "has no doubt grown a bit weary of fighting something of a lone battle." But Meyer's concern was not assuaged by Geiseman's gentle response. He wrote to Schulz a few days later about what he called the "Lindemann debacle," reporting that he had discussed the whole matter with President Pfotenhauer, who shared Schulz's view.[12]

Meanwhile, Meyer had apparently forwarded Lindemann's plan to at least some other officers of the Synod. F. J. Lankenau wrote him on October 19, accusing Lindemann of being a "faultfinder" and criticizing the document at nearly every point, asserting that everything "good" in the document was already being done by the Synod. His contempt for Lindemann was clear:

> I heard that Paul Miller is also in with the movement. I was also told that he is pushing Paul Lindemann as THE MAN OF THE HOUR.—But as I told the brother that gave me this information, are these men that are criticising [*sic*] Synod's administration so severely showing such a great superiority over others in their work?

> Dear Lorry, I see breakers ahead. We need a safe man at the helm, or it may mean the wrecking of the ship; and I feel that the safest man we can possibly find at this crucial hour is the present captain of the ship.

He signed the letter "very sincerely and most confidentially." So Lankenau, at least, seems to have seen Lindemann's proposal as an effort to undermine the reelection of President Pfotenhauer at the next summer's convention—a view which, while an overreaction, would prove to be prescient as to the ultimate result of the *American Lutheran* series.[13]

Now Lindemann, in consultation with his associates, decided to take another tack. He wrote to the Synod officials who had been suggested for the now cancelled meeting and sent them a copy of the plan; he assumed that if they read it, "they will accord it their hearty approval and thus make the meeting proposed unnecessary." He assured them that they "had in mind nothing which might in any way jeopardize the peace and harmony of the Church" and intended "to conduct ... discussion along the most evangelical lines and without reference to personalities." He enclosed, in addition to the plan itself, a "list of editorials and subjects which we hope to treat and also an excerpt from the opening editorial." He then asked each recipient whether he "could be persuaded to write an article on any topic which might be related to the topics mentioned."[14]

Lindemann sent a copy of this letter to Meyer, with an apology that "our correspondence terminated as it did." He asked Meyer if he would be willing to contribute an article on the financial situation of the Synod to the proposed series. He listed the names of others who would be approached to contribute articles, names which he said "no doubt will quiet any misgivings regarding the character of our plan."[15]

Lankenau was one of those approached by Lindemann, and he promptly wrote to Meyer for advice. "How much am I supposed to know of the Plan Lindemann submitted to his board?" he asked. And "what do you think of the request that I write an article for the series?" The proposed articles seem reasonable enough if done "in the proper way, but many of them may set off charges of dynamite." Or "do I see too darkly?"[16]

Meyer immediately wrote back to warn against contributing any articles to the series, since they "might be misconstrued." He suggested to Lankenau that Lindemann's "original plan and the one outlined in his letter are not in harmony with one another"—strongly implying that Lindemann was misrepresenting his intentions in his request for an article from Lankenau. This was an unfair accusation, since the two documents had quite different purposes. The original plan had been a quite detailed "in house" proposal of the topics Lindemann hoped to address, while the summary sent to Lankenau (and several others) was mostly a list of proposed titles of articles. Nonetheless, Meyer took it as further evidence that Lindemann could not be trusted, and so his advice was clear: "To Dr. Lankenau I would say, if you do write, write guardedly; to my dear friend Lankenau I would say, don't write at all." Lankenau then sent a very diplomatic letter to Lindemann, pleading that he had too many "irons in the fire" to be able to contribute to the *American Lutheran*.[17]

Knowing that John W. Behnken had also received a letter from Lindemann soliciting an article, Meyer took it upon himself to write to Behnken, warning him against the request. He enclosed a copy of some of his previous correspondence with Lindemann because "you ought to know what has preceded so that you would be in a position to give him an intelligent answer." He clearly hinted that Behnken also ought to decline to contribute, and that is what he did. It may well be that Meyer offered similar warnings to others who had been asked by Lindemann to contribute the series. In the end, E. J. Friedrich was the only synodical official (he was then professor of homiletics at the seminary in St. Louis) who wrote an article.[18]

Despite the opposition from St. Louis, the planned series began to run in January 1935 under the title "Today and Tomorrow." Lindemann toned down the language a bit from his memo to the ALPB board, but he was still clear about the purpose of the series:

> There must be today on the part of the Church an earnest self-examination, both personal and organizational. There must be a pitiless analysis not along sentimental lines, but based upon cold scientific standards. Are we functioning up to our possibilities? If not, why not? If the influence of the Church is waning, why is it waning? ... If there is less response to our message than formerly, why this new unresponsiveness? ...

> The AMERICAN LUTHERAN wants to be helpful. ... Our campaign for the next six months is designed to be absolutely objective and is to be carried on in a soundly evangelical spirit. ... We want to throw open the columns of the AMERICAN LUTHERAN for a free discussion of our pressing problems. ... On one thing, however, we are all agreed; we all love Christ and want to further His cause.[19]

But it soon became clear that Lindemann's "evangelical spirit" had considerable impatience with what he saw as irrelevant issues that too often occupied the concern of Missouri Synod Lutherans. The very first piece after the opening editorial threw down the gauntlet:

> Let us stop dissipating time and energies in trivialities. Is it essential to know who wrote the Book of Joshua? Can I afford to expend my force in fulminations against a brother who takes his exercise at the Y. M. C. A.? Cannot I use my time to better advantage than in a critical analysis of the Boy Scout movement? Am I making a contribution in the battle that is raging when I write learned essays trying to find a violation of Scriptural principles in life insurance? ... Let us stop playing our own little hose on the bonfire in our own backyard and help put out the fire that is consuming the world.[20]

Over the next six months, the series "Today and Tomorrow" covered a remarkable range of topics. There were articles about home missions, the urban church, and the church's responsibility to youth. The series also tackled social problems; an article by Edgar Witte brought a stern rebuke from one reader, Julius Kretzmann, who insisted that such topics were not really the field of expertise of pastors. Even the language used, he complained, suggested that the writer's thoughts had been "partly assimilated, if not greatly appropriated, from the thinking, phraseology and philosophy of ... the so-called 'New Dealers' who are in almost dictatorial control of our present government."[21]

Other articles were more spiritual in nature, calling for renewal and a new focus on the means of grace and the care of souls. Herbert F. Lindemann, son of the editor, advocated the preaching of a gospel of sacrifice. The cross of Christ, he wrote, "means living a life that is a direct contradiction to everything our civilization stands for. It requires a return, strangely enough, to the ancient principles of Poverty, Chastity, and Obedience." With regard to poverty, the church must preach stewardship and "be more of a guide to the people's giving than she has." With regard to chastity, the church must "advise the world in the tones of the Baptist that men are bound to observe the only rule of morality that has any validity or purpose: that human bodies are meant to be temples of the Holy Ghost." She must do this even though "pagan indifference to sexual matters has made inroads into the Church." With regard to obedience, we must recognize that "the world today is suffering from the excesses of liberty, economic, sexual, and even religious. ... All this is thoroughly pagan and quite different from the idea of subjection to a God and service to fellowmen."[22]

As the series came to an end, Otto Pannkoke offered "An Attempt to Outline a Progressive Programme." He made several specific proposals about education, home missions, and church organization, and then called for spiritual renewal in the Synod:

> One of the most significant phenomena in our Synod today is the tense, nervous search for a new certainty. ...
>
> We have the renewed zeal for orthodoxy in its extremest, harshest form. It believes that the isolation from and condemnation of every other Lutheran is the road to win God's favor. We have the liturgical movement. We have the growing emphasis on Scripture reading which in sections borders on Bibliolatry. ...
>
> The road to freedom and victory lies in none of these directions. It lies solely and alone in placing into the very center of our Church's thought, life and work: the vital, living, dynamic, transforming experience of faith in the Christ of the Damascus Road, in the Christ of the monastery cell.

Such faith, he wrote, will transform every aspect of the church's life.[23]

The final installment of the series was in the June 1935 issue, and Lindemann led with an editorial looking forward to the convention in Cleveland. It was clear that he hoped for a change:

> The affairs of the kingdom of God are never unimportant, but the Cleveland convention falls in a period of seething social and economic turmoil and spiritual bankruptcy, of rapid and revolutionary changes in the mode and thought of life. The world in which the church must function differs from what it was even three years ago. ... Policies that were workable and effective even a decade ago do not seem to meet the exigencies of the present hour.

By the end of it, "Today and Tomorrow" had taken up some 80 pages of the *American Lutheran* over six months. Lindemann and his colleagues now waited to see what impact their "movement" might have on the Synod. Events that summer would indeed usher in significant changes, both for the Synod and for ALPB.[24]

Opposition

"An un-Lutheran spirit"

"Today and Tomorrow" got the immediate attention of many throughout the Synod. In March 1935, Geiseman made a trip to St. Louis; he reported to Lindemann that "all the boys down there seem to be reading the American Lutheran." He had spent an evening with Lorry Meyer, and he hoped that he had "persuaded him that it would be at least wise for him to keep his mouth shut and not to oppose our program if he cannot heartily approve it." Geiseman, always the optimist, continued to believe that "in the deepest depths of his own heart [Meyer] sees precisely what we see and feels exactly as we feel, but the old official complex makes him believe it to be necessary to rise in defense of the organization."[25]

He also reported that Theodore Graebner seemed to be "particularly well pleased with the missionary programs outlined in the March issue." Prof. Richard Caemmerer was "very enthusiastic about our program." He did offer one caution:

> The only real criticism which might have meaning to it that has come to my ears thus far has been ... that sometimes our language in the various articles has not always been as expressive of love as it might be but leaning in the direction of the caustic. This will, of course, be wise for us to try and avoid, for, after all, the more objective we can keep the matter and the more our articles are filled with the spirit of love, the better will they succeed in persuading others.[26]

But there were also harshly negative reactions to the series. In March 1935, the Synod's board of directors received a letter complaining about a "clubbing arrangement" that involved the *American Lutheran*, the *Walther League Messenger*, and *Lutheran Witness*. This agreement provided a joint subscription to the three magazines for a single price, an offer apparently aimed primarily at libraries. The writer of the letter, however, took it as synodical approval of the two unofficial publications. The minutes of the board of directors meeting recorded that "no action was taken, although several board members expressed their earnest disapproval of some of the articles in the 'American Lutheran,' which certainly do not represent the position of the Missouri Synod."[27]

But J. E. Seuel, manager of Concordia Publishing House, unilaterally decided to discontinue the joint subscription arrangement "in accordance with the position of the Board, as he understood it"—and furthermore, he told the two independent publications that CPH would no longer be able to purchase advertising in their pages. The *American Lutheran* editorial board protested, but the Synod board of directors "held that Mr. Seuel was right in his interpretation of the Board's attitude, since quite a few letters are received, objecting to articles in this publication and voicing their displeasure." The board agreed that the clubbing offer gave the impression that the *American Lutheran* and the *Walther League Messenger* were official synodical publications, and it formally resolved that the arrangement should be discontinued; it left the question of advertising, however, to the discretion of Concordia Publishing House.[28]

One of the most virulent protests came from an Illinois pastor, Alex Guebert, who sent a "Timely Warning and Admonition" to the officers and other leaders of the Synod, accusing the *American Lutheran*—and Lindemann in particular—of "an un-Lutheran spirit and dangerous tendencies ... which [call] for official action." The editorial board of the *American Lutheran* felt compelled to respond to this vehement attack. In a four-page letter to the same officials who had received Guebert's "Timely Warning," the board addressed the "charges so grave and so unjustified."

> We believe that the AMERICAN LUTHERAN has made and is making a worthy contribution to the life of our Church. It is sincerely seeking to further the interests of Christ's kingdom. It is an open forum for the expression of opinion and practical questions concerning the Church. Honest differences of opinion regarding the propositions it presents are natural, but it can hardly permit an attack on its Lutheranism and doctrinal orthodoxy to pass unnoticed and unrebuked. With honest and sincere hearts we enlist your continued support of the cause that we represent in order that the kingdom of Christ may prosper and the truth may prevail upon earth.[29]

Still another harsh response came from William M. Oesch, the pastor who had criticized the alleged unionism practiced in the European tour of 1927. Oesch had continued to read the *American Lutheran* closely, looking for further signs of unorthodoxy. By 1935, he had accepted a call to serve two congregations in London affiliated with the Missouri Synod, and in April of that year he wrote again to Lindemann: "Permit me to call your attention to the fact that both the February and March issues of the 'American Lutheran' contain evident approaches to false doctrine, if not directly false doctrine." He cited three specific articles. The first was an editorial by Lindemann which "does not clearly state that doctrinal controversies within the Lutheran Church in America should be relegated into the background, but it allows the reader to make this conclusion, and this, to my mind, is worse than frankly stating such a unionistic opinion."[30]

The second was Herbert Lindemann's essay on the traditional monastic values. In his advocacy for a re-appropriation of poverty, chastity and obedience to address "the new paganism," Oesch charged, Lindemann revealed himself as a "theological stripling who does not know the first thing about dividing Law and Gospel." "How can you publish such revolting stuff in your magazine?" he demanded.[31]

He took strongest issue, however, with Edgar Witte's "The Challenge of the Church and the Present Social Order." Despite the title, Witte's essay did not embrace the platform of the social gospel movement; indeed, he insisted that the "advocacy of specific reforms ... is not the church's business." But he also argued that the church's "task in this age [is] to resume her ancient role as a builder of sentiments, a creator of atmospheres, an architect of attitudes and an arbitrer [*sic*] of values."[32]

This, Oesch insisted, is not Lutheranism. "I have been observing with growing grief for years that you are heading more and more toward Cryptocalvinism," which he described as the effort "to influence people by moralistic measures and great comprehensive schemes." He then attacked other aspects of the *American Lutheran* through its history:

> Some of your publicity ideals were unsound; ... some of your sponsoring of liturgical reforms was precipitate and done without a real understanding of what is endangering the Church. ... This is not a wholesale condemnation of your Magazine. But the best features can never excuse one iota of false doctrine. A unionistic attitude was always evident to the keen observer in the News Columns of your Magazine and in the American Lutheran Tours.

He concluded with a stern admonition: "This Lenten time ought to remind you of what the Saviour did <u>for</u> us all and ought to cause you to sincerely repent of every guilt incurred through false and misleading statements and so change the tenor of your activities that such things cannot recur."[33]

Adolf Meyer responded quite graciously to Oesch's criticism, addressing his response to "Brother Oesch":

> I know that you have always been a friend of the AMERICAN LUTHERAN and the Publicity Bureau, and in that spirit of helping not only our organization but the Church at large you have written as you did. I am sincerely sorry that you were disturbed by certain articles which have appeared from time to time in our publication. May I only say this that our editorial policy is well defined along the established lines of Biblical Christianity emphasizing those things which we conscientiously feel make for the progress of Zion. ...
>
> I prayerfully trust that my letter will bring you to a closer realization of our aims, and that before you misjudge our message you will investigate its source and purpose.

But no such luck. Oesch wrote a scathing 8-page reply:

> If you think the well-meaning commonplace of your reply contribute [*sic*] anything to the debate you are mistaken. ... All the theologians who in course of Church History have ruined the orthodox church have invariably claimed they meant well and that they did not mean to depart from orthodox principles But they did, anyway.

The rest of the letter reiterated Oesch's criticisms and added several more. He assured Meyer that he was sending copies of his rant to the president of the Synod, all the vice presidents, and the entire St. Louis faculty.[34]

The ALPB and the *American Lutheran* also faced regular criticism from the Wisconsin Synod. John Brenner, one of the early editors of Wisconsin's *Northwestern Lutheran* and president of that synod from 1933 to 1953, had disparaged the whole idea of publicity for the church as early as 1925. "No one can object when a congregation in a proper manner announces its services in the newspaper," he wrote. "But it is a different thing when we practically force our invitation and our literature indiscriminately upon all the people of our community." As time went on, the Wisconsin Synod would become increasingly concerned that the *American Lutheran*'s positions on church fellowship and liturgical matters underscored what Wisconsin viewed as the doctrinal problems in the Missouri Synod that would ultimately lead to the breaking of fellowship between the two groups.[35]

The accusations against the *American Lutheran* would continue as conservative opposition to the Bureau festered; but what appeared to be a sea change in Synod leadership was about to complicate matters considerably.

1935 Convention

"there was very much electioneering or propaganda"

When the delegates gathered for the 1935 Missouri Synod convention in Cleveland, there was an undercurrent of support for change. The ALPB's *American Lutheran* had been among the most vocal advocates for new directions, though the magazine had refrained from criticizing any individuals. Still, from the point of view of many of the old guard, the magazine's articles were a key factor in preparing the field for what was about to happen.

President Pfotenhauer had been in office for 24 years. He was only the fifth man to hold the office in the Synod's nearly 90-year history, and he had served longer than any previous president. Born in Germany, he was still more comfortable in German than in English. He represented a strong connection to the Synod's history—he himself had sat at the feet of the great C.F.W. Walther. While it was generally expected that Pfotenhauer would be elected to yet another term, there was a movement afoot to choose instead John W. Behnken, first vice president of the Synod. Behnken was a Texan by birth, a former president of the Texas District and the long-time pastor of Holy Trinity Lutheran Church in Houston. English was his native tongue, and he had a reputation as a fine preacher and evangelist. Behnken would recount:

> As the 1935 convention approached, the members of my church council wanted to know whether there was anything to the rumor that I would be elected President. I assured them that it wouldn't happen, since I had been reliably informed on my visit to St. Louis that spring for the noonday services that synodical leaders had persuaded Dr. Pfotenhauer not to refuse reelection. With Dr. Pfotenhauer available, I informed the church council, the matter was settled as far as I was concerned.[36]

But it was not settled as far as some others were concerned. On the second morning of the convention, the first ballot for president was cast. President Pfotenhauer received 263 votes—just four short of the majority required for election. Behnken received 157; three others received a handful of votes (including Paul Lindemann, at 14). On the next ballot, Pfotenhauer received 253 and Behnken 206, with the other three remaining far behind. The third ballot brought a shock: Pfotenhauer and Behnken were virtually tied, 259 to 257. On the fourth ballot, Behnken pulled ahead, receiving an absolute majority and making him the new president of the Synod.

At this distance, it is impossible to reconstruct precisely what was happening here—and indeed, accounting for any election is always a matter of interpretation. It seems clear, however, that there was considerable "politicking" going on in the hallways of the convention. Behnken would later write, in a passage ultimately omitted from his autobiography:

> In all honesty, I must say that if I had known at the time of the Cleveland convention what I learned about five years later, I would not have accepted the Presidency. From a man, whose reliability I cannot doubt, I learned that there was very much electioneering or propaganda. This occurred in the lobby and had also taken place through the mails. It is hardly believable that anyone would resort to such political tactics and maneuverings, against or for a candidate, in church elections. But it happened. ... May God graciously preserve our Synod from practices which would make a political football out of our elections. Where this is done the church body is on slippery paths, and these lead downward.[37]

Did ALPB personnel play a role in the alleged electioneering in Cleveland? Again, after more than seven decades it is impossible to know. The "Today and Tomorrow" series in the *American Lutheran* had certainly encouraged those who thought it was time for a change in the administration of the Synod. Behnken, though never associated with ALPB, was thought to be sympathetic to many of the concerns and goals for which the *American Lutheran* had argued. Many of those associated with the Pfotenhauer administration took the magazine's criticisms quite personally, believing that the magazine's staff was deliberately seeking to undermine the president. On the other hand, there appears to be no archival evidence (despite the existence of considerable correspondence by ALPB principals) for Bureau involvement in the kind of electioneering described by Behnken.

Controversy continues

"the fear ... which has been so prominent in our Synodical life"

Hoping that the new administration might be more sympathetic to the *American Lutheran*, Paul Lindemann wrote to the Synod board of directors, asking them to rescind the earlier decision about the clubbing arrangement with *Lutheran Witness* and *Walther League Messenger*, and he then met in person with the board that summer. The board informed him that they had received several letters of protest about the *American Lutheran* and that "in the judgment of members of the Board itself a number of articles and expressions in the magazine were of such a nature that they did not reflect the position of our Synod in doctrine and practice." The minutes suggest a rather robust discussion:

> The Board made due allowance for the fact that the editor is a very busy man and also so far removed from the place of publication that a careful supervision of all articles is rendered rather difficult. Nevertheless, the fact remains that the magazine, especially since it is sent out with the 'Witness,' is looked upon by many as an official paper of Synod and should therefore be most careful in avoiding any appearance of deviating from our synodical policies. Pastor Lindemann repeatedly declared that he would personally censor all articles before they are published. It was therefore <u>resolved</u>, in the face of these assurances of Pastor Lindemann, that the execution of the resolution of the Board, to discontinue the clubbing arrangement, be suspended.[38]

Theodore Graebner, as editor of *Lutheran Witness*, also got into the act (though apparently not publicly). Prior to the board meeting, he had written to E. J. Gallmeyer, a lay member of the board of directors, with what he called "very plain talk":

> Concordia Publishing House makes a club arrangement with W. L. Messenger and Amer. Luth. They never asked me, and when the club arrangement was declared void, last spring, they did not ask me. Now, as editor of the Witness I am reminded of a solemn duty that I have to help settle this matter. ...
>
> The American Lutheran has had articles that I would not write nor subscribe to. Knowing that this is an imperfect world, I refused to go into a seizure about it. I even continue to write for the paper. Others complained and accused P.L. [Paul Lindemann] of false doctrine. It is mentioned at a meeting of the Board of Directors. Acting on the fear complex which has been so prominent in our Synodical life, they pronounced adverse opinion on the club arrangement and C.P.H. ads. Really, the matter did not concern them any more than the price of bananas in Mexico or the age of consent in Thibet [*sic*]. What happened? Mr. Seuel takes the hint and cuts off friendly relation [*sic*] with the American Lutheran. To top it off, a Chicago Conference demands that the declaration be made that it was for doctrinal reasons that the American Lutheran has been disavowed. ...
>
> I don't want to see the new administration saddled with the wrecks that were left by the old. Furthermore, I don't want the Board of Directors to continue to busy itself with affairs that do not concern it. The doctrinal errors of the American Lutheran belong before the presidium, not before the Board of Directors. ...
>
> Now, however sensible the above may read to you, do not be surprised when heavy guns will be lined up to make this Board suffer for the sins of the fathers.[39]

Graebner was right about the "heavy guns." In October, Synod board member Albert H. Ahlbrand complained that, despite Lindemann's assurances, another offensive article had appeared in the *American Lutheran*. President Behnken, attempting to calm the troubled waters, reported that he had personally been in touch with *American*

Lutheran representatives in New York and had been assured that "they would be careful in their editorial policy."[40]

But protests continued. Guebert's conference in Northern Illinois wrote to Behnken, Concordia Publishing House, and the seminary president, formally complaining about the clubbing arrangement. Behnken reported to the Synod board of directors that he had spoken personally with Guebert, reiterating that Paul Lindemann had assured him he would "avoid further offence." Apparently the board then followed Graebner's advice and washed their hands of the controversy; the clubbing arrangement continued.[41]

Several weeks after the election upset, Lorry Meyer submitted a rather defensive article to the *American Lutheran*. "Much that has been written about our remissness in missionary activities in the various papers circulating throughout Synod is only too true," he acknowledged. "But the cure for our present tendency towards mission stagnation is not regimentation, nor mechanization, nor centralization, but *spiritualization*." Meyer acknowledged that the Synod's leadership, being human, had likely made mistakes; both the board of directors and the various executive staff would freely admit this.

> But it is also true that the members of the Board of Directors are keenly alive to the overwhelming issues and realities forced upon the Church by an upheaval in the economic, social, and political world. Their hours of wrestling with God in prayer for wisdom and guidance are not published in big bold headlines. And even though a conservative Board in these days of change does not always follow the lead of a more daring school of thought, who knoweth whether such conservative leaders have not been sent to the Kingdom for such a time as this.[42]

As for the new administration, Behnken at first seemed willing to give the *American Lutheran* the benefit of the doubt, but he soon realized that controversy about the magazine was not going to go away and he was going to need to be very careful. Adolf Meyer wrote to the president within a few months of his election, inviting him to contribute regular articles to the *American Lutheran*. Behnken ignored him at first, but Meyer was persistent; at last in October 1936 Behnken responded that his "letters regarding proposed articles in the American Lutheran were duly received." He politely declined, and his refusal sheds significant light on how the magazine was perceived among the leaders of the Synod. While he told Meyer he wasn't averse to his request, "you are fully aware of the opposition which the American Lutheran has had to experience." He cited the accusations by Oesch and others, the protests from the Synodical Conference, and the controversy over the clubbing arrangement. "All of these things will convince you that the American Lutheran is now under closer observation than ever before."

> All of these things make me hesitate. I am asking myself seriously whether it would be wise (not whether it would be right) to be a regular contributor to such a 'free-lance' paper, when it is very evident that some are taking serious objection to it. I am not arguing whether they would be justified in their objections. That's another matter. ...

Now I have spoken very frankly. I plead with you to regard this as confidential. I feel that absolutely no harm is done, and no one will be offended, since they do not know it, if I postpone such contributions for the American Lutheran until some later date. I realize full well that you have the interests of the Kingdom, and of our dear Missouri Synod, at heart, and I believe that because of this you will understand my negative answer all the better.

Of course, "some later date" never came.[43]

A few months later, Behnken offered a gentle rebuke to the ALPB. The Bureau had sent a mailing to subscribers over the signature of J. F. E. Nickelsburg, urging them to renew their Bureau membership and *American Lutheran* subscription. The sheet featured a photo of Behnken, with a reprint of a piece he had written for the *Lutheran Witness* in which he advocated aggressive evangelism—using "all legitimate means to testify for Christ." Behnken's reference was not specifically to the ALPB, but it seemed in line with what the Bureau had long advocated.

The mailer fell into the hands of Lorry Meyer, who thought it inappropriate. He passed it on to Behnken with a note: "I think this is using the picture (which, by the way, I think is not so good, I like your other one much better) and the name of the President of our Synod 'in vain.'" Behnken immediately wrote to Nickelsburg:

> Just by chance I got hold of a letter ... in which you request prompt renewal of membership and magazine subscriptions.
>
> I am very sorry to note that you have displayed my picture as you did. You are well aware that I am in full accord with your purpose of 'dignified publicity, wide distribution of tracts, the placing of Lutheran publications into libraries and reading rooms, and the sponsoring of a National Lutheran Publicity Week,' but I doubt the wisdom of displaying the picture of the president of Synod on such an appeal for membership. I feel that it will receive much unfavorable comment and fear that it may serve as a boomerang for your cause rather than to serve the purpose which you intended to serve.
>
> Of course the thing is done now and cannot be changed. However, I felt that I should write you in very straightforward manner about it, for I believe that that is what you want, and again, I believe that you will understand.

Perhaps to mitigate his rebuke, Behnken enclosed a small contribution to the Free Tract Fund, along with his "kindest personal greetings."[44]

Liturgical renewal

"the liturgy did not get half a chance"

The *American Lutheran*'s interest in liturgical matters did not begin with F. R. Webber's "Fine Arts in the Service of the Church" column. From the very first years of publication, Lindemann had made the case for "church decorum"—a rubric under which he criticized a good many things about the liturgical life of Lutherans:

> The church may be dirty, the furniture in bad repair, the carpet torn, the organ out of tune, the hymn-books ragged, the windows filthy. Services start at any old hour, deacons and ushers are late; the pastor rushes about in last minute attention to details; there is loud conversation and laughter in the vestibule and even in the pews; the singing is weak and draggy. ... The liturgy itself is in its rendition often a thing of horror. Not infrequently it is atrociously played by the organist and murdered vocally by the congregation. ... All in all, the beauty of the service has not been enhanced by the liturgy because the liturgy did not get half a chance.

Most of the magazine's early articles on worship reflected the magazine's committed purpose of addressing "practical church work."[45]

In the 1930s, however, the *American Lutheran*'s interest in worship developed into a larger vision of liturgical renewal. Perhaps this reflected the "liturgical movement" that was taking root in many churches during the mid-20th century. Jeffrey Zetto has suggested that Paul Lindemann's interest in liturgy may have increased when he was elected first vice president of the English District in 1930, giving him more opportunities to worship in other congregations than is usually possible for a parish pastor. But others were also raising the banner for liturgical renewal; Theodore Graebner, for example, referred in 1935 to the Synod's "liturgical chaos."[46]

In 1925, a group of east coast pastors led by Berthold von Schenk, then pastor of St. John the Baptist Lutheran Church in Hoboken, NJ, founded the Liturgical Society of St. James. St. John the Baptist was a declining congregation in what von Schenk would call a "near-slum area" with an average attendance of fewer than a half-dozen. Von Schenk had sought this call with the specific intent of attempting to revitalize it in accord with his own vision of liturgical renewal. He was installed in January 1925 and within a year had banded together with a handful of colleagues to form the Society. The group flew under the radar for a few years, but in 1933 it sponsored a conference at von Schenk's congregation, attended by perhaps 20 pastors. One of the attendees was F. R. Webber.

This was apparently the first direct contact that Webber had with the Society, though he had no doubt heard of the group; von Schenk had come onto the ALPB board in 1929, and Webber knew him at least by reputation. Webber wrote an extended report in his column in the *American Lutheran* in June 1933 which suggested something of the liturgical ferment that was taking place in Lutheranism.

> For several years we have noted a widespread interest in liturgical matters. Letters have come from men in every part of the country, not only of our own Synod, but from men of various Synods. They have expressed a lively interest in liturgics. In a number of cases they have spoken of certain improvements that have been made.

... Along with this has come a liturgical awakening. Men have come to realize that we have a rich liturgical heritage, and that we have not been using it in the past as fully as we might.

Webber was cautious in describing the conference—no doubt aware that there was, in many quarters of the Synod, a visceral dislike of anything "high church":

> Pastor von Schenk and his congregation are careful not to conduct a form of service that is merely an imitation of the Roman Catholics or the Anglo-Catholic branch of the Church of England. Pastor von Schenk, and the other pastors who are associated with him in the Society of St. James, have done exhaustive work in order to discover just what is really old Lutheran tradition. They lay stress upon the principle that any such service must be built only upon a conservatively Lutheran basis. ... Nothing is done merely because it is 'nice' or 'pretty.' It must be based upon early Lutheran tradition, and it must have a meaning.

But Webber was clearly impressed by what he saw. He noted that von Schenk's congregation had experienced a remarkable turnaround, now numbering over 300 communicants. They "report 2,200 communions per year, exceeding in this respect, every other congregation in Synod insofar as we can ascertain."[47]

That last statistic reflected the fact that von Schenk had instituted the weekly celebration of the Eucharist as part of his renewal program. There were many planks in the platform of the Lutheran liturgical movement, but the centrality of the Eucharist was at its heart. This was expressed the next year at the second liturgical conference of the Society, when von Schenk offered "a brief explanation of our main objective":

> It is our main objective to *foster the Liturgical Life*. The liturgical life is nourished through the prayers of the Church and its divinely appointed means of grace. ... The neglect of the Holy Eucharist in the life of the average parish is certainly pitiful and tragic, to say the least. There are large churches in which the Sacrament is celebrated only once a month. In some of our churches it is the custom of the minister to dismiss the congregation after the sermon, before the preface, before the sanctus, before the great moment when the very words of Jesus are spoken, before the faithful kneel to receive the precious body and blood of the sacrificed Saviour. ... It is not unusual to-day that two-thirds of the assembled congregation leave before the Communion.[48]

Webber's account of the 1933 conference vigorously defended the concept of *adiaphora*—the conviction that specific matters of liturgical usage are ultimately "things indifferent," and that the Lutheran confessions "permit liberty in these things." Nevertheless, a "true Lutheran ought ... to work toward a better way, so that all things be done decently and in order."[49]

Not all writers in the *American Lutheran* were sympathetic with liturgical renewal. Edgar F. Witte, for example, accused the liturgical reformers of being like Nero fiddling while Rome burned. They are, he wrote, "the exemplification of those who busy themselves with inconsequentials and infinitesimals when the world is tumbling down about their ears." Lutherans have "no need for ... the props and costumes of ancient priests."[50]

Editor Paul Lindemann took a more moderate position. In a 1934 editorial, he took note of the increasing interest in liturgy across denominational lines. He applauded those giving attention to liturgical studies, insisting they "should not be discouraged and hampered in their work by the half-baked judgments and deprecating opinions that are based either on ignorance or prejudice." Lutheranism's liturgical heritage has been allowed to "fall into disuse and to be replaced by ecclesiastical crudities and vulgarities and by insipid sentimentalities borrowed from the hip, hip, hurrah meeting house 'services' of the American sects." Lindemann was a cautious reformer, however, and he warned advocates of liturgical reform to avoid "excesses and extravagances that will from the outset prejudice their case and ... nullify all possibilities of beneficial influence." Still, he committed the *American Lutheran* to the discussion of liturgical renewal.[51]

This did not always proceed as he hoped, and the next year he admitted the conversation had sometimes been "acrimonious." The *American Lutheran*, he said, has "tried to avoid taking sides" and has opened its pages to writers of varying opinions. "But the proponents of both extremes have accused us of being favorable to the other side" and "the demand has been insistent that the *American Lutheran* declare its sentiments editorially."[52]

Lindemann prefaced his remarks by noting that he wrote as a pastor, not a liturgical expert—but a pastor who has long worn cassock and surplice, had a vested choir, and used the Common Service, complete with chants. The *American Lutheran,* he wrote, is "wholeheartedly out of sympathy with the cynical and oftentimes ribald and wholesale condemnation of the liturgical movement," and yet it is also "out of sympathy with the precipitate introduction of liturgical practices that are bound to arouse the resentment and antagonism of the people."[53]

Lindemann's chief concern was that "liturgical extremists" were undercutting the importance of preaching. He was convinced that "the appreciation and veneration for the blessed Sacrament is at a shamefully low ebb in our circles and that nothing must be left undone to reestablish its blessed value in the hearts of our people. But we are disquieted by the pomp and ceremony" that goes along with it in some congregations. "Can we not avoid both extremes?"

> Well, there is our position. Are we liturgical-minded or not? Honestly we do not know. The reader will probably judge us according to his personal predilections. This we do know, however, that the cause of Jesus Christ must be preeminent in the thinking and striving of all of us. ... Personal likes and dislikes must be submerged if they threaten to divert us from our prime objective.

So Lindemann's view can best be described as moderate sympathy with many aspects of the liturgical movement, a resistance to what he saw as "excesses," and a commitment to "reestablishing [the Eucharist's] blessed value in the hearts of our people."[54]

Striving for frequent communion

"every opportunity to commune"

Genuine liturgical renewal, of course, is not about "pomp and ceremony," but finds its center in a renewed love for the Sacrament; as the liturgical movement matured, it focused increasingly on weekly celebration and frequent reception of communion. This was not a practice entirely without precedent in the Missouri Synod; the 19th century professor of liturgics Friedrich Lochner had advocated Holy Communion as the "chief service" each Sunday, and the respected and influential early 20th century theologian Franz Pieper had commented that "the more or less frequent use of the Lord's Supper [is] one of the thermometers of the spiritual life of a congregation."[55]

The ALPB had actually been ahead of the curve on this issue. A tract published in 1920, apparently written by Pr. J. N. H. Jahn and one of the Bureau's most frequently requested resources, was entitled "This Do! How Often?" It quoted Luther's insistence in the introduction to the Small Catechism that a Christian will "seek or desire the Lord's Supper at least some four times a year." But it noted that even receiving four times a year was "the exception rather than the rule" in the Synod. It outlined a series of reasons why some Christians resist coming to the Lord's Table, and answered each objection. While the tract didn't quite advocate more frequent celebrations of the Eucharist, it was clear on more frequent reception:

> A Christian will not and cannot be satisfied with appearing at the Lord's Table once or twice, or even four times a year. Knowing himself a sinner, striving after holiness, meeting with opposition having tasted of the sweet grace offered him in the Sacrament, he will do as he does in regard to hearing of the Word: **Avail himself of every opportunity to commune.** [emphasis in the original]

Of course, the observation that "even four times a year" is insufficient is a *de facto* argument for offering the Sacrament more often than quarterly.[56]

But actual practice in the parishes of the Synod was quite different, and the *American Lutheran* began to call for change. It began with Fred Lindemann's two-part essay entitled "At the Lord's Table." He began with a statistical observation: when one compares the number of communicant members with the number of reported communions, it appears that in 1935 the average Missouri Synod Lutheran communed only 2.18 times. "How far we have drifted from what our Lord had in mind when He instituted [the] Supper on the night before His death! The figures reveal an appalling spiritual coldness." He suggested that the Synod's preoccupation with teaching doctrine had led it to neglect practice.[57]

Lindemann argued that one reason for the "coldness" was another practical issue—that of the general practice within the Synod of the pastor not communing himself. Thus most pastors themselves received the Eucharist only at pastoral conferences or conventions. "Can pastors who commune only rarely speak persuasively and convincingly of the necessity of frequent communion? Should isolation from other pastors keep them from enjoying the blessing?" There may be other reasons, he wrote, but they are all only symptoms of "one and only one failing. At bottom lies the incontrovertible fact that Holy Communion does not occupy the place in our religious life which the Lord plainly intended." Lindemann spoke of his own experience:

> The writer had a very happy youth. ... But he is inclined to grow bitter when he thinks back upon his earlier communion experiences. The question of worthiness was the one string harped upon constantly. At least it seemed so to him. Yes, the Body and the Blood were received as a seal of forgiveness, but only by the worthy. Are you worthy? What the Lord intended to be the happiest moments of the Christian's life became an occasion for fear and torture of conscience to be postponed until the 'This do!' compelled compliance at intervals. ... The full joy of Holy Communion came only with the realization of doing it in remembrance of the Saviour.

The only way to increase frequency of reception, Lindemann concluded, was "if a heartfelt desire and joyous anticipation can be created in the hearts of men and women." The Lord clearly "wanted His disciples to do this often and in all circumstances."[58]

Lindemann was the most persistent writer on the topic of communion frequency, but the whole editorial board was in general agreement. A 1941 editorial noted that the Federal Council of Churches had begun a campaign for "World-Wide Communion." The literature for the campaign, the writer noted, said "not one word ... concerning the Real Presence of Christ or of the fact that in and with the reception of the bread and wine we have the true Body and Blood of Christ, and with it the sure forgiveness of sins." Still, the editorial appreciated the fact that these memorialists "have come to a realization of the necessity of frequent Communion for a live church experience." It does, the editor went on, cause one to ponder why Lutherans, who "believe that in our celebration of the Holy Sacrament we have something very precious and sacred," have not shown such "zeal and fervor in pushing our Communion as those who for so many years have esteemed the Holy Eucharist but lightly."[59]

But it was Fred Lindemann whose passion was the centrality of the Eucharist, and he began to advocate a weekly celebration. His first public statement came in a book of communion sermons he published in 1937 entitled *In Remembrance of Me*. The addresses were published by Lutheran Press, an independent company closely aligned with the ALPB; it had printed many items for the ALPB, and would shortly be taken over by the Bureau. Lindemann was criticized for his advocacy of what seemed a strange notion to many Lutherans, and he took to the pages of the *American Lutheran* in 1938 to defend his position. He began by remarking that many had thanked him for his presentation, but some (always "men not in the active ministry") had accused him of "legalism" and "extremism."

> The sentence which seemed to cause grave shaking of heads did not appear in the *American Lutheran*. It was unearthed from a volume of 140 pages and reads: 'If we are sincere in our appreciation of the Sacrament, we must strive toward the ideal that every member commune every week.' A single sentence may be eliminated from a manuscript by running a line through it. But if a single sentence is instrumental in bringing the real issue before us, there is reason for rejoicing that it was not eliminated.

No one thinks it "extreme," Lindemann mused, when a pastor suggests that people ought to come to church every week, though weekly church attendance has no more Biblical warrant than weekly reception of the Eucharist. As for "legalism," many misquote Luther to suggest that a real Christian will receive quarterly, but any such standard is "legalistic," whether the standard be weekly, quarterly, or annually. The real issue for Lindemann was that Christians need the blessing of the Sacrament. [60]

"Why not face the issue squarely?" he asked the next month. "That the Church has operated largely with nickels and dimes for centuries is no argument for the continuation of the arrangement." Yet he was adamant that simply increasing the number of celebrations was not the answer; rather "our purpose must be to elevate the Sacrament again to that place in the lives of our Christians which the Lord intended for it."

> We must begin by preaching so, that Holy Communion becomes to our people the loftiest, sweetest, happiest experience of their lives, as the personal application of the Gospel proclaimed and applied generally in the sermon. Then they will come of their own accord and demand that we pastors administer the Sacrament more frequently.

He concluded by relating the experience of an unnamed church (no doubt his own congregation, Trinity Lutheran in Long Island City, NY) as it moved over the course of some years from offering the Eucharist every other month to a weekly celebration, with nearly all members communing each week. "Today the only people who leave after the sermon are visitors from other Lutheran churches," he wrote, "usually from the Middle West."[61]

Notes

1. Paul Lindemann, "Plan for the American Lutheran Covering the Issues from October, 1934, to May or June, 1935." Meyer Papers, Box 1, Folder 1.
2. Ibid. Lindemann would expand on this theme in his book *Ambassadors for Christ* (St. Louis: Concordia Publishing House, 1935).
3. Ibid.
4. Ibid.

5. Lawrence Meyer to Paul Schulz, 8 Oct.1934. Meyer Papers, Box 1, Folder 1.

6. Paul Lindemann to O. A. Geiseman, 8 Oct. 1934, O. A. Geiseman Papers, Box 8, Folder 5, Concordia Historical Institute (hereafter cited as Geiseman Papers).

7. Ibid.

8. O. A. Geiseman to Paul Lindeman, 10 Oct. 1934, Geiseman Papers, Box 8, Folder 5.

9. Paul Lindemann to Lawrence Meyer, 8 Oct. 1934, Geiseman Papers, Box 8, Folder 5.

10. Paul Schulz to Lawrence Meyer, 12 Oct. 1934, Meyer Papers, Box 1, Folder 1. Friedrich was at this time professor of homiletics at Concordia Seminary; his precise association with the *American Lutheran* is unclear, though he would later serve on its editorial board.

11. Lawrence Meyer to Paul Lindemann, 11 Oct. 1934, Meyer Papers, Box 1, Folder 1.

12. O. A. Geiseman to Lawrence Meyer, 12 Oct. 1934, Meyer Papers, Box 1, Folder 1; Lawrence Meyer to Paul Schulz, 15 Oct. 1934, Meyer Papers, Box 1, Folder 1.

13. F. J. Lankenau to L. Meyer, 19 Oct. 1934, Meyer Papers, Box 1, Folder 1.

14. Paul Lindemann to F. J. Lankenau, 30 Oct. 1934, Meyer Papers, Box 1, Folder 1. While this is the only letter in the file, it appears that substantially the same letter was sent to Behnken, Fuerbringer and Schulz.

15. Paul Lindemann to Lawrence Meyer, 30 Oct. 1934, Meyer Papers, Box 1, Folder 1.

16. F. J. Lankenau to Lawrence Meyer, 1 Nov. 1, 1934, Meyer Papers, Box 1, Folder 1.

17. Lawrence Meyer to F. J. Lankenau, 5 Nov. 1934, and F. J. Lankenau to Paul Lindemann, 10 Nov. 1934, Meyer Papers, Box 1, Folder 1.

18. Lawrence Meyer to John W. Behnken, 2 Nov. 1934, Meyer Papers, Box 1, Folder 1.

19. "Today and Tomorrow," *AL* 18, no. 1 (Jan. 1935), 2-3.

20. Ibid., 4.

21. Julius C. Kretzmann "Another Letter," *AL* 18, no. 4 (Apr. 1935), 12.

22. Herbert Lindemann, "Some Old Virtues for the New Paganism," *AL* 18, no. 2 (Feb. 1935), 13-14.

23. O. H. Pannkoke, "An Attempt to Outline a Progressive Programme," *AL* 18, no. 6 (June 1935), 10.

24. "The Cleveland Convention," *AL* 18, no. 6 (June 1935), 3.

25. O.A. Geiseman to Paul Lindemann, 26 Mar. 1935, Geiseman Papers, Box 8, Folder 5.

26. Ibid.

27. Minutes, Synod Board of Directors, Item 350318-K, 18 Mar. 1935, CHI.

28. Minutes, Synod Board of Directors, Item 350516-A, 16 May 1935, CHI.

29. "To the Officers and Visitors of Synod," 10 June 1935, Geiseman Papers, Box 8, Folder 5.

30. William Oesch to Paul Lindemann, 11 Apr. 1935, Behnken Papers, Box 4, Folder 38.

31. Ibid.

32. Edgar R. Witte, "The Challenge to the Church in the Present Social Order," *AL* 18, no. 3 (Mar. 1935), 15.

33. William M. Oesch to Paul Lindemann, 11 Apr. 1935, Behnken Papers, Box 4, Folder 38.

34. Adolf F. Meyer to William M. Oesch, 24 June 1935, William M. Oesch to Adolf Meyer, 26 Dec. 1935, Behnken Papers, Box 4, Folder 38.

35. "The Radio Church," *Northwestern Lutheran* 9 (Jan 8, 1922), 8; cited by Mark Braun, "John W. O. Brenner," *WELS Historical Institute Journal* 27, no. 1 (April 2009), 31.

36. John W. Behnken, *This I Recall* (St. Louis: Concordia Publishing House, 1964), 47.

37. John W. Behnkan, "First Draft" of *This I Recall* quoted in John C. Wohlrabe, Jr., "The Missouri Synod's Unity Attempts during the Pfotenhauer Presidency, 1911-1935." Master of Sacred Theology thesis, Concordia Seminary, St. Louis, 1982. Wohlrabe indicated that this "first draft" was at that time in the possession of William J. Schmelder.

38. Minutes, Synod Board of Directors, Item 350826-W, 26-29 August 1935, CHI.

39. Thedore Graebner to E. J. Gallmeyer, 12 August 1935, Graebner Papers, Box 67, Folder 5.

40. Minutes, Synod Board of Directors, Item 351030-RR, 29-30 Oct. 1935, CHI.

41. Minutes, Synod Board of Directors, Item 351217-EE, 17 Dec. 1935, CHI.

42. Lawrence Meyer, "Whither Away," *AL*, 18, no. 11 (Nov. 1935), 12.

43. John W. Behnken to Adolf Meyer, 1 Oct. 1936, Behnken Papers, Box 4, Folder 38.

44. John W. Behnken to J. F. E. Nickelsburg, 18 Dec. 1936, Behnken Papers, Box 4, Folder 38.

45. "Church Decorum," *AL*, 10, no.3 (Mar. 1927), 2.

46. Jeffrey Zetto, "Aspects of Liturgical Theology in the Liturgical Movement in the Lutheran Church—Missouri Synod, 1930-1960," (ThD diss., Christ Seminary—Seminex, 1982); Theodore Graebner, "Our Liturgical Chaos" in *The Problem of Lutheran Union and Other Essays* (St. Louis: Concordia Publishing House, 1935), 135-166.

47. F. R. Webber, "A Liturgical Conference," *AL* 16, no. 6 (June 1933), 9-10.

48. Berthold von Schenk, "The Task of the St. James Society," *Pro Ecclesia Lutherana* 2, no. 1 (1934), 5.

49. Webber, 10.

50. Edgar F. Witte, "Nero Fiddles," *AL* 17, no. 5 (May 1934), 8.

51. "Liturgical Forms," *AL* 17, no. 2 (Feb. 1934), 4.

52. "The Liturgical Question," *AL* 18, no. 11 (Nov. 1935), 6.

53. Ibid., 7.

54. Ibid.

55. Quoted in Zetto. Zetto's dissertation is the most complete study of the mid-20th century liturgical movement in the LCMS.

56. "This Do! How Often? A Communion Tract," ALPB, ca. 1920.

57. Fred H. Lindemann, "At the Lord's Table," *AL* 19, no. 9 (Sept. 1936), 7.

58. Fred H. Lindemann, "At the Lord's Table—II" *AL* 19, no. 10 (Oct. 1936), 10.

59. "World-Wide Communion," *AL* 24, no. 3 (Mar. 1941), 4.

60. Fred H. Lindemann, "What Is Extreme and Legalistic?" *AL* 21, no. 10 (Oct. 1938), 9-10.

61. Fred H. Lindemann, "Evangelical Striving for Frequent Communion," *AL* 21, no. 11 (Nov. 1938), 10-11.

Chapter 6

A Moment of Crisis

W hen Paul Lindemann was elected president of the LCMS's English District in 1936, he was already dealing with serious health issues. A 1934 surgery had apparently been successful, but it was now impossible for him to make the trip from St. Paul to New York for the annual editorial staff meeting, so Adolf Meyer traveled to St. Paul instead. In 1937, the staff meeting had to be cancelled when Lindemann required another surgery for a "very pronounced duodenal deformity." Through much of 1937 and 1938, Lindemann was unable to contribute much to the *American Lutheran*, and Meyer took on increasing responsibility. Still, Lindemann's death on December 12, 1938, came as a shock to all those who had admired his ministry in its many facets.[1]

Lindemann's legacy
"We could ill afford to lose him"

Lindemann's funeral was the occasion of an unfortunate incident which, in the words of Jack Treon Robinson, "made a deep and lasting wound in the hearts and minds" of Lindemann's friends and colleagues in the ALPB. Lindemann's widow and their son, Herbert Lindemann, asked O. P. Kretzmann to preach the funeral sermon. When they learned that several Missouri Synod officials, including President Behnken, would be present, they invited Behnken and Martin Walker, vice president of the English District and one of the founders of the ALPB, to make brief addresses after the funeral. The problem arose with the arrival of Dr. Michael Reu, a personal friend of Lindemann's and a professor at the American Lutheran Church's Wartburg Seminary. Herbert Lindemann invited Reu to speak as well. When Behnken heard of this, he protested; for synod officials to speak at the same service with the ALC professor would, in his view, constitute unionism. Robinson related what happened next:

> On the morning of the funeral about ten prominent clergymen of the Missouri Synod, including Dr. Behnken, gathered in the living room of the home of the deceased and discussed, debated, and finally argued over the prospects of Dr. Reu speaking at the funeral. After the space of about two hours, Herbert Lindemann and his mother decided that the dispute had gone far enough. They announced that if Dr. Reu did not speak then no one would offer a special address after the service. Dr. Behnken would not capitulate and the funeral service ended without anyone making a special address.

The hard feelings left by this incident may well have been a factor in the *American Lutheran*'s increasing passion for inter-Lutheran fellowship.[2]

The January 1939 issue of the *American Lutheran* announced Lindemann's death. It led with two editorials he had written prior to his death. One celebrated the 25th anniversary of the ALPB, rejoicing that many things the Bureau had advocated "have become common practice," then adding prophetically that the ALPB would celebrate its anniversary "[consecrating] itself to new endeavors in the great task of holding aloft the light of Christ's cross in the ever deepening darkness of this world."[3]

The rest of the issue was devoted to tributes to Lindemann. ALPB president A. F. Bobzin set the tone:

> Great as the loss sustained by the American Lutheran Publicity Bureau, the Church's loss is greater. For Pastor Paul Lindemann was a man singularly endowed with a Kingdom vision. Combining a childlike trust in Jesus, his Savior, with a deep fervency to proclaim the love of his Savior, he lived and preached and taught and wrote this Gospel of Salvation. ... We believe that he was chosen of God to do a particular work and endowed of God with necessary equipment.[4]

O. A. Geiseman, in a "While It Is Day" column twice its usual length, offered an expansive eulogy:

> [Lindemann] was the beloved pastor and eloquent preacher of a large and widely-scattered metropolitan congregation composed of heterogeneous groups gained by years of painstaking missionary labors. He was the cheering friend, the ready helper of the lowly and needy. He was the widely applauded editor of the *American Lutheran*, the very person with whom this publication and the American Lutheran Publicity

Bureau had become identified as with no other. He was the popular leader of the English District of the Missouri Synod who knew how to employ the able talents and energies of his official associates by soliciting their whole-hearted co-operation and by planning with them for the advancement of Christ's cause. He was the respected counselor in pastoral conferences and Synodical gatherings. None enjoyed the love and regard of other Lutheran bodies more fully than he did. ... [He] was a man after God's own heart. He was a pillar of strength in the Church because he was a sound theologian who stood foursquare on the Word of God.

Geiseman praised his friend's editorial courage:

He had no desire to fill official positions or serve on important committees. ... This very attitude gave him a freedom of thought and speech which not only enabled but actually impelled him to express his views frankly and fearlessly. He never stopped to worry how this might affect him personally. He never tried to be subtle or ambiguous. He spoke and wrote in a forthright manner. ... Sometimes this made him the object of vehement criticism. ... When he advocated new methods of Church work gauged to modern needs, [his opponents] suspected it as a manifestation of modern liberalism. When he criticized the functionings of his Church, they wrote it down as an evidence of disloyalty. When he counseled love in relationship to Christians in other bodies, they feared doctrinal indifferentism. He was well aware of this, but so long as it was not true he was content that his judges should bear the responsibility and blissfully went about his tasks undeterred by opposition or suspicion.[5]

There were also quotations from 20 years of Lindemann's editorials, along with tributes from an array of pastors and other church leaders. An excerpt from Kretzmann's funeral sermon was included, as well as a biographical sketch of Lindemann. Perhaps the most succinct epitaph came from Theodore Graebner: "He was a rare combination of high courage and aggressiveness with gentleness and humility. With our lack of insight into God's plans we say that we could ill afford to lose him."[6]

Facing the future

"That cause is bigger than any of its servants"

Lindemann's death was a moment of crisis for the American Lutheran Publicity Bureau. Since the Bureau's founding he had been a key figure, and for most of that quarter century he was the voice of the ALPB through the pages of the *American Lutheran*. When an emergency meeting of the board of directors convened to discuss how to proceed, Fred Lindemann argued that the *American Lutheran* was so closely identified with his brother that the magazine should now be discontinued. Adolf Meyer and others disagreed, arguing that Lindemann himself would want the *American Lutheran* to live on and that it was a vital part of the ALPB's ministry. In the end this view carried the day. "We are sobered by the sense of heavy loss," Meyer wrote in the next issue. "But

Paul Lindemann was only an instrument in the hands of God. He served a cause. That cause is bigger than any of its servants."[7]

Perhaps to respect Fred Lindemann's feelings, the ALPB board decided not to name a new editor. Instead, they appointed an editorial board consisting of Meyer, Lindemann, Geiseman, Arthur Brunn, O. P. Kretzmann, and George Koenig, with Meyer as "managing editor" (a title he had held for some years, but which also meant he would be the *de facto* chair of the editorial board). All members of this board would contribute editorials, and the whole group would review and approve all editorials; they would be published unsigned, and so would express the official position of the *American Lutheran*. Contributions from others would be welcomed, but if published they would not necessarily reflect the opinion of the magazine. "There are many practical questions on which even sincere followers of the Lord do not see eye to eye," Meyer wrote. "There should be a place in our great Church where such differences can be aired"—provided only that "the material offered helps the cause for which the AMERICAN LUTHERAN stands."[8]

In the February 1939 issue Meyer introduced the new editorial board. Arthur Brunn had been on the ALPB board of directors for many years, Meyer wrote, and he is "an experienced and widely respected churchman with knowledge of synodical problems and frequent opportunities of inter-synodical church contacts." While Meyer didn't mention it, Brunn was also president of the Synod's Atlantic District. O. A. Geiseman, already a regular contributor to the *American Lutheran*, "is known for his fearless honesty and respected for the courage of his convictions. Lutherans of various synodical bodies will rejoice in his willingness to serve in directing the policies of the AMERICAN LUTHERAN." George Koenig was the first managing editor of the magazine, and so has "been in close touch with the editorial problems of our official organ from the beginning." O. P. Kretzmann is "so well known that we hesitate to comment upon his exceptional abilities." Executive director of the International Walther League and editor of *The Cresset*, he will "contribute that spiritual note ... which every religious magazine welcomes." Finally, Fred Lindemann is indeed "a real Lindemann" with a particular heart for "young pastors in the field. ... [He] will be widely read and loved in the pages of the AMERICAN LUTHERAN." In addition to the editorial board members, Meyer assured readers that F. R. Webber would continue to edit the "Fine Arts Department" with complete editorial latitude "even where the editors do not share his viewpoint."[9]

It was an illustrious group, though quite a collection of strong personalities and not always an easy bunch to coordinate. Meyer would later recall Kretzmann's remark: "Ade, I sympathize with you in having to ride these 'bucking broncos' every month. When I receive [my copy], I say under my breath—'The <u>American Lutheran</u>—The monthly Miracle.'"[10]

The new editorial board met almost immediately. Geiseman was not present, but Meyer wrote him with the details of their meeting. Geiseman applauded the direction the ALPB was taking with the magazine, but he raised one caution:

> I believe that before any one individual is made responsible for the perpetuation of the American Lutheran its finances should be brought into better shape. Lindy had become so accustomed to thinking of it as a struggling sheet and was more than surprised each morning when he awoke and discovered that it had not as yet breathed its last. This was because he had grown up with it from scratch, and, therefore, never came to realize what an important function it was playing in the life of the church. He saw its empty treasuries and its precarious existence. A definite effort ought to be made by either an editorial board or by representatives of The American Lutheran Publicity Bureau to put the American Lutheran on a sound financial basis.[11]

Geiseman's regular column had provoked discussion at the initial editorial meeting. Some felt that separating Geiseman's contribution from those of the other editorial writers might "be placing [his] editorial material in a secondary and inferior position." Geiseman, however, was not concerned about that.

> It is honestly my opinion that we ought not discontinue the column. ... My contacts with quite a few pastors of the Ohio Synod when I spoke at Columbus; or the Iowa Synod when I spoke at Dubuque; and of our own group as I met them on my western trip last summer have given me reason to believe that many of the men read the 'While It Is Day' column. I think the heading is a very good one and since we have just begun to establish something of a following for it, it would seem to me to be rather unwise to throw it in the ash can at this time.

Geiseman's comment indicates that the *American Lutheran* had by this time developed a significant readership beyond the Missouri Synod. Meyer responded that continuing the column in its present form was perfectly fine with him, and the rest of the editorial board readily agreed.[12]

The state of Christendom

"Protestantism today is shaken"

The spirit of Paul Lindemann continued to find expression in the magazine over the next several months. Meyer immediately announced "a most important series" by O. P. Kretzmann on "The State of Visible Christendom." Kretzmann introduced the series by referring to the late editor's "profound insight into the problems of Christendom in the first half of the twentieth century."

> It was the custom of Paul Lindemann to talk freely and often with younger men who came to visit him. Especially during the last five years of his life a small group gathered more or less regularly to discuss the problems of the Church with him. At

these meetings he said very little, but when he spoke it was impossible not to feel the tremendous power of a unified philosophy of life and an integrated view of the work of the Church. ... From these conferences this series of articles has grown. ... If there is any good in them, it shall be a memorial to our sainted editor.[13]

Kretzman outlined the tremendous political, social and cultural changes that had taken place in the world during the past century. He spoke particularly of the rise of totalitarianism, and argued that the church must "protest against the persecution of all minorities. ... Today it may be the Jew. Tomorrow it may be the Lutheran." He cautioned that Christians must beware of being swept away by easy solutions, for social problems are always rooted in the human heart.

> We recently heard a churchman say that the removal of a dozen men from the world-scene would promptly put an end to the world's difficulties. Like most simple solutions of the problems of man, that is wrong. The men who now occupy the center of the world stage are almost as completely and helplessly pawns in the grip of dark forces beyond their understanding and control than the most bewildered worker who suddenly finds himself unwanted in the world's labor market. ...

The task before the church is indeed daunting:

> It is impossible to deny that the world in 1939, politically, socially, and culturally, presents a picture of almost unrelieved darkness. Man's vaulting ambitions have again ended in dust and ashes. Science and education have left him helpless and alone. Once more man faces the inevitable blank wall at the end of his mistakes.

But "the more subtle the approach of sin becomes, the more the moral sensitivity of the Church must be sharpened."[14]

Kretzmann then discussed the state of the church as it faces these challenges. He outlined the rise and fall of modernism, which he saw as rooted in the teaching of Schleiermacher. This had been a serious problem for the Protestant churches, but now seems to be on the decline. Yet Protestantism "has come upon a time of judgment and waiting. It is puzzled and bewildered," and this has "brought about a tremendous revival of interest in the doctrine of the Church."[15]

It is unfortunate, he admitted, that in America this interest "so often expresses itself in movements toward immediate, external, organizational union. Protestantism has not yet learned the distinction between the visible and invisible Church." But fortunately, there is now a vision of unity and catholicity which is leading toward "a desire for the agreement in doctrine and practice," a hopeful and positive sign. While "Protestantism today is shaken, thoughtful, sobered, waiting," it may yet again in our time make a valuable contribution to Christian thought and life."[16]

Reading this series, one is struck with the clarity with which Kretzmann saw the challenges and realities of his day, and the prescience of his analysis and predictions. It is significant that his perspective, by his own admission, reflected years of conversation with Paul Lindemann and others in his circle. This group included, in addition to Kretzmann, O. A. Geiseman, Henry F. Wind, Fred Lindemann, Herbert Lindemann, A. B. Kretzmann, E. B. Glabe, B. H. Hemmeter, and W. E. Hohenstein—several of whom were also closely involved with ALPB in one way or another. They continued to meet after Paul Lindemann's death. Their discussions had originally begun, according to Geiseman, with an investigation of what Scripture actually teaches about unionism, particularly the question of whether the Synod's teaching was in fact Biblical. This had led to a wider conversation about the doctrine of the Church. They were not content simply to accept the views they had been taught; in 1940, for instance, they invited ALC theologian Michael Reu to meet with them for a day of discussion on the subject "What Is the Church?" They were developing a point of view that was rather foreign to the conservative Missouri Synod, but one which would undergird the work and the priorities of the *American Lutheran* and the ALPB in the decades to come.[17]

Celebrating an anniversary

"we enter upon the new era with grateful hearts"

Lindemann's death had coincided with the 25th anniversary of the ALPB, and the issue after the January memorial was filled with historical reminiscences. An editorial, presumably by Meyer, wondered whether the time and money expended by the Bureau over a quarter-century had brought about any benefit. "Has it reached any worthwhile objectives? Is it nearer the goals set twenty-five years ago?" To answer the question, he perused the files. He recalled the days "when F. C. Lang or Theodore Lamprecht covered the deficit" of the *American Lutheran* so that the magazine could keep going. But he found many goals had been accomplished. Methods originally advocated by the Bureau "are employed quite generally today." Furthermore, the "Lutheran Church is known better and more favorably." The Bureau's encouragement of congregational newsletters has led to "a most gratifying increase in the number of parish papers, many of them excellent as to content and appearance." The economic crisis of the 1930s "brought a decided shrinkage"; but the Bureau then "urged the use of the mimeograph, which has become a permanent and indispensable fixture in the church office." And, of course, the tract ministry has had a tremendous impact. Tens of millions have brought the gospel to "boys in the trenches, ... the sick and dying in the hospitals, the forsaken and hopeless and despondent, men and women far from God. ... How much light and comfort and saving knowledge our tracts must have brought."[18]

Meyer cited the contribution of F. R. Webber to the improvement of "the architectural [and] ecclesiastical atmosphere" of Lutheran churches. He noted the usefulness of the *American Lutheran* as a "clearing house" for ideas about practical church work.

He remembered the Bureau's role in advocating for an improved home mission policy. "Any number of proposals which were adopted by the Synod appeared in our magazine years before." In sum, yes, the Bureau's ministry—and especially the *American Lutheran*—has had a substantial impact.

> The *American Lutheran* is the only church paper which lends itself to the free discussion of theories and ideas. ... This service was made possible by the magazine's refusal to be intimidated by opposition. It insisted on a man's right to say what he had to say, and if it was worth hearing it insisted on the magazine's right to print it, even if the editor did not agree with the opinions expressed. And how opinions did change! ... Some who were violent opponents and believed the *American Lutheran* to be an evil influence have become its staunchest friends and supporters. They were big enough to tell us frankly when they disagreed and therefore big enough to admit that the magazine had won their confidence and that they had changed their minds.

> So we enter upon the new era with grateful hearts that our Lord permitted the Bureau to render service to His Church. Our prayer is that He would breathe upon the smoldering fire of our devotion and fan it into the flaming heat of earlier days.[19]

The anniversary was also the occasion for a special ALPB fundraising appeal entitled "Forward Again!" The publicity for the $5,000 campaign particularly stressed the importance of the *American Lutheran*'s role as "an 'open forum' to the Lutheran public." The Bureau promised to continue its "vital, progressive, and far-reaching policies." It solicited memberships ranging from "Regular" at two dollars to "Benefactor" at $100, with a note that all memberships include a subscription to the *American Lutheran*.[20]

Another anniversary year project of the Bureau was the development of a "Lutheran presence" at the 1939/1940 New York World's Fair. The fair featured a "Temple of Religion," intended as a kind of testimony to religion as "a fundamental need of modern civilization," emphasizing "a spirit of tolerance and freedom for all religious views" and promoting "the freedom of religion as the foundation of all freedom." Various religious groups took turns offering presentations at the Temple of Religion. Lutheran Day was sponsored in part by ALPB, offering "a program of outstanding speakers and musical talent similar to the Lutheran Day observance held annually in the metropolitan area" and featuring their old regulars, Walter A. Maier as speaker and Edward Rechlin at the organ. The event drew some 7,000, "the largest religious assembly the World's Fair has seen."[21]

The ALPB's J. F. E. Nickelsburg also chaired the "Lutheran Fair Bureau," with offices adjoining those of ALPB at 1819 Broadway. This program kept a list of Lutheran families in the New York area who were willing to host visiting Lutherans in their homes. ALPB friends were cordially invited, when they visited the World's Fair, to stop by the offices of the Bureau "with its displays of tracts, publicity materials, and other interesting helps for church members."[22]

The Bureau's work at the fair did not go unrecognized; the October 1940 issue of the *American Lutheran* featured on its cover a photograph of the bronze plaque noting a "Special Award of Merit" presented to the ALPB by the World Fair's directors. "Of religious groups in the nation," the magazine crowed, "the American Lutheran Publicity Bureau alone received the Bronze Plaque of Merit for being first in its class!"[23]

Longing for Lutheran unity

"the time has come for some plain speech"

Since 1872, the Missouri Synod had been in fellowship with the other members of the Synodical Conference. This body's membership had fluctuated over the years, but by 1920 it had stabilized and now consisted of the Missouri Synod, the Wisconsin Synod, the Norwegian Synod (later to be known as the Evangelical Lutheran Synod), and the Slovak Evangelical Lutheran Church. These were all groups based in the Midwest, conservative in their theology, and insistent that the only acceptable basis for any fellowship (including joint prayer and cooperative work) was complete agreement in doctrine and confession.

But the Missouri Synod, by far the largest of these groups, had grown more open to discussion with other Lutherans, and some other synods—particularly the conservative German heritage synods of Ohio, Iowa and Buffalo—had made recurring attempts to establish fellowship with Missouri. Some promising conversations during the 1920s between Buffalo, Ohio, Iowa, Missouri and Wisconsin had collapsed in 1929, but one result was the drafting of "A Brief Statement of the Doctrinal Position of the Missouri Synod," approved by the 1932 Synod convention as the basis for future doctrinal discussions.

The Ohio, Iowa and Buffalo synods had united in 1930 to form the American Lutheran Church (ALC). The new body was eager to continue discussions with the Missouri Synod, and conversations proceeded on the basis of "A Brief Statement." By 1938, agreement had nearly been reached; the ALC members of the negotiating committee accepted "A Brief Statement" but then offered the so-called "Sandusky Declaration," intended as a clarification of certain matters. If Missouri could accept these statements, then "the American Lutheran Church stands ready officially to declare itself in doctrinal agreement with the honorable Synod of Missouri and to enter into pulpit and altar fellowship with it."[24]

The 1938 Missouri Synod convention had responded cautiously, thanking God "for the guidance of the Holy Spirit by which the points of agreement have been reached" but emphasizing that "under the most favorable circumstances much time and effort may be required before any union may be reached." The convention authorized continued discussion, leaving the next formal steps somewhat open-ended: "If, by the grace of God, fellowship can be established, this fact is to be announced by the President of Synod. Until then no action is to be taken by any of our pastors or congregations which would overlook the fact that we are not yet united."[25]

Adolf Meyer attended that convention as a delegate, and he reported his reaction in the *American Lutheran*:

> The loyal members of our Missouri Synod who are also friends of true Lutheran union were cheered by the conservative report of our committee in presenting the matter of possible closer affiliation with the American Lutheran Church. ... In walking among the delegates before and after sessions, we were impressed by the impatience of the laymen who were anxious to cast their ballot in favor of the resolution as it was finally adopted. ...

The magazine took the same position in September, in an editorial probably written by the ailing Lindemann, as it "hailed with sincere joy and deep gratitude to God the great news that [the Synod] has unanimously adopted the report of the Committee on Lutheran Union ... looking towards the elimination of doctrinal differences and eventual fellowship and union [with the ALC]." Yet the editorial was realistic:

> We may be certain that the devil is opposed to any movement which may bring health and strength to the Church of Christ and that he will make serious attempts to frustrate the plans that look toward a more unified campaign of the forces of light against the powers of darkness. He may call into his services the premature and ill-advised actions of thoughtless enthusiasts on both sides, or he may utilize the fears and prejudices of those who have come to accept strife and division as the normal status of the Church and regard all pacific moves with suspicion. ... We shall have to do much earnest praying during the next few years that God may foster and bless the project of Lutheran unity ...[26]

Earnest praying, but also earnest advocating. ALPB personnel had always been more committed to Lutheran unity than some others in the Synod. In part this can be attributed to the fact that the center of gravity of the ALPB's ministry was in New York, where there was generally a greater willingness to step across synodical lines when it seemed salutary to do so. The ALPB, while clearly rooted in the Missouri Synod, had frequently reached out to other Lutherans over the years.

Now the Synod itself, after decades of discussion with the groups recently united in the American Lutheran Church, seemed to be taking at least baby steps toward that body. Lindemann emphasized the care with which these steps had been taken. He insisted that in the convention's action "there was no tendency to ignore or minimize or gloss over existing differences." No, the opening toward the ALC was made "only after the most careful and thoroughgoing deliberation upon all the doctrinal points at issue." Lindemann affirmed that "expediency must never replace principle," but also that progress must not be hampered by "traditional predilections and inherited prejudices."

This action of Synod "may easily prove to be one of the momentous movements in modern Lutheran church history," and in the view of the *American Lutheran*, this was "a great step forward."[27]

After Lindemann's death, the *American Lutheran* offered an ever-increasing stream of editorials and articles advocating cooperation and discussion with other Lutherans. In February 1939, the magazine acknowledged that "only complete agreement concerning the full counsel of God for the salvation of man can form a lasting and God-pleasing basis for eventual [Lutheran] unity." But how is that agreement to come about? The 1938 convention had urged "free conferences" between LCMS and ALC pastors around the country; the *American Lutheran* now urged that such conferences include laity as well as clergy and be widely publicized so that the laity of the church are kept informed.[28]

The next month an editorial called attention to a recent statement by the Augustana Synod's Conrad Bergendoff, who objected to what he described as Missouri's "method of attaining fellowship which consists in one party offering a document [e.g., "A Brief Statement"] to the other to be signed on the dotted line." The editorial agreed with Bergendoff, arguing that "no one in the Missouri Synod should insist that ... discussion must begin on the basis of a statement already formulated by the Missouri Synod or one of its leaders."[29]

O. A. Geiseman joined the fray two months later, counseling understanding and compassion for other Lutherans rather than condemnation and criticism. The Missouri Synod's history, he wrote, has given it a unique ability to "preserve a strong and sound doctrinal position." But it must avoid arrogance and self-righteousness:

> Let us be ready to confess that we have only too often failed to show a proper understanding of the difficulties under which others have labored ... and that even in our own work the actual practise [*sic*] has not been uniformly good in all of our individual parishes. If we are ready to confess our failures and to meet others in that humble spirit, they recognizing their difficulties and shortcomings may be all the more ready to confess on their part. ... We promise ourselves much more blessed results from such an approach to unity than from one in which the bitterness of one's attitude and suspicion is made a measure of one's orthodoxy and depth of Christian sincerity.[30]

The most shocking and unanticipated contribution came in Theodore Graebner's 1939 article "Lutheran Union: A Plea for Sanity and Clarity." As editor of the *Lutheran Witness* and a professor at the seminary, Graebner was a synodical official; his publishing his views in the *American Lutheran* indicated that he was not representing the view of the Synod but speaking as an individual. But he had never been known as an avid supporter of unity efforts. Just four years before he had published *The Problem of Lutheran Union*, a vigorous defense of the Missouri Synod's traditional opposition to unionism. He had admitted that other synods, even the ULCA, may have soundly

Lutheran doctrinal statements, but the real problem is that none of the other Synods (outside the Synodical Conference) actually value and maintain doctrinal agreement within themselves. Thus any fellowship with them raises the question of just with whom Missouri would actually be in fellowship and ran the risk of becoming "tolerant of false doctrine through such new associations."[31]

But in his 1939 *American Lutheran* article, Graebner struck a quite different note. One of the unexplored mysteries of LCMS history is Theodore Graebner's apparent change of perspective during these years, but this article gives at least some hints. He had been fully supportive of the Synod's rapprochement with the ALC and was astonished at the vehemence of the reaction to it by many—including the ALPB's old nemesis William Oesch, whose self-published *The Crucible*, sent to all Missouri Synod pastors, was sharply critical of the 1938 action.

Even more troubling, Missouri's partners in the Synodical Conference were fiercely opposed to the increased openness to the ALC. They had kept up a steady drumbeat of concern about the Missouri/ALC discussions through the 1930s, and after the 1938 convention action, the criticism came quickly. "Further negotiations [with the ALC] for establishing church fellowship," said Wisconsin, "would involve a denial of the truth and would cause confusion and disturbance in the Church and ought therefore to be suspended for the time being." The reaction of the Norwegian Synod had been equally negative.[32]

Graebner charged that the opposition to the 1938 statement "is based on the major premise that no sentence or phrase can be declared acceptable so long as standing by itself it permits of an evil interpretation."

> This implies, of course, that any omission will be viewed as intentional, as a denial of some truth. ... [The implication is] that 'here error can hide,' 'here false doctrine finds protection,' if it is not the direct insinuation that on the one part there has been an attempt to hide, cunningly, some traditional heresy while the other party is either too dull to see how the church is being hoodwinked or has too little regard for divine truth to insist on a better statement. ...

> A little more sanity! A little more clarity! We are all for orthodoxy, but in contending for the authority of Scripture, let us not overlook the thirteenth chapter of First Corinthians. And in fighting for the Lutheran Confessions let us not overlook that portion ... which is entitled The Eighth Commandment. Let us defend our neighbor, speak well of him, and put the best construction on everything.[33]

The *American Lutheran* editors had solicited this article from Graebner, and they called attention to it on the first page of that issue. Graebner's words have "needed to be said." The other Synodical Conference members have placed the question of fellowship "into an atmosphere of suspicion and distrust which is neither Lutheran nor Scriptural.

The law of love has been violated time and again." Graebner has "performed a distinct service ... by placing his finger directly on the fundamental error in these attitudes."[34]

An editorial in the next issue was even more forceful, declaring "the time has come for some plain speech regarding efforts to prevent a God-pleasing settlement of the differences separating Lutheran bodies."

> We have gradually become convinced that there are people who have set themselves to prevent any kind of settlement, God-pleasing or otherwise. ...
>
> We have grown extremely tired of a certain group of defenders of the faith. They are constantly being offended and other people are always giving offense. Perhaps we might take time out to declare that we are offended by their utterly loveless approach to the subject of union, by the atmosphere of suspicion in which God's will cannot be done. The attitude of these men sickens a child of God all the more because it is assumed over against everybody, even leading theologians of our own Synod.[35]

A second article by Graebner appeared, provocatively titled "Not a Sect—Yet." In it he discerned "a strongly sectarian tendency" among opponents of the agreement, revealed both in their arguments and in their spirit. He described his own history with regard to Lutheran unity:

> There need be no misgivings as to the writer's attitude on this or any church union movement. He has not become untrue to the conviction, held for the greater part of a lifetime, that any attempt to gloss over doctrinal differences is not only contrary to Scripture but must be distasteful (as fundamentally hypocritical) to any one who hates sham and pretense. I suppose I have done my share to place the Missouri Synod on record against unionism. ... My observations and my experiences ... have taught me that if one is to bear witness against unionism it is necessary to sacrifice friendships, income, academic honors, and to be misunderstood even by some who have on their own account made sacrifices for the truth. But I have just as little regard for a fanaticism which continues to heave cudgels at church bodies which have publicly declared their acceptance of the same truth which we profess, or who are midst great difficulties working their way towards a better appreciation of conservative Lutheran principles.[36]

Graebner's articles were immediately attacked from a new source—this time from within the Synod. In January 1940, Minnesota pastor Paul H. Burgdorf began publishing the *Confessional Lutheran*. Burgdorf didn't mention Graebner by name, but he alluded to the December 1939 article, titling his own response "Lutheran Union: A Case of Sanity and Charity Plus." He responded critically to each of Graebner's points.[37]

Then he turned his guns on *American Lutheran* itself. The magazine's claim to be an "open forum" Burgdorf found specious. Ever since it had become an "instrument of propaganda for a totalitarian Lutheran church," the magazine had given up any semblance of such openness. His evidence was the fact that an article on unionism had been submitted to the *American Lutheran* but the editor had refused to print it; the article, he said, was written by "no one less than one of [*American Lutheran's*] own associate editors [apparently F. R. Webber], whose special department had regularly appeared in this organ for quite a number of years." It can be readily seen, Burgdorf argued, "that the open forum of 'The American Lutheran' is not so very open.'"[38]

The *American Lutheran* did print an article harshly critical of Graebner by George O. Lillegard, a Norwegian Synod pastor. But in introducing the article, the editors noted that Lillegard's reply "is an almost complete demonstration of the truth of Dr. Graebner's statements." Right from the first paragraph, his language "move[s] the discussion into an atmosphere of suspicion and distrust which is in sharp contrast to the judicial restraint of Dr. Graebner's articles." Noting that Lillegard had sarcastically remarked that the *American Lutheran* was an advocate for union "for which they have been laboring so long," the editors owned up to the charge:

> Yes, we have labored long for Lutheran Union and shall continue to do so. We believe that the removal of schism in the Church is a duty which cannot be avoided or ignored. Not to labor for Lutheran Union is to fly in the face of the divine will for the Church on earth. So long as there is schism and false doctrine anywhere, it remains for us to testify against it and, as God gives grace and power, to remove it from the body of the Church.[39]

To Burgdorf, however, this was simply more evidence of the *American Lutheran's* intolerance of other opinions. The May *Confessional Lutheran* reported that Lillegard's article had been "rewritten by its editorial staff" and that "extensive and important portions" were omitted. Burgdorf then proceeded to print what he claimed was the entire article, with the portions omitted by the *American Lutheran* in capital letters so that readers might judge for themselves whether the editing had been fair. (Oddly enough, the article printed in *Confessional Lutheran* seems to be entirely different from the one in the *American Lutheran*.)[40]

Burgdorf also took after Graebner's "Not a Sect—Yet" in an essay asking "What Is a Sect?" Attributed to "F. R. W." (apparently Webber), the article asked:

> When then does an orthodox church body become a sect? The moment she is willing, for sweet charity's sake, to tolerate some doctrinal agreement which does not declare in emphatic, unambiguous language that man cannot keep the Law, that Jesus Christ kept it perfectly in our stead, and that we are saved only by His blood and His perfect righteousness. Such statements have been strangely lacking in certain journals of late.[41]

The *Confessional Lutheran* would continue its attacks on what it perceived as unionism for a couple of decades, often specifically targeting the *American Lutheran*. In 1942, the magazine began identifying itself as the organ of the "Confessional Lutheran Publicity Bureau." Whether this was much of an actual organization or not is questionable; the point was that Burgdorf and his associates were setting themselves up to be the conservative counterpart to the ALPB and the *American Lutheran*. For its part, the *American Lutheran* simply ignored Burgdorf, and continued to enthusiastically advocate Lutheran unity.

Notes

1. Paul Lindemann to O. A. Geiseman, 30 Apr. 1937. Geiseman Papers, Box 8, Folder 5.
2. Jack Treon Robinson, "The Spirit of Triumphalism in the Lutheran Church—Missouri Synod: The Role of the 'A Statement' of 1945 in the Missouri Synod" (PhD diss., Vanderbilt University, 1972), 205-206. Robinson indicates that his account came in a personal interview with Herbert Lindemann and was confirmed by another Missouri Synod pastor who asked not to be named.
3. "A. L. P. B. Celebrates Twenty-Fifth Anniversary," *AL* 22, no. 1 (Jan. 1939), 4.
4. Ibid., 5.
5. O. A. Geiseman, "While It Is Day: A Tribute to A Dear Friend, A Christian Gentleman, A Faithful Pastor, A Churchman of Vision," *AL* 22, no. 1 (Jan. 1939), 6-7.
6. *AL* 22, no. 1 (Jan. 1939), 11.
7. "The American Lutheran Faces the Future," *AL* 22, no. 2 (Feb. 1939), 3.
8. Ibid.
9. Ibid., 6.
10. Meyer, "Autobiography," 21.
11. O. A. Geiseman to Adolf Meyer, 10 Jan. 1939, Geiseman Papers, Box 10, Folder 1.
12. Adolf Meyer to O. A. Geiseman, 4 Jan.1939; O. A. Geiseman to Adolf Meyer, 10 Jan. 1939, Geiseman papers, Box 10, File 1.
13. O. P. Kretzmann, "The State of Visible Christendom," *AL* 22, no. 3 (Mar. 1939), 13-14.
14. O. P. Kretzmann, "The State of Visible Christendom: II—The Scaffolding of the Church," *AL* 22, no. 4 (Apr. 1939), 7-8; "The State of Visible Christendom: III—The Scaffolding of the Church [*sic*]," *AL* 22, no. 5 (May 1939), 6; "The State of Visible Christendom: IV—Cultural Change," *AL* 22, no. 6 (June 1939), 10.
15. O. P. Kretzmann, "The State of Visible Christendom: [VI]—Protestantism in 1939," *AL* 22, no. 9 (Sept. 1939), 9-10.
16. Ibid.
17. O. A. Geiseman to M. Reu, 11 Dec. 1940, Geiseman Papers, Box 12, Folder 2.
18. "The American Lutheran Faces the Future," *AL* 22, no. 2 (Feb. 1939), 2-5.
19. Ibid, 6.
20. "Forward Again!" n.d., American Lutheran Publicity Bureau File, CHI.
21. "Religion at the World's Fair," *AL* 22, no. 10 (Oct. 1939), 21; August F. Brunn, "Religion at the New York World's Fair," *AL* 22, no. 4 (Apr. 1939), 12. For further information on the Temple of Religion, see J. Terry Todd, "The Temple of Religion and the Politics of Religious Pluralism: Judeo-Christian America at the 1939-40 New York World's Fair" in Courtney Bender and Pamela E. Klassen, eds., *After Pluralism: Reimagining Religious Engagement* (New York: Columbia University Press, 2010), 201-222
22. Brunn, 12.
23. "American Lutheran Publicity Bureau Honored," *AL* 23, no. 10 (Oct. 1940), 3.
24. "Sandusky Declaration of American Lutheran Church, 1938," in Richard C. Wolf, *Documents of Lutheran Unity in America* (Philadelphia: Fortress Press, 1966), 398.
25. "Statement on Pulpit and Altar Fellowship with American Lutheran Church, 1938" in Wolf, 399-400.
26. Adolf Meyer, "Convention Impressions," *AL* 21, no. 7 (July 1938), 6; "Progress Towards Lutheran Union," *AL* 21, no. 9 (Sept. 1938), 3.
27. Ibid.
28. "Let Us Meet and Discuss," *AL* 22, no. 2 (Feb. 1939), 7.
29. "Objection," *AL* 22, no. 3 (Mar. 1939), 3.

30. O. A. Geiseman, "While It Is Day," *AL* 22, no. 5 (May 1939), 5.

31. Theodore Graebner, *The Problem of Lutheran Union and Other Essays* (St. Louis: Concordia Publishing House, 1935), 19-20.

32. "Wisconsin Synod Reaction to Missouri-Ohio Agreement, 1939," in Wolf, 403.

33. Theodore Graebner, "Lutheran Union: A Plea for Sanity and Charity," *AL* 22, no. 12 (Dec. 1939), 7-9.

34. "A Needed Voice," *AL* 22, no. 12 (Dec. 1939), 3.

35. "Unionism or Separatism," *AL* 23, no. 1 (Jan. 1940), 4.

36. "Not a Sect—Yet," *AL* 23, no. 2 (Jan. 1940), 7-8.

37. "Lutheran Union? A Case of Sanity and Charity Plus—," *Confessional Lutheran* 1, no. 1 (Jan. 1940), 2-4.

38. "An Open Forum?" *Confessional Lutheran* 1, no. 1 (Jan. 1940), 4.

39. "A Needed Voice—III," *AL* 23, no. 3 (Mar. 1940), 5-6.

40. George O. Lillegard, "In Non-Essentials, Liberty," *Confessional Lutheran* 1, no. 5 (May 1940), 27-31.

41. "What Is a Sect?" *Confessional Lutheran* 1, no. 2 (Feb. 1940), 6.

Chapter 7

LUTHERAN UNITY

T heodore Graebner's two articles on Lutheran unity had elicited angry responses from Paul Burgdorf's *Confessional Lutheran* and others, but the reaction did not stop the *American Lutheran*'s increasing attention to the subject; soon more significant criticism would emerge, both from Missouri's partners in the Synodical Conference and from official figures within the Missouri Synod itself.

Cooperation in externals

"not my kind of orthodoxy"

One aspect of the debate on Lutheran unity was the question of "cooperation in externals." Missouri had departed from her Synodical Conference colleagues by agreeing to work, on a very limited basis and on matters restricted to "external" concerns, with synods with whom she was not in fellowship. The Synod had taken this position as early as the camp pastor controversy during World War I, but there had never been a clear statement of just what qualified as "externals." The *American Lutheran* waded into this issue in February 1941 with an article by William Arndt considering the question of how much intersynodical cooperation might be appropriate on the foreign mission field. He spoke of the "serious crisis" facing foreign missions which, because of the war in Europe, had been cut off from their sponsoring churches. Arndt noted that the Lutheran World Convention—a group in which Missouri did not participate—had set up a commission to aid these "orphan missions." He argued that the Synod "can with a good conscience participate in this endeavor." At the end of Arndt's article was an editorial note: "The above ... begins a series of articles from Lutheran leaders, who discuss possible benefits of cooperation between the various Synods of the Lutheran Church in their fields."[1]

But the magazine had its own opinion, and the next issue featured a full editorial on the matter. The question was framed as a concern of the laity, who are generally "united in supporting their clergy regarding doctrinal matters."

> There is one thing, however, which constantly irritates sincere laymen to the point of rebellion:—Where there is no question of compromising the truth they find the work for which Christ suffered and died is hindered purely because of the tradition of non-cooperation between Lutheran synods. Where man's stubbornness and jealousy blocks the way of Christ's plan, one cannot blame the Lutheran layman for his dissatisfaction.

The editorial then endorsed the position of Dr. Arndt expressed in the previous issue and called attention to an article in the current issue by Henry F. Wind, president of Associated Lutheran Charities, on the question of cooperation in the field of human welfare ministries.[2]

Wind pulled no punches. The inability of synods to work together on these ministries despite their doctrinal differences, he wrote, is a sin and a shame. "No compromise of disputed points of principle or doctrine is involved," he insisted, "only a casting aside of old jealousies, old prejudices, old fears, old misconceptions. And that 'casting aside,' by the way, must be done not only by the 'non-cooperative' Missourians, but by men of all synods." Wind would soon join the editorial board of the *American Lutheran*.[3]

A few months later, the editors asked Theodore Graebner to tackle the question head on. He agreed to "try to outline the meaning and limitations of 'cooperation in externals' between church bodies not yet in fellowship with each other" in a three-part series of articles. He began by searching for some official pronouncement, but could find nothing beyond an essay by H. G. Hartner in 1936. It was "official" only in the sense that it was a paper delivered to the South Nebraska District, and thereafter published in their reports; this implied that it had "passed the censorship of the faculty of Concordia Seminary, St. Louis." Hartner had allowed that there were situations where cooperation was acceptable—matters that were "external"—but he had explicitly excluded joint operation of educational and charitable work, religious journalism and missionary education. Graebner could not agree with Hartner's approach. First, he criticized the very use of the word "externals"; after all, preaching and baptism are "external acts," yet no one would call them "externals" of church work. Better, he wrote, to think in terms of "essential" and "non-essential." "Essential" are those specific matters that Christ has assigned to the church—preaching, instructing, administering the sacraments, exercising church discipline, worship. But the church also does many things which, though good and salutary, are not "essential" to its mission. So "externals" properly speaking are these things that are not "essential"; they "begin where there is no implication of unity of doctrine. ... Externals are all those matters which have not been specifically assigned to the church as her definite mission."[4]

He then offered several examples of his own. The first, perhaps a bit tongue in cheek, suggested a corner on which sat four buildings: a Lutheran church, a Catholic church, a Christian Science church, and a Masonic temple. In that block "a dance hall has been making night hideous and flaunting vice in the face of decent citizens." Surely the four groups could cooperate together in protesting the problem without any compromise of doctrinal integrity.[5]

As for Dr. Wind's argument for cooperation in welfare work, Graebner was not quite so certain. He acknowledged, however, that Wind knew a lot more about the field than he did, and he was willing to accept his judgment in such matters. Graebner offered several more examples of what he deemed appropriate intersynodical cooperation. He cited organizations such as the American Lutheran Statistical Association and the Lutheran Editor's Association (of which he was a member)—groups whose work is "far on the periphery" of the church's activity as far as "the divinely commissioned work of the church is concerned." Surely there is no violation of confessional standards if Missourians join in organizations that present musical performances of Haydn's *Creation* or Handel's *Messiah*. And why should Missourians not contribute chapters to books, or give lectures at academic events, sponsored by other synods? To the fear that orthodoxy "may be threatened by personal contacts" of this nature, his reply was that "an orthodoxy which demands avoidance of every appearance of willingness to remove hindrances to unity, is not my kind of orthodoxy. ... There is no concession here to any unscriptural principle."[6]

Prayer fellowship
"the greatest single source of misunderstanding"

An even more contentious issue was "prayer fellowship"—the practice of praying with other Christians with whom Missouri had not realized doctrinal unity. In June 1940, the *American Lutheran* published an article by Edward Fendt, professor of systematic theology at the ALC's Capital University, expressing appreciation for Graebner's articles—for "their evangelical tenor, the faithfulness to genuinely Lutheran principles, the strong motive to let truth dispel error." Graebner's approach, he said, left him "hopeful and confident."[7]

But Fendt admitted that there was one question "for which we have no satisfactory answer: why do the men of Missouri continue to refuse to pray with fellow Lutherans?" He had put his finger on a continuing point of tension. Missouri and the other members of the Synodical Conference saw prayer fellowship as unionism (along with pulpit and altar fellowship). This view had been argued forthrightly by Friedrich Bente in 1905, and then by Franz Pieper in 1924. Pieper argued that "to pray with [false teachers] or to partake of the Lord's Supper with them would mean to consent to, and to become 'partakers of their evil works.'"[8]

Within Missouri, however, there were divergent opinions. Controversy had erupted in 1923 when Adolph Brux, a Synod missionary in India, had been a houseguest of Presbyterian colleagues and had accepted the invitation to join in their table devotions, including prayer. When he returned to the United States in 1931, he came under fire for praying with these fellow missionaries. In his own defense, Brux had prepared a paper evaluating Missouri's practice in which he concluded that it "goes beyond what a sound interpretation of these Bible passages [cited to support the practice] warrants." He did not convince the Board of Foreign Missions, and they terminated his service. He subsequently resigned from the ministry of the Missouri Synod. The question of prayer fellowship, however, continued to stir up dissension within the Synod.[9]

The *American Lutheran* alluded to this matter editorially in August 1940. It quoted an editorial in the Norwegian Synod's *Lutheran Sentinel* which had warned of "a spirit of indifference to a sound doctrinal basis." The *Sentinel* writer had criticized those whose attitude seemed to be "'Let us forget the [Lutheran Church] fathers and get back to Scripture.'" The *American Lutheran* pondered this, and related a pertinent anecdote from an unspecified intersynodical gathering:

> A truly great theologian read an exegetical paper on some passages from Scripture which were frequently adduced against praying with Lutheran pastors of another synod. He proved to the satisfaction of a number that the passages did not apply. At this point a brother, whose sincerity we do not doubt, arose and made the plea that if all passages from Holy Writ were taken from under our feet, we have nothing left on which we base our position on prayer-fellowship. It may not have been intended to sound as it did, but it seemed to argue that we have a position to maintain and therefore we must not admit that certain passages from God's Word do not say what they must say if we are to maintain our position.

The *Sentinel*'s view, the *American Lutheran* observed, suggested that a plea for basing doctrine on the Bible made the man a "unionist." Furthermore, the *Sentinel* wrote with an "acrid, loveless tone which characterizes the very approach to the question in some quarters."[10]

In January 1941, President Behnken agreed to attend a meeting called by the American Lutheran Conference's Commission on Church Unity, held in Columbus,

OH. The purpose was to discuss refugee resettlement and other practical matters arising out of the war in Europe. Behnken made it very clear that he was attending "unofficially." But the meeting had included prayer, and Behnken immediately came under criticism, especially from the Wisconsin Synod.

With that in the background, the question of prayer fellowship came up at the Synod convention in 1941 in Ft. Wayne. While the delegates agreed to continue negotiations with the American Lutheran Church, the convention again cautioned:

> That in the meantime it be understood that no pulpit-, altar-, or prayer-fellowship has been established between us and the American Lutheran Church, and until such fellowship has been officially declared by the synods concerned, no action is to be taken by any of our pastors or congregations which ignores the fact that we are not yet united.

Geiseman's column in the *American Lutheran* referred to the action as the "low point" of the Ft. Wayne convention. Prayer fellowship, he wrote, was a matter "on which the understanding and viewpoint of a very large number of our pastors has changed appreciably during recent years as a result of careful Bible study and conference discussions."[11]

In November 1941, the editors called prayer fellowship "the greatest single source of misunderstanding" with the American Lutheran Church. ALC members "feel that refusal of prayer fellowship is an unwarranted insult carrying the implication that they are not Christians or that they are not earnestly desirous of the guidance of God the Holy Spirit in such conferences." This has become "a very sore spot in our intersynodical relations. It should be faced candidly and fearlessly. It requires a humble re-examination of our attitudes in the light of the Word of God."[12]

In 1942, Behnken was again invited to an intersynodical meeting in Columbus called by the National Lutheran Council for May 15. In this instance he agreed to go, but in his acceptance he issued a caveat: "For obvious reasons—and I hope this will not be misunderstood or misinterpreted—we are not taking part in the devotional worship and shall be present for only the business meeting." Clearly Behnken was walking a very fine line here; he believed that Missouri's presence at this meeting was vital, but he was wary of the criticism, both from partners in the Synodical Conference and from some in the Missouri Synod, about his participation in any meeting that included prayer.[13]

But the *American Lutheran* was impatient about the whole issue, and in July 1942 the magazine published an "anonymous" letter (actually written by Herbert Lindemann, son of the late editor) over the pseudonym "Simplicissimus." Lindemann posed as a simple man who was confused. He had been taught by his confirmation pastor that "members of the Christian brotherhood were to be found in every Christian denomination, and that it was our duty to rejoice in the tie of faith which bound all believers together in the Body of Christ." Yet now he reads that the president of his church body has refused to take part in devotions with other Lutherans "for obvious reasons." "Dear Mr. Editor," he wrote, "what were these obvious reasons?"

> Why ... did Missouri's representatives refuse to participate? Did they think the assembly was un-Christian? Why then were they at Columbus at all? What were these obvious reasons? To me they are not obvious at all. Will someone please enlighten me? ...

> When a man refuses to pray with me, I conclude that he thinks there is something wrong with my worship. ... If he refuses on the ground that I am not always correct in everything I say, he is taking an untenable position. If he is looking for such a person to pray with, he will have to pray alone until he gets to Heaven.[14]

President Behnken was furious when he saw the letter. He immediately wrote to Adolf Meyer, with copies to the full editorial board. "More than I can put into words," he wrote, "do I regret that the American Lutheran has done this." Had the letter's criticism been directed at him personally, he would keep silent, but "this is an attack upon the President of the Missouri Synod."

> Perhaps I would say nothing if this had appeared in the periodicals of one of the other Lutheran bodies. That has happened. Perhaps the 'Letter' was written by someone not within our Synod. I cannot know. It is anonymous. But I cannot understand how brethren of mine can permit the printing of such an anonymous attack upon the President of their Synod in the American Lutheran without even giving him a hearing. To what will this lead? O how those who are not friendly to our cause will rejoice! May God have mercy upon us!

He signed his letter to Meyer, "Yours with a heavy heart."[15]

Meyer immediately responded, expressing his regret that Behnken was "so deeply disturbed." He told the President that Herbert Lindemann was the author of the letter, and that it was an editorial decision, not Lindemann's request, to withhold his name. He offered Behnken the opportunity to respond, but he did not apologize for printing the letter. "Men everywhere are asking questions similar to those in the letter of Herbert Lindemann's," he explained. "These men will demand an answer sooner or later." Meyer acknowledged that sometimes the *American Lutheran* printed pieces that "hurt personal feelings," but that its purpose was to air issues needing "intelligent discussion" when such discussion "helps the cause of our Saviour. And if it aids Jesus then certainly it must aid also the cause of our Synod."[16]

Behnken was not mollified by Meyer's letter—far from it. He was "somewhat surprised that ... you are ready to call this a matter of hurting 'personal feelings.'" Since this letter was "an attack upon an official of the church," printing it was "unwarranted and unjustifiable, and certainly a very unwise thing," and if Meyer thinks he was serving the cause of the Savior, "I fear that you have an altogether wrong conception." He also regretted that Meyer had revealed the author's name, for "I wish that I did not know it at all." And as for Behnken writing a response, "I am sure that, after you give the matter thorough thought, you would not want the president of your Synod to do anything like that."[17]

Meyer stuck to his guns. He wrote that he had "rather expected" Behnken's answer, and that in fact he had decided a response from Behnken would be unwise. Furthermore, he had decided that the editorial board itself would print a response to "Simplicissimus." But still he refused to apologize for the letter itself. If church members believe their leaders are wrong, he asked, can they not say so? "I do know that in the Catholic Church it is considered wrong for any Catholic to criticize the action of the Pope.— But we are not Catholic." There was apparently no further response from Behnken.[18]

Other members of the editorial board wrote directly to Behnken. Henry Wind was conciliatory. While he regretted that the president had been offended, he had reread the Simplicissimus letter and still believed it was "simply attempting to discuss the question of prayer-fellowship and related issues without involving personalities." He assured Behnken that the editors would take up the matter when they met in August.[19]

Arthur Brunn, who had resigned as president of the Atlantic District the year before when he was elected one of the vice presidents of the Synod, was more sympathetic to Behnken. He had not seen the Lindemann letter before it was published, apparently because it had been mislaid in his office. "I believe that the entire matter of prayer-fellowship must be restudied," he wrote, "but certainly Herbert Lindemann's approach is reprehensible." Still, he believed that Lindemann was not "finding fault with you either personally nor as the president of Synod, but simply used the Columbus incident as a hook on which he hung his disagreement" with Synod about prayer fellowship.[20]

The editorial staff convened August 10, with nearly everyone involved in the magazine present: members of the editorial board—Meyer, Brunn, Geiseman, Kretzmann, Fred Lindemann, and Wind (E. J. Friedrich, who had joined the board the previous year along with Wind, was unable to be present); J. F. E. Nickelsburg, the business manager, was there, as were contributing editors A. W. Brustat and William F. Bruening. F. R. Webber was present for one session only.

The group immediately took up the controversy about the Lindemann letter, and the minutes of the meeting suggest that the discussion was long and heated. Brunn had been asked to draft an editorial in response to "Simplicissimus," which he presented to the group. After some discussion, he "agreed to make certain changes which would more clearly express the editorial opinion." It was agreed that President Behnken "should be supported as having acted at Columbus in accordance with the letter of the Ft. Wayne resolution but not with the spirit." Brunn strongly defended Dr. Behnken, arguing that the president was simply "interested in keeping peace, that he does not want to give the impression to the outside that the Missouri Synod is not united, and [desires] that discussion be carried on outside of public print."[21]

Geiseman had written a statement on prayer fellowship, and the group discussed it. But Brunn asked, "Are we clear in our mind just what prayer-fellowship is?" He argued that "we ought to be clear before we go further in the matter." Theodore Graebner not too subtly had suggested that his willingness to continue to support and recommend the *American Lutheran* might have to be reconsidered if more articles of that nature were forthcoming. He had also proposed a meeting between the editorial boards of the two publications "out of which should come a joint statement on issues involved." Kretzmann thought such a meeting would be useful, but "we should be clear in our own minds on the subject."[22]

Geiseman then proposed a series of articles for the *American Lutheran* which, after setting some context, would take up unionism and prayer fellowship. Brunn "raised the question whether or not the work of the [Bureau] should be jeopardized by the pursuit of the policy of the magazine, [i.e.] the discussion of controversial subjects. He felt that the Bureau might make enemies." Meyer replied that the "real work of the Bureau" is "the furthering of the Kingdom," and that work is best served by continuing to be a forum for discussion within the pages of the magazine. Others agreed, pointing out that only an independent voice like the *American Lutheran*—one not subject to Synod's censorship—was able to offer constructive criticism of the Synod's policies and actions. It was finally agreed that the publishing of controversial articles was already within the magazine's policy, and there was no reason to change that policy. Brunn then urged that the editorial board accept the proposal to meet with their counterparts at *Lutheran Witness*, but he thought Dr. Behnken should also be included in the conversation.[23]

After a lunch break, there was more discussion both of Geiseman's proposal for an editorial series and the request for a meeting with the editors of the *Lutheran Witness*. Lindemann argued that any such meeting would be "tantamount to asking for [their] approval," which "would be dangerous and might lead to an 'unofficial censorship.'" But Geiseman and others believed they couldn't afford politically to turn down the invitation; some even argued that they might be able to influence Graebner at such a meeting. In the end, the consensus was that Meyer write to Graebner "expressing pleasure and interest over the invitation to hold a joint meeting."[24]

Geiseman's editorial on prayer fellowship was approved, with minor changes. His proposed series, however, was set aside in favor of an alternative proposal by Kretzmann entitled "The Problem of Lutheran Union: An Editorial Program." The group also discussed briefly what to do about the criticisms of the *Confessional Lutheran*, and the conclusion was unanimous: "Continue to ignore them."[25]

There were decisions about several other matters made at this meeting. It was agreed to suspend temporarily Webber's "Fine Arts Department" and to invite Webber instead to contribute a regular "page emphasizing the spiritual welfare of the boys in the service." It was decided to institute a column on Biblical archeology, to be edited by A. W. Brustat. Fred Lindemann was asked to reinstate his "Churchman's Digest" column, which had presented clippings from a variety of other Lutheran magazines. J. F. E. Nickelsburg was commended for his twenty-five years of service to the ALPB.[26]

The very next issue of the *American Lutheran* printed the editorial response to "Simplicissimus" agreed upon by the editorial staff. It recounted the events referred to in the letter and acknowledged that Dr. Behnken "could not enter into prayer-fellowship with others, no matter at all what his personal conviction may have been." It regretted that anyone might have taken the letter as a criticism of the president; that was certainly not what the editors had in mind. The real "question at issue" is "whether or not prayer-fellowship falls into the same category with pulpit- and altar-fellowship." The editorial noted that there was a difference of opinion in the Synod about this, and that the issues needed to be studied without "raising accusations, casting doubts, and criticizing the acts of others." The *American Lutheran*, it said, "plans to add its contribution to this study."[27]

The problem of Lutheran unity
"we have failed God in the greater task"

The editors wasted no time. In September 1942 the lead editorial was essentially Kretzmann's proposal: "The Problem of Lutheran Unity: An Editorial Program." The editorial listed seven statements summarizing "the convictions of the editorial staff"; they were, in fact, a summary of seven articles to come. Some of the statements in this opening précis were rather brief—just two or three sentences; others were more extensive, with a general statement followed by several sub-points. The articles themselves were unsigned; presumably each was agreed to by the whole editorial board.[28]

The first article, printed the following month, was an appraisal of the state of Lutheranism in the United States. After briefly tracing the doctrinal history of Lutheranism since the Reformation, the essay noted a steady trend in the direction of orthodoxy even in the more liberal Lutheran synods. The church isn't yet where it needs to be, but progress has been made, and it is the challenge of "every member of the Lutheran church" to continue to fight for sound Lutheranism.[29]

The second installment was a re-affirmation of the Lutheran principle of *sola scriptura*, but the author took it in a rather unexpected direction. He recalled Luther's courageous insistence that "councils can err," and that only the Word of God is a reliable source of truth. He suggested that those who refuse to pray with members of other synods are following the modern equivalent of councils which are in error. The general rule about prayer is expressed in Schwan's exposition of the Small Catechism: "All believers are in Christ the children of one Father, and should, therefore, pray for and with each other." If there are to be exceptions, "they must have their basis and reason in Scripture." The writer also criticized the oft-heard statement that praying with those of other synods "causes offense" to some, and so should be avoided on those grounds. It is indeed wrong to "give offense," he wrote, "but no less serious is it to *take* offense. ... Only weak Christians take offense when none is given."[30]

The third article argued that agreement on the authority of Scripture and subscription to the Lutheran confessions was all that was required for Lutheran unity. The editorial did not mention Missouri's 1932 "Brief Statement," but there is little doubt that was what was meant when it criticized "new confessional statements."

> What the Lutheran Church of America needs more than an endless line of new documents is sincerity of faith and purpose within each group, complete confidence on the part of one group in the sincerity of those in another group, plus a generous measure of patience and love to help each other achieve the richest and fullest spiritual development so that we can all, individually and collectively, contribute most fully to the glory of God, the welfare of men, and the upbuilding of our Lord's kingdom.[31]

This was the last straw for some Missouri Synod conservatives, who began to complain both to the editors of *American Lutheran* and to President Behnken. J. Theodore Mueller, a professor at St. Louis, was typical when he wrote to Behnken that "something should be done about it. The American Lutheran should not determine the policy in the union matter." He suggested that Behnken convene a special meeting of the district presidents to discuss what to do.[32]

Homiletics professor John H. C. Fritz, who had been one of the founders of the ALPB, also wrote to Behnken "with great heartache" about the December article. "The whole line of argument," he insisted, "is wrong." He was appalled that "on the Editorial Board we find a Vice-President of Synod [Brunn], a member of the Board of Directors of Synod [Geiseman], a former member of the St. Louis Faculty [Friedrich], and the President of our Valparaiso University [Kretzmann]." Such officials surely ought to uphold the policy of Synod.[33]

Behnken responded to each correspondent by agreeing with the concern, but lamenting that he had to be very circumspect in light of Synod's 1935 refusal to bring independent publications like the *American Lutheran* under Synod control. He usually suggested that individuals might write to the editors directly. Several of them did, sending copies to Behnken. Fritz's letter to Adolf Meyer was forthright: "I deplore the attitude which your Editorial Board takes toward church unity. ... Every student of history ... knows where such a conciliatory attitude as you have taken leads: The truth always suffers as a result."[34]

Despite the controversy, the series on Lutheran unity continued. The fourth article, picking up on a then-current patriotic slogan, "They shall not march alone," deplored the idea that the Missouri Synod should "march alone" in meeting the great tasks looming, especially after the war. It confessed that "we have failed God in the greater task which He had assigned to us," and argued that we would fail God once again "if we fail *now* earnestly to seek the establishment of peace and unity among the scattered forces of Lutheranism in America."[35]

The editors at last turned to the still controversial question of prayer fellowship. They argued that the Biblical passages used to defend the refusal to pray with other Christians were really speaking about prayer with non-Christians. For the Lutherans of the Missouri Synod, the entire question had been mostly theoretical as long as linguistic isolation made it unlikely that prayer with other Christians would ever take place; but now this has become "one of the truly urgent problems of this day." The position of the *American Lutheran* was clear: To pray with another Christian "to the true God in the name of Jesus Christ for a God-pleasing purpose dare under no circumstance be declared to be wrong and sinful, but should rather be regarded as a Christian duty."[36]

When the editorial board met in February 1943, the increasingly vocal reaction to the editorial series was on everyone's mind. Arthur Brunn, who was under tremendous pressure from some of his colleagues, immediately raised the question of whether the series should be abandoned. There were "too many insurmountable objects ... to expect that such Unity might be accomplished in our generation." But the others pushed back. O. P. Kretzmann insisted that the subject was more important than ever. E. J. Friedrich argued that the series was having much more impact than might be evident, and that the "thinking men" in the Synod are reading and absorbing the arguments in the *American Lutheran*. After extended discussion, a formal motion was approved: "that ... we must go forward and strive toward our common goal, the closer relation of Lutheran Bodies on the basis of Scripture."[37]

The next day the board met with *Lutheran Witness* staff members Theodore Graebner, W. G. Polack, and George V. Schick. Graebner was asked to moderate the conversation. He began by expressing appreciation for the cordial relationship between the two magazines. His hope for the meeting was that they could cooperate on some of the significant issues facing the church, particularly post-war planning and Lutheran unity. As the meeting progressed, it became clear that one motive of the *Witness* staff was to encourage the *American Lutheran* to print articles which, because of the Synod's censorship, could not appear in *Lutheran Witness*. Graebner specifically urged a continuing treatment of prayer fellowship.[38]

Both Graebner and Polack acknowledged that the ULCA "as consisted [*sic*] today is different than in 1918," and that a Missouri Synod pastor could in many cases, with a clear conscience, "dismiss one of his members" to a ULCA congregation. This assertion was something of a bombshell, as first Fred Lindemann and then others expressed their astonishment that nothing of this nature had ever been hinted at in the *Lutheran Witness*. Friedrich said he was at a loss to understand why it fell to an unofficial periodical like the *American Lutheran* to advocate such opinions if, in fact, they were held by persons in authority in the Synod. This, he suggested, is one reason for "much of the distrust in the minds of many of our clergy." Graebner's rather weak reply was that many of Missouri's pastors were still quite legalistic. The meeting no doubt left the staff of the *American Lutheran* puzzled and yet encouraged that they had some support in St. Louis.[39]

The final two articles came after the editorial board discussion. In what must be counted a gem of eighth commandment generosity, the March edition reflected on the series so far and noted "the thoughtful, brotherly reaction of pastors and laymen of all branches of the Church, even when they sincerely felt that they were unable to agree on all the statements made in our editorial series." It admitted that, just as there were some obstacles to unity within the Synodical Conference, so there were similar obstacles within other groups. But having said all this, the writer concluded, "we affirm our conviction that the first hurdle in the road to Lutheran unity lies in our attitudes."

> Our separation is our own fault. Confessing our faults to one another and ad-monishing one another we shall march steadily toward the vision of a truly united Lutheran Church which shall be and will be, please God, a light bright and true in our dark world.[40]

The final essay summarized the series, reiterating the importance of Lutheran unity in the context of the current world crisis. The church also faces a crisis, an urgent and immediate task. Lutheran unity, while desirable, "is not an end in itself. It is a means to an end. The final purpose must always be the greater building of the Kingdom." There were no doubt those in St. Louis who breathed a sigh of relief when the *American Lutheran*'s controversial editorial series came to its conclusion, but it soon became clear that the controversy was only beginning.[41]

A controversial letter

"Talk, talk, talk!"

Ernest J. Gallmeyer was a business executive in Ft. Wayne, IN. He was also the president of the Lutheran Layman's League and a member of the Synod board of directors. In the spring of 1943, he wrote a letter to the editor of the *Lutheran Witness* complaining that the "ecclesiastics" had completely botched the important task of Lutheran unity and suggesting that perhaps it was time for the laity to take over so that something could be accomplished.

Theodore Graebner replied to him in a letter dated June 12. Your letter, Graebner wrote, was typeset and ready to be printed. "However—there's a however." The staff of the *Lutheran Witness* was enthusiastic about the letter, but "the Censorship bids us consider the possible effects and the implications which this article has" in its implication that there are no remaining significant differences among Lutheran synods. "So, for the present, it will stay on the galleys."[42]

But Graebner had already made it clear that he thought the *American Lutheran* could get away with things the *Lutheran Witness* could not, and he took it upon himself to send the letter to Adolf Meyer. Meyer, he reported to Gallmeyer, had agreed to publish the letter, and O. P Kretzmann would be in touch with Gallmeyer to discuss the matter.[43]

And so, in the August issue of the *American Lutheran*, Gallmeyer's letter was printed in full. It was a no-holds-barred attack on Missouri's foot-dragging.

> In recent years we have again approached the matter of union with Lutheran brethren of other synods. The possibility of such a heart-warming cooperation with those of the household of faith seems again doomed. Talk, talk, talk! Is it quite fair that we alone sit in judgment on the program? No we seemingly do not furnish the leadership which maps out a program, but rather we content ourselves with sitting on the sidelines and deciding how far wrong the other fellow is.

> Everywhere there is an expression on the part of the laity of the hope that shortly these ecclesiastical debates may end. ... Yes, the laymen of the Church are becoming impatient—impatient at the aloofness—impatient at the dilatory technique—impatient at the ineffectualness.

The *American Lutheran* added a note identifying Gallmeyer's positions with the Lutheran Layman's League and the Synod board of directors.[44]

Once again President Behnken was furious. On September 29 he wrote a letter to the editors of the *American Lutheran*.

> In all sincerity I want to request you to refrain from soliciting and publishing letters or statements from laymen such as the letter from Mr. E. J. Gallmeyer. This grieved me very much personally and I know that it has offended many throughout our Synod.[45]

Behnken also wrote directly to Gallmeyer, asking that he "withdraw" his letter. Gallmeyer was about to do so, but Geiseman talked him out of it. "You have made yourself guilty of no false doctrine," he wrote. "I cannot even remotely conceive that anyone should ask you to withdraw the statement." He insisted that Gallmeyer had the right to express his opinion, and that "the most [anyone] can say is that he doesn't agree with you." E. J. Friedrich, too, encouraged Gallmeyer, telling him that he had "heard many fine comments about your letter out here, both from pastors and laymen." He found Behnken's request disturbing, though it was "in line with an unfortunate official attitude and policy developed in recent years."[46]

Meyer assured the president that his concern would be given due consideration by the editorial board—though he had already heard from most of its members and it was clear that they were not of a mind to accede to Behnken's request. Meyer also had to take a proactive step. The *American Lutheran* had in June announced a new series on the question of Lutheran unity which would include a number of statements from laity.

The October issue, already in the mail, included the first installment of these statements, along with an editorial highlighting them. He wanted Behnken to understand that this issue had been completed prior to his letter, and that the collection of "letters from laymen" was not meant as a provocative response to the president's request. Furthermore, the statements in the October issue had in fact been solicited by the magazine, whereas Gallmeyer's letter was submitted by him, not requested by the editors.

Meyer sent a copy of Behnken's letter and his reply to each member of the editorial board, along with a lengthy memo outlining his own thoughts. "I do not remember any request so revolutionary in its demands to have come from any official of Synod." President Pfotenhauer was "supposed to have been much more conservative as a stand-patter than Behnken," and yet Pfotenhauer "kept his hands strictly off the AMERICAN LUTHERAN." Behnken has taken a much more reactionary stance.[47]

A week later Meyer wrote again to the editorial board with some further reflections. He did not want "to have an open fight with the President of our body," and wondered if perhaps a face-to-face meeting of the entire staff with Behnken might be useful to "try to talk sense to him." At the same time, he expressed his frustration at Graebner, who had printed an editorial about the Gallmeyer letter in the *Lutheran Witness*, along with four articles on "obstacles to union." These had appeared in the *Lutheran Witness* prior to the publication of Gallmeyer's letter in the *American Lutheran*, and Graebner's editorial tried to explain the whole sequence of events—but in Meyer's opinion, Graebner was "again guilty of twisting the facts and straddling the issue." What particularly peeved him was Graebner's statement that the *Witness* staff had thought Gallmeyer's was "a voice that should, must be heard," but that they had believed (and "our faculty censorship agreed") that the letter should be accompanied by articles responding to his allegations. At no point, Meyer told his editorial colleagues, had Graebner ever said any such thing when he suggested that the *American Lutheran* publish Gallmeyer's letter. As a result, the *Witness* published defenses of the Synod's policy before Gallmeyer's criticism had appeared in print. Meyer disgustedly said he had more important things to do than engage in another controversy with Graebner, but suggested that other board members who had occasion to encounter Graebner might feel free to challenge his statement.[48]

Meyer also quoted a letter written by Graebner to Gallmeyer (which Gallmeyer had forwarded on to Meyer for the editorial board's information only) in which he confessed to "speeding up the machinery" in order to get the editorial into the *Lutheran Witness* so quickly. The *Witness* staff, Graebner said, was very pleased with the presentation "and finds fault only with the rather generous treatment of the American Lutheran which really laid an egg if there was ever one laid, by printing your letter when it was out of season." One can readily see why Meyer was skeptical of working with Graebner.[49]

The other members of the editorial board generally shared Meyer's opinion. Friedrich was particularly incensed.

Behnken's recent letter reminds me of the prolonged chastening which I had to endure at his hands for about three months after Paul Lindemann's funeral. I was still at the seminary at that time. The controversy ended with this exhortation from him: 'Professor Friedrich, be careful in the future not to criticize the President of Synod.' To me this was a new doctrine. Now it is being elevated to the position of a dogma.

Friedrich said it was time to "take the bull by the horns." "It will not be a pleasant task, but it has to be done." His preference was for a unanimous statement by the editors refusing Behnken's request, though he recognized that this would put Brunn on the spot. If such a declaration was not feasible, then each editor should write to Behnken and tell him what he thinks.[50]

In the end, it was agreed that Behnken would be invited to meet with Meyer and others to discuss his concerns. The meeting took place at the ALPB offices in New York November 13; in addition to Behnken and Meyer, participants included Arthur Brunn, ALPB president August Bobzin and A. W. Brustat. The meeting appears to have been cordial; Behnken insisted that he had no desire to censor, formally or informally, the *American Lutheran*. He confessed that he did not favor the *American Lutheran's* approach to Lutheran unity, largely because he saw it as "hanging our dirty linen on the line for the rest of the world to see," but he was not protesting the magazine's right to its opinion. He reiterated his disagreement with the decision to publish Gallmeyer's letter, and he hoped that any future articles or letters would avoid "attacks made against Synod and the fathers." He also made it very clear that he did not personally approve of the *Confessional Lutheran*, even if some seemed to think it reflected his views. Meyer typed up a summary of the meeting and sent it off to Behnken, who suggested a few changes in wording to better reflect his opinion; Meyer then incorporated Behnken's requested changes and sent the summary to the whole editorial board.[51]

When the board met in January 1944, about half the meeting was devoted to an official response to Behnken's September letter. A statement of policy was drafted by Brunn:

1. The staff assumes joint responsibility for all articles which appear under the heading "editorials."
2. Within the limits of Scriptural truth the editors of special columns have freedom of expression
3. The "Open Forum" is conducted to give desirable opportunity for free expression and exchange opinion within the limits of Scriptural truth, since official publications of the church can not meet this need.
4. Neither the editorial staff nor the ALPB by publication necessarily endorses the views and opinions expressed in the Open Forum.
5. The editorial staff reserves the right to refuse publication of any contributed article.

Meyer suggested that the policy should be approved by the ALPB board before being disseminated further, and it was so agreed. Presumably the board approved it, for on

February 17 Meyer sent the policy to Behnken as the editorial board's official response to his September 30 request.[52]

Behnken, however, did not think the policy responsive to his request. He appreciated their sharing it with him, but he had asked "that letters of a certain specific type be not solicited and published," and he was disappointed that they hadn't given a direct answer. "I am of the opinion that the real issue was evaded. Perhaps I have no business to expect a direct reply." Meyer responded with assurances that there was no intention of evasion; the editors believed that point 3 was in fact a direct reply, since Gallmeyer's letter had not been "solicited" and was thus in the nature of an "Open Forum" contribution. The editors had agreed, however, to publish "a permanent statement of open forum policy to appear regularly at the head of that column. ... Perhaps this will do more than anything else to clear the atmosphere."[53]

And there the matter lay, at least for the moment. The editorial board, believing that they had responded adequately to President Behnken's concern, agreed to continue the current series on Lutheran unity. The collection of "voices of the laity"—begun in October but temporarily suspended while conversations were going on with Behnken— was completed in March 1944. The series took up some other topics as well; there was an article advocating that Missouri join the National Lutheran Council, and another which traced with appreciation the "trend toward confessionalism" in Lutheran bodies outside the Missouri Synod.[54]

In June, right on the cusp of the Synod convention in Saginaw, MI, the magazine published an editorial entitled "The Problem of Lutheran Unity at Saginaw." Noting that "greater progress [toward unity] has been made during the past three years than in any comparable period in the recent history of Lutheranism in America," the editorial urged the delegates to Saginaw to continue on that path. "We know that the discussions will be conducted scripturally and charitably. It is our conviction that the Saginaw Convention will mark another step forward in our progress toward true Lutheran Unity."[55]

The Saginaw convention did not go quite as far as the editors had hoped, but the *American Lutheran*'s analysis of the convention's actions, headlined "Lutheran Collaboration at Saginaw," put the very best construction on things. The convention had resolved that "we ... do not direct our officers to make application for membership in the National Lutheran Council," but the *American Lutheran* noted that this did not *prevent* the Synod from applying for membership. It "merely states that Synod does not direct the officers to make application." The editorial argued that the need for cooperation in post-war reconstruction would inevitably push Missouri into a closer relationship with the NLC; if the delegates were not quite ready at Saginaw to join the Council, it was because the idea was before them for the first time and many simply did not understand what they were being asked to do. "In the light of circumstances," the editorial concluded, "the resolutions may be regarded optimistically. ... [T]he door is wide open for the fullest co-operation possible."[56]

Notes

1. W. Arndt, "Foreign Missions and Intersynodical Cooperation," *AL* 24, no. 2 (Feb. 1941), 10-11.

2. "Hindering Christ," *AL* 24, no. 3 (Mar. 1941), 3.

3. "Lutheran Union and Human Welfare," *AL* 24, no. 3 (Mar. 1941), 6.

4. Theodore Graebner, "Cooperation in Externals," *AL* 25, no. 1 (Jan. 1942), 7.

5. Ibid., 8.

6. Theodore Graebner, "Cooperation in Externals—III," *AL* 25, no. 3 (Mar. 1942), 7-8.

7. Edward C. Fendt, "American Lutheranism in 1940," *AL* 23, no 6 (June 1940), 6.

8. *Oregon and Washington District Proceedings, 1924*; cited in Mark E. Braun, *A Tale of Two Synods: Events that Led to the Split between Wisconsin and Missouri*, 2nd ed. (Milwaukee, WI: Northwestern Publishing House, 2003), 133.

9. Adolph Brux, *Christian Prayer-Fellowship and Unionism: An Investigation of our Synodical Position with Respect to Prayer-Fellowship with Christians of Other Denominations* (Racine, WI, 1935); cited in Braun, 134.

10. "Imitate Their Faith," *AL* 23, no 8 (Aug. 1940), 3.

11. *Proceedings of the Thirty-eighth Regular Convention of the Ev. Lutheran Synod of Missouri, Ohio, and Other States ... Ft. Wayne, Ind. ... 1941* (St. Louis, 1941), 303, cited in Richard C. Wolf, *Documents of Lutheran Unity in America* (Philadelphia: Fortress Press, 1966), 408; O. A. Geiseman, "While It Is Day," *AL* 24, no. 8 (Aug. 1941), 5.

12. "Tragic Misunderstandings," *AL* 24, no. 11 (Nov. 1941), 3.

13. Behnken's caveat was expressed in a letter, apparently to Synod pastors, quoted in *AL* 25, no. 7 (July 1942), 11.

14. "A Letter," *AL* 25, no. 7 (July 1942), 11.

15. J. W. Behnken to Adolf Meyer, 10 July 1942, Behnken Papers, Box 4, Folder 38.

16. Adolf Meyer to J. W. Behnken, 15 July 1942, Behnken Papers, Box 4, Folder 38.

17. J. W. Behnken to Adolf Meyer, 17 July 1942, Behnken Papers, Box 4, Folder 38.

18. Adolf Meyer to J. W. Behnken, 20 July 1942, Behnken Papers, Box 4, Folder 38.

19. Henry Wind to J. W. Behnke, 17 July 1942, Behnken Papers, Box 4, Folder 38.

20. Arthur Brunn to J. W. Behnke, 17 July 1942, Behnken Papers, Box 4, Folder 38.

21. Minutes, Editorial Staff of *American Lutheran*, 10 August 1942, Geiseman Papers, Box 21, Folder 2.

22. Ibid.; Theodore Graebner to A. F. Meyer, 15 June 1942, Graebner Papers, Box 121, Folder 2.

23. Minutes, Editorial Staff of *American Lutheran*, 10 August 1942, Geiseman Papers, Box 21, Folder 3.

24. Ibid.

25. Ibid.

26. Ibid.

27. "The Letter of Simplicissiumus," *AL* 25, no. 8 (Aug. 1942), 3-4.

28. "The Problem of Lutheran Unity: An Editorial Program," *AL* 25, no. 9 (Sept. 1942), 3.

29. "The Problem of Lutheran Unity: Present-Day Lutheranism in America—an Appraisal," *AL* 25, no. 10 (Oct. 1942), 8.

30. H. C. Schwann, *Dr. Martin Luther's Small Catechism* (St. Louis: Concordia Publishing House, 1912), 112; "The Problem of Lutheran Unity: Are We the Same?" *AL* 25, no. 11 (Nov. 1942), 10.

31. "The Problem of Lutheran Unity: Confessional Statements and Lutheran Unity," *AL* 25, no. 12 (Dec. 1942), 21.

32. J. Theodore Mueller to John W. Behnken, 4 Jan. 1943 [misdated 1942], Behnken Papers, Box 3, Folder 37.

33. John H. C. Fritz to John W. Behnken, 28 Dec. 1942, Behnken Papers, Box 3, Folder 37.

34. John H. C. Fritz to Adolf Meyer, 11 Jan. 1943, Behnken Papers, Box 3, Folder 37.

35. "The Problem of Lutheran Unity: Must We March Alone?" *AL* 26, no. 1 (Jan. 1943), 10.

36. "The Problem of Lutheran Unity: Prayer Fellowship and Unionism," *AL* 26, no. 2 (Feb. 1943), 7.

37. "Notes taken during the meeting of the Editorial Board of the 'American Lutheran,' February 25th, 1943, at Chicago," Geiseman Papers, Box 21, Folder 3.

38. "Notes of Joint Meeting, Feb. 26, 1943," Geiseman Papers, Box 21, Folder 3.

39. Ibid.

40. "The Problem of Lutheran Unity: Are We All Good Lutherans?" *AL* 26, no. 3 (Mar. 1943), 6-8.

41. "The Problem of Lutheran Unity: Looking Ahead" *AL* 26, no. 5 (May 1943), 6.

42. Theodore Graebner to E. J. Gallmeyer, 12 June 1943, Geiseman Papers, Box 20, File 4.

43. Ibid.

44. "A Letter," *AL* 26, no. 8 (Aug. 1943), 8.

45. John W. Behnken to Editors of the American Lutheran, 30 Sept. 1943, Behnken Papers, Box 4, Folder 37.

46. O. A. Geiseman to E. J. Gallmeyer, 21 Sept. 1943, Geiseman Papers, Box 20, Folder 4; E. J. Friedrich to E. J. Gallmeyer, 24 Sept. 1943, Geiseman Papers, Box 5, Folder 2.

47. Adolf Meyer, "Editorial Bulletin," 8 Oct. 1943, Geiseman Papers, Box 20, Folder 4.

48. Adolf Meyer, "Editorial Bulletin," 14 Oct. 1943, Geiseman Papers, Box 20, Folder 4.

49. Ibid.

50. E. J. Friedrich to Adolf Meyer, 10 Oct. 1943, Geiseman Papers, Box 20, Folder 4.

51. Adolf Meyer to Editorial Staff of the AMERICAN LUTHERAN, 3 1943, Geiseman Papers, Box 20, Folder 4.

52. Minutes, *AL* Editorial Board, 20-21 Jan. 1944, Geiseman Papers, Box 21, File 3.

53. John W. Behnken to Adolf Meyer, 25 Feb. 1944, and Adolf Meyer to John W. Behnken, 2 Mar. 1944, Behnken Papers, Box 4, Folder 37.

54. "The Problem of Lutheran Unity: The Trend Toward Confessionalism in the Lutheran Church of America," *AL* 27, no. 5 (May 1944), 8-10; "The National Lutheran Council and the Missouri Synod," *AL* 27, no. 4 (Apr. 1944), 5-7.

55. "The Problem of Lutheran Unity at Saginaw," *AL* 27, no. 6 (June 1944), 4.

56. "Lutheran Collaboration at Saginaw," *AL* 27, no. 8 (Aug. 1944), 3-4.

Chapter 8

THE WAR YEARS

While Lutheran unity had become the top priority of the *American Lutheran*, the magazine's interests (and the ALPB's) were hardly confined to that topic. As the crisis in Europe deepened and America at last entered the war, the *American Lutheran* gave more attention to secular events—the war itself, and the coming need for reconstruction, but also domestic issues such as the deepening racial crisis in America. It consciously moved away from an exclusive focus on "practical church work" and began to "make space for doctrine," explaining that the Synod's doctrinal disputes had in fact become a practical matter because they were inhibiting the evangelical mission of the church. Beyond the *American Lutheran*, the Bureau's ministry included the Child Evangelism Campaign and the publication of its first full-length book.

A Manual of Practical Church Work
"preachers will find little theory in this book"

"Shall We Publish a Book?" That was the question raised by an *American Lutheran* editorial in June 1941. The Bureau had received numerous letters wondering if it might be possible to produce an index of articles from the magazine. There was some consideration given to such a project, but the task seemed overwhelming—and the result not very useful unless a subscriber had saved every issue from the beginning. So an alternative proposal was considered.

> It would be possible to clip all worthwhile articles and editorials from past issues of the AMERICAN LUTHERAN and by an improved offset process reproduce such articles in book form. Such a book, if carefully edited, should prove to be an invaluable aid to all men in the Lutheran ministry. ... The proposed volume would be, in short, a book on practical church work as actually lived in practice throughout the years of the AMERICAN LUTHERAN magazine's existence.

"Is such a volume wanted?" the editor asked, and he urged people to write indicating their interest "immediately after reading this editorial."[1]

The response was positive and the project went forward under the direction of Adolf Meyer, who enlisted members of his congregation to help with the "cutting and pasting." The result was a remarkable assortment of articles covering the whole gamut of the *American Lutheran*'s interests through the years, published in 1942 as *Manual of Practical Church Work*. It was quite literally a collection of clipped articles. The preface issued a disclaimer:

> Readers may find certain pages resembling a pasted scrap-book, and others which carry articles referring to some past event. In editing the book it was impossible to eliminate all past dates. It was felt, however, that the pastor who purchases the "Manual of Practical Church Work" will care little where the scissors cut as long as he can find therein some practical help for a more efficient operation of his church.

The editor warned that "preachers will find little theory in this book," but the ideas presented have been tested by thousands of pastors, and the book "gives an accurate idea as to the contents of the monthly AMERICAN LUTHERAN magazine."[2]

The articles chosen for the book dealt with publicity, stewardship, Christian education, church finance, men's and women's organizations. Several of Fred Lindemann's reflections on Holy Communion were included, as were some of F. R. Webber's columns on church architecture and other liturgical matters. While the book was not explicitly organized by topic, articles on a specific theme were generally in proximity to each other. There was an extensive index that included titles and topics, but no indication of the issue of the *American Lutheran* from which each article came.

Manual of Practical Church Work was published under the imprint of the Lutheran Press. This entity was independent of the ALPB, though through the late 1930s its titles were frequently advertised in the pages of the *American Lutheran*. The December 1941 issue of the *American Lutheran,* however, announced that "the Business Department of the American Lutheran Publicity Bureau has acquired the stock and publication rights of the Lutheran Press." Then in May 1942 there is reference in the minutes to "the Lutheran Press matter." The following month a motion was approved that "the Business department of the American Lutheran Publicity Bureau be discontinued and that the Lutheran Press be continued and supervised by a special committee of three." It was agreed that the Lutheran Press accounts would be kept separate from those of the Bureau itself, and that "it shall be the general policy that the Lutheran Press shall publish and sell material which will help pastors, churches, and church societies to carry out the objects of the American Lutheran Publicity Bureau and its official organ, the American Lutheran." It was also agreed that when publications of the Lutheran Press were advertised in the *American Lutheran*, the Lutheran Press would pay the going rate, less a fifteen percent discount. This seems to have been simply an accounting device to keep the Lutheran Press financially discrete from the Bureau's other ministries, even though the Bureau had taken it over. The Lutheran Press Committee was composed of three members of the ALPB board, and the full board had "full authority to establish rules and regulations" regarding the Lutheran Press.[3]

It appears the *Manual of Practical Church Work* was the first item published by the Bureau under the Lutheran Press imprint. The book ran to 384 pages, sold for $2.50, and went through at least four editions from 1942 to 1945. By 1950 it was out of print; there was some discussion about another printing, but the board believed the book had served its purpose and no further editions were published. *Manual of Practical Church Work* was also the Bureau's first book-length publication, and while it would be several years before the next, the *Manual* was a harbinger of what was to come.

The *American Lutheran*'s changing mission
"make space for doctrine"

As the *American Lutheran* began its twenty-fifth year, it was apparent that there had been a gradual but fundamental shift in the magazine's self-understanding. The first editorial in volume 25 noted that shift. The *American Lutheran* had begun as a magazine of practical church work, but it had become a venue for an open forum on a variety of issues beyond the practical. The editors may not always agree with articles published, but they "stand ready to defend to the death a man's right to present his thoughts in the AMERICAN LUTHERAN just as long as the Word of God is not violated."[4]

Six months later the editor acknowledged the shift even more explicitly in an editorial entitled "Make Space for Doctrine."

> The AMERICAN LUTHERAN has always been a magazine of practical church work. We have published numerous articles advocating better publicity, systematic financial programs, fine arts in the service of the church, etc. Our emphasis has been upon the practical. The time has come, however, when a universal understanding of disputed doctrinal theses becomes a most practical matter. The pew as well as the pulpit must

know the basic issues which are preventing the progress of the Kingdom as far as the Lutheran Church is concerned.

This only stated overtly what had already been happening; the magazine had often published articles that touched on matters of doctrine, particularly church fellowship and sacramental theology. The "magazine of practical church work" was now an open forum, tackling just about any controversy in the church's life.[5]

But having stated the policy so clearly, some on the staff had second thoughts. The next month's editorial meeting included the long discussion [see above, p. 110] sparked by Brunn's concern that the magazine's "pursuit of ... controversial subjects" was endangering the ALPB's larger mission. The group had ultimately agreed that the *American Lutheran* was already "opening its columns to controversial articles, and that therefore it is not making a departure from established policy," but the question continued to come up in various ways (particularly from Brunn, who, since his election as a vice president of the Synod, was increasingly sensitive to the Behnken administration). At the next meeting, for instance, he raised the question of whether there was any point in continuing the emphasis on Lutheran unity since there were so many "insurmountable object[s]." The editorial board insisted that "we must go forward" and "continue [our] open forum policy," but they agreed that the magazine "will not lend its pages to personal attacks."[6]

One change in the editorial personnel of the *American Lutheran* in this period would prove to be quite significant. In February 1945, the magazine announced that contributing editor William Bruening would be leaving the editorial staff to accept a new call in Washington, DC. He would be succeeded by Oswald C. J. Hoffman, then professor of Greek and Latin at Concordia College in Bronxville, NY. Hoffman's immediate assignment would be to edit the "Service Department," the feature in the *American Lutheran* that focused on practical suggestions for parish ministry; he would soon become a significant influence on the magazine and a widely-known figure in the Synod—particularly when he succeeded Walter A. Maier as primary speaker on "The Lutheran Hour."

A new name for the Synod

"It was hard enough before"

In the 1940s, the name of the church body the ALPB primarily served was still officially "The Evangelical Lutheran Synod of Missouri, Ohio and Other States" (the modifier "German" had been dropped when the name was officially translated into English after World War I). As early as 1931, the *American Lutheran* had published proposals that the name be changed to be more in keeping with the 20th century reality of a church no longer geographically confined. A 1932 editorial had placed the magazine clearly on the side of a "widespread and growing sentiment in our Synod for a change in our official name." The Synod was now "national in the scope of its work," Paul Lindemann had written, and our name makes us appear "like an interloper who has strayed far afield." He had admitted that "the supply of names expressive of national character has been pretty well exhausted," but suggested that he personally favored one proffered by Otto Pannkoke: "The Evangelical Lutheran Church in America."[7]

The magazine had run more than a dozen articles or letters on the topic over the next decade, most advocating a change. Finally in 1942, President Behnken appointed a committee to consider a name change, and the *American Lutheran* came rushing into the fray. The April 1942 issue reprinted the editorial from ten years before, along with excerpts from several letters that had been received in response to it. Over the next several months, a series of articles urged a change.

The issue came to a head in 1944 when the Synod convention in Saginaw submitted to congregations a constitutional amendment changing the name of the Synod to "The Lutheran Church, Missouri Synod." This was not the direction the *American Lutheran* had in mind, and the magazine took the unprecedented step of urging congregations to vote "no" on the proposed amendment. The proposed name "puts our great church body in the category of a small isolated state group." Furthermore, the "unnecessary appendage of Missouri Synod is not confessional." The editors hoped that "the miracle will occur and that one third of the voting congregations of our Synod will send in a dissenting vote."[8]

They found support for their position from an unlikely source. Ade Meyer had become friends with Rachel McDowell, religious news editor for the *New York Times*. He asked her to write about the issue for the *American Lutheran*. McDowell was a Presbyterian, but she was obviously an authority on press coverage of churches, and she pulled no punches in lamenting the proposed change. If it is approved, she said, "I will give up my hope of trying to make my editors understand that you are a national church. It was hard enough before."[9]

Meyer's desired miracle did occur, however, and the congregations rejected the name. The 1947 Synod convention in Chicago proposed instead "Lutheran Church—Missouri Synod" (a change, the *American Lutheran* noted, which amounted to substituting "a dash for a comma"). The editors were appalled. "Is it wise policy for a convention of Synod to disregard such an overwhelming voice of its constituent congregations?" It may be, they suspected, that the congregations now "will throw up their hands and say 'What's the use of voting about the name in any manner, shape or form, because the voice of the congregation is not being listened to anyway?'" But the editors hoped otherwise, urging that congregations "patiently but firmly insist that our church carry a name which adequately describes its confessional heritage and its geographical scope in world-wide church work." They once again urged congregations to vote against the proposal, but to no avail; the proposal was approved by the congregations, and their church body was now the Lutheran Church—Missouri Synod.[10]

Liturgical kerfuffles
"such an avalanche of protest"

The *American Lutheran* continued to promote liturgical renewal in the 1940s. The focus had turned away from the early emphasis on "church decorum" to a more theologically sophisticated discussion of the centrality of the Eucharist, especially in the writings of Fred Lindemann. But in 1943 Lindemann wrote an editorial which picked up and expanded on the earlier theme of decorum, and the result was a piece which, in Ade Meyer's words, did "a great deal to disturb the clergy throughout the entire country." "Never before," Meyer told the other editors, "has any article in the AMERICAN LUTHERAN (not even the printing of the letter of 'Simplicissimus') brought forth such an avalanche of protest"—even among "those who had been our friends."[11]

Lindemann's editorial—which, as was the practice, had been read and approved by all the other members of the editorial board, and then published unsigned—was entitled "The Minister Disturbs Our Worship." It was a caustic criticism of pastors who inject their own personalities and preferences into their liturgical leadership. A Lutheran pastor, he wrote, presumably has "some measure of understanding" of liturgical principles, but too often a worshiper is unable "to concentrate on drawing near to God because the minister disturbed us" by "violating many liturgical principles which are the result of the Church's experience through almost two thousand years." Lindemann's complaints were those of a man with well-developed and precise liturgical sympathies; he criticized pastors who sat in the wrong place, or faced the wrong direction, or made inappropriately superfluous instructive comments ("Why could he not follow the simple wording of the rubrics when announcing the lesson?").[12]

These were, many readers thought, trifling matters in a time of war (though Lindemann had suggested that precisely because it was a time of war, worshipers need all the more to be able to "draw near to God" without the impediment of "liturgical outrages"). But one remark almost in passing elicited a sharp response from W. G. Polack, editor of the recently published *Lutheran Hymnal*. Lindemann had taken a swipe at the new book. "Bad enough that we should be led through part of the Order of the Communion and then be sent home without the Sacrament," he groused. "Bad enough that our new hymnal sanctions such a departure from liturgical usage." Polack took issue with Lindemann's insinuation:

> To say, as your editorial does, that this [service without Communion] is a 'departure from liturgical usage' is going too far. Everyone who has looked into the past liturgical usage of the Lutheran Church knows that that statement is not true. I well understand the position of some of the brethren who feel that Holy Communion ought to be administered in our churches every Sunday but several centuries of experience have shown that this simply cannot be done in the average congregation nor is it ever advisable to use means to force people to attend the Sacrament.

Polack's letter was published (without editorial comment) in the *American Lutheran*.[13]

Despite the "avalanche of protest," this turned out to be a tempest in a teapot—though it pointed to an issue that would be of continuing significance for the ALPB. At the heart of the controversy was the question of what it means to be "Lutheran," and it touched both on liturgical usages and sacramental doctrine. It would not be long before the *Confessional Lutheran* would begin to oppose the "pernicious leaven" of the liturgical movement within Missouri.[14]

Child Evangelism Campaign

"my heart rejoiced at the news"

In 1943 the ALPB launched what it called the "Child Evangelism Campaign." The idea was spawned at a board meeting that June when one of the lay members of the board asked for the floor. His words, as recalled later by ALPB president August Bobzin, were passionate:

> Brethren I was in court the other day and saw a young man of 18 being arraigned for a serious offence. His mother was present and terribly distraught for she sensed the serious consequences to her son. The judge asked the young man whether he had ever gone to church and Sunday School or had any religious training, to all of which the young fellow replied with a sullen 'No!' Brethren, I can't erase that scene from my mind. It has done something to me. What is our Church in America doing about the 17 million boys and girls who are without the Gospel today?

A. W. Brustat, who agreed to chair the campaign, would describe the meeting as "one of the most Spirit-filled which it was my privilege to attend." Bobzin agreed:

> Something happened to the men in that room. Man after man, clergyman and layman spoke. The foundation thought always was 'what can we do to put God into the life and education of American youth? What can we do to awaken our Church to this huge responsibility?' ... Before the meeting was adjourned every man present had spoken, and the speech of the men had about it something of the breath of the Great Commission Jesus gave to His Church on the Mount of Ascension.[15]

The centerpiece of the campaign was an effort to promote Christian education, particularly the Sunday school, with a goal of enrolling these unchurched children (all 17 million of them!) in Sunday school that fall. While many in the LCMS still complained that the Sunday school was inferior to the Christian day school, the popular American institution was being widely adopted by Synod congregations, and it became the primary emphasis of the Child Evangelism Campaign.

The campaign was not without its skeptics among the editors of the *American Lutheran*. Discussion of the plan took up much of an evening session of the editorial staff meeting that summer. Fred Lindemann, Kretzmann and Geiseman thought the intentions were good, but they were not convinced the Sunday school was an effective means of religious education. Meyer, Nickelsburg, and Bobzin (who was present as president of the Bureau) believed it was the best vehicle for the campaign available in most congregations. Lindemann went so far as to state that literature encouraging Sunday school attendance might "do more harm than good" since many parents were already convinced that Sunday school as an institution was a failure. Despite the debate, it was acknowledged that the ALPB board had launched the program, and that settled the matter; several suggestions were passed on from the editors to the Child Evangelism Committee regarding possible resources and emphases.[16]

The first public announcement of the campaign came in the August issue of the *American Lutheran*, which featured on its cover a brief note from President Roosevelt to Brustat: "I wish we might have in this country a general revival of religion. ... To this end I wish that every American child might be enrolled in a Sunday School." September's cover printed a handwritten note from New York Giants manager Mel Ott, testifying that "the Sunday School has been a powerful influence in my life ... both in our little family circle, as well as in my work as a baseball player and manager of a great team." That issue also offered complete details about the campaign, as well as resources and suggestions for how to publicize and carry out the program in one's own community.[17]

The next few issues continued the promotion. In October, there were two pages of letters of endorsement from a variety of leaders in church and society. LCMS president Behnken was pleased to be able to commend the Bureau. "To tell you that my heart rejoiced at the news ... is expressing it mildly," he wrote—though in a nod to the anti-Sunday school crowd, he described the campaign as one to enroll "millions of unchurched children into Christian Schools and Sunday Schools." Letters were also printed from FBI director J. Edgar Hoover, a collection of members of Congress and governors, and the presidents of several other Lutheran synods.[18]

After its dramatic start, however, the Child Evangelism Campaign quietly fizzled out. There was virtually no mention of it in 1944, but by 1945 the campaign had morphed into a "National Sunday School Week" each September. An editorial in the *American Lutheran* defended this new emphasis against those who continued to criticize the Sunday school movement:

> Granted that the Sunday School has shortcomings, still it remains the only means in many localities for the Christian teaching of our youth. Let us stop belittling the Sunday School or for that matter any of the other religious instruction institutions and use what we have as never before.

The Bureau would continue to sponsor National Sunday School Week for many years, providing resources and suggestions for increasing enrollment and generally improving the quality of the program.[19]

Attitudes toward Germany and the war

"We must refrain, therefore, from malicious joy"

The *American Lutheran* had been strangely silent about the developing situation in Germany during the 1930s—unlike some other voices within the Synod. The *Walther League Messenger*, for example, had been generally favorable toward Adolf Hitler. In an editorial entitled "Hitler Shows the Way," Walter A. Maier had condemned the American "newspapers which are dominated by Jewish influence [which] have systematically antagonized [Hitler's] reforms." Hitler, Maier went on, had demonstrated how to repudiate "atheistic communism ... immorality ... pornographic literature ... nudist colonies" and other "rampant social evils." Maier would, by 1939, become a sharp critic of the German regime.[20]

It is possible that some leaders in the ALPB had similar views during the 1930s. As late as 1937, a laudatory analysis of Hitler's regime had been published by the Lutheran Press (which had not yet been absorbed by the ALPB, though it was a frequent advertiser in the *American Lutheran*). Entitled *Christ versus Hitler*, the book by William Kraft presented itself as "a true and unbiased account" of the situation in Germany. Kraft had spent considerable time in Germany, and he claimed to have observed Hitler at close range; he judged him "a pious, God-fearing man and a convinced Christian." As for the Jews, Kraft insisted "I do not know of any serious offenses against them." "What their future lot will be," he wrote, "nobody knows; but this much is certain: they will never regain control of the press, the theatre, or of banking, commerce and industry under the present regime." He spoke also of the racial situation in America: "Whatever our view may be on the racial problem, the genuine value of the purity of race cannot be denied." He called "absolutely ridiculous" the assertion that the Nazi regime had been making "a systematic attack on the church in Germany."[21]

These views are astonishing to later generations, but they were not unusual among Americans in the 1930s, particularly among German American Lutherans. Still, it seems that among the leadership of the Bureau, there was at first suspicion and then outright hostility toward Hitler's regime. A 1936 editorial asked, "Do European Conditions Affect Us?" While the focus was primarily on the church situation rather than political or social matters, the writer (presumably Paul Lindemann) had a realistic view of the situation:

> Germany's religious influence even before the war was primarily destructive and modernistic and the strife engendered in the Church by the Nazi decrees seems to have paralyzed at least temporarily its influence. There seems to be evidence that some prominent German churchmen are playing politics rather than tending to their ecclesiastical knitting.

Lindemann was likely referring here to the pro-Nazi *Deutsche Christen*, rather than the opposition group that had issued the Barmen Declaration in 1934.[22]

In 1938, editorial board member O. P. Kretzmann founded the *Cresset*, with a staff of associate and contributing editors that included his *American Lutheran* colleagues Paul Lindemann, E. J. Friedrich, and O. A. Geiseman. The *Cresset* quickly became the most consistently anti-Fascist voice within the Synod. About the same time, the *American Lutheran* made its first direct comment on the German situation:

> The baneful influence of Nazi rule on the church life of Germany can no longer be denied. ... [The] reports that come from unprejudiced sources seem to establish the fact that the Church is gravely imperiled. In the face of the incontrovertible evidence of suppression and actual persecution one becomes somewhat weary of the American defenders of Nazism who vehemently seek to justify Adolf Hitler's church policy.

Hitler would continue to have his defenders among Lutherans, but after 1938 the *American Lutheran* would be unfailingly critical of the Nazi regime.[23]

America would not enter the war until the attack on Pearl Harbor in December 1941, but war clouds were on the horizon and preparations were being made many months before that day of infamy. President Roosevelt signed the Selective Training and Service Act in September 1940, giving America its first peacetime conscription. Remembering the success of its war tract series two decades earlier, the ALPB prepared to increase its tract production to meet the needs of military chaplains. The *American Lutheran* tackled the sensitive issue of conscientious objection, asserting that it was right for the government to provide that option for those who conscientiously refuse to take part in war. On the other hand, "the conscientious objector has no right to foist his convictions on others" and "he must not demand that the Church agree with him in his contention, unless he can prove from the Bible that his contention is right."[24]

Editorially, the *American Lutheran* was cautious about America's entering the war and insistent on the church's unique role. In November 1941, on the eve of the Pearl Harbor attack, New York's Mayor Fiorello La Guardia, whom President Roosevelt had appointed director of the Office of Civilian Defense, wrote a letter to clergy across America requesting that they preach a sermon on November 16 extolling the role of religion in supporting democracy. The *American Lutheran* was astounded—as were many clergy from across the spectrum of U. S. churches. Perhaps most critical was Charles Clayton Morrison, editor of the liberal Protestant *Christian Century*. The *American Lutheran* quoted him approvingly:

> This is an unspeakable insult to the clergy of the United States. Who would have imagined that an agency of the American Government would go so far as to tell preachers what to preach and actually to provide the outline of a model sermon for them to follow? Hitler and Goebbels never went further. Totalitarianism is already here.

The *American Lutheran* editorial argued that not only was the request inappropriate, the content of the proposed sermon was not one that could ever be preached from a

Lutheran pulpit. "Readers looked in vain for any reference to Jesus Christ. The Saviour of the world was ignored completely. ... To preach it would have been tantamount to a denial of the faith. ... The refusal of the Lutheran Church must be immediate and clearly decisive." The editorial spoke scornfully of what it called the "war party" among American churchmen, particularly citing the Episcopal Bishop of New York, William Manning, who "has been preaching a war policy for America."[25]

But after war was declared, the *American Lutheran* left no doubt about its support for the allied cause. The magazine immediately began two new features: F. R. Webber's "Our Boys in the Service" and Lambert Brose's "Chaplain's Corner." Brose, director of public relations for the Synod's Army and Navy Commission, focused on the ministry of military chaplains with special emphasis on how those at home could support that ministry.

In July 1942, the *American Lutheran*'s cover portrayed an American flag in full color with the caption, "United We Stand." An accompanying editorial urged "unanimous support" from Lutherans in purchasing war bonds. "Let us as citizens of this country labor for the preservation of its freedom, manfully fight for it, and if necessary, willingly shed our blood for it." In November 1943, an *American Lutheran* editorial proclaimed, "More Chaplains Needed," and urged Lutheran clergy to consider serving. The "Service Department" suggested how local churches might support and care for their members in the military. Geiseman's column often addressed war issues. Noting that most pastors were being called upon to meet with young men headed off to battle, he urged a reconceptualization of how those conversations might proceed:

> It seems to us that our Christian boys who go into military service should not only be told to shun such evils as gambling, drinking, and immoral sex relationships, but they should be instructed particularly to have a heart for many of those who are to be their buddies in arms and who have never yet in life enjoyed the privilege of Christian training. Our Lutheran boys ought count it a part of their responsibility to take such uninstructed boys by the hand and lead them to God and to Christ. Every one of our men ought be encouraged, before donning the uniform, to become the right hand man of the chaplain. ... A word of encouragement to each boy before leaving for the service may go a long way toward helping him realize to the fullest his possibilities as a spokesman for Christ while under arms.[26]

The magazine also made clear that its earlier opposition to La Guardia's ill-conceived request did not mean Lutheran congregations should be reluctant to cooperate with civilian defense efforts; rather pastors and congregations should gladly "offer the facilities of parish houses, school halls, church basements, and the like for use as shelters and temporary relief quarters in cases of emergency." An April 1942 editorial offered a sober reflection on the duty of the church in wartime:

> When the church does her duty by the individual, she will do many things which will result in strengthening the nation for war, even if this should not be intended.

Other things she must say may be condemned by some as having a depressing effect on the nation's morale for war. But she must be true to herself and to her Head. The Church must always be the Church. The morale that is based on hatred of the enemy or upon self-righteous nationalism must be counteracted.[27]

Within a few months, the editors were thinking already about the church's responsibility in a post-war world. Noting that allied leaders were planning for the massive humanitarian needs that would face Europe when the fighting ceased, an editorial in July 1942 suggested that relief work might provide an opportunity for Christian missionary work. "The church," it advised, "ought, therefore, be getting ready now to avail itself of such probably unprecedented opportunity for the spread of the Gospel." The church should be gathering funds and recruiting "an army of qualified missionaries which could be put to work immediately for the good of men the minute the war is ended."[28]

But as the war dragged on, Geiseman took a more sober view. In 1943 he cautioned his readers not to believe that "the world will be one of peace when the war comes to a close." Even when the war is over, he wrote, "the battle between men, with all of its attendant heartaches and sorrows, rages on. There is conflict between races, between classes, between husbands and wives in many homes." These things are a "perpetual concomitant of human life," and they are no less appalling than the ravages of war.[29]

As the war drew to a close, the *American Lutheran* continued to echo Geiseman's profound insight. In April 1945 the magazine quoted at length from Karl Barth (while noting that "we do not subscribe to all of [Barth's] theological premises"), who urged caution and a measure of realistic self-assessment in thinking about how to deal with Germany after the war.

> Dr. Barth stressed that the destruction of the Nazi state will place an obligation on the victors not only of passing judgment on the German people, but of bearing a share of 'man's common responsibility for rebelling against divine law.' He said:
>
> 'Our disobedience against the eternal law is no less real than the Germans'. We must refrain, therefore, from malicious joy, nor must we pass from fear of the Germans to pity for them. Our attitude must combine respect and sympathy as well as dread, since Germany's end is meant to teach us, too, that God's law cannot be flouted.'

Barth, the editorial noted, has shown "common sense and excellent Christian counsel."[30]

Not long after the war's end, the magazine printed a disturbing "Report from Germany" by Chaplain George L. Steinbeck. He told a moving story about his praying with a dying German boy, which astonished the boy's mother and others in the village because they had been taught "to fear and hate all Americans who had been pictured to them as blood-thirsty killers guilty of rape and mutilation of children." He then related a horrific experience:

In recent weeks I have also had the personal opportunity to see horrors and atrocities on the part of the Germans which I would have found most difficult to believe—had I not seen them! In one place we overran one of the Nazi concentration camps full of emaciated, starving, starved and dead Poles, Czechs, French, Russian and other 'slave laborers.' This particular camp was called the 'Camp of Death' because to it were sent those who were so emaciated, sick and weak that they could no longer work in nearby factories. ... At any rate, our Medics were called upon to evacuate the living from among the dead. The filth and stench was terrific. The Chicago Stockyards smell like gardenia in comparison! Bodies stacked like cordwood under the stairs; most of the survivors had diarrhea, and there were no sanitary facilities. ... I could tell you more, but if you're not sick now you probably would be by the time I finished. As it is now, I don't know just how much of this will get by the censor. But it's a matter of record now and the full story will probably have broken in the papers by the time this reaches you. It's simply one of these things which I have been hearing and read about but couldn't make myself believe.[31]

Adolf Meyer would later recall that "as far as I know we were the first Lutheran publication to tell the story of this Nazi horror."[32]

Race relations

"racial segregation in the Church ... cries to the high heavens!"

Even as the United States fought the evils of Nazi Germany, racial unrest was bubbling beneath the surface at home. After the war, the irony of African American soldiers battling against a harshly racist regime when they were regarded as second-class citizens at home would fuel a rapidly growing civil rights movement. But already during the war, the *American Lutheran* had begun to call attention to the need for Christians to confront issues of racial inequality. In May 1944, a letter to the editor from one Delvin Ressel reported on a new organization in St. Louis called the St. Louis Lutheran Society for Better Race Relations. Its founders, he wrote, were "convinced that present race relations in the Church constitute a real and serious problem." Presiding over the new interracial group was the Rev. Andrew Schulze, the (white) pastor of the (predominantly African American) St. Philip's Lutheran Church.[33]

Two months later Pr. Schulze himself contributed an "Open Forum" piece entitled "Racial Segregation in Society in General." Comparing America's racial segregation to Hitler's persecution of Jews and the caste system in India, Schulze noted that "the breaking down of the system [of racial segregation] is everywhere apparent." This is only right, he argued; after all, "racial segregation is in open opposition to the democratic ideology that our soldiers, sailors, and marines are told at every turn they are fighting to uphold." But it is also clear that segregation is harmful to those discriminated against, and that as Christians, our obligation is to "help keep hurts away from our neighbor for the sake of his earthly and temporal comfort" because only by doing so may we "win and keep him for Christ and for heaven." Schulze wrote again in October at Meyer's invitation. "Racial segregation in society in general is wrong," he asserted, "but racial segregation in the Church, of all places, cries to the high heavens! ... It is contrary to Christian love, and obviously unjust. It gives offense in the very house of God."[34]

Schulze would become, over the next several years, one of the most important voices for racial equality in the Missouri Synod. He was the moving force behind the Lutheran Human Relations Association of America, founded in 1953. Years later Schulze would reflect on the role of the *American Lutheran* and the ALPB in the struggle for civil rights:

> The *American Lutheran* ... was published by the American Lutheran Publicity Bureau, an independent organization that had its membership and area of concern largely within the Missouri Synod. The ALPB was both progressive and at the same time more socially and politically liberal than the Synod itself. This attitude was reflected in the editorial policy of the *American Lutheran*, also as that policy pertained to the race issue. In the ... early forties, when I sent an article on the church and the race issue to the *American Lutheran*, not only was it published, but the editor, the Rev. Adolf F. Meyer, wrote encouraging me to send them more materials for publication; and this I did. Many articles and book reviews written by men like the Rev. Clemonce Sabourin, the pastor of Mount Zion Church in Harlem, as well as sustaining editorials, were presented by the magazine.

The struggle for civil rights became a consistent focus throughout the rest of the magazine's existence. [35]

True to its commitment to be an "open forum," the magazine was willing occasionally to print pieces that took a reactionary point of view on civil rights. An "Open Forum" essay by Theodore Schliepsick explained "How the South Feels." He insisted that there was "not one passage in Scripture which insists on equality for all men." Perhaps in a century things will be different, but for now, "the South will stick to segregation." But from the 1940s on, most of the *American Lutheran's* articles—and all its editorial comment—would be strongly supportive of the civil rights movement.[36]

Promotions, Programs, Anniversaries
"our magazine was a true pioneer"

While tackling the challenges of depression, war and racial unrest, the Bureau and the *American Lutheran* also tended to more mundane matters. J. F. E. Nickelsburg had for some years been concerned about the secularization and commercialization of Christmas—especially the lack of Christ-centered Christmas cards available from commercial card companies. At his urging the ALPB began to offer a line of Christmas cards that might be more suitable for Christians. In February 1940, he reported that the

Bureau had sold more than "100,000 cards with Christ-centered messages"—making this "one of the most successful undertakings conducted by the Bureau." He added that commercial card companies had also reported a substantial increase in requests for "religious cards."[37]

The tract ministry continued unabated. Nickelsburg proudly announced that a half-million tracts had been distributed during 1940, and the anticipated goal for 1941 was a million. Two tracts originally published in the Bureau's first year, "Why Go to Church?" and "What the Lutheran Church Stands For," were still in print and among the most popular sellers. But new titles continued to be produced, including "Wearing the Cross," "The Bible Church," and "Why Doesn't the Church Leave Me Alone?" The latter was described as "a new type of tract"—one which, rather than seeking to "contain the whole Gospel" in a single tract, offered a streamlined text directing people to the Bible and the church. The goal was "a tract of very few words, illustrated with pen sketches, which shows briefly what the Lord Jesus Christ offers through his Church and urges [the reader] to investigate." In 1942 the Bureau modestly aimed to place one of its tracts in every home in America.[38]

The *American Lutheran* continued to offer new ideas and suggestions. Noting that Catholic churches were generally kept open during the week, a February 1942 editorial by Ade Meyer advocated an "open church" policy. "Is there any good reason why Lutheran churches should not be open during the week for meditation and prayer? It can be done! It is being done!" He offered suggestions as well for how to address questions of security and expense, insisting that having the church open can be a vital ministry to one's community:

> We believe that especially in this day when modern living conditions provide so little privacy in the apartment home, that there are many burdened hearts which seek a place where they can meditate and pray to their God without interruption. Amidst the present sorrows of war the quiet peace found within the church's walls may help to bring healing and comfort to many a wounded heart.[39]

The ALPB also experimented with outdoor advertising, offering billboards and posters that could be erected along highways or in other public places. To demonstrate the possibilities, the Bureau itself in 1942 paid for a 23-foot billboard in the heart of Times Square in New York, which the *American Lutheran* called "the busiest spot in this troubled world." The text read: "A Changeless Christ for a Changing World. Times Which Try Men's Souls. Pray. Go to Church. Build up Your Faith, Courage and Strength. The Lutheran Church Invites You." The Times Square billboard was the subject of a press release from Religious News Service, and it was covered as well by the secular press in New York. The *New York Times* printed a photo of the billboard the day after it went up, reporting that it was one of some 200 similar signs erected around the metropolitan area, and that others had been posted elsewhere in the country. The *American Lutheran* urged readers to use similar means "to reach the travelers on the highways of your community."[40]

The Bureau continued to take pride in its reputation as a resource for information of all kinds, especially in the New York area. A promotional piece in the *American Lutheran* in 1941 outlined the services ALPB was asked to provide:

> 1819 Broadway, Columbus Circle, New York, has not only become the Lutheran Center of the Metropolitan area, but the headquarters of the A-L-P-B has also become more and more the Information Bureau of national Lutheran activities. Visitors from many states and from abroad, visit the Bureau offices, seek information as to travel plans, sightseeing, lodging, etc. 10% of our daily mail consists of 'information-please.' From January 1st this year to September 1st our telephone switchboard had 1,581 calls. 'Information-please,' included such questions as: 'address of Pastor So and So,' 'hours of services,' 'locations of churches,' 'institutions,' 'lot numbers in Lutheran cemetery,' 'what is the rule in Lutheran Churches, in regard to marriages,' 'baby adoption,' 'employment,' 'baptism certificates,' and what not.

While this kind of service was neither an official nor a major part of the ALPB ministry, it did suggest the Bureau's growing reputation as the "go-to" source for people seeking a wide range of information about Lutheranism.[41]

The January 1942 issue of the *American Lutheran* took note of the fact that the magazine was marking its 25th anniversary. It included a message from ALPB President August Bobzin:

> As we cast a reflecting glance over these past years we immediately become aware of human weaknesses. We wistfully wish that some issues of the magazine could be done over again. We are not unaware that our AMERICAN LUTHERAN was another human institution attended by the frailties that are part of all of us. Yet with forgivable pride we are thinking of some other things. We remember that our magazine was a true pioneer in the Church and has not lost its pioneering spirit. We recall the important blows which these pages put in for causes that were truly worthwhile. We think of the many ways in which the magazine was helpful to Pastors and churches. ...

> Particularly are we humbly grateful to be able to state one other thing, the main thing. It has been our policy that we were willing to open the pages of the AMERICAN LUTHERAN to any article written in the spirit of love and helpfulness that would foster the interests of the church. We adhered to that policy. We have no other today.

But soon the *American Lutheran's* efforts to foster a "spirit of love and helpfulness" would precipitate a major crisis in the Missouri Synod.[42]

Notes

1. "Shall We Publish a Book?" *AL* 24, no. 7 (July 1941), 4.
2. "Preface," *Manual of Practical Church Work* (New York: Lutheran Press, 1942).
3. Minutes, ALPB Board, 18 May 1942, 15 June 1942, Graebner Papers, Box 121, file 1.
4. "Volume XXV, Number 1," *AL* 25, no. 1 (Jan. 1942), 3.
5. "Give Space for Doctrine," *AL* 25, no 7 (July 1942), 3-4.
6. Minutes, *AL* Editorial Board, 10 Aug. 1942 and 25 Feb. 1943, Geiseman Papers, Box 20, Folder 4.
7. "Shall We Have a New Name?" *AL* 15, no. 10 (Oct. 1932), 4.
8. "Vote Now," *AL* 27, no. 10 (Oct. 1944), 3.
9. Rachel K. McDowell, "Advice from a Friend," *AL* 28, no. 2 (Feb. 1945), 11.
10. "Change of Name," *AL* 30, no. 11 (Nov. 1947), 3.
11. "Editorial Bulletin," 4 June 1943. Geiseman Papers, Box 21, Folder 2.
12. "The Minister Disturbs Our Worship," *AL* 26, no. 5 (May 1943), 3-4.
13. Ibid.; "A Letter," *AL* 26, no. 7 (July 1943), 9.
14. See, for example, "Sacramentalism and the Union Movement," *Confessional Lutheran* 10, no. 2 (Dec. 1949), 142.
15. Aug. F. Bobzin, "An Important Meeting," *AL* 26, no. 9 (Sep. 1943), 14; A. W. Brustat, "To the Members of the Board, the Vice-presidents, and the Editorial Staff of the American Lutheran Publicity Bureau," [ca. June 1943], Graebner Papers, Box 121, Folder 1.
16. "Editorial Bulletin: Report of the Editorial Conference at Lutherland July 29th and 30th, 1943," Geiseman Papers, Box 20, Folder 4.
17. *AL* 26, no. 8 (Aug. 1943), 1; *AL* 26, no 9 (Sep. 1943), 1-4, 14-17.
18. *AL* 26, no 10 (Oct. 1943), 14-15.
19. "National Sunday School Week," *AL* 28, no. 5 (May 1945), 3-4.
20. Walter A. Maier, "Hitler Shows the Way," *Walther League Messenger* 41 (Apr. 1933), 461; quoted in Pahl, 172-175.
21. Walter Kraft, *Christ versus Hitler* (New York: Lutheran Press, 1937), 37, 47, 61, 65, 133-34.
22. "Do European Conditions Affect Us?" *AL* 19, no. 12 (Dec. 1936), 5.
23. "Editorial Musings," *AL* 21, no. 2 (Feb. 1938), 7. On Missouri Synod Lutherans and Hitler, see Dean Wayne Kohlhoff, "Missouri Synod Lutherans and the Image of Germany, 1914-1945" (PhD diss., University of Chicago, 1973). See also Jon Pahl, *Hopes and Dreams of All*, chapters 6 and 7; and Kenneth C. Barnes, "American Lutherans and the Third Reich" in Betty Rogers Rubenstein and Michael Berenbaum, eds., *What Kind of God? Essays in Honor of Richard L. Rubenstein* (Lanham, MD: University Press of America, 1995), 187-199.
24. "Just Wars," *AL* 24, no. 1 (Jan. 1941), 4.
25. "The State Tells Us What to Preach," *AL* 24, no. 12 (Dec. 1941), 4.
26. "Does that Star-Spangled Banner Yet Wave?" *AL* 25, no. 7 (July 1942), 4; "More Chaplains Needed," *AL* 26, no. 11 (Nov. 1943), 3; "The Local Congregation and the Man on Foreign Soils," *AL* 26, no. 12 (Dec. 1943), 16; O. A. Geiseman, "While It Is Day," *AL* 26 no. 4 (Apr. 1943), 5.
27. "Civilian Defense," *AL* 25, no. 3 (Mar. 1942), 5; "The Church in Time of War," *AL* 25, no. 4 (Apr. 1942), 4.
28. "War-Aims and the Church," 25, no. 7 (July 1942), 3.
29. O. A. Geiseman, "While It Is Day," *AL* 26, no. 11 (Nov. 1943), 5.
30. "Treatment of Germans," *AL* 28, no. 4 (Apr. 1945), 4.
31. George L. Steinbeck, "Report from Germany," *AL* 28, no 8 (Aug. 1945), 13, 18.
32. Meyer, "Autobiography," 31.
33. Delvin Ressel, "Attacking the Race Problem in the Church," *AL* 27, no. 5 (May 1944), 17.
34. Andrew Schulze, "Racial Segregation in Society in General," *AL* 27, no. 7 (July 1944), 9-10; "Racial Segregation in the Church," *AL* 27, no. 10 (Oct. 1944), 9.
35. Andrew Schulze, *Race Against Time: A History of Race Relations in the Lutheran Church—Missouri Synod from the Perspective of the Author's Involvement 1920-1970* (Valparaiso, IN: The Lutheran Human Relations Association of America, 1972), 106. On Schulze's life and ministry, see Kathryn M. Galchutt, "Career of Andrew Schulze, 1924-1968: Lutherans and Race in the Civil Rights Era" (PhD diss., Marquette University, 2002).

36. Theodore Schliepsick, "How the South Feels," *AL* 27, no. 10 (Oct. 1944), 9.

37. J. F. E. Nickelsburg, "The A.L.P.B. Report," *AL* 24, no. 2 (Feb. 1941), 13.

38. "A New Departure in Tracts," *AL* 25, no. 2 (Feb. 1942), 5.

39. "Open Church," *AL* 25, no. 2 (Feb. 1942), 3.

40. *NYT*, 12 Mar. 1942, 40; "American Lutheran Publicity Bureau Tells the World," *AL* 25, no. 4 (Apr. 1942), 3

41. "INFORMATION—Please," *AL* 24, no. 12 (Dec.1941), 14.

42. A. F. Bobzin, "In Passing," *AL* 25, no. 1 (Jan. 1942), 5.

Chapter 9

"A Statement"

T he November 1945 edition of the *American Lutheran* contained this notice: "The following 'Statement' and accompanying letter was sent to all pastors of the Missouri Synod. For the present the American Lutheran withholds comment." There followed what was originally called simply "A Statement" (though it became known more commonly as the "Statement of the 44" because of the number of signatories, all pastors in the Synod, several of them men of some prominence). The document precipitated one of the most contentious episodes in the Synod's history, one still viewed—many decades later—in sharply different ways. Whatever else may be said about the controversy, the *American Lutheran*'s "withholding comment" was a bit disingenuous, for the editors were hardly objective bystanders. Not only were personnel of the magazine and of the ALPB among the signers of "A Statement," they were instrumental in its genesis.

The genesis of "A Statement"

"we discussed our present status quite thoroughly"

By late 1944, Americans were anticipating an end to the long world war. In St. Louis the mayor invited representatives of different churches to plan a community celebration when peace came at last. When the LCMS representative informed the mayor that the

Synod could not participate in a service of worship, it was agreed that the celebration would be designed as a civic event. In May 1945, the Axis powers surrendered and the St. Louis celebration of "V-E Day" was scheduled. The mayor was to preside, and clergy representatives from five different religious groups were invited to speak for five minutes each. The Missouri Synod was represented by Dr. Richard Caemmerer, professor of homiletics at Concordia Seminary. His participation was approved by the St. Louis pastoral conference. The other speakers included a Roman Catholic priest, a rabbi, a Presbyterian, and an African American Protestant pastor. All the addresses were primarily of a civic nature; Caemmerer, for instance, "stressed the significance of V-E Day as a reminder of undone tasks and the need for continued vitality of citizenship." Another Missouri Synod pastor had been asked to give the benediction, but when concerns were expressed by fellow pastors that this would cross the line into participation in a unionistic service, he bowed out and Caemmerer took his place. Instead of offering a prayer, Caemmerer closed the meeting by reading portions of Lincoln's Second Inaugural Address.[1]

Nevertheless, some were offended at Caemmerer's participation, and letters were sent to Synod officials charging him with "violation of God's Word and the Synod's constitution." For other Synod members—so argued Jack Treon Robinson, whose 1972 dissertation is the most complete account of the events surrounding "A Statement"—this attack on Caemmerer was the last straw, and discussion began about how to make their concerns known. The result was the document drafted by a group of Missouri Synod pastors who met in Chicago in September 1945.[2]

Who initiated this meeting is a matter of some confusion. Robinson interviewed E. J. Friedrich and O. P. Kretzmann, and at least one of them told him the idea originated in a meeting between them and O. A. Geiseman in Chicago in April 1945, where they agreed to convene a gathering in Chicago September 6-7. The date was set to coincide with a meeting of the *American Lutheran* editorial board (all three were members of that board, and they anticipated the rest of the editorial staff would participate). There are some inconsistencies in this account. Robinson believed that a key precipitating factor in calling the September meeting was the Caemmerer incident. The V-E Day event, however, took place in May, weeks after the alleged April meeting.

On the other hand, Adolf Meyer claimed a much more significant role for the *American Lutheran* editors. "It was our Editorial Staff," he wrote in his autobiography, "which had invited people to meet with us and which had formulated and adopted this Statement." In a 1981 letter to Henry Lieske, he went even further: "I had called a large meeting of the (1945) staff of the American Lutheran in Chicago—asking MANY of our contributing editors to attend."[3]

That was almost certainly an overstatement. Archival evidence appears to suggest that the plan for this meeting originated somewhat later than Friedrich's and/or

Kretzmann's recollection, and that it was the idea of Kretzmann, Geiseman, Henry Wind, and Adolf Meyer—all members of the editorial staff of the *American Lutheran*. In July 1945, Kretzmann wrote to Friedrich, "I was at a meeting with Ade, Hank and Geise in Fort Wayne last week and we discussed our present status quite thoroughly. Out of this meeting a number of suggestions have come." The first was a request that Friedrich call "a meeting of men interested in the problem of Lutheran unity just as quickly as possible." Kretzmann listed 33 names discussed by the group, but added that they thought it might be best to limit the number to 25. He suggested that they seek some laymen to "finance the expenses at least of those who must come from some distance." He told Friedrich that they had "agreed that you and I should get together in order to plan the program." As for the date for this proposed meeting, he suggested September 6-7 in Chicago because the Social Work Institute would be meeting the following week at Valparaiso. Kretzmann's letter didn't mention the *American Lutheran* editorial board meeting (scheduled for September 5, not September 3-4, as Friedrich and/or Kretzmann recalled to Robinson), but that was likely also a factor in setting the date. Indeed, a list sent by Friedrich to Meyer of "Men Announced to Date for the Chicago Meeting" categorized the prospective attendees as "American Lutheran Staff" and "Others."[4]

Perhaps there had been earlier discussion between Friedrich and others, though the archival evidence should be given greater weight than recollections 30 years or more after the fact. Whatever the timing of specific conversations about such a meeting may have been, Friedrich quickly agreed to chair the planning committee. On August 4 he wrote to Ade Meyer, confirming the September 6-7 date. He told Meyer that about 45 men would be invited, including the entire *American Lutheran* editorial staff; he hoped that, since the meeting coincided with the editorial board meeting, the magazine's budget could cover the costs of those coming from the East.[5]

Friedrich also drafted the letter of invitation, dated August 9:

May I take a little of your time for a matter of tremendous importance in the life of our Church? It has been causing many of us great concern, and I welcome this opportunity to unburden my soul by telling you about it and asking your help.

In recent years, especially since the Saginaw Convention, a strange and pernicious spirit, utterly at variance with the fundamental concepts of the gospel and the genius of the Lutheran Church, has lifted its ugly head in more than one area of our beloved Synod. This spirit has its origin in a wrong approach to the Holy Scriptures and in a tragic misconception of the very essence of the gospel and the nature, functions and mission of the Church. It is characterized by barren, negative attitudes, unevangelical techniques in dealing with the problems of the individual and the Church, unsympathetic legalistic practices, a self-complacent and separatistic narrowness, and an utter disregard for the fundamental law of Christian love. One need not be a prophet to forecast what the results will be if this unevangelical and intolerant spirit is left unrestrained and to its own devices. Spiritual life will be blighted. The organism of the Church will be paralized [*sic*]. Ecclesiastical persecution will occur with increasing frequency. The onward march of the Gospel will be obstructed. ...

During the past year this alarming phenomenon in our synodical life has been the topic of many discussions. ... But invariably the question arose, What can be done?

Several groups in different parts of the country have arrived at the same answer: We must, to begin with, arrange a meeting of kindred minds to study the situation.

At the request of several of these groups, I have consented to call such a meeting. ... This will be nothing revolutionary or iconoclastic. On the contrary, our meeting is to be sane and soundly Lutheran, evangelical, positive and constructive. It is our desire to keep it on a high spiritual level.

He then extended a "hearty invitation" to attend, suggested that meals and lodging would be provided and that travel assistance would be available to those more than 400 miles from Chicago, and asked for a prompt response.[6]

Some 49 persons received the letter. There had been careful discussion about whether to invite President Behnken; the group decided that it would put him in an awkward position, since whether he attended or declined, one faction or another in the Synod would be critical. There was also disagreement about whether to invite Theodore Graebner. Kretzmann was in favor and Geiseman opposed, so they left it to Friedrich. Graebner was invited, and he would turn out to be one of the key defenders of "A Statement" in the controversy that ensued.[7]

Most of those invited responded positively. As might be expected, word of the proposed meeting quickly got out beyond the invitees, and rumors began to fly. Behnken later told Friedrich that he had been stopped in the train station in Chicago by a pastor in the Northern Illinois District who "told him that a meeting of a revolutionary group in the synod was going to be held in Chicago after Labor Day." Some were convinced that this group was planning to attempt to unseat Behnken at the 1947 convention.[8]

When the meeting finally took place, there were 42 clergymen present (as well as a layman, W. C. Dickmeyer, who, along with E. J. Gallmeyer and a few others recruited by Kretzmann, had underwritten the meeting financially). A good number of them were associated with the *American Lutheran* or with the Bureau itself. ALPB president August Bobzin was there, as were most of the editorial staff of the magazine (Meyer, Brunn, Geiseman, Fred Lindemann, William F. Bruening, Friedrich, Brustat, Hoffman, Kretzmann; Henry Wind was unable to attend but would ask that his name be included among the signers). Theodore Graebner was a national vice president of ALPB, a largely honorary post, though he had also written frequently for the magazine. Several others in attendance were past contributors to the *American Lutheran*. It may be that others present were contributing editors, board members or vice presidents of ALPB; we do not have complete information about who was serving in those capacities during this period. It would be safe to say, however, that at least a third and perhaps more of those present had a direct association with ALPB and the *American Lutheran*.[9]

The editorial staff meeting convened in Room 12 of the Hotel Stevens in Chicago on September 5—the same room where "the 44" would meet the next day. The morning session took up the usual business—a review of the past year's magazine, plans for the coming months. The afternoon session turned to what was about to take place. Four pastors had been asked to prepare papers for the meeting of "the 44," including Geiseman and Kretzmann. Both shared their papers with the others on the editorial staff that afternoon, and discussion followed. The staff expressed "unanimity of agreement on the two papers." There was talk of publishing these essays (and the other two by William Arndt and Richard Caemmerer) in the *American Lutheran*. In the minutes of the meeting, there is a question mark beside this point, apparently indicating that no decision was made about this proposal; in the end the essays were not published.[10]

The larger group convened the next morning. E. J. Friedrich opened with an address in which he suggested that the session was not primarily intended to be a discussion of Lutheran union (despite that focus in the original planning in Ft. Wayne), but its purpose was "the unhampered spread of the Gospel in Christian love." Certain decisions about procedure were made; August Bernthal was chosen to chair the conference, and August Brustat was named secretary. The four essays prepared were read, and copies were distributed.

The first paper was presented by William Arndt and was entitled, "The Application of the Law of Love in the Practical Life of the Church." Arndt, a professor at Concordia Seminary, argued that the "law of love" must be the key motivation for the Christian's relationship with those who "fall into doctrinal errors." The traditional Missourian view, based on Romans 16.17, was that such persons should be avoided, but Arndt argued that even in extreme cases, the law of love must be observed. Similar principles apply when dealing with other church bodies that are in error, or with "our own brethren who are super-zealous, extreme in their conservative, too narrow in their outlook." This will mean "abstaining from name-calling" and from "impugning the motives of these brethren." The law of love particularly applies to fellow Lutherans, no matter what their synod. Even if they must be admonished for their errors, love demands that "the language of rebuke ... be couched in such terms that our deep love ... will become manifest and with God's help they may be won for the truth."[11]

Caemmerer's brief paper, "Doctrines and Life, and Their Application to Synodical Attitudes," argued that Christian doctrine is not a "static body of information with influence only on the intelligence"; rather the Holy Spirit uses Christian doctrine to bring individuals to faith—and particularly to a new life. A Christian's evangelical witness and teaching arises out of this new life of love, not out of "recitation of Christian doctrine unapplied to life."[12]

Kretzmann's "Organization and Church" was also brief, but it engendered the most discussion. He cited the traditional distinction between the *una sancta*—the true church which is invisible, and which, in Missouri Synod thought, subsists in the congregation—and the *ecclesia representativa,* the "organized union of congregations" such as the Synod. Recently the latter has "moved into the center of thought and life" in a destructive and dangerous way, leading to "a demand for a rigid organizational loyalty" which "tends to narrow our horizons, to multiply authoritative traditions, to becloud our vision of the Body of Christ, to engender suspicion of all other groups within Christendom." It also makes it "difficult, if not impossible, to exercise any appreciable influence upon those who are in need of our testimony."[13]

The final paper was Geiseman's "Protest and Appeal." He apparently anticipated that it might be endorsed by the others and serve as a statement of the whole group; that was not to be the case, but it did provide a kind of model for what would emerge from the meeting. Geiseman observed that "a new spirit is beginning to obtrude itself upon the life and thought of our Synod," a spirit that is neither that of New Testament Christianity nor of the founders of the Missouri Synod. It "lays claim to a special degree of orthodoxy"—more like Rome than the Lutheran Reformation—which "neglects the principle of Christian love." It is a "new, strange, unbiblical and unLutheran spirit of legalism" which "begets the necessity of going on and of becoming ever more loveless, severe, and tyrannical." He appealed, first, to those who have been "infected" with this spirit to change their hearts; second, to leaders of the Synod to do all in their power "to the end that this new and strange spirit may be eradicated from our midst"; and third, to all pastors and congregations to "be on their guard ... lest they be robbed of the right of private judgment."[14]

The discussion was robust and not always harmonious. Robinson reported, based on his interviews, that there was a sharp disagreement between Arndt and Geiseman about the interpretation of Romans 16.17 which led to Geiseman's threatening to walk out. Kretzmann and Friedrich prevailed on him to stay, and ultimately Arndt accepted Geiseman's understanding of the passage.[15]

The group appointed a committee consisting of the four essayists and five others (including Friedrich) to propose a definite recommendation. They met until late that night, taking into consideration all four papers and the points made in the discussion, and then asked Kretzmann to draft a document embodying their consensus. The result was unanimously approved by the whole group the next morning and was published as "A Statement." Robinson's analysis suggested that it was "an accurate compend of the various concerns voiced at the meeting" in both the papers and discussion, and "not the expression of just one individual. It belonged to the group."[16]

"A Statement" consisted of twelve positive affirmations, coupled in most cases with a negative statement beginning "We therefore deplore ..." Most of the affirmative statements were non-controversial; it was what the group "deplored" that raised the wrath of more conservative Missourians. So, for example, the first statement affirmed "our unswerving loyalty to the great evangelical heritage of historic Lutheranism." It would be hard for any Lutheran to disagree with that sentiment. But it also "deplore[d] any and every tendency which would limit the power of our heritage, reduce it to narrow legalism, and confine it by manmade traditions." The statement doesn't name names, but the obvious implication is that, in the view of the signers, some in the synod were guilty of such "narrow legalism."[17]

The document then addressed more specific issues. It deplored "a tendency in our Synod to substitute human judgments, Synodical resolutions, or other sources of authority for the supreme authority of Scripture." This certainly was a veiled reference to the 1932 "Brief Statement of the Doctrinal Position of the Missouri Synod," which had been given a kind of semi-confessional status by the Synod in 1938. While the issue of "Lutheran union" may not have been specifically discussed, the matter of "Lutheran unity" pervaded the Statement, as it condemned the loveless attitude which "has been expressed in suspicions of brethren, in the impugning of motives, and in the condemnation of all who have expressed differing opinions concerning some of the problems confronting our Church today."[18]

The statement criticized Missouri's traditional exegesis of Romans 16.17, which "does not apply to the present situation in the Lutheran Church of America." It deplored the "new and improper emphasis on the Synodical organization" at the expense of the *una sancta* and the local congregation. It tackled head on the contentious issues of prayer fellowship and unionism, insisting that "any two or more Christians may pray together to the Triune God in the name of Jesus Christ if the purpose for which they meet and pray is right according to the Word of God." The term "unionism" should properly be applied "only to acts in which a clear and unmistakable denial of Scriptural truth or approval of error is involved" and not "to any and every contact between Christians of different denominations." It criticized those who would claim to "take offense" at the words or actions of others as a cover for their own prejudices, and it asserted that church fellowship "is possible without complete agreement in details of doctrine and practice which have never been considered divisive in the Lutheran Church." The final statement affirmed that God has "richly, singularly, and undeservedly blessed our beloved Synod" and pledged to make every effort to continue to build the Synod in the future.[19]

Before adjourning, the group in Chicago voted to send copies of "A Statement" to every pastor in the Synod. They appointed a "Continuation Committee" of five to "work out all further details" and empowered it to act on behalf of the group. This committee included Friedrich, Kretzmann and Geiseman (all members of the *American*

Lutheran editorial board). The other two, A. R. Kretzmann and B. H. Hemmeter, had both written for the magazine and had been part of the group of pastors who had met regularly with Paul Lindemann until his death.

Most of these positions had been standard fare in articles in the *American Lutheran* for a decade or more, and the text of "A Statement" clearly shows the influence of the magazine's editorial board. Yet the *American Lutheran* was remarkably silent in the weeks immediately following the issuance of "A Statement." The text and the cover letter were printed in the November issue, but there was no editorial comment, either then or in subsequent months. Geiseman did write about the gathering itself in the November issue, calling it "a memorable meeting." He summarized its genesis and its "three-fold purpose": to emphasize the authority of the Word of God, to lift up the "principle of love in the life and work of the church as distinguished from the spirit of lovelessness," and to clarify the theological distinction between the congregation and the "man-made organization" of synodical bodies. He explained the genuine intention of those who had attended in Chicago:

> The men present tried to summarize their discussions in a statement, and resolved to send a copy thereof to every pastor within Synod. It is to be hoped that the discussion of this statement will bring as much profit and blessing to the individual pastors in the various parts of synod as they meet with one another in smaller circles or larger gatherings and discuss the same, as it did to the men who were responsible for drafting it.[20]

That hope would turn out to be remarkably naïve. There was strongly negative reaction to "A Statement," both from Synod leaders and from many pastors. This led the *American Lutheran* editors, in a meeting February 14, 1946, to agree "not to publicize the 'Statement' but rather to treat the basic issues involved in an objective manner editorially and also by special articles."[21]

The aftermath

"What has happened to the Forty-Four?"

A few days after the Chicago meeting, E. J. Friedrich wrote to President Behnken, telling him what had transpired and enclosing a copy of "A Statement." It arrived in Behnken's hands during a meeting of the Synod board of directors, and he read it to the group. He then handed the letter to Paul Schulz, the Springfield, IL, pastor who had been hostile toward the *American Lutheran* at least since the "Today and Tomorrow" controversy ten years before. Schulz took it to one of the Synod's secretarial staff and asked her to make a copy, being sure that she spelled all the names correctly.[22]

Behnken was about to leave for Europe, and he telephoned Friedrich and asked that distribution of "A Statement" be postponed until he returned. Friedrich believed that this would be to break faith with the decisions of the Chicago group; the others on the Continuation Committee agreed, so he informed Behnken that this would not be possible. A few days later, Friedrich received a telegram:

IN THE INTEREST OF SYNODS WELFARE ITS PRESIDENT AND VICEPRESIDENTS MEETING IN CHICAGO OCTOBER 2ND PROTEST AGAINST THE SENDING OUT OF A CHICAGO STATEMENT AT THIS TIME AND REQUEST THAT THE ENTIRE SITUATION UNDERLYING THE STATEMENT BE DISCUSSED WITH THEM.

The telegram was signed by Behnken and by Arthur Brunn, identified as "Secretary."[23]

Brunn, of course, was a member of the editorial board of the *American Lutheran* (as well as a member of the ALPB's board of directors for several years, though it isn't clear whether he was still serving in 1945). He had been present in Chicago and had signed "A Statement." But he was also second vice president of the Synod, and shortly after the Chicago meeting he telegraphed Friedrich insisting that his name be removed. The pressure on Brunn was intense, and it would lead to his resignation from the staff of the magazine a few months later.[24]

"A Statement" was mailed, along with a cover letter, to every pastor in the Synod in early October. The reaction was swift and heavy. Some expressed gratitude for what the group had done, but the negative comments seem to have been much more voluminous. Robinson quoted a letter from A. T. Kretzmann as typical of the criticism:

Received your communication and statement yesterday. I read the letter first, and was distinctly shocked to find that you and forty other brethren in Synod could have been so unbrotherly as to claim that 'in more than one area of our beloved Synod' there is being manifested 'a pernicious spirit utterly at variance with the fundamental concepts of the Gospel' ... and yet in a loveless and unbrotherly manner have failed to reveal the identity of the men who supposedly have shown this anti-Christian spirit and have failed to give proof so that these men might defend themselves. To my knowledge there has never been a time in the history of our Synod when men of such high standing in the Synod have so utterly disregarded the law of Christian love in dealing with offenses allegedly committed by brethren in the faith.

In addition to many complaints about the "unbrotherly" accusations, there were charges that the group had denied the Scriptural positions of the Synod. Some demanded that the professors from Concordia Seminary who had signed the statement be dismissed.[25]

When Behnken returned from Europe, he decided that something must be done about the furor caused by "A Statement." He, along with other Synod officials, met with the Continuation Committee in December and again in January. Friedrich would report that President Behnken was "belligerent in his attitude." He urged the Continuation Committee to retract the statement and to meet with the "Confessional Lutheran group"—thus identifying that magazine which had been started in opposition to the *American Lutheran* as the primary center of opposition to "A Statement." The Continuation Committee informed Behnken that retraction was "out of the question" and that they would not under any circumstances meet with the *Confessional Lutheran* group "because we have not accused them and have not dealt with them." They did agree that the entire group of signers would meet with the praesidium (Behnken and the several vice presidents) and the district presidents in St. Louis, February 14-15, with the understanding that it would be a closed meeting "for brotherly discussion and not a judicial procedure" against the signers. There was also a "gentlemen's agreement" to discourage all "propaganda for or against the Statement" until after that meeting.[26]

Most of the signers (about five were absent) arrived early in St. Louis and met all day on February 13. Different individuals had been asked by the Continuation Committee to write brief essays elaborating on each of the twelve theses, and these were read and discussed at length by the group. They also strategized about how best to approach the next day's meeting.

When the larger group convened February 14, much of the day was taken up with reading the ten essays. The praesidium had a brief meeting following the afternoon session, though there's no record of what was discussed. The *American Lutheran* editorial board met over the dinner hour, and its second item of business was to "accept the resignation of Dr. Arthur Brunn, with sincere regret." There is no comment in the minutes about what provoked Brunn's resignation, nor whether it had been presented that day or previously; the timing suggests, however, that Brunn may have been pressured to resign from the board by the other members of the praesidium that afternoon. Meyer would later recall that Brunn resigned because he wanted to "be neutral in the furor caused by the issuance of the STATEMENT by the 44"; of course that does not mean that he was not pressured by other Missouri Synod leaders, and it reinforces the close connection that was assumed between "A Statement" and the *American Lutheran*.[27]

The signers of "A Statement" were convinced the praesidium had decided that afternoon to try to discredit them before the district presidents during the evening meeting, and indeed that evening session, in Robinson's words, "became bellicose," with several members of the praesidium making sharp and accusatory comments.[28]

The signers met at 9:30 p.m., after the larger meeting had adjourned, to discuss how to proceed. Following that discussion, the Continuation Committee drafted three resolutions, which were then approved by the whole group of signers at an early meeting on February 15. Friedrich presented the resolutions to the Synod officials when they convened a short time later. The first asked that, in preparation for the Synod's approaching centennial, pastors and congregations be invited to "re-study" several issues: *sola scriptura* and legalism, unionism and separatism, the law of love, Romans 16.17-18, prayer fellowship, and what is divisive of fellowship. The second proposed that Behnken appoint ten men "to represent opinions differing or contrary from the theses of the Statement" who would meet with ten of the signers for further discussion. The third called for the papers presented at this meeting to be duplicated and given to the praesidium and district presidents, with the understanding that after thirty days they might be more widely circulated.[29]

These resolutions were approved by whole group, and they were implemented to a greater or lesser degree. The essays were mimeographed and sent to the praesidium and district presidents; they were subsequently published in book form as *Speaking the Truth in Love: Essays related to A Statement, Chicago, Nineteen forty-five*. President Behnken asked the faculty at St. Louis to prepare guidelines for discussion of the matters agreed to in the first resolution, but this did not happen in a timely manner and was never really completed.[30]

The third resolution led to three meetings of the so-called "Ten and Ten" in August, September, and November of 1946. These meetings were not productive for several reasons, and were not continued. There was then a series of meetings between the Continuation Committee and the various Synod officials (members of the praesidium, Lorry Meyer, and the St. Louis faculty members who had signed "A Statement" were present in different combinations at each meeting), resulting in an agreement that "'A Statement' and the accompanying letter be withdrawn as a basis of discussion so that the issues involved may be studied objectively on the basis of theses prepared under the auspices of the President of Synod." It was emphasized that this "withdrawal" did not mean that the signers were retracting the statement. It was also agreed that:

> 1) The signers will no longer exist or function as a group; 2) the Continuation Committee will be disbanded; 3) the Statement as such will no longer be promoted by [the signers]; 4) nothing will be done to push the sale of 'Speaking the Truth in Love.'

Despite this agreement, "A Statement" continued to be regularly condemned by conservatives within the Synod. At both the 1947 and 1950 Synod conventions, there were memorials (none of them approved) to repudiate the document or to discipline its signers.[31]

The aftermath of "A Statement" continued to have an impact on the *American Lutheran* and its personnel. When the editorial board met in May 1946, the affair was still much on everyone's mind. The ALPB board of directors had been invited to join the editorial board the first evening of their meeting for a testimonial dinner honoring Brunn for his long years of service. In the editorial board meeting that afternoon, there was again discussion of Brunn's abrupt resignation, and it was agreed that "not too much be said" at the dinner. There was also an extended discussion of the current state of the magazine, including some pointed self-criticism. ALPB president Bobzin complained that the magazine was sometimes "amateurish." Henry Wind believed that "at the present time we are not crusading for anything definite; hence the lack of pep and power." O. P. Kretzmann observed that the magazine had been responsible for many accomplishments, particularly with respect to Lutheran unity, but in light of "A Statement," that now seemed to be "out of our hands."[32]

This led to a wide-ranging discussion about where the magazine was headed. Wind and Geiseman argued that "A Statement" should be addressed directly, but others disagreed. It was finally resolved to publish a "series of editorial articles on the subject matter of the statement (but not mentioning the statement)." The discussion moved on to other ideas for the future, but it kept circling back to "A Statement." Fred Lindemann regretted that the magazine had not followed up on its initial printing of the document with explanatory articles. Kretzmann reminded him that many of the editors had spoken "all over" in support of "A Statement," but Lindemann replied, "We published nothing. The opposition did. We agreed to limit ourselves. The policy was not wise." Several other topics were then addressed, but at the end of the meeting "A Statement" came up yet again, with Kretzmann suggesting that some articles be written "around the Chicago Statement in terms of the Laity." It was agreed that Kretzmann and Geiseman would prepare some suggested articles and authors for consideration.[33]

But while several of the themes from "A Statement" would continue to be addressed by the *American Lutheran*—particularly those related to Lutheran unity—virtually nothing in the magazine would refer specifically to the controversial document and its aftermath. In February 1948, a reader would write, asking for some follow-up information: "We know what has happened to the Statement. Could you answer a question? What has happened to the Forty-Four?" The response came as an "Editor's Comment" (written by Oswald Hoffman):

> The Forty-Four was a group bound together only by a common desire to speak the truth in love. Members of the group at the Chicago Convention agreed that the Forty-Four no longer exist as a group since their purpose has been achieved: to secure Synod-wide discussion of the issues raised in the Chicago 'Statement.' By official resolution, Synod has decided to conduct such discussion in pastoral conferences and in our congregations. These discussions must be based solely on the Word of God, without regard for one-sided or purely traditional viewpoints. Only if so conducted will they result in a greater dedication to preaching the Gospel and in a more evangelical spirit throughout the church.

With that comment, reference in the *American Lutheran* to "A Statement" came to an end. For many conservatives in the Synod, however, the close association of ALPB leaders and editors with the "Statement of the 44" would color their view of the Bureau and its magazine for decades to come.[34]

Lutheran unity

"our gentlemanly attitude has gotten us exactly nowhere"

Lutheran unity continued to preoccupy the editors of the *American Lutheran* even as the reactions to "A Statement" ran their course. In the late 1940s, one focus of this concern was Missouri's careful dance with the National Lutheran Council. Since its formation in 1918, the Council had been sometimes condemned and often ignored by the Missouri Synod; in the 1940s, however, attitudes were beginning to change. At the Synod's 1944 convention in Saginaw, proposals to join the NLC had been defeated, but over the next few years the *American Lutheran* continued to beat the drum for LCMS participation.

Sometimes this advocacy was couched in indirect terms. A 1945 editorial entitled "The Missing One-Third" took note of the San Francisco Conference on International Organization, a meeting of allied nations whose purpose was to draft the United Nations Charter. Wire services, the editorial said, had carried an article about Lutherans who "were praying for a God pleasing culmination" of the conference and pleading for "the guarantee of Religious Freedom throughout Europe." These Lutherans, though, were those who were members of the NLC, and the wire service report had made clear that these sentiments represented "two-thirds of all Lutheran church members in the United States." Those who read these reports in their newspapers, the editors suggested, "must wonder about the missing one-third. 'Were not the Lutherans outside of the National Lutheran Council praying for the welfare of the world?'" Surely they were—so "Why can't we say so? What would be wrong if our voice were joined with the National Lutheran Council in such statements?"[35]

Within the editorial board, there were discussions about how openly to advocate for a closer relationship to the National Lutheran Council. Some believed it was important to continue to stump for Missouri's membership in the NLC; others favored an approach which, while advocating Lutheran unity, did not endorse specific proposals. But as the 1947 LCMS convention approached, the former perspective won out. The Chicago convention would celebrate the Synod's centennial, and the editorial board decided to publish a series of open letters to the clergy and laity of the Synod with that anniversary as its theme.

The first letter began by observing that 1947 "will be a year of judgment and decision and promise" for the LCMS. The centennial celebration must be undertaken in "honesty and humility." It recounted the Synod's history, praising its founders as men who were "thoroughly trained, highly intelligent, and deeply committed to the task of recovering a Christianity which would be pure and undefiled by the mud and silt of the faithless centuries." They were not perfect, of course, but they are still to be honored. "Certainly the first part of our Centennial commemoration should be a *Te Deum* for these saints and prophets—great under God—who have gone before us."[36]

The second letter, however, emphasized the need for change:

It is blasphemous arrogance to transfer to a human organization qualities and attributes which belong to the Word alone. More than that, it almost inevitably leads to disaster; it persuades men and women to demand unchangeability of an organization which by its very nature is unable to meet that requirement. The result is either a dead rigidity or, when the inevitable changes become evident, a hopeless defeatism.

"We have been fearful of some changes," the editorial lamented, "and have, therefore, denounced all change. It is an old and tragic story," one which leads to "ecclesiastical senility."[37]

The third letter addressed the laity of the church among whom "there is a widespread restlessness and dissatisfaction." They see "how bad and how needy the world is and they seem to feel that the Church is not fully aware of the lateness of the hour and the immediate need for decisive, courageous and adventurous action." Recent years have seen several controversies over doctrine, but the attitude seems to be "Keep it away from the laity. They must not know what is going on, and, above all, they must not be permitted to decide on the merits of the case."

Certainly one of the great results of our centennial self-examination would be a resolution by our laymen to devote themselves, individually and collectively, to a thorough study of the problems of the church, both doctrinal and practical, and then join their pastors in finding intelligent and Scriptural solutions for them.

This third installment ended with a promise that the next month would take up the "relationship of the Missouri Synod to other bodies in visible Christendom, especially to other Lutheran synods."[38]

But that was not to be. The editorial in question, the fourth of the series, was drafted by E. J. Friedrich, and it apparently advocated for Missouri's participation in the NLC. It was ready to go to press when the editors received a letter from President Behnken, dated April 27. Someone who had the galleys of the May issue had read Friedrich's editorial to him, and it "fills my heart with deep concern."

I want to plead with you good men not to let that go into print. The effects, if it is printed, will be most disturbing. I want to plead with you in all sincerity rather to put forth every effort to quiet the troubled waters.

In a former letter to you I requested that whenever matters are to be printed which effect [*sic*] our church's welfare, you folks might be so kind as to discuss the matter with me before going to print. I have been informed that one of your members was to talk to me personally. To date this has not taken place though I have asked both

Pastor Adolf Meyer and Dr. O. P. Kretzmann that such a meeting might be arranged. I sincerely wish that there might be a thorough understanding.

Behnken closed the letter "in the hope that my fervent plea may be heeded."[39]

This letter led to a flurry of phone calls and correspondence among the editors. Meyer immediately wrote to Behnken, with copies to the other editors. He was respectful, but pulled no punches:

> I was surprised to receive your communication of April 22nd. ... As you know our AMERICAN LUTHERAN staff has during the past months gone out of its way repeatedly in order to aid you in preserving peace within the Church. As you also know our gentlemanly attitude has gotten us exactly nowhere. There has been no corresponding reaction among the leaders of the Confessional Lutheran group. Since their publication is permitted to come out carrying the most fantastic charges which certainly irritate and disturb a large number of our people in our Synod I cannot understand why you protest such a restrained and charitable editorial as we have on the press for the May American Lutheran.

Meyer told Behnken the editorial staff meeting had discussed the editorial carefully and prayerfully, and each member was "fully convinced that it would be in the Church's interest to say the things recorded in the editorial." Furthermore, they believed that this editorial would in fact "in general strengthen the support of our officials."[40]

As for the editorial's stance on the NLC, Meyer insisted it was nothing new but in fact simply reiterated what the magazine had been saying since before the 1944 Saginaw convention. He suggested that Behnken call O. P. Kretzmann to discuss his concerns personally, but since the editorial had been approved by the entire editorial board, "I have no choice in withdrawing the text unless they so direct." In a note appended to the copy of this letter he sent to the editors, he asked them to contact Kretzmann immediately with their vote as to whether or not they should pull the editorial. To Kretzmann he wrote:

> Ossie [Hoffman] and I both agree that if [Behnken] would agree to play ball our way that then we might hold up the editorial at the last minute and change it so that Behnken's party would achieve the things that the AMERICAN LUTHERAN has in mind. But if this is not what he means by reaching a thorough understanding then Ossie and I at least are in favor of printing the editorial.[41]

There is no record of what transpired between Kretzmann and Behnken, but it seems to have convinced Meyer, in consultation with Kretzmann and Hoffman, to hold off on the editorial. He wrote to all the editors and reported that the following night letter would be sent to Behnken:

> Conference with several editors resulted in decision to postpone open letter until June stop following explanation will be published in May issue [quote] Our readers will

recall the announcement in the April issue that our Open letter this month would consider the problem of Lutheran fellowship. The letter was written, endorsed by the entire editorial staff, and set up in galley proof. The letter came to the attention of our synodical authorities. The president of the Missouri Synod has expressed his misgivings about the open expression of our position in the matter. In keeping with our editorial policy the letter advocated full membership in the National Lutheran Council. The editorial board is now conferring with the President of Synod and will announce the result of the deliberation in the June issue. Unless it can be demonstrated that the publication of the editorial will be harmful to the cause of confessional Lutheranism in American and in the world, the editors will print the open letter in the June issue of the American Lutheran. We consider the issue a matter of conscience and basic for the future of the Lutheran Church in American and in the world unquote consider meeting of editors with you imperative before May 15.

When the proposed note appeared in the May issue, however, it had been toned down considerably. The reference to "synodical authorities" was eliminated; instead readers were told, "Because some of our friends who chanced to see the galley suggested a different approach we have postponed printing of the editorial in order that they may have an opportunity to present their views."[42]

Probably it was Behnken's response to the telegram that led to the more temperate public announcement, for Meyer subsequently thanked him for his "very fine letters of April 30th. I appreciated the spirit in which all of them were written." He went on to offer his own reassurance:

> I do wish you to know that the staff of the AMERICAN LUTHERAN is doing everything possible to cooperate with you even though we may not agree with your viewpoint. We have literally stopped the AMERICAN LUTHERAN in its printing, held up the edition for an entire week and revised about six pages in order to make the alteration necessary to comply with your request. In addition to the amount of money involved, and, of course, the amount of editorial staff work, there is the inconvenience caused to our entire subscription list. We are willing to do this, however, because we are very sincere in our desire to do nothing which would hurt the progress of Christ's Kingdom.

Meyer proposed a meeting with Behnken on May 15, reminding him in the process that the ALPB had agreed to take on the task of coordinating publicity for the centennial celebration.[43]

A few days later Friedrich wrote to Kretzmann, informing him that he would be unable to be present for the May 15 meeting—a disappointment, he said, not only because he regretted missing the conversation with Behnken but because "I had been looking forward to an opportunity of discussing recent developments in regard to the Agreement with you and the rest of the Continuation Committee" (an interesting statement, given the agreement four months earlier that the Continuation Committee would be disbanded). He did, however, want to express his opinion that the "Open Letter" editorial should be "published just as it is," at least unless "Dr. Behnken can convince you that certain expressions should be toned down." Then he added:

> As far as my editorial on the National Lutheran Council is concerned, do with it whatever you please. I am aware of the fact that certain statements, and perhaps even entire paragraphs, may have to be eliminated for diplomatic reasons. ... There is a possibility, of course, that the entire editorial is unsatisfactory. If that is the case, do not hesitate to throw it into the waste-basket.[44]

Friedrich recounted to Kretzmann the discussion of the NLC at the recent College of Presidents meeting (which he attended as president of the Colorado District). Time for discussion had been divided between those for and against membership. He reported that several members had spoken in favor, but when time came for the opponents, "Lorry [Meyer] monopolized almost all the time." Friedrich's comment illustrates the significance of the fact that some of those involved with the *American Lutheran* and ALPB were also in positions of authority in the Synod, which gave the magazine access to a good amount of insider information.[45]

There was apparently no record kept of the May 15 meeting, but it did result in the editorial on the NLC being "thrown in the waste-basket," at least for the time being. The series continued in the June issue with Part IV which explained that "The AMERICAN LUTHERAN has decided not to enter upon a detailed discussion of some of the issues which will be presented to the convention." Instead, the magazine would discuss the "broad background for these issues."

> While it is always difficult to look clearly into the future, the convention should know that our generation will continue to live in a suffering world. War and its inevitable bleak aftermath of maladjustments, broken lives, economic disaster, and psychological aberrations will bring more suffering and sorrow to our world than we like to imagine. The whips of God are still whistling through the universe in judgment.

There was not a word about the National Lutheran Council, nor about Lutheran unity.[46]

But though Behnken's pleas had kept Friedrich's editorial from the *American Lutheran*, the magazine hardly folded on the larger questions. The final installment of the "Open Letter" was a review of the action of the Synod convention in Chicago. It was cautiously optimistic, particularly on the issue of Lutheran unity. While the advances "were not as great as some might have asked," there was progress nonetheless as the Synod "demonstrated a growing awareness of its tremendous responsibility in the field of Lutheran fellowship and unity."[47]

Behind the scenes, however, no such caution was being exercised. The editorial board meetings continued to talk about how best to press for Lutheran unity. At their September meeting, the editors had lunch with Carl Lund-Quist, an Augustana Synod pastor who was serving as executive secretary of the Division of Public Relations of the NLC. The November issue then introduced a new feature entitled "One Lutheran Voice," edited jointly by Lund-Quist and Oswald Hoffman. The column would, the magazine announced, "give a well rounded picture of Lutheran events in all synods of America and bodies beyond, as well as a Lutheran interpretation of world events." The editors would serve "not so much as reporters but rather as news analysts."[48]

The September 1947 editorial board meeting also agreed that a revised version of Friedrich's article on the National Lutheran Council should be published (though that doesn't appear to have happened). They met with W. G. Polack, associate editor of the *Lutheran Witness*. He passed along several pieces of advice from Theodore Graebner, who could not be present—advice that reflected both Graebner's continuing evolution on the issues facing the Synod, and his behind-the-scenes support for the mission of the *American Lutheran*. Graebner urged that they "[not] permit Behnken to put the American Lutheran on the same plane with the Confessional Lutheran representing opposite extremes." Furthermore, they must "safeguard [their] independence" and "[not] allow the Presidium's veto or censorship of what you write." Graebner stressed that the biggest danger to the Missouri Synod "is not unionism but separatism of the Wisconsin, Norwegian and anti-44 men."[49]

The editors had also arranged another meeting with Dr. Behnken. The conversation this time was not about Lutheran union, but about the follow-up to "A Statement," demonstrating once again the close connection between the *American Lutheran* staff and the controversial 1945 document. The editors pressed the president on the matter of the guidelines that were supposed to have been published to facilitate discussion of the issues raised by the signers of "A Statement." He responded that one such document had already been published, and others were in the pipeline. At the end of the conversation, Behnken again appealed to the editors "not [to] ruffle or disturb the peaceful waters of Synod." The minutes of the meeting record that "the American Lutheran staff made no promises or commitments to Dr. Behnken in any way, manner or form."[50]

Notes

1. Theodore Graebner, *Prayer Fellowship* (St. Louis: Concordia Publishing House, 1945), 28-29.

2. Jack Treon Robinson, "The Spirit of Triumphalism in the Missouri Synod" (PhD diss., Vanderbilt University, 1972), 207-208. Robinson's dissertation is the most complete account of this episode. Though clearly written from the perspective of one who viewed "A Statement" as a salutary and constructive attempt, his use of the archival materials is thorough and informative.

3. Meyer, "Autobiography," 31; Adolf Meyer to Henry L. Lieske, 14 Sept. 1981, Lieske Research Collection on the Moderate Movement in the Lutheran Church—Missouri Synod, PA" 245, Subgroup II, Box 8, Folder 2, Lieske Correspondence A-W, 1980-1983, ELCA Archives (hereafter cited as Lieske Collection).

4. O. P. Kretzmann to E. J. Friedrich, 12 July 1945, and E. J. Friedrich to Adolf Meyer, 4 Aug. 1945, E. J. Friedrich Papers, Box 1, Folder 1, Concordia Historical Institute (hereafter cited as Friedrich Papers).

5. E. J. Friedrich to Adolf Meyer, 4 Aug. 1945, Friedrich Papers, Box 1, Folder 1.

6. E. J. Friedrich to F. H. Lindemann, 9 Aug. 1945, Friedrich Papers, Box 1, Folder 1. The same letter was sent to each invitee.

7. Interview with E. J. Friedrich, cited in Robinson, 211-212.

8. Ibid., 217.

9. Robinson, 247, explains the apparent contradiction between the number present and the number signing; see also "Minutes of the Informal Conference of Missouri Synod Pastors (Assembled on Sept. 6 and 7, 1945. Room 12, Hotel Stevens, Chicago)," Friedrich papers, Box 1, Folder 1.

10. Minutes, *AL* Editorial Board, 5 Sept. 1945, Geiseman Papers, Box 21, Folder 2.

11. William Arndt, "The Application of the Law of Love in the Practical Life of the Church," Lieske Collection, Subgroup II, Box 6, Folder 9, Greater Chicago Area, 1944-47, 1968, n.d.

12. Richard Caemmerer, "Doctrines and Life, and Their Application to Synodical Attitudes," ibid.

13. O. P. Kretzmann, "Organization and Church," ibid.

14. O. A. Geiseman, "Protest and Appeal," ibid.

15. Robinson, 234-235. This disagreement is not mentioned in the minutes of the meeting.

16. Robinson, 238-239.

17. "A Statement." The full text of the statement has been often reprinted and is widely available, e.g.: Robinson, 240; *AL* 28, no. 11 (Nov. 1945), 4; Carl S. Meyer, *Moving Frontiers: Readings in the History of the Lutheran Church—Missouri Synod* (St. Louis: Concordia Publishing House, 1964), 422-424.

18. Ibid.

19. Ibid.

20. O. A. Geiseman, "While It Is Day," *AL* 28, no. 11 (Nov. 1945), 5.

21. "Decisions Reached at the Editorial Staff Meeting February 14th, 5:30 to 7:30 P.M.," Geiseman Papers, Box 21, Folder 2.

22. Robinson, 250. This story was told to Robinson by Friedrich, who heard it directly from the secretary involved.

23. Ibid., 251-252.

24. Ibid., 245.

25. A. T. Kretzmann to E. J. Friedrich, 12 Oct. 1945. Thomas Coates Papers, Concordia Historical Institute. Quoted in Robinson, 257.

26. "Meetings of the 44 Signers Held at St. Louis, February 13-14, 1946," Concordia Historical Institute; E. J. Friedrich to signers of "A Statement," Jan. 23, 1946, quoted in Robinson, 274.

27. Robinson, 278; Meyer, "Autobiography," 33.

28. Robinson, 279, citing minutes of the "Meeting of the Praesidium, the District Presidents, and the Signers of the Statement, February 14-15, 1946 in Holy Cross Hall, St. Louis, Missouri."

29. Ibid., 282-283.

30. *Speaking the Truth in Love: Essays related to A Statement, Chicago, 1945* (Chicago: Willow Press, 1946); Robinson, 294. Robinson suggests that the failure was due in part to the St. Louis faculty's decision to ask the faculty of Concordia Theological Seminary in Springfield, IL, to join them in this endeavor, and it was very difficult for the two faculties to agree on the points of discussion.

31. E. J. Friedrich to signers of "A Statement," January 16, 1947. Quoted in Robinson, 302-305.

32. Minutes, *AL* Editorial Board, 6-7 May 1946, Geiseman Papers, Box 21, Folder 2.

33. Ibid.

34. "Open Forum," *AL* 31, no. 2 (Feb. 1948), 16.

35. "The Missing One-Third," *AL* 28, no. 6 (June 1945), 4.

36. "An Open Letter," *AL* 30, no. 1 (Jan. 1947), 3-4.

37. "An Open Letter to the Clergy and Laity of the Missouri Synod—II," *AL* 30, no. 2 (Feb. 1947), 3-4.

38. "An Open Letter to the Clergy and Laity of the Missouri Synod—III," *AL* 30, no. 3 (Mar. 1947), 3-4.

39. John W. Behnken to Editors of the American Lutheran, 22 Apr. 1947, Geiseman Papers, Box 20, Folder 4.

40. Adolf Meyer to John W. Behnken, 24 Apr. 1947, Geiseman Papers, Box 20, Folder 4.

41. Ibid.

42. Adolf Meyer to "All Editors of the American Lutheran," 27 Apr. 1947, Geiseman Papers, Box 20, Folder 4; "Open Letter Editorial Postponed," AL 30, no. 5 (May 1947), 4.

43. Adolf Meyer to John W. Behnken, 4 May 1947, Geiseman Papers, Box 20, Folder 4.
44. E. J. Friedrich to O. P. Kretzmann, 12 May 1947, Geiseman Papers, Box 4, Folder 3.
45. Ibid.
46. "An Open Letter to the Clergy and Laity of the Missouri Synod—IV," *AL* 30, no. 6 (June 1947), 3.
47. "An Open Letter to the Clergy and Laity of the Missouri Synod—VI," *AL* 30, no 9 (Sept. 1947), 3.
48. "One Lutheran Voice," *AL* 30, no. 11 (Nov. 1947), 4.
49. Minutes, *AL* Editorial Board, 25-26 Sept. 1947, Geiseman Papers, Box 21, Folder 3.
50. Ibid.

Chapter 10

CATHOLICS, COMMUNISTS, COMMUNION

W hile the debate over "A Statement" was the most dramatic issue faced by the ALPB during the post-war period, there were many other controversies. The perceived threat of Roman Catholicism, hysterical fears about Communism and the reaction known as McCarthyism, contention over liturgical renewal—these were the topics that filled the pages of the *American Lutheran* and enlivened other ALPB ministries in the postwar years. Significant personnel changes were also afoot, both at the *American Lutheran* and in the ALPB itself.

The truth about Catholicism

"The Word of God or the Word of Man?"

Lutheran suspicion of the Roman Catholic Church was certainly nothing new. In the United States, it had been reinforced and stoked by a deep-seated strain of anti-Catholicism—in the words of Arthur Schlesinger, Sr., "the deepest bias in the history of the American people."[1] In the post-war years, this anti-Catholicism erupted anew among

American Protestants. The *Christian Century* published a series of articles by Harold Fey with titles such as "Catholicism Invades Rural America" and "Can Catholicism Win America?" Paul Blanshard's widely-read *American Freedom and Catholic Power* warned about the dangers Catholicism posed to American democracy. His subsequent book, *Communism, Democracy, and Catholic Power*, went even further, suggesting a "fundamental resemblance between the Vatican and the Kremlin."[2]

Anti-Catholic rhetoric appeared also in the publications of the ALPB. As early as 1944, discussion within the editorial staff reflected a fear of "Catholic power." The *American Lutheran* planned a series entitled "10 Great Questions Confronting Lutheranism in the next 25 Years," and one of the issues proposed by O. P. Kretzmann was "The Dangers of Roman Catholicism." As it turned out, the concept for this series was changed somewhat, and discussion of Catholicism was dropped from the final version; that did not end the matter, however.[3]

The October 1945 *American Lutheran* announced the publication by the ALPB's Lutheran Press of "a timely and important pamphlet" entitled "The Split between Roman Catholicism and Christ." It "presents only historical facts," the magazine insisted, "facts presented in as favorable a light as Roman Catholic books themselves can present them. Side by side with the word of the Roman Church has been printed the Word of God." The 24-page booklet listed no author, but Adolf Meyer later wrote that he and Oswald Hoffman had "worked out the text together." The pamphlet was needed, he wrote, because "the Roman Church was openly and defiantly boasting that it could take over America. Our people were asking for answers to their many claims of being the only true church with the only right teaching."[4]

The opening paragraphs asserted that the Roman Catholic Church had begun deviating from "the Original Christian Church" in the early centuries, while the church of the Reformation had remained true to the Word of God. After the Roman Empire "made [Christianity] a state religion," things deteriorated rapidly. "How quickly did the churchmen of Rome acquire the presumption, arrogance and avarice of their imperialist colleagues in the civil government! How readily they forgot Christ and adopted the methods of Caesar!"[5]

The booklet's pages contained two columns, one headed "The Word of Rome," the other "The Word of God." The items listed included the usual Protestant objections to Catholicism—purgatory, Papal authority, indulgences, Marian dogma. In several cases the quotations used to explain "The Word of Rome" were not from official documents but popular Catholic literature. "The Word of God" column contained Biblical proof texts, allegedly disproving the Catholic doctrine in question. At the end of each page, in large print, the question was posed: "Which Will You Choose—The Word of God or The Word of Man?" The booklet concluded with this dire warning:

We stand at the beginning of a new era. The great war has ended. Atomic energy has been released for good or ill. Social, economic, and political forces are energetically seeing expression in the world.

Will America take its place in this new world in the spirit of Jesus Christ to set men free, or in the spirit of Roman Catholicism to enslave them? ...

The issue is clear: Will you follow Christ or will you follow a man who pretends to speak for Christ? Will you choose the freedom of Christ or the dictatorship of Rome? **The Word of God or the Word of Man?**[6]

As might be expected, this booklet stirred up a good deal of controversy and criticism. An editorial in the *American Lutheran* defended the tract. It does not malign Roman Catholics; "we shall always endeavor to speak the truth in love." Suggesting that the criticism had been specifically focused on the booklet's explication of the Catholic view of marriage, the editorial quoted from a "Question and Answer" feature in a national Roman Catholic monthly publication in which queries were printed about the validity of marriages outside the church; the answers given explained Catholic doctrine and policy, citing Pius X's 1908 decree restricting valid marriages to those "contracted before the parish priest or the local ordinary." For the *American Lutheran* editorial, this "speaks for itself. No further editorial comment is needed." It then offered more editorial comment. This decree is a "subterfuge" by which the Roman Catholic Church is "making itself party to the scourge of divorce which, in violation of the laws of God and man, is sweeping the world." It is a "travesty upon the holy ordinance of matrimony."[7]

This strident criticism of the Roman Catholic Church was followed by an article by William Dallman in the June 1946 *American Lutheran* entitled "Why Lutheran—not Catholic." He asserted that "*The Pope* curses justification by faith without the deeds of the law. ... He teaches salvation by good works." Dallman listed a series of contrasts between what "the Bible teaches" and what "the Pope teaches"—indulgences, the Eucharist (including the sacrifice of the mass, transubstantiation, various Eucharistic practices), the saints and Mary, the Bible, purgatory, confession, celibacy, "monkery," and much more. He concluded with a diatribe on the danger of Catholic power in the United States—citing, for instance, the presence of some cabinet members and congressmen at the recent consecration of the new Roman Catholic bishop of Columbus, OH. "What business had they there?" Dallman demanded.[8]

The danger of Roman Catholicism was often a topic of discussion at editorial staff meetings during this period. At the May 1946 meeting, August W. Brustat was asked to write editorials on "Romanism"; he was hesitant, he said, "because of the possible rejection in view of the polemical nature of the editorials" he would be bound to write. Ade Meyer responded that they had a duty to "witness to the truth." He added that "it might be well to call attention to Protestantism's spinelessness and that Rome will win unless we have the zeal they have."[9]

In November 1946, the *American Lutheran* published a promotion for a long list of materials available on "the Catholic issue" from the Lutheran Press. It began with a quotation from an unnamed "national magazine":

> Why does the United States continue to maintain an ambassador at the Vatican, [a claim not actually technically true; the American envoy did not have ambassadorial rank] despite protests by nearly every Protestant denomination? Why do moving pictures increasingly extol Catholic priests, Catholic churches, Catholic customs? Why, in short, is the power and influence of the Catholic Church so painfully evident, when the population of the United States is only 16% Roman Catholic?

The list of materials included titles like "Rome Stoops to Conquer" and "How the Catholic Church Helped Hitler to Power."[10]

A second edition of "The Split Between Roman Catholicism and Christ" was printed in 1947, then a third in 1949. The tract was translated into Portuguese at the request of a pastor in Brazil. It went through several additional printings over the next years. In 1950, the ALPB board was informed that "classified ads had been placed in approximately fifty small town newspapers, largely in the state of Texas," promoting the tract.[11]

After the Second Vatican Council, the ALPB stopped circulating this vehemently anti-Catholic booklet. In 1984, one Dante Rosso sent the Bureau a Spanish translation of the piece he had made, requesting permission to reproduce and circulate it in South America. Glenn Stone, at that time the ALPB's executive director, responded:

> Our board of directors has withdrawn the English version of this piece from circulation, and we take the position that we do not want it used as the basis of any translated publications. Our reason is that we feel that the scholarship on which the original was based is partially outdated. The booklet, for example, takes no account of the second Vatican Council and recent restatements and reinterpretations of Roman Catholicism. ... To continue to use this booklet without major changes, in the light of this new situation, would both weaken the impact of its message—and, not a small matter, would also be Christianly unfair to the Roman Catholic Church.

Stone acknowledged that the work was not copyrighted, and was thus in the public domain; but he insisted that if Mr. Rosso should choose to translate and circulate the work, "it must in no circumstances be identified with 'The Lutheran Press'" since that is "one of the titles under which we have conducted our ministry, and we do not want to be associated with further use of this booklet in its present form." Well into the 21st century, certain groups and individuals have continued to reproduce the booklet without ALPB permission.[12]

In 1951, President Truman nominated General Mark Clark to be the U. S. Ambassador to the Vatican. There had been no official U. S. representation in the Vatican since 1867, though Myron Charles Taylor had served as personal envoy to the Holy See for Presidents Roosevelt and Truman. The proposal to establish full diplomatic relations provoked intense opposition from Protestant leaders, including officials of the National Council of Churches, President Franklin Clark Fry of the ULCA, and the editors of *Christian Century*. President Behnken also issued a statement protesting the appointment. ALPB president John Kavasch sent Truman a telegram on behalf of the Bureau, which then was printed on the cover of the *American Lutheran*:

> By your nomination of a first ambassador to the Vatican you are opening the door to conflict between Roman Catholics and Protestants in our country, and are leading the way in the surrender of the principle of separation of Church and State that is basic to freedom of religion and worship so highly coveted by all true Americans.
>
> The fact that Communism has made its greatest inroads in Roman Catholic countries of Europe disproves the assertion that the United States of America needs the political support of the Roman See in the battle against Communist aggression. You must know that the majority of Americans consider it undemocratic and un-American for you ... to give diplomatic standing to one church group over against all other church groups that total larger numerical strength. ... [The] creation of such a diplomatic post is discriminatory, and is in violation of the Constitution of the United States of America.[13]

The *American Lutheran* made a more extensive argument in an editorial. It quoted Behnken's statement, noting that the editors "unanimously associate themselves" with his sentiments. In an unusual foray into partisan politics, they speculated on Truman's motivation:

> Was he trying to embarrass the Republican party on the eve of [the presidential election of] 1952? Was he trying to curry favor with the Roman Catholic authorities in the metropolitan centers where 'the Roman Catholic vote' is particularly valuable to politicians? Was he trying to assure that his own candidate would receive the Democratic Presidential nomination by thus deliberately jeopardizing the chances of Senators like Douglas, Fulbright, Kefauver and McMahon? Whatever his reason, the President made a grave mistake.

The editors urged readers to contact their members of Congress and tell them "that they must not endorse and repeat the President's error."[14]

The Bureau itself set up a "Special Committee on the Vatican Ambassadorship" which reported at the January 1952 board of directors meeting that it had sent a mailing of materials to Synod clergy; it "had been most favorably received and ... numerous requests for additional materials had been received." A week before that meeting, Clark had asked that his name be withdrawn, and while Truman indicated that he intended to submit another nominee, he never did.[15]

On the other hand, an article in the *American Lutheran* in February 1952 reported with some surprise that there seemed to have been a "turning to the Bible" within the

Roman Catholic Church. The author, James V. Claypool, doubted Roman Catholic claims that they had faithfully taught the Bible all along, but he observed that the Roman Catholic attitude toward Scripture "is not nearly as narrow as Protestants ordinarily think."

> The Catholics have rediscovered the Bible, and continue to rediscover it day by day. There exists among these Christian brethren an active impulse toward Bible reading for its devotional value. No one can tell how far it will go. But to us Protestants it is another summons to take more faithfully and devotedly a 'new turn' into the pages of our own Bibles.

It is striking that the magazine could print a reference to Roman Catholics as "Christian brethren" even as it continued to speak of the "split between Roman Catholicism and Christ." The ALPB attitude toward the Roman Catholic Church would gradually soften over the next few years, and then change dramatically after the Second Vatican Council.[16]

Anti-Communist hysteria

"anti-God, anti-Christ, anti-Scripture"

At mid-century, America was in the grip of another fear—that of a Communist conspiracy threatening the Western way of life. Fed by the politics of the Cold War, politicians like Senator Joseph McCarthy (R-WI) made a career of looking for Communist influence in various American institutions of government, education and religion. For a time, the *American Lutheran* got caught up in this controversy.

August W. Brustat had been an ALPB stalwart for several years—first as a board member who had chaired the 25th Anniversary Fund Appeal and the original Child Evangelism Campaign, then as a member of the editorial board of the *American Lutheran*. He was also a staunch anti-Communist. In 1949 he was called as pastor of Trinity Lutheran Church in Scarsdale, NY, and he promptly became involved in a controversial effort to remove books deemed subversive from the local high school curriculum.

Brustat began a six-part *American Lutheran* series on "The Communist Conspiracy" in April 1951. The introductory essay quoted FBI director J. Edgar Hoover:

> The known, card-carrying Communist is not our sole menace. The individual whose name does not appear on party rolls but who does the party's dirty work, who acts as an apologist for the party and who rises in its defense and spear-heads its campaigns in numerous fronts, is a greater menace. These are the 'Communist sympathizers,' 'fellow travelers,' and 'Communist stooges.' ... Whether they be innocent, gullible, or wilful [sic] makes little difference because they further the cause of Communism and weaken American democracy.[17]

The next article discussed the Communist infiltration in public education, alleging that many widely-used textbooks "are in reality Communist propaganda." Brustat noted, for instance, that a popular English literature textbook contained poems by the African American poet Langston Hughes, who was "affiliated with from 71 to 80 Communist-front organizations." The anthology was edited by the "pro-Communist" Louis Untermeyer.[18]

Next Brustat took up Communist infiltration of religion. "In the widest, most vicious, most subtle and diabolical of all uprisings against the cause of Christ this earth has probably ever witnessed," he wrote, Christians now face "unprecedented modes and techniques of persecution in this anti-God, anti-Christ, anti-Scripture campaign conducted by Communism." He reported at length on the persecution of Christians in the Soviet Union and other Communist countries.[19]

He then turned to allegations of Communist infiltration of various American religious organizations and publications. He listed American churchmen whom he accused of "supporting the atheistic cause of Communism"—something he found "utterly unbelievable and unspeakably tragic." The series concluded with a long list of things that Christians can (and should) do to fight the Communist threat. One of his suggestions was to "ask your pastor and denominational officials where they stand" on the issue of Communism. "If they have Marxist sympathies—either they resign or you find a Church which preaches the Gospel."[20]

Paul Blanshard's *Communism, Democracy, and Catholic Power* was published in 1951, and Brustat reviewed it for the *American Lutheran*. Blanshard's book, he wrote, offers a "sterling analysis" of the inevitable conflict between American democracy and the "two enemies of freedom"—Communism and Romanism. By this time voices had begun to be raised against the tactics of McCarthy and other members of Congress who were enthusiastically investigating Communist infiltration in American life—voices which included some prominent American churchmen. Brustat could not understand their criticism; in his view, the investigating committees were doing important work. Sometimes, he admitted, mistakes may be made in this process; but if someone should be falsely accused, "an apology is quickly forthcoming."[21]

The next month Brustat overtly praised McCarthy in a review of his book *McCarthyism: The Fight for America*. Brustat admitted the senator was a controversial figure, but insisted that "his fearless exposé of Communist infiltration in government has brought the wrath of the Communists and their sympathizers and fellow-travellers upon his head." The book is "a fair, frank open report" which has "more than vindicated" McCarthy as a courageous "citizen and public servant."[22]

This was too much for some readers of the *American Lutheran*, who wrote to protest Brustat's opinions. "I can hardly imagine the writer being serious," wrote Art Simon, "and refuse to believe that other members of the editorial board concur in this opinion." McCarthy and others have unearthed very few "avowed Communists," but "in the meantime, how many reputations have been needless marred by slander or innuendo?" Pauline C. Hemmeter agreed: "Guilt by association has never been a Christian or American tradition," yet that is precisely what McCarthy and others have offered.[23]

A young LCMS pastor named Martin Marty, who would become one of the most eminent American church historians of the 20th century, also protested Brustat's articles. "It is unfortunate that the frustration [Brustat] has seen in his own community in presenting his political views should find expression in your magazine," Marty wrote. He hoped that in the future the *American Lutheran* would "confine itself to the realm in which it excels, churchmanship," and either omit "articles of this nature" or exhibit "a more serious regard for their accuracy and fairness."[24]

Brustat wrote a vigorous response to his critics. "The fact of the matter," he insisted, "is that too many clergymen, especially among the Protestants and Jews, have wittingly and unwittingly collaborated with Communists to an alarming degree"—and "names could be mentioned." Furthermore, the number of Americans who, under the influence of "a slanted press," criticize the Congressional investigations "is appalling and tragic." "The Church better busy herself with this menacing problem, or her voice in America may likewise be silenced here as it has been in so many places dominated by the Kremlin."[25]

Perhaps reflecting discomfort by the other editors with Brustat's position, his response was immediately followed by two statements from other Lutherans—one from the ULCA's Board of Education and the other from Conrad Bergendoff, president of Augustana College—which defended academic freedom and obliquely criticized those who "have become almost hysterical" in investigating possible subversion. That same month, Ade Meyer commented in passing in a letter to Geiseman, "I think we have now had enough on the subject of communism."[26]

Martin Marty wrote again a few months later, this time offering a more extended reflection on the "religious threat in McCarthyism." In Marty's view, McCarthyism represented a worldview at odds with Christianity. The senator represented, in the words of the *Christian Science Monitor*, "an ideological certainty which demands rigid conformity." Like Communism itself, Marty wrote, McCarthyism offers "false claims and oversimplifications of history," as well as "a self-righteous view of man incompatible with the Christian view." For McCarthy, a person is "either 'good' or 'bad.'" This is not the Christian understanding. "Where does acknowledgement of error and sin come in? Christianity says the 'mess' is in us—and not only in Washington." No, Marty concluded, the church must not, in its opposition to Communism, fall off the horse on the other side. "The message of the Cross will be obscured if the Church's concern be tied to the negative alternatives of McCarthyism and Communism." Rather the church must be "simply pro-Christ, endeavoring to view truth, history, and freedom in the light of the truth given by the Spirit of Christ."[27]

Perhaps the other editors agreed with Marty's critique, or perhaps, like Meyer, they were simply weary of the matter. In one sense the issue had run its course, as McCarthy was increasingly denounced and ultimately censured by the Senate. In any event, there was little further discussion of the issue in the *American Lutheran*. Brustat continued for several years to write and lecture about the Communist threat, but other than occasional glowing reviews of anti-Communist books, his writings did not appear in the ALPB's magazine.

The Eucharist

"There is only one way—the Sacrament"

In the postwar period, the *American Lutheran* gave increasing attention to a principal goal of the liturgical movement: restoring the centrality of the Eucharist to Lutheran worship. Fred Lindemann continued to be the primary spokesman on this topic. It sometimes seemed as if for Lindemann, the deterioration of the Sacrament in Lutheran life and practice was to blame for nearly every ill that beset the church. In one editorial staff meeting, Lindemann made the comment (the precise context is not clear in the minutes) that "there is only one way—the Sacrament"; Brustat, who was keeping the minutes, noted parenthetically, "For his tombstone."[28]

Lindemann's 1943 editorial "The Minister Disturbs Our Worship" had provoked a letter of protest from W. G. Polack, who took issue with Lindemann's statement that a service without Holy Communion was a "departure from liturgical usage." "Everyone who has looked into the past liturgical usage of the Lutheran Church," Polack had written, "knows [that] is not true." Polack's letter had been printed without comment, but several months later Lindemann at last returned fire. "If this were a contest of wits," he wrote, "and not an attempt to get at the truth, here would be the place to claim a foul."[29]

Polack had insisted that weekly communion "simply cannot be done in the average congregation." Lindemann noted that the average size of Missouri Synod congregations was 182 communicants, which "does not absolutely eliminate even a weekly celebration." The real problem, he argued, isn't the logistical one, but simply "the indifference of Christians" to the joy of the Sacrament.[30]

In 1944 there appeared a little book by Berthold von Schenk entitled *The Presence: An Approach to the Holy Communion*. Von Schenk had at one time been a member of the ALPB board of directors (though he was apparently not still serving in 1944). His approach to the Eucharist was almost mystical, quite unlike the typical Lutheran dogmatic treatment. Lindemann was asked to review the book. Von Schenk's meditations, he wrote, "are echoes of what the saints in all ages have thought and felt. If the sound of the echo is strange to our ears, it must be that we have been deaf to the voices that may be heard down the centuries."[31]

But so enthusiastic was Lindemann about the book that he wrote an article separate from the review, published in the same issue, pleading for a "reading without prejudice."

> The author courageously makes the attempt to express on the cold printed page emotions and reactions that can never be adequately put into words. ... He must have anticipated that he will not be understood by many and be misunderstood by some, yet he offers what he has found, not counting the cost. It is nothing new, though new to many of this generation. ... In a sense, this volume may be the test whether [the reader] retains the ability to recognize independent thought and to give fair consideration.[32]

Lindemann went on for nearly four full pages, anticipating negative reactions to von Schenk's book and offering explanations and support. He particularly applauded von Schenk's effort to disconnect the Eucharist from the concept of "worthiness."

> The all-important word now is Worthiness. Before appearing at the Lord's Table one must rouse oneself to a proper appreciation of sinfulness. By ten o'clock on that first Sunday of the month one must be a miserable sinner. The journey to the pastor's study for registration really serves no purpose, but the inconvenience is a penitential act. ... The preparatory address may not be pleasant to the Old Man, but one must be worthy and that requires preparation. The more crushed one feels the more worthy. ... Fortunately, one need not submit to this kind of spiritual exercise too frequently. It's over with now until the first Sunday of the second or third month.

But in taking to heart von Schenk's more mystical approach, "new life will surge through the dead bones of the Church. Individual lives will be lived in the Presence and be the happier and more joyful and more fruitful and holier for it."[33]

Lindemann really got himself into hot water, though, with an article entitled "The Lord's Supper and the Church." His approach in this essay was to point out an important difference between preaching and the Sacrament. The former is public, "directed to the whole world." Non-Christians are permitted, even welcomed, to hear the proclaimed Word. The Sacrament, on the other hand, is restricted to Christians. It is thus the "line of demarcation" between the church and the world. When a service does not include the Sacrament, "there is nothing to impress upon the believer that he is separated from the unbeliever who sat with him and heard the same sermon." Thus "the Church needs the Lord's Supper. ... Wherever the Sacrament falls into decay and disuse, the boundary line between Church and world becomes indistinct." Furthermore, "there is no surer sign that a congregation or a church body is dying than the failure to assign to the Lord's Supper the place intended for it by our Lord."[34]

Lindemann argued that "an over-emphasis ... on the spoken and printed Word at the expense of the Visible Word" produces a church afflicted with "listlessness, coldness, indifference, pride, half-heartedness, worldliness." The church attempts to address these symptoms by "[competing] with the world on the entertainment level of a club. We have choirs that sing well. We have excellent organists. We work hard to produce good sermons." As a result "many of the people believe that their hunger for the Word can be satisfied at home and over the radio. ... They have been given to understand that all the audible Word can give they have in the printed Word."[35]

The remedy, Lindemann argued, is to "restore the Lord's Supper to its rightful place." What "makes the Church" is "not purity of doctrine, not intellectual faithfulness to the printed Word, not faith on man's part, but the Presence of Christ"—and that is what is given in the Sacrament. The Lord's Supper is the "heart of the Church," and "when the heart stops beating, the body dies."[36]

This article was called to the LCMS president's attention by Rev. H. A. Grueber of Milwaukee. Behnken responded to Grueber (inappropriately, one must think):

> May I say with reference to the article that I had not read it until your letter arrived? I must say that I've not gotten time to read much in the AMERICAN LUTHERAN. I do not make it a practice of reading Pastor Lindemann's articles. He is by no means the man that his brother Paul was. His record in the ministry is certainly less than an impressive one. Some of his troubles and difficulties which he has experienced trace back to the fact that he has tried to carry the idea of communion every Sunday as a 'must' into his congregational activities.

The same day Behnken wrote to Adolf Meyer with a personal plea:

> The March issue ... carries an article 'The Lord's Supper and the Church' ... [which] definitely touches matters of doctrine. I am very much surprised that this is published. If that is Lutheran doctrine then surely my ministry as far as preaching on the Lord's Supper is concerned and as far as teaching catechumens is concerned has been a complete failure. I am not the only one who feels that way about it. One of our very fine pastors, who has been a real leader in our church's work, informed me that he was simply 'sick at heart' when he read this article. I know that our Lutheran Church has not taught this. I know that this is not Luther's teaching. I know that it has not been the teaching at Concordia Seminary, etc.

Since the *American Lutheran* is not under Synodical censorship, he went on, it is "all the more important that you as Managing Editor ... exercise every precaution not to permit articles of such a nature to be published."[37]

Meyer responded graciously, indicating that he wanted to discuss the matter with Lindemann before saying anything further. At the editorial staff meeting a few days later—a meeting at which Lindemann was not present—it was resolved that Meyer tell Behnken the editors are "shocked at the charge of heresy" and ask him to point out what specifically he finds objectionable.[38]

If there was further correspondence about this matter, it doesn't appear to have survived. But Lindemann's ideas continued to be controversial. Later that year, he published two books on the Eucharist. One of them, *Thy King Cometh*, was a collection of sermons demonstrating how a pastor might preach about the Eucharist on various Sundays of the church year. The other, *Til He Comes*, was a historical and theological treatment of the Eucharist; most of its chapters were originally published in the *American Lutheran* (including the one that so exercised Behnken).[39]

While Lindemann was by far the most prolific writer on the Eucharist in the *American Lutheran*, he was not the only one. A 1946 issue again took up the propriety of pastors communing themselves, offering articles arguing both in favor (by Harold Schweigert) and against (by Rudolph Norden). This was an issue closely related to Lindemann's concern for frequent communion; in his view, the very rare opportunities for most pastors to receive communion (primarily at pastoral conferences) meant that pastors themselves did not experience the power of regular reception. Allowing self-communion of pastors was thus a key to encouraging more frequent celebrations. An editorial note made clear that "neither the editorial staff nor the American Lutheran Publicity Bureau necessarily endorses the opinions expressed by the writers."[40]

Lindemann's nephew, Herbert Lindemann, also wrote on the topic of the Eucharist. In July 1950, he contributed a two-part essay urging pastors to preach regularly about the Sacrament. "A great many of our people see no particular reason for communing except that Christ commanded it," he observed. "The fault rests squarely on the clergy" for their failure to preach winsomely about "a deeper appreciation of and love for the Blessed Sacrament of the Altar."[41]

If Fred Lindemann's views were more advanced than those of the other editors, his colleagues nevertheless generally agreed with his direction. An editorial in January 1946, commenting on the recently revived liturgical journal *Una Sancta*, asked the question, "Why Liturgical Movements?"

> Lutherans generally have lost the art of worship. The atmosphere of reverent adoration and joyful worship is rare. ... Today the Eucharist of the Apostolic Church and the post-Reformation Lutheran Church is usually 'celebrated' as a recent bereavement would be observed. There may be an awful solemnity and an oppressive seriousness, but no joy on the faces or in the voices of the people. ... As long as a liturgical movement aims to preserve Lutheran piety in our modern anti-Christian culture and seeks to recapture for our people the art of worship, it deserves the wholehearted support of every devout child of God.

While cautious about "occasional orgies in ceremony and rite indulged in by some who personally tend toward showmanship," the magazine continued to highlight the importance of Lutheran liturgy, particularly the crucial role of the Eucharist in Christian life. "A Lutheran who is not interested in the Liturgy of his Church ... is an incongruity and out of step with the Augsburg Confession."[42]

Personnel changes

"More of a heartache than an inspiration"

The post-war period saw significant changes in personnel, both in the ALPB and the *American Lutheran*. Oswald C. J. Hoffman had been named a contributing editor of the magazine in 1945, and he quickly became such a vital member of the team that he was invited to be a member of the editorial board; August W. Brustat, who had been for some time an assistant editor in the "Bible and Spade Department," was also added to the board.

Frederick Roth Webber, who had contributed to the magazine since 1922 and had initiated the "Fine Arts in the Service of the Church" column in 1931, ended his association with ALPB around this time. At the editorial board meeting in 1944, Meyer reported that Webber "seems a bit sour on us," but it was agreed to leave his name on the magazine's masthead as editor of the Fine Arts Department. The following year it was decided that "his name be stricken from the masthead and that the Managing Editor gently break the news to him."[43]

It is not clear just what was going on here. Webber, though a longtime and pro-lific contributor, had never become closely involved with the mission of the *American Lutheran*; he was apparently drifting more into the orbit of the *Confessional Lutheran* group. He did not attend editorial staff meetings and does not seem to have been per-sonally intimate with others on the staff. His departure from the magazine, however, had a salutary result when Arthur Carl Piepkorn was added to the staff as editor of what would now be called the "Ecclesiastical Arts Department." Piepkorn's initial column was quite generous to Webber. To him, Piepkorn wrote, "must go the lion's share of the credit for the very great improvement in the application of the fine arts to the Lutheran Church and its services during the period between the two World Wars."

> His uncompromising loyalty to the Church of the Augsburg Confession and its doctrine, his impatience with sham and dishonesty in any form, his humility and modesty, his flawless esthetic taste, his impeccable judgment in matters of art and design, his titanic erudition, his encyclopedic memory for detail, his sure-handed scholarship utterly free from pedantic pretense—all these combined to fit him uniquely for the task which he discharged with such consistent competence.

Piepkorn would continue to be closely involved with the *American Lutheran* until 1962.[44]

Even more important to the future of the Bureau was the decision to call an executive director. Since Arthur Herbert's resignation as executive secretary in 1924, the ALPB had been an organization directed primarily by volunteers. J. F. E. Nickelsburg had long been employed as business manager (though his specific job title and responsibilities had changed through the years), and there had been one or more paid secretaries to handle the office work. But in the post-war years, it became clear the ALPB needed a salaried executive who could give closer attention to program development and generally oversee the Bureau's ministry.

The search for such a person, however, was no easier than it had been in the 1920s. In 1946, there was discussion with a Pastor H. Heuer about taking the position; he was even introduced to the *American Lutheran* editorial staff meeting by the Bureau president, August Bobzin. A few months later it was reported that Heuer "could not accept our call because of an overseas appointment." At least two other pastors were offered the position but declined. The 1947 editorial staff meeting discussed several other possible names; one of them was a young pastor named Theodore Wittrock, and it was he who ultimately accepted the position. Wittrock was born in Kansas in 1920, the son of an LCMS pastor. He had graduated from Concordia Seminary in 1946, served as missionary-at-large in Southern California and then as pastor of two California congregations. He accepted the call to be executive secretary of the ALPB, and he began that ministry in January 1948. He would serve the Bureau in this capacity for some twenty-one years.

Another significant change came in 1951, when August F. Bobzin stepped down as president of the ALPB. Bobzin had first joined the board in 1928 and had served as president for nearly twenty-one years—three times as long as any previous president (and longer than any of his successors to date). He had seen the Bureau through many crises through the years. He regularly attended editorial staff meetings of the *American Lutheran*, providing a strong connection between the ALPB board and the editorially independent magazine they published. His resignation came because he had accepted the position of chairman of the Synod's Board for European Affairs, and he felt he could not do justice to both positions (in addition to his responsibilities as pastor of Lutheran Church of the Resurrection in Flushing, NY). Bobzin would remain on the ALPB board for several years after stepping down as president. His successor as president was John A. Kavasch, pastor of Calvary Lutheran Church in Verona, NJ.

The *American Lutheran* edition of March 1953 led with an editorial announcing another significant change. After nearly four decades, the irrepressible J. F. E. Nickelsburg was retiring—"not at sixty-five, not at seventy, or even at seventy-five, but at the ripe old age of seventy-nine years." Ade Meyer claimed that "the ALPB was born because J. F. E. Nickelsburg was willing to give up his business position, and with the aid of an old secondhand desk, a battered typewriter, office help, and a very small salary," go to work for the fledgling Bureau. He lauded Nickelsburg's evangelical spirit; even beyond his work for the Bureau, Nickelsburg "carried on his own private publicity bureau for the Lutheran Church." "Whether he got paid or not made no difference. He felt compelled to broadcast by every and any available means of communication the message of Christ his Lord and of his beloved Lutheran Church."[45]

Nickelsburg had indeed been a key figure in the Bureau almost since its inception. From its very first issue he had been the business manager of the *American Lutheran*. At meetings of the editorial staff, he consistently urged that the magazine be designed to appeal to laity as well as clergy. He had served as a member of the board of directors since 1915—certainly the longest tenure of any director before or since—and in 1951 was named one of the regional vice presidents of the Bureau. In his retirement, he continued to serve on the board and to edit the "News Briefly Told" section of the *American Lutheran*; the latter responsibility he kept up until the *American Lutheran* suspended publication in 1966 to be replaced by *Lutheran Forum*. Nickelsburg died the next year at the age of 92.[46]

One final change came later in 1953, when the ALPB board decided it was time for a complete reorganization of the editorial staff of the *American Lutheran*. When Paul Lindemann died in 1938, responsibility for the magazine had been given to an editorial board, originally consisting of Adolf Meyer, Arthur Brunn, O. A. Geiseman, O. P. Kretzmann, George Koenig and Fred Lindemann, with Meyer coordinating the group as managing editor. This arrangement had supposedly been temporary, but it had gone on now for more than a dozen years. The personnel had changed somewhat, but Meyer, Geiseman, Kretzmann and Lindemann were still the core of the board. In 1953, the other members were August Brustat, Oswald Hoffman, Henry Wind, Arthur Carl Piepkorn, and E. J. Friedrich.

It was not always a comfortable arrangement. Shortly after the 1951 staff meeting, Meyer wrote to Brustat, who typically took the minutes at these meetings:

> Although it seemed for one-and-a-half days as though our editorial staff meetings were to run off smoothly, the final hour of our sessions on Friday served to dash such hopes to the ground. This sort of thing has now happened at quite a few of our meetings with the result that the hearts of the men are depressed and the united spirit of the staff is greatly jeopardized.

Meyer observed that Brustat's minutes had never revealed this tension, but now he felt that "the time has come when for the honest reflection of what transpires in our meetings this should definitely be included so as to present a true and correct picture of what actually transpired."[47]

Meyer's letter to Brustat didn't say so, but the difficulty revolved around Fred Lindemann, whose mercurial personality often grated on some of the others. It was not a new problem. Lindemann had thought the magazine should cease publication after his brother's death, and he never quite got over the feeling that the magazine did not meet his brother's standards. He often insisted that the magazine was too timid, particularly in the wake of the controversy about "A Statement" and in addressing attacks from the *Confessional Lutheran* and others. He was generally supported in this view by Kretzmann, though the latter was less acerbic in expressing his opinion.

As early as 1942, Geiseman had written to Meyer about "all the fireworks in the Editorial Staff during the past year or two." Geiseman wondered if he were to blame for it, since Lindemann seemed to target him in particular. He recalled an incident where Lindemann had sharply criticized a proposed editorial at a previous meeting:

> Just how blindly prejudiced an individual can be may be seen from the passionate manner in which Fred tore apart the editorial which was written by O. P. but which mistakenly bore my initials. I know that no good can be achieved for the kingdom of God by attitudes of strife, bickering and jealousy, and I would rather not be a partner to any such situation, for I am sure the devil gets more fun out of it than does the Lord. ... If it will contribute to the elimination of things which certainly are not good, I will be equally glad to have the men who voted me on, vote me off again.

Meyer emphatically replied that he wanted Geiseman to continue; he had, he wrote, made that very clear to Lindemann.[48]

Tensions continued, however, and in 1944 Lindemann threatened to resign from the editorial board. Geiseman pleaded with Meyer to accept the resignation and move on:

> If you want my advice I would say, let's be very grateful for this resignation and accept it without argumentation. I think we ought to give Fred a page or a column to conduct in the magazine, leave with him also if he wants it the task of reviewing the books ... but don't let's keep him on the editorial staff. He has demonstrated, in my judgment, that he is not qualified emotionally to serve on a consultative or collaborative group. Why should we deliberately insist on keeping someone in our midst who is forever rocking the boat? ... I suppose we could not satisfy him unless we all resigned and allowed him to be the editorial staff.

While Lindemann "has a good mind and a facile pen," Geiseman concluded, "his inability to control his emotions disqualifies him."[49]

It isn't clear just what happened next, but Lindemann continued to serve on the editorial board. In January 1952, Geiseman again pleaded with Meyer:

> I agree with Hank [Wind] that the meetings of the editorial staff over the past several years too often have been more of a heartache than an inspiration, due primarily to the negative and, in my judgment, uncalled for critical attitudes of a personal nature on the part of Fred. At one meeting he would direct his barbs at one member of the staff. At another meeting they would strike some other member. This has greatly disturbed the spirit of peace and harmony and taken the note of joy out of meetings which lose their purpose if they do not give the individuals a lift and knit them together more closely.[50]

Apparently it was Wind who suggested that the ALPB board "dissolve the present editorial staff and ... appoint a new staff with [Meyer] as the responsible editor." The idea had been broached initially at the September 1951 editorial staff meeting, where a motion that Meyer be appointed editor was approved, but then reconsidered and tabled. Some members of the staff seem to have shared their concerns with the ALPB board.[51]

It was two years before action was taken, but in November 1953, the board of directors agreed to reorganize the editorial responsibilities. Meyer emphatically asked that he be relieved of responsibility. After some consideration, the board informed him that they could find no one else acceptable to them and asked him to assume the title of editor, with full authority to organize a staff as he saw fit. (While the minutes from that meeting are missing, a memo from President Kavasch quotes one rather sardonic sentence from them: "In spite of Dr. Adolf F. Meyer's urgent request that he be relieved of all responsibility of editing the AMERICAN LUTHERAN the Board of Directors unanimously elected him as editor of the magazine.") As managing editor since 1926—and particularly since Paul Lindemann's death in 1938—Meyer had very much put his stamp on the *American Lutheran*. Now with the title "editor" and the mandate to reorganize the staff as he wished, Meyer took charge of the magazine in a more assertive way.[52]

His first task was to recruit a small group of "editorial associates," as well as a larger group of "contributors." He intended to use the editorial associates in much the same way as the editorial board had functioned in the past; they would meet at least annually and be his closest collaborators, both in writing editorials and in setting editorial policy (in consultation with the ALPB board's Magazine Committee). Meyer outlined his plans confidentially to Geiseman, the colleague on whom he had come to rely the most. His intent, he said, was to streamline the staff. He wanted to eliminate the title of "managing editor" and ask Wittrock to act simply as "business manager." He wanted to limit the editorial associates to three—Geiseman, Hoffman, and Piepkorn.[53]

This obviously had the potential for hurt feelings among the others who had been on the editorial board. Geiseman urged that Kretzmann be included, despite his close relationship to Fred Lindemann which "has repeatedly caused him either to side with the recalcitrant member or to acquiesce in his tirades by silence." But Meyer didn't think he could invite Kretzmann without also inviting Henry Wind. He intended instead to ask both Kretzmann and Wind to be among the contributors. His letter to Geiseman said nothing about including Fred Lindemann in either capacity, though he would later tell Kretzmann that he, Wind, and Lindemann had all been invited to serve as contributors.[54]

In a carefully worded letter to Kretzmann, Meyer explained that the Bureau's magazine committee had authorized only three editorial associates (not mentioning that this was at his recommendation!). Geiseman, Hoffman and Piepkorn were selected after long discussion, since they were "the men who had produced regularly during the past year."

> In discussing your name I told the boys the only reason you had not contributed was due to the fact that you were overburdened with a terrific job [president of Valparaiso University]. ... I told them that I certainly wished to have your continued counsel and assistance in the formation of particular policy, for consultation in emergencies, and in the setting up of magazine program. The magazine committee of the ALPB made it very clear that as editor I could call in any of the Contributors for any purpose that I might wish. ...

> Incidentally I am asking ALL of the former members of our staff (including, of course, Fred) to serve as contributors. You were the only one, however, that I specifically stated I wanted to work with me as outlined above.[55]

Despite Meyer's diplomatic approach, Kretzmann was miffed. After assuring Meyer that the reorganization "has my full approval," he admitted that "the manner in which [it] was effected was viewed by me with some regret and concern."

> I am always a little disturbed when I see major decisions made by a group of men who are far removed from the heart and life of the Missouri Synod as New York City. I am, of course, perfectly willing to accept your and Ossie's judgment in such matters, but concerning some of the rest of the brethren I have my grave and continuing doubts. In addition, I was somewhat disturbed by the fact that the reorganization was effected at a time when several of us whose names appeared on the masthead were under fire from certain quarters. I believe that it would have been far better to take a closer look at some of the implications of the disappearance of our names from the masthead at this particular juncture in the history of the Missouri Synod. Certainly The AMERICAN LUTHERAN has done absolutely nothing (except in Geise's column) to counteract directly and effectively the viciousness that has appeared lately in such publications as the "Lutheran Loyalty" and "The Confessional Lutheran."

> I hope that you will not interpret these last few sentences as reflecting an attitude of bitterness. It is merely to tell you very honestly how I feel about matters at the present moment. ... [We] have definitely gone downhill in the cause for which we fought eight and ten years ago. I am certain, too, that Paul Lindemann would not have approved of the course of inaction which we have so largely adopted during the past years. As you know, too, I have felt for some time that The AMERICAN LUTHERAN instead of being a brave, free, courageous, and independent organ of thought has been more and more a slight deviation from the official party line. While this may be desirable in terms of certain immediate objectives, in the long run I do not believe that we shall be serving the Kingdom as effectively as we did years ago when we spoke out on the great issues confronting Christendom in our time.

In light of all this, Kretzmann declined the offer to be listed as a contributor. He promised that Meyer could count on him "for any assistance which I may be able to give" and that he would "continue to write just as much as possible but will look for other avenues for publication." He reiterated that though he had no bitterness, he thought the "manner in which the reorganization was effected ... was exceedingly unfortunate."[56]

Kretzmann sent copies of his letter to all members of the editorial board. Geiseman, who often played the role of mediator during *American Lutheran* staff conflicts, managed to coax Kretzmann to reconsider. The January 1954 issue of the *American Lutheran* carried a new masthead which named Meyer as editor, Wittrock as business manager, Geiseman, Hoffman and Piepkorn as editorial associates, and a list of thirty-seven contributors. O. P. Kretzmann, Henry Wind, E. J. Friedrich, and August Brustat were among them; Fred Lindemann was not.

Notes

1. Cited in John Tracy Ellis, *American Catholicism*, 2nd ed. (Chicago: University of Chicago Press, 1969), 151.

2. Harold E. Fey, "Can Catholicism Win America," *Christian Century* 61 (29 Nov. 1944), 1378-80; "Catholicism Invades Rural America," *Christian Century* 62 (10 Jan. 1945), 44-47; Paul Blanshard, *American Freedom and Catholic Power* (Boston: Beacon Press, 1950); Paul Blanshard, *Communism, Democracy, and Catholic Power* (Boston: Beacon Press, 1951). For a good overview of anti-Catholic prejudice in postwar America, see John T. McGreevy, *Catholicism and American Freedom: A History* (New York: W. W. Norton & Co., 2003).

3. Minutes, *AL* Editorial Board, 26-27 Oct. 1944, Geiseman Papers, Box 21, Folder 2.

4. *AL* 28, no. 10 (Oct. 1945), 4; Meyer, "Autobiography," 31.

5. "The Split Between Roman Catholicism and Christ" (Lutheran Press, 1948).

6. Ibid.

7. "Maligning the Roman Catholics," *AL* 31, no. 10 (Oct. 1948), 4.

8. William Dallmann, "Why Lutheran—Not Catholic," *AL* 28, no. 6 (June 1946), 6-8.

9. Minutes, *AL* Editorial Board, 6-7 May 1946, Geiseman Papers, Box 21, Folder 2.

10. "Is There a Catholic Issue?" *AL* 31, no. 11 (Nov. 1948), 21.

11. "Highlights of March A.L.P.B. Board Meeting," *AL* 30, no. 4 (Apr. 1947), 23; "Highlights of A.L.P.B. Board Meeting," *AL* 32, no. 6 (June 1949), 11; "Highlights of ALPB Board Meeting," *AL* 33, no. 2 (Feb. 1950), 10; "Highlights of the ALPB Board Meeting," *AL* 33, no. 12 (Dec. 1950), 24.

12. Glenn C. Stone to Dante N. Rosso, 24 Oct. 1984, American Lutheran Publicity Bureau Collection, Box 36, Folder 2a, Gettysburg Seminary Archives (hereafter cited as Gettysburg Collection).

13. "Copy of Telegram Sent to President Truman by Rev. John A. Kavasch," *AL* 34, no. 11 (Nov. 1951), front cover.

14. "The President's Mistake," *AL* 33, no. 11 (Nov. 1951), 5-6.

15. "Board Briefs," *AL* 34, no. 2 (Feb. 1953), 22. For an excellent analysis of Protestant opposition to the appointment of a Vatican ambassador, see F. William O'Brien, "General Clark's Nomination as Ambassador to the Vatican: American Reaction," *Catholic Historical Review* 44, no. 4 (Jan. 1959), 421-439. An American ambassador to the Vatican was finally nominated by President Reagan and confirmed by the Senate in 1984.

16. James V. Claypool, "The 'New Turn,'" *AL* 34, no. 3 (Feb. 1953), 8-9,19.

17. August W. Brustat, "The Communist Conspiracy: The Pattern," *AL* 34, no. 4 (Apr. 1951), 9. The quote from Hoover appeared in *Newsweek*, June 9, 1947.

18. August W. Brustat, "The Communist Conspiracy: II. In Education," *AL* 34, no. 6 (June, 1951), 7.

19. August W. Brustat, "The Communist Conspiracy: III. Against Religion," *AL* 34, no. 9 (Sept. 1951), 10.

20. August W. Brustat, "The Communist Conspiracy: III. In Religion (3)," *AL* 34, no. 11 (Nov. 1951), 24, and "The Communist Conspiracy: III. In Religion (4)," *AL* 34, no. 12 (Dec. 1951), 9.

21. August W. Brustat, Review of *Communism, Democracy, and Catholic Power*, *AL* 34, no. 9 (Sept. 1951), 18, and "Investigating Communism in Education," *AL* 36, no. 4 (Apr. 1953), 30.

22. August W. Brustat, Review of *McCarthyism: The Fight for America*, *AL* 36, no. 5 (May 1953), 19.

23. "Open Forum," *AL* 36, no. 6 (June 1953), 12-13.

24. "Open Forum," *AL* 36, no. 8 (Aug. 1953), 7-8.

25. August W. Brustat, "Some Thoughts on Communist Attitudes," *AL* 36, no. 8 (Aug. 1953), 9-10.

26. Conrad Bergendoff, "Toward a Right Way of Thinking," *AL* 36, no. 8 (Aug. 1953), 10; Adolf Meyer to O. A. Geiseman, 19 August 1953, Geiseman Papers, Box 10, Folder 1.

27. Martin E. Marty, "Religious Threat in McCarthyism," AL 37, no. 5 (May 1954), 24.

28. Minutes, *AL* Editorial Board, 21 Nov 1946, Geiseman Papers, Box 21, Folder 2.

29. Fred H. Lindemann, "Discussions on the Lord's Supper," *AL* 27, no 2 (Feb. 1944), 7.

30. Ibid.

31. Fred H. Lindemann, "Book Review," *AL* 29, no. 5 (May 1946), 23.

32. Fred H. Lindemann, "A Plea for Reading Without Prejudice," *AL* 29, no 5 (May 1946), 9.

33. Ibid., 29.

34. Fred H. Lindemann, "The Lord's Supper and the Church," *AL* 35, no. 3 (Mar. 1948), 10.

35. Ibid., 10-11.

36. Ibid., 24.

37. John W. Behnken to H. A. Grueber, 27 Mar. 1948, and John W. Behnken to Adolf F. Meyer, 27 Mar. 1948, Behnken Papers, Box 4, Folder 38.

38. Minutes, *AL* Editorial Board, 8-9 Apr. 1948, Geiseman Papers, Box 21, Folder 2.

39. Fred H. Lindemann, *Thy King Cometh* (New York: Ernst Kaufmann, Inc., 1948); *Til He Come* (New York: Ernst Kaufmann, Inc., 1948).

40. Harold F. Schweigert and Rudolph Norden, "Self-Communion," *AL* 29, no. 10 (Oct. 1946), 6-9.

41. Herbert Lindemann, "Preaching About the Sacrament," *AL* 33, no. 7 (July 1950), 7.

42. "Why Liturgical Movements?" *AL* 29, no. 1 (Jan. 1946), 3; "Is Lutheran Liturgy Important?" *AL* 35, no. 4 (Apr. 1951), 3.

43. Minutes, *AL* Editorial Board, 26-27 Oct. 1944 and 5 Sept. 1945, Geiseman Papers, Box 21, Folder 2.

44. Arthur Carl Piepkorn, "The Ecclesiastical Arts: By Way of Introduction," *AL* 30, no. 1 (Jan. 1947), 7.

45. "J. F. E. Nickelsburg Retires," *AL* 36, no. 3 (March 1953), 3.

46. For a detailed account of Nickelsburg's work with the ALPB, see Alan Graebner, "Meet 'Mr. Lutheran Publicity': A Tribute to J. F. E. Nickelsburg," *AL* 47, no. 7 (July 1964), 6ff.

47. Adolf F. Meyer to A. W. Brustat, 24 Sept. 1951, Geiseman Papers, Box 10, Folder 1.

48. O. A. Geiseman to Adolf Meyer, 4 June 1942, Geiseman Papers, Box 10, Folder 1.

49. O. A. Geiseman to Adolf Meyer, 12 Jan. 1944. Geiseman Papers, Box 10, Folder 1.

50. O. A. Geiseman to Adolf Meyer, 25 Jan. 1952, Geiseman Papers, Box 10, Folder 1.

51. Ibid.; Minutes, *AL* Editorial Board, 20-21 Sept. 1951, Geiseman Papers, Box 21, Folder 2.

52. John Kavasch memo, n.d., Geiseman Papers, Box 10, Folder 1.

53. Adolf Meyer to O. A. Geiseman, 5 Nov. 1953, Geiseman Papers, Box 10, Folder 1.

54. O. A. Geiseman to Adolf Meyer, 9 Nov. 1953, Geiseman Papers, Box 10, Folder 1.

55. Adolf Meyer to O. P. Kretzmann, 23 Nov. 1953, Geiseman Papers, Box 10, Folder 1.

56. O. P. Kretzmann to Adolf Meyer, 10 Dec. 1953, Geiseman Papers, Box 10, Folder 1.

Chapter 11

The 1950s

T he 1950s saw significant changes for the ALPB. With Theodore Wittrock as executive director and John Kavasch as president, the Bureau worked more intentionally at developing resources for local congregations, including a popular evangelism program and widely-used "Reformation emphasis" materials. A reorganization of the *American Lutheran* editorial staff gave a new focus as well as a facelift to the magazine, which continued to advocate for Lutheran unity and to discuss the church's role in addressing social problems. An important milestone came in 1954, when the Bureau celebrated its 40th anniversary.

The new *American Lutheran*
"no fundamental change"

Adolf Meyer hadn't sought the position of editor of the *American Lutheran*, but he responded to the call with enthusiasm. Less than a month after assuming the helm, Meyer wrote the first of a series of "editorial bulletins" to his newly named editorial associates and contributors, expressing his gratitude that "almost the entire list of men whom I approached accepted their appointments." He announced a meeting of the editorial associates to be held in February "to review magazine policy and program," inviting the contributors to offer their suggestions prior to that meeting. He enclosed a questionnaire so that the contributors might indicate areas of interest to them. He did not intend to compete with other Synod magazines, he told them, but to offer "new approaches in the operation of all phases of the church's work."[1]

The February meeting was an auspicious beginning; one of the editorial associates told Meyer "this was the best session which the AMERICAN LUTHERAN had convened." Meyer summarized the conversation for the contributors. The editorial associates had decided to publish a series on "The Problem of Moving Clergymen into New Parishes." They had met with ALPB president John Kavasch, who had "presented in considerable detail certain programs of the ALPB"; the group in turn assured him of their cooperation in "presenting such programs to our readers." They had decided to phase out some features of the magazine, and agreed that gradual changes to the physical layout of the magazine would be made (though a new masthead appeared immediately, replacing the banner that had graced the magazine since 1926 with a more contemporary font and logo). They had endorsed Wittrock's plan for a subscription campaign.[2]

Most significantly, they had agreed on a statement of policy for the *American Lutheran*. The magazine had been accused of departing from the "practical church work" emphasis of its founding editor. This new statement of policy, Meyer insisted, continues to follow Paul Lindemann's principles. "There will be no fundamental change in the editorial policy while the present Editorial Board is in charge."[3]

The ten-point statement was published on the cover of the April issue of the magazine—entitled "Re-Statement of Editorial Policy," to emphasize the theme of continuity:

It is our purpose:

1. To bring the Sacred Scriptures, as the source and norm of Christian doctrine and practice, to bear upon the opportunities and problems of our time.

2. To help the Church in its efforts to equip itself for intelligent action in evangelizing the world and in deepening the spiritual life of its membership.

3. To inform Lutherans regarding the problems confronting the Church and to suggest possible solutions.

4. To point out possible improvements in the Church's approach to its own problems where they affect the Church's first objective of proclaiming the Gospel of Christ.

5. To help remove man made obstructions which tend to impede the Church in its task of proclaiming the Gospel to all men.

6. To help our American neighbors better to understand Lutheran doctrine and practice.

7. To suggest to our Lutheran constituency tested methods by which they can help the people of their communities to understand Lutheranism more fully.

8. To stimulate action by local congregations and their members in the responsible exercise of their privileges as members of the Christian Church.

9. To present news of events important to Lutheranism, digests of current expressions of Christian thought, and reviews of important new books.

10. To encourage the unhindered exchange of viewpoint inherent in the freedom of the Christian man.[4]

An accompanying editorial reiterated that the statement was "true in every detail to the program which has guided the American Lutheran Publicity Bureau since its founding forty years ago." The magazine had always "striven conscientiously to advance the program of mission work both at home and abroad." It had "tried to face problems frankly and fearlessly even when some believed that a situation was too delicate for public discussion." And it had "sought to keep the church alert to the perpetual danger of having human opinion take the place of divine authority in the church." Such a commitment will "not win the approval of all," but the *American Lutheran* "has had reason to be proud both of its friends and of its opponents."[5]

The Sharing Christ Plan

"our people will respond"

Through the 1940s, the Bureau's work was focused on the *American Lutheran*, the tract ministry, and the annual National Lutheran Publicity Week and National Sunday School Week emphases. Now reinvigorated with a full-time executive director and a new president, the ALPB began a new emphasis on congregational resources. One of the most successful was an evangelism program called the "Sharing Christ Plan." It had originated at Calvary Lutheran Church in Verona, NJ, where John Kavasch was pastor; the concept was sparked by Fred Engelman, one of Calvary's elders, who would soon join the Bureau's board of directors.

The Sharing Christ Plan was introduced to the readers of the *American Lutheran* in 1953 with a lengthy explanatory article by Kavasch. He and Engelman had designed it to coincide with the ALPB's National Lutheran Publicity Week, the week prior to Ash Wednesday and a time when many congregations had already been encouraged to think about evangelism. Taking its basic concept from the popular "every member canvass" stewardship strategy, the program entailed visiting every household in the parish, with a special emphasis on inactive members, non-member parents of Sunday school and confirmation class students, and other prospective members.

Engelman was a retailer (he owned a sportswear firm), and he brought his sales experience to the Sharing Christ Plan—indeed, at Calvary Lutheran Church he had insisted that at least one or two other persons with sales experience serve on the program's coordinating committee. The plan called for distributing to every household a packet containing a prayer candle and wooden candle holder (made by members in the congregation with woodworking talents), a prayer card with special prayers for the success of the program, and other materials (including ALPB tracts) aimed at encouraging attendance at Sunday and special services during Lent. Callers were trained and assigned to visit members of one of the targeted groups; their instructions and the materials in their packets were specific to the families they were visiting. The program, Kavasch wrote, utilizes a successful stewardship model and "puts it to work in the effort to reach the people on the church prospect list." The article was illustrated with photos of some of the explanatory pieces produced by his congregation, all of which, "as well as additional materials for publicizing the gospel of Christ," could be ordered through the ALPB.[6]

The program was remarkably successful, at least in the East. In 1955, the second year after its introduction, some 75 congregations in the Atlantic District of the LCMS took part in the Sharing Christ Plan. The reports from those congregations indicated that they had experienced on average a 50% increase in church attendance at Ash Wednesday and Lenten services. Pr. Victor Albers, assistant executive secretary of missions and stewardship for the Atlantic District, summarized the results: "The Sharing Christ Plan ... has worked in all kinds of parishes and has demonstrated that our people will respond to a 'doing program.'"[7]

The Bureau continued to promote the Sharing Christ Plan for several years. It was recommended for use in the congregations of the Synod by evangelism officials in 1956, and then was formally commended by the Synod convention in June of that year. In May 1957, the *American Lutheran* published letters testifying to the program's success in congregations in California, Ohio, Iowa, Florida and Illinois. An editorial noted that "one of the large purposes of the American Lutheran Publicity Bureau is to give direction and aid, particularly to those pastors engaged in the difficult program of planting and establishing congregations." The Sharing Christ Plan has "brought real and lasting results." In 1957 alone, "almost 1,000,000 items, ranging from miniature gold crosses to doorknob hangers, candles, tracts and Lenten triptychs were distributed in connection with the Sharing Christ Plan." In 1956 a follow-up "Easter to Pentecost Church Attendance Crusade" was inaugurated, with thematic or programmatic suggestions for each Sunday as well as an Ascension Day service, "a neglected festival in need of re-emphasis." The program would end with a "climactic celebration of Pentecost" which is "an opportune time for receiving new members." The plan was revised in 1960 and marketed as the "New Sharing Christ Program." It was also supplemented by the "Fishermen's Club Plan," an effort to bring Sunday School students into the evangelism effort.[8]

Reformation Week

"the living Christ is the sure Hope"

Another emphasis promoted by the ALPB during the 1950s was Reformation Week, an annual focus on the teaching of Luther and the Reformers. This should be seen in the context of the escalating anti-Catholic rhetoric in the culture and the church during this period, exhibited in ALPB materials such as "The Split Between Roman Catholicism and Christ." The Bureau established a "Reformation Week Committee" in 1950, and they unveiled the program that fall. Theodore Wittrock urged that "more planning and effort" could turn Reformation Day into a week-long emphasis—or perhaps two weeks, or even the whole month of October! Wittrock offered numerous suggestions for congregational programs and services, newspaper and radio publicity, and ALPB tracts and other resources (including "The Split"). The October issue of the *American Lutheran* offered a dramatization of Luther's life that could be presented as part of Reformation celebrations.[9]

Each year brought new ideas and resources. In October 1951, the *American Lutheran* offered an article on how to use "The Split" in an adult Bible class; the author enthusiastically claimed that this topic resulted in a threefold increase in attendance in his parish. In the September 1953 issue, John Kavasch explained "How to Use Reformation Week Materials in a Confirmation Class Training Program." Kavasch's plan taught confirmands the basics of Reformation history and doctrine using a frankly apologetic approach. Second year students, for instance, would include a class on "Personal discernment … by contrast with Roman Catholic teaching." One of the resources suggested was a new ALPB tract, "The Assumption of the Virgin Mary—a New 'Dogma'" which will "help [students] to know that the Roman Church is still making new doctrines not found in the Bible."[10]

Though the 1953 Louis de Rochemont Associates film *Martin Luther* did not have an official ALPB connection, *American Lutheran* editorial associate Oswald Hoffman was an advisor in its production and the *American Lutheran* promoted it enthusiastically. The magazine was particularly pleased that the film was the product of cooperation between five Lutheran church bodies (including the Missouri Synod) and an inter-Lutheran agency. *Martin Luther* soon became a staple in ALPB's suggestions for Reformation Week, and the Bureau obtained permission to sell 16 mm prints of the film for congregational use.

In 1955, the Reformation Week theme was "The Message of the Reformation Must Live Today." A six-page brochure proposed a week-long preaching mission leading up to Reformation Day that would include a screening of *Martin Luther*. It offered poster-sized copies of "A Lutheran Manifesto" which outlined in ten statements basic Lutheran doctrine with a twist that highlighted its relevance for the Cold War era. For example:

8. The advent of the atomic age has not shortened the hand of God nor removed Christ from His throne as Ruler of the world and Head of His Church …

10. In the midst of insecurity and amid the false hopes of this present time, the living Christ is the sure Hope of all such as believe and trust in him.

The manifesto, the ALPB suggested, might be "placed on the outside of the church door in a brief ceremony fifteen minutes before the service, or immediately after the service." The Bureau advised sending a news story on the church door ceremony to the local newspaper, since "this should be a news worthy item in most communities."[11]

By 1959 "Reformation Week" had become "Reformation Month," with a comprehensive four-week program that included four sermons on Reformation themes, four lectures on the history of the church and a variety of other new resources. The most popular proved to be "God's Man of Faith," the story of Luther in comic book format, with text by John Tietjen and illustrations by George Evans. Intended primarily for school children, the ALPB was confident that "many a mother and father, older sister and brother" will also read the booklet. The final page summarized the importance of Luther's story:

We must make sure we appreciate the blessings God has given us. We ought to thank God for them and make sure that we do not ever lose them or let anyone take them away from us. We should be eager to share them with other people by inviting them to believe in Christ as we do. But, above all, we must make sure that, like Luther, we, too, are God's men and women of faith.

Well into the 1960s, the Reformation emphasis continued to be an annual ALPB promotion.[12]

A bold stance on race

"No Jim Crow Chariot!"

As racial unrest continued to simmer in America, the *American Lutheran* became ever more resolute in addressing the issue from a Christian perspective. Paul G. Amt celebrated "Advances on the Racial Front" in a 1950 article. He highlighted the move toward integration of "Negro work" into the district structure of the LCMS, the increased openness of "some of our Synodical Concordias to our Negro youth," and organizations like the St. Louis Lutheran Society for Better Race Relations. He lauded the *American Lutheran*, which "has long ago opened its columns to a thorough airing of the subject from every point of view." Yet he called for much more. The church must "throw aside all subterfuge and launch forth with a vital program of education in race relations." Even more important, there is "one disheartening trend in our circles that must be more vigorously challenged and finally checked"—namely, the tendency of congregations to move out "when the racial complexion of their neighborhoods changes." Despite its progress, the church has only "touched the hem of the garment" in terms of "Negro evangelism" and better race relations.[13]

Richard Klopf, pastor of St. John's Lutheran Church in Brooklyn, argued in 1951 that Lutheran congregations, particularly in urban settings, must find ways to "assimilate the Negro" into their membership. He met head on the arguments of some who would argue that white members simply "cannot be changed, their prejudices are too deeply rooted." Klopf insisted that indeed people *can* be changed—that the whole mission of the church is to change people. He told the story of his own parish and its resolve not to relocate but to remain in its neighborhood even as the demographics changed—first with waves of Italian and Jewish residents, followed by African Americans. The latter group, he said, provide "a tremendous opportunity." He noted with dismay that while most blacks are Protestant, "there are more Negroes in two Roman Catholic parishes in New York City than there are in all of American Lutheranism." Clearly, he said, the church must be stirred to evangelistic action. It won't always be easy, but it can be done—as his parish has demonstrated.

> But have there been no problems? Of course there have been, problems arising from the 'weak spots in some people's Christianity.' Human relations will always be a struggle. … [But] human relations for the Christian become the joyous anticipation of the blessedness which will be his in the perfect society of heaven.

Kopf's article featured a photograph of his marvelously integrated confirmation class.[14]

In 1954, the *American Lutheran* called the Supreme Court's *Brown v. Board of Education* ruling "a decision which Christians can enthusiastically commend"—and one which "conforms to the policy and practice of the Lutheran Church at her best." The editors admitted that not all Lutherans "have been able as mature Christians to shed completely the prejudices that we acquired in the process of growing up," and this has led in some places to "deplorable action at the parochial level."

> Old and irrational prejudices die hard. It will take more than a decision of the Supreme Court to kill them. We are frankly afraid that they may induce some Lutherans, in violation of the Fourth Commandment, to join in conspiring with reactionaries to nullify or evade the law by some of the dubious subterfuges that have been suggested. It is not impossible that some Lutherans, in sincere but short-sighted simplicity, may believe that they see an opportunity for educational evangelism in the establishment of segregated Lutheran day schools and high schools which would attract children of parents who do not want their offspring to associate with Negroes.

"We feel with unalterable firmness," the editorial concluded, "that for the sake of the Church and for the sake of Christ Himself such prejudices must not be allowed to prevail and such courses of action must not be undertaken."[15]

A few months later, another editorial entitled "No Jim Crow Chariot!" was clear about the duty of the church: "The evangelist Philip, knowing the Lord's command, did not set up a Jim Crow chariot on the famous ride to the stream where the Ethiopian was baptized." While segregation may continue for a while in some parts of society, there is "no longer any possible excuse for its existence anywhere in the Church—if there ever was an excuse for it there!"[16]

In December 1955, the magazine published another article by Pr. Klopf entitled "The Interracial Church." This one featured photos of black and white communicants kneeling together at the altar and of completely integrated Sunday school classes where (the caption pointed out) "white and colored children" were being taught cooperatively by "white and colored teachers." "At this we can only rejoice," the editor wrote. "God speed the day when the last vestige of rebellious racial pride in the Church will have been conquered by the love with which God has loved us all!"[17]

Lutheran unity

"a God-pleasing unity among Lutherans"

Though the editors of the *American Lutheran* had acquiesced to President Behnken's request to back off from their full-throttled advocacy of joining the National Lutheran Council, the magazine continued to beat the drum for Lutheran unity. They were jubilant when, in May 1949, a meeting of the presidents of Missouri Synod colleges expressed "profound distress over Lutheran disunity" and requested President Behnken to work with other church body presidents "to form a national inter-Lutheran committee for the purpose of arranging ... free conferences of Lutheran pastors and laymen" toward the end of bringing about "unity of Christian faith and fellowship." The editors saw this action as a sign that "all of a sudden, apparently without advance warning, God [has] placed the subject [of unity] squarely before all Lutheran bodies of America."[18]

An even more auspicious sign, the editors continued, was "a vast and growing 'ground swell' among the laymen of all Lutheran bodies for the FACTS regarding the problem of Lutheran unity." For that reason, the *American Lutheran* "feels ... that it may best serve its readers and the Lutheran Church at large by devoting a large part of its pages during the next twelve months to a factual presentation of the various problems involved" in attaining "a God-pleasing unity among Lutherans." The editors also admitted a secondary agenda: offering "information regarding possible Missouri Synod membership in the National Lutheran Council."[19]

But the unity movement in American Lutheranism was moving very rapidly, and the LCMS was being left behind. Early in 1949, a "Committee of 34" established by the eight member churches of NLC had met in Minneapolis. They proposed a plan that envisioned organic merger of the eight bodies, or at least a federation which would be a kind of intermediate step toward such a merger. The LCMS, since it was not a member of the NLC, was not invited to the meeting. When the proposal was released, the *American Lutheran* was not impressed. "Well intentioned as these men undoubtedly were," the editors wrote, "their published plan represents an organizational monstrosity. The worst feature is that its effect, if not its purpose, will be to make the National Lutheran Council an agency for union." Reading between the lines of the editorial, it is likely that the editors viewed this movement as a setback to their hopes for pushing Missouri to join the National Lutheran Council.[20]

The editors also expressed some resentment that these meetings had excluded Missouri. Though Missouri, they wrote, had often been jokingly called "isolationists," this new development leads one to wonder just who the isolationists are. The resolution of the college presidents calling for a free conference had essentially been spurned by the National Lutheran Council in favor of their own process, and yet only such a free conference offered that possibility of a wider unity in which Missouri might take part. The editors noted, however, that their endorsement of such a strategy "is predicated upon the assumption that all free conferences be opened with prayer"; the magazine "cannot support any plan which does not include the asking of Divine guidance and blessing."[21]

The promised emphasis on Lutheran unity unfolded with each issue of the magazine over the next several months. As the 1950 Synod convention prepared to consider the possibility of membership in the National Lutheran Council, Adolf Meyer wrote to Paul Empie, the NLC's executive director, asking a series of questions about the program and direction of the agency, as well as the history of its relations with the Missouri Synod. Empie admitted that such questions to some extent were a matter of opinion, but he provided a lengthy response which was then printed in the *American Lutheran* in June 1950. Empie's forthright answers made for fascinating reading. He suggested, for example, that frictions in the NLC's program—both in its relationships with Missouri and among member bodies of the NLC—"often result not from policy but rather where personalities have a tendency to rub each other the wrong way." Meyer had asked whether Missouri's presence, if she were to join the NLC, would be an irritant rather than a constructive contribution—a concern that had been expressed by the LCMS committee charged with studying possible membership in the NLC. Empie was frank to say that the group operated on the principle of majority vote, and no single body could have veto power; certainly Missouri could be an irritant "if it should sit on the side-lines and criticize the work in areas where it does not co-operate." On the other hand, Empie was optimistic about the contribution Missouri might make:

> My own feeling is that wherever the Lutheran Church—Missouri Synod should participate wholeheartedly, its point of view would frequently prevail, for it would find in the National Lutheran Council kindred spirits on many subjects; yet, if church bodies participate in good faith, they must accept a majority decision. ... The whole

history of the National Lutheran Council has been one of experience demonstrating how church bodies can work together for common objectives without compromise of their principles at the same time they respect the position of others and move toward mutual understanding.[22]

When the Synod convention that summer turned down a proposal to apply for membership in the NLC "at this time," the *American Lutheran* tried to put the best face on it. In the light of an apparent movement toward some kind of deeper unity or even union among the NLC bodies, "practically everyone in attendance at the convention was convinced that the time was inopportune for Missouri Synod entrance into the Council." The editorial took a slap, however, at the "somewhat left-handed and poorly organized report of the committee which ... recommended such negative action." The magazine rejoiced that the convention voted to "continue a policy of cooperation" with the Council.[23]

Even more encouraging, the editorial continued, was the convention's overwhelming vote to approve the "Common Confession," a statement developed by a joint committee of the Missouri Synod and the American Lutheran Church. This statement—which still needed to be affirmed by the ALC—was "a forward step for conservative Lutheranism" that was accomplished by the "efforts of those who witnessed in a brotherly way to the truth held by the Missouri Synod rather than ... the intransigent spirit which sometimes has been mistaken for true 'Missourianism.'"[24]

Despite its enthusiasm for Lutheran unity, the *American Lutheran* was much more cautious about the wider ecumenical movement. When the National Council of Churches was formed in 1950, the constituting convention's presiding officer was Franklin Clark Fry, president of the United Lutheran Church in America. Noting that the ULCA was one of three Lutheran bodies who had become charter members of the NCC, the *American Lutheran* reminded readers that "the majority of Lutherans in America belong to churches not holding, or even considering, membership in the National Council."

> Naturally, it is to be expected that the non-cooperating Lutheran churches will be charged with the now familiar failings of stupidity, lethargy, nationalism, isolationism, separatism, etc. If we are to judge by past performance, these charges will originate largely in the Lutheran bodies now members of the Council. This situation, too, ought to be viewed dispassionately without recrimination or resort to the usual slogan method of argumentation. Simply pinning a brand on a person or organization proves nothing—and solves nothing.

"It is easy to poke fun at a ponderous assembly" like the NCC's constituting convention, the editorial admitted, and it behooves non-participating Lutherans to try to understand just what the Council is all about; but the editors admitted to some skepticism. The business of the church, they wrote, is "to bring the Gospel of Jesus Christ to those who do not yet know Him." "How the National Council will do this work—or undo it—will be the real test of its worth."[25]

Lutheran disunity

"the sin of separatism"

Even as a new day was dawning for Lutheran unity, events were unfolding within the Synodical Conference which would ultimately lead to its demise. The most problematic points of contention were Missouri's modification of its view of prayer fellowship, its continuing discussions with the ALC, and its cooperation in externals with the bodies in the NLC (particularly on military chaplaincy). In the view of the other synods, Missouri was taking (or at least moving toward) positions that the Synodical Conference had long rejected.

At the Wisconsin Synod centennial convention in 1949, attendees heard an essay by one of the WELS seminary professors, Max Lehninger, in which he criticized certain "men in our sister Synod, Missouri" who by their actions "show Missouri [to be] in fellowship with men of other bodies with whom she did not have fellowship for the past 50-75 years." Lehninger complained that despite Wisconsin's protests, the "responsible officials" in Missouri have by their silence continued to condone such practices. These remarks were reported in the *Badger Lutheran*, and they came to the attention of the *American Lutheran* editors.[26]

The *American Lutheran* issued a sharp criticism of the Wisconsin professor. "If this report ... accurately reflects the attitude of the Wisconsin Synod," the editors asserted, "we have here a perfect example of the sin of separatism, a sin certainly no less deadly and destructive of true unity than the sin of 'unionism.'"

> [These] are the marks of this sin: An unyielding insistence that the position of our party (one's own) is the only scriptural position, down to the minutest detail; unsparing denunciation of all who dare to differ; refusal even to meet with those who are suspected of holding differing views in friendly gathering, lest testimony be dulled and eyes be drained of 'perception against the lurking danger of compromise.'

If the professor's position is in fact scriptural, "then we certainly have misread Scripture these many years."[27]

In February 1950, the magazine published an article by Theodore Graebner, who had recently retired as editor of the *Lutheran Witness*, entitled "What Price Patience?" An editorial called special attention to Graebner's article, observing that "for many Lutherans of the Missouri Synod, membership in the Synodical Conference is becoming as much of a problem as possible membership in the National Lutheran Council." The magazine offered "to open its columns to a frank discussion of the present situation within the Synodical Conference."[28]

Graebner's article was a gem of righteous indignation. "Do you hear that faint rasping sound somewhere in the middle distance?" he began. "It is the sharpening of the knives for the cutting of the throat" of the recent proposals for Missouri/ALC church fellowship. Graebner attacked recent editorials in the Wisconsin Synod's *Theological Quarterly*. The editor "apparently has forgotten that the Synodical Conference ... in its first constitution announced the purpose of 'uniting all Lutheran synods of America into one orthodox American Lutheran Church.'" But Wisconsin has condemned every effort by Missouri to foster unity "ever since our Synod resolved that meetings held for the purpose of removing doctrinal differences might be opened with prayer without violating the principle of prayer fellowship." Missouri, he said, has bent over backward to address Wisconsin's objections, but the result has simply been that "we are making a laughing-stock of conservative Lutheran theology." He suggested that perhaps the Wisconsin Synod should simply "resign its membership in the Synodical Conference." That need not mean that all relations between Wisconsin and Missouri would be severed; but it would mean that Wisconsin would "no longer [be compelled] to help frustrate every move for a larger fellowship which we may initiate now or in the future."

> Nor on the other hand, would we be held responsible by other Lutherans for the teachings and spirit of those who speak for the Wisconsin Synod. What is needed is not a divorce necessarily, but a new arrangement of the kind by virtue of which husbands sometimes insert a note in the county paper. 'After this date I am no longer responsible for my wife's debts.'[29]

The article brought a flood of letters to the *American Lutheran*—most of them appreciative ("Just about the most amusing piece of writing I have read in a decade— were it not so sadly and realistically true," wrote E. J. Bernthal). True to its commitment to "frank discussion," the magazine printed a scathing reply by a Norwegian Synod professor, Norman Madson—at least it printed some of it. The piece was prefaced by an editorial note that the *American Lutheran* would print any response "provided such expression is consonant with Christian love and the accepted ethics of journalism"— which meant they would not "publish violent personal attacks upon an individual, or supposed statements, unsubstantiated otherwise, of people long since dead." They were therefore publishing Prof. Madson's remarks "with proper excisions." Madson severely criticized Graebner's article, calling him "an incompetent witness." The editors of the *American Lutheran* provided several footnotes refuting or disputing Madson's charges.[30]

By late 1950, the *American Lutheran* had essentially given up on the Synodical Conference. At the editorial board meeting that October, the minutes made it clear:

> Regarding the Wisconsin Synod, it was decided, after varying viewpoints were expressed, that, while we must look to the break-up of the Synodical Conference as an organization to pave the way for a wider Lutheran fellowship, we are not to express

that thought per se publicly, but to strengthen the hand of our 'friends' and look at the rest as 'Methodists' who are in error, appealing them to return to the Word of God and not human opinion.

The prediction of the Synodical Conference break-up would come true, though not for another decade.[31]

In the meanwhile, relations between Missouri and the other members of the Synodical Conference continued to deteriorate, and in its convention in the summer of 1953, the Wisconsin Synod declared itself to be *in status confessionis* ("in a state of protest") in its relationship with Missouri. The *American Lutheran* referred to this as "a bombshell" and blamed it on the recalcitrant attitude of Wisconsin's leaders who had forced Wisconsin into an "unhappy position." Wisconsin was essentially demanding that Missouri reverse certain decisions it had made, or face a break with Wisconsin. "Holding a gun on a man is serious business," the *American Lutheran* said. "The Wisconsin Synod's leadership is going to have to answer some serious questions in the days to come." The editorial hoped that an honest self-evaluation by Wisconsin might lead to "new and stronger ties" between the two synods.[32]

O. A. Geiseman's analysis was less optimistic, though he attempted to put the best construction on things. He acknowledged that the situation "as it now prevails between the Wisconsin Synod and our own is very bad"—indeed, it has "so sickened some of the simple Christians ... who have been loyal members of the Lutheran Church all their lives" that "they have come to feel ashamed even to admit they are Lutherans." He acknowledged that there are "many fine evangelical pastors within the Wisconsin Synod who can hardly be happy with or proud of some of the positions held and attitudes manifested by some men within their own synod." He gently suggested that a root cause of the strife was that the Wisconsin Synod had still not passed through "the period of transition through which our people began to pass during and immediately after the first world war," leaving Wisconsin in a position of "social isolation." The only way to make sense of the current situation is to realize that church bodies "are composed of human beings" and that "prejudices of long standing must be reckoned with." In the end, Geiseman predicted, this situation would lead to a realignment among American Lutherans, with one extreme "[moving] farther and farther down into the dark pit from which some of the other Protestant groups in America are now trying to emerge"; another becoming "a kind of Lutheranism which preaches the Gospel as though it were the law"; and a third group "who will take their position squarely on the foundation of the prophets and the apostles with Jesus Christ as the chief cornerstone and ... the accepted confessions of the church as a true and correct exposition of the Scripture."[33]

As the 1954 meeting of the Synodical Conference approached, literature about the issues in dispute was being distributed furiously. One of these pieces was an 8-page tract, "Prayer Fellowship," published by the WELS to defend its position. The *American Lutheran* attacked it forthrightly. Most of the issues in dispute, the editors opined, "can be discussed in an atmosphere of mutual respect" and need not be seen as divisive—but not this one. The tract, they wrote, expresses a position that is so extreme that it is held only by "a small but vocal Missouri Synod group."[34]

The 1954 meeting brought no resolution to the conflict over Missouri's alleged "unionism." As a result, the Norwegian Synod the next year suspended its fellowship with the Missouri Synod (though it remained, for a time, a member of the Synodical Conference). The Wisconsin Synod did not immediately follow suit, though Edward Reim, chair of Wisconsin's Doctrinal Unity Commission, commended the Norwegian Synod and prayed "God grant that we do as well when the time for our decision comes." O. A. Geiseman, reflecting in the *American Lutheran* on the ongoing strife with Wisconsin, suggested that "we would do well to allow the controversies between the Wisconsin Synod and ourselves to lie dormant for a time" since "it is impossible ... to carry on in the Spirit of Christ and to make sound reason prevail in an atmosphere which is charged with temper and emotion gone wild."[35]

But the controversies did not lie dormant, and in 1961 the Wisconsin Synod formally suspended its fellowship with Missouri. The *American Lutheran* responded soberly and sadly. Wisconsin's repudiation of Missouri now lays upon the LCMS "the responsibility of proving to itself, to other Lutherans, and to Christendom that Lutheran orthodoxy, firmly held and intelligently practiced, is not essentially disruptive but a unifying force around which loyal followers of Christ can rally." The editors were optimistic that Missouri was up to the challenge.[36]

The ALPB's 40th Anniversary

"a wonderful and heartening experience"

As 1954 approached, the ALPB prepared to celebrate its 40th anniversary. The January 1954 issue of the *American Lutheran* kicked off the public celebration with a four-page compilation by J. F. E. Nickelsburg of "dates and events in the history of the ALPB." But the real thrust of the anniversary observance was a "40th Anniversary Appeal" that sought to raise $100,000 for the work of the Bureau.

This was the first major special fundraising effort the Bureau had attempted since the 1920s. The 1953 synodical convention had commended the work of the Bureau and encouraged congregations to support its work. The Synod board of directors had then granted permission for the appeal, with the understanding that it be "restricted to [the Bureau's] friends and users of its materials." The September 1954 *American Lutheran* introduced the program to readers. Taking as its theme "More for Christ," the appeal was co-chaired by Ade Meyer and Oswald Hoffman, assisted by a network of district and regional directors. President Kavasch offered three reasons why congregations and individuals should support the Bureau's ministry: its record of achievement and its fine "economy of operation" were the first two ("As one close to the administration of the Bureau puts it, the ALPB will do a million dollar job with one hundred thousand dollars)." More to the point, the ALPB "receives no financial subsidy from Synod" but depends on congregational and individual contributions.[37]

The funds raised, Kavasch wrote, would be used for several specific programs: the Free Gospel Tract Fund, free materials for mission congregations, a revised edition of the *Manual of Practical Church Work*, development of new outdoor posters and other materials, a proposed series of workshops for local congregations. Perhaps most interesting stated purpose was "mobility of action on vital issues." Under this rubric, Kavasch recalled the Bureau's activity in protesting the proposed U. S. Ambassador to the Vatican. The ALPB's independence allowed it "to alert the church in great haste." Contributions to the 40th anniversary fund "will help place the Bureau in position for ready and effective witness that will pay great dividends in many ways."[38]

How successful was the 40th Anniversary Appeal? It's difficult to know. ALPB board minutes are missing for this period, and while a notice in the December 1954 *American Lutheran* suggested that financial results should be known within a couple of months, there was no subsequent report in the magazine. The December comment, however, proclaimed that the program "was a wonderful and heartening experience for the members of the board and for all those who have, through the years, given so generously of their time and talents to our work." "It was evident," the report said, "that the Bureau had won the respect and confidence of the brethren and their support of our larger plans do to MORE FOR CHRIST."[39]

Notes

1. Adolf Meyer, "Editorial Bulletin #1," 18 Dec. 1953, Geiseman Papers, Box 21, Folder 2.
2. Adolf Meyer, "Editorial Bulletin #4," 26 Feb. 1954, Geiseman Papers, Box 21, Folder 2.
3. Ibid.
4. "Re-Statement of Editorial Policy," *AL* 37, no. 4 (Apr. 1954), 1.
5. "Editorial: Re-Statement of Editorial Policy" *AL* 37, no. 4 (Apr. 1954), 4-5.
6. John A. Kavasch, "The Sharing Christ Plan," *AL* 36, no. 12 (Dec. 1953), 6-9.
7. John A. Kavasch, "The Sharing Christ Plan Report," *AL* 38, no. 6 (June 1955), 6-8.
8. "The American Lutheran Publicity Bureau Serves Again," *AL* 40, no. 5 (May 1957), 4; "Church Attendance Crusade: A Program for Easter Sunday and for the Fifty Days after Easter, April 1 to May 20, 1956," n.d., ALPB Archives.
9. John A. Kavasch, "A Reformation Week Dramatization," *AL* 33, no. 10 (Oct. 1950), 14.
10. Arthur F. Steinke, "Using 'The Split' in a Bible Class," *AL* 34, no. 10 (Oct. 1951), 14; John A. Kavasch, "How to Use Reformation Week Materials in a Confirmation Class Training Program," *AL* 36, no. 9 (Sep. 1953), 13.
11. "Reformation Week October 23-30, 1955," n.d., ALPB Archives.
12. "New Twelve-Page Booklet," *AL* 42, no. 9 (Sept. 1959), 4.
13. Paul G. Amt, "Advances on the Racial Front," *AL* 33, no. 5 (May 1950), 9ff.

14. Richard Klopf, "It Can Be Done," *AL* 35, no. 12 (Dec. 1952), 7.

15. "Lutherans and the Non-Segregation Decision," *AL* 37, no. 9 (Sep. 1954), 3-4.

16. "No Jim Crow Chariot," *AL* 38, no. 7 (July 1955), 4.

17. Richard Klopf, "The Interracial Church," *AL* 38, no. 12 (Dec. 1955), 69; "The Church's Report Card on Integration," *AL* 38, no. 12 (Dec. 1955), 4.

18. "Lutheran Union in the Air," *AL* 32, no. 6 (June 1949), 3.

19. "'We Want the Facts,'" *AL* 32, no. 5 (June 1949), 4.

20. "Things Have Been Happening," *AL* 32, no. 7 (July 1949), 3.

21. "Who Are the Isolationists?" *AL* 32, no. 7 (July 1949), 4-5.

22. "Editorials," *AL* 33, no. 6 (June 1950), 4.

23. "The Voice of Jesus Christ," *AL* 33, no. 8 (Aug. 1950), 3.

24. Ibid., 4.

25. "The National Council of Churches," *AL* 34, no. 1 (Jan. 1951), 3-4.

26. Quoted in "The Sin of Separation," *AL* 32, no. 12 (Dec. 1949), 3.

27. Ibid., 4.

28. "Freedom of Speech," *AL* 33, no. 3 (Mar. 1950), 4.

29. Theodore Graebner, "What Price Patience?" *AL* 33, no. 3 (Mar. 1950), 7.

30. "Open Forum," *AL* 33, no. 5 (May 1950), 8; "Norman Madson, "What Price Union?" *AL* 33, no. 5 (May 1950), 7.

31. Minutes, *AL* Editorial Board, 10-11 Oct. 1950, Geiseman Papers, Box 21, Folder 2.

32. "The Wisconsin Synod," *AL* 34, no. 11 (Nov. 1953), 3.

33. O. A. Geiseman, "While It Is Day," *AL* 36, no. 10 (Oct. 1953), 21-22.

34. "'Prayer Fellowship,'" *AL* 37, no. 8 (Aug. 1954), 3.

35. *Northwestern Lutheran*, July 10, 1955, 215ff., quoted in J. Herbert Larson and Juul B. Madson, *Built on the Rock* (Mankato, MN: Evangelical Lutheran Synod, 1992), 102; O. A. Geiseman, "While It Is Day," *AL* 38, no. 1 (Jan. 1955), 7.

36. "Explosive Year," *AL* 45, no. 1 (Jan. 1962), 5.

37. John A. Kavasch, "The American Lutheran Publicity Bureau Today," *AL* 37, no. 9 (Sep. 1954), 11-12.

38. Ibid., 13.

39. "Report on 40th Anniversary Appeal," *AL* 37, no. 12 (Dec. 1954), 6.

Chapter 12

Facing a New Day

As the ALPB was developing new resources for congregations, the *American Lutheran* continued to challenge and stretch the thinking of its readers, lay and clergy alike. Members of the National Lutheran Council were moving toward two separate mergers which did not include the LCMS, so the magazine's advocacy of Lutheran unity turned toward the possibility of the Missouri Synod's joining the Lutheran World Federation. In a shift away from the almost knee-jerk anti-Catholicism of the past, the *American Lutheran* offered a symposium on what it might mean for a Roman Catholic to be elected President of the United States, and it even began to speak of the "catholicity" of Lutheranism. Meanwhile, another significant ALPB transition loomed when Adolf Meyer asked to be relieved of his responsibilities as editor.

Congregational resources
"*I didn't plan to be an embezzler!*"
Ted Wittrock's call as full-time executive secretary of the ALPB in 1948 had allowed the Bureau to expand significantly its resources for congregations. The Sharing Christ

Plan and Reformation Week programs were increasingly popular. The *American Lutheran* also began to include some special features intended to increase lay readership. A column specifically aimed at church council members, written by Ralph Richman and entitled "Church Council Chit-Chat," began in October 1950 and was promoted as an incentive for congregations to buy subscriptions for their own lay leaders. At year's end in 1956, Wittrock reported that this had led to some 800 new subscriptions, bringing the circulation to a new high. The magazine offered other articles of interest to congregational leaders, such as a 1957 symposium on "Fair Remuneration for the Servants of the Church" (a theme the magazine had first broached as early as 1920).[1]

But Wittrock believed additional help was needed to continue expanding the Bureau's program, and he sought to hire an assistant. He approached Paul John Thielo, a New York native who was at that time a student at Concordia Seminary. Thielo was interested in the ALPB's ministry, but there were no financial resources for an additional staff person and Thielo took a call to Concordia College in Portland, OR. Two years later, however, Wittrock approached Thielo again, reporting that he now had funding lined up and inviting him to come to work for ALPB. "Ted made the position seem quite romantic," Thielo later wrote, "and the pay was better." In June 1958, he resigned from Concordia College, moved back to New York, and started with ALPB that summer as assistant executive secretary. He would be a key contributor to several of the Bureau's projects over the next few years.[2]

Paul Lindemann had emphasized stewardship as something other than simply fundraising, and the *American Lutheran* had published many articles on the topic in the 1920s and 1930s. The subject had receded somewhat in the magazine's pages, though there were still some popular stewardship tracts available from the Bureau. But in 1957 a more comprehensive stewardship program was offered under the theme of a "Spiritual Life Crusade." Each year the program was supplemented with new resources. In 1960, for instance, the Bureau introduced "Seek the Lord First," a filmstrip which discussed "first-fruit, generous, proportionate giving." It also offered a phonograph record in which principles of Christian stewardship were explained:

> Rev. Scott reads a letter he received from Douglas and Dorothy Neal, long-time members of his church, who did not understand the Christian stewardship of money. Biblical principles on the grace of giving are clearly and simply presented as Rev. Scott tells how the Neals learned that Christian giving is FROM blessings which God gives rather than TO a budget or man-made goal.

A leader's guide was included in the packet, as well as a "pocket-size flip chart" for use in "every member visitation" presentations—all for $10, with a "satisfaction guaranteed" promise.[3]

The following year the Bureau published a series of new tracts entitled "The pressure *is on*," "It's in *your* hands," and "I was an embezzler ... and didn't realize it." The latter brochure explained what it meant by the provocative title:

> This is what happened. From earliest childhood I admired and wanted nice things—at first, pretty toys and games; later, fancy clothes and a car; then, the latest and best of household furnishing and gadgets. To get what I wanted was a very big thing in my life.
>
> I didn't plan to be an embezzler! I didn't plan to steal! I didn't realize just what I was doing. In fact, I thought I was a good Christian. Then it happened. Through our home devotions, our pastor's sermons, and our Church's Every Member Visit, my eyes were really opened. I discovered that my life was badly out of line with the pattern of thankful living as a redeemed child of God. I was selfish! I was thinking too much of myself and my own pleasure. ...
>
> To my amazement I actually discovered that I was not an owner at all. I was merely a **manager** of what God entrusted to me for a short period of time. ...
>
> There's no use kidding,—I was an embezzler! But God in His grace and mercy opened my eyes![4]

During this period, the Bureau also published a few small books aimed at providing help of various kinds for congregations. Waldo Werning's *How to Raise Men and Money in the Church: A Plan for Effective Church Financing* was released by the ALPB in 1957, billed as "a manual to help your stewardship committee." The next year a book on evangelism was published, reprinting several articles from the *American Lutheran* by Concordia Seminary professor Arthur M. Vincent.[5]

A popular addition to the Bureau's congregational resources was the 1960 filmstrip "Lutheran Liturgy in Slow Motion," intended to be used in small group settings such as confirmation or membership classes. The script was written by Paul Malte, at the time a graduate student at Concordia Seminary, with color graphics provided by Richard Caemmerer, Jr., then artist in residence at Valparaiso University. A companion phonograph record included music arranged by Concordia Seminary's Robert Bergt; it was narrated by Walter Grotrian of the LCMS's radio station KFUO. The entire project was coordinated by Paul John Thielo. The accompanying leader's guide offered salient suggestions for how to present the material (including "completely dark room, good ventilation, visibility of the screen, finesse of mechanical operation, and <u>prior preparation</u>" [emphasis in original]).[6]

The filmstrip was based on the Order for Holy Communion, and it assumed that the Sacrament would be a regular part of the Lutheran liturgy. It led the viewer through each part of the liturgy in *The Lutheran Hymnal.* "As the strip is unreeled," proclaimed the brochure advertising it, "it is almost impossible to remain uninformed about the church. Now you will know what happens in church and why it happens."

The presentation moved from an opening affirmation—"When we worship, exciting things happen"—to a conclusion proclaiming that "through the living liturgy we have experienced the splendor of God's greatness, glory, and grace."[7]

In 1961, the Bureau released an album set of two LP phonograph records entitled "The Best in Lutheran Hymns." The recording featured a selection of hymns, mostly oriented toward the church's liturgical year, performed by the Concordia Seminary Cantata Chorus and Brass Ensemble. The ensemble was directed by Robert Bergt, who described the collection as "a 'little canon' of great Lutheran chorales coming to us from the period when storm and stress ... brought about orthodox expression of biblical truths in hymnody."[8]

The Bureau had actively publicized the Lutheran Film Associates' 1953 production *Martin Luther*, and it played a similar role with another LFA film in 1961. *Question 7* told the fictional story of a young East German boy, a pastor's son, dealing with tremendous pressure by the Communist government to renounce his faith and join the Communist party. The *American Lutheran* published several articles and editorials lauding the film, noting that it had been widely acclaimed by sources as diverse as Billy Graham, the National Council of Churches, and the Roman Catholic National Legion of Decency. "When 'Question 7' opens in your neighborhood," the editors urged, "go see it. Pull your friends away from their television sets to see it with you."[9]

In 1958, the Bureau and the Lutheran Layman's League joined forces to launch a new evangelism campaign called "Tell Three." The program encouraged Lutheran laymen to share three tracts, one each to "an unchurched friend," a "former or lax church member," and a "Christian with a burden." The LLL produced the tracts in cooperation with the ALPB, and the campaign was promoted in the *American Lutheran*. The League hoped that the program would bring rich results, but even more important was its goal to "make the individual Lutheran Christian realize his responsibility and privilege as a member of the body of Christ." The campaign was followed up the next year with "Tell Three More." The *American Lutheran* supplemented this campaign by introducing a new evangelism column, "Now Then We Are Ambassadors," written by Waldo J. Werning."[10]

Still another ALPB initiative during this period was the development of materials designed to encourage young people to consider church vocations. A multi-page brochure entitled "Where Do I Go from Here?" advised youth that "vast opportunities in many fields clamor to claim your life," but "you will fail in life if you do not know what life is for. Your life will become empty, unhappy, frustrating if it does not fulfill its purpose." A series of photos suggested that there are many ways to serve God—as business man [*sic*], musician, surveyor, doctor, farmer. This was certainly in keeping with the Lutheran doctrine of vocation. But then it raised the question: "[W]hat about a full-time church vocation?" It briefly explained the "job description" of a pastor, a parochial school teacher, a deaconess, and a church social worker, with photos showing such people at their work. On each page it asked, "Will you fit into this picture?" A companion piece directed at adult leaders was entitled "Counseling for Church Vocations: Practical Suggestions for Pastors and Counselors." Each brochure concluded with the caption: "Church Vocations: A service project of the American Lutheran Publicity Bureau."[11]

Lutheran World Federation

"one of the hottest and most caustic editorials"

When the Lutheran World Federation was formed in 1952, the Missouri Synod had taken no part in the discussions. The new body, however, invited the Synod to consider membership, and so a committee was established in June 1953 to study the issue and report to the 1956 convention. The committee was directed to have its report in the hands of congregations by January 1, 1955; it failed to do so, pleading the "complexity and delicacy" of its assignment. The report was finally ready a year later—just six months before the convention was to meet. The recommendation was that the Synod "respectfully decline the invitation."

The *American Lutheran* was furious—both at the recommendation and at the long delay. The committee, an editorial fumed, "has certainly handled the 'complexity and delicacy' of its task with all the finesse of a locomotive running wild through a crowded railroad station." It "has in a sense declared war on the Lutheran World Federation and asks the Synod to do likewise." The editorial listed several specific objections to the "unabashedly tendentious" report—a document which, "is literally filled with assumptions and interpretations which responsible leaders of the Lutheran World Federation will almost certainly disavow."[12]

The editors acknowledged that the committee could have raised "some serious questions" but instead it "has challenged the whole basis of the organization" and thus "invites Lutherans all over the world to challenge its conclusions."

> The committee will not be disappointed. In the next issue, THE AMERICAN LUTHERAN will present a serious interpretation of the Lutheran World Federation constitution which takes direct issue with the judgments of the committee. These men who will challenge the committee's interpretation are European theologians of recognized acumen—and are at the same time friends of The Lutheran Church—Missouri Synod and what it stands for. Their judgment should carry at least as much weight as that of the three-man committee, none of whom had any part in framing the documents which they have so harshly judged—or so brashly misjudged.

In short, the editors raged, "this report ... ought to be consigned to the limbo reserved for documents that in pretending to have proved everything, proved nothing."[13]

Ade Meyer would later describe this editorial as "one of the hottest and most caustic editorials in the history of the *American Lutheran*"—but he obviously enjoyed the ensuing reaction:

We received heated letters ... accusing us of all kind of things. (GREAT DAYS). In succeeding issues we ran a series of articles by distinguished German theologians who were good friends of Missouri Synod, whose witness countered point by point the statements by the Three-Man Committee.

A letter from a group of South Dakota pastors, for example, criticized the editorial, claiming that it had been a "loveless" criticism. "I have a very high regard for the three brethren who were members of the committee, and consider them as personal friends," Meyer responded. "I believe that they, and the rank and file of our readers, recognize that, while we take violent disagreement to their report, our objections are offered out of loyalty to our Synod and to Christ." The copy of this letter at Concordia Historical Institute is apparently one sent by J. R. Sheppard, the spokesman for this group, to President Behnken. Meyer's letter to Sheppard had been signed in his absence by his secretary; Sheppard called attention to this: "The 'J' below and to the right of the signature shows that it is not a personal signature, therefore the letter loses its personal force and value." Apparently Pr. Sheppard was not satisfied with Meyer's response.[14]

When the convention met that summer, the report of the committee was adopted overwhelmingly—after President Behnken had stepped out of the chair to plead from the floor that the Synod decline the LWF invitation. The *American Lutheran* described this with the comment that "the report was accepted without giving it the discussion explicitly intended by the resolution adopted by Synod [in 1953]." But the editors noted that Dr. Behnken had "assured the delegates that the door was not closed to future discussions leading to a possible solution of doctrinal differences"—and indeed, the committee resolution itself had expressed willingness for future discussion. The *American Lutheran* staff resolved to keep the heat on.[15]

At the editorial staff meeting a few months later, there was discussion of how best the magazine could continue to raise the issue of the LWF. Concern was expressed about "the tone of editorials" that had been published on the matter, and it was agreed that "the charitable approach" would be taken in the future. Several topics for those future editorials and articles were outlined.[16]

This led ultimately to a decision to offer a symposium of various views on LCMS membership in the Federation. Unfortunately, it was difficult to find LWF opponents to participate. President Behnken flatly refused to write about his own views, and seems to have suggested that he thought the symposium was a bad idea. Adolf Meyer responded carefully:

I discussed the matter with Dr. [Oswald] Hoffmann and both of us honestly and sincerely feel that this symposium in its presentation should serve the interests of Christ's Church throughout the world, and, of course, the interests of the Lutheran Church—Missouri Synod. Several years ago, when we expressed ourselves regarding the Lutheran World Federation, you admonished me in St. Paul that we had gone about this matter in the wrong way. I wish you to know, Dr. Behnken, that I took your advice seriously to heart. Perhaps you have noticed how the AMERICAN LUTHERAN since that time has been very careful in handling the Lutheran World Federation question. I do wish to assure you that even though we have very sincere convictions as to how our church can best serve in connection with the L.W.F., that in the forthcoming symposium we have the determination that all opinions presented will be treated with the utmost fairness. More that that, we are genuinely concerned that the opinions of those who oppose membership should receive a fair hearing.

But such a fair hearing would only be possible if opponents were willing to participate. Meyer listed several "prominent men" who had declined his invitation. He asked Behnken if he might confidentially suggest other possible contributors.[17]

Whether or not Behnken made any suggestions, in the end the symposium did offer a number of diverse opinions. There were twenty contributors over five months. Most were LCMS pastors, but there were some unexpected writers. A couple of laywomen offered their views—up to that point a voice seldom heard in the *American Lutheran*. Swedish Bishop Bo Giertz, widely admired by conservative Lutherans in America, weighed in, as did other Lutheran church leaders from Europe and Australia. The comments were heavily weighted in favor of LCMS participation in the LWF—only four of the twenty were overtly opposed—but that was not for want of trying to get opposing viewpoints. The editors made clear at the beginning of each installment that the articles "were solicited from men and women whose considered opinions are presented without regard for their sympathy with or opposition to previous editorial expressions" of the magazine.[18]

Many of the writers stressed the contribution that the LCMS could make by joining. "It would be a boundless spiritual blessing for Lutheranism," Bishop Giertz wrote, "if The Lutheran Church—Missouri Synod were to join the Lutheran World Federation." He painted a bleak picture of "the continuing conflict *within* Lutheranism between … classical faith and the currents which would attenuate it in the direction of a relativized Word, a dulled Christological confession, and … an evolutionary attitude toward religion." Giertz acknowledged his admiration for Missouri's ability to combine "theological conservatism with an energetic practical Church life," and he thought LCMS participation in the LWF would help nurture "a possibility of working for a sound development in loyalty to the Word of God."[19]

Illinois state legislator (later U. S. Senator) Paul Simon took the opposite approach. Perhaps Missouri's presence would benefit the LWF, but he saw the greater issue being how membership would benefit Missouri. "We need help in ridding ourselves of a sinful provincialism," Simon mused. "To work in cooperation with fellow-Lutherans throughout the world, to listen to their viewpoints, this is something we need. We need the glasses of a world vision to solve the myopia of provincialism—and the LWF can help give us those glasses."[20]

Those who opposed membership did so on the expected basis of eschewing participation in a body where there is not doctrinal agreement. Mark J. Steege, a professor at the Springfield seminary, was typical in his conviction (and generous in his admission):

> [The] Lutheran World Federation is rendering a distinct benefit to many Lutheran bodies. We thank God for that. But we have greater reason to thank God for having so guided us these many years that no argument, no appeal, no promise could sway us from our soundly Scriptural position that church union is proper only when doctrinal unity has been established. The latter must ever be our goal. Until it is achieved, the former can do us and others no lasting good.[21]

But for many of the contributors, Steege's position was precisely the problem. Paul L. Maier, son of the late frequent ALPB and "Lutheran Hour" speaker Walter A. Maier, admitted that a LWF-sponsored scholarship had enabled him to study in Europe, and this would disqualify him from serving as a juror if the LWF were on trial. But "at the bar of world Lutheran opinion ... it is not the LWF, but the attitude represented by the Lutheran Church—Missouri Synod which is on trial." He raised a sharp question: "*Why is it that our synodical conscience seems continually so burdened by reservation rather than by responsibility?*" In refusing LWF membership, Maier argued, we fail to listen and we fail to speak. This is "not merely a case of responsibility outweighing reservation. The reservation is itself ill-founded, and becomes a progressively expensive luxury."[22]

It was left to young historian Martin Marty to offer the sharpest critique of Missouri's reservations. He suggested that the Synod's explanations would shortly bring it to "the point described by Talleyrand: 'If we go on explaining we shall cease to understand one another.'" What we need, Marty suggested, is not explanations but a sermon—which he then proceeded to preach:

> The Missouri Synod is not a member of the Federation because it has not found a way. It has not found a way because it does not want to. It does not want to because it compounds a predictably negative response to calls for Christian unity with official institutional *hybris* and widespread constituent apathy. ... When it realizes ... that its evasion of the whole ecumenical impulse may well be *the* sin of its part of the Church in our time; that it is as much to be pitied as censured for what it is missing in the exhilarating life of the wider Christian community—it shall find a way. ...

> And if the day comes that it changes its present course, pray God that instead of strutting to applause ... [we] shall have the decency and be given the grace to come on our knees. For it is love, the kind that could break barriers and reconcile to man God at Calvary, that can reconcile man to man, Christian to Christian, Lutheran to Lutheran.

"Love," Marty concluded, "will find a way. Then we need no longer explain. Then we shall understand each other."[23]

A Roman Catholic president

"important questions for all Americans"

In 1928 the *American Lutheran* had hinted (not very obliquely) that Lutherans ought not vote for Democrat Al Smith because he was a Roman Catholic, and well into the 1950s ALPB publications warned about the dangers—theological and political—of Roman Catholicism. As late as 1959, an editorial questioned whether Americans should consider voting for a Roman Catholic candidate for president. While normally a person's religion should not be a factor, "we cannot altogether discount or overlook the fact that Romanists do have an allegiance to a foreign Church-State Potentate—the Pope at Rome."[24]

But as the 1950s drew to a close, old clarities began to be questioned. In early 1960, the *American Lutheran* acknowledged that Sen. John F. Kennedy appeared to be the front-runner for the presidential nomination of the Democrats. Furthermore, in the event that Kennedy were not the nominee, both major parties had a number of Roman Catholics on the "short list" for the vice presidential nomination. Thus "there exists a very real possibility that both national parties will present slates with a Roman Catholic as candidate for one of the two top executive spots."[25]

The editorial (unsigned but probably written by Piepkorn) mused that the "sentiment against a Roman Catholic president persists." The magazine proposed to offer a symposium that would discuss the question—not with any idea of "trying to influence our readers' political decisions" but simply to discuss "the fundamental issues inasfar [*sic*] as these have an authentically religious significance." The editorial admitted that those questioning the wisdom of electing a Roman Catholic president have raised "important questions for all Americans," and the *American Lutheran* editors "do not profess to have all the answers. We are certain that a poll of our masthead contributors, like a poll of our readers, would produce a wide variety of responses." The symposium would be offered, therefore, "to assist our readers—and ourselves—in this process" by inviting "Lutherans from a broad continuum of backgrounds ... to give their considered opinion."[26]

The symposium began with the April 1960 issue and continued each month through September. By the time it was over, some twenty-nine contributors had offered their "considered opinions"—which indeed were all over the map (in every sense of that phrase). The majority were pastors, but there were some significant and interesting lay voices as well. Paul Simon wrote somewhat reluctantly because he thought that even to have the discussion "violates the spirit of our constitution." Voting for or against a candidate on the basis of religion shows "a basic misunderstanding of democracy."[27]

Another lay response was by George Lindbeck, the Yale professor of historical theology who would soon play a key ecumenical role as a Protestant observer at Vatican II. Lindbeck thought the controversy was largely the result of ignorance on the part of Protestants. Modern American Roman Catholics "generally show little hesitation in opposing the Vatican on political issues." Indeed, Roman Catholic theologians are clearly "transforming the meaning" of traditional Catholic teaching on church and state, and there is little reason other than "blind prejudice" to be concerned about electing a Roman Catholic president.[28]

On the other hand, the ALPB's own Julius Nickelsburg emerged from his retirement to offer a word of concern. While acknowledging that the U. S. Constitution plainly states that a citizen's religion is no bar to holding office, Nickelsburg quoted a recent statement by Pope John XXIII (applicable, he admitted, only to the Diocese of Rome, but with "implications for Roman Catholics everywhere") forbidding Catholics "to enact ... laws harmful to the Church" or "to read publications inspired by Protestantism, illuminism, existentialism, atheism or materialism." While he didn't say it in so many words, Nickelsburg was clearly concerned about the influence such decrees might have on an American president.

The opinions from pastors and academics were also very much divided. Martin Marty argued that there would be a Catholic president—either this year or at some later time—and he suggested that the best strategy was simply to see what happens. "After four years we may decide never to repeat the experiment or we may decide that Protestant fears were unfounded." Others took a more definitive stand. Gerhard Lenski, the influential pastor of Grace Lutheran Church in Washington, DC, referred to Jaroslav Pelikan's book *The Riddle of Roman Catholicism* (Abingdon Press, 1959). If Catholicism is a riddle to an intellectual giant like Pelikan, Lenski mused, it is very much more so to the rest of us. Electing a Roman Catholic would be an "uncertainty" too big to risk "in days like these," and Americans should avoid it when they go to the polls.[29]

But Alfred P. Klausler, a staffer for the Walther League, had quite a different certainty. "I would vote for a Roman Catholic," he wrote, "providing his platform for future action agreed with what I felt was best for my country." He admitted to being a registered Democrat, though he wasn't so enthusiastic about Kennedy because of the senator's "rather equivocal attitude toward ... the late, unlamented Senator Joseph McCarthy." Nonetheless, he was most disturbed by "the intolerance and even rabid bigotry [toward the possibility of a Catholic President] displayed by Protestants in general, Lutherans in particular." He suspected that "Lutherans and Protestants use the hue and cry about the Vatican to disguise their ineptness in good politics and their social unconcern."[30]

In October, with Kennedy now officially the nominee, the editors summarized the discussion:

> One irate reader ... whose letter was not printed because it did not measure up to our request for 'strong reaction expressed in a temperate and wholesome way,' suggested that Roman Catholic journals give up defending Kennedy's candidacy; the American Lutheran had done it for them. Actually, the self-declared Democrats among the contributors to the Symposium who supported the choice of a Roman

Catholic for president stated quite frankly their reservations about Senator Kennedy as a candidate. Yet it is true that a substantial majority of the contributors saw no major obstacles to supporting a presidential candidate who was a Roman Catholic.

Still, the editors felt some ambivalence. With regard to Kennedy himself, they had no question; his "frank and open support of the traditional American principles of separation of church and state should make it clear that as far as the present candidate is concerned there is no religious issue." And yet, the editorial continued, Kennedy's position is at odds with that of his church, and until the church itself makes some official statement that its traditional church-state doctrines do not apply in the American context, "we will have to raise the same discussion every time a Roman Catholic seeks the presidential office."[31]

The *American Lutheran* editors believed that the symposium had made an important contribution, and yet when the dust settled, they seemed to have second thoughts. A reflection on the election's results in the January 1961 issue had a rather negative tone. Kennedy's nomination, the editorial argued, "was a masterpiece of clever maneuvering." Once he was nominated, the "religious issue" was "soft-pedaled" and Kennedy "pounded home his personal adherence to the traditional American policy of separation of church and state" and "repudiated the traditional position of his own church." Efforts like the *American Lutheran*'s "to discuss the 'religious issue' in an objective way were found to be naïve in the rough and tumble action of a political campaign." In the editors' view, Kennedy won because "many Roman Catholic voters switched their allegiance ... because of the 'religious issue.'" They did not think this boded well for the future of American politics.[32]

Reclaiming catholicity

"what the Lutheran Church really is"

At the same time the *American Lutheran* was debating the pros and cons of a Catholic president, there was a reappraisal going on of the concept of "catholicity." One aspect of this was a growing interest in the Roman Catholic Church itself, which seemed to be undergoing significant changes of its own; another was an increasing awareness of a "Lutheran catholicity" that embraced, rather than eschewed, Lutheranism's connection to its catholic roots.

In February 1960, Richard Koenig, a young pastor who would become a major player in the ALPB's publication program, wrote a rave review of Jaroslav Pelikan's *The Riddle of Roman Catholicism*. The "riddle," Pelikan argued, is the contradictory character of the Roman church. "How can one institution," Pelikan asked, "include ... both the Pontifical Institute of Medieval Studies and the Shrine of Our Lady of Guadalupe?" In Koenig's view, Pelikan's book itself pointed to the answer to the riddle, which is "to understand and appreciate" the Roman Catholic Church. Koenig commended Pelikan's "honest admission of Protestant weakness and debts to Roman Catholicism." He offers "an unqualified affirmation of the aims of the ecumenical movement"—not with any "surrendering to Rome" but "an honest probing of the unity we now have and the unity we seek." Protestantism, Koenig wrote, "and especially the Lutheran Church—Missouri Synod, has scarcely heard more prophetically evangelical summons. We can only pray that everyone in our own communion listen to what this man says to us."[33]

A few months later, the ALPB published two new tracts written by Walter Bouman, at that time pastor of St. Matthew Lutheran Church in Albany, NY. These companion pieces were entitled "What a Roman Catholic Should Know about the Lutheran Church" and "What a Protestant Should Know about the Lutheran Church." As the titles suggest, Bouman argued that Lutheranism was neither Roman Catholic nor Protestant—and yet it was "catholic." In fact, the former tract appeared first as an article in the *American Lutheran*, where it was entitled "Lutheran Catholicity."

Bouman argued that the term "catholic" must not be allowed to refer only to the Roman Church—indeed, if anything, the word belongs more justifiably to Lutheranism. "Neither history nor theology support the assumption that ... catholic faith and worship are found in the Roman church. Nor do history and theology support the assumption that Lutheranism is less than catholic." The 16th century Lutherans, Bouman insisted, in their Augsburg Confession "made quite explicit their adherence to the holy catholic faith."[34]

Lutherans are not only catholic in faith, "but also in that which is most intimately related to faith: in sacramental life and worship." Bouman outlined in some detail Lutheran sacramental teaching on Holy Baptism, the Eucharist, and private absolution, and then added that Lutherans are "not unwilling to call ordination a sacrament" (citing *Apology* XIII). He went on to explain why Lutherans do not regard confirmation, matrimony and extreme unction as sacraments. But his conclusion was that Lutherans are, in faith and worship, faithful to the standard for catholicity articulated by Vincent of Lérins in the fifth century: "What is believed everywhere, always and by everyone."[35]

Indeed, Bouman suggested, in most respects the Lutheran Church is truer to that standard than the Roman Church itself. He outlined specific areas of practice where Lutherans depart from Roman Catholics (vernacular worship, married clergy, church structure, popular piety, etc.), and argued that Lutheran practice is more faithful to the early church. Lutherans, he claimed, have "sought to determine apostolic and catholic principle—granting freedom where this is indicated, accepting apostolic authority where this is evident." Lutheranism "invites the careful scrutiny and seeks the sincere fellowship of all who desire to be truly catholic Christians."[36]

The other tract was published in the *American Lutheran* some months later, addressed to "the interested Protestant who wants to know for himself what the Lutheran

Church really is and what it teaches." Here Bouman addressed Protestants who think the Lutheran Church "too catholic." He defended the use of the ancient creeds, described the Lutheran confessions, and justified Lutheranism's respect for and acceptance of "tradition" in its worship.[37]

In these articles and tracts, the *American Lutheran* and the ALPB were turning in a new direction—one that would continue in the following years as the Bureau began overtly identifying itself with the cause of what came to be known as "evangelical catholic Lutheranism."

Other concerns

"NO NEW SYMBOLS!"

In addition to its symposia on the Lutheran World Federation and the possibility of a Roman Catholic president, the *American Lutheran* offered an eclectic variety of articles and editorials on matters mundane and controversial. August Brunn, for example, advocated the use of newly marketed telephone answering devices to provide a telephone prayer service. This ministry would "bring a daily inspirational message, at any hour of the day or night." Brunn reported positive responses from several different cities where the "Dial-A-Prayer" had been instituted. In Pittsburgh, "all newspapers have given feature articles to the program, and all major hotels have placed a card with the number into their guest rooms." In short, "a modern invention has opened still another way to bring the Gospel of Redemption into the homes and hearts of men everywhere."[38]

A 1960 editorial renewed the *American Lutheran*'s longstanding campaign to keep church doors unlocked. It began with the story of the Episcopal Church of the Ascension in Manhattan, whose doors had been perpetually open for thirty years. The rector who had made that decision, now a retired bishop, had said that "to close the doors would take the heart out of this holy place." The editorial (likely written by Adolf Meyer, for whom this had long been a crusade) agreed:

> Well, how about it? Are the doors to *your* church open right now? If not, why not? Can the passerby find a welcome to the sanctuary of your house of worship regardless of the day of the week or the hour of the day? Suppose a real crisis came into your life today. Wouldn't it be helpful to go to the place 'where His honor dwelleth' and talk over your problem with the all-knowing and loving God? But would you be permitted to enter?

The editorial took note of the usual concern about vandalism, but thought that fear was "out of proportion" and could easily be dealt with. The Church of the Ascension, for instance, had not had any such problem "since the golden candelabra have been replaced by wooden ones." The pastor of an Omaha church that remained unlocked reported no problem "unless you regard the incident of a cold, homeless traveler sleeping between the pews [on] a winter night as belonging in that category."[39]

In March 1960, the magazine offered a lengthy evaluation of the newly published *Service Book and Hymnal*, authorized by the several church bodies about to form the American Lutheran Church and the Lutheran Church in America. An introductory editorial lamented that the LCMS had not been involved in this project—due to "very complicated factors." Yet the magazine's extended review of this book that would not be used in the Missouri Synod reflected the ALPB's increasing involvement with and service to Lutherans beyond the LCMS.[40]

The *American Lutheran* did not shy away from criticizing the Synod when it felt it necessary. The 1956 synodical convention had passed a controversial resolution: "That we reject any and every interpretation of documents approved by Synod which would be in disagreement with the Holy Scriptures, the Lutheran Confessions, and the *Brief Statement*." The latter reference, which seemed to elevate the document by Franz Pieper approved by the Synod in 1932 to confessional status, was the sticking point. The resolution, the editors wrote, "appears worse to us every time we reflect on it." It attempts "to absolutize what is at best a transient formulation of opinion and to exalt it to the level of another symbolical document." Such formulations may have their place "to clarify specific issues in controversy," but "with each passing year *A Brief Statement* has become less and less relevant." It was simply "a valiant effort to produce a document which would heal an old breach but which failed to do so." The gist of the editorial was apparent in its title: "NO NEW SYMBOLS!"[41]

The role of "A Brief Statement" in the Synod's life took another turn in 1959, however, when the synodical convention meeting in San Francisco approved what came to be known as "Resolution 9." This action affirmed that "every doctrinal statement of a confessional nature adopted by Synod as a true exposition of the Holy Scriptures is to be regarded as public doctrine (*publica doctrina*) in Synod" and decreed that all pastors, teachers and professors "are held to teach and act in harmony with such statements." The *American Lutheran* was disgusted with what it called "a totally unnecessary note of discord." "Obviously, a church convention should not set up a straw man to see whether he can be knocked down. There is far greater doctrinal unanimity in the Missouri Synod than would appear from this debate." The resolution "did not deserve the attention it received."[42]

The golden anniversary

"the ALPB will continue its work ... in new dimensions"

As the new decade unfolded, the Bureau was preparing to observe its golden anniversary. The celebration of a half-century of ministry was fairly low-key; there was an anniversary offering, but it was not as heavily promoted as the 40th anniversary drive had been, and there was little in the way of other anniversary promotions. The Bureau offered congregations who provided financial support to the ALPB a collection of blurbs that could be inserted in weekly bulletins recognizing the occasion and briefly depicting the importance of the ministry. Two sermons were distributed, one by Meyer and one by Wittrock, touting the importance of what the Bureau was doing.

The *American Lutheran* printed the sermon preached by William F. Bruening at a special service commemorating the anniversary held at Village Lutheran Church in Bronxville, NY. Bruening had long been associated with the ALPB, and he was at the time a member of the LCMS board of directors. Taking as his text Psalm 68.11, "The Lord gave the Word; great was the company of them that published it," Bruening suggested that the ALPB's ministry was always part of a gracious plan, a work which God had "put into the minds and hearts of the founding fathers of this Bureau to PUBLISH HIS WORD, and in the hearts and minds of those who have continued this work since."[43]

In Bruening's estimation, the Bureau's "publishing the Word" had helped to rescue the Missouri Synod from serious trouble at three different points in its history. The first was its influence in the transition from German to English during World War I and after, when the Synod "almost foundered on the shoals of language isolationism." The second was in the 1940s, when the Synod was "in grave danger of locking itself out of the Christian community by synodical and organizational isolationism." The third was in the recent days, when "there were forces at work in Synod which were attempting to force our church into a theological isolationism which, many of us believe, would have reduced our beloved Synod to a sect."[44]

But the Bureau, Bruening insisted, dare not rest on its laurels, for the "challenge of publishing the Word that God has given us is as great today as it ever was."

> In a day when it is still the only Word that can change the hearts of men, we dedicate ourselves anew to the propagation of that Word, by the old methods which have been developed in the past, through the printed page, tracts, the radio, TV, and through every means still to be invented, perchance to publish that Word even in the unexplored regions of infinite space that seem to be opening up to us, so that we may continue to be among those to whom God has given His Word and also among the multitudes who will continue to publish it.[45]

Perhaps the most important contribution to the golden anniversary celebration was a five-part series on the history of the ALPB, published in the *American Lutheran*. The first three installments were written by Alan Graebner, a grandson of Theodore Graebner, who was then doing doctoral work at Columbia University. Graebner's dissertation, ultimately completed the following year, was entitled "The Acculturation of an Immigrant Lutheran Church: The Lutheran Church—Missouri Synod, 1917-1929." In the course of his project, he had done considerable research on the early history of the ALPB, which he rightly identified as being instrumental in accelerating the Synod's process of Americanization. Graebner's three articles in the *American Lutheran* took the Bureau through its first three decades.[46]

The series was continued by Alfred Klausler, the editor of the Walther League publication *Arena* and a contributing editor of the *American Lutheran*; he was also executive secretary of the Associated Church Press. Klausler surveyed the work of the Bureau during the past twenty years and then wrote about its mission in "a new era"— an era which, he suggested, has much in common with the time when the ALPB was founded. He quoted a recent book review in the *American Lutheran* of Martin Marty's *The New Shape of American Religion*. Written by Richard Koenig, the review had struck a somber note. "We have fallen on evil days," Koenig observed. "There are demonic forces at work within our culture which we are only vaguely beginning to comprehend." Klausler took that comment as an indication of what the future held for the ALPB:

> On this note of almost frightened frustration the survey of the ALPB's fifth decade ends. There is still more work for the ALPB. Truth to tell, judging by its past work and its understanding of the needs and problems of the time, the ALPB will continue its work, undoubtedly in new dimensions but dimensions whose spiritual framework would be easily recognized by the honorable founders who faced the disrupted world of 1914.[47]

A new editor

"it would be in the best interests of the magazine"

Adolf Meyer had begun his association with the ALPB the same week he was installed in his first parish back in 1923. He had been managing editor of the *American Lutheran* from 1926 until 1954, then editor through the 1950s. As the new decade dawned, however, he became firm in his resolve to give up the editorial reins. His pastorate at St. Mark's in Yonkers was becoming more demanding, and it seemed wise to leave the unpaid position with the Bureau he had held for nearly four decades. He took up the issue with the editorial staff (including the Bureau's president, John Kavasch) in 1959, suggesting that he would like to be replaced as editor—or, alternatively, perhaps the Bureau could appoint a new managing editor to assume some of the responsibility for the magazine. After considerable discussion, it was agreed to recommend to the ALPB board that the position of managing editor be offered to John Tietjen, the young pastor of Calvary Lutheran Church in Leonia, NJ. Tietjen had graduated from Concordia Seminary (where he had roomed with ALPB assistant executive director Paul John Thielo) and then earned a PhD at Union Seminary in New York, writing a dissertation subsequently published as *Which Way to Lutheran Unity?*[48]

Tietjen accepted the position and it worked out well. In May 1961, Meyer announced his intent to retire in December and recommended that Tietjen succeed him. Tietjen, however, protested that he was not able to assume the editorial post that quickly, and asked that Meyer stay a while longer. At length Meyer agreed to remain through 1962 if necessary, though he clearly preferred to lay down his responsibilities sooner. Meanwhile, Oswald Hoffman had resigned as an editorial associate (though he promised to continue to contribute as time permitted), and at Meyer's suggestion Norman Temme had joined the group of editorial associates.

These new arrangements were made public in the August 1961 issue. Meyer wrote that for several years he had believed "it would be in the best interests of the magazine to appoint a younger man to the position of editor who would have the opportunity of introducing new programs which might better serve the Church of Jesus Christ." He revealed that the ALPB Board had finally agreed that he "be permitted to lay aside full editorial responsibilities as of January 1962, with the understanding that he continue on the staff as 'consulting editor.'" He then announced that, effective with that issue, John Tietjen "has been elevated to the position of 'Executive Editor,' and as such will assume immediately many of the functions and responsibilities which belong to full editorship." Meyer offered a valedictory word:

> The editor wishes to take this opportunity to thank his entire staff, especially his editorial associates, who have given so much of their time to counsel and support him in editing The American Lutheran. ...
>
> The great strength of The American Lutheran Magazine has always been its readers. Our readers are invited to submit not only 'letters to the editor,' but articles for possible publication. Our magazine honestly wishes to portray and reflect the constructive ideas of our people who are 'doing things'—ideas which will best serve the larger interests of the Lord's Church.

Tietjen took charge in January 1962, and Meyer, while still listed on the masthead as "consulting editor," relinquished the major role he had played in the magazine for some thirty-six years. Changes were coming, though—both for Tietjen and for the ALPB—that would make the new editor's tenure very short.[49]

Notes

1. Minutes, *AL* Editorial Board, 17 Dec. 1956, Geiseman Papers, Box 21, Folder 2.

2. Paul John Thielo, with Dick Williams, *A Rewarding Life* (privately published, 2014), 57-58.

3. "Out of Darkness Into Light," 1960, ALPB Archives.

4. "I was an embezzler ... and didn't realize it!" 1961, ALPB Archives.

5. Waldo W. Werning, *How to Raise Men and Money in the Church: A Plan for Effective Church Financing* (New York: ALPB, 1957); Arthur M. Vincent, *The Christian Witness* (New York: ALPB, 1958).

6. "The Lutheran Liturgy in Slow Motion," Leader's Guide, n.d., ALPB Archives.

7. "The Lutheran Liturgy in Slow Motion," Promotional Brochure, n.d.; ibid., ALPB Archives.

8. Quoted in publicity brochure for "Through the Church Year with the Best in Lutheran Hymns: 40th Anniversary Edition CD & Hymn Guide," 2001, ALPB archives.

9. "'Question 7' Ready for Release," *AL* 44, no. 9 (Sept. 1961), 4.

10. "LLL Launches 'Tell Three' Tract Mission," *AL* 41, no. 1 (Jan. 1958), 14-15; "Now Then We Are Ambassadors," *AL* 41, no. 1 (Jan. 1958), 4-5.

11. "Where Do I Go from Here?" n.d., ALPB Archives.

12. "A Three-Man Committee Report," *AL* 39, no. 1 (Jan. 1956), 5.

13. Ibid., 5-6.

14. Meyer, "Autobiography," 47; Adolf F. Meyer to J. R. Sheppard, 18 Mar. 1956, Behnken Papers, Box 4, Folder 38.

15. "Highlights of the 43rd Convention of the Lutheran Church—Missouri Synod," *AL* 39, no. 7 (July 1956), 3.

16. "Minutes, American Lutheran Magazine Meeting," 17 Dec. 1956. Geiseman Papers, Box 21, Folder 2.

17. Adolf Meyer to J. W. Behnken, 10 June 1958, Behnken Papers, Box 4, Folder 38.

18. "Symposium Re Lutheran World Federation," *AL* 41, no. 8 (Aug. 1958), 6.

19. Bo Harald Gietz, "Symposium Re Lutheran World Federation: A Swedish Bishop Speaks," *AL* 41, no. 12 (Dec. 1958), 8.

20. Paul Simon, "Symposium Re Lutheran World Federation: A Lutheran Legislator," *AL* 41, no. 8 (Aug. 1958), 6.

21. Mark J. Steege, ""Symposium Re Lutheran World Federation: A Lutheran Seminary Professor," *AL* 41, no. 9 (Sept. 1958), 11.

22. Paul L. Maier, "Symposium Re Lutheran World Federation: A Lutheran Pastor," *AL* 41, no. 8 (Aug. 1958), 11.

23. Martin E. Marty, "Symposium Re Lutheran World Federation: A Lutheran Pastor," *AL* 41, no. 9 (Sept. 1958), 11.

24. "Shall We Elect a Roman Catholic President?" *AL* 42, no. 9 (Sept. 1959), 4.

25. "Symposium on 'A Roman Catholic President,' *AL* 43, no. 2 (Feb. 1960), 3.

26. Ibid., 4.

27. Paul Simon, "Symposium on a Roman Catholic President," *AL* 43, no. 4 (Apr. 1960), 8.

28. George Lindbeck, "Symposium on a Roman Catholic President," *AL* 43, no. 7 (July 1960), 16.

29. Martin E. Marty, "Symposium on a Roman Catholic President," *AL* 43, no. 4 (Apr. 1960), 9; Gerhard E. Lenski, "Symposium on a Roman Catholic President," *AL* 43, no. 4 (Apr. 1960), 8.

30. Alfred P. Klausler, "Symposium on a Roman Catholic President," *AL* 43, no. 5 (May 1960), 13.

31. "Yes and No: An Editorial summary and Appraisal of the 'Symposium on a Roman Catholic President,'" *AL* 43, no. 10 (Oct. 1960), 3-5.

32. "A Year of Decision," *AL* 44, no. 1 (Jan. 1961), 3-4.

33. Richard E. Koenig, "The Riddle of Roman Catholicism: A Review Article," *AL* 43, no. 2 (Feb. 1960), 10-11.

34. Walter R. Bouman, "Lutheran Catholicity," *AL* 43, no. 10 (Oct. 1960), 7.

35. Ibid., 8.

36. Ibid., 26.

37. Walter Bouman, "What a Protestant Should Know about the Lutheran Church," *AL* 44, no. 10 (Oct. 1961), 7ff.

38. August F. Brunn, "The Telephone Prayer Service," *AL* 41, no. 4 (Apr. 1958), 12.

39. "Throw the Keys Away?" *AL* 43, no. 3 (Mar. 1960), 4.

40. "The 'Service Book and Hymnal of the Lutheran Church in American,'" *AL* 43, no. 3 (Mar. 1960), 3.

41. "NO NEW SYMBOLS!" *AL* 40, no. 7 (July 1957), 3-4.

42. "San Francisco Convention," *AL* 42, no. 8 (Aug. 1959), 4.

43. William F. Bruening, "The Word Was Published," *AL* 47, no. 3 (Mar. 1964), 17.

44. Ibid., 17-18.

45. Ibid., 25.

46. Alan Graebner, "50 Years of the A.L.P.B.: Part I—Organized for Lutheran Publicity," *AL* 46, no. 8 (Aug. 1963), 14-6; "Part II—Proponent of Missions to Americans," *AL* 46, no. 9 (Sept. 1963), 14-15; "Part III—An Era of Rapid Social Change," *AL* 46, no. 10 (Oct. 1963), 14-15.

47. Alfred P. Klausler, "50 Years of the A.L.P.B.: Part I—The ALPB Accepts the New Challenge," *AL* 46, no. 12 (Dec. 1963), 21.

48. John H. Tietjen, *Which Way to Lutheran Unity? A history of efforts to unite the Lutherans of America* (St. Louis: Concordia Publishing House, 1966).

49. "Staff Changes," *AL* 44, no. 8 (Aug. 1961), 4-5.

Chapter 13

THE SIXTH DECADE

W hen Ade Meyer retired from the *American Lutheran*, he had been associated with the magazine for well over three decades. It had become not merely an independent voice within the Missouri Synod but the primary voice of the ALPB—hardly the only aspect of the Bureau's program, but certainly the most widely known. Meyer admitted he left the ministry to which he had devoted so many years with "gratitude and relief." John Tietjen's willingness to take over, he wrote, "is an answer to prayer. God has been gracious and good in giving the American Lutheran Publicity Bureau such an able and deeply consecrated scholar to carry forward the program of its official organ."[1]

Editor Tietjen
"Wowie, this is really something!"
The new editor quickly gave the *American Lutheran* a facelift. A new first page featured a striking logo, a *Christus Rex* figure superimposed on a globe with the ALPB's slogan—"A Changeless Christ for a Changing World"—at the top. Articles were set in a

new typeface, not dramatically different but fresher and more contemporary looking. "In presenting the 'Changeless Christ' even a magazine's format has to change occasionally to keep pace with 'a changing world,' " Tietjen wrote. "We hope you like the new look."[2]

O. A. Geiseman liked it very much indeed. He had been intending to be in touch with Tietjen, but "now since the lady has appeared in her new and enchanting dress, I must write you."

> Wowie, this is really something! I don't know whether these ideas for improvement sprang out of your own brain or out of collaboration with other men's brains, but it matters not where they came from. I think the change is wonderful. I think it is going to be hard for people to take a look at the outside of the American Lutheran without wanting to peek on the inside and see what sort of material would appear in such attractive garb.

> Let me also tell you that in my opinion the inside of the magazine, the contents, have been vigorous and vitalizing. I am sure that the Lord meant well with the future of the American Lutheran when He put it into your hands.

Geiseman also hoped that there might be "other young men like yourself hiding in the woods somewhere" who might be enlisted into service with the *American Lutheran*. He prayed that Tietjen would have "many years of opportunity to serve in editorial capacity."[3]

The magazine under Tietjen continued to offer firm and sometimes controversial opinions. When the 1959 Synod convention in San Francisco had approved "Resolution 9," Meyer had suggested that it was something of a straw man whose importance was overblown. Now Tietjen argued that the resolution had gone much too far. The confessional standard for the Synod, he insisted, was spelled out in Article II of the constitution, pledging the Synod to the Scriptures and the Lutheran confessional writings. For Tietjen, that was sufficient:

> Other documents can be perfectly in accord with the Scripture but not therefore automatically become confessional standards. They ought never be imposed as confessional standards, certainly not by a mere resolution at a synodical convention. They cannot become a confessional standard until they are willingly subscribed by those who are to teach according to them. ...

> Unless we are willing to become a Lutheran sect, 'Missouri' Lutheranism had better mean true Lutheranism and not a special variety of Lutheranism.

The LCMS can "best stand for true Lutheranism," he argued, "by vigorously and conscientiously measuring itself according to the universal Lutheran confessional standard."[4]

Nonetheless, Tietjen did not advocate immediately rescinding "Resolution 9." Rather he supported petitions submitted by the Atlantic and English Districts asking for a commission of theologians to study the matter and report back to the 1965 convention. That process, Tietjen argued, would allow for "calm and reasoned discussion" rather than a hasty decision in the pressure of a brief convention. His sympathies were clear, however; in the same issue, he printed a six-page report from the English District explaining their opposition to Resolution 9.

Tietjen reviewed the Synod convention in Cleveland that summer with enthusiastic optimism. It was, he wrote, "the beginning of a new era." He gave kudos to a somewhat unlikely person—President John Behnken, whose request not to be re-elected was "the surprise of the convention." While the *American Lutheran* had always spoken respectfully of Behnken, private correspondence and editorial board minutes had frequently revealed frustration with his policies and decisions. But Tietjen (who, after all, had not been privy to much of the conflict) was effusive in his praise:

> Due recognition for starting the new era must be given to the man who served the synod as president for the past 27 years, Dr. John W. Behnken. Under his leadership and with his encouragement the Missouri Synod took a firm stand against the efforts of a very small but extremely vocal minority to turn back the clock of history and commit the synod to a policy of theological obscurantism and ecclesiastical isolationism.

"It takes a big man with a big heart to know when to lay down the mantle of leadership," Tietjen summarized. He offered the magazine's "heartiest congratulations" to the new president, Oliver R. Harms.[5]

The knottiest problem at Cleveland had been what to do about "Resolution 9." The delegates had declared the controversial action of the previous convention to be unconstitutional because, in their view, it had added to the confessional commitment of the Synod without going through the required process for doing so (i.e., without a constitutional amendment approved by the congregations). This, in the view of the *American Lutheran*, was a wise decision which "re-endorsed the Lutheran confessional principle."[6]

It wasn't the new editor alone who was enthusiastic about the Cleveland convention; O. A. Geiseman, in what would prove to be his last "While It Is Day" column, called it "a Hallelujah Convention," one which "quite obviously brought to a close a specific era in the history of the Lutheran Church—Missouri Synod." In his view, the convention had at last put to rest the controversy about church fellowship that had been plaguing the Synod for decades. He traced the history of the controversy, scorning the conservative view expressed, he said, by "a brother ... at one of the open hearings" in Cleveland: "'It is not wrong if you pray with a non-Lutheran neighbor in his home where no one can see you but if you do this in public it is sinful.'" Thankfully, Geiseman wrote, the Cleveland convention would have none of this. Still, Geiseman warned against resting easy. "Satan has no intentions of abandoning efforts to confuse and destroy the Church." He then offered a prescient prediction of what was to come:

> If the problem of Christian fellowship consumed much of the church's energy and time in the past three or four decades, it is probable that the Doctrine of "the

Word," which is vastly more serious and more complex, will be with the church in the decades which lie ahead.[7]

Three years later, the *American Lutheran* was still optimistic. At the Synod convention in Detroit, the re-election of President Harms on the first ballot and several actions demonstrating a new openness to relationships with other Lutherans "[sustain] the judgment we made three years ago. The Missouri Synod is indeed living in a new era. ... Though the synod is still not sure exactly how to go forward, at Detroit it resolved that there is no turning back."[8]

The state of Lutheranism

"alien norms have apparently conquered parochial life"

The very first issue of the *American Lutheran* under Tietjen offered a challenging and provocative article by Walter Bouman on "The Mission of the Lutheran Church to America." Bouman's essay, first presented to a conference of Lutheran clergy the previous year in Teaneck, NJ, expressed a "sense of urgency" in considering the issue raised by the title. The "religious atmosphere" in the contemporary American scene, he wrote, had four dimensions: Roman Catholicism, the ecumenical movement among Protestants (which he called the "'great new fact' of our era"), the "resurgence of religious Judaism," and the development of "what Martin Marty has called 'Religion in General'" (i.e., the "secularization, nationalization and domestication of unique, particular Christian witness"). "Does Lutheranism," Bouman asked, "present a fifth alternative? Does it possess a theological tradition which more accurately reflects the human condition and the divine Word spoken to that condition?" Bouman was not optimistic, for "an honest appraisal of our present situation" suggests that contemporary American Lutheranism "is theologically sterile, organizationally sectarian and parochially stale."[9]

The theological sterility, he argued, is due to the fact that "theology has been relegated to the side-lines—frightened or drowned out of the denominational seminaries, all but banished from pastoral concerns."

> [T]he alarming fact is that most pastors (in Missouri) are operating with a theology that begins and ends with the Synodical Catechism. We find ourselves speaking in clichés which have little relation to reality, with labels that are inaccurate to say the least, with misunderstood or misapplied concepts, with heresies and alien imports that we do not recognize as such, with irrelevant proclamation and disobedient life. ... We do not want our private little theological worlds (and they are *little*) to be 'disturbed' by the troubling necessity to hear, to think, to bow before the Word. ... We refuse to read—as one district official wrote me—because we might be contaminated by heresy! ... Do we need documentation for this indictment? Attend dull conferences, listen

to insipid preaching, note the deterioration of parish life, examine actual teaching at every level of the Church, look at publishers lists and denominational periodicals, give scrutiny to your own habits of study, to the routine of your ministry—and I'm certain you will find ample documentation.

Bouman doubted one could even speak of "the Lutheran *Church* in America" in any meaningful sense since "there is no more doctrinal unity within Missouri than in the rest of American Lutheranism." Yet "we continue to pursue the very course which must frustrate our mission." Parishes are focused on "mere activity," fund-raising, gimmickry. There is "liturgical chaos and deformity."

> True, 'rites or ceremonies, instituted by men,' need not be everywhere alike. But while this may mean that ushers can wear morning coats or sport shirts, that the Church can be round or cruciform, that one may kneel, sit or stand according to personal necessity or parish usage, it does not mean that one can be Lutheran and liturgical 'schwarmer' at the same time. We find a seminary president describing himself as a 'Southern Baptist' liturgically—a liturgical leader (reputedly) introducing any practice as long as he 'likes it' (the essence of 'schwarmerei')—a leading educator advocating an annual Eucharist (because the Passover was celebrated only once a year). All this is evidence that something more basic is at stake than variety within a universal tradition.

The parish, in short, has become a "religious country club," a "painted corpse."[10]

In the next issue, Bouman issued a "call to be catholic and evangelical" (another foreshadowing of how the ALPB would soon come to describe its own mission). By "catholic," Bouman wrote, we generally understand "some continuation of the Western Christian tradition," but he preferred to substitute for "evangelical" the term "apostolic." Lutheranism's call to be catholic and apostolic describes its identity and its universality. He then outlined what he thought those concepts mean for theology and parish life.[11]

With regard to theology, Bouman decried "the alien influences which have shaped our development up to the 20th century." Alluding to a quote from C. S. Lewis, he insisted that "if you are headed in the wrong direction, it won't do to proceed." That is where American Lutheranism stands. We are called now to focus on the Third Article of the Creed—which is to say, "on the Church, its nature, its ministry, its means of grace, its eschatological expectation. ... These are the areas of catholic and apostolic concern." This might "rescue the pastoral office from its bondage to the American way of life."[12]

He also charged that "alien norms have apparently conquered parochial life." The solution is, first, "understanding ourselves and living as the *worshipping* Body of Christ." This means taking much more seriously the Sacrament of Holy Baptism, but especially it requires that we "restore the Holy Eucharist, with all its rich theological content, to an apostolic and catholic place in the life of the parish." This means the Eucharist must be "*the* service of the Church on Sundays, Feasts and Festivals," with the goal that "all 'examined and absolved' Christians will receive at every celebration."[13]

The biggest obstacle, Bouman concluded, is that we are simply unwilling to do more than "nod in pious agreement" and then "excuse ourselves by saying that our *people* aren't ready." But it is the vocation of pastors "to make them ready." "This is not a matter for majority vote. This is a matter of fidelity to the Scriptures and the Confessions—and to the apostolic and catholic norm embodied in them." Thus Bouman anticipated the ALPB's mission in the years to come: an advocacy of an evangelical catholic Lutheranism offering a robust theological and sacramental life as an alternative to both the impulse toward sectarianism and the embrace of liberal Protestantism.[14]

Lutheran identity

"a model for Lutherans to follow and a goal to strive to achieve"

Tietjen also launched a seven-part series on the theme "What is Lutheran?" He saw this as an urgent inquiry in a time of ecumenical *rapprochement*. A "truly Lutheran consciousness will serve the cause of church unity. For genuine Lutheranism is genuinely ecumenical." But Lutherans, having "emerged from the cultural and language barriers," are now in danger of becoming just another Protestant group. "*Lutherans are in fact already in the process of doing so*," he lamented. "The theology and the practice of many a Lutheran parish are not too distinguishable from what you will find in the more conservative and evangelical churches of Protestantism." He hoped that the forthcoming articles would "sketch an ideal Lutheranism as a model for Lutherans to follow and a goal to strive to achieve."[15]

The series began with Arthur Carl Piepkorn asking the basic question: "What Is the Lutheran Church?" He found in the Lutheran confessions, especially the ecumenical creeds and the Augsburg Confession, the defining center of Lutheranism—a church "evangelical in her unqualified commitment to the Gospel of God's reconciling and redeeming act of grace in Christ, and catholic in her deliberately willed continuity with the past ... 'on prophets and apostles built with Christ the Cornerstone.'"[16]

In subsequent installments, Richard Caemmerer asked "What Is Lutheran in Faith and Life?" He insisted that, contrary to Lutheranism's reputation of putting works in opposition to faith, the genuine Lutheran teaching is that "truly good works proceed from God, are done with love for people, and they are done in our daily relation toward others." He acknowledged that this doesn't always seem to work out in real life.[17]

George W. Hoyer addressed "What is Lutheran in Worship?" He recognized that while the Lutheran confessions do not demand "absolute uniformity in the expression of worship," there are limits to this diversity:

The chief service of worship, the service that is the standard for all others and their center, the service that will self-evidently, obviously be celebrated each Lord's Day and holy day, is The Holy Communion, in which both Scripture and Sacrament move men to adoration of God.

While 16th century Lutherans "realized that it was *possible* for Christians ... to drop all the inherited forms of worship ... they recognized also that it was not *expedient*." "Real catholicity," he concluded, "is within the grasp of the Lutheran Church." Lutherans have, by God's grace, restored "purity of doctrine," and they also have "the purity of the Sacrament by the grace of God. What remains is to practice its Sacrament."[18]

Other writers discussed "what is Lutheran" in missions and evangelism (William Hillmer), in education (Harry Coiner) and in church government (Andrew Weyermann). The series concluded with Walter Bouman considering "What Is Lutheran in Theology?" Bouman insisted that the heart of Lutheran theology is the "antithesis between Law and Gospel." But this insight "is never a possession which can be enshrined in eternally valid formulas, memorized by generations of seminary students, rehearsed in mindless fashion by the occupants of Lutheran pulpits." Rather Lutherans must bring this conviction into engagement with the world, interpreting "our contemporary experience in terms of the wrath of God—and then [proclaiming] that Christ is God-for-us."[19]

These essays by seven different theologians had two underlying themes in common. First, the writers insisted that Lutherans did not repudiate but rather embraced an identity as evangelical and catholic. Second, they argued that Lutherans have a vital calling to be engaged in the world—a vocation to proclaim the Gospel to all, inviting all into the fellowship of the church where through the means of grace, as Luther put it, God "daily and abundantly forgives all my sins." These two themes—Lutheranism as evangelical and catholic, and Lutheranism as engagement in the world—would more and more characterize the interests of the ALPB.

Embracing ecumenism

"This is God's work"

Spurred on both by the rapidly changing situation in the Roman Catholic church and the escalating ecumenical fervor among American Protestants, the *American Lutheran* now brought the ecumenical movement front and center before its readers. In April 1962 a new column appeared, written by Richard Koenig and entitled "One Church." The feature, Koenig promised, would focus on "the emergence of an ecumenical consciousness and the concomitant movement toward unity of the churches," but he assured readers that he was "emphatically not committed to the idea of 'union at any price.' Simply because one takes cognizance of the ecumenical movement ... does not mean that one is uncritical of efforts to unite the Churches."[20]

Over the next few years, Koenig discussed a wide variety of ecumenical topics—the World Council of Churches, the Student Christian Movement, the Lutheran World Federation, the Second Vatican Council. He wrote occasionally about ecumenically significant figures such as Karl Barth. In 1965 he began asking non-Lutheran writers to contribute to the column; this did not really get off the ground, and the column itself came to an end in June of that year. Koenig's role in the magazine would increase however, as he had recently been named one of two new editorial associates.

The most significant ecumenical event of the early 1960s was the Second Vatican Council. On the eve of the Council, the *American Lutheran* was interested in, but also somewhat skeptical about, what might happen. A lengthy editorial stressed that "despite its name, it will not be a genuinely ecumenical council in the sense in which the term applies to the first seven councils. It will be a denominational council, concerned with the affairs of one denomination." It predicted (a bit sarcastically!) that the council would be "distinguished by pomp and pageantry that in our times can probably not be rivaled even by the most glamorous ceremonies of the few surviving monarchies."[21]

Despite these critical comments, the editorial praised the inclusion of non-Catholic observers. It outlined the topics said to be on the agenda, but acknowledged that no one can "be wholly sure what will happen at the Council, not even the Pope and the Curia." No matter how carefully managed things are, it is possible that the Council may "embark on an unanticipated course with such ultimate unanimity that a sagacious Pope would have little choice but to concur."[22]

Be that as it may, the editorial noted that both the Pope and many non-Catholic church leaders (including "a number of German Lutheran bishops") have asked Christians to pray for the Council, and "we feel that such prayers are in order." God "can accomplish more than men can imagine or even hope for. Let us not hinder His work by our scepticism [*sic*], our little faith, or our prayerlessness."[23]

By the end of the Council's first session, the *American Lutheran*'s enthusiasm had grown considerably. In just the opening weeks, the editor wrote, the Council has "affected the whole Roman Catholic Church so profoundly that it can never again be quite the same as it was, either in the eyes of its own constituency or in the eyes of those who observe it from without." For starters, "the exemplary courtesy and consideration ... shown to the delegate-observers from the other denominations of Christendom cannot fail to have consequences in the attitude which Roman Catholics ... will take toward their fellow-Christians." Furthermore, "the naïve myth of the monolithic uniformity of the Roman Catholic Church, already cracked by the events of the past decade, has received a shattering blow."[24]

The editorial outlined the Council's decisions, including its "evangelical emphasis on the love of God for the whole world" and "its concern with problems of human beings in national and international society." It expressed cautious optimism about the relatively restrained "Mariological developments" in the Council and enthusiasm about Cardinal Bea's addressing ecumenical observers as brothers in Christ. It lauded the initial actions on liturgical renewal, and yet offered a caution for Lutherans:

> Lutherans must sternly resist the temptation to belittle what is accomplished or to gloat patronizingly over divisions and the persistence of error. Those of us who have had the mass in the vernacular and the Holy Communion under both kinds for over four hundred years are in peril of becoming a bit smug. ... The Pharisee who lurks uncomfortably close to the surface in all of us needs to be reminded that the triumphs which grace has won in our own midst are often equally scanty.

The editorial concluded with an admonition: "Precisely because it is a conclave of brothers in Christ, Vatican II continues in the current recess to need our intercessions."[25]

Beyond the editorial comments, the *American Lutheran* published substantive articles discussing the Council from various perspectives. F. Dean Lueking put the Council in historical perspective, tracing Luther's attitude toward early church councils and his eagerness in the 16th century for a council to be called that would bring about the reform of the church. Because the Council of Trent and the First Vatican Council had in fact "widened the breach" between Roman Catholics and Protestants, many Protestants had viewed the calling of a new council with "mixed emotions"; but the "time table" for Christian unity "is not set by human hands. This is God's work."[26]

A few months later Tietjen published the text of an address by Jaroslav Pelikan on the radio program *The Catholic Hour*—"an example," the editor noted, "of the kind of purposeful dialogue Lutherans can engage in with Roman Catholics." Pelikan spoke about "Tradition" in the church—often viewed as a dividing line between Catholics and Protestants, but in Pelikan's view a thorny problem for both:

> I might note that we who have been working to instill the idea of tradition into American Protestantism have sometimes been inclined to blame the Reformation for destroying the feeling of continuity in our churches and people, but we need only look at Roman Catholicism in the United States to recognize that it is principally a cultural phenomenon, not a religious one, that we face. In Protestant piety, 'the old-time-religion' is the religion of the nineteenth century revivals, and in Roman Catholicism the so-called 'old ways' of devotion are the tabernacle piety of very recent generations! Even the theologians of the Roman Catholic Church have frequently ... preferred the precise formulas of St. Thomas Aquinas to the less conventional thought and language of the great Fathers of the early centuries. For that matter, they have preferred the formulas of the catechism and the textbook of dogma to the works of St. Thomas himself.

Pelikan was therefore encouraged that "the leaders of the Council have wisely and persistently warned against the equation of the Catholic tradition with the forms it acquired" during the medieval period. He hoped that the Council "can catch the vision of the Church Catholic and of her unity-in-diversity." It may indeed be "our common Tradition that will reunite us in that Christ to Whom the Tradition bears witness and under Whose judgment and sovereignty the Church stands."[27]

Lutheran unity

"No stumbling blocks have appeared"

The cause of Lutheran unity underwent a sea change in the early 1960s. Two significant mergers brought eight different synods into two large church bodies, the American Lutheran Church and the Lutheran Church in America. The Missouri Synod was not a part of either of these mergers, and yet she was profoundly influenced by them—and Missouri's ongoing discussions with the [former] American Lutheran Church brought the Synod into almost immediate conversation with its successor, the new ALC.

At the same time, the growing estrangement between Missouri and her former allies in the Synodical Conference freed Missouri for closer fellowship with other Lutheran bodies. When the Wisconsin Synod suspended fellowship with Missouri in 1961, the Synodical Conference itself seemed to be irrelevant. Both WELS and the Evangelical Lutheran Synod withdrew in 1962, leaving the Synodical Conference with Missouri and the tiny [Slovak] Synod of Evangelical Lutheran Churches as the only members. The *American Lutheran* suggested that it was time to face reality. Insisting that Missouri had not "departed from 'the historical doctrinal position of the Conference'" (as WELS and ELS claimed), the magazine argued that the two departing synods were "guilty of separation." "Though there will no doubt be sentimental pleas to continue [the Synodical Conference]," the magazine editorialized, "the time has come to dissolve it." The Synodical Conference would in fact limp along until 1967, when it at last formally dissolved.[28]

The *American Lutheran*, while lamenting these developments, was not entirely unhappy that the LCMS was free from the "albatross" of the Synodical Conference. Noting that the Wisconsin Synod convention had encouraged its Commission on Doctrinal Matters to continue to attend inter-Lutheran meetings as observers, the editors rather hoped they wouldn't. The idea is "commendable" on the surface, the magazine admitted, and it might even be that WELS representatives would "discover, as countless members of the Missouri Synod have, that there are many more confessionally orthodox Lutherans around than they had imagined." Still, the Missouri Synod has in the past often been hindered in its relationships with other Lutherans by Wisconsin Synod objections, and Wisconsin's attendance at meetings might be motivated by "a desire to continue to hold the Missouri Synod in check." To the editors, that would be unacceptable. "It is high time for Missouri to do what it ought to do and not what Wisconsin wants it to do."[29]

What Missouri "ought to do," the *American Lutheran* believed, was cooperate in every way possible with the two newly-formed bodies. And the best way to do that would be to participate in the discussions aiming to form a new body to replace the old National Lutheran Council. This the Synod agreed to do at its 1962 convention, an action that the *American Lutheran* warmly welcomed. The new LCA had already voted to join the discussion, and the new ALC was expected to do so that fall. "We stand on the threshold of a new era in the relations of Lutherans to each other," the magazine proclaimed.[30]

As the conversations continued, the *American Lutheran* kept its readers informed—but it realized that Missouri's ultimate involvement in what was to be named the "Lutheran Council in the United States of America" (LCUSA) would not come easily. "Progress on the new inter-Lutheran agency continues at a steady pace," an editorial noted in early 1964. "No stumbling blocks have appeared." And yet "it is by no means certain that The Lutheran Church—Missouri Synod will adopt the constitution of the proposed agency. Loud and strident voices will be raised against Missouri Synod participation, and there will be strenuous efforts to keep Missouri out."[31]

Two months later Richard Koenig expressed frustration that Missouri's leaders had not kept the Synod informed of the negotiations, and he criticized them for insisting that they had as yet made no commitment to LCUSA. They are "playing a dangerous game," Koenig warned, since those planning the new organization have already "paid a price in order to gain or pave the way for Missouri admission."

> [Many features] of the proposed constitution are directly the result of Missouri's insistence or presence in the Council. To hold that the Missouri Synod is not committed after all of the concessions it has won, wrung or received from the other Lutherans is difficult, if not impossible.[32]

Still, Koenig was pleased with the progress that was being made. Rather than criticize shortcomings of the LCUSA proposal, "American Lutherans should accept it as a gift from the Lord of the Church who will overrule our shortsightedness and ineptitude even as He uses us, often in spite of ourselves, to let His Kingdom come." If we can do this, Koenig concluded, it "can be the beginning of the greatest hour in Lutheranism's history in the new world."[33]

As the 1965 synodical convention approached, the *American Lutheran* strongly endorsed Missouri's participation in LCUSA. Predicting that the proposal would be approved with a surprising ease, the magazine urged a unanimous vote. Such a step entailed some risks, to be sure. "But the time has come for the risks to be taken in the faith that the Spirit of God is at work molding the Lutheran Church into a more effective instrument for the preaching of Christ."[34]

At the Detroit convention, the Synod did in fact agree to participate in LCUSA—not unanimously, but overwhelmingly (in part due to the support of former president

John Behnken). This was "one of the most important decisions" made at Detroit, the *American Lutheran* reported, and it "represents a major breakthrough in efforts to bring about Lutheran unity in America." The new agency is "a reflection of the unity which already exists in American Lutheranism" and it "could serve a major role in the future course of Lutheran union."[35]

A more practical aspect of Lutheran unity was often discussed in the pages of the *American Lutheran*, sometimes with great frustration. The magazine "has long felt that a common official hymnal and service-book for all of America's Lutherans is a primary desideratum," the magazine editorialized in early 1964. It found "alarming" the Synod's apparent rush toward developing a new hymnal in isolation from other Lutherans and urged the Synod's Commission on Worship, Liturgics and Hymnology to "redouble their efforts to achieve real intersynodical cooperation ... in the production of a single Lutheran hymnal"—ideally within the next twenty-five years.[36]

The magazine took up the subject again a few months later. It noted that the *Service Book and Hymnal* had been introduced only six years previously and was now widely used in the ALC and LCA; those churches obviously would not be ready for another new hymnal for several years. If Missouri went ahead and published a new hymnal now, "there will not be an all-Lutheran hymnal by the late 1980's or even the year 2000." Missouri ought to be content with publishing some supplementary materials and work with the other bodies toward a goal of a unified hymnal and service book. This would require that the 1965 Detroit convention "put the brakes" on the commission's desire to produce a new hymnal for Missouri.[37]

It soon became clear that the commission was in fact pushing for a new hymnal, to be completed within three years. The *American Lutheran* protested vigorously. The commission, it said, had been authorized only to "revise" the 1941 *Lutheran Hymnal*, but they are planning an entirely new volume. It is certainly true that the 1941 book is out of date, and the commission has given valid reasons to produce a new one. "But are they compelling [reasons] in the light of the Lutheran unity situation in America? ... A common Lutheran hymnal is essential as an expression of Lutheran unity and as an instrument to bring it about." Again the editor urged the Synod convention to stop the plans for a new book.[38]

The *American Lutheran* was therefore pleased when the Detroit convention authorized the appointment of representatives to meet with other Lutherans and discuss a possible joint Lutheran hymnal, in effect side-tracking the plans of the commission.

> In many ways the convention's hymnal resolution is as important for the cause of Lutheran unity as its decision to enter LCUSA. The AMERICAN LUTHERAN hopes that the other Lutheran church bodies in America will recognize the significance of the action and will grasp the hand which the synod has now extended. ... We hope they will not hesitate. No doubt the work to produce a single book of

worship will take a while ... [but] the possibilities for both worship and unity are exciting.

The other bodies responded favorably to the invitation extended by Missouri, and the significant result was the establishment in 1966 of the Inter-Lutheran Commission on Worship.[39]

Despite this dramatic new development, the Synod's commission some months later announced that it planned to proceed with what it called an "interim hymnal." The editor of the *American Lutheran* was outraged. "We couldn't believe it," the editorial said. "We wouldn't believe it!" "The action of the Commission is simply incredible. It flies in the face of a specific action of a synodical convention." After rehearsing the progression of events at some length, he reiterated the importance of the pan-Lutheran project. "We are not opposed to the publication of worship materials on an experimental basis in the interim until a common Lutheran hymnal can be published." But the kind of substantive book the commission envisions "will help to delay" any joint project. The commission members, the editorial concluded, "are not a law unto themselves," and it urged readers to write both to the commission and to the Synod president in protest of the commission's plans. In the end, the commission contented itself with publishing supplementary materials, and the projected "interim hymnal" never appeared.[40]

Interpreting the Bible

"a book which is—humanly speaking—far from letter perfect"

O. A. Geiseman's final column in 1962 had predicted that the doctrine of the Word would become the new focus of controversy in the Missouri Synod. As if in preparation for that battle, John Tietjen asked Robert H. Smith to write a series of articles on Biblical interpretation. Smith was then pastor of the Lutheran Church of our Redeemer in Chappaqua, NY, but would soon join the faculty of Concordia Seminary; he would later be among the faculty who left Concordia to form Christ Seminary—Seminex.

The introductory editorial noted that there had been ongoing debate on how to interpret the Bible in the light of "efforts to apply the historical critical method." The debate had been taking place among Lutheran scholars for some time, the editor wrote, but Biblical interpretation is "not simply a question for theologians and pastors"; the laity need also "to know what the debate is all about." The goal of the series was to "bring the light of understanding to what is a complex and confusing subject" so that the Bible might "continue to be the source and norm of faith for Lutherans."[41]

Smith's series took a very long view of Biblical interpretation. In the opening article, he introduced what he called the "Biblical renaissance" in the 20th century. He suggested that it was in part a result of the ecumenical movement, especially the flowering of Biblical scholarship among Roman Catholics. There is now, he wrote, "a growing consensus that the proper scholarly approach to Sacred Scriptures is the rigorous application of the historical-critical method." The older methods of interpretation, Smith suggested, dealt with what the text *means* for contemporary Christians, while the historical-critical method deals with what the text *meant* for its writers. What is really needed now is a method that addresses both questions.[42]

In subsequent articles, Smith traced the history of interpretation—a history, he said, "did not begin in Marburg, Basel, Cambridge and Chicago in the 19th and 20th centuries but in Antioch, Alexandria, Caesarea and Constantinople in the 2nd and 3rd and 4th centuries." An entire article was devoted to Luther as interpreter. He argued that the Reformer's hermeneutical principal was strongly Christological:

> The Bible is the cradle or manger in which Christ is laid. He is swaddled in Scripture. It is only a slight and simple word, said Luther, but Christ is in it. Take out Christ and what is left? Nothing!

> The heart of the Bible is the kerygma, the prophetic and apostolic proclamation, the Gospel, the announcement and the offer of God's pardon and absolution for the sake of Jesus Christ. That message of redemption in Jesus Christ is the heart of the New Testament and the heart of the entire Bible.

Luther, Smith argued, was really in a sense "the father of modern Biblical exegesis."[43]

He summarized the state of Biblical scholarship in the 20th century. He briefly explained the significance of the liberal scholars of the 19th and early 20th century, and noted the sea change after World War I which "shattered the foundations of liberalism." Twentieth century scholarship, he said, "has been seeking a new theology, neither liberal nor orthodox, which can recover the Bible as the Word of God." He devoted a few paragraphs each to Karl Barth, Rudolf Bultmann, and Oscar Cullman, noting their important insights and contributions but insisting that each was caught in the theological pessimism that arose after the war. "Younger men," he wrote, "have a different outlook and are introducing shifts in Biblical interpretation." Their "one great question" is, "How can we apprehend Jesus and the Bible in such a way that they are not distorted or domesticated and so that we may become the sons of God and disciples of Jesus."[44]

In what would be the final issue of the *American Lutheran*, Smith began to explain the tools of the historical critical method. He discussed textual criticism, outlining its history and purpose—and noting that throughout its development, there had been churchmen who accused the textual critics of undermining the Word of God. Smith portrayed these churchmen as seriously wrong-headed. After all, without the textual scholars, "when we read Paul, how could we be sure we were reading the Apostle and not a pious and orthodox—or impious and unorthodox—corrector of the 2nd or 3rd or 4th century?" Returning to Luther's manger analogy, Smith argued that the recognition and study of thousands of textual variants is in fact a good and salutary thing:

Contrary to human expectation and intelligence it pleased God to reconcile the world to Himself through One laid as an infant in a rude, rough manger. And it should occasion neither surprise nor offense but only gratitude that Almighty God in His wise providence was pleased to offer us the Christ and reconciliation in Christ through a book which is—humanly speaking—far from letter perfect.[45]

Smith apparently intended to write additional articles on other contemporary approaches to Biblical interpretation, but the December 1966 issue brought the *American Lutheran*'s 49-year run to a close. When its successor, *Lutheran Forum*, was inaugurated in January 1967, the Smith series was not continued—though the issue of how to interpret the Bible would soon become a major matter of contention in the Missouri Synod.

Notes

1. Adolf Meyer, "Our New Editor," *AL* 45, no. 1 (Jan. 1962), 5.
2. "Our New Look," *AL* 45, no. 4 (Apr. 1962), 6.
3. O. A. Geiseman to John Tietjen, 23 Apr. 1962, Geiseman Papers, Box 15, Folder 2.
4. "Resolution 9," *AL* 45, no. 4 (Apr. 1962), 5-6.
5. "The Beginning of a New Era," *AL* 45, no. 8 (Aug. 1962), 3; "Cleveland in Retrospect," *AL* 45, no. 8 (Aug. 1962), 4.
6. Ibid.
7. O. A. Geiseman, "While It Is Day," *AL* 45, no. 8 (Aug. 1962), 7-8.
8. "No Turning Back," *AL* 48, no. 8 (Aug. 1965), 4.
9. Walter R. Bouman, "The Mission of the Lutheran Church to America," *AL* 45, no. 4 (Apr. 1962), 8.
10. Ibid., 9-10.
11. Walter R. Bouman, "The Mission of the Lutheran Church to America—II," *AL* 45, no. 5 (May 1962), 10.
12. Ibid., 11-12.
13. Ibid., 25.
14. Ibid., 26.
15. "What Does It Mean to Be Lutheran?" *AL* 47, no. 2 (Feb. 1964), 5.
16. Arthur Carl Piepkorn, "What Is the Lutheran Church?" *AL* 47, no. 2 (Feb. 1964), 8ff.
17. Richard R. Caemmerer, "What Is Lutheran in Faith and Life?" *AL* 47, no. 4 (Apr. 1964), 6ff.
18. George W. Hoyer, "What is Lutheran in Worship?" *AL* 47, no. 6 (June 1964), 7-9.
19. Walter R. Bouman, "What Is Lutheran in Theology?" *AL* 48, no. 12 (Dec. 1965), 10ff.
20. Richard Koenig, "One Church," *AL* 45, no. 4 (Apr. 1962), 22.
21. "The Coming Roman Catholic Council," *AL* 45, no. 10 (Oct. 1962), 4.
22. Ibid.
23. Ibid.
24. "Vatican II: Progress Report," *AL* 46, no. 2 (Feb. 1963), 4.
25. Ibid., 7.
26. F. Dean Lueking, "The Second Vatican Council in Historical Perspective," *AL* 46, no. 2 (Feb. 1963), 10.
27. Jaroslav J. Pelikan, "The Church and the Council: A Non-Catholic View," *AL* 46, no. 11 (Nov. 1963), 10-12.
28. "A Dead End for the Synodical Conference," *AL* 46, no. 10 (Oct. 1963), 5.
29. "Will the Albatross Remain?" *AL* 46, no. 10 (Oct. 1963), 5.
30. "The Beginning of a New Era," *AL* 45, no. 8 (Aug. 1962), 3.
31. "Lutheran Council in the United States of America," *AL* 47, no. 3 (Mar. 1964), 5.

32. Richard E. Koenig, "Missouri and the Lutheran Council in the USA," *AL* 47, no. 5 (May 1964), 10.

33. Ibid., 11f.

34. "Missouri's Conciliar Experiment," *AL* 48, no. 4 (Apr. 1965), 5.

35. "No Turning Back," *AL* 48, no. 8 (Aug. 1965), 4.

36. "Think It Over," *AL* 47, no. 3 (Mar. 1964), 3-5.

37. "Time to Put on the Brakes," *AL* 47, no. 10 (Oct. 1964), 5.

38. "The Progress that Must Be Stopped," *AL* 48, no 3 (Mar. 1965), 4.

39. "No Turning Back," *AL* 48, no. 8 (Aug. 1965), 5-6.

40. "Can You Believe It?" *AL* 49, no. 9 (Sept. 1966), 3-5.

41. "Our New Series on Bible Interpretation," *AL* 49, no. 2 (Feb. 1966), 4-5.

42. Robert H. Smith, "The Biblical Renaissance," *AL* 49, no. 2 (Feb. 1966), 7-8.

43. Robert H. Smith, "The Study of the Bible in the Ancient Church," *AL* 49, no. 4 (Apr. 1966), 6;
"Luther's Interpretation of the Bible," *AL* 49, no. 6 (June 1966), 26.

44. Robert H. Smith, "Biblical Scholarship Today," *AL* 49, no. 10 (Oct. 1966), 9.

45. Robert H. Smith, "Criticism of the Biblical Text," *AL* 49, no. 12 (Dec. 1966), 22.

Chapter 14

CHURCH AND SOCIETY

John Tietjen's editorial boldness was not confined to questions of Lutheran identity and ecumenical relations. The most significant social issue of those years, civil rights, was always front and center on the *American Lutheran*'s agenda. An early series of articles under Tietjen's leadership took as its theme "The Church Battles the World," and it tackled a range of subjects from communism to contemporary entertainment. Another series focused on the increasingly contentious matter of the role of women in church and society. The early 1960s also saw numerous new resources offered by the ALPB, even as the Bureau faced yet another financial crisis and more leadership changes.

Combatting prejudice
"fling all expediency to the winds"
In 1963, the infamous church bombing in Birmingham, AL, which killed four young girls outraged the nation. The *American Lutheran* lauded nine Missouri Synod pastors

in the city who read a bold message from their pulpits the following Sunday, decrying violence and insisting that "the Church is not a segregated community. We are one in Christ. The members of our congregations, as part of the body of Christ, therefore, have no right to segregate any member of the body." The editorial particularly noted that Edgar Homrighausen, president of the LCMS's Southern District, had himself signed the statement and "was convinced both that the stand taken was Scripturally right and that the majority of Lutherans in Birmingham would accept it." The LCMS College of Presidents had also supported the action. To all of them "the AMERICAN LUTHERAN pays tribute."[1]

A 1965 editorial commented on "Lutherans and the Selma Struggle." Most Lutherans, if they knew of Selma at all, knew it as the site of a small Lutheran preparatory school and college for Negro youth operated by the Synodical Conference. But recently "Selma got on the map in a way that caught Lutherans, as well as others, by surprise." After summarizing the voter registration efforts spearheaded by Martin Luther King Jr.'s Southern Christian Leadership Conference, the editorial noted that "Lutherans were active in their support" of the Selma efforts. Some two dozen Lutheran pastors from around the country had joined King in Selma, two-thirds of them from the Missouri Synod—"possibly aroused to action by a strange sequence of events involving Missouri Synod pastors several days before."[2]

The incident to which the editorial referred had involved the Rev. Joseph Ellwanger, pastor of the predominantly black St. Paul's Lutheran Church in Birmingham. Ellwanger, whose father, Walter Ellwanger, had recently retired as president of the Alabama Lutheran Academy and College in Selma, led a group of some 72 white citizens intending to march on the Selma courthouse to support the registration efforts. Prior to the march he was confronted by another LCMS clergyman, James Rongstad, pastor of St. John's Lutheran Church in Selma, a white congregation. Rongstad "urged Pastor Ellwanger to leave Selma's problems to the people of Selma." When the group reached the courthouse, Ellwanger was handed a telegram from his district president, Homrighausen, stating that Ellwanger did not have his support and was not representing the Lutheran Church—Missouri Synod. The *American Lutheran* was appalled:

> We are certain that Dr. Homrighausen did not intend his act to be interpreted as a defense of the status quo in Selma and the South. Nevertheless the net effect of his telegram was to identify him with those white citizens of Alabama who refuse to recognize thousands in their state as full-fledged American citizens.

The editor insisted (perhaps too optimistically) that all Lutherans "agree on the goals; justice, equality, brotherhood for all citizens of the United States." But as to the means, "opinion is divided." This makes it even more important that Lutherans be in communication with one another. The editor revealed that in fact Ellwanger and Homrighausen had been in "brotherly consultation" prior to the incident, and both were aware of what the other intended to do.[3]

Noting that the LCA had officially endorsed civil disobedience, and the ALC had explicitly "identified itself with civil rights marches and demonstrations," the editor sighed that "it may be the Missouri Synod's destiny to agree to disagree on methods and procedures." At the very least, though, Lutherans must respect each person's right to act in accord with conscience. The editorial called for further consultation as soon as possible:

> We recommend that a conference be called that will involve the top leadership of Synod and the districts most directly involved as well as the Lutheran leaders, both clergy and laity, in civil rights movements. It is imperative that this meeting of the minds be held prior to the Detroit Convention of the Synod in June because this subject will be certain to come up there in one way or another.

When such a consultation took place in Birmingham in May, the *American Lutheran* claimed that Homrighausen had convened it "in response to an appeal for such a conference by the AMERICAN LUTHERAN."[4]

The magazine left little doubt as to where it stood. In May 1965, an editorial insisted that "the time is now for Christians everywhere to repent of their part in the oppression that 'keeps the Negro in his place' and be what the Spirit of the Lord calls them to be: liberators of the oppressed." Acknowledging that the "challenge is particularly difficult for Christians in the deep south" where "support of demonstrations is exceedingly unpopular—and dangerous," Tietjen nonetheless insisted that the "time is long overdue for Christians everywhere to fling all expediency to the winds and to identify all the way with the Negro struggle." It is true that this "way lies the Cross, as it did for our Lord," but "the disciple is called to follow in his Master's steps."[5]

The *American Lutheran* also began to back away from the casual anti-Semitism of earlier years. The turning point was an article by Arthur Carl Piepkorn in 1964. Piepkorn's interest in the subject was sparked by his involvement with the Lutheran Human Relations Association of America, an organization founded by Andrew Schulze to promote interracial harmony and racial justice.

> From my association with [the LHRAA] I recalled frequent evidences of a distaste for antisemitism [*sic*] in that group. People interested in human rights soon discover that prejudice tends to be of a piece. Antisemitism, 'that oldest and most comprehensive of modern neuroses' (James Parkes), is often coupled with a determination to deny civil rights to Negroes, Puerto Ricans, Orientals, and American Indians.

Entitled "The Lutheran's Image of the Jews," Piepkorn's article was originally presented as a paper at a symposium cosponsored by Concordia Seminary and the Anti-Defamation League. He had done a good deal of research in various Lutheran publications, trying to determine just what contemporary attitudes might be. He concluded that LCMS materials "do not come out very favorably." The problem wasn't so much overt prejudice as "sins of omission." Writers did not distinguish between "the Jews of the first century and the Jews of today," and did not clearly condemn anti-Semitism. Piepkorn was encouraged, however, by a study finding that Lutheran seminarians showed little inclination toward this prejudice. Nonetheless, he believed there was much still to be done. "Where any of us has been personally guilty of prejudice in his thoughts and words and actions where others are involved," he concluded, "let him be ready to say: 'Forgive us, our Father, for we have sinned.'"[6]

There were additional symposia on Lutheran/Jewish relations at Concordia Seminary over the next few years, and the *American Lutheran* continued to publish the papers presented there. Then, in the wake of Vatican II's statement which absolved the Jewish people of "corporate responsibility for the crucifixion" of Jesus, the magazine discussed an international Lutheran gathering in Logumkloster, Denmark. The conference had made specific recommendations to Lutheran churches about combatting anti-Semitism which "merit the careful attention of responsible Lutheran groups in America."[7]

In July 1966, the magazine made note of *Christian Beliefs and Anti-Semitism* by Charles Glock and Rodney Stark. The two sociologists found that there was a direct correlation between a church's orthodoxy and the prevalence of anti-Semitism among its members. In comparing various denominations, the study ranked the Missouri Synod as particularly anti-Semitic. The *American Lutheran* editor wasn't entirely convinced, suggesting there were methodological problems in the survey. Nevertheless, he insisted that the report was worthy of careful study, and "Lutherans particularly must face up to it squarely." At the very least, the study "ought to shatter any remaining complacency about the existence of anti-Semitism among us."[8]

Other social issues

"a task in which the theologian and the pastor must join hands"

Racism was not the only social issue given attention by the *American Lutheran* during this era. The first article in the series "The Church Battles the World" discussed the "threat of world communism." Ralph Moellering, student pastor at the Lutheran Chapel at the University of California in Berkeley, took quite a different approach from that of August W. Brustat a decade earlier. Acknowledging that "the Communist drive toward world domination is the gravest threat in our time," Moellering claimed that the complexity of the threat often leads Christians to fall victim to the "many brands of irresponsible anti-Communism running rampant in our country today which cast suspicion on anyone who does not conform to their own definition of 'one hundred per cent' Americanism." Some "misguided zealots" engage in "ill-conceived crusades" against the United Nations or the National Council of Churches, but this "can only give aid and comfort to the enemy who rejoices over our internal strife and stupidity." Moellering suggested a five-point program to constructively "deter the insidious growth of Communism," including educational programs in congregations, an emphasis on racial justice in church and society, hospitality extended to international students and visitors, and "prophetic voices ... in the pulpit and in our religious journals." In the end, he wrote, the church's answer to communism "is uttered in faith." "The final decision pertaining to the destiny of the human race will not be made in the Kremlin or in the Pentagon" but in the promise of Christ.[9]

Another writer discussed the matter of "family life." David S. Schuller surveyed recent statistics and studies of a variety of issues related to marriage, family, and sexuality—premarital sex, marital infidelity, divorce, abortion. This was new territory for the *American Lutheran*; the only previous discussion of this nature seems to have been an article about venereal disease among American soldiers in 1947 and a series on "Courtship and Marriage" in 1953. Schuller's article was a description of the changing sexual mores, followed by some recommendations that began with a call to arms:

> To a generation bred on the assumption that there are no absolutes, the church must again proclaim a sense of values grounded in God's revelation of Himself. The church must be ruthless in her own examination. She must be sure that she is dealing with unchanging values and not with cultural fixtures which have achieved an air of sanctity over the centuries. ... Here is a task in which the theologian and the pastor must join hands.

He offered a list of "short-range objectives" proposed by a recent Conference on Church and Family Life (include sex education in Christian education curriculum, offer support to parents in discussing sensitive matters with their children). One of these was particularly interesting: "Keep communication open with persons with sex problems (one area discussed, for example, was homosexuals)." This seems to be the first mention of homosexuality in an ALPB publication; it would not be the last.[10]

Sometimes the *American Lutheran* veered a little too close to "politics"—at least in the opinion of some readers. A 1964 editorial took up "moral issues in the Presidential election." The editor expressed concern about "right-wing extremist" support for the candidacy of Sen. Barry Goldwater, and for what he saw as a watering down of the civil rights plank in the Republican platform as compared with that of 1960. These are moral issues that should be of concern to Christians, he went on, along with "world peace, nuclear war, poverty, human freedom, government power and authority." "The Church has no business in politics," but "Christian pastors should not leave their people without counsel and advice on political issues that are also moral issues."[11]

Some readers apparently took the editorial as a partisan endorsement of President Lyndon Johnson over Sen. Goldwater, but Tietjen insisted that they had "found more in our previous editorial than was actually there." The editorial had simply "pointed out that a number of political issues in the campaign are also moral issues. ... The purpose of the editorial was to urge [Lutherans] to become more involved." He cited some "moral issues" on which President Johnson might be criticized, and reiterated that the magazine had not made an endorsement and would not do so. But he offered some "question guidelines for making a choice on Election day." "Which of the candidates espouses the programs and policies that will foster the genuine well-being of the nation and international peace and good-will? Which of the candidates will be more likely to follow our Christian aspiration for justice for all members of society?"[12]

The intersection of church and society sometimes came to the forefront in unexpected ways during the 1960s. In 1965 a controversy arose when leaders of the Walther League invited folk singer Pete Seeger to be part of the program at their international convention. The invitation was condemned by what the *American Lutheran* called "an extremist right-wing news commentator in Southern California" on the grounds that Seeger was an alleged communist. In the face of the complaints, both the International Walther League Board and the Synod's Board for Young People's Work supported the League's decision to invite Seeger. This, the *American Lutheran* editorialized, was a "profile in courage."

> The Walther League Board members have actually done the rest of the Missouri Synod a service. ... If the synod had capitulated to the radical right on this issue, it would have lived to rue the day. Our synod has been harassed enough as it is by the destructive criticism that has been coming from its extremists. ...
>
> There is no point in trying to protect [our young people] from the problem. This is their world, too. They have enjoyed Pete Seeger's music and identified with it long before Walther League officials asked him to perform. They will sing along with him for an hour or so. ... But the real highlight of their convention will be the hours of Bible study, spiritual discussions, and worship.

The storm over Seeger is likely not over, the editorial concluded. But "the courageous stand of the Walther League will spare us all a worse storm in the future."[13]

Women in the church
"an open discussion of the subject"

Betty Friedan's *The Feminine Mystique* was published in 1963, sparking what is sometimes called "second-wave feminism" in the United States (the "first wave" having been the campaign for women's suffrage in the late 19th and early 20th centuries). As conversations about women in society swirled, churches also began to reevaluate the role of women. In the Missouri Synod of the 1960s, women were generally excluded from many aspects of church life. In most congregations, women were not eligible to vote or to serve on governing bodies. The one exception, at least in some congregations, was that women were permitted to vote to extend a call to a pastor—the theory being that he would equally be their pastor, and so they had a right to be involved in the process of calling him.

In January 1966, the *American Lutheran* announced a series of articles on women in the church. An introductory editorial noted that there had been "major change in the role of women in our society" which has "opened up all kinds of areas which were previously privileged male sanctuary." In the church, too, women were insisting that "in Christ there is neither male nor female."

> An increasing number of women find the average church women's society unsatisfying. They are not content to play a role limited to Sunday School teaching, sewing layettes, and serving suppers, as important as they may recognize those tasks to be. Many a woman is still content to let the men 'run the church,' though more and more women—and men, too—cannot understand why they should be deprived of the right to vote in church affairs and to serve on church boards.

"We hope we can be of service to the church," the editorial concluded, "by stimulating an open discussion of the subject."[14]

Most of the articles in the series were written by women, a fact unusual enough that the editor called attention to it. Two introductory articles—interestingly, both by members of the LCA rather than the LCMS—set the stage. Catherine W. Herzel described the social changes that have impacted women in recent years, particularly the large-scaled entry of women into the workforce. This has had two significant results. In the first place, many women have taken jobs for economic reasons that are not particularly creative or rewarding; what they now need from the church is opportunities "that reaffirm the value and worth of the human spirit." Second, working women have much less control over their own time, and so "scheduling of church services and activities may need overhauling."[15]

In the same issue, Robert E. Huldschiner agreed that "the story of the 'typical church woman' has to be rewritten." He quoted "a lady in Los Angeles":

> 'The woman's auxiliary was a wonderful outlet for women who didn't have much to do. That's changing. More and more one notices that church women's organizations are gearing their programs to younger women, and younger, active women are getting involved in retreats and conferences.'

He noted that in the LCA, the "official women's organization" (Lutheran Church Women) had been going in a new direction. He quoted Lois Leffler, an LCW official: "Perhaps our most important educational job right now is to help men and women see themselves in the role of a responsible laity. Our program is an education for partnership."[16]

Paul Jacobs, president of the California and Nevada District, tried to clarify the official position of the Synod on women's suffrage in the church. The 1965 LCMS convention had approved a resolution which included the words: "God forbids women publicly to preach and teach the Word to men and to hold any office or vote in the Church where this involves exercising authority over men with respect to the public administration of the Office of the Keys. ... We consider woman suffrage in the Church as contrary to Scripture only when it violates the above mentioned scriptural principles." Jacobs insisted the resolution clearly "permits congregations to extend the right of vote to women in the Voting Assembly of the congregation" and that it is "for each congregation to determine the degree of woman suffrage which it desires to extend to the women, keeping in mind the restrictions which the Resolution imposes upon the congregations of the Synod."[17]

Another article offered a startling (to some) idea. In "Ordain Women?" LaVonne Althouse, editor of the LCA's *Lutheran Church Women*, noted that most of the European Lutheran churches had been ordaining women for some time (the *American Lutheran* had reported on this debate in Europe as early as 1953). She then examined the scriptural arguments used to oppose the ordination of women and found them lacking, citing, for example, Paul's insistence in Galatians 3.28 that in Christ there is neither male nor female. She acknowledged some possible practical issues in ordaining women, and yet argued that similar issues had been dealt with satisfactorily as women entered many vocations traditionally restricted to men. She stopped just short of advocating the ordination of women, but she clearly was pointing in that direction:

> Whether or not we are able to accept a challenge of that magnitude ... new possibilities exist for women's service to the church today. Integrity in all relationships and obedience to our Lord require that we make it possible for women to equip themselves for any service they can potentially give and to serve in any capacity they can fill. If God is Lord of creation, if he gives gifts according to his good pleasure, and if he has called us as men and women into a new relationship in Jesus Christ, no other course is open to us.[18]

Worship and the Eucharist

"not some special dessert for use on select occasions"

Fred Lindemann was no longer around to beat the ALPB drum for a piety and practice centered on the Eucharist, but there were others who took up the cause. Glenn Stone was a young pastor who would soon play a major role in the Bureau, but at this time he was assistant pastor at the Lutheran Church of the Good Shepherd in Roosevelt, NY, and the editor of *Una Sancta*, a journal devoted to theology and liturgy. In October

1962, the *American Lutheran* published his paper, "The Sacrament of the Altar and the Church's Mission."

Stone began by observing that there was a "rising tide of sacramental interest" and that frequency of celebration of the Eucharist was increasing dramatically. It was also a time when newly-merged church bodies were heavily focused on home missions. This raised the question of the sacramental life of mission congregations. Were these "special situations" where frequent communion simply wasn't realistic? Stone insisted that was not the case.

> The place that the Sacrament of the Altar ought to hold in the life of our American mission congregations is really no different from the place it ought to hold in any other congregation. If it be urged that the mission situation involves special circumstances which require us to adapt our theories about church life to practical reality, it must be answered that any of our 'old established' congregations actually face a greater mission challenge than the newly developed suburban parishes, which are largely occupied in gathering in transfers, or 'converting' those already Christian than winning the non-Christian.[19]

The question of frequency, Stone insisted, is more a question of theology than of mission strategy. When we organize a congregation, what is it we are forming? The confessional answer is clear: it is, according to the Augsburg Confession, "the congregation of saints, in which the Gospel is rightly taught and the Sacraments are rightly administered." He then surveyed various understandings of the church, emphasizing especially the church as the "Body of Christ"—terminology which draws a close correlation between the church and the "Body of Christ" received in the Eucharist.[20]

Stone next considered the relationship between Word and Sacrament. Often in Lutheranism, he mused, they have been viewed as somewhat parallel "vehicles of grace," so that the Sacrament is regarded as redundant in a service when there has already been preaching. But Stone argued that they in fact have quite different purposes, recognized by Luther himself.

> In Luther's view, preaching is critically important, but in the final analysis, both the content and goal of preaching is the testament or gift which is in the Sacrament. The preaching calls men to the Sacrament (as Luther also points out in the *Formula Missae*), interprets it, sets forth the new covenant, prepares men to receive it; the Sacrament completes the preaching, provides the content of that to which the preaching summons, is the actual communion of the new covenant.

In Stone's view, then, Word and Sacrament are complementary channels of God's grace, so "it is wrong to split up the Means of Grace and think of them apart from each other."[21]

Stone considered what it is that is unique about the Sacrament of the Altar, and why it is essential to the Church:

It creates *koinonia*. Preaching calls men into the fellowship, Baptism incorporates them into it, but it is a fellowship already existing by virtue of the Sacrament of the Altar. The full expression of one's participation in this fellowship is not seen until one receives the Holy Communion. The Sacrament of the Altar creates this communion by virtue of the fact that to it alone is attached the Real Presence of the Body and Blood of Christ. ... Christ takes form in the gathering itself because it is here that whole and entire He enters into each member, bodily as well as spiritually, and thus unites them into one.[22]

For Stone, the implication was clear: "There ought to be the celebration of the Holy Communion every time there is parakletic preaching, that is, the kind of preaching that is done (or ought to be done) at the regular Sunday and holy day celebrations of the liturgy." He allowed that there were other kinds of assemblies—evangelistic meetings, for instance—where preaching alone might be appropriate, with no celebration of the Sacrament. But "any regular liturgical assembly of the Church which omits either [preaching or Sacrament] must *in principle* be considered incomplete." Does this mean that several hundred years of Lutheran services without the Sacrament were in vain? That isn't the case, of course; and yet "is it possible that much of the recurring weakness and irrelevance of what we call 'the Church' can be traced to our unwillingness to be fully THE CHURCH?"

> Let us recognize our weaknesses and deficiencies so that the Church can grow into the measure of the stature of the fullness of Christ. It may yet be that a true application of the 'Protestant principle' of self-criticism will help us to realize our catholicity.[23]

The *American Lutheran* also tackled Eucharistic practice, challenging attitudes and usages which had come to be generally accepted. Melvin Kieschnick, a missionary in Hong Kong, wrote a column in which he confessed to a sinful thought one Sunday night when he felt gladness that "we didn't celebrate Holy Communion today." His "devil-implanted feeling" arose because that morning at his church there had been a large group of international visitors, including two who were members of the Batak Church in Indonesia (a member of the Lutheran World Federation, but not in fellowship with the Missouri Synod).

> But had we celebrated the Lord's Supper, that blessed means of grace and living expression of fellowship, on this Sunday morning would we have invited these brothers to join us? And if word had gotten out that the local pastor had actually invited (mind you, *invited*) them to attend he would have to be prepared to give some explanations.

This situation, he went on, had happened many times, and he always felt some angst when visitors included Lutherans from other synods. He acknowledged that "the solution is not to simply say that whoever attends our services is eligible (a bad word!) to attend the Lord's Supper." But he urged that Missouri Synod Lutherans "repent, and restudy and beseech" Christ to lead his people into closer unity. He prayed that the Holy Spirit might work "so that even with non-Missouri guests present at our church services our hearts will cry out with joy and anticipation, 'With desire have I desired to eat this meal with you.'"[24]

Kieschnick's plea was underscored by Tietjen in an editorial entitled "Communing at Lutheran Altars: When and by Whom?" He briefly spoke of the Galesburg Rule, a principle articulated by Lutherans of the old General Council in the 19th century: "Lutheran altars are for Lutheran communicants only." This standard "came to be the general practice among all Lutheran groups in America." But then Tietjen asked a pointed question: "Are the Lutheran altars of Missouri Synod congregations reserved for Missouri Synod communicants only? Some people think so." On the other hand, he went on, many Missouri Synod congregations "are accustomed to communing members of other Lutheran church bodies" and simply do not believe that "either the Galesburg Rule or the principle of close communion is meant to apply to fellow Lutherans."[25]

But Kieschnick's column, Tietjen noted, raised another issue—the reality that there "are ever so many Lutheran congregations, outside of the United States and within it ... where on any given Sunday morning a Lutheran will not be able to receive the Sacrament of Holy Communion." Indeed, most Lutherans are not able to receive in their congregation on any given Sunday.

> Perhaps many a Lutheran congregation should make a 'Sunday Night Confession' and explain to the Lord of the Church why it chose not to make use of the Means He provided to receive His grace and power to come into communion with Him. Lutherans the world over need to recognize the Sacrament of Holy Communion for what it is: the Bread of Life and the Cup of Salvation for which they should hunger and thirst as they do for daily food and not some special dessert for use on select occasions.

Weekly Eucharist may not solve Kieschnick's problem, "but it might require us all to find more adequate solutions to the problem of exhibiting the church's fellowship amidst a divided Christendom."[26]

A 1965 article by Lawrence Martin, an Ohio pastor, tackled yet another aspect of the Eucharist: the use of the chalice. Martin began by recalling some secular experiences of "drinking from a common vessel"—boyhood hikes where all drank from the same canteen, high school football teams where all drank from the same dipper, sharing a flask of whiskey with friends at the Rose Bowl game. These occasions were "frequently quite a meaningful ritual." Yet in the church, after "Pasteur's discovery of bacteria, a germ scare swept through congregations and denominations." He recounted the invention of small communion glasses in the early 20th century and their promotion by glass companies. He marveled at how "in one fell swoop, the germ question became a Tower of Babel destroying over 1900 years of sacred practice."[27]

Martin cited recent scientific studies demonstrating the safety of the common cup from a health perspective (particularly as opposed to the bacteria potential in individual cups handled multiple times prior to their use). He also considered the deeper meaning of the large-scale movement among Lutherans and others away from the use of the chalice. In Martin's view, this shift came about because of two factors. First, he observed that God's people have always been "of a rebellious mind, destroying or manipulating both the holy means or the holy context of God's outreach"—citing as examples the Biblical Tower of Babel and the golden calf. Just as troubling, though, was his suspicion that the use of the individual communion glass represents "our refusal to come to terms with all that God has done to make us one with Him *and* the neighbors in the new world given to us in Jesus Christ." Rejection of the chalice in favor of individual glasses demonstrates "a Hindu-like spiritualism which is more concerned with the private, vertical relationship to God, at the expense of the suffering neighbor in the world." For all these reasons, he concluded, Lutherans ought to insist on the use of the chalice and "drink of this cup of joy."[28]

In August 1966, just a few months before the *American Lutheran* would cease publication, the magazine led with an editorial strongly advocating that the Eucharist be offered each week as the main liturgy. "Why Settle for Half a Service?" Tietjen asked, lamenting that, while the Eucharist was being offered "with increasing frequency," for most Lutherans the Sunday service was simply "a truncated version of the church's historic liturgy." Weekly communion is not simply to be defended on historical or liturgical grounds, but "from our understanding of the Incarnation as the Word of God made flesh, from our conception of the church as the covenant community created by the blood of the Cross ... from our appreciation of Word and Sacrament as means by which God works among us with His grace." For too long the "burden of proof" for offering weekly Eucharist has been placed on the advocates of the practice, but "actually [it] should be on those who make the chief service of Christian worship something other than the full service of Word and Sacrament." It is they who are following a practice that is less than truly Lutheran. "Like the Lutheran confessors before us we need to instruct God's people with greater diligence concerning the holy sacrament, why it was instituted, and how it is to be used. And we need to offer it to them."[29]

New directions

"Lutheranism—evangelical, confessional, catholic, and ecumenical"

In addition to publishing the *American Lutheran*, the Bureau continued to expand its programs and resources for congregations. In 1962, several new resources were introduced for congregational use during Lent. One example was a "Lenten Triptych"; two panels contained Lenten prayers for morning and evening, while the third left space for a schedule of the congregation's Lenten and Easter services. Another was a Lenten prayer booklet, intended for distribution on Ash Wednesday.

That same year the U. S. Supreme Court decided (*Engel v. Vitale*) that a voluntary prayer composed by the New York State Board of Regents for use in public school classrooms was unconstitutional—thus ending the common practice of opening public school sessions with prayer. The ALPB responded by producing a "Silent Prayer Bookmark" which students could carry to school. The bookmark contained a prayer written by Edward Stammel, pastor of Trinity Lutheran Church in Hicksville, NY—a prayer which students might use privately and silently to begin their day. The ALPB was awarded a Freedoms Foundation award for this resource, which, the Foundation said, was "an outstanding achievement in bringing about a better understanding of the American way of life."[30]

Another award-winning resource was introduced in 1965. The "Closer to God through Regular Worship" program provided a dozen tracts urging the importance of church attendance. The campaign suggested mailing one tract to every member during the week prior to the first Sunday of the month. The tract for January, for example, tapped into the theme of "New Year Resolutions":

TIRED OF NEW YEAR'S RESOLUTIONS?—SO IS HE!

If we're tired of making New Year's resolutions imagine how tired Christ is ... of seeing them broken.

Yet, he loves us. He died to give us another chance.

This is our new chance, a new year ... a good time to resolve to worship Him every Sunday, not just some Sundays ... a time to resolve to really worship and praise HIM for His goodness and love ... a time to resolve to receive Holy Communion more often in this coming year.

And a time to ask Him to give us the strength to keep our New Year's Resolution this time ... to Worship Him that liveth forever."

Each tract had a striking color graphic—"To see it is to want to pick it up and read it," enthused the *American Lutheran*. The program received an Award of Excellence from the Religious Public Relations Council, and it was endorsed by the evangelism departments of not only the LCMS, but the ALC and LCA as well. Two years later it was replaced by a series entitled "New Life through Regular Worship," with themes coordinated with the 450th anniversary of the Reformation.[31]

The *American Lutheran* had offered many articles on worship over the years, and about 1965 the Bureau decided to publish a collection of reprints of some of the "most useful and representative." This project was originally conceived by Paul John Thielo when he was assistant executive secretary of the Bureau in 1958, but it was not until he had left the Bureau to accept a call to develop a mission congregation,

All Saints in Brookville, NY, that it came to fruition. "I realized the absolute necessity for reprinting many of these articles for help and guidelines in maintaining truly Lutheran parishes," he wrote. The core of the 58-page book, published as *Christian Worship*, consisted of columns written by Arthur Carl Piepkorn in 1947-48, but there were also articles by Fred Lindemann, Frederick Roth Webber, Milton Rudnick, and Walter Buszin, published between 1934 and 1958. Thielo's introduction expressed his deep appreciation for the magazine's sometimes controversial liturgical emphasis over the years: "May the American Lutheran continue in our times to do brave things for Christ and his Church."[32]

There were personnel changes within the ALPB board during this period. John Kavasch, who had served as president through the 1950s, turned the reins over to Pr. Rudolph P. F. Ressmeyer in 1961. Ressmeyer had a long and deep connection with the Bureau; his grandfather, Henry Ressmeyer, had been one of the founders, and his father, Pr. Rudolph S. Ressmeyer, had been employed briefly as field secretary in the 1920s. The younger Ressmeyer served as president for only three years, though he continued on the board until the 1980s. He was succeeded in 1964 by Fred Engelman, the layman who had helped create the "Sharing Christ Plan." Engelman had been a member of the board for more than a decade, and now became the first lay president in thirty years.

There were also staff changes at the *American Lutheran*. When Tietjen took over as editor, there were three editorial associates—O. A. Geiseman, Arthur Carl Piepkorn, and Norman Temme. Geiseman died later that year; he had been a member of the magazine's staff for some twenty-six years, and had made many other contributions to the life of the church. A few years after his death, the ALPB published a collection of his "While It Is Day" columns, edited by F. Dean Lueking, Geiseman's successor at Grace Lutheran Church in River Forest, IL.[33]

Tietjen invited Jaroslav Pelikan to fill the vacancy left by Geiseman's death. Pelikan was a rising star in academia, having recently been named Titus Street Professor of Ecclesiastical History at Yale University; he served on the *American Lutheran* staff for two years, then found it necessary to resign (though he continued as a contributing editor). Tietjen also appointed Pr. John S. Damm, assistant pastor at Grace Lutheran, Teaneck, NJ, as managing editor; he would assist in the technical aspects of production, enabling the editors "to devote more attention to the planning and production of editorials and articles."[34]

Following Pelikan's resignation in 1965, Tietjen announced that two new editorial associates had come on board, both of whom had been associated with the magazine as contributors for several years. F. Dean Lueking brought an interest in missions; he had recently written a history of foreign missions of the Missouri Synod. Richard Koenig was pastor of Immanuel Lutheran Church in Amherst, MA, campus pastor for several nearby colleges, and a regular contributor to and columnist for the magazine. Both would remain associated with the ALPB and its ministries for years to come.

Change is always challenging in many ways, and as the ALPB's publications and programs grew in the 1960s, a new financial crisis arose. In January 1966, the *American Lutheran* published "an urgent appeal." Readers were warned that a "serious financial crisis" put the "very existence of the AMERICAN LUTHERAN in jeopardy." The editor explained that the ALPB had been running with an increasing deficit for the past three years, and the expense of the magazine was one of the primary reasons for the financial hole. "We need to increase our magazine receipts by some $12,000 annually," he wrote, "or cease to publish." He pleaded the magazine's cause, noting that "even those who do not agree with some phases of its editorial position have valued its role as a forum where new ideas and controversial views can find expression." He gave a hint as to the *American Lutheran's* future:

> Editorially we intend to keep on calling them as we see them as we stand for genuine Lutheranism—evangelical, confessional, catholic, and ecumenical. We are carefully considering ways and means of transforming our magazine into a journal that speaks with an independent voice to and for all Lutherans in America.[35]

He then outlined a plan for raising the financial support necessary. The magazine would *not* raise the subscription price, but would redouble its efforts to expand the subscription base. It would invite readers to become patrons, contributing gifts over and above their subscription fees. Finally, it would seek some "financial angels" to make significant major contributions. He pleaded for help: "Good reader, this editorial is not 'crying wolf.' We appeal to you for help because we must."[36]

Four months later, the magazine reported that "the financial situation of the ALPB has improved considerably" but "we are not yet out of the woods." That issue attached an envelope to be used for additional contributions. Then in July the news was good: "The ink is black." The ALPB had completed its fiscal year without adding to the deficit. "The Bureau must now find ways to reduce the deficits built up over the last three years," but the board "is looking to the future with optimism and vision."[37]

The end of an era

"step boldly into the future"

The November 1966 issue of the *American Lutheran* made an announcement that must have come as a shock to its readers—some of whom had no doubt been subscribers since the first issue 49 years earlier. The ALPB board had decided to "step boldly into the future" by expanding its magazine publication program. This first public announcement suggested that the *American Lutheran* would be continuing under a different name as "an independent journalistic voice to all of Lutheranism in America as it has spoken in the past to The Lutheran Church—Missouri Synod." It sounded as though the only substantive changes would be the new name and, for the first time, a full-time salaried editor. An editorial the next month, however, was closer to the mark: "The ALPB has authorized what is in actuality a new magazine with a new name. Take note of it. Next month in place of the AMERICAN LUTHERAN you will receive LUTHERAN FORUM." *Lutheran Forum* would in fact be a new publication entirely, with the January issue designated Volume 1, Number 1 (though for its first ten years it would include on its masthead the words "Continuing the *American Lutheran* 1918-1966").[38]

These final issues did not spill much ink recounting the long and distinguished history of the *American Lutheran*. There was no mention of the founding editor, Paul Lindemann, or his successor, Adolf Meyer. There were no references to names that had graced the pages of the magazine, some of them over decades, as editors, writers and columnists: F. R. Webber, O. A. Geiseman, J. F. E. Nickelsberg, E. J. Friedrich, O. P. Kretzmann, Arthur Carl Piepkorn, Fred Lindemann, Theodore Graebner, and many others. The regular columns in the magazine had been phased out earlier that year.

The one exception was a humor column first begun in 1951 under the pseudonym "Imaprea Chertoo." In the final issue, that feature included an editorial note explaining that it had been written for all these years by the Rev. Detlaf A. Kraft, pastor of St. John Lutheran Church, Flushing, NY. Kraft's help had been solicited by Ade Meyer who, he wrote, had "long admired the Simeon Stylites column carried by the *Christian Century*" and who asked Kraft to try his hand at something in a similar vein. Kraft had discussed many things, but particularly his experiences as a pastor—generally with gentle humor, usually describing experiences with which most pastors could identify. His columns, the closing editorial revelation noted, "have often cheered and sometimes wrung our hearts."[39]

One article in the penultimate issue pointed in the direction that the Bureau and its publications were headed. C. J. Curtis, pastor of Immanuel Lutheran Church in Chicago, offered a thoughtful essay entitled "Evangelical Catholicity." He began with a strong assertion:

> Evangelical catholicity is the foundation for the promotion of Christian unity and the ecumenical understanding of the doctrines of the church. Without catholicity there will be neither an adequate, ecumenical church nor a complete, ecumenical theology. The Protestant must enhance and cultivate his catholic vision. The Roman, Greek, and Anglo-Catholic must grasp anew and revivify his evangelicity. Evangelicity and catholicity are essential for the future of the one church and promotion of Christian unity.

The *American Lutheran* had been linking these two concepts in one way or another for some years, but now Curtis provided a clear phrase and a cogent description.[40]

Curtis sketched out the meaning of the two terms—"catholicity" as the "sum total of actual Christian congregations, but also the mystical universality of the whole church"; "evangelicity" as "the central message of the gospel:—the redeeming power of God." While the Reformation is often considered a "violent and irrational defection from true catholicity" and "the ardent and truly biblical embrace of genuine evangelicity," this understanding must be challenged. Both concepts must be embraced, for "neither evangelicity nor catholicity is sufficient unto itself. In truth, there is no autonomous evangelicity or autonomous catholicity. There is only one, true, evangelical catholicity." For Lutherans and other descendants of the Reformers, he wrote, the term "Protestant" has a negative implication—the protest "against errors, evil, superstition, and spiritual oppression." But "a more appropriate name would certainly be that of 'Evangelical Catholics'—evangelical, because of the sole authority of the Bible as the supreme norm of Christian faith and theology, and catholic because Protestants are one branch of the one holy catholic church."[41]

As the *American Lutheran* prepared to give way to *Lutheran Forum*, this admonition to understand Lutherans as "evangelical catholics" foretold the direction that the ALPB would be moving over the next decade. Editor Tietjen's final editorial lauded his successor, Glenn Stone, as "a deeply confessional Lutheran, an evangelical Christian, an ecumenical and catholic churchman." He expressed his joy and confidence that "the magazine is in good hands."[42]

Notes

1. "Nine Brave Men in Birmingham," *AL* 46, no. 12 (Dec. 1963), 4-5.
2. "Lutherans and the Selma Struggle," *AL* 48, no. 4 (Apr. 1965), 4.
3. Ibid.
4. Ibid.; "Alabama 'Think Session' on Race Relations," *AL* 48, no. 7 (July 1965), 3.
5. "What About Demonstrations?" *AL* 48, no. 5 (May 1965), 7-8.
6. Arthur Carl Piepkorn, "The Lutheran's Image of the Jew," *AL* 47, no. 7 (July 1964), 16-19.
7. "The Jewish Question," *AL* 49, no. 2 (Feb. 1966), 5.
8. "Christian Beliefs and Anti-Semitism," *AL* 49, no. 7 (July 1966), 4.
9. Ralph L. Moellering, "The Christian Responsibility Toward the Threat of World Communism," *AL* 45, no. 3 (Mar. 1962), 7ff.
10. S. Schuller, "Family Life," *AL* 45, no. 6 (June 1962), 6ff. The article's author is listed as S. Schuller, "Associate Professor in the Department of Practical Theology at Concordia Seminary." Very likely the author's name was misprinted; almost certainly it was David S. Schuller, to whom the description seems to apply.
11. "Moral Issues in the Presidential Election," *AL* 47, no. 9 (Sept. 1964), 5.
12. "The Presidential Election," *AL* 47, no. 10 (Oct. 1964), 4.
13. "The Walther League's Profile in Courage," *AL* 48, no. 5 (May 1965), 7.
14. "The Role of Women in the Church," *AL* 49, no. 1 (Jan. 1966), 5.
15. Catherine W. Herzel, "Women and the Church," *AL* 49, no. 1 (Jan. 1966), 6ff.
16. Robert E. Huldschiner, "The Changing Look of Church Women," *AL* 49, no. 1 (Jan. 1966), 10ff.
17. Paul E. Jacobs, "Woman Suffrage and the Detroit Resolution," *AL* 49, no. 6 (July 1966), 10ff.
18. LaVonne Althouse, "Ordain Women?" *AL* 49, no. 10 (Oct. 1966), 22.

19. Glenn C. Stone, "The Sacrament of the Altar and The Church's Mission: Part I—The Nature of the Church," *AL* 45, no. 10 (Oct. 1962), 6.

20. Glenn C. Stone, "The Sacrament of the Altar and The Church's Mission: Part II—The Sacrament and the Church," *AL* 45, no. 11 (Nov. 1962), 12.

21. Ibid., 13, 15.

22. Ibid., 15-16.

23. Glenn C. Stone, "The Sacrament of the Altar and The Church's Mission: Part III—The Nature of the Church," *AL* 45, no. 10 (Oct. 1962), 6.

24. Melvin Kieschnick, "The Church Abroad: Sunday Night Confession," *AL* 47, no. 12 (Dec. 1964), 16ff.

25. "Communing at Lutheran Altars: When and By Whom?" *AL* 47, no. 12 (Dec. 1964), 5.

26. Ibid.

27. Lawrence E. Martin, "This Cup Is the New Testament," *AL* 48, no. 11 (Nov. 1965), 6-7.

28. Ibid., 7ff.

29. "Why Settle for Half a Service?" *AL* 49, no. 8 (Aug. 1966), 4.

30. "Congratulations to Our Publisher," *AL* 46, no. 6 (June 1963), 5.

31. "We Applaud and Commend," *AL* 48, no. 1 (Jan. 1965), 7.

32. Paul John Thielo, ed. *Christian Worship* (New York: ALPB, ca. 1965), 2.

33. O. A. Geiseman and F. Dean Lueking, *While It Is Day: A Geiseman Reader* (New York: ALPB, 1968).

34. "... And a New Managing Editor," *AL* 46, no. 3 (Mar. 1963), 5.

35. "To Our Readers—An Urgent Appeal," *AL* 49, no. 1 (Jan. 1966), 3-4.

36. Ibid., 4.

37. "Our Plea for Help," *AL* 49, no. 5 (May 1966), 5; "The Ink Is Black," *AL* 49, no. 7 (July 1966), 4.

38. "A Bold Step into the Future," *AL* 49, no. 11 (Nov. 1966), 5; "*Lutheran Forum* Is the Name; Meet the Editor," *AL* 49, no. 12 (Dec. 1966), 5.

39. Meyer, "Autobiography," 41; "That Man Thomas," *AL* 49, no. 12 (Dec. 1966), 15.

40. C. J. Curtis, "Evangelical Catholicity," *AL* 49, no. 11 (Nov. 1966), 12. The term "evangelical catholics" was not new in the 1960s; the usage apparently first arose among some German theologians in the 19th century, was later popularized by Swedish Archbishop Nathan Söderblom, and had appeared occasionally in American Lutheran writings earlier in the twentieth century.

41. Ibid., 22ff.

42. "*Lutheran Forum* Is the Name: Meet the Editor," *AL* 49, no. 12 (Dec. 1966), 5.

Henry P. Eckhardt, founding president of the ALPB. Image courtesy of Concordia Historical Institute, St. Louis, Missouri.

Julius F. E. Nickelsburg, longtime ALPB business manager. Image courtesy of Dr. George Nickelsburg.

First issue of the *American Lutheran,* January 1918. ALPB Archives.

The *Brooklyn Daily Eagle*, 13 Oct 1914, reports the permanent organizational meeting of the ALPB. Image courtesy of Newspapers.com.

The Glories of the Lutheran Church

By ARTHUR BRUNN

Has the Lutheran Church anything of which she can glory, not for the purpose of self-exaltation, but on the ground of which she can appeal to her members for staunch, self-sacrificing support? Has the Lutheran Church anything distinctively her own, anything worthy of the support and the loyal attachment of her members? Would it be a great loss to society, to the world, if the Lutheran Church would go down?

The great divisions in the visible church have often been deplored. Denominationalism has been condemned as hindering the outward growth of the church. The divisions in the Protestant Church particularly, are often described as growing out of narrow-minded bigotry, petty bickerings between theologians and preachers in which the common man has no interest. Forces are at work, and are hailed with great joy by many, which would cut down all denominational lines and create one union church, a League of Churches. The result of this tendency, already apparent, is the great indifference as to doctrinal values among the common people. The ease with which people today change their church membership from one denomination to another clearly shows, that there is no appreciation of doctrine.

If any denomination ceases to have any distinctive doctrine to which it adheres for conscience's sake, then that denomination has no right before God or man to exist. If it is not a matter of conscience, but only a matter of

THIS DO! HOW OFTEN?

A COMMUNION TRACT

"O sweet and loving word in the ear of a sinner, that thou, my Lord God, shouldst invite the poor and needy to the participation of thy most holy body and blood!"

"What meaneth this so gracious a condescension and this so loving invitation?"—Thomas a Kempis.

"If a person does not seek or desire the Lord's Supper at least some four times a year, it is to be feared that he despises the Sacrament and is not a Christian, just as he is not a Christian who refuses to believe or hear the Gospel." Thus writes Luther in his introduction to the Small Catechism. If Luther is right then it must be feared that a goodly number of people within our congregations despise the Sacrament and are no longer Christians. The records show that a congregation averaging even four communions per member for the year is rather the exception than the rule. Is Luther right? Should "some four times a year" be the very least a Christian partakes of Holy Communion? Or is once or twice sufficient?

The Lord has laid down no law prescribing just how often He wants His Christians to appear at His Table. All He commanded was: "This do in remembrance of me." "This do as oft as ye drink it in remembrance of me." He has commanded merely that it be done, that together with the consecrated bread and wine His body and His blood be received.

Two of the earliest ALPB tracts: Arthur Brunn's "The Glories of the Lutheran Church," ca. 1916; Fred Lindemann's communion tract, ca. 1920. ALPB Archives.

Two of the ALPB's "War Tracts" series, ca. 1917: William Schoenfield's "Lutherans and the War" and W. H. T. Dau's "Going Over?" ALPB Archives.

Lutherans and the War

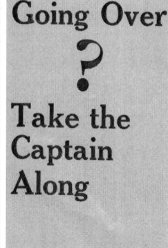

Going Over ?

Take the Captain Along

Published by the
AMERICAN LUTHERAN PUBLICITY BUREAU
234 East 62nd Street, N. Y. City
35c per 100 and postage

Paul Lindemann, first editor of the *American Lutheran*, 1918-1938.
Image courtesy of Concordia Historical Institute, St. Louis, Missouri.

Adolf F. Meyer, *American Lutheran* managing editor, 1938-1954, and then editor, 1954-1962. Image courtesy of William and Marie Meyer.

Editorial staff of the *American Lutheran*, ca. 1944.
Left to right, standing: Fred Lindemann, E. J. Friedrich, August W. Brustat, William F. Bruenning,
Arthur Brunn; *seated*, O. A. Geiseman, Adolf Meyer, O. P. Kretzmann. ALPB Archives.

August F. Bobzin, 1949;
ALPB president, 1931-1951.
ALPB Archives.

Fred H. Lindemann, longtime ALPB board
& *American Lutheran* editorial board member.
Image courtesy of Jim Lindemann.

J. F. E. Nickelsburg represents the ALPB at the 1947 LCMS Convention. ALPB Archives.

J. F. E. Nickelsburg and ALPB president John Kavasch, ca. 1958. ALPB Archives.

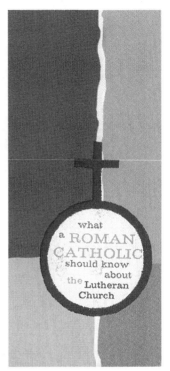

Materials offered by ALPB for its "Reformation Emphasis, 1950s and 1960s." ALPB Archives.

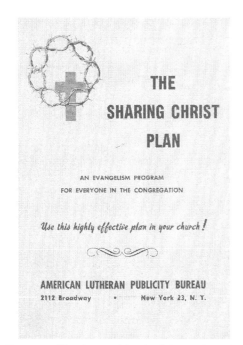

Promotional brochure and doorknob hanger from the "Sharing Christ Plan" in the 1950s. ALPB Archives.

The New Sharing Christ Plan Committee reviews materials for the 1960 campaign. *Left to right:* Fred Engelman, Paul John Thielo, John Kavasch, Theodore Wittrock, Rudolph P. F. Ressmeyer. ALPB Archives.

Theodore Wittrock,
ALPB executive secretary, 1948-1969.
Image courtesy of Concordia Historical
Institute, St. Louis, Missouri.

Glenn C. Stone, ALPB executive director,
1973-1986, and *Lutheran Forum* editor,
1965-1971 and 1972-1988.
Image courtesy of ELCA Archives.

Richard E. Koenig,
first editor of *Forum Letter*, 1972-1974.
Image courtesy of ELCA Archives.

Richard John Neuhaus,
Forum Letter editor, 1974-1990.
Image courtesy of ELCA Archives.

ALPB executive committee visits "headquarters" in Delhi, New York, 1993.
Left to right: Frederick J. Schumacher (executive director), Dorothy A. Zelenko (treasurer), Hans Quitmeyer (president), and James Corgee (vice president). ALPB Archives.

Donna K. Roche, ALPB office manager, and Martin A. Christiansen, *Lutheran Forum* managing editor, look at a *Lutheran Forum* issue, 1993. ALPB Archives.

Paul R. Hinlicky, *Lutheran Forum* editor,
1988-1993, and ALPB executive director,
1989-1993. Image courtesy of ELCA Archives.

Russell E. Saltzman, *Forum Letter* editor,
1990-2009. Image courtesy ELCA Archives.

Leonard R. Klein, *Lutheran Forum*
editor, 1993-1996. Image courtesy
of Dorothy A. Zelenko.

Ronald B. Bagnall, *Lutheran Forum*
editor, 1996-2006. Image courtesy
of Dorothy A. Zelenko.

Dorothy A. Zelenko supervising the mailing of the first volume of *For All the Saints*
at St. Matthew's Lutheran Church, White Plains, New York, 1994.
Image courtesy of Frederick J. Schumacher.

ALPB board of directors and staff, 1993. *Standing, left to right:* Paul R. Hinlicky, Donna K. Roche,
Robert Wollenburg, Phillip Max Johnson, Leonard R. Klein, Lois Bowman-Hines,
William Weicher, Theodore Wittrock, Martin A. Christiansen, Frederick J. Schumacher.
Seated, left to right: Ruth Zerner, Glenn C. Stone, Dorothy A. Zelenko, Hans Quitmeyer,
James Corgee, Connie Seddon. ALPB Archives.

Frederick J. Schumacher presents a gift of appreciation to Dorothy A. Zelenko, 1997. ALPB Archives.

Three *Forum Letter* editors, 2009: *Left to right:* Richard John Neuhaus, Richard O. Johnson and Russell E. Saltzman. ALPB Archives.

The two final ALPB tract series. The "Lutheran Identity" series, released in 1994, consisted
of five tracts written by Christa Klein, Glenn C. Stone, Phillip Max Johnson and Eric Gritsch.
The "Christian Sexual Morality" series included ten tracts written by Phillip Max Johnson
and Rebecca Frey, published in 1998 and 2000. ALPB Archives.

Lutheran Forum issue for Lent, 1980,
promoting the *Forum*/Graymoor proposal
for closer Lutheran/Roman Catholic relations.
ALPB Archives.

Lutheran Forum issue for Reformation, 2007,
first issue by Sarah Hinlicky Wilson.
ALPB Archives.

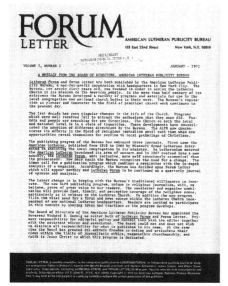

Initial issue of *Forum Letter*, January 1972.
ALPB Archives.

Forum Letter, January 2011.
ALPB Archives.

Sarah Hinlicky Wilson,
editor of *Lutheran Forum*, 2009-present.
Image courtesy of Sarah Hinlicky Wilson.

Paul R. Sauer,
ALPB executive director, 2015-present.
Image courtesy of Paul R. Sauer.

John R. Hannah, ALPB president 2005-
present. Image courtesy of John R. Hannah.

ALPB Centennial bronze medal:
"What Would Luther Do? Today!"
Image courtesy of Frederick J. Schumacher.

Chapter 15

New Occasions, New Duties

T he 1960s were a time of great change for American Lutheranism. A series of mergers over several decades had resulted in the consolidation of most Lutherans into three bodies: the American Lutheran Church, the Lutheran Church in America, and the Lutheran Church—Missouri Synod. Efforts toward further unity had led to the formation of the Lutheran Council in the USA, inaugurated January 1, 1967, with all three of these taking part. There was great optimism that the more comprehensive Lutheran unity long advocated by the ALPB was emerging. But was there still a role for the Bureau in these new circumstances?

The founding of *Lutheran Forum*
"the ALPB ran out of mission"

With the new configuration of American Lutheranism, the ALPB began to consider just what its mission in the last third of the 20th century might be. Many of the Bureau's original programs in the areas of public relations, stewardship and evangelism had been adopted over the years by the Missouri Synod itself. Some wondered about the continued need for the *American Lutheran*. It had focused heavily on the goal of Lutheran union, and now that objective seemed on the verge of attainment. In a 1978 interview, John Tietjen recalled the Bureau's wrestling with its future:

> And then ... the ALPB ran out of mission. ... I remember attending a lot of meetings of the ALPB board, in which we simply asked the question of purpose. What are we here for? We tried all sorts of things to justify our existence. ... But the ALPB was in search of a mission and finally came to a proper conclusion, that the mission that it had left was the publication of a journal, a journal of opinion, which was so very necessary within the Missouri Synod. What we decided to do was to broaden that to make it all Lutheran, make it pan-Lutheran.

Tietjen wondered whether the board would have made the same decision had they known how things were going to develop in Missouri, with "the emergence of a group that was to lead the Missouri Synod back to isolation." But that was hindsight; in 1966, the board decided to refocus the ALPB's identity, transforming it from an independent voice within the LCMS to an independent voice within the broader Lutheran community. Other aspects of the Bureau's ministry would continue, but the publication of a "journal of opinion" soon became its primary mission.[1]

It was quickly agreed that the *American Lutheran* should cease publication and a new magazine take its place. There were three factors at work here. One was Tietjen's resignation as editor of the *American Lutheran* to take a public relations post in the new LCUSA—a position he believed was offered him because of his visibility at the *American Lutheran*. The Bureau thus faced the very practical need to think about new staff.

Secondly, the *National Lutheran*, magazine of the NLC, would cease publication when the Council went out of existence at the end of 1966. There had been discussion months earlier about a merger of the *National Lutheran* and the *American Lutheran,* but it had not panned out. There was strong feeling in favor of continuing an independent publication. An unsigned and undated memo in the ALPB files made the argument:

> The future holds so much of promise and challenge for the Lutheran Church that it is difficult to imagine that the next period of her life in America can be adequately served without a publication which plays the kind of part that these two extra-synodical publications have played. It is our concern for the ongoing shape of Lutheran unity and the practical cooperation based on it which leads us to propose a new publication which shall in some sense succeed these two independent voices within the Lutheran Church of the United States. ... We believe there is a need for a magazine that will speak for the Lutheranism that is coming to be; that can be, God willing, but has not yet emerged. Indeed, there is need for a publication to speak for the Lutheran Church—unhyphenated—that already exists.[2]

Minutes of the ALPB board are missing from this period, so the precise sequence of events is unclear; but by September 1966, the decision had been made to appoint

Glenn Stone, editor of the *National Lutheran*, to edit the yet unnamed successor to the *American Lutheran*—and that suggests the third factor: the board's decision to broaden the ALPB constituency beyond the Missouri Synod. Stone was an LCA pastor, formerly of the Augustana Synod, and his appointment as editor reflected the board's commitment to become a truly "inter-Lutheran" independent ministry, unaffiliated with any of the church bodies but serving them all. Minutes do exist from a meeting September 27, 1966, of a group "to plan for new publication." Present were Stone, Tietjen, Wittrock, Ruth Taylor (advertising director for the *American Lutheran*), and Pr. James Lokken (recently hired by the ALPB as editorial assistant). These minutes note that Stone, "as of January 1, 1967, will be the editor of the successor publication to the AMERICAN LUTHERAN."[3]

Most of the conversation at this meeting focused on the mundane matters of promotion, advertising, and budget. Stone read a draft of a statement of purpose (perhaps the undated and unsigned memo cited above). Whoever was taking minutes at this meeting summarized:

> There was general agreement concerning the objectives and purposes for this indepen-
> dent Lutheran journal: that it should attempt to interpret and promote cooperative
> Lutheran activity and to speak for all Lutheranism to other Christians; that it could
> provide the neutral ground on which all Lutherans could meet journalistically and
> be of service to congregations and their leaders by sharing ideas for the nurture of
> the faith and life of the church.[4]

They agreed that the magazine should have a "new format that would reinforce the idea that this will be a completely new magazine, and free the editor from any previously established pattern." They also agreed that the publication should have a new name, and by the end of October, the new publication was being called *Lutheran Forum*. Stone indicated that none of the regular columns in the *American Lutheran* would be carried over, but he planned to retain the four current editorial associates (Richard Koenig, Arthur Carl Piepkorn, Dean Lueking, and Norman Temme) and to recruit an advisory board of 12 to 20 members.[5]

Plans for the new publication proceeded with remarkable speed. While *Lutheran Forum* was not a formal merger of *American Lutheran* and *National Lutheran*, in the latter publication's final issue John Tietjen commended the new magazine to readers:

> By selecting Pastor Stone as editor the ALPB expresses the intention of continuing
> the interests and concerns of both the *American Lutheran* and The NATIONAL
> LUTHERAN—and hopefully also the present subscribers to both publications—in
> a completely new magazine. Because of the new Lutheran Council there is need for a
> journal that will address itself not primarily to the work of a single Lutheran Church
> but to all of Lutheranism in America. There is need for an independent journal that
> will speak responsibly and critically concerning the programs and policies of the

new Council and of its participating churches. *Lutheran Forum* intends to be such a journal. ... I hope that you will take advantage of this opportunity to become a charter subscriber.[6]

Unfortunately, subscribers to the *National Lutheran* did not jump on the band-wagon as enthusiastically as Tietjen had hoped. *Lutheran Forum* began its publication with a reported subscription list of 7,400—considerably more than the *American Lutheran*'s 5,076 in 1966, and yet the *National Lutheran* had boasted a subscriber base of nearly 15,000. There was a slight increase in the number of subscribers the next year, but then over the next few years the number would decline to around 5,000 and stay at that level for several years. As an inter-Lutheran publication, it was reaching a much smaller percentage of potential readers than had the LCMS-oriented *American Lutheran*. A 1972 analysis would show that 48% of *Lutheran Forum*'s readers were in the Missouri Synod—by far the largest segment of the readership. Progress was slow in expanding the base to the other Lutheran bodies.

The publication began with a somewhat different staff configuration than Stone had projected in September. Stone was the editor, and James A. Lokken was editorial assistant. Lokken had been serving an ALC parish in South Dakota when he came on board at ALPB in late 1966 to help launch *Lutheran Forum*. He and Stone were the only paid editorial staff. There were five editorial associates—four of them Missouri Synod pastors. Richard E. Koenig had a sterling LCMS pedigree, and he was serving on the ALPB board of directors. Dean Lueking, like Koenig, had been an editorial associate of the *American Lutheran* under Tietjen. Norman L. Temme had been direc-tor of public relations for the LCMS in New York until 1966; he now was working in a similar capacity with the American Bible Society and serving as associate pastor at Village Lutheran Church, Bronxville, NY. John H. Tietjen was now head of commu-nications for LCUSA. The one non-Missourian in this group was Philip A. Johnson, an LCA pastor who had served for several years as public relations director for the NLC; earlier in his ministry, as pastor of Salem Lutheran Church in Chicago, he had spearheaded efforts to integrate a racially tense section of Chicago's South side. There were also 16 contributing editors listed on the masthead. ALPB executive secretary Theodore Wittrock served as business manager for *Lutheran Forum*, and Ruth Taylor managed the advertising.

Stone's editorial in the inaugural issue of *Lutheran Forum* laid out both the history and the intended future:

> [*Lutheran Forum*'s] stage is set by the disappearance of two publications which had largely fulfilled their reasons for being. The stage of development in the Church's life of which *The National Lutheran* was a primary journalistic interpreter has been superseded: the half century of the National Lutheran Council is over. The magazine which carried its banner ended with it.

The circumstances calling for the death of *The American Lutheran* were not quite so clear-cut. Yet many sensed that it had also come to a critical turning point. Its very name proclaimed it a harbinger of the 'Americanization' of the Lutheran Church. Born during a World War which hastened the day of that cultural acclimatization, it maintained a prophetic voice within the church body it primarily served, calling for a creative application of the Lutheran tradition to the realities of the new society into which this Church had been transplanted. But its task too had been largely fulfilled. Its Church had 'bought' much of that for which it stood. ...

LUTHERAN FORUM appears because of new factors on the Lutheran scene. This is a time of new breakthroughs in Lutheran cooperation. The dead-end roads of a century of inter-church relationships appear to have been largely bypassed; yet Lutheran unity has not yet achieved full expression. ...

Its name is descriptive of the kind of role LUTHERAN FORUM seeks to play. This magazine recognizes the variety within Lutheranism and seeks to reflect that richness of life; it recognizes also the uniting foundations, the common ground which makes discussion possible and the existence of tensions fruitful. ...

This does not mean that LUTHERAN FORUM itself has no unique point of view. It has a vision of the Church, its nature and its role in our time which in fact shapes what this magazine is and will become. ...

Perhaps the one word that best characterizes our vision is *wholeness*, a quality we seek to encourage in Lutheran life, in self-understanding as well as in mission and service. We seek to foster a national and international concept of the Lutheran Church in a spirit of comprehensive catholicity. ...

We want to serve as an independent, responsibly critical voice in comment upon the policies and programs of the Church; to interpret its life with insight and interest; to provide a common ground upon which all Lutherans may meet, in order to exchange ideas, air issues and promote consensus; to speak from a Lutheran standpoint to other Christians and those outside the Church in many areas where our Church's voice should be heart, and to provide a means whereby Lutherans may be helped to listen creatively to others.[7]

But "responsibly critical voices" generally stir things up, and *Lutheran Forum* wasted no time on that score. Stone's introductory editorial was followed immediately by another which criticized the direction of the intersynodical committee planning for the 450th anniversary of the Reformation. The committee's proposals, he wrote, don't go much beyond pageants and projects. Modern Lutherans want to follow the Reformers who "joyfully trumpeted the Gospel with the exciting relevance" for "their own time, but end up by making the Reformation a list of congregational 'projects.'" Instead, he continued, Lutherans should work on two goals: "a mighty clamor from congregations, conferences and councils for the declaration of pulpit and altar fellowship" and "appropriate initiative toward transferring additional areas of work to the Lutheran Council in the U.S.A." The editorial got the immediate attention of the wider Lutheran world; LCUSA's news service issued a press release headlined, "New 'Lutheran Forum' Critical of Reformation Observances."[8]

The first issues demonstrated the scope of Stone's interests. *Lutheran Forum* pondered the future of Lutheranism, with essays by William Lazareth (then academic dean at the LCA's Lutheran Theological Seminary at Philadelphia), Jerald Brauer (University of Chicago historian), and John Tietjen. Subsequent issues discussed Lutheranism in Australia, the arms race, the churches and the civil rights movement, 19th century Lutheran attitudes toward slavery, anti-Semitism in the church. A California pastor wrote a heart-wrenching reflection on why he was considering demitting the ministry. An art professor wrote about "controversial crucifixions." *Lutheran Forum* offered a remarkable potpourri of articles about dozens of different subjects.

One regular feature was the "Editor's Ambo," and Stone's editorial homilies were also diverse. He lamented the divided state of Lutheranism on the eve of the 450th anniversary of the Reformation. He urged the Lutheran World Federation to take the lead in the resettlement of Palestinian refugees. He approved of Lutheran dialogue with other churches but noted that it must move from discussion to action. He called for immediate negotiations to end the war in Vietnam and promised that *Lutheran Forum* would be "dealing increasingly with the issue of peace." He advocated, as an ecumenical gesture toward the Orthodox, that the *filioque* clause—that ancient cause of controversy and division between Eastern and Western Christianity—be deleted from the Nicene Creed in forthcoming Lutheran liturgical materials. *Lutheran Forum* editorials, like those in the *American Lutheran*, discussed controversial issues in church and society, and they did so forthrightly and often courageously.[9]

Controversy could be expected each month from Richard John Neuhaus, whose regular column in *Lutheran Forum* usually discussed political or social issues. Originally unnamed, the column soon was called simply "Neuhaus," and then in 1970 became "A Voice in the Church." Stone told Neuhaus that he thought such a name "would be more descriptive of [the column's] role in the FORUM." His explanation seems to suggest that Neuhaus himself was evidence that there are a variety of opinions in the church, and that *Lutheran Forum* was committed to airing diverse voices (and perhaps, at least subliminally, Neuhaus was being compared to a certain New Testament character described as "a voice in the wilderness").[10]

The concept of giving voice to different opinions was an important part of Stone's vision for *Lutheran Forum*. Each issue included a section called "Open Forum"—generally letters to the editor in response to articles, but Stone gave individual writers somewhat more space than is often typical for such features.

A regular part of *Lutheran Forum* for several years was a last page column entitled "On the Way to the Forum" and written by Eric Modean, head of the news bureau of the NLC and then LCUSA. Writing under the pseudonym "Moses Dean," Modean acknowledged that the lofty statement of purpose of the magazine would not reflect the editorial position of his column. "On the Way" would be dedicated instead to "facts, fancies and foibles." With apologies to Stephen Decatur, the author declared: "Our opinion! May it always be in the right; but our opinion, right or wrong!" Those opinions were not particularly momentous, but they provided a light and humorous commentary on a wide range of topics. ("And then there's the story about the cannibal chief standing alongside a steaming cauldron and complaining to the chef: 'Have you noticed that since the ecumenical movement began, all missionaries taste alike?'") "On the Way to the Forum" was taken over in January 1969 by James Lokken, who used the pseudonym "Klokker" and continued the humorous patter.[11]

A voice for students

"student thinking can be communicated to the church"

In the 1960s, a student movement was emerging on campuses across the United States. Among Lutheran students, conversations were underway between the Lutheran Student Association of America (LSAA), which included students from the ALC and the LCA, and the LCMS's Gamma Delta. The two would merge in 1969 to become the Lutheran Student Movement USA. LSAA's magazine *Frontiers* had folded in 1966 because of financial problems, and the two student groups had appointed a joint committee to consider publication alternatives.

Almost as soon as *Lutheran Forum* began, LSAA president Richard Magnus approached the ALPB about the magazine becoming a voice for campus concerns. After some months of conversation, both student organizations voted to establish a relationship with *Lutheran Forum*. The student groups would "recognize" *Lutheran Forum* and recommend it to their members; in return, *Lutheran Forum* would add to the editorial board two students, one from each organization. The journal would encourage submissions from the campus community. A special student subscription rate would be offered; the promotional work would be done by *Lutheran Forum* but funded with contributions from LSAA and Gamma Delta. With those parameters agreed upon, the relationship was approved and announced. Stone was quoted in a LCUSA news release:

> It is recognized that the kinds of issues we are interested in [at *Lutheran Forum*] are also those that affect the Lutheran student community, both as churchmen and as students. The Forum will provide a means whereby student thinking can be communicated to the church-at-large, and by which wider Lutheran thinking on important ecclesiastical and moral issues can be shared by the student community.

Gregory Shaffer, a student at Amherst College in Amherst, MA, was appointed by LSAA to sit on the *Lutheran Forum* editorial board, and Pamela Schmidt, a student at the University of Colorado, Boulder, was named to represent Gamma Delta.[12]

The February 1968 issue of *Lutheran Forum* included a brief editorial note, "Welcome, students!" The new arrangement, it explained, was "based on the assumption that the issues that engage all thinking Lutherans largely overlap those which are of importance to Lutherans on college and university campuses." The editor promised that occasional issues of *Lutheran Forum* would "include much campus-oriented material," but that every number "will continue to focus on concerns pertinent to every Lutheran—on or off campus." Well into the 1970s, *Lutheran Forum* would dedicate one issue a year to an emphasis on higher education.[13]

Fire!

"some extra hot items"

In the pre-dawn hours of February 13, 1968, a fire broke out in the Park Avenue South building where the ALPB's offices were housed. Its origin was never determined, but it did significant damage both to the ALPB and the adjacent offices of Lutheran World Relief. The most serious loss was in the area where the Bureau stored its tracts and other materials; some 98% of the inventory was destroyed. Also lost were dozens of orders of Lenten resources that were packaged and ready to ship, and because the records of those orders were also destroyed, the ALPB had no way of notifying its customers of the disaster. The Bureau office itself also suffered significant smoke and water damage.

The next issue of *Lutheran Forum* tried to put the best construction on the tragedy, announcing that on that February morning the ALPB "had some extra hot items in its stock and shipping room." The most important effect of the fire was to eliminate, at least for the present, the tract ministry that had been such a significant part of the ALPB's program for decades. In retrospect, that was perhaps not such a terrible thing. Years later Glenn Stone would note that tracts were really in decline as a means of communication; in any event, church publishing houses had long been offering a tract ministry that had rendered the ALPB's program superfluous. The fire thus had the result of helping the Bureau focus even more clearly on its journalistic ministry; fortunately, the fire did not destroy subscription records and other materials related to *Lutheran Forum*, and "with only minor interruption" the magazine continued its operation. There soon appeared another silver lining to the disastrous fire: the insurance settlement had the salutary effect of stabilizing, at least for the moment, the ALPB's budget.[14]

There were changes in the personnel of the ALPB during this period. Fred Engelman, president since 1964, stepped down in 1969. Ted Wittrock, who had served as executive secretary of the Bureau since 1948, resigned that same year to accept a call to Redeemer Lutheran Church in the Bronx; he was promptly elected to the ALPB board and succeeded Engelman as president. Three years later Wittrock was followed by John H. Leonard, an advertising executive and active layman at St. Mark's Lutheran Church in Yonkers, NY, where Adolf Meyer had been longtime pastor.

ALPB and the Missouri wars

"they have politicized theological discussion"

As the ALPB turned in a self-consciously inter-Lutheran direction, the Lutheran Church—Missouri Synod was entering a period of great contention, even convulsion. Through the early 1960s, Missouri had cautiously begun warmer relationships with other Lutherans—a goal which the ALPB had long advocated. The LCMS had not only joined LCUSA, it was moving toward sharing altar and pulpit fellowship with the American Lutheran Church.

But a burgeoning conservative reaction was showing its strength as the 1969 convention in Denver approached. Many feared that one casualty would be the movement toward unity with the ALC. Over the next decade, the growing conflict in the LCMS would be the most dramatic story in American Lutheranism, dividing congregations and families and ultimately leading to a significant exodus of pastors and congregations from the Synod. It was not unexpected, then, that the ALPB and its publications would have to grapple with the unfolding crisis.

Neuhaus's column in July 1968 called it "the testing of Missouri." Since the 1967 convention, he mused, "warning signals have multiplied. ... At almost every level of its life, the Synod is permeated by the smell of fear. As one synodical official says privately, 'We're all running scared.'" Neuhaus tied the Missouri conflict to the general cultural situation:

> In the Church as in the nation, insecurity cries out for law and order, even if control must be purchased at the price of sacrificing the values by which we profess to live. If official Missouri smells of fear, the ranks of the right detect the sweet smell of success. ... The chosen weapons are suspicion of 'those other' Lutherans and fear of change.[15]

Editor Stone took a less apocalyptic stance in January 1969. He recalled that *Lutheran Forum* had urged Missouri to approve fellowship with ALC in 1967, fearing that if the proposal were postponed, "the interval would be used by an archly reactionary clique within the synod to bring about its defeat." Stone regretted that his prediction had come true, and now "reports from reliable sources indicate that the [conservative opponents of fellowship] will attempt to assume control of the synod at Denver by electing candidates meeting its approval and carrying out a thorough purge of what it considers 'liberals.'" Stone feared that many in the Synod might just decide that approving fellowship with the ALC simply wouldn't be worth the internal fight.[16]

In the June 1969 issue, the last before the Denver convention, Stone pled again for approval of the fellowship agreement, as did O. P. Kretzmann, now chancellor of Valparaiso University, and ALC vice president David Preus. Stone argued that the debate on fellowship would be the most important matter in Denver. Neuhaus was not sanguine about the outcome:

> Those who style themselves the conservatives of 'old Missouri' charge that synodical leadership is less than honest in denying that there have been significant changes in synodical teaching and practice. There is truth in the charge. Those who are most angry, however, are largely responsible for the sorry state of theological exchange in Missouri. They have politicized theological discussion by establishing benchmarks of orthodoxy by which everyone is to be rated on a spectrum ranging from conservative to radical. The name of the game is labeling rather than listening, categorizing rather than understanding, purging rather than persuading. This is the same strategy used by fundamentalists in other American churches to force quarrels and divisions a half century and more past.

As it happened, the Denver delegates did approve the fellowship proposal; but far more significant in the long run was the defeat of LCMS president Oliver Harms, who had led the Synod in new directions, and the election of Dr. J. A. O. Preus, president of Concordia Theological Seminary in Springfield, IL, candidate of the conservatives. The ALC fellowship proposal was adopted despite Preus's opposition, but it was apparent that the Missouri Synod's movement toward closer relations with other Lutherans was about to be slowed—and, many feared, reversed.[17]

Lutheran Forum's coverage of the Denver convention was written by Richard Koenig. He had been a delegate to the convention, and he described the defeat of Harms by Preus as "two of the darkest days I have spent as a minister of the Lutheran Church—Missouri Synod."

> The emotion that gripped many of us was simple fear—not for ourselves but for the church body we love and the many great Christians who serve in it. The fear was, first, that the direction followed by the Synod since World War II toward a richer evangelicalism, a beginning ecumenism, the support of responsible freedom for Christian scholars and a ministry to the whole man in a world of sudden social change would be halted and reversed. Secondly, there was the darker fear that those who elected Preus in order to see heads roll would be granted their wish.[18]

Koenig praised many of the other actions of the convention—approval of ALC fellowship, rejection of a resolution to withdraw from LCUSA, granting of congregational voting rights for women. He suggested that these more "progressive" actions represented the real feelings of the convention delegates; the defeat of President Harms, he said, was the result of "scare tactics and character assassination." "If the presidential election had been held on Wednesday [i.e., later in the week], there is no doubt that President Harms would have won by a two-to-one majority."[19]

Still, Koenig was open to being surprised. "If movements toward reconciliation and progress are forthcoming, Missouri under Preus will unite to give its best to Lutheranism and the world." For now, Koenig urged, "let us pray ... [that Preus] will lead his synod into new and fruitful paths." Koenig's cautious optimism was echoed by Stone. While "Missouri's waters" may be muddy, Stone wrote, that is "perhaps not an unmixed curse."

> The mud of the great river is finally deposited in the delta where it builds some of earth's most fertile soil. The variety within an essential confessional unity that is Lutheranism can yet congeal into a wholeness in which the Gospel can grow and bring forth fruit a hundredfold.[20]

But within a few months, *Lutheran Forum* was singing a different tune. President Preus claims things are settling down, Stone editorialized in December, but "the evidence indicates otherwise."

> Those who led a partly-successful *putsch* of the previous administration and who are completely unreconciled to Christian fellowship with brother Lutherans in the American Lutheran Church, having had a taste of blood, already appear to be sharpening their weapons for further ritual sacrifices. On their list, it appears, are those district presidents who support fellowship and otherwise stand for a more evangelical church body. Certain of them have already had the dubious honor of having their pictures published and their 'sins' catalogued in print.

Stone catalogued several other attempts to oust various officials, some successful, as well as Preus's refusal to reappoint others whose terms were up. This policy of what Preus himself had called "head chopping" "can only lead to increased fear, suspicion and polarization in the LC-MS."[21]

Not much was said about the Missouri situation over the next year as *Lutheran Forum* focused on other matters. But in March 1971, Neuhaus wrote a column entitled "Missouri's gift" which really stirred the pot. He admitted that he had "never believed the Missouri Synod to be 'the true visible Church on earth,' as my father believed and his father before him." Nevertheless, he had valued Missouri as "one of the few church bodies left where theological debate is possible, where theology is not denigrated as an indulgence of idle academics." He lamented that the Synod had long been "in theological captivity to Franz Pieper and in institutional captivity to the activist boosters of the religious prosperity of the 1950s." For some of this he blamed former president Oliver Harms:

> Oliver Harms is, I believe, a good and honorable man with engaging personal qualities, but his presidency must be judged a failure in important respects. His critics were right: he did ignore the seriousness of disagreements within the synod; efficiency was more important than direction; troubling questions were evaded; the tone was that of an uncertain trumpet.[22]

Neuhaus had hoped that Preus might revive "serious theological reflection," but that did not appear to be happening. "Nothing is definite until all the returns are in," he wrote, "but to date the returns continue to be depressing."

> Preus calls for calm, says we should not air our family quarrels in public, and then turns to the secular press to sow vicious suspicions about the Lutheran loyalty of his critics. He has invoked the darker side of the synod's life; called forth from the deep every ancient grudge, revived the smart of almost forgotten resentments. ... Preus now has the zealous support of the nest of vipers who produce *Christian News*.[23]

Neuhaus then turned his attention to a "fact-finding committee" which had recently been appointed to investigate charges of doctrinal deviation among the faculty at Concordia Seminary. Preus, he wrote, "has unleashed his sleuths. ... Faculty members are encouraged to inform on their absent colleagues who are then confronted with charges from anonymous sources."

> The faculty submits to the investigation only 'under protest,' but it submits. There is talk about who might have to go, about how much blood is required to slake the thirst of the Inquisition. Perhaps it is expedient that one man (maybe two, maybe three) should go for the sake of the school. ... From a faculty of 50, Preus has split off his support group of five. They are a strange mixture of incompetence, sycophancy, emotional instability.[24]

Neuhaus had toned down the column prior to its publication, following a heated meeting with Stone, Koenig, and Lueking. The argument revolved around questions of strategy, with Koenig and Lueking concerned that Neuhaus's strident language would make matters worse. A few days after this conversation, Neuhaus wrote to Koenig, with copies to the others:

> I hope you will be pleased by the substantial difference in tone as a result of some changes. I am indebted to you and Dean for taking the piece so seriously and pointing out possible improvements. At the same time, I have no doubt you might still dissent from some of the statements in the revised column, and I am equally sure that this is attributable to an honorable difference in our judgments both about what is happening in the Synod and about the best way to address the current problems we face in common.

> I believe it important that we publicly evidence among ourselves that evangelical openness to dissent that we advocate for the rest of the church. ...

> Threats to cut off personal relations over disagreements of judgment or suggestions that the Forum should not publish views disagreeable to those whose devotion make the Forum possible, should be odious to us. I am confident that in a more reflective moment we would all be of one mind on this.[25]

The article "prompted an unusually vigorous response"—much of it positive, but some quite angry. Stone received a furious letter from Martin Scharlemann, one of the faculty minority at Concordia Seminary who supported the Preus investigation. "Any journal that is willing to print a scurrilous article such as Neuhaus' 'Missouri's Gift' is not welcome in either my home or my office. The irresponsibility ... is really quite beyond belief." Stone, who always tried to respond graciously to his critics, replied a few days later:

> Your chagrin over the Neuhaus article in the March issue is naturally understandable. Frankly, I was quite unhappy with it for several reasons myself. Nevertheless, I do not conceive of myself as a censor of Neuhaus's opinions—or those of any other writer in the FORUM.
>
> Far less understandable is your decision to cancel. ... Neuhaus' column is provocative, expressing strong opinions, stepping on toes from time to time. ... Am I to believe that you were willing to get a magazine which printed Neuhaus' column when other toes were being pinched, but were moved to cancel only when yours were injured? Furthermore, am I to believe that the presence of Neuhaus cancels out for you all the other material which is printed in the FORUM, and which has induced you to remain a subscriber for several years? Is that not to give much too much credit and weight to Richard John Neuhaus?

Scharlemann responded quite snippily, "Dear Stone: ... To read [your letter] is to be confirmed in the conclusion of the ethical sogginess that pervades your decisions. ... It will be a relief to live without Lutheran Forum. "[26]

Some of the negative response came from unanticipated quarters. John Tietjen wrote to "object to the statements [about the minority faculty] as unworthy of the journal because they are intemperate and judgmental in their description of brothers in the faith." Neuhaus responded personally, saying that he understood the letter reflected Tietjen's responsibilities as president of the seminary, but he stood by the column as "legitimate journalistic comment."[27]

Stone's response to Tietjen was longer. Like Neuhaus, he recognized Tietjen's responsibility as president to support his faculty—even those with whom he might disagree. But he defended Neuhaus's column—both its accuracy and its publication in *Lutheran Forum*:

> Whether Richard's charges are warranted or not is a difficult matter to prove, since it is essentially a matter of his personal reactions to the men alluded to. For myself, a recent experience in trying to communicate with one of the five referred to in Richard's article [apparently Scharlemann] lends credence in my mind to the term 'emotionally unstable' if used with reference to that person. ...
>
> I am, frankly, less sure about your comments in your capacity as an editorial associate of the FORUM. ... [Our] magazine has never shrunk from controversy and from

attempting, within the limits of our resources, to expose all the factors in situations with which it has dealt. ... Obviously, you are very close to the situation ... but from where I sit Richard's estimate of the situation did not look like an unreasonable one.

Not long after this incident, Tietjen resigned as an editorial associate. In his 1978 interview, he noted that his continued association with *Lutheran Forum* "was causing me problems."[28]

The most ominous reaction came from J. A. O. Preus, who wrote directly to Neuhaus on May 12. While the comments about Oliver Harms "were in exceedingly poor taste," the comments about the five seminary professors "are in clear violation of the Eighth Commandment and of the law of love, to say nothing about synodical procedures." Preus asked "in brotherly love and out of concern for the fraternity which we have in Christ" that Neuhaus apologize individually to each person concerned, and publish the apology in *Lutheran Forum*.[29]

Neuhaus's response was acerbic:

I regret that you are unhappy with the column in the Forum, but your unhappiness is, of course, quite understandable. As you no doubt noticed, the burden of the column is critical of your presidential actions and only in passing is it critical of President Harms and the five professors. Your response also to the main argument would be of genuine interest.

Permit me to express my sincere appreciation of your solicitude for the reputations of members of the synod, and the hope that equal anxiety is demonstrated when other members including myself, are criticized from other quarters.

He enclosed a "clarification" he had written that would be published in the August/September issue. He also suggested, since Preus seemed to be impugning the integrity of his ministry, that Neuhaus's ecclesiastical supervisor, Atlantic District president Rudolph P. F. Ressmeyer (a long-time ALPB board member) be part of any continued conversation.[30]

In the response to be published, Neuhaus acknowledged that "some have suggested that my comments exceeded the bounds of propriety or even of Christian ethics." Noting that the "very nature of journalistic opinion [is] to provoke agreement and disagreement," he nonetheless offered "some clarification." First, he did not intend to attack former president Harms; he wished he had said Harms "minimized" rather than "ignored" the disagreements within the Synod. On the other hand, he found it striking that Preus would protest his comment about Harms when he had been among those "most instrumental in undermining President Harms' leadership and removing him from office, and now seem set on reversing the achievements of his administration." He admitted his description of the faculty minority at Concordia had been harsh, but he insisted that he made it "reluctantly, sadly and with love." Still, he admitted, "both content and style [of the column] reflect the imperfections of the author and

I am grateful for those who, in a spirit of constructive criticism, have provoked the above clarifications." [31]

Unsatisfied, Preus wrote again to Neuhaus on June 2. Apparently the president had a sense that this second letter may have been a little shrill, so he sat on it for several days, then asked his secretary to re-type a somewhat toned down version. The revision, dated June 23, was still blistering:

> I cannot judge your heart, but it appears to me that your recent letter to the Forum constitutes an explanation for why you said what you did and also adds a certain amount of insult to injury … but does not constitute an apology. …
>
> I must therefore reiterate my request to you that you make an apology. … You have broken the law of God. You have not only broken the Eighth Commandment but you have broken the spirit of the Scripture.[32]

But Neuhaus had already left on a three-month trip to Africa, and would not receive the letter until he returned in September. Preus had sent a copy of his letter to Ressmeyer, who telephoned Preus to inform him that Neuhaus was out of the country. He then wrote a lengthy private response to Preus. He began by noting that, as the Milwaukee convention of the LCMS approached, the whole Synod was praying "but we're probably not all praying for the same thing." His own prayers, Ressmeyer wrote, are that Preus "will be more open to those who dissent from your views." "You have a tendency to over-react (as you have freely admitted to me on several occasions)," Ressmeyer said. "I believe that you owe an apology to the now rather numerous brethren whom you have publicly opposed," including *Lutheran Forum*.[33]

Ressmeyer then tried to explain the purpose of *Lutheran Forum* and to defend the ministry of the ALPB:

> The very nature of <u>Lutheran Forum</u> invites legitimate controversy. Its function is to serve as an independent Lutheran forum for the exchange of ideas and the hearing of varying views on matters that affect all Lutherans in the U.S.A. You said to me over the phone that it shouldn't be messing in the internal affairs of the Missouri Synod. I don't quite understand that. Are our 'internal' affairs above scrutiny? That which affects the life and work of the whole Synod, as well as our fellow Lutherans in other synods, can hardly be called 'internal.' Are we so sure we're right that we don't want or need the criticism of our brothers?
>
> When I explained to you the role played by the Board of Directors of the American Lutheran Publicity Bureau in the publication of <u>Lutheran Forum</u>, your response was, 'That's a lousy way to run a journal.' Perhaps you're right. But I suppose it really depends on your viewpoint. I've been a member of the Board of Directors of the ALPB for sixteen years. What was true of the <u>American Lutheran</u> is also true of its successor, <u>Lutheran Forum</u>. The board merely sets the broad scope of the magazine and neither plans nor censors its contents. The editor determines editorial content,

writers, etc. Over the years it has contained both approval and disapproval of the positions taken by various people, groups, church bodies, and society as a whole. That's its function. It follows no 'party line.' It does not report news, as such, but is a journal of opinion. Of course it has an obligation as a Christian publication not to distort the views of those on whom it comments, but it has every right to disagree even with the church leaders. Of course it has an obligation to maintain the character and integrity of those with whom its writers disagree. The writers however have the privilege of speaking their minds and run the risk of rebuttal.

Noting that they had agreed to put off further conversation about Neuhaus until his return from Africa, Ressmeyer lamented "how difficult you make it for me to confront men like Neuhaus with fractures of the Eighth Commandment" when Preus himself had "made judgments in print" and questioned "the motives and integrity of many fine, loyal members of the Synod."[34]

When Neuhaus returned in September, he found a brief note from Preus, enclosing a copy of the June 23 letter and asking for a response within a week. Neuhaus sent it on to Ressmeyer, writing that he didn't know whether to interpret it "as simply intemperate language or as the bringing of grave charges" but that he thought it would best be handled through Ressmeyer's office. He sent a copy of this letter to Preus, along with a cover letter expressing "deep regret that yours of June 23 supplies no basis for personal dialogue through which misunderstandings may be resolved." Preus immediately responded:

> You apparently do not yet seem to realize the enormity of the wrong which you have committed. Do not have any question as to whether I am using 'simply intemperate language' or bringing 'grave charges.' I am bringing grave charges against you. ...
>
> Likewise, I think it is seemingly out of character for one who showed such great courage in writing articles for you now to take shelter beneath the wings of your district president.
>
> The matter is between you and me. You are herewith once more admonished to write a proper letter of apology, with copy to me, to the men involved, suitable for printing in the Lutheran Forum. I will give you one week from the receipt of this letter to do this or I will take up the matter with your district president in a thoroughly and completely official way.[35]

Neuhaus, likely with advice and counsel from Ressmeyer, made another stab at an apology. He wrote to Preus on October 9:

> With reference to your letter of October 5, please be assured that I deeply regret any personal hurt to you or others and any misunderstanding occasioned by my article. ... I am sorry for whatever may be untrue in my analysis of our synodical troubles and equally sorry for whatever may be true. ... Please be certain of my continued prayer that your leadership may yet be transformed into the healing ministry our

synod requires if we are to turn from internal squabbles toward the urgent mission of Christ's Church in our time.

This was certainly not the surrender that Preus had demanded; nonetheless, he responded graciously. "You have acted in a brotherly and Christian manner. ... Thank you for your prayers for our church."[36]

The apology, if it can be called that, was subsequently printed in the November *Lutheran Forum,* since "it concerns a matter which originally appeared in our pages." But it would be Neuhaus's last contribution for a while; in January there was a change in editors at *Lutheran Forum*, and without public explanation, Neuhaus's column was dropped. Probably Neuhaus himself asked to be relieved. There were many things going on in his personal life at that time, including the final illness of his father (who would die in February 1972). Clergy and Laity Concerned about Vietnam, an organization Neuhaus had co-founded and in which he had been a leader, was moving in a direction that Neuhuas opposed, and he felt, perhaps with some resentment, that he needed to step down from his leadership role. His final full column for *Lutheran Forum* was entitled "The loneliness of the long-distance radical," and it carried an undertone of weariness. He would return two years later as the controversial editor of ALPB's *Forum Letter.*[37]

Financial crisis

"entirely unrelated to the implied threats of the Preus letter"

Right at this time *Lutheran Forum* faced a new financial crisis. The ALPB had helped to support the magazine in its beginning by obtaining grants from the fraternal organization Lutheran Brotherhood. The grants had totaled $75,000 over four years, and had been gratefully acknowledged by Stone in the pages of *Lutheran Forum* (most recently in the April 1971 issue), though he had not published the amount. This came to the attention of J. A. O. Preus when he received a memorial approved by Redeemer Lutheran Church in Wayzata, MN, accusing Lutheran Brotherhood of supporting *Lutheran Forum*'s "politically biased and prejudiced propaganda."[38]

Preus was furious; his grandfather had been insurance commissioner for the state of Minnesota and one of the founders of the company that became Lutheran Brotherhood, and the president was outraged that the company was funding a publication that had been so critical of him. On June 18, 1971, Preus took up the issue in "Brother to Brother," a newsletter sent to all pastors and teachers in the Synod (and this particular issue was also sent to all lay delegates to the forthcoming convention). After expressing his sympathy for a couple of dissident conservative groups in the Synod (the Federation of Authentic Lutherans and the publisher of *Affirm*), Preus fulminated:

The March [*sic*] issue of the *Lutheran Forum* tells us that the Lutheran Brotherhood Insurance Company has made a generous contribution to the *Forum*. The *Forum* is published by the American Lutheran Publicity Bureau. Further information from the Lutheran Brotherhood indicates that this insurance company has given $75,000 to the *Lutheran Forum*. Recent articles in this journal have been so pejorative and have so tragically fractured the Eighth Commandment that your president himself felt it necessary to admonish one of our pastors who had written an article viciously attacking five of our seminary professors.

"This matter," Preus added ominously, "at the present time is in the hands of this man's District president." Preus soon received a concerned phone call from Lutheran Brotherhood's CEO, Arley Bjella. He noted that the grants had been made prior to Preus's election and insisted that he was completely unaware of the articles in question. Preus suggested that Bjella make a public statement disavowing the articles and making it clear that no further funds would be going to *Lutheran Forum*. Bjella wrote to Preus with the requested statement; it was duly publicized in Missouri Synod channels, and the matter was regarded as closed.[39]

But Stone received so many questions about Preus's allegation that he felt compelled to respond editorially. The grants from Lutheran Brotherhood, he explained, had been made because the organization believed in the value of an independent publication like *Lutheran Forum*. He admitted that *Lutheran Forum* had "both blamed and praised" various church presidents and others for one thing or another; but this was the first time a "prominent figure has ever sought to punish us by seeking a cutoff of our funding."

> As it happens, when the insurance society authorized its fourth grant to us late last year, we were informed that it would be the final such grant. This, we understand, is in line with Lutheran Brotherhood's usual policy to make grants only during the initial stages of a project. ... So our readers should be assured that the funding of the Brotherhood subsidy is entirely unrelated to the implied threats of the Preus letter.

Stone concluded by observing that "the ability of a church leader to communicate his views widely at church expense ... only underscores the need for independent publications in which less exalted churchmen may also have a say." Years later, he was still convinced that Preus had tried directly to stop any future funding of *Lutheran Forum* by Lutheran Brotherhood, though he did not think it was a factor in that funding coming to an end.[40]

The loss of Lutheran Brotherhood support left the ALPB's magazine in a real financial bind, and the editorial board of *Lutheran Forum* struggled with how to continue. They discussed several options, which they then presented to the ALPB board. The plan favored by the editorial board was to suspend *Lutheran Forum* and instead launch a pan-Lutheran newspaper with a tabloid format. They envisioned a bi-weekly paper, modeled after the *National Catholic Reporter*, whose target audience would be

Lutheran laity and clergy (offered in bulk subscriptions) from all Lutheran bodies. The group acknowledged that this may be "just a bit 'too late,'" that the tabloid medium may have passed its prime as a means of church communication; on the other hand, they noted that such an endeavor had never been given a "full scale try in Lutheranism."[41]

Several other options discussed by the editorial board were summarized in their report to the ALPB board. First, *Lutheran Forum* could be replaced by a bi-weekly newsletter, a format which, they said, "seems to be in high vogue." It would contain "succinct, summarizing information, along with behind-the-scenes insight and astute interpretation of trends and events." Second, *Lutheran Forum* might continue in its present form, reducing publication to ten issues annually. This option, they noted, would require both increased fundraising and increased circulation. Or, third, some combination of options might be tried. Perhaps a monthly supplement could be included with *Lutheran Forum* that would fulfill the need for that "succinct, summarizing information"; or perhaps *Lutheran Forum* could become a quarterly publication, with a newsletter supplement the other eight months. Finally, ALPB could decide to cease all periodical publication, either turning *Lutheran Forum* over to some other publisher, or finding some other periodical that would fulfill existing *Lutheran Forum* subscriptions.[42]

At the ALPB board meeting in May 1971, there was spirited discussion of these options. While the minutes are missing, it appears that a general direction was approved, with details to be worked out over the summer. The board was clear that they would not abandon the field of religious journalism, which had become the most important component of the ALPB's ministry. But they also realized that a change needed to be made, and so in the end they approved a modification of the "combination" option. Effective in January, *Lutheran Forum* would become a quarterly journal, to be supplemented by a newsletter, *Forum Letter*, which would be published monthly (not merely in the "off months" of the journal). Glenn Stone, who had been a full-time employee, would step down as editor of *Lutheran Forum*. He would be replaced by Richard Koenig, who would edit both publications but on a part-time basis. Koenig would cease publication of his own personal newsletter, *Missouri—Free, United, Evangelical*, and urge his readers to subscribe to the new *Forum* package. Stone would continue to assist as needed on an hourly basis until he accepted some other call.[43]

In the final issue of *Missouri—Free, United, Evangelical*, Koenig described his personal hopes for the new "*Forum* package":

> 'Forum Letter' and <u>Lutheran Forum</u> will seek to address issues within Lutheranism from the perspective of what the editor and his associates hope will come to be seen as 'progressive confessionalism,' the conviction that the Lutheran heritage is a bridge, not a barricade, to the future. ... 'Forum Letter' and <u>Lutheran Forum</u> will serve as at least one voice for moderates, moderates not only in the LC-MS but in all Lutheran bodies. ... [They] will seek to encourage the growth of progressive confessionalism

within all segments of American Lutheranism. Problems within the LC-MS will naturally receive extensive coverage and analysis because of the crisis in which the Synod finds itself. With editorial associates of the caliber serving 'Forum Letter' and Lutheran Forum, a wider, more varied, and we believe more helpful treatment of these and other issues will be obtained.[44]

The beginnings of *Forum Letter*
"I have literally measured the inches"

A prototype of *Forum Letter* was mailed to all subscribers in July 1971, consisting of an eight-page report by Stone on the LCMS's Milwaukee convention. He pulled no punches. The convention had been a "brass-knuckled battle" between moderates and conservatives. It was the "logical culmination of the conservative tide that began to flow at New York in 1967." While moderates managed to "beat back the major conservative onslaught," it was "a bit closer to the real Armageddon" than Richard Koenig had predicted in his pre-convention *Lutheran Forum* article. He ended on an optimistic note:

> This convention made it clear that repression, hard-lining, legalistic discipline will not be supported by the Missouri majority. The Word will take its course, and will bring peace and unity, not by might or power, but by the Spirit. If that fact is not recognized, Missouri will have neither peace nor unity.[45]

Stone's lively account—part narrative, part analysis—set the tone for what would become *Forum Letter*'s reportorial style. In the August/September issue of *Lutheran Forum,* he explained that this was "the first of what we hope will be periodic special reports on events and trends of interest to our readers. Our plan is to issue such newsletters on a regular schedule beginning next January."[46]

The first regular issue of *Forum Letter* rolled off the press in January 1972. It opened with a statement from the ALPB board of directors:

> The last decade has seen singular changes in the life of the Church. Programs which were well received fail to attract the enthusiasm that they once did. Pastors and people are searching for new directions. The Church on both the local and national level is in a state of transition. These developments have necessitated the adoption of different directions by the Bureau. The ALPB now concentrates its efforts in the field of religious journalism until such time when new opportunities reveal themselves for service to local gatherings of Christians.

> The publishing program of the Bureau has embraced three journals. First came the *American Lutheran*, published from 1918 to 1966 by Missouri Synod Lutherans interested in assisting the local congregation in its ministry. As Lutheranism matured the *American Lutheran* broadened its area of concern and in 1967 evolved into a new monthly, the *Lutheran Forum*, more inclusive, more self consciously ecumenical

than its predecessor. Now once again the Bureau recognizes the need for a change. The times call for a publication program which combines a newsletter with the in-depth analysis of a magazine. Accordingly, the Bureau has decided upon Forum Letter which will appear monthly and *Lutheran Forum* to be continued as a quarterly journal of opinion and analysis.

The latest change is in keeping with the Bureau's traditional willingness to innovate. ... The newsletter and magazine combination will provide fast, timely, and perceptive coverage of the religious scene, particularly as it relates to the Lutheran Church. In addition the new program fills the vital need for a forum and news source within the Lutheran Church independent of any national Lutheran headquarters.[47]

That first issue concentrated on major questions facing American Lutheranism in 1972. It discussed the status of the fellowship relationship in effect since 1966 between the ALC and the LCMS; LCMS district presidents were polled to get a sense of what that relationship was looking like "on the ground" (the answer was "spotty"). A second piece reported on the continuing "moderate/conservative struggle" in the LCMS. The LCA was not ignored in this issue, as Koenig analyzed the work to date of its Commission on Function and Structure. But he raised the question of whether the LCA might be "thinking too narrowly" and "missing a *kairos*, an opportune moment in Lutheran history." Isn't it possible, he wondered, "to imagine conversations looking to a new Lutheran Church" in which even the LCMS might participate? Koenig's musings were a strong echo of the ALPB's longstanding advocacy for Lutheran unity—and a prescient foreshadowing of a Lutheran merger still some sixteen years in the future.[48]

Forum Letter covered all three large Lutheran church bodies. There were interviews with prominent Lutheran leaders, including LCA president Robert Marshall, ALC president Kent Knutson, and, after Knutson's death, his successor, David Preus. There was extensive reporting on denominational conventions and other meetings, often with very frank "behind the scenes" glimpses. One report described what appeared to be LCMS president Preus's "abrupt change of direction" regarding relationships to other Lutheran bodies; *Forum Letter* asked a "prominent LC-MS official" to characterize ALC and LCA response, and the official exclaimed, "Disgust!"[49]

But *Forum Letter* also continued to represent ALPB's longtime concern with congregational life. Koenig surveyed a hundred readers about the status of traditional Lenten midweek services and found that they were alive and well—often now couched in the structure of "Lutheran vespers" but "showing greater inclination toward the use of film, drama and even dance." The survey also showed "the growing popularity of the Easter Vigil" (though Koenig felt it necessary to explain to readers just what that is), "accompanied by what appears to be a lessening number of Easter sunrise services."[50]

After six months of the newsletter, Koenig reported to the ALPB board that he was pleased with the progress of the new *Forum* package. The publications "are attracting the attention of people and making an impact," he wrote. "I find that we are being denounced by the right people and, what is more important, praised by the right people as well." The biggest criticism, he admitted, is that there had been too much coverage of the struggle in the Missouri Synod. "I am highly sensitive about this, since I'm faced somewhat with a dilemma." Koenig had been personally conflicted about Missouri's situation; it had been the focus of the newsletter he had edited prior to establishing *Forum Letter*, and many readers subscribed because they wanted his independent view of the crisis. The situation keeps changing rapidly, he wrote, and he was trying to cover it responsibly while "diligently [trying to keep] the amount of space devoted to this issue to a minimum."[51]

In a memo the following day to his associate editors, Koenig was more forthright:

I do not think that the Missouri Synod struggle is the be-all and end-all either of my own personal ministry or the ministry of the FORUM. However, it continues to attract national attention, once again this week receiving a long treatment in the New York <u>Times</u> and in national magazines. It would seem to be absurd to avoid giving our own comments and reporting of an event of that notoriety. ... If the ALC or LCA were threatened by schism, I would watch that story with a great deal of interest and concern. I think by measuring the amount of space I have been giving to this, I am not overdoing it so far. I have literally measured the inches ... to make sure that balance is preserved.[52]

Already there was awareness of the differing needs and expectations of different camps among Lutherans. In analyzing why some who had initially subscribed were not renewing, Koenig told the board that some ALC and LCA "midwestern types ... don't identify as closely with the FORUM as Missouri people do or as the Eastern seaboard ALC and LCA people do." To the associate editors, he was again more direct:

Now, are we making an impact? ... I am not sure how to answer it. I know that we are a potent force within the Lutheran Church—Missouri Synod. I know that we are read by President Marshall and other people in the LCA establishment. I know too that ALC leaders read us. I'm not sure that the man in the field regards us as essential. I think our approach is still too clerical and too fuzzy for us to have an image in the minds of many people as the kind of progressive publication we want to be. I hope we can have time to develop and not be put to the wall before we are finished with our year of experimentation. ... It isn't the easiest of all situations. We tried to work out a full time arrangement, but the money simply was not there. Our problems will be severe if we cannot find someone to be a managing editor who is close to the office. ... I'm hoping that the Board is able to solve some of these problems.[53]

Forum Letter's first year ended with a somber article about the grave illness of ALC President Kent Knutson. Koenig had interviewed him for the October issue, and he clearly regarded Knutson as a significant voice in American Lutheranism. "Many people have been attracted to him for his quiet, evangelical style of leadership," Koenig wrote. "Lutherans of all persuasion looked to him and the ALC for help in bringing all Lutherans together." As if in anticipation of the worst, Koenig opened the December issue with an extended quote from a Christmas sermon by Knutson (who would die in March 1973): "Life is more tragic than it sometimes seems and he has borne it all. And so we love this man Jesus and call him Immanuel—God with us. But the dimension that rises to the top in this hour is the God of hope."[54]

Notes

1. John H. Tietjen, interview by Margaret E. Schulze, transcript, 14 Oct. 1978, Archives of Cooperative Lutheranism, Lutheran Council in the USA, Oral History Collection, ELCA Archives, 12, 16-17.

2. Unsigned and undated memo, Gettysburg ALPB Collection, Box 5, Folder 6.

3. Minutes of "Meeting to Plan for New Publication to Succeed the AMERICAN LUTHERAN," 27 Sept. 1966, Gettysburg ALPB Collection, Box 5, Folder 6.

4. Ibid.

5. Ibid.

6. *National Lutheran* 34, no. 12 (Dec. 1966), 2.

7. *LF* 1, no. 1 (Jan. 1967), 20.

8. Ibid., 21; "New 'Lutheran Forum' Critical of Reformation Observances," Lutheran Council in the United States of America, [*News Releases*]—*News Bureau, Lutheran Council in the United States of America* (New York: News Bureau, LCUSA), #67-2 (12 Jan. 1967).

9. Glenn Stone, "Editor's Ambo" in *LF* 1, no. 1 (Jan. 1967), 21; no. 3 (Mar. 1967), 25; no. 4 (Apr. 1967), 12; no. 8 (Aug. 1967), 14; no. 10 (Oct. 1967), 21; No. 11 (Nov. 1967), 12-13.

10. Glenn Stone to Richard John Neuhaus, Nov. 26, 1969, ALPB Archives

11. "On the Way to the Forum," *LF* 1, no. 1 (Jan. 1967), 38; *LF* 1, no. 8 (Aug. 1967), 30.

12. "2 Student Groups to Use Lutheran Forum as Outlet," Lutheran Council in the United States of America, [*News Releases*]—*News Bureau, Lutheran Council in the United States of America* (New York: News Bureau, LCUSA), #67-105 (29 Nov. 1967).

13. "Welcome, students!" *LF* 2, no. 2 (Feb. 1968), 17.

14. "Fire!" *LF* 2, no. 4 (Apr. 1968), 11; Glenn Stone and Theodore Wittrock, interview by Fred Schumacher, tape recording, 20 May 1993, ALPB Archives.

15. Richard John Neuhaus, "The testing of Missouri," *LF* 2, no. 7 (July 1968), 19.

16. Glenn C. Stone, "Denver and after: the fellowship question," *LF* 3, no. 1 (Jan. 1969), 16-17.

17. Richard John Neuhaus, "A modest view of Missouri," *LF* 3, no. 6 (June 1969), 13.

18. Richard E. Koenig, "Missouri, A. D., is different," *LF* 3, no. 9 (Sept. 1969), 4.

19. Ibid., 5.

20. Ibid., 7; Glenn C. Stone, "Missouri's waters are muddy," *LF* 3, no. 9 (Sept. 1969), 22-23.

21. Glenn C. Stone, "Unsettled Missouri," *LF* 3, no. 12 (Dec. 1969), 14.

22. Richard John Neuhaus, "Missouri's gift," *LF* 5, no. 3 (Mar. 1971), 22.

23. Ibid.

24. Ibid., 23.

25. Richard John Neuhaus to Richard Koenig, 3 Mar. 1971, ALPB Archives.

26. "Open Forum: 'More on Missouri's gift,' *LF* 5, no 7 (Aug./Sept. 1971), 19; Martin Scharlemann to Glenn Stone, 6 Apr. 1971; Glenn Stone to Martin Scharlemann, 12 Apr. 1971; Martin Scharlemann to Glenn Stone, 13 Apr. 1971, ALPB Archives.

27. John Tietjen to Glenn Stone, 20 May 1971; Richard John Neuhaus to John Tietjen, 27 May 1971, ALPB Archives.

28. Glenn Stone to John Tietjen, 9 June 1971; John Tietjen interview, 15, ALPB Archives.

29. J. A. O. Preus to Richard John Neuhaus, 12 May 1971. Office of the President: Preus Administration, 1969-1981, Series 1, Box 9, Folder 45, CHI (hereafter cited as Preus Papers).

30. Richard John Neuhaus to Jacob Preus, 20 May 1971, Preus Papers, Series 1, Box 9, Folder 45.

31. "More on 'Missouri's gift,'" *LF* 5, no. 7 (Aug./Sept. 1971), 19.

32. J. A. O. Preus to Richard John Neuhaus, 23 June 1971, Preus Papers, Series 1, Box 9, Folder 45.

33. Rudolph Ressmeyer to J. A. O. Preus, ca. July 1971, Preus Papers, Series 1, Box 9, Folder 45.

34. Ibid.

35. Richard John Neuhaus to J. A. O. Preus, 27 Sept. 1971, Preus Papers, Series 1, Box 9, Folder 45.

36. Richard John Neuhaus to J. A. O. Preus, 9 Oct. 1971, J. A. O. Preus to Richard John Neuhaus, 22 Oct. 1971, Preus Papers, Series 1, Box 9, Folder 45.

37. Richard John Neuhaus, "Neuhaus' apology," *LF* 5, no. 11 (Nov. 1971), 22, and "The loneliness of the long-distance radical," *LF* 5, no. 11 (Nov. 1971), 18.

38. "Memorial Re: Lutheran Brotherhood Grant to Lutheran Forum," Preus Papers, Series 1, Box 9, Folder 45.

39. "From the Desk of the President: Brother to Brother," 18 June 1971, ELCA Archives, Henry L. Lieske Research Collection on the Moderate Movement in the Lutheran Church—Missouri Synod, Series 4, Subseries 1, Box 4.

40. Glenn C. Stone, "Brother to brother to brother," *LF* 5, no. 8 (Oct. 1971), 4; Stone and Wittrock interview.

41. Glenn Stone, "The Future of the Forum: Five Alternatives," ca. 1971, ALPB Archives.

42. Ibid.

43. Minutes, ALPB Board of Directors, 13 May 1971.

44. *Missouri—Free, United, Evangelical*, Letter #21 (14 Nov. 1971), 1, ELCA Archives, Henry L. Lieske Research Collection on the Moderate Movement in the Lutheran Church—Missouri Synod, Series 4, Subseries 1, Box 4.

45. *Forum Letter* prototype, n.d. [July 1971], ALPB Archives.

46. "New and views," *LF* 5, no. 7 (Aug./Sept. 1971), 3.

47. *Forum Letter* 1, no. 1 (Jan. 1972), 1.

48. Ibid., 7.

49. *FL* 1, no. 2 (Feb. 1972), 4.

50. *FL* 1, no. 3 (Mar. 1972), 3.

51. Dick Koenig to Board of Directors and Editors, 14 June 1972, Gettysburg ALPB Collection, Box 28, Folder 2a.

52. Dick Koenig to R. Bagnall, N. Kretzmann, J. Lokken, G. Stone, 15 June 1972, Gettysburg ALPB Collection, Box 28, Folder 2a.

53. Dick Koenig to Board of Directors and Editors; ibid.

54. *FL* 1, no. 12 (Dec. 1972), 1-2. Knutson died several weeks later.

Chapter 16

Serving All Lutherans

T he ALPB had gone through a major transition as the *American Lutheran* morphed into *Lutheran Forum*, and then *Forum Letter* was added to the mix. There was a growing sense that these changes were being made somewhat haphazardly, without a clear plan. The board had affirmed their commitment to religious journalism, but was the *Forum* package to be the only component of the Bureau's ministry? And how could the Bureau withstand the increasing criticism of its ministry by some in high places in the various Lutheran bodies, as well as the vitriolic hostility from the ultraconservative wing of the LCMS?

A reconfigured staff
"More needed than ever"
These questions led to a reconsideration of the Bureau's staff, which was currently in a state of disarray. Richard Koenig was editing both *Lutheran Forum* and *Forum Letter*, but he was also pastor of Immanuel Lutheran Church in Amherst, MA, and could not regularly attend to routine administrative matters in New York. The Bureau had been without an executive secretary since Ted Wittrock had stepped down in 1969. Administrative tasks since then had been assumed by Glenn Stone, with the assistance of secretary Elly Pfeifer. Stone had continued to volunteer since his resignation (minutes from the March

1972 board meeting indicate he was "still coming in daily," but would be available only through April). Meanwhile Ronald Bagnall, who had been assistant editor of *Lutheran Forum*, submitted his resignation when he took a call in Wyndanch, NY.[1]

The board decided to offer Koenig a full-time position as editor, with the understanding that he would also take charge of administration and promotional activities. Members were convinced the ALPB had a responsibility to oppose the rightward drift of the Missouri Synod, and Koenig's long history as analyst and critic of the Missouri wars made him the ideal candidate for the job—though board member Robert Madigan wondered "whether the financial arrangements were feasible and whether the ultimate impact on the Missouri Synod would be worthwhile."[2]

Koenig agonized over the offer. In a lengthy memo to the board, he reiterated his commitment to the Bureau's publications, which are "more needed than ever." But he, too, was concerned about the financial feasibility of the proposal. He outlined in detail his family responsibilities (one child about to start college, another in high school). He observed that, with the promotional responsibilities, he was effectively being asked to raise his own salary—a task for which he didn't feel suited. He proposed two alternatives: (1) the board could hire a managing editor to do the administrative tasks, while Koenig continued as editor; or (2) the board could replace Koenig entirely with someone who could more adequately fill the position as it had been defined, and at the salary offered.[3]

The board's search committee came back with a counter offer: Koenig would remain as part-time editor (and retain his pastorate in Amherst) and Stone would be hired through the end of 1972—"and hopefully beyond"—to handle the administrative and promotional tasks, as well as the physical layout of the publications. Stone had now indicated he could probably be available at least that long, though proposed restructuring being discussed by the LCA might result in an editorial job being offered him. Koenig pronounced himself "delighted" at this new proposal, and the full board gave its approval.[4]

A long-range plan

"'A Changeless Christ for a Changing World' remains our motto"

With the staffing issue settled for the present, the ALPB turned to larger questions. In November 1972, Koenig urged the board to develop "a comprehensive plan for the future of the ALPB." They agreed and asked Glenn Stone to draft a paper for discussion. Stone gave them a fifteen-page analysis of the history of the ALPB's ministry, its present state, and some possible future directions. He suggested that the Bureau's long-time slogan, "A Changeless Christ for a Changing World," was a good summary of the ALPB's two-fold concern "for the building up of the Body of Christ, its internal strengthening, cleansing, inspiration" but always "for the sake of a strong, pure, relevant witness to the world in word and deed."[5]

The ALPB, Stone noted, had for many years been primarily associated with the Missouri Synod. Its image had long been one of "progressivism" in the sense that it was concerned with "new methods of church work." It had claimed to be primarily concerned with "practical church work," with an emphasis on the printed word. It had often been identified with specific program emphases—"campaigns, promotions, limited achievable goals pursued through carefully designated steps, perhaps even 'gimmicks' from time to time."[6]

He then took a shot at formulating a statement of what the ALPB "actually is now and is on the way to becoming":

> American Lutheran Publicity Bureau is an organization of Lutherans, both lay and clergy, organized as a not-for-profit religious corporation, intimately concerned with the Lutheran churches but independent of their control. It serves as a vehicle of communication within Lutheranism concerning all subjects which may be of topical interest to Lutherans, but with special attention to the areas of church renewal, interchurch relations and the social responsibility of Christians. It publishes two periodicals which, taken together, present both current information and penetrating analysis concerning both church life and events in the contemporary world that impinge on the Church and its members.

He observed that the Bureau's identification with the LCMS was proving tough to shake. The board was overwhelmingly LCMS, financial support came primarily from LCMS congregations and individuals, and editorial attention had been focused on internal LCMS events. A slow transition was being made ("about half of our readers are now 'non-Missouri'"), but the board hadn't been very successful in efforts "to promote an 'inter-Lutheran' identity." A disadvantage of this attempted "broadening" had been that the ALPB now had a "precariously narrow" institutional base.[7]

The progressive image of the Bureau, he noted, was not entirely accurate, and some persons within each of the Lutheran church bodies might "consider us much too cautious." The ALPB in fact desires "to be open, experimental and adaptive, but ... with a sense of continuity, avoiding radical breaks and strongly rooted in the ageless essence of the Church." A changeless Christ for a changing world.[8]

The "practical church work" aspect of the ALPB had receded, and the Bureau had become "more theological." Perhaps, he suggested, the Bureau should be "more alert" to possible new programmatic initiatives. As for the continued preoccupation in ALPB publications with the LCMS, the Bureau must "cheerfully acknowledge" that the LCMS strife is indeed a matter of great import and interest to the entire Lutheran community. Still, the Bureau must not let the debate "so monopolize our concern that we give the impression of being a one issue organization." This, he mused, is currently "our biggest internal question."[9]

Stone outlined three general directions that the ALPB might take. The first would be simply to disband—to acknowledge that the "ALPB is outmoded," its original ministry has been taken over by others, and there is no longer a financial base to support an independent agency. If this direction were to be taken, much better to go out of existence in a deliberate and carefully planned way.[10]

The second direction would be to continue the present program. This would declare that the *Forum* package is "the most needed thing that we can do right now for the Church, and it is something in which we have experience and expertise." While there might be tweaking to be done—expanding board membership, doing more intentional fundraising, perhaps increasing the publication schedule of *Lutheran Forum*—there need be no radical change.[11]

The third possibility would be an aggressive expansion of the program. Some possible areas to consider: resuming the tract ministry, offering a wider range of services (thematic conferences, seminars on parish renewal, a consultative service on public relations, a "practical church work" newsletter). Such expanded programs might "make at least a modest profit which would be applied to our Forum program."[12]

Whatever the board may decide, he concluded, we must "sharpen in our own minds our image of ... what we are about," and then "move vigorously and boldly" ahead. "And let us not forget to seek the guidance of God's Spirit upon our discussions, decisions and actions."[13]

Stone's paper was discussed over the next few board meetings. It was clear that the option of disbanding the ALPB would not be considered. In the end, the board opted to continue the present program, but the discussion led to some immediate decisions—including yet another reorganization of staffing. Stone now agreed to return to work full time for the Bureau; at the same time, Koenig was finding it increasingly burdensome to be editing two different publications while serving his parish. The board therefore appointed Stone as editor of *Lutheran Forum* at the "fulltime salary" of $12,000 (including housing, pension and benefits), while Koenig continued to edit *Forum Letter* (without stipend). Stone's job responsibilities would include the administrative needs of the Bureau (in 1974 he would be given the titles "executive secretary" and "managing editor" in addition to "editor"). The board also agreed to expand its membership to broaden the representation of Lutheran church bodies, and several specific names were suggested. Finally, Koenig and Stone were asked to prepare a draft statement of "the aims of the ALPB" for the board's consideration.[14]

The requested statement was brought to the next board meeting, but it did not pass muster. Entitled "New Forms for the Old Gospel in a Time of Change," the document began with the remarkably wooden statement, "Lutheranism is part of the 'organized Church.' We affirm its organizational character without apology or embarrassment." After some discussion, Stone and Koenig were sent back to the drawing board.[15]

The second attempt fared better, but it still did not get the board's approval. Entitled "For Unity and Mission: Serving All Lutherans," the draft focused on the Bureau's commitment to Lutheran unity. It noted—perhaps too polemically for the board—that there were currently "two alternative approaches pursued by some Lutherans today." Some "would draw the lines more sharply between varieties of Lutherans," while others "would by-pass Lutheran confessional integrity and Lutheran unity as irrelevant or unnecessary." The ALPB "consciously and clearly takes its stand" against both approaches. But just what that stand might be was left unsaid, and the board asked for yet another draft.[16]

The third time was the charm, and with only minor tweaking the new draft, now titled "Serving All Lutherans: Together, in Christ, for Others," was approved by the board that summer. It offered a clear statement of how the Bureau understood its ministry as it approached its 60th anniversary:

> American Lutheran Publicity Bureau is a membership organization which supports the movement toward Lutheran unity. We believe that a united approach by Lutherans to their joint mission is crucial to the growth and strength of the Lutheran Church. ...

> For 60 years, ALPB has assisted Lutherans to carry on their mission. We are keenly aware of the changing circumstances, the new challenges and obstacles, which constantly arise for the Church. Trusting in the living Christ who is 'the same yesterday, today and forever,' we seek to provide new tools to help the Church speak to the new times. 'A Changeless Christ for a Changing World' remains our motto.

> Today ALPB serves the Lutheran Church in its struggle for unity and pursuit of mission primarily through two publications. LUTHERAN FORUM provides a voice for Lutherans across church body lines, in which they can discuss common issues. FORUM LETTER reports and interprets events and movements which influence or reflect the common aspirations and institutions of Lutherans. The editors are charged with serving the broad goals of the ALPB, but are given freedom to serve those ends creatively and vigorously.

The statement concluded by inviting the "participation and support of all who share our vision of service for the unity and mission of the Church."[17]

Three aspects of this statement deserve comment. First, the reference to "membership organization" was inserted at the board meeting, probably at the urging of Nazareth Magarian, an attorney who had recently joined the board and who noted that the ALPB articles of incorporation so identified the Bureau. In New York, "membership organization" had some specific legal implications, requiring formal membership classes, annual membership meetings, and several other things that had not been true of the Bureau for decades. Magarian was asked to prepare new legal documents which would eliminate the description of the ALPB as a "membership organization." From henceforth legally the "members" of the ALPB would be the members of the board of directors.

Second, the statement is striking in its clear affirmation that the Bureau serves "the Lutheran Church"—no reference to individual church bodies; indeed, it serves

Lutherans "across church body lines"—and that its primary focus is the "movement toward Lutheran unity." This had been true for some time, of course, but the 1973 document is the first time it was clearly stated as the policy of the Bureau.

Third, the comment about the role of the publications and the editors attempted to define the sometimes rather fuzzy relationship between the board and its editors. This had been an issue since the early days of the *American Lutheran*. The publications had never really "spoken for" the board in a direct sense, and there had been little board oversight over editorial content. Still, the *American Lutheran* for decades had often been identified as "the ALPB"; that was even truer with the *Forum* package, since it was now pretty much the *only* program of the Bureau. The policy statement attempted to articulate that relationship in a formal way.

Thunder on the far right

"the misleading statements, innuendo, the outright lies"

Glenn Stone's discussion paper had suggested that the view of the Bureau as "progressive" wasn't entirely accurate, but there had always been those on the conservative end of Missouri's political spectrum who would disagree. The ALPB and its *American Lutheran* magazine had come under attack thirty years before from Paul Burgdorf's *Confessional Lutheran*. The board at that time had wisely decided simply to ignore the criticism. The *Confessional Lutheran* continued publication until 1969, but after 1962 it was increasingly eclipsed as the voice of Missouri's extreme right by Herman Otten's *Lutheran News*. Otten was a graduate of Concordia Seminary, where he had been a thorn in the side of many faculty and other students whom he accused of "liberalism." The seminary faculty had declined to certify him for ordination, but he nonetheless received a call to Trinity Lutheran Church in New Haven, MO, and would serve as pastor there for more than five decades. *Lutheran News* began as a ten-page newsletter and soon became a tabloid-style newspaper; the name was changed to *Christian News* in 1968. Otten's first issue explained his purpose and his methodology:

> During the past few years various publications of major Lutheran bodies in America have published articles which have expressed views contrary to the historic position of the Lutheran Church ... [while] conservatives have been repeatedly denied opportunity to answer certain attacks upon basic doctrines. ...

> This newsletter will print a few of the facts which are being suppressed. ... We shall photographically reproduce much of the material with as little comment as necessary. The facts should speak for themselves.

From that issue onward, Otten did indeed "photographically reproduce" material from other publications—generally without seeking permission from the copyright holder to do so.[18]

The ALPB came into Otten's sights quite early. In April 1963, he complained that the ALPB was permitted to have a display table at the 1962 Synod convention while a conservative group was not. From that time on, the ALPB, its publications and its personnel, were frequent targets of the paper. For years, the ALPB ignored Otten, but when in 1973 he attacked *Forum Letter* editor Richard Koenig and accused *Lutheran Forum* of "radical anti-Christian theology," Glenn Stone responded in *Forum Letter* to "the misleading statements, innuendo, the outright lies contained in a single paragraph" of Otten's article. Noting that Otten's accusations appeared in "the same issue containing copyrighted FORUM material which *Christian News* illegally prints without permission," Stone corrected one by one the false statements made by Otten. "One does not 'prove' to a partisan that he is guilty of slander by distortion and misrepresentation," he concluded. "Many have tried it in the ten years the *Christian News* has been in business. None have succeeded. We doubt that this one will either." He was right about that; in response Otten simply reprinted Stone's words in *Forum Letter* with a note that "what we said ... is correct." Subsequent ALPB editors and board members generally refused to respond to *Christian News.*[19]

Controversy and criticism

"how can dissent within the church be voiced?"

Criticism of the ALPB was not restricted to the extreme right in the LCMS. For more than thirty years, there were detractors and critics within the leadership of the Missouri Synod. As the Bureau expanded its ministry to the wider Lutheran community, ALPB publications would find themselves under fire from leaders in the ALC and LCA as well. This was perhaps not unexpected, since an independent voice sometimes ruffles the feathers of just about everybody. But in the 1970s, as J. A. O. Preus strengthened his hold on the LCMS, it was still the LCMS leadership that offered the most consistent denunciation.

One example was a discussion in the LCMS Council of Presidents in early 1972 over the propriety of Rudolph Ressmeyer's membership on the board of the ALPB. Ressmeyer had served on the board since 1955 and was its president for a few years in the early 1960s. In 1967 he was elected president of the Atlantic District. At the March 1972 meeting of the Council of Presidents, one of his colleagues suggested that he resign from the board. Ressmeyer asked for an opportunity to respond, but time ran out before he could do so. He subsequently wrote a letter to the presidents "to say what I would have said to you in person." Ressmeyer began by stating forthrightly that he did not intend to resign from the board. He traced the history of the ALPB, noting the many ways that it had positively influenced in the Synod over its history. He described the transition from the *American Lutheran* to the new publications, and the reasons for the change. The board, he said, has only ever had one editorial policy: "to provide a free forum for the exchange of opinions currently held in Lutheranism today." While members of the board "often disagree with what appears" in the publications, they are convinced that the free exchange of ideas "is both helpful and necessary in the church." He admitted that he had on occasion spoken with the editors and writers, urging them not to write intemperately and not to repeat rumors without substantiation. Editor Richard Koenig, he insisted, "is deeply devoted to the Holy Scriptures, the Confessions, and to the Synod. ... He is seeking to promote the validity of a third option to fundamentalism and liberalism." The real issue, he concluded, is much broader: "how can dissent within the church be voiced in a responsible, constructive and God-pleasing manner?"[20]

Koenig steps down

"somebody has to keep 'carrying the torch'"

As the 1973 LCMS convention in New Orleans approached, *Lutheran Forum* published a three-part series by Koenig entitled, "What's behind the showdown in the LCMS?" He traced the history of the Synod's "traditions"—from the Saxon immigration in the 19th century, through the period when the Synod "turned moderate," and then the "conservative reaction" of the 1960s. It was a helpful survey, both for those within the Synod and for other Lutherans who were puzzled by what was happening. The ALPB reprinted the three articles as a stand-alone piece, with a special price for bulk copies— clearly hoping that congregations would distribute the analysis to all their members. Koenig had again been sober, yet hopeful:

> Even if Preus were re-elected, an outcome in considerable doubt at the present time, his election would mean the restoration of the old Missouri—the Missouri of doctrinal rigidity, isolation, suspicion of others and fear of itself—on the official level only. The Missouri of the parish in the majority of instances would continue to exhibit the change which the synod underwent and approved after 1938. ... In the end ... moderate Missouri will again assert itself and claim the future.[21]

Koenig's naïve optimism quickly evaporated after the so-called "Battle of New Orleans." "The shock of New Orleans is already rolling across the country," he reported. "Everywhere moderate pastors and congregations are reassessing their situation and deliberating on what response to make toward the drastically altered church body they now must live in."[22]

Over the next few months *Forum Letter* reported on developments in the wake of New Orleans: the organization of Evangelical Lutherans in Mission (ELIM) as the voice for moderates in Missouri, the continued turmoil over the faculty and leadership of Concordia Seminary. It kept its eye as well on the rest of the Lutheran scene, with articles on the ALC and LCA, LCUSA, the Inter-Lutheran Commission on Worship, and other Lutheran institutions and agencies. It also commented on various social issues—war and peace, conflict in the Middle East, contemporary film and other arts.

But Richard Koenig was becoming weary and a bit discouraged. In January 1974, he wrote a lengthy letter to Glenn Stone, reflecting on the new reality in American Lutheranism and how that might impact the mission of ALPB. He observed that the "moderates" in the Missouri Synod now seem to feel "there is no point in continuing any political or theological struggle" because "the conservatives have won a total and complete victory." The desire in Missouri for Lutheran unity has also "just about died out." This meant, Koenig suggested, that the ALPB must go in a very different direction:

> To continue to concentrate on the Missouri Synod is to speak to an audience which no longer is present. To continue to push for Lutheran unity is quixotic. I would believe that ALPB would serve its readership best if it would return to an emphasis on the practical ministry in a new form.

Koenig believed he was not the person to lead the publications in a new direction and suggested that the "advantage to ALPB at this time could be very great if I were to resign."[23]

Stone replied that the emergence of ELIM and their *Missouri in Perspective* publication in fact relieved *Forum Letter* of covering the "basic, nitty-gritty, tit-for-tat" details in Missouri, and thus freed ALPB to focus on the broader picture of Lutheran unity—which, he insisted, was not a dead issue. Indeed, there is an even greater "need for an inter-Lutheran perspective, which stands outside the church bodies and views the whole scene as one." The pursuit of that unity, he argued, is not quixotic "except in the sense that the 'impossible dream' still compels one to push on against all odds."

> In this area, I see our role as engaging in a kind of guerilla [sic] warfare. Wherever anyone is busy building the 'walls of Zion' as a defense against other Lutherans, our job is to undermine those 'walls,' to peck away wherever possible at self-satisfaction and the inertia of rest. This may mean encouraging local Lutheran interchange even where it is not possible on a national level. ... It may mean even such simple things as learning from each other, entirely outside of structures—LUTHERAN FORUM itself being the structure which, because it is read by different Lutherans, becomes the vehicle of interchange. ...
>
> Frankly, I feel I have been involved in minority causes for most of my ministry. I still think that during the 'dark night,' somebody has to keep 'carrying the torch.'

Stone urged Koenig to continue as editor for at least another year. He offered to remove the burden of the physical production of *Forum Letter*, either by moving the production to the ALPB office or by hiring someone in Amherst (where Koenig lived) to handle those matters, and he volunteered to act as "co-editor" of *Forum Letter*. Koenig at length agreed to continue.[24]

But four months later, Koenig insisted on resigning, citing reasons "personal, professional, and family." In his letter of resignation, he again noted that his own involvement with the LCMS had caused *Forum Letter* to be "locked in ... in a certain way." He suggested that *Forum Letter* should be "revamped and that the institutional side of Lutheranism be played down in the interest of new perspectives and opinion and human interest stories." In his final issue (June 1974) Koenig explained to readers that two and a half years of monthly deadlines had "taken their toll." But "to be candid," he added, "there are other reasons."

> The purpose of FORUM LETTER is to offer readers report and opinion on events and issues affecting Lutheranism both in the U.S.A. and abroad. In so doing, FORUM LETTER aimed at serving the vision of one, united Lutheran Church. ... Where we thought we saw Lutheranism succumbing to reactionary forces, we reported it and commented sometimes at length. Where we saw possibilities, we tried to highlight them and inspire those who love their Church to turn them into realities.

> As exciting as it all was (and there *is* plenty going on in Lutheranism that is exciting), there comes a time when other perspectives are needed to focus in a fresh way on what Lutheranism is and what it can be.

Glenn Stone was named acting editor, and for the next few months *Forum Letter* continued along the same path blazed by Richard Koenig. At the same time, however, the ALPB board was having more discussion about the mission and purpose of its publications, and that issue was necessarily connected to the choice of a new editor. [25]

The hiring of Neuhaus

"he is responsible, so help him, for everything that appears"

As the board considered who would succeed Koenig at *Forum Letter*, Richard John Neuhaus quickly emerged as the primary candidate. In addition to his previous contribution as a columnist in *Lutheran Forum*, he had considerable editorial experience. He was at that time senior editor of *Worldview*, a journal published by the Council on Religion and International Affairs; he had previously edited *Una Sancta*, the Lutheran-oriented journal focusing on liturgy and theology, and *Church Renewal*, a bimonthly newsletter directed at a Lutheran audience. These were all topics that were relevant to the ALPB's traditional concerns. He also had continued to contribute to *Lutheran Forum*, even after his column was discontinued. With all this in mind, the search committee settled on Neuhaus.

Some board members, perhaps remembering the 1971 controversy over "Missouri's gift," were not so sure it was a wise move. Stone wrote to Neuhaus on August 16, 1974, inviting him to attend the next board meeting.

> I believe that the board is positively disposed toward your candidacy, but that they have some questions about the approach, style and intended audience you would envision for FORUM LETTER. As an example, I enclose a copy of a statement ... by [board member] Bob Madigan. This ... is not endorsed in all points by all board

members. Nevertheless it may illustrate the kinds of questions that would be asked of you by some board members at the Sept. 18 meeting.[26]

The document by Madigan proposed a new approach for *Forum Letter*. It should, he argued, "be <u>interesting and readable</u> with as much human interest material as possible," aimed at "the <u>interest level of an involved layman.</u>" But perhaps more to the point:

> It no longer should be a passionate, partisan protagonist in the LC-MS battle or any other struggle. Rather it should be a readable letter <u>observing</u> and <u>interpreting</u> the present day scene for those interested in Pan-Lutheranism. ... [It] should give <u>even handed treatment</u> to those opposing views—it must be journalistically even handed. Readership interest would be enhanced by regular (though not monthly) airing of other points of view <u>in the Letter itself.</u> This might be done through quotes from those on the other side, by brief occasional Letters to the Editor or by guest columnists <u>in the Letter itself.</u>

Neuhaus's meeting with the board apparently assuaged concerns by board members, for they voted unanimously to appoint him as the next editor of *Forum Letter*. To be clear about the division of responsibilities, the minutes recorded that Glenn Stone would be executive secretary of the ALPB (though the title would shortly be changed to executive director), editor of *Lutheran Forum*, associate editor of *Forum Letter*, and managing editor of both; Neuhaus would be editor of *Forum Letter* and associate editor of *Lutheran Forum*.[27]

In Neuhaus's first issue (November 1974), he rather whimsically introduced himself to the readers:

> Born the sixth son of eight children in a Canadian parsonage, Richard John Neuhaus was educated, so to speak, in Texas and the Midwest and since 1961 has been a pastor of the Church of St. John the Evangelist in the Black and Puerto Rican Williamsburg section of Brooklyn, N.Y. (In distinction from the more famous Cathedral of St. John the Divine, the parish is frequently referred to as St. John the Mundane.) He is also senior editor of Worldview, the monthly journal published by the Carnegie-endowed Council on Religion and International Affairs. He is a founder or board member of organizations such as Clergy and Laity Concerned About Vietnam, National SANE and Bread for the World, and served as liaison between Martin Luther King and the peace movement until Dr. King's death in 1968. ... There are other things, but the point is he is responsible, so help him, for everything that appears in FORUM LETTER, unless the item appears over another name. In cooperation with Pastor Glenn Stone, editor of LUTHERAN FORUM, he hopes to develop the distinguished tradition established by Pastor Richard Koenig. ... So help him.

Neuhaus would become the most audible "public voice" of ALPB for the next several years. He did not, however, fulfill Koenig's hope for "changing the FORUM'S image from a polemical publication to something more constructive" or Madigan's desire for *Forum Letter* to be "journalistically even handed."[28]

Forum Letter

"So much for conventional thought-slots"

Neuhaus almost immediately asked the board if *Forum Letter* might be expanded from eight to twelve pages. What lay behind this request (besides Neuhaus's having a lot to say) was a realization that the continuing crisis in the Missouri Synod was going to require extensive coverage. Executive director Stone told the board that the budget would allow for every other issue to be expanded to twelve pages, but some board members believed a more concise publication was better in keeping with the newsletter concept. There was also the ongoing concern, voiced by Koenig when he resigned, that *Forum Letter* must not be preoccupied with the LCMS. The board decided to keep *Forum Letter* at eight pages, but gave Neuhaus permission to publish occasional four-page supplements that would focus more intently on the Missouri situation.[29]

Neuhaus's first issue of *Forum Letter* opened, not with more commentary on the LCMS, but with a report by James Lokken on the recent convention of the American Lutheran Church. Lokken, who had left the ALPB in 1968 to work for the Liturgical Conference in Washington, DC, was admiring:

> The ALC emerges in 1974 as the strongest, if not the largest, Lutheran body in America. Internally unified, its leadership is competent and dedicated. It seems able to address theological, social and ethical questions with intelligence, if not with unanimity. The ALC maintains a middle-of-the-road position between Missouri and the LCA, and remains the likely catalyst for Lutheran unity in the United States.[30]

But if anyone thought that the new regime at *Forum Letter* would either abbreviate or tone down the coverage of the Missouri Synod conflict, Neuhaus's article which followed Lokken's report quickly set them straight. Entitled "'As Missouri Turns': Year Six, Episode Four" (a not-so-veiled allusion to a contemporary television soap opera, *As the World Turns*), Neuhaus contemplated just what the "question" is about Missouri:

> Some say it is: Can the tide of liberalism in the late 20th century be turned back by a staunch defense of Lutheran orthodoxy? Others suggest: Can two inveterate church wreckers, brothers from a rival Lutheran dynasty, capture a conservative evangelical church body and transform it into a sect? Or: Can a body for 130 years schizophrenically divided between being Church and being sect find survival, if not happiness, under the rule of the Gospel?

He then took six of the expanded issue's twelve pages to bring readers up to date on the rapidly developing situation in the LCMS. In the next issue, it was four pages out of eight; in the next few issues, typically three or four pages were devoted to the Missouri crisis.[31]

In May 1975, "As Missouri Turns" was moved out of the regular pages of *Forum Letter* to become the separate "occasional supplement" suggested by the board. But the "occasions" seemed to be almost constant. "As Missouri Turns" appeared in May, June,

August (that month the "supplement" took over the entire issue) and September, and then every issue thereafter until June 1976. Then Neuhaus announced that "As Missouri Turns" was coming to an end—primarily, he would say, because the title was "being outpaced by events, since many members of the cast are moving beyond Missouri." He contemplated some possible titles which would continue to play on the title of some popular television show (he quipped that he was considering "The Preus Is Right" or perhaps "The Little Rascals").[32]

In July 1976, *Forum Letter* included a supplement called "The Continuing Crisis." Neuhaus assured readers that only the name was changing. "The subject matter, sorry to say, remains much the same." This supplement appeared at least every other month for two years. It covered the unfolding development of the Association of Evangelical Lutheran Churches (AELC), the reactions within the LCMS, and other matters in the aftermath of the Missouri civil war.[33]

Then, in June 1978, Neuhaus remarked that the earlier name change had been made to allow treatment of "other issues as well," and so he would now indeed take up another issue—the role of women in the church. From that time on, "The Continuing Crisis" seldom dealt with the LCMS. It discussed ecumenism, liturgical matters, and other topics; it seemed essentially to be a way for Neuhaus to get the extra four pages when he had more to say about one topic or another. The last regular installment in the series, Number 18, appeared in January 1979. "The Continuing Crisis" made one final appearance in August 1981, with a special report by Charles Austin on the LCMS convention that elected Ralph Bohlmann to succeed J. A. O. Preus as president. The LCMS, Austin concluded is not "the contentious, politicized denomination" of the 1970s; the sad cost of that newfound unity, however, is that Missouri "is going its own way" while the other Lutheran bodies "are heading in a different direction."[34]

Forum Letter discussed much more than the Missouri Synod's turmoil. Its range of concerns paralleled that of *Lutheran Forum*: liturgical developments, institutional issues in all the major Lutheran church bodies, ecumenical relationships, and social concerns—particularly abortion. Nearly every issue had some reference to that topic. Sometimes it was just a passing comment or brief review of a book on the subject, but often there was more extensive commentary. It was, Neuhaus averred, "the issue that will not go away." In an essay with that title in 1978, he admitted that what he was about to say might result in the loss of some subscribers, but "the issue is infinitely more important than a few cancellations." He insisted that that pro-abortion advocacy "is not a liberal cause but a regressive movement that exploits women and men, disdains the poor and weak, and restricts the boundaries of the human community." The churches' witness, he thundered (quoting Robert Jenson of Gettysburg Seminary), has been "contemptible":

> Contemptible because it is a cowardly evasion of controversy. Contemptible because
> it prefers conformity to honest examination of conscience. Contemptible because

it abandons Christian principle in subservience to fashionable secular opinion. Contemptible because it assumes that we good Americans, backed up by 'the law of the land,' are incapable of the horrors perpetrated by other people at other times.

"Contemptible," he concluded, "and, for those who love the Church, pitiable."[35]

His treatment of homosexuality, an issue just beginning to be discussed openly in the church, was more nuanced. While not sympathetic to changing traditional Christian teaching, he believed the issue belonged to the sphere of pastoral discretion. "Sometimes the better part of wisdom is to leave things to implicit trust, common sense and an encompassing awareness of human frailty," he advised. After all, "Christian doctrine is not challenged by the acknowledgement that, on this and other scores, Christians fall short of their calling. We all live by forgiveness." He criticized those who "insist upon approval [of homosexuality] by official fiat," yet he also blasted the Missouri Synod's "usual macho bombast, recruiting a few Bible passages to shore up its prejudices."[36]

Three years later, he still insisted that "some issues do not lend themselves to formal rule-making."

> An all-out debate ... would almost certainly play into the hands of reactionaries and witch-hunters who view the issue as a litmus test of orthodoxy. As it is today, some synod and seminary examining committees are reported to ask more earnest questions about sexual orientation than about theological competence. In a community of saints and sinners—where we are all and always both—ambiguity is sometimes an essential part of love. There is no ethical nor theological warrant to compromise the Church's traditional teaching on sex, marriage and family. At the same time, there should be no compromise of pastoral and episcopal space for discretion and forgiveness with respect to the homosexual or heterosexual. The ancient distinction between private sin and public scandal still has much to recommend it, but always within the context of a call to holiness.[37]

Despite his insistence that Christians must be engaged in social issues and his own willingness to share his opinions on everything from abortion to foreign policy, Neuhaus was adamant that this was not the primary task of the church:

> We Christians need to emphasize the importance of political engagement. But for those who are engaged or want to be engaged, it is perhaps as important to prophesy against the idolatrous primacy of politics in contemporary culture. Recently I spent several hours with a Lutheran bishop who is based in the Midwest. We discussed his leadership in church renewal, in preaching, liturgy, ministry among the poor. Then, turning to the Church's political role, he declared emphatically, 'That's where I really want to make a difference, in the real world.' Alas. The statement is the sadder for his being among the best of our Lutheran leaders. ... Our trouble is that we believe the lies we are told about the primacy of politics. 'And that's the way it is, May 30th, 1980,' concludes Walter Cronkite. Nonsense. 'All the News That's Fit to Print,' banners the *New York Times*. Nonsense. ... The way it is, the real news, what's hap-

pening—it's people muddling through with sin and grace, glimpsing glory through their tears, sighing faith's assent to the Gospel claim, offering and being offered in the eucharistic bread and wine of human hope. If we do not believe that this is 'the real world,' then we and all the worlds there are are surely lost.[38]

Neuhaus began running a series of page-long articles entitled "Renewing Lutheran Worship," written by Larry Bailey and Leonard Klein, both LCMS pastors in New York (though both would soon join the exodus into the AELC). The series was focused on the work of the Inter-Lutheran Commission on Worship, and it began by giving a brief history of that group. Several installments reviewed the ILCW's proposed Eucharistic prayers. The authors fervently hoped the prayers would be widely used, and yet suggested that the prayers as worded "participate too much in the spirit of the classroom"—good theology, but "in prayers ... irksome."[39]

This series continued as a regular feature in *Forum Letter* until the end of 1982, more than 50 essays altogether. Besides discussing the various ILCW proposals, and then the final product, *Lutheran Book of Worship*, Bailey and Klein took up a variety of other liturgical matters: the weekly Eucharist, vestments, doctrine and practice in the liturgy, and much more. These brief articles were concise, provocative, and pastorally sensitive—an excellent resource for busy pastors.

On the question of Lutheran unity, Neuhaus was cautious. The AELC issued a "Call to Lutheran Union," inviting the much larger LCA and ALC to begin conversations with the goal of merger. Neuhaus's immediate reaction was that the AELC—a church body he himself had joined, though with little enthusiasm—was "behaving in a rather silly manner." He criticized most of the arguments for a pan-Lutheran merger.

> Lutheran union in North America <u>was</u> an ecumenically compelling vision for many; the organic union of two-thirds of North American Lutheranism is not. ... Who in the world would be impressed by the fact that there are only three rather than four or five major Lutheran jurisdictions in North America? ... The singly most compelling objection is that the Call is utterly beside the point in view of the great ecumenical mandate and opportunity of this moment: the healing of the breach of the 16th century. ... It would, in our opinion, be a great shame to permit ourselves to be distracted by a proposal so confused, so time-consuming, and finally so trivial in result."[40]

He was also cautious in his evaluation of ecumenical rapprochement. While enthusiastic about warming relationships between Lutherans and Roman Catholics, he was not convinced about the wisdom of closer ties with American Protestant denominations. In 1982, as some Lutherans and Episcopalians were moving toward interim Eucharistic sharing, Neuhaus printed a letter from Yale theologian George Lindbeck about the proposal, together with his response. Neuhaus had "seemed puzzled," Lindbeck wrote, "when we talked recently, about my enthusiasm for the proposed agreement," and then he outlined in some detail the reasons for his enthusiasm. "I am clearly not the first to applaud [the agreement]," Neuhaus replied, "and I'm not standing on my chair to cheer, but I do applaud." He expressed his concern about the Missouri Synod being left out of the agreement. "The days of 'waiting for Missouri' are past," he admitted, "and that is both necessary and sad. But this does not mean the rest of us should go off on an ecumenical romp as though Missouri no longer exists." He then noted his own ambivalence about drawing closer to the Episcopal Church:

> I think the Episcopalians can be insufferable. We all manage that at times, but it seems to come more naturally to them. Doctrinally vacuous, evangelistically anemic, stylistically precious and ecumenically pretentious, I cannot say it is my favorite church body. Nonetheless, some of my best friends, etc. A much more important 'nonetheless' is your point that Episcopalianism in this country is not the same thing as the global Anglican communion. Although I do not share your pessimistic reading of John Paul's ecumenical leadership, I readily agree that the Lutheran-Anglican connection could contribute strongly to the quest for unity, especially in relations with Rome and the Orthodox.

In sum, he wrote, if the agreement is approved by all sides, it will be "a step both ominous and exhilarating" and "once taken, what we Lutherans mean by fellowship will never be the same. The sound you hear ... is applause; sober but sincere."[41]

Neuhaus did not suffer fools gladly, and he took great delight in excoriating silliness wherever it appeared in the church. He dubbed a "question and answer" column in the LCA's *Lutheran* magazine "the most consistent source of popular misinformation about worship and the sacraments in American Lutheranism." He lambasted Fortress Press for "inventing instant traditions in order to inflate the market"—the case in point being the hawking of "Friar Tuck clergy shirts in color." He noted that in the Fortress ads, women were shown in dull browns, while the men were in brighter colors; "among clergy, as among birds, apparently chromaticity is related to the chromosomes." A flood of protests from readers who liked the shirts led him to admit that his opposition to the colored shirts was not theological but aesthetic: "It is merely a question a taste, and I certainly did not mean to offend the slobs who disagree."[42]

Neuhaus's social views were by this time causing consternation among many of his old friends and allies from the anti-war and civil rights struggles. He addressed the concern in 1979:

> Wherever I go, the question is asked whether I am more radical or more conservative than I was in the 60's. ... I am generally disinclined to bore people with intellectual autobiography. ... But, since some of you ask (others should feel free to skip what follows), herewith a brief response. During the '60's I was viewed as an unqualified liberal or even radical. ... Those were the years of intense engagement in civil rights, urban change issues and the antiwar movement. Faced with the same issues, <u>I hope I would, in general, do now what I did then.</u> I was not then as comfortable with the labels applied to me as were those who—whether in approval or opposition—applied them.

He recounted a 1967 article he had written for *Commonweal* which had "ruptured friendships with many friends on the left. One always knew, but it was painful to experience, the truth that <u>there is also a liberal party line</u> that it is deemed treason to violate."

> So have I moved left or right, or at all? In terms of conventional thought-slots, the movement appears to be rightward. So much for conventional thought-slots. Comparing, say, 1965 with 1979, it is not surprising that I see clear continuity. I was then and am now <u>a pragmatist economically, a liberal politically and a conservative culturally.</u> ... Politically, I was in 1965 and am now a liberal democrat (also with a big D). So much am I committed to democratic pluralism that I am prepared to argue that it is supported by, if not required by, a Christian theology of human nature and history. ...
>
> I am, first and last, a Christian of catholic persuasion, a pastor and a churchman held accountable by a tradition of faith. That is a very liberating awareness because it means you need not be, cannot be, fitted into any secular school of thought.[43]

Resources, old and new

"returning to production of tracts"

The 1970s conversations about the Bureau's mission led the ALPB to offer new resources beyond just the *Forum* package. One such effort was a return, on a limited yet significant basis, to the publication of tracts. Despite the destruction by fire of nearly the whole inventory, the Bureau had continued to receive inquiries about the availability of certain tracts. Glenn Stone raised with the board in October 1972 the possibility of "returning to production of tracts on a limited basis." The idea was discussed over the next few meetings and information was gathered about potential cost. Finally in September 1974, the board authorized the reprinting of four of the most popular tracts: "Lutheran Church Worship," "The Lutheran Church Invites You," "The Lord's Supper," and "What Does Church Membership Mean."[44]

One of the Bureau's early programs had been a "Lutheran lecture lyceum." It gradually morphed into the annual "Luther Day" events featuring Walter A. Maier and other Lutheran speakers, but that program had run its course by the end of the 1930s (with one brief reprise in 1949). Now the concept was resurrected with an annual dinner in the New York area featuring a prominent Lutheran speaker. The first "Inter-Lutheran Forum" was held in 1975, with LCA President Robert Marshall speaking on "The Issues Facing All Lutherans Today." The evening was a success, and over the next several years a variety of "big name" Lutherans (and occasionally others) were the speakers: ALC president David Preus (1976, "Contemporary Lutheran Perspectives"), historian Martin Marty (1977, "Lutherans: Born Again?"), sociologist Peter Berger (1978, "A Lutheran View of the Elephant"), ecumenists Dr. George Lindbeck and Fr. John Hotchkin (1979, "Fifteen Years of Roman Catholic/Lutheran Dialogue: What Are the Next Steps?"), Lutheran World Ministries director Paul Wee (1980, "Lutheran

Unity and the Heavenly Banquet"), LCA bishop James Crumley (1982, "Toward a New Lutheran Church: The Process and the Issues"), and Dr. William Lazareth (1983, "Luther's Living Legacy"). Often these addresses were printed in *Lutheran Forum* or made available for purchase on tape.

Frequently the dinner included some other celebration or recognition. At the first dinner in 1975, special honor was paid to Richard Koenig for his many years of service to the ALPB. A similar recognition was given in 1976 to Chester Edelmann, longtime treasurer of the Bureau. This became more formal in 1977 with the creation of the "Lutheran Forum Award," presented to an individual in recognition of distinguished contributions to Lutheran unity. The first award that year was given to Adolf Meyer, former editor of the *American Lutheran*; subsequent awards were made to Robert Marshall (1978), Paul Empie (1979, posthumously), Eugene Brand (1980), and E. Clifford Nelson (1982).

Developing a forum

"the 'controversial' nature of the FORUM"

But the Bureau's primary focus continued to be the *Forum* package. The board sought ways to expand *Lutheran Forum* to "serve the broad goals" of the ALPB. One proposal was to work with the church and society agencies of the various church bodies to produce a regular supplement focusing on Christian social responsibility.

Event, a monthly social issues magazine published by the ALC, had suspended publication in 1974. Church and society staff had dreamed of an inter-Lutheran publication focused on their concerns, but various obstacles had arisen. LCMS officials believed the current turmoil in the synod would make their participation difficult. The LCA was unwilling to consider the idea unless both the ALC and the LCMS bought in. It appeared that the idea of a joint venture was dead in the water.

At this point Byron Schmid, a staff member of LCUSA, began to think about another approach. He conceived of three options; the one he preferred was a regular social issues supplement to *Lutheran Forum*. He approached Glenn Stone, who reported the conversation to the ALPB board in May 1974. Discussion went on for several months, with program units of the ALC, the LCA, and LCUSA participating.

The proposal envisioned the participating groups financing a 16-page supplement to *Lutheran Forum* six times a year. An advisory committee would be responsible for editing the supplement. The ALPB would increase publication of *Lutheran Forum* from four to six issues annually and would provide reprints of the supplement at the request of any of the participating groups. The church bodies would publicize *Lutheran Forum* and provide ALPB with access to certain of their mailing lists for publicity purposes.

Stone met in July 1974 with representatives from ALC, LCA, LCMS and LCUSA. While LCUSA and ALC representatives were enthusiastic about the proposal, the LCA response was lukewarm. The LCMS representatives were favorable but apprehensive about the political realities in their church body—though LCUSA's involvement would technically keep the LCMS in the mix, since Missouri was a LCUSA member. Things were progressing so smoothly that Stone announced to subscribers that, beginning in January 1975, each issue of *Lutheran Forum* would include a special section devoted to Christian social concerns, and that the section was "being developed with the cooperation of 'church and society' staff people in two of the church bodies."[45]

But it all came unraveled that fall—for unanticipated reasons. The LCA pulled out of the negotiations when the management committee of their Division for Mission in North America decided to postpone action. Charles Lutz, the ALC's church and society staff person, was flabbergasted. "We can explain to our boards and others concerned why LCMS is not along," he wrote to his LCA counterpart, Franklin Jensen. "We don't know what to say concerning LCA." Jensen replied that his management committee wanted to consider the possibility of using existing LCA media for communication about social issues. After all, he noted, the *Lutheran* had a current circulation of over half a million, and so would reach considerably more readers. Stone would report "rumors that the 'controversial' nature of the FORUM" played a significant part in the decision.[46]

Lutz insisted that the ALC, LCUSA and ALPB would go it alone if necessary. In mid-October, Stone met with the ALC and LCUSA representatives to plot out possible topics and guest editors for the first six issues of what they were now calling "*Lutheran Forum*'s Public Issue." But then it became apparent that ALC President David Preus was not on board. He argued that the proposal had become essentially an ALC project, and that if that were the case, it would be better to keep it "in house." He also believed that *Lutheran Forum* had a "political image" which could harm ALC/LCMS relations; the ALC, he told Stone personally, was hoping to play a reconciling role with respect to the Missouri Synod, and ALC involvement with the ALPB in this project might "give unnecessary offense." Preus had also been peeved with the report on the ALC's national convention in the November 1974 *Forum Letter* which suggested that the ALC was making its hunger appeal a low priority, and Stone hinted that this hadn't helped the situation.[47]

And so the proposal was dead. LCUSA had approved participation and funding, but with both the LCA and the ALC bowing out, that approval became moot. This was an embarrassing moment for the Bureau for several reasons. On October 4, Stone had written a letter to patrons of the *Forum* publications informing them of the new social concerns section, along with the announcement that *Lutheran Forum* would be expanding from a quarterly to a bi-monthly publication. The disintegration of the proposed social issues section meant that the bi-monthly publication plan was not financially feasible, and *Lutheran Forum* remained a quarterly. It was ironic that ALPB, so long an advocate for inter-Lutheran cooperation, was now viewed as too controversial to be welcomed as a partner in a cooperative venture. The incident also revealed that not just the LCMS but both the LCA and the ALC were still quite a way from seriously considering concrete cooperative projects—and certainly not if those projects involved the ALPB.

Una Sancta
"a Lutheran and Catholic vision"

A more successful effort addressed another of the ALPB's longtime concerns, that of liturgical renewal. *Una Sancta* was a journal with roots in the 1930s. It had gone through several incarnations through the years; its focus had been on liturgical matters (though more recently it had also discussed the church's response to various social issues—a linkage that had also been true, for example, of the Oxford Movement in England). *Una Sancta* had a succession of editors through the years, several of whom had ALPB connections (including Arthur Carl Piepkorn, Glenn Stone, and Richard John Neuhaus). The most recent version of the magazine had ceased publication in 1969.

In 1975, there was conversation among several people, including Stone, about the possibility of resurrecting the journal yet again. They believed that the active work of the Inter-Lutheran Commission on Worship, which was working toward what would become the *Lutheran Book of Worship,* made it imperative that there be some forum for wider discussion of liturgical goals. Stone suggested doing this in conjunction with *Lutheran Forum.* He proposed adding two issues per year to *Lutheran Forum*'s publication schedule which would be devoted to liturgical concerns. The ALPB board was interested, but thought it not financially feasible; they suggested instead that there be a regular section in each issue.

Stone convened a group to make specific plans. Those involved included LCA pastors John Cochran, Ronald Bagnall, John Halborg and Louis Smith; LCMS pastors Larry Bailey, Leonard Klein and Raymond Schulze; Deacon Thomas Dorris and Dr. Gail Ramshaw Schmidt. The proposal they developed called for a quarterly 12-page supplement to *Lutheran Forum* that would be bound within the journal (paginated differently, to make clear that it was technically not part of *Lutheran Forum*) and mailed to all *Lutheran Forum* subscribers. It would have its own editor and an editorial committee which would include the editor of *Lutheran Forum.* The ALPB would handle all business and subscription matters, and the editor of *Lutheran Forum* would have final editorial authority. The ALPB board agreed in principle to this plan in June 1976.[48]

Stone, Cochran and Klein began trying to raise funds; Stone had estimated the cost would be about $5,000 per year and had recommended that they not proceed without two years' funding in hand. Raising the money proved to be slow going. In 1977 Klein wrote to contributors, apologizing that nothing had yet been published. He told them that they hoped to proceed with a single supplement in the fall of 1978, but he acknowledged that this was not what had been proposed and he offered to return the contribution of anyone who asked.[49]

In December 1977, the board authorized a one-time issue, with the expectation that this might attract enough interest and support to continue the supplement. Edited by Klein, *Una Sancta*'s new iteration appeared in the Reformation 1978 issue of *Lutheran Forum*. The editor hoped that it could be "issued occasionally" and invited readers to help underwrite its future. That first edition led with an article by Robert Wilken on "Lutheran Catholicity":

> This is not the place to chronicle the ins and outs of Una Sancta's history nor the shifts in Lutheran consciousness over the last several decades. Let it simply be said that the time is ripe for a renewal of Una Sancta's original vision which was no less a Lutheran and Catholic vision than that which marked its life when it was devoted primarily to the renewal of the liturgy and the Church's social responsibility. For a genuine and authentic mark of Catholic Christianity is, and always has been, the cultivation not only of the public worship of the Church but a nurturing of the inner life.

The supplement also included an article by Gordon Lathrop advocating weekly Eucharist, a historical sketch by Aubrey Bougher about the movement toward more frequent communion in the LCA, an account of liturgical renewal at Zion Church, Wausau, WI, by Dale Hansen, and a defense of the true Lutheran character of the new *Lutheran Book of Worship* by Leonard Klein.[50]

Una Sancta proved to be a success. Another edition appeared the following year, and then again in 1979—this time without the differently numbered pages. By 1983 it was referred to as the "Annual *Una Sancta* Supplement," and then in 1985 as the "Annual *Una Sancta* Issue of *Lutheran Forum*." It continued as a more or less annual feature until 1993, and then as an occasional theme—though liturgical matters were discussed in nearly every issue of *Lutheran Forum*.

Notes

1. Minutes, ALPB Board of Directors, 6 Mar. 1972.
2. Minutes, ALPB Board of Directors, 24 Mar. 1972.
3. R. Koenig to Board of Directors, 23 Mar. 1972.
4. Minutes, ALPB Board of Directors, 4 May 1972.
5. Minutes, ALPB Board of Directors, 28 Nov. 1972; Glenn Stone, "A Study Paper," (29 Jan. 1973), 2, ALPB Archives.
6. Ibid., 3.
7. Ibid., 4-5.
8. Ibid., 6.
9. Ibid., 7-8.
10. Ibid., 10.
11. Ibid., 11.
12. Ibid., 13-14.

13. Ibid., 16.

14. Minutes, ALPB Board of Directors, 18 Feb. 1973.

15. Minutes, ALPB Board of Directors, 3 April 1973.

16. Minutes, ALPB Board of Directors, 6 June 1973.

17. Minutes, ALPB Board of Directors, 1 Aug. 1973.

18. *Lutheran News* 1, no. 1 (15 Dec. 1962), 1. For a more extensive discussion of Herman Otten's early life and career, see chapter one of James C. Burkee, *Power, Politics, and the Missouri Synod: A Conflict that Changed American Christianity* (Minneapolis: Fortress Press, 2011).

19. *FL* 2, no. 6 (June 1973), 6-7; *Christian News* 6, no. 26 (25 June 1973), 9.

20. Rudolph Ressmeyer to Council of Presidents, n.d. [ca. Mar. 1972], ALPB Archives.

21. Richard E. Koenig, "What's behind the showdown in the in the LCMS? Conservative reaction: 1965-1969," *Lutheran Forum* 7, no. 2 (May 1973), 21.

22. *FL* 2, no. 7 (July 1973), 6.

23. Richard Koenig to Glenn Stone, 4 Jan. 1974, Gettysburg ALPB Collection, Box 29, Folder 2e.

24. Glenn Stone to Richard Koenig, 17 Jan. 1974, Gettysburg ALPB Collection, Box 29, Folder 2e.

25. Richard Koenig to John Leonard, 17 May 1974, Gettysburg ALPB Collection, Box 29, Folder 2c; *FL* 3, no. 6 (June 1974), 1.

26. Glenn Stone to Richard John Neuhaus, 16 Aug. 1974, Gettysburg ALPB Collection Box 29, Folder 2b.

27. Draft memo by Bob Madigan appended to Minutes, ALPB Board of Directors, 14 August 1974; Minutes, ALPB Board of Directors, 18 Sept. 1974.

28. *FL* 3, no. 11 (Nov. 1974), 12.

29. Minutes, ALPB Board of Directors, 18 Feb. 1975.

30. *FL* 3, no. 10/11 (Oct./Nov. 1974), 5.

31. Ibid.

32. *FL* 5, no. 6 (June 1976), 7.

33. "The Continuing Crisis: A supplement to *Forum Letter*," *FL* 5, no. 7 (July 1976), CC-1.

34. Charles Austin, "Those Strange Missourians," "The Continuing Crisis Revisited: A supplement to *Forum Letter*," *FL* 10, no. 8 (21 Aug. 1981), CC-4.

35. *FL* 7, no. 2 (24 Feb. 1978), 3-5.

36. Ibid., 7.

37. *FL* 12, no. 3 (1 Apr. 1983), 3.

38. *FL* 9, no. 5 (30 May 1980), 8.

39. Larry Bailey and Leonard Klein, "Renewing Lutheran Worship Installment #5," *FL* 5, no. 5 (May 1976), 7.

40. "The Continuing Crisis Number 13: A supplement to FORUM LETTER," FL 7, no. 2 (24 Feb. 1978), CC-4.

41. *FL* 11, no. 7 (30 July 1982), 1-4.

42. *FL* 7, no. 4 (28 Apr. 1978), 7; *FL* 8, no. 6 (29 June 29, 1979), 5; *FL* 8, no. 7 (17 Aug. 1979), 8.

43. *FL* 8, no. 3 (30 Mar. 1979), 2-4.

44. Minutes, ALPB Board of Directors, 18 Sept. 1974.

45. Glenn Stone to "Patrons of Lutheran Forum/Forum Letter," 4 Oct. 1974, Gettysburg ALPB Collection, Box 29, Folder 2b.

46. Charles Lutz to Franklin Jensen and Russell Long, 7 Oct. 1974; Franklin Jensen to Charles Lutz, 15 Oct. 1974; Glenn Stone to "Interested parties," 1 Nov. 1974, Gettysburg ALPB Collection, Box 5, Folder 3a.

47. "Record of Meeting, Advisory Editorial Committee for LUTHERAN FORUM'S PUBLIC ISSUE," 17-18 October 1974; Glenn Stone to Richard J. Neuhaus, 20 Nov. 1974, Gettysburg ALPB Collection, Box 5, Folder 3a.

48. "Una Sancta: A Proposal for a Journal of Theology and Liturgy," [undated, ca. 1976], 6, Gettysburg ALPB Collection, Box 2, Folder 4; Minutes, ALPB Board of Directors, 8 June 1976.

49. Leonard Klein to "Dear Friend," 21 Dec. 1977, Gettysburg ALPB Collection, Box 2, Folder 3a.

50. Robert Wilken, "Una Sancta: Lutheran Catholicity," *LF* 12, no. 3 (Reformation 1978), S3.

Chapter 17

WIDENING CONCERNS

With Glenn Stone back at the helm of *Lutheran Forum* and Richard John Neuhaus firmly in place as editor of *Forum Letter*, the two publications settled into an editorial pattern that would remain stable for several years. The ALPB board, meanwhile, turned its attention to other matters—subscription numbers, advertising revenue, the tract program, the quincentennial of Luther's birth, a new statement of purpose. The Bureau was also involved in an ambitious ecumenical initiative with the Graymoor Institute.

Forging a new identity
"unity among Lutherans and all Christians"

The discovery that the ALPB had no current constitution led to further review of its legal documents. An amendment to the stated purpose of the ALPB in its articles of incorporation and bylaws was approved in 1975:

> To proclaim the Gospel of Jesus Christ according to the teachings of the Holy Scriptures and the confessions of the Lutheran Church; to make known the doctrines, practices, history and life of the Lutheran Church; to work for and support the movement for unity among Lutherans and all Christians; to promote and strengthen Lutheran cooperative mission and ministry; to facilitate exchange of ideas and

information among Lutherans and other Christians. To accomplish these purposes the Bureau shall publish appropriate literature and engage in such other activities as it deems useful, all to be accomplished without profit.

The policy statement adopted by the board two years previously had emphasized the need for Lutheran unity, but here there was overt support for unity "among Lutherans and all Christians." This new ecumenism would become an increasingly important focus in ALPB publications.[1]

Discussion of the legal documents went on for some months. The board considered changing the corporate name of the Bureau to something more in keeping with its present ministry. In the end, they decided not to do so, but agreed that in some circumstances it was appropriate to use *Lutheran Forum* when referring to the Bureau's ministries, implying that programs sponsored by *Lutheran Forum* were *de facto* programs of the ALPB. Amendments to the articles of incorporation were approved in May 1977 and accepted by the state in May 1979.[2]

Efforts to broaden the constituency continued, but by the end of 1976 the board's membership was still more than half Missouri Synod. Two months later, four new board members were elected who were LCA or ALC, bringing the total membership closer to parity among the church bodies. In contrast, of those who responded to a survey of readers mailed with *Forum Letter* earlier that year, 40% were LCA, 34% LCMS, 23% ALC, and 3% other. In 1979, Stone told the board that circulation had reached "an all-time high" (at that point around 5,300) and estimated that the publications "reach about 25% of active Lutheran clergy."[3]

The resumption of the tract ministry appeared to be successful. The first reprinting of four tracts had sold out in two months, and a second was being planned. An older series of tracts designed for use during Lent was also reprinted. A tract on the liturgical year was redesigned based on changes being recommended by the Inter-Lutheran Commission on Worship. Stone would report in 1975 that since the resumption of the tract ministry, some 416,000 pieces had been sold; to the delight of the board, the treasurer's report for 1977 revealed that income from the sale of tracts had been $2000 more than anticipated.[4]

The board also reprised other projects and emphases of earlier years. The ALPB had sponsored New York City concerts by the St. Olaf College Choir in the 1920s and again in 1972; now they agreed to do so again in 1980, with Lutheran Community Services as a co-sponsor. Ticket sales filled about 70% of Avery Fischer Hall, and the ALPB realized some $3,000 in profit from the event. The Bureau sponsored the choir's concert again in 1985.[5]

A stewardship program was proposed in 1977 by board member John Leonard. The "Thank You Envelope Plan" had been developed at St. Mark's Lutheran Church in Yonkers and had significantly increased income in that parish; Leonard hoped that the

ALPB might make it available to other congregations. The board was intrigued, and the concept was developed over the next three years. Finally published in 1980, it was described as "a new program designed to help Christians grow in the grace of gratitude and to enable parishes to raise 'new money' for a variety of causes." Unfortunately, it was not as successful as the board had hoped, and only a handful of congregations ordered the materials.[6]

Another change of office location took place in 1980, when Gustavus Adolphus Lutheran Church, the Bureau's home since 1971, asked for a prohibitive rent increase. Space at the existing rental cost was offered at St. Luke's Lutheran Church on 46th Street in Manhattan, and the move was accomplished in December of that year.

The presidency of the ALPB changed hands several times during these years. John H. Leonard served until 1976, at which time he was succeeded by Harold Midtbo. Midtbo was an executive with Exxon, and he was the first non-Missouri Synod Lutheran to serve as president of the Bureau. The next president was Pr. George Matzat, pastor of St. Peter's Lutheran Church, Huntington, NY, who served from 1979 to 1983. He was followed by Pr. Richard Pankow, pastor of Lutheran Church of the Good Shepherd in Brooklyn, who was president from 1983 to 1985. Pankow in turn was followed by Dr. Leonard Roellig, a physicist and administrator at City College of New York.

Controversy over Neuhaus

"There he goes again"

Lutheran Forum/Forum Letter remained the most significant aspect of the ALPB's program, but there was continued disagreement about *Forum Letter* under Neuhaus. There were several things that got readers—and board members—riled up. One was the issue of abortion. Since the 1973 Supreme Court ruling on *Roe v. Wade*, the topic had been a contentious one in America, not least within the churches. Both *Lutheran Forum* and *Forum Letter* had consistently taken a pro-life stance, but it was Neuhaus's increasingly vocal opposition to abortion that rankled some subscribers. In 1980, he tackled the criticism head on:

> 'There he goes again.' Among the most frequent criticisms this LETTER receives is that too much attention is paid the abortion debate. As one friendly correspondent put it recently, 'Everyone knows where you stand by now, so why not just let the subject rest for a while?' Why not? For the same reason that in years past and still today one could not be quiet about racial discrimination in Church and society. For the same reason one could not be silent about the shameful indifference of the Church to ministry among the poor, in the inner city and elsewhere. For the same reason that, during the Vietnam years and since, one could not desist from pressing the moral issues posed by America's foreign policy. ... I am persuaded that the issues involved in the abortion debate engage the most urgent moral questions facing our

society today. The core question is, to put it quite simply, How do we define the human community for which we accept collective responsibility?[7]

But while his emphasis on abortion may have been the most frequent criticism directed at Neuhaus, it was not the only one. Some thought he was unfair to women; while he didn't quite oppose the ordination of women, he thought there were "troubling questions" about the arguments being made in support. Others, particularly some of his old friends and political allies, were convinced that Neuhaus had made a radical shift in his political allegiances. In November 1981 Neuhaus published an open letter to him by "a long-time friend," Pr. Ralph Moellering. Moellering was "puzzled by some of your interpretations, affirmations and critiques in recent years." "Perhaps it should not be surprising then that some of your erstwhile cohorts are inquiring: 'What happened to Dick Neuhaus? What sort of psychological-sociological-ecclesiastical factors have produced this transformation?'"[8]

Neuhaus insisted that he was in fact "a good deal more radical now that I have ever been." He admitted his perspectives had changed. "Newman wrote, 'Growth is the only evidence of life,' and I hope I've grown." Many of those who ask about his change, he went on, "are refugees from the radicalism of the '60s who are pained that an erstwhile cohort has not joined them in exile." But "we are all together in [an] exile" which "has little to do with the politics of the principalities and powers. ... I believe we must resist those, whether of the left or of the right, who would realign the Church by political definitions of reality. ... You and I are pledged to a catholicity that is the opposite of that." He mused that it was his vocation, or his fate, "to spend a great deal of time on matters political." He hoped that his lengthy response would help "explain how and why I'm doing that and thus answers, in part, the question of what has happened to Dick Neuhaus. So far."[9]

In May 1978, the board spent ninety minutes discussing the "philosophy and direction" of its publications (though unfortunately the secretary did not summarize the discussion). The conversation continued in a desultory fashion over the next several months, but in 1980 a "Committee to Review and Evaluate Publications" was appointed, consisting of board members Cecile Johnson, Rudy Ressmeyer, and James Solheim. They surveyed readers who had not renewed subscriptions, examined various documents about the history of the two publications, and met with the editors.

They reported, first, that *Forum Letter* "is read more thoroughly because of its format and style of writing," but suggested that "some topics are dealt with more extensively than necessary." In general, the committee thought the *Letter* "is pretty well fulfilling its purposes." On the other hand, they had some suggestions about *Lutheran Forum*. Its contents seemed "too parochial," aimed at "a certain set of clergy" rather than a more general lay/clergy audience. They thought the layout and graphics were not up to contemporary standards, and that articles tended to be "excessively wordy." They proposed several questions that the board might consider about how both publications might be improved. But they also insisted that "the editors are, indeed, to be commended for their very good work, given the limitations imposed by limited budgets and time."[10]

The report was discussed at the May 1980 board meeting, and the result was the appointment of another task force, largely composed of non-board members, "to advise the board on the future needs of the Church in the area of independent journalism." While there are some minutes missing over the next couple of years, it does not appear that this task force ever actually materialized, and in 1982 the board asked board members Gail Ramshaw Schmidt, William Gentz and Leonard Roellig "to evaluate the last two years" of the publications. They reported they were pleased with changes in *Lutheran Forum*, finding the appearance good, the layout attractive. They appreciated the new *Una Sancta* section, and wondered if other regular sections on different topics might be considered. They wondered if "the topics and tone of the articles could be somewhat more controversial," but hastily added that they did not "advocate any radical change."[11]

As for *Forum Letter*, however, there was much disagreement. The committee could only report and summarize the contradictory opinions:

> This is the livelier of the publications, personally read more. This is the peripheral publication, only cursorily scanned. The topics are healthily broadening. The topics are too far removed from one's life to be interesting. The gossip aspect is appreciated. The gossip aspect is boring. The pithiness of the writing and the succinct nature of the reviews make it useful and snappy reading. The brevity too often allows for topics to be presented superficially and to be praised or condemned without stated cause.

It finally seemed to boil down to how one felt about Neuhaus. Perhaps the most trenchant comment in the report was that "the ALPB must continually ask whether its purpose lies in supporting such personal journalism, whether the editor is Richard John Neuhaus or someone else." The board went into executive session to discuss the report, asking the president to relay a summary of the conversation privately to Neuhaus and Stone. It would be just a year later that another major controversy over Neuhaus would erupt, causing the board yet more anxiety over their support of "such personal journalism."[12]

The Forum/Graymoor proposal
"Healing the breach of the 16th century"

In 1978, ALPB personnel were instrumental in an ambitious ecumenical project that came to be known as the "Forum/Graymoor Proposal." It began in February 1978 with an informal meeting between the staffs of *Lutheran Forum* and the Graymoor Ecumenical Institute, an independent Roman Catholic organization dedicated to ecumenical dialogue. The purpose was to develop a plan tying together the 450th anniversary of the Augsburg Confession in 1980 and the Week of Prayer for Christian Unity (a special focus of Graymoor), with the hope of fostering Lutheran/Roman Catholic dialogue in parishes across the United States. Neuhaus was a prime mover in this project, and he served as the group's unofficial secretary.

They met for several hours in a wide-ranging discussion. They proposed that the theme for this observance might be "healing the breach of the 16th century" (a phrase likely coined by Neuhaus). Neuhaus summarized the conversation:

> 450 years after the Augsburg Confession, is the division still necessary? If division is not necessary, is it permissible? These questions are given new urgency and substance by the results of the RC-Luth theological dialogue. The danger is that the studies issuing from the dialogue will simply gather dust rather than playing their role in carrying us on to the next stage of ecumenical engagement.

Those present believed that Graymoor and the ALPB had a "distinct advantage of relative freedom" as independent groups which were "less limited in taking new initiatives." Their goal was to engage thousands of Roman Catholics and Lutherans in local communities in a study of the official Lutheran/Roman Catholic dialogues to date. They hoped this study would tackle "reunion, or 'reintegration,' of the Church in the West, mutual recognition of baptism, eucharist, ministry, and other matters relevant to healing the breach of the 16th century."[13]

An expanded group met in April; it included eight Lutherans (five of them with strong ALPB connections) and seven Roman Catholics (including noted theologian Avery Dulles and a representative from the National Conference of Catholic Bishops). This conversation led to plans for a series of regional gatherings in the fall of 1979, a local dialogue program that would begin in January 1980 (in connection with the Week of Prayer for Christian Unity), and an encouragement of "practical cooperation and significant interaction" at the local level during Lent and Easter of 1980.[14]

They also agreed to develop resources for local use. The primary piece would be a summary of the Lutheran/Roman Catholic dialogues; this was ultimately published as *Exploring the Faith We Share*, edited by Glenn Stone and Graymoor's Charles La-Fontaine, with a forward by Dulles and Lutheran ecumenist George Lindbeck. The group hoped to have all materials issued jointly by Catholic and Lutheran publishers, but neither Fortress Press nor Augsburg Publishing House agreed to take part, so the book was issued by Paulist Press alone. They also produced a leader's guide and a set of study guides based on the book.[15]

They contacted Lutheran and Roman Catholic leaders, seeking their support. The response was generally positive, though with some hesitation. ALC president David Preus was, of Lutheran leaders, the most supportive. The LCA's Robert Marshall was encouraging, but he believed that the LCA's constitution prevented him from directly supporting any initiatives that were not "officially LCA." Not unexpectedly, LCMS president J. A. O. Preus was most reticent. He wrote to Neuhaus that "grassroots ecumenical engagement between Lutherans and Roman Catholics has much to commend itself," but thought it more appropriate that any such program be channeled through LCUSA "rather than turning the project over to an independent and unofficial journal which does not represent any of our churches."[16]

Neuhaus responded to Preus by reiterating that the role of Graymoor and *Lutheran Forum* was "simply initiating and catalytic in nature," and they expected "local churches, colleges, and informal groups would 'do their own thing.'" Given Preus's vehement anti-communism, Neuhaus wisely refrained from using the tongue-in-cheek description (based on an inaccurate quotation of a Maoist saying) that was common among the Forum/Graymoor committee: they hoped to "let a thousand flowers bloom." He suggested that Preus push LCUSA to "launch a program encouraging grassroots engagement." There was apparently no further response from Preus.[17]

Remarkably, Preus would later write to an Illinois Roman Catholic monsignor who had invited him to take part in a Lutheran/Roman Catholic event that he "knew very little" about the Forum/Graymoor proposal, and he took a gratuitous swipe at Neuhaus:

> From what I can determine, it is the result of the efforts of a Roman Catholic priest, unknown to me, and one Reverend Richard Neuhaus of New York City, who is presently listed on the clergy rosters of both the Lutheran Church—Missouri Synod and the Association of Evangelical Lutheran Churches. This is an unrealistic position and one which cannot continue indefinitely. ... Pastor Neuhaus has never been authorized by The Lutheran Church—Missouri Synod ... to plan and promote any kind of Lutheran/Roman Catholic Dialogues, or anything else for that matter. ... Neuhaus and his Catholic counterpart have set up the agenda for these meetings but have acted entirely on their own, without receiving the consent or approval of responsible parties within the Lutheran Church—Missouri Synod.

The letter fell into Neuhaus's hands, and he naturally printed excerpts in *Forum Letter* and then excoriated Preus's "disingenuity." He pointed out that Preus, like all the Lutheran presidents, had in fact been kept fully informed about the proposal for some two years. There is, of course, "nothing new or particularly interesting about inaccuracies in statements by Jacob Preus." These comments did nothing to improve the ALPB's reputation among conservative Missouri Synod Lutherans.[18]

Despite Preus's resistance, some LCMS district presidents were among the bishops and judicatory heads of both communions who were excited about the proposal. By the time it was publicly announced in 1979, nearly 40 Roman Catholic bishops and more than 50 Lutheran synod and district presidents had endorsed the project. The announcement had originally been planned for Reformation Day in 1978, but with the deaths of Popes Paul VI and John Paul I and the election of Pope John Paul

II dominating the religious news, the planners decided to hold off until the Week of Prayer for Christian Unity in January 1979.

All of this raised some hackles among members of the ALPB board. At the September meeting in 1978, someone asked "why the board had not been previously apprised of the project." Stone explained that it had originally not been conceived as an ALPB project *per se*, but an editorial emphasis of the publications. He "acknowledged that it had grown in dimensions beyond what was originally expected," but he assured them that he anticipated no impact on the ALPB's budget.[19]

At the next meeting, Stone and Neuhaus gave the board a complete report on the proposal's history and development. The board then endorsed the proposal in principle, with the understanding that the editors would provide them with a written document for discussion at the next meeting. They considered "possible production of materials by ALPB for use in the dialogues contemplated" by the plan. Unfortunately, the minutes of that next meeting have been lost, but over the next several months the board received rosy reports on the impact the program was having across the church.[20]

Though the board did not become closely involved in the details of the proposal, the ALPB promoted it in several ways. First and most important, the Bureau gave it continuing publicity through *Forum Letter* and *Lutheran Forum*. In June 1979, for example, *Forum Letter* included a special supplement entitled "Suggestions for Roman Catholic—Lutheran Interaction at the Local Level," written by Graymoor's Thaddeus Horgan. It included information on how to order copies of the five volumes of *Lutherans and Catholics in Dialogue* that had been published at that time; further suggestions were included in the September issue. Neuhaus also wrote frequently about Roman Catholic/Lutheran ecumenism, sometimes going so far as to speak of "efforts toward reunion."[21]

Lutheran Forum highlighted the proposal in the Lent 1979 issue, with an editorial offering "Questions and Answers about the Forum/Graymoor Proposal." That issue also printed a letter from Pr. Paul Meyer, raising cautions about the emphasis on the Lutheran/Roman Catholic relationship. Neuhaus addressed Meyer's concerns:

> We are not returning to Rome, nor is Rome capitulating to Wittenberg. We are neither prodigals nor conquerors. We are sinners all, seeking to be more obedient to what you rightly describe as Christ's work of Christian unity. Unity is not possible without humility. Humility about our ability to undo the evils of the past and build better for the future. Humility in acknowledging our need for the gifts others can offer. Most of all, we need the humility that breaks the demonic sense of satisfaction with ourselves, the fatal feeling of self-sufficiency that elevates our concern for 'our Church' above his will for his church.[22]

The Lent 1980 issue of *Lutheran Forum* focused almost entirely on Lutheran/Roman Catholic matters, with a striking cover photograph of a Montana church sign advertising "Prince of Peace Lutheran Church" and "John XXIII Catholic Church" above the words "Everyone Welcome." Beneath the photo was the caption, "Signs of Spring?" Inside was an article on the two congregations in Missoula who shared not only a building but a Christian education program and occasional joint services.[23]

The next issue included several articles on the Augsburg Confession from an ecumenical perspective. It included the text of a statement on the Augustana, "All One Under Christ," issued by the Joint Roman Catholic/Lutheran Commission of the Vatican Secretariat for Promoting Christian Unity and the Lutheran World Federation. It also contained an essay by Roman Catholic ecumenist George Tavard on "The Augustana and the Ecumenical Future." The Bureau offered a cassette tape of a lecture by Walter Bouman entitled "The Augsburg Confession and Our Ecumenical Mission" and a six-page reprint from *Lutheran Forum* containing the Lindbeck and Hotchkin presentations. The Bureau ultimately served as a "joint sponsor" of *Exploring the Faith We Share*, giving at least a nominal Lutheran imprimatur to the book published by Paulist Press.[24]

Stone recruited and corresponded with more than a hundred Lutheran coordinators of the project around the country, supplying them with a stream of information such as the names of local Roman Catholic ecumenical officials in their area with whom they might work. Many of them were present in Lombard, IL, in October 1979, when an organization called "Partners in Reconciliation" was launched under the leadership of LCA pastor Jack Lundin and others. It was conceived as "a clearing-house for ideas and materials in furtherance of the 'Year of the Augsburg Confession' emphasis." While not directly related to the ALPB, this group's newsletter, *ReConciLe*, was distributed as a supplement to *Forum Letter* beginning in December of that year. Edited by Bob Hale, the usually bimonthly supplement reported on what various individuals and groups were doing around the country to promote Roman Catholic/ Lutheran reconciliation.

At the end of the Forum/Graymoor proposal's "year," Lundin, Stone, Neuhaus, and a few others met in Chicago and decided that Partners in Reconciliation should be reconstituted as "an association of Lutherans for evangelical-catholic unity." *ReConciLe* would continue as a publication independent of *Forum Letter*; it struggled along through 1981, but it became apparent that the enterprise was "financially prohibitive." In 1982, the offices of Partners in Reconciliation moved to New York, with the same address as ALPB, and Neuhaus became the new editor of *ReConciLe* (with Glenn Stone as managing editor). Now published quarterly, the newsletter was mailed separately to the subscription list that had been built by Partners in Reconciliation, but it also became a regular supplement to *Forum Letter*. The first issue under the new arrangement stated that "RECONCILE is published quarterly by American Lutheran Publicity Bureau in behalf of PARTNERS IN RECONCILIATION."[25]

Under Neuhaus's editorship, what had been a newsy roundup of ecumenical events and programs became a platform for more substantive essays—sometimes controversial. The December 1983 issue, for example, was a four-page essay on "Abortion and the

Unity of Christians"; January 1984 took up "Women's Ordination as an Ecumenical Issue." That appears to be the final issue of *ReConciLe*, though no reference appeared in *Forum Letter* or the ALPB board minutes accounting for the supplement's demise.

The Luther quincentennial
"God's Man of Faith"

With a successful "Year of the Augsburg Confession" coming to an end, the ALPB began planning for the 1983 celebration of the quincentennial of Luther's birth. A commemorative 7-inch plate was designed, in consultation with Bing and Grøndahl Porcelain, Ltd. of Copenhagen, depicting Luther preaching in an intimate setting at the Wartburg Castle. Bing and Grøndahl were also commissioned to produce a set of Luther commemorative trays. To round out the commemorative collection, the board engaged Celebration Arts to design and produce a Luther medallion. All these items sold reasonably well; by May 1983, there had been orders for 1585 medals, 1214 plates, and 1041 trays.[26]

Another quincentennial resource was the republication of the Luther comic book, *God's Man of Faith: The life and teachings of Martin Luther*. Originally produced as part of the Reformation Week resources in 1959, the piece had been out of print for years, and rights to it had been transferred to Concordia Publishing House. Concordia agreed to return the rights to the Bureau, and Stone set to work updating the language, both to tone down the pre-Vatican II triumphalism of 1959 and to reflect more inclusive language. By 1983 the booklet was ready for publication, and it found a sizable audience.

Still another Luther year resource was a sound recording entitled "Music of the Reformation." Produced by Pro Arte Records of Minneapolis, it featured the East German Desden Kreuzchor, with the well-known German tenor Peter Schreier as soloist. Available on either vinyl record or cassette tape, the set included a historical introduction to the music and reproductions of some of the original scores. The ALPB became the primary distributor of the recording.

All these Luther year materials were quite successful; in March 1984, the board was told that the various projects had netted $34,711, "far overmatching losses in the publications program" and providing an "unusually large annual surplus" in the ALPB's budget for the year.[27]

The *60 Minutes* kerfuffle
"tidal wave of reaction"

In 1983, a very public controversy erupted over *Forum Letter* editor Richard John Neuhaus which led to some heated discussion among ALPB leaders and cost the

ALPB publications some subscribers and supporters. Neuhaus had been a founder of the Institute on Religion and Democracy (IRD), a Christian think tank focused on the involvement of American churches in international affairs. The group decried what it claimed was inappropriate channeling of church funds to Marxist regimes in Latin America and elsewhere by various denominations and other organizations such as the National and World Councils of Churches.

The IRD's media campaign began with a January 1983 article in *Reader's Digest* entitled "Do You Know Where Your Church Offerings Go?" in which IRD founder David Jessup accused the United Methodist Church of using church money to support "pro-Soviet totalitarian movements." The second blow came later that month, with a story on the popular CBS news magazine *60 Minutes* entitled "The Gospel According to Whom?" Among those interviewed by Morley Safer was Richard John Neuhaus. The clips of his interview used in the broadcast were brief, but Neuhaus's words were sharp:

> What worries me most—indeed, outrages me most—is when the Church starts telling lies. ... The height of hypocrisy is to pretend that in painting a rosy picture of the sufferings of the poor, in making excuses for those who oppress the poor, that one is speaking on behalf of the poor. So we have religious leaders who go to countries which are massively repressive regimes, in which Christians are in jail, are being tortured, have been killed by the thousands. And they go to those countries, and our religious dignitaries consort with the persecutors of the Church of Christ. This is evil; this is wrong. This discredits the Church as social witness, it undermines any elementary notion of justice.

Others from IRD interviewed on the program were more outspoken than Neuhaus; United Methodist pastor Ed Robb accused the ecumenical agencies of producing "propaganda ... for a pro-Marxist cause." Neuhaus was more nuanced, admitting that "for the most part" money donated to churches for meeting human need was being used in appropriate ways.[28]

The ecumenical and denominational agencies responded immediately, protesting that the *Reader's Digest* and *60 Minutes* stories were hit pieces by an irresponsible right-wing group. In the furor that unfolded over the next weeks, Neuhaus seemed to be particularly targeted. Within days of the CBS broadcast, he was fired as senior editor of *Worldview*. He was accused of willful deception by ALC president David Preus and Lutheran World Ministries executive Paul Wee.[29]

Responding to what he called the "tidal wave of reaction," Neuhaus defended himself in the pages of *Forum Letter*. He noted that the program had aired only a few minutes of what had been a two-hour interview. He considered the criticism that his language may have been ill-chosen, but concluded that in fact "lying is precisely what has been done by church leaders who consort with the persecutors of the Church and then try to deny or belittle the existence of such persecution." He insisted that there was ample documentation for all charges made against the ecumenical and denominational agencies. "Does anyone really believe that billion-dollar enterprises like the *Digest* and CBS, with their rafts of high-priced lawyers, are going to expose themselves to libel suits?" Of course, both offered "highly editorialized stories," not a "fair and balanced overview," but that is the nature of journalism.[30]

But the "reaction of the councils and their controlling member churches to date," he suggested, "has been just that, reaction. ... [T]here have been invitations withdrawn, slanderous allegations, threats to my livelihood." Church leaders have engaged in what "was, in the Nixon era, called stonewalling." Neuhaus regretted that David Preus and James Crumley had both signed a letter defending the councils against the allegations. "One can sympathize with the pressures for establishment solidarity, but it is still very disappointing." While opining that the National Council of Churches "may have outlived its usefulness," Neuhaus argued that the World Council "is a chief bearer of the ecumenical imperative and promise." What is called for is "critical self-examination," an acknowledgement that "something is deeply wrong." The goal, he insisted, is "a revitalized ecumenical vision and an enhanced credibility of the churches' witness to the world."[31]

But the "tidal wave of reaction" was far from over, and the ALPB board itself caught the wave. At the March 1983 board meeting, there was a "special order" on the agenda. The minutes reflect the turmoil of the conversation:

> Due to the controversy arising from the '60 Minutes' program on the National and World Councils of Churches, in which Pastor Richard Neuhaus participated, the board decided to open up a discussion about Pastor Neuhaus as our writer of FORUM LETTER and about the LETTER in general. Pastor Stone gave an historical overview of the LETTER, which has always functioned independently of the board, and of the writers, who enjoy editorial freedom. Pastor [George] Matzat [president of the board] focused on the issue at hand, heightened by the '60 Minutes' controversy, that the LETTER is seen by some to be disturbingly idiosyncratic and too narrow for us to continue to support in the way we have been supporting it. Several board members spoke of Pr. Neuhaus' identification with both ALPB and the Institute for Religion and Democracy, but others urged that the discussion remain focused on the LETTER. Several board members dealt with the nature of personal journalism and [wondered] whether Pr. Neuhaus has become too personal in his handling of topics and disrespectful of opposing opinion.

Neuhaus (who was present for all of this) responded that he was willing to attend any board meeting where *Forum Letter* was discussed. He said that he viewed *Forum Letter* as part of his ministry, and that while he certainly would maintain his personal opinions, he was committed to being "journalistically fair." After lengthy and heated discussion, it was agreed to continue the matter at the next meeting.[32]

In May, the board took up the matter again—first hearing a letter of resignation from a newly elected board member because he did not wish "to become involved in the situation concerning FORUM LETTER and Richard John Neuhaus." While there was apparently reluctance to remove Neuhaus from his editorial role, the board discussed several other possibilities, including adding a second editor or changing the format or frequency of the publication. In the end, a committee was appointed to "explore alternatives and report back" in September.[33]

Much of the September meeting was devoted to the report of this special committee. After some tweaking, their recommendations were adopted. They called for an editorial advisory committee of five members (three of them board members) to "serve as a vehicle for suggestions and advice to Pastor Neuhaus relating to his editorship" of *Forum Letter*. Neuhaus was further directed to devote two pages of each issue to an "op-ed" section written by guest writers, edited by himself and Stone. There were board members who, perhaps hoping that Neuhaus would be asked to step down, expressed disappointment that "this proposal was less far-reaching than they expected." But in the end the board agreed to the proposal that would keep the editor but provide a greater variety of opinions in *Forum Letter*.[34]

The board's actions, however, didn't have much effect. The advisory committee was established and had its first meeting in March 1984, but it doesn't appear to have met after that. The desired "op-ed" feature didn't appear in *Forum Letter* until June 1984. It seldom exceeded a single page, the topics were never particularly controversial, and those asked to contribute tended to have views compatible with Neuhaus's. Newly elected ALPB president Richard Pankow wrote to Stone in August that he was "disappointed in the so called op-ed sections of the letter. I do not think that the subject matter or the authors are of sufficient interest or stimulation to offer an alternative view" to that of Neuhaus. The minutes of the next few board meetings are missing, and there is no indication of what further conversation about this matter took place, if any. The feature would continue until February 1987, but it never accomplished the purpose of presenting an "alternative view" to that of the editor.[35]

The most serious fall-out from this whole affair was an apparent diminishing of both readership and support for the ALPB *Forum* package. In March 1984 Glenn Stone reported to the board that subscriptions had dropped by some 300 (about 5%), leaving the publications with the lowest circulation in ten years. A survey revealed that there were three reasons. Some dropped their subscriptions, they reported, because of the cost, and others because they just had "too much to read." But a significant number specifically cited displeasure with Neuhaus's appearance on *60 Minutes*.[36]

Notes

1. Minutes, ALPB Board of Directors, 10 Sept. 1975.
2. Minutes, ALPB Board of Directors, 24 May 1977 and 22 May 1979.
3. Glenn Stone to ALPB Board of Directors, 2 Dec. 1976; Minutes, ALPB Board of Directors, 22 Feb. 1977; "Forum Letter Questionnaire Data" n.d. [ca. May 1976]; Minutes, ALPB Board of Directors, 25 Sept. 1979. This was not technically an "all-time high" since the initial subscription list, inherited from the *American Lutheran* and the *National Lutheran*, had approached 7,400, but it had dropped below 5,000 after the transition was complete.
4. Minutes, ALPB Board of Directors, 18 Feb. 1975, 25 Nov. 1975, 22 Feb. 1977, 24 May 1977.
5. Minutes, ALPB Board of Directors 26 Feb. 1980.
6. "The THANK YOU ENVELOPE Plan," *LF* 14, no. 4 (Advent 1980), 5.
7. "Protecting the Vulnerable," *FL* 9, no. 1 (25 Jan. 1980), 6.
8. *FL* 10, no. 11 (30 Nov. 1981), 1-2.
9. Ibid., 2-5.
10. Memo "To ALPB Board of Directors from Committee to Review and Evaluate Publications," 15 May 1980, ALPB Archives.
11. Minutes, ALPB Board of Directors, 27 May 1980; "Report of Review Committee," appended to Minutes, ALPB Board of Directors, 23 Mar. 1982.
12. "Report of Review Committee."
13. Richard Neuhaus to "Those attending 23 February meeting and those invited to meet Monday, April 3," 27 Feb. 1978, Gettysburg ALPB Collection, Box 1, Folder 1d. This copy appears to be a rough draft of the memo.
14. "To Heal the Breach of the XVI Century: A proposed program of Lutheran/Roman Catholic Interaction" [report prepared by Thaddeus Horgan], 13 Dec. 1978, Gettysburg ALPB Collection, Box 1, Folder 1b.
15. Glenn C. Stone and Charles LaFontaine, *Exploring the Faith We Share* (New York: Paulist Press, 1980).
16. J. A. O. Preus to Richard Neuhaus, 28 June 1978, Gettysburg ALPB Collection, Box 1, Folder 1d.
17. Richard John Neuhaus to J. A. O. Preus, 7 July 1978, Gettysburg ALPB Collection, Box 1, Folder 1d.
18. *FL* 9, no. 6 (June 20, 1980), 3-4.
19. Minutes, ALPB Board of Directors, 26 Sept. 1978.
20. Minutes, ALPB Board of Directors, 28 Nov. 1978.
21. *FL* 9, no. 1 (25 Jan. 1980), 1.
22. "An exchange of letters on 'healing the breach,'" *LF* 13, no. 1 (Lent 1980), 5, 17.
23. Terry Knight, "Parish Ecumenism in a Montana Valley," *LF* 14, no. 1 (Lent 1980), 15-16.
24. *LF* 13, no 2 (Pentecost 1980), 6-20.
25. *ReConciLe* 3, no. 2 (Apr. 1982), 4.
26. Minutes, ALPB Board of Directors, 24 May 1983.
27. Minutes, ALPB Board of Directors, 27 Mar. 1984.
28. Transcript of "The Gospel According to Whom," *60 Minutes*, Volume 15, Number 19, broadcast 23 Jan. 1983, ALPB Archives.
29. Randy Boyagoda, *Richard John Neuhaus: A Life in the Public Square* (New York: Image, 2015), 427-428, note 18.
30. *FL* 12, no. 2 (25 Feb. 1983), 3-4.
31. Ibid., 5-6.
32. Minutes, ALPB Board of Directors, 22 March 1983.
33. Minutes, ALPB Board of Directors, 24 May 1983.
34. Minutes, ALPB Board of Directors, 27 Sept. 1983.
35. Richard C. Pankow to Glenn Stone, 30 Aug. 1984, ALPB Archives.
36. Minutes, ALPB Board of Directors, 27 Mar. 1984.

Chapter 18

TROUBLED WATERS

During the 1980s, both *Lutheran Forum* and *Forum Letter* turned their attention to the inexorable march toward the merger that would establish the Evangelical Lutheran Church in America. There were significant changes at the ALPB during this period, with a new statement of purpose, a new executive director, and another serious financial crisis. The board also dealt with renewed controversies about *Forum Letter* editor Richard John Neuhaus.

Toward a new church

"a merger of confusions"

In the summer of 1982, the LCA, the ALC and the AELC all approved the formation of the Commission for a New Lutheran Church (CNLC). LCA bishop James Crumley was the speaker at the ALPB's 7th Inter-Lutheran Forum dinner in New York that fall, and his address, "Toward a New Lutheran Church," was subsequently published in *Lutheran Forum*. Crumley sketched out what he believed were the basic elements that must be part of the new church plan. The new body, he said, must be a confessional church, ecumenical in its orientation. It must be "pastoral in all it does" and "have as broad a participation of its members as possible." It must be "socially sensitive" but also "efficient and effective." God, he concluded, is giving Lutherans "a marvelous opportunity. ... Let us pray and work with all of our might that what God asks of us may truly take place as we give ourselves to the task."[1]

The most extensive ALPB commentary on the proposed merger came in *Forum Letter*. In April 1983, Richard John Neuhaus posed what he called "One and Nine Questions Toward a New Church." The document was, he wrote, "an editorial statement of LUTHERAN FORUM, but many people contributed to it."

> First we brainstormed with a small group, then we sent out the results to a wide range of theologians, pastors, bishops and laypeople in the churches. The responses we received were very positive indeed. They came also with suggestions and criticisms, and we have taken these into account, producing a final draft that is significantly different from the first. The statement has, of course, no official status and should be judged on its own merits.

He promised that forthcoming issues would contain commentary on each point, and invited responses. But he was honest about the endeavor:

> You may detect in all this a measure of skepticism with respect to talk about a 'new church.' You would be right. A 'new' church, understood literally, would be a sect. The goal, we believe, is the renewal of our part of the one church of Christ. We also concur entirely with John Tietjen: ... 'We need to guard against the notion that the act of forming a new church is going to be the renewal for which we long. The church we form can be a detriment to or an instrument of renewal. ... Renewal is a continuing process, not an end to be achieved by forming a new church.'[2]

The "one question," the overarching question, was "Will this proposal strengthen the church in the gift and work of Word and Sacrament?" Beneath this most important question, and issuing from it, were the "nine questions":

I. WILL THIS PROPOSAL ENHANCE THE PREACHING OF THE GOSPEL?

II. WILL THIS PROPOSAL ENHANCE THE PRACTICE AND UNDERSTANDING OF BAPTISM AND EUCHARIST?

III. WILL THIS PROPOSAL HELP DEEPEN THE DEVOTION AND DISCIPLESHIP OF BELIEVERS?

IV. WILL THIS PROPOSAL CONTRIBUTE TO VITALIZING CHURCH LEADERSHIP?

V. WILL THIS PROPOSAL STRENGTHEN THE THEOLOGICAL INTEGRITY OF OUR COMMUNITY?

VI. WILL THIS PROPOSAL HELP ANIMATE THE FULLNESS OF MINISTRIES IN THE CHURCH?

VII. WILL THIS PROPOSAL HELP ADVANCE THE EVANGELIZATION OF ALL PEOPLE?

VIII. WILL THIS PROPOSAL MAKE MORE CREDIBLE AND EFFECTIVE
THE WITNESS AND WORK OF CHRISTIANS IN SOCIETY?

IX. WILL THIS PROPOSAL STRENGTHEN LUTHERANISM'S GIFT
TO THE WHOLE BODY OF CHRIST?

Each of the questions was accompanied by an explanation of four or five sentences, further fleshing out the concerns the drafters wished to highlight. "We pray this statement will help inform the continuing conversation and debate," it concluded, "among all who look for a new church that is a church renewed."[3]

Over the next several months, Neuhaus wrote his commentaries on each of the questions posed. His approach was to analyze the documents coming out of the CNLC by comparing them to the "One and Nine." For example, the second question—"Will this proposal enhance the practice and understanding of Baptism and Eucharist?"—was elucidated in the original document as follows:

> A renewed church will lift up Baptism as new birth and therefore the source of dignity and ministry of all who belong to the community of faith. A renewed church will advance the catholic practice, confessional imperative and ecumenical consensus that the Eucharist is the chief service of the people of God. As a Eucharistic community exercising its baptismal gift and vocation, a renewed church will be reconciled and reconciling through the personal and corporate practice of confession and absolution.[4]

When Neuhaus offered his reflections on this question, the Task Force on Theology of the CNLC had recently released its final working draft. He found the report "a generally admirable statement," but with some reservations. On confession and absolution, he said, the task force was "especially weak, saying only: 'Confession, including private confession, has been important in Lutheran tradition.'" "That's it," Neuhaus groused, "no more than a past tense reference in passing. The ongoing significance of Baptism as reconciliation ... is quite entirely ignored."[5]

When it came to the centrality of Eucharist, for so many years a significant emphasis of the ALPB publications, Neuhaus found the task force report woefully inadequate. It falls "far short of what is implicit and explicit in LBW." He acknowledged and lamented the political realities. "Viewed as the striking of a deal among American Lutherans who have different views on these matters," he conceded, perhaps the task force report is "an advance." But "as a statement of an ideal for a new Church that is a Church renewed, it leaves a great deal to be desired."[6]

And that was pretty much how he viewed most of the concerns touched upon in the "One and Nine Questions." "There is ... very little church in much talk about the 'new church,'" Neuhaus complained. He was particularly incensed at what he regarded as "a flaccid confessional subscription." "It would be outrageous," he fumed, if this "permitted Missouri to posture as the champion of confessional integrity." Given reports that many on the commission were inclined to draft a "new confession for a new church" to replace the 16th century Lutheran documents, he groused that the "flaccid subscription" proposed by the task force might be interpreted as "somewhat gratifying."[7]

Neuhaus viewed the direction of the CNLC as a rejection of what had been a growing consciousness of the Lutheran identity as "evangelical catholics" and Lutheranism as "a reforming movement within and for the whole Church." This important task of continued confessional renewal is, "sorry to say, not yet clearly articulated or embraced in the proposals for the new church." Indeed, "the feeling grows that there is little renewal to be expected from the merger process," and it appears that "the new church will be only a merger of confusions."[8]

As the process continued, Neuhaus became increasingly pessimistic. In the spring of 1984, there was a much-publicized vote in the CNLC on a motion to eliminate language referring to God as "Father, Son and Holy Spirit" in the new church's statement of faith and substitute "the triune God." After much discussion, it was defeated on a vote of 33 to 30. That such a proposal would be taken seriously, Neuhaus wrote, "says something profoundly disturbing to many about the seriousness of our confessional commitment to the Catholic faith." He claimed not to be the only one disturbed; indeed, there are "distinguished theologians in the merging churches [who] are privately and sometimes publicly expressing concern that the merger process may be leading American Lutheranism into apostasy, in the most solemn meaning of that term." Some bishops and staff members of the merging bodies "hastened to publicly 'correct the impression'" left by Neuhaus's comments. They argued that the issue was not the doctrine of the Trinity, but the words used to articulate it. Neuhaus would have none of it. "The words are the doctrine. There is no meaning apart from words; more specifically 'Triune' has no meaning apart from 'Father, Son and Holy Spirit.'"[9]

By June 1986, Neuhaus had reluctantly concluded that the merger process should be scrapped entirely. He was hearing from many church leaders that they were gravely concerned over many aspects of the proposal—particularly the profound theological questions about the nature of the church, the ministry, and confessional commitment, as well as the controversial quota system. "Let us say it plainly," Neuhaus wrote. "We are persuaded that the merger process should be suspended. ... We plead with ALC and LCA leaders who have also reached this decision to speak out now while, please God, there is still time."[10]

Lutheran Forum avoided polemics, offering instead sober discussion of the issues at stake in the merger. Editor Glenn Stone suggested, albeit with "some hesitancy," that the new church be called "The Evangelical Catholic Church (Lutheran)."

> As far as we know, the two terms [evangelical and catholic] were first linked by a Lutheran, Archbishop Nathan Söderblom, more than half a century ago. We might as well claim it.

In calling ourselves evangelical catholic, we would be forced to understand for ourselves and interpret for others both sides of the equation, as well as our distinctive linking of them. It would be a salutary exercise in coming to terms with our heritage in all its complexity and—incidentally—a public relations coup.[11]

But while Stone's public comments on the merger were more irenic than Neuhaus's, he, too, had grave concerns. In 1986, when the three church bodies were all facing votes on the merger, he admitted that he wasn't sure how he would vote if he were a delegate to one of the conventions. He found himself "skeptical and uncertain." He expressed his uneasiness, and then confessed that his "ears will be open and my mind active during one of the most interesting—and perhaps unsettling—summers of my life."[12]

The controversial Pastor Neuhaus
"like Zeus sitting atop Mount Olympus"

Neuhaus's coverage of events leading up to the merger embroiled him in yet another controversy. The 1984 AELC convention met in Chicago, and Neuhaus (who was not present) subsequently wrote a scathing report in *Forum Letter*. The AELC had elected Pr. Will Herzfeld to succeed William Kohn as bishop. Herzfeld, an African-American, indicated that he saw himself as "a bishop for people of color." Neuhaus wrote:

> This note was struck so incessantly that some delegates of non-color began to mumble about whether they still belonged to the AELC. One bishop confronted Bishop Herzfeld in a smaller meeting and said, 'Will, some of us are wondering whether there is still a place for us in this Church.' At which, it is reported, Bishop Herzfeld 'went white' and assured all and sundry that he will be bishop for all and sundry.[13]

Then Neuhaus reported a comment allegedly made publicly by the new bishop:

> Bishop Herzfeld told the convention how, when he was engaged with companionable strangers in nude bathing at Esalen [a humanistic retreat and conference center in Big Sur, CA] and a game of what is rather inelegantly called 'grab-ass' got underway, he definitely detected the reluctance of white folks to mix it up with Blacks, which goes to show how deeply racism is rooted in our culture. And there were other colorful stories of this sort. ... True, some delegates thought the stories and, indeed, the mood of the meeting somewhat off color, but they were sharply reminded that they'd been running things long enough and had better get used to an inclusive church.[14]

The firestorm began immediately, with complaints that Neuhaus's article had been inaccurate at several points, or that, even if it was not inaccurate, the criticism of Herzfeld was out of bounds. In the next issue Neuhaus defended his report.

> Should we have published ... the indecorous remarks made by an AELC leader at its recent Chicago convention? The question has been raised and deserves a serious

answer. First, we published only after much thought and consultation. That does not mean we made the right decision; it does mean we did not make it lightly. Second, the remarks we reported were not private but were made publicly to a plenary session of the convention. Third, the remarks were not an aberrant indiscretion but typical of a style of leadership consistently asserted. Conclusion: Had we not published the remarks, we would have been remiss in not conveying a critical dimension of the Chicago meeting's tone and direction. We regret that some people may have been offended by the report. We respectfully suggest that any cause for offense lies in the event itself and not in its being reported.

Neuhaus asserted that "the AELC ... is possessed of a theological, pastoral and ecumenical seriousness" that the Chicago convention did not reflect, and his hope was that shining the light on the Chicago incidents would help to rectify the problem.[15]

These comments only further inflamed the situation—as did the unauthorized reprinting and wide distribution of the original article in Herman Otten's *Christian News*. There were phone calls among several AELC leaders; John Tietjen, who had been elected vice president of the AELC, was asked to compose a letter of response which was then released over the signatures of Tietjen and the AELC bishops.[16]

The letter accused Neuhaus of inaccuracy at several points and denied most of what he had written about Bishop Herzfeld:

> The bishop did not 'announce that he viewed himself as "a bishop for people of color."' This remark was made by someone else about him. The report of remarks made by Bishop Herzfeld in regard to a nude bathing scene was not correct. Bishop Hertzfeld has clarified the matter. He referred to a touch football game among the men of the group who were not strangers but fellow civil rights workers.

The AELC leaders allowed that any editor "has the right to express his feelings and opinions, but we feel the need to correct these factual errors." A copy was sent to the ALPB's president, Richard Pankow, and to Neuhaus; a cover letter requested that "you use the good offices of the Board of Directors of the American Lutheran Publicity Bureau to assure publication of the requested retraction and apology."[17]

A harsher, more personal letter came from Tietjen to Neuhaus himself. "Since in my judgment the [AELC leaders'] letter does not say all that needs to be said," Tietjen said, he felt it necessary to write.

> For some time now I have been disturbed by your reporting in <u>Forum Letter</u>. We are treated regularly to innuendo and snide comments based on unnamed sources. I picture you like Zeus sitting atop Mount Olympus ... hurling thunderbolts at those of us who sully our hands with honest work. ...

> With the October 26 issue ... you have gone much too far. You have damaged the good name of the AELC, its people, and its leaders, especially Bishop Will Herzfeld. ... Faced with criticism, you respond ... not by apologizing for your errors in fact

and the consequent damage but by making the AELC convention responsible for your false report of it! ...

My reaction when I read your report ... is instructive. Instinctively, I crumpled it in my hands and threw it in the waste basket. That tells you what I think of <u>Forum Letter.</u> I have put it in the same category as <u>Christian News</u>, a publication I refuse to read.

Tietjen asked to be removed from the mailing list since "I can't trust the truthfulness of anything else in your publication." He sent a copy to Glenn Stone with a cover letter demanding to know "what you as executive director and the ALPB Board of Directors plan to do" about the situation and making it clear he expected an apology from Neuhaus. "Since none of us is infallible," Tietjen wrote, "it isn't all that difficult for an editor to say, 'I made a mistake and I'm sorry.' If the editor won't do it, then the publisher has to assume the responsibility."[18]

Neuhaus, however, firmly believed he was right, and he had no intention of apologizing. He told Tietjen that he was "grieved by the tone and content of your letter." He regretted Tietjen's cancellation of his subscription—and rather puckishly added that he had received "an almost identically worded statement from Jack Preus many years back, although I'm glad to say that I know he continued to read the Letter." He said that he had "checked and rechecked" his information, and found no reason to correct anything further (beyond a minor correction about the opening sermon he had already made in the November issue). Neuhaus then expressed disappointment at Tietjen's "attempt in your letter to Glenn to divide the editors of Forum and bring the pressure of the ALPB board upon us"—an action Neuhaus found "thoroughly unworthy of you, John—as a person and as a former editor who ought to understand the meaning of editorial integrity." He assured Tietjen that he continued "to hold you in high regard. ... I am among the many who gratefully acknowledge you as a gift of God to the Church." He asked for Tietjen's forgiveness "where I have been responsible for any misunderstandings or hard feelings between us."[19]

Neuhaus also wrote to the AELC bishops. His six-page letter to them began by regretting that "you have chosen to exacerbate the embarrassment occasioned by the convention of the AELC."

Be assured I am not averse to being taught and corrected, especially by bishops. I am keenly aware that I have much to learn and many faults that need correcting. At the same time, you will understand that I must try to speak clearly and, if need be, critically when the facts and my own conscience leave no choice. In responding to your actions, I pray I may address you respectfully and in a manner that contributes to the healing of whatever has been hurt or broken.

He responded at length to each of the points made by the bishops, defending what he had written and insisting that his portrayal was accurate according to "the people present at the convention with whom I have discussed this." While he did not name his sources, he described them as "people of good judgment and deep devotion to the AELC." "In all of this, brothers," he wrote, "it seems to me that you have overreacted in a manner that is likely to prove to be counterproductive."

> I can understand your public relations anxieties, but I wonder if your reaction does not reflect the deep insecurities which have marked AELC over the years. ... In what other church body can you imagine its Council of Bishops collectively responding in such a way to a press report? I do not recall anything quite comparable from our days back in the Missouri Synod.

"I am sorry this response has gone on so long," he concluded. "But please permit me to observe that you are the people who elected to prolong the matter."[20]

Neuhaus also felt compelled to respond in print to the AELC leaders' widely distributed letter. He noted that he had already corrected the matter of what was said in the sermon at the convention. He would not, however, apologize for what he had said about Herzfeld.

> 'Bishop Herzfeld has clarified the matter. He referred to a touch football game among the men of the group who were not strangers but fellow civil rights workers.' We are glad that Bishop Herzfeld has clarified the matter. It is, however, an after-the-fact clarification. We were reporting on what happened at the Chicago convention, and in the course of doing so carefully checked the facts with those who were present. We are now told that there exist, after all, tapes of the pertinent convention sessions. Regrettably, we have been informed that these tapes are not available for examination. It is reasonable to think that the tapes might help in settling some disputes about what actually happened in Chicago. Regrettable too is a letter from AELC officialdom calling for some undefined, but clearly punitive, action against your editor. Happily, the publisher of FORUM is not in the business of censorship to protect church leaders from critical comment.

There was no further comment on the matter in *Forum Letter*.[21]

No doubt this was a topic for considerable conversation at the ALPB board meeting of March 25, 1985; unfortunately, the minutes are incomplete, so the upshot of that conversation is unknown, but after the meeting Stone responded to Tietjen's December letter. "The appropriate committee ... charged with the responsibility of liaison with the editors of ALPB publications has met," he told Tietjen. "The issue which you raised has been presented to the committee."

> To respond briefly and to the point: ALPB accords freedom to the editors of its publications to comment on events, issues, ideas and individuals in the church. Whether or not any of us would have evaluated the mood and tone of the AELC convention as did Richard, on the basis of the reports he received, we support his right to evaluate it as he did. Beyond the matter of editorial judgment is the question of the factuality of certain items in the report. If the information printed is shown to be false, we

would of course insist upon a retraction. Richard has issued corrections of a couple of minor points in the article. Neither he nor we have received any evidence that there is anything further which requires the kind of response you have asked for.

He noted that the tapes of the convention could clarify the matter once and for all, and asked if Tietjen might "prevail upon those who control them to allow Richard (and, if you like, our committee) to listen to those tapes?" He assured Tietjen that if the tapes reveal "falsity in the FORUM LETTER report, Richard has assured us that he will retract and apologize—and so will we." The tapes were not forthcoming, and no retraction was ever printed.[22]

Issues and answers
"a great deal ... is up for grabs"

There were many issues besides the proposed merger roiling American Lutherans during the 1980s. In January 1986, ALC president David Preus startled Lutheran ecumenists when he proposed a "course correction" in Lutheran ecumenical relations. Dialogue between Lutherans and three Reformed churches (Reformed Church in America, United Presbyterian Church USA, and Cumberland Presbyterian Church) had led to *An Invitation to Action*. Preus proposed that the ALC accept the recommendations of the dialogue and declare pulpit and altar fellowship with the Reformed bodies.

Lutheran Forum had just published a lengthy critique of *An Invitation to Action* by Joseph F. Anderson arguing that the recommendations should be tabled when they came to the Lutheran church conventions in the summer of 1986. Following Preus's proposal, Glenn Stone declared that the magazine was "in substantial agreement" with Anderson's position. "The case for Lutheran fellowship with the Reformed," he wrote, "is not proven." But he urged that "the debate kicked off by Bishop Preus continue vigorously." As if to encourage that debate, the next issue of *Lutheran Forum* included an article by Paul Kuenning urging adoption of the recommendations, calling Preus's proposal "both prudent and evangelical."[23]

Forum Letter was sharper in its criticism. Preus's proposal, Neuhaus wrote, "has thrown top LCA leadership into consternation, has raised serious problems for the merger and, most important, has proposed a fundamental change in the theological and ecumenical self-understanding of Lutheranism." It "has come as a severe shock to George Lindbeck and other veterans of ecumenical dialogue," who generally regarded *Invitation to Action* as evasive and theologically problematic. Approval of full communion between Lutherans and the Reformed churches "would indicate either doctrinal indifferentism, which is odious, or the existence of doctrinal agreement, which is false."[24]

As the church conventions approached, both the ALC's *Lutheran Standard* and the LCA's *Lutheran* published articles (by Walter Wietzke and Robert Fischer respectively) urging adoption of the recommendations—and specifically rebutting the arguments that had been made against them in the ALPB publications. Neuhaus fought back, countering each of their points with his own analysis and convictions.

> Wietzke suggests Reformed and Lutherans now affirm 'the real presence' in the Lord's Supper. But it matters not even if we talk about the really <u>really</u> real presence. Some Christians claim to encounter the real presence in listening to Robert Schuller or attending their therapy groups. And surely they are right, for the cosmic Christ is really present everywhere. Confessional Lutheranism speaks about the <u>body and blood</u> of Christ truly given and received. ... Even the Leuenberg Agreement (1973) between Lutherans and Reformed in Germany tried to preserve this Lutheran and thoroughly catholic understanding. *Invitation* says it 'affirms' Leuenberg, but any such understanding of the Lord's Supper is really, truly and substantially absent from the document Wietzke and Fischer defend.[25]

The ALC convention nevertheless overwhelmingly approved *An Invitation to Action*'s recommendations, and full communion was declared with the Reformed bodies. Neuhaus's criticism was withering. He ridiculed the way the Eucharist had been celebrated at the convention—using "those little plastic disposable cups, the kind you get jelly in on the cafeteria line."

> 'The common cup,' explained Pr Kathy Sukke, who was in charge of worship arrangements, 'is a health issue. I had five colds one year using common cup.' Health aside, she said, there were not enough volunteers to wash 1500 individual glasses. Hence the plastic jelly cups with their eminently practical disposability in those big Hefty Bags.

"So much for official statements on communion practices," he sighed, "not to mention what in ecumenical dialogues we Lutherans claim to 'believe, teach and confess' about the Presence."[26]

The LCA convention did not consider the recommendations; its executive committee had instead recommended continued dialogue with the hope of one day achieving full communion. A floor amendment ultimately approved nudged the LCA closer to the ALC's action, with a call for occasional joint Eucharistic services with the Reformed. Neuhaus admitted that the strong majority in the ALC coupled with the apparent agreement among many in the LCA suggested that the ELCA would end up declaring full communion with the Reformed. "After the conventions of August it is not true that everything is up for grabs," he wrote. "But a great deal of what is constitutive of historic Lutheranism is up for grabs."[27]

Something else "up for grabs" was the sensitive issue of homosexuality. *Forum Letter* had argued in the past that questions of sexuality and the church were best dealt with pastorally rather than legislatively, but in 1986 Neuhaus wrote that "for better and for worse, homosexuality is on the Church's agenda in a manner quite unprecedented."

The occasion was the LCA's "Report on Issues Relating to Homosexuality," released in 1986. Neuhaus was not impressed.

> The theological sections of the document [exhibit] a complete absence of reference to the third article of the creed, to sanctification, discipleship, and growth in grace. A more unvarnished version of what Bonhoeffer called 'cheap grace' can be imagined only with difficulty. For that matter, the treatment of creation and sexuality is devoid of any reference to two thousand years of Christian reflection on the subject. The only thing we know for sure from the Old Testament is that God is in favor of 'sexual equality,' an expression that doubtless would have puzzled the scriptural writers. The recommended bibliography of 17 books might, with one exception (Helmut Thielicke), have been proposed by the National Gay Task Force on Religion. A veritable library of studies and alternative arguments is simply ignored. It is this propagandistic character of the Report, combined with a Phil Donahue penchant for cultural-sexual clichés, that finally makes the report so tacky and so unpersuasive.[28]

While the report didn't say so specifically, Neuhaus believed the thrust of its argument was to support the ordination of "declared and active homosexuals." Looking to the future, he thought it unlikely that the ELCA would adopt such a policy, "at least not in the very near future." But they would not do so for "the least edifying of reasons"—fear of a storm of protest.

> Instead, what may very well happen is that the argument of this Report will be quietly accepted. Then some seminaries, ministry committees and bishops will discreetly look the other way when it comes to the question of homosexuality, as indeed some look the other way now. Those who insist that the new acceptance should be officially stated in policy will be told, 'The people aren't ready for that yet.' The condescending assumption will be that of course 'we' know there is nothing wrong with ordaining gays and lesbians but 'they,' the ordinary people, still need to be 'educated.' ... Thus carelessness in thought will be compounded by cowardice and mendacity in practice. There has to be a better way.[29]

A few months later, Neuhaus noted a recent Roman Catholic statement, "The Pastoral Care of Homosexual Persons." It is "almost everything that the current LCA report on homosexuality is not—theologically informed, ethically coherent, commonsensically astute, and centered in sin and grace." He suggested that Lutherans study the Roman Catholic statement as a complement to the LCA document.[30]

The ALPB's longstanding interest in liturgical matters was expressed in many other articles beyond the annual *Una Sancta* issue of *Lutheran Forum*. In the Lent 1986 issue, a new column by Robert Hale appeared for the first time. Hale, a television newscaster from Kentucky, noted that Luther-Northwestern Seminary had recently abandoned the common cup in its chapel. He called attention to Lawrence Martin's 1965 article on the chalice in the *American Lutheran*—particularly noting Martin's citation of a scientific study which had demonstrated that the chalice posed little health risk. He received a swift response from officials at the seminary, who accused him of relying "on the popular press for your information. ... Just some more of the same old thing from the FORUM." Furthermore, they said they couldn't find the study to which Martin had referred, and "hinted the reference was a fabrication." Two issues later, Hale admitted that he had been preparing to eat crow, but then, with the help of his son, found the article in question (the citation in the original Martin article had been incorrect), and was happy to provide it.[31]

Meanwhile, Frank Senn, then pastor of Church of the Holy Spirit in Lincoln-shire, IL, argued passionately in *Lutheran Forum* for the use of the common cup at the Eucharist. He looked at the history of the chalice, considered the modern concerns about public health, discussed theological, ethical and cultural issues, but in the end his conclusion was clear:

> Let those with colds or contagious diseases show courtesy toward other communicants by dipping the bread in the cup. And let love respect those who cannot partake of the cup. But let all others 'take and drink' and so experience the new community in Christ. The Eucharist effects Christian fellowship not just when the cup is on the altar, but when it is shared.[32]

Senn's article engendered much debate, showing that the chalice continued to be controversial among Lutherans. In the next issue, Leigh Jordahl, a professor at Luther College, while admitting that he had no problem with the common cup, argued that it simply wasn't that important and "it's time to get off the common cup debate." The following issue's "Open Forum" continued the conversation with contributions from four readers (most of them opposing Jordahl) and a somewhat longer article by Roger Bates Kronmann, arguing that abandoning the chalice "violates both Scripture and the Church's traditional practice."

Jordahl and Senn went head to head in the Reformation 1987 issue. Jordahl noted that he had received "several letters, all favorable. ... The unfavorable letters went directly to the FORUM." He accused Senn of being "wrongheaded in treating restoration of the common cup as a virtually non-negotiable goal of liturgical renewal." Senn responded that he didn't "mind being called wrongheaded about matters on which I recognize my point of view." He insisted that he had "never regarded the restoration (or even the retention) of the common cup as a non-negotiable goal of liturgical renewal." But that does not mean it is unimportant.

> If our only concern is to do what is popularly pleasing, we wouldn't need liturgical study or any other kind of study. A simple show of hands would suffice to establish practice. But the Lutheran tradition has taken theology more seriously than this. Our theology, in fact, has come in the form of confessional propositions. Confes-

sional propositions in my article include these: that catholic tradition should not be set aside for reasons less weighty than the clear proclamation of the Gospel; that irrational fears should not be given into but dealt with in truth and love; that the Church is a body and not just a bunch of individuals; that we cannot treat some members of the body as lepers were treated in Jesus' day just because they happen to have a communicable disease; ... and that following a Lord whose own body and blood were defiled on the cross might entail a willingness to risk defilement ourselves.

"I can no more make people drink out of the same cup than I can make them spend a day passing out food at an inner city food pantry," Senn observed, "but that doesn't mean that the confession should not be made. Making the confession does not necessarily mean that practices are non-negotiable."[33]

Refocusing the ALPB's mission

"an independent, critical perspective"

The mid-1980s found the Bureau struggling once again, both financially and programmatically. The budget surplus in 1983 had allowed for an increase in salaries for both executive director Stone and office manager Ellie (Pfeifer) Spangenberg, but that increase, combined with canceled subscriptions in the wake of the Neuhaus controversy, led to a 1984 deficit of more than $10,000. Stone's salary was reduced by 40%, with the understanding that he would work for the Bureau three days per week—an offer he made because he had been hired as a part-time editorial assistant for the *Lutheran*, the magazine of the LCA. The board again began to think seriously about its purpose and mission.[34]

The board conducted another telephone survey of subscribers; it found that many readers distinguished between *Lutheran Forum* as a "respected scholarly publication," while they saw *Forum Letter* as a "gossip sheet." The survey revealed little sentiment, however, for separating the two publications or eliminating either of them; indeed, "most subscribers were enthusiastic" about the package.[35]

In January 1986, the board had a "wide-ranging discussion" about the Bureau's program and mission. The minutes recorded several points that were raised by Board members:

(i) Importance of parish support materials such as tracts, especially in outreach to 'new' Lutherans.

(ii) The focus on Lutheran unity in the old policy statement is unduly limited in the light of present needs and activities of ALPB.

(iii) Need for more articles in the publications directed to laity.

(iv) Results of last year's telephone survey showed that our readers want reports and information that is independent from and supplements the official publications. The FORUM publications have an ability to provide coverage and viewpoints which simply cannot be duplicated elsewhere.

(v) Need for understanding of ALPB history in looking to the future.

The executive director was asked to draft a new "statement of policy" for the board's consideration.[36]

Stone's proposal came to the board for discussion two months later and was adopted (with one amendment). More concise than the 1973 statement, it showed the Bureau's shifting understanding of its own mission:

> The American Lutheran Publicity Bureau exists to provide an independent, critical perspective of matters of interest to American Lutherans. While firmly grounded in ties of faith and that unity received from God through Jesus Christ, the major ALPB publications—LUTHERAN FORUM and FORUM LETTER—offer opportunities for debate and commentary among the diverse elements of American Lutheranism. Through its efforts, the ALPB makes known Lutheran doctrine, supports Lutheran unity, and promotes cooperative Lutheran mission, ministry and ecumenical relationships.

The most obvious difference between this statement and the earlier one is the treatment of Lutheran unity. That concern had dominated the earlier three-paragraph statement but now was reduced to a couple of phrases. The opening words here, suggesting that the ALPB's purpose is to offer "an independent, critical perspective," is also an interesting change; neither "independent" nor "critical" appeared in the 1973 statement. Also of note is an altered description of the relationship of the Bureau itself to the *Forum* publications. In 1973, the board specifically emphasized the editorial freedom of the two publications; now that freedom (though it certainly still existed) received no emphasis—allowing the inference that "the major ALPB publications" were in fact speaking for the Bureau.[37]

The discussion of the statement, however, was somewhat subdued since at that meeting the board got some unexpected news: Glenn Stone was resigning as executive director. He had agreed to go to work full time for the *Lutheran* and would begin in September, less than four months away. He had served the ALPB as executive director and editor of *Lutheran Forum* for nearly 20 years. Stone told the board he was willing to continue to edit *Lutheran Forum*, but he could not take on any tasks beyond that. The board accepted his resignation with regret and agreed to accept his offer to continue as editor of *Lutheran Forum*.

Over the next weeks, the seriousness of the situation began to sink in. Income had continued to decline—hardly the best backdrop for hiring a new executive director. The board in June authorized a fundraising drive to address the issue, but in August board member (and immediate past president) Richard Pankow wondered how they could meet payroll that month. The problem was exacerbated by the illness of Chester Edelmann, long-time treasurer of ALPB; he had relinquished the job title to Ted Wittrock, but he was still serving as assistant treasurer. It was he who prepared the financial reports, but he had been unable to do so for some months. Board minutes contain repeated frustration about the need for a cash flow projection.

In November 1986, Wittrock reported that as of the end of October, the year's deficit amounted to $7,804.56, while the Bureau's net worth was only $5,068.41. The Bureau was being kept afloat only by a couple of significant donations and bequests—including Glenn Stone's returning a portion of his salary. In spite of the dire situation, Dr. Thomas Sluberski, an LCMS clergyman and faculty member at Concordia College in Bronxville, NY, agreed to accept the board's call to become the ALPB's new executive secretary, effective January 15, 1987.[38]

The birth of the ELCA

"rather asthmatic, wheezing through preordained decisions"

The conventions of the LCA, ALC and AELC did approve the merger during the summer of 1986, and the constituting convention for the Evangelical Lutheran Church in America was set for the following spring. There was not much discussion of the new church in the ALPB publications during the intervening months; one reason is that Neuhaus fell behind in writing *Forum Letter*, and there were only six issues of the newsletter between September 1986 and June 1987. But most of the decisions having been made, there wasn't much to discuss; there was a "wait and see" attitude.

The constituting convention itself was covered for *Forum Letter* by ALPB board member Russell Saltzman. He described the assembly as "rather asthmatic, wheezing through preordained decisions punctuated by coughing fits called elections." He was unimpressed by the opening worship—"a bit hokey"—and by the preacher, New York pastor Barbara Lundblad, whose "hermeneutical equation linking secular justice to the doctrine of justification might have raised the eyebrows of any theologians who happened to be in attendance."[39]

The election for bishop also elicited some sharp comments. He quoted one observer whom he quoted as saying, "It'll be a tall guy with white hair" (an allusion to the expectation by many that the race was primarily between ALC president David Preus and the LCA's Minnesota Synod bishop Herbert Chilstrom). On the first ballot Preus led, followed by Chilstrom, then by William Lazareth (whom Neuhaus had essentially endorsed in *Forum Letter* a few months earlier). But Saltzman was flummoxed by the fourth name on the nominating ballot, Barbara Lundblad—who, in the elaborate procedure adopted by the convention, remained in the running for several ballots. "Only six years out of seminary," he wrote, "it seemed a remarkable thing for Lundblad's name to stay in until the seventh ballot." But she "was the women's candidate and her support was hard to the core. ... She clearly was the feminist symbol of an organized band of delegates dedicated to her, most of whom were females from both coasts."[40]

Chilstrom was ultimately elected, and Saltzman had gracious words to say both about the new bishop ("a mediator and a sensitive pastoral presence") and Preus (in defeat "a class act"). Still, he was not encouraged about the future. "And so decisions, big and little, have been made," he concluded. "The atmosphere at Columbus was not in any sense euphoric. It was determined. The feeling was, 'We are going to make this work.'"[41]

There were two interesting postscripts to *Forum Letter*'s coverage of the convention. First, Saltzman's report prompted Lundblad to publish a response, printed in a format resembling *Forum Letter* but called instead "Opinion Letter." She did so, she wrote, because she knew "full well the folly of responding to FORUM"; she had many colleagues who "submitted long, carefully crafted responses to [Neuhaus] only to receive back a postcard with one line, usually something like, 'Dear _____, People with such fuzzy thinking ought never submit it to print.'" She charged that Saltzman's "sarcasm surpasses that of Neuhaus"—sarcasm being "a hallmark of FORUM's style." She blasted Saltzman's criticisms of her and accused *Forum Letter* of a "pervasively negative portrayal of women."[42]

Neuhaus graciously took note of the piece ("in which ire is tempered with good humor"), suggesting that readers who wanted a copy might send a self-addressed stamped envelope to Lundblad. But he also published a response by Leonard Klein, pastor of Christ Lutheran Church, in York, PA. Klein defended *Forum Letter*, calling it "the closest thing we have to a free press in all of American Lutheranism." He excoriated Lundblad's critique which, he said, "makes no effort to respond to the substance of the issues raised." "Even extreme feminists no doubt have a role to play in the ELCA," he admitted, "but that role does not include redesigning the church in their image, or attempting to silence those who have a different understanding of the Christian reality."[43]

The other postscript came years later, in 1992, when Augsburg Fortress published *Anatomy of a Merger: People, Dynamics, and Decisions that Shaped the ELCA* by Edgar Trexler, editor of the *Lutheran*. Someone noticed that a good many phrases, words, even entire sentences from Saltzman's report in *Forum Letter* appeared verbatim in Trexler's book without attribution. Paul Hinlicky, at that time editor of *Lutheran Forum*, printed a page giving examples in parallel columns, with a headline: "What's Going On Here? You Decide." He invited readers to cast a vote, choosing from these options:

Contemporary instances of divine inspiration, even verbal dictation, are not as unusual as one might think.

Imitation is the sincerest form of flattery.

Monkey see, monkey do.

Editors of house organs are above the law, above ethics, and in any case, do the little known Forum Letter *a favor by spreading its ideas without accreditation, since, naming* FL *as the source would be the kiss of death, at least in a delimited geographical area in the environs of O'Hare airport (where, however, none of the usual rules apply).*

He invited readers to send their votes to the chair of the advisory committee of the *Lutheran.* Trexler made no public comment.[44]

Chilstrom vs. Neuhaus

"I accept your apology"

Thomas Sluberski had just come on board as executive director when yet another controversy about Neuhaus arose. Prior to the ELCA's constituting convention in the spring of 1987, *Forum Letter* had included a rundown on potential candidates for bishop of the new church. Neuhaus viewed the most likely candidates as David Preus ("an unlikely champion of the confessional identity and mission that is required ... in the critical years ahead"), Martin Marty (whose "largely uncritical identification with oldline liberal Protestantism raises serious questions about his understanding of the ecumenical responsibilities of Lutheranism"), H. George Anderson ("word is he has definitely declared he is not interested in the position"), William Lazareth ("eminently qualified" but "at best a dark horse"). And then there was Herbert Chilstrom, bishop of the LCA's Minnesota Synod.

Chilstrom, in the judgment of many, poses all the problems posed by David Preus. In addition, he is sharply criticized for being 'trendy' on most of the issues that come down the religio-cultural turnpike, and having an ALC pastor as his wife is thought to be a neat formula too clever by half.[45]

Chilstrom was miffed at this characterization, and he expressed his unhappiness to Glenn Stone. Stone suggested to Neuhaus that he try to repair the damage; Neuhaus sent Chilstrom something of an apology:

One problem is that, at least as a general rule, when you get to know people personally, and to like them, it is a powerful inhibiting factor with respect to any public comment. If I knew you better, it is more than possible that I would have had a different angle. ... As it is, I had to form my judgment on the basis of reading what you have written and said, plus impressions from public reports and private conversations with people familiar with you and your work. ...

With regard to your wife being an ALC pastor, I do regret using the expression 'too clever by half.' Glenn [Stone] points out that readers might infer from that a deliberate calculation on your part. I should have said 'too neat by half' or simply 'too pat.' As you are undoubtedly aware, people have remarked on the fact that an

LCA bishop married to an ALC pastor seems to anticipate neatly the merger. But I apologize for my unfortunate choice of words and will do so also in a forthcoming issue of the Letter.

I am truly sorry that you felt abused by the reference in the article. And I do hope that I will have the benefit of getting know you better in the future.

A few days later, Chilstrom was elected bishop. Shortly after the election he wrote a terse response to Neuhaus which showed a serious misinterpretation of Neuhaus's letter:

Thank you for your letter. I accept your apology. I am grateful to Glenn Stone for his willingness to speak to you. I respect your desire not to know me on a more personal and informal level or to learn about my positions on various matters through direct conversation.[46]

But if Chilstrom was miffed, his wife, the Rev. Corinne Chilstrom, was downright furious. She wrote an angry letter to each individual member of the ALPB board, with a copy to Neuhaus. "This cannot go unchallenged," she thundered.

I am more than 'his wife.' I am a child of God, a person with a name and with a call from God to ordained ministry in the American Lutheran Church. To suggest that my call to ministry is nothing more than a maneuvering device to promote my husband's career is a falsehood, to say the least. It is also demeaning to me and is an insult to God who has called me.

"Are you going to allow this?" she demanded. "What will you as a board member do to make this right? I will wait for your reply."[47]

Sluberski immediately wrote to each board member, asking them not to respond "to any letter you might receive in regards to the FORUM LETTER" until after the May board meeting. At that meeting, Sluberski reported that Neuhaus had responded to "a letter from Corinne Chilstrom." He may have been referring to Neuhaus's letter to Herbert Chilstrom, which was written before Corinne Chilstrom's letter had been received; if Neuhaus replied directly to Corinne Chilstrom, the letter has apparently not survived. Nonetheless, there was extensive discussion by the board; a motion was made to allow Corinne Chilstrom to respond in *Forum Letter*, but it was defeated. The next day president Leonard Roellig sent a laconic note to Pr. Chilstrom on behalf of the board: "The members of the Board ... are in receipt of your comments on a recent issue of Forum Letter. We wish to thank you for your letter and we are sorry that you felt hurt by comments in Forum Letter."[48]

Neuhaus now tried again to mollify the Chilstroms. In the July *Forum Letter*, he fulfilled his promise to apologize in print—sort of.

In the days prior to [the constituting convention in] Columbus, Bp Herbert Chilstrom protested forcefully—and his wife, Pr Corinne Chilstrom, protested yet more forcefully—Forum Letter's comment on his candidacy. For the record, we did not say and we did not mean to say that the LCA bishop-husband and ALC pastor-wife arrangement was calculated to advance his candidacy. Had we meant to say that, we would have said it. Our point was that many people gave that arrangement as a reason for supporting Chilstrom and we thought that "too clever by half." There were no doubt many good reasons for voting for Chilstrom, but anticipatory merger by marriage was not one of them. In any event, the publishing board of Forum has a long-standing policy of preserving editorial independence and integrity, and we, for our part, intend to support the leadership of Bp Chilstrom as fully as we are able.

It may be that Neuhaus was still smarting from Corinne Chilstrom's letter, or perhaps from Herbert Chilstrom's snippy reply to his attempt to make amends, and this turned what was promised as an "apology" into "this is what I meant, obviously."[49]

In any event, he did try again personally to mend fences with the newly elected bishop. "Please permit me first to deal with the recent unpleasantness," he wrote on June 3, "and then see if we cannot get back to a more cordial and constructive conversation."

> You state in your letter of May 12: 'I respect your desire not to know me on a more personal and informal level.' ... I am afraid you have misunderstood quite entirely. In my letter of 29 April I say precisely the opposite. The last sentence reads: 'And I do hope that I will have the benefit of getting to know you better in the future.' That continues to be—indeed it is increasingly—my hope.
>
> My letter was written, of course, before I was aware of your wife's most unfortunate letter to the publishing board of Forum. That letter can hardly be interpreted as anything other than a demand for the exercise of censorship. Such a demand is, I believe, inappropriate, unconstructive and wrong in principle. I am pleased but not surprised that it is rejected by the board. ...
>
> I recognize that Pastor Corinne Chilstrom's letter is not from you and I do not know whether you approved of it. But you and she have very publicly declared your partnership in the ministry on which you have entered, and I therefore cannot help but think that there is a measure of shared responsibility in this matter.

He congratulated Chilstrom on his election and assured him that "at our house you are already remembered each day by name in evening prayer." He acknowledged that it was "quite possible that in the months and years ahead I will be publicly critical of your leadership on this question or that," but he promised that he would "strive always to be respectful, informed and fair." He concluded with a standing invitation to share a meal whenever Chilstrom might be in New York.[50]

There were a few more letters over the summer that finally resulted in Neuhaus having dinner in a Chicago restaurant with both Chilstroms and an evident thaw in their relationship. Neuhaus (who had picked up the tab for dinner) thanked them (the salutation was "Dear Herb and Corinne") for "a graciously memorable evening." "I believe that I understand better the directions in which you hope to lead the ELCA," he wrote, "and, again, assure you of my desire to be helpful. I expect there will be occasions for our recalling our agreement that friendship and support do not preclude disagreement from time to time." He also made an intriguing comment: "I am thinking very carefully about what you said with respect to Forum Letter, and I trust that the consequences of your good counsel will be evident to you in future issues."[51]

Chilstrom responded warmly ("Dear Richard"), thanked Neuhaus for treating them to dinner, and looked forward to another opportunity to share a meal. There continued to be, however, underlying unhappiness about Neuhaus. Some months later David Brown, bishop of the ELCA's Northeastern Iowa Synod, wrote an appreciative letter to Neuhaus about an article in *Forum Letter*. He sent a copy to Chilstrom, who responded:

> Thanks for sharing with me a copy of your letter to Richard Neuhaus. I did not read that issue of the Forum Newsletter. In fact, I have not read the Newsletter for some time. As [Rocky Mountain Synod bishop] Wayne Weissenbuehler puts it, 'He's so damn predictable!' In the midst of a lot of gossipy claptrap Richard often says things we need to hear in the church. I once asked him why he uses his fine intellectual skills to indulge in that kind of thing. 'Because it sells subscriptions,' was his reply.[52]

In public, though, Chilstrom was gracious toward Neuhaus and the Bureau. When the board resumed its Inter-Lutheran Forum series (which had been on hiatus since 1983), Chilstrom agreed to be the speaker—though as it turned out, his message was not quite what the board expected. His address, "The Role of the Church in Shaping Our Common Life," defended the importance of the church's "public ministry." Taking a few oblique shots at criticisms in the ALPB publications of the church's social issue advocacy, he argued that the ELCA "must negotiate between the temptations at both extremes—to be silent because we can never know enough, or to [speak] beyond our level of competence." The address, Neuhaus wrote, "was received politely by a large and otherwise enthusiastic audience."[53]

Notes

1. James R. Crumley, Jr., "Toward a New Church: The Process and the Issues," *LF* 17, no. 1 (Lent 1983), 14-16.
2. *FL* 12, no. 4 (29 Apr. 1983), 1.
3. Ibid., 7-8.
4. Ibid., 7.
5. *FL* 12, no. 8 (26 Aug. 1983), 1.
6. Ibid., 2.
7. *FL* 12, no. 11 (25 Nov. 1983), 3.

8. *FL* 13, no. 3 (23 Mar. 1984), 1-3.

9. Edgar R. Trexler, *Anatomy of a Merger: People, Dynamics, and Decisions that Shaped the ELCA* (Minneapolis: Augsburg, 1991), 60; *FL* 13, no. 4 (20 Apr. 1984), 1; *FL* 13, no. 6 (22 June 1984), 3.

10. *FL* 15, no. 5 (6 June 1986), 3.

11. "Editor's Ambo: How Excellent a Name," *LF* 19, no. 2 (Pentecost 1985), 4.

12. "A Summer of Discontent," *LF* 20, no. 2 (Pentecost 1986), 4.

13. *FL* 13, no. 10 (26 Oct. 1984), 1.

14. Ibid., 1-2.

15. *FL*, 13, no. 11 (23 Nov. 1984), 6.

16. There are several drafts of this letter in Tietjen's papers in the ELCA archives, including two rather different documents that both appear to be "final drafts." One of these, dated 17 Dec. 1984, is addressed to "All AELC Pastors, Teachers and Synod/District Bishops of the ALC and the LCA"; the other, much longer, is dated only Dec. 1984, and addressed "Dear Sisters and Brothers in Christ," yet it bears the signatures of five AELC leaders (Bishops Walter Grumm, Harold Heche, Rudolph Ressmeyer, Robert Studtmann, and Vice-President Tietjen), while the first has only their typed names. It may be that the longer version was sent to selected leaders, while the shorter one was more of an "open letter." It appears that the latter is the one sent to Neuhaus and to ALPB board members. In any event, the two letters covered essentially the same matters.

17. Walter Grumm, Harold Heche, Rudolph Ressmeyer, Robert Studtmann and John Tietjen, to All AELC Pastors, Teachers, and Synod/District Bishops of the ALC and the LCA, 17 Dec. 1984, John H. Tietjen Papers, Box 15, ELCA Archives (hereafter cited as Tietjen Papers); Walter Grumm, Harold Heche, Rudolph Ressmeyer, Robert Studtmann and John Tietjen, to Richard Pankow, 12 Dec. 1984, Tietjen Papers, Box 15.

18. John Tietjen to Richard John Neuhaus, 20 Dec. 1984; John Tietjen to Glenn Stone, 20 Dec. 1984, Tietjen Papers, Box 15.

19. Richard John Neuhaus to John Tietjen, 27 Dec. 1984, Tietjen Papers, Box 15.

20. Richard John Neuhaus to John Tietjen, n.d. [shortly after 18 Dec. 1984]; Richard John Neuhaus to The Council of Bishops, AELC, n.d. [shortly after 18 Dec. 1984], Tietjen Papers, Box 15.

21. *FL* 14, no 1 (25 Jan. 1985), 5.

22. Glenn C. Stone to John Tietjen, 15 Apr. 1983, Tietjen Papers, Box 15.

23. Joseph F. Anderson, "What Is Wrong with This Picture?" *LF* 19, no. 4 (Advent 1985), 20-30; "Shall We Have a Preus-ian Union?" *LF* 20, no. 1 (Lent 1986), 4; Paul P. Kuenning, "The Conflict Over Lutheran Ecumenical Priorities," *LF* 20, no. 2 (Pentecost 1986), 14-20.

24. *FL* 15, no. 2 (28 Feb. 1986), 1-2; *FL* 15, no. 3 (4 Apr. 1986), 3.

25. *FL* 15, no. 7 (8 Aug. 1986), 3.

26. *FL* 15, no 8 (16 Sept. 1986), 3.

27. Ibid., 6.

28. *FL* 15, no. 9 (14 Nov. 1986), 1, 4.

29. Ibid., 5-6.

30. *FL* 15, no. 12 (27 Mar. 1987), 8.

31. Robert S. Hale, "A Sweet Cup of Water," *LF* 20, no. 1 (Lent 1986), 28; "The Game of One-Cupsmanship," *LF* 20, no. 4 (Advent 1986), 24.

32. Frank C. Senn, "The Cup of Salvation: Take and Drink," *LF* 20, no. 3 (Reformation 1986), 26.

33. Leigh Jordahl, "The Cup and Common Sense," *LF* 21, no. 3 (Reformation 1987), 6; Frank C. Senn, "The Cup and Confession," *LF* 21, no. 3 (Reformation 1987), 7.

34. Minutes, ALPB Board of Directors, 26 Mar. 1985.

35. Ibid.

36. Minutes, ALPB Board of Directors, 7 Jan. 1986.

37. Minutes, ALPB Board of Directors, 20 May 1986.

38. Minutes, ALPB Board of Directors, 26 Nov. 1986.

39. *FL* 16, no. 2 (12 June 1987), 1.

40. Ibid., 2.

41. Ibid., 8.

42. Barbara Lundblad, "Opinion Letter," July 1987, ALPB Archives.

43. *FL* 16, no. 6 (23 Oct. 1987), 8; *FL* 16, no. 7 (27 Nov. 1987), 7-8.

44. "What's Going On Here? You Decide," *LF* 26, no. 3 (Aug. 1992), 45.

45. *FL* 15, no. 12 (25 Mar. 1987), 3.

46. Richard John Neuhaus to Herbert W. Chilstrom, 29 Apr. 1987; Herbert W. Chilstrom to Richard John Neuhaus, 12 May 1987, Herbert W. Chilstrom Papers, Box 5, ELCA Archives (hereafter cited as Chilstrom Papers).

47. Corinne Chilstrom to Dorothy Zelenko, 28 Apr. 1987, ALPB Archives.

48. Thomas Sluberski to ALPB Board Members, 4 May 1987; Minutes, ALPB Board of Directors, 19 May 1987; Leonard Roellig to Corinne Chilstrom, 20 May 1987, ALPB Archives.

49. *FL* 16, no. 3 (3 July 1987), 2.

50. Richard John Neuhaus to Herbert W. Chilstrom, 3 June 1987, Chilstrom Papers, Box 5.

51. Richard John Neuhaus to Herbert and Corinne Chilstrom, 8 Oct. 1987, Chilstrom Papers, Box 5.

52. Herbert W. Chilstrom to L. David Brown, 22 Aug. 1988, Chilstrom Papers, Box 5.

53. Herbert W. Chilstrom, "The Role of the Church in Shaping our Common Life," Chilstrom Papers, Box 5; *FL*, 17, no. 12 (8 Jan. 1989), 1.

Chapter 19

Calling the Church to Faithfulness

The Neuhaus/Chilstrom brouhaha was only one challenge facing the ALPB in the late 1980s. Financial struggles, conflict within the board of directors over the purpose and tone of its publications, some rather angry resignations from the board, anxiety about the direction of the new ELCA and the Bureau's responsibility in addressing it—all these things made for continued turbulence for the ALPB. Nevertheless, there were also some exciting and creative new initiatives as the Bureau adjusted to a very new situation in American Lutheranism.

Editorial change
"my tone would be more urgent"
The Bureau had seldom been a financially secure operation, but now another crisis developed. The 1986 fiscal year showed a loss of more than $2,500. The death of assistant treasurer Chester Edelmann necessitated some regrouping in the ALPB's financial management and reporting. An emergency appeal for funds that summer brought in some $13,000, but the Christmas appeal, a regular ALPB program for many years, was not as successful as usual—perhaps because of the summer appeal. Samples of the

Forum package were sent to all LCA and ALC pastors, hoping to increase circulation, but the best that could be said is that the "mailings have paid for themselves in terms of response."[1]

Glenn Stone was now editing *Lutheran Forum* in a year-to-year appointment. In September 1987, Stone indicated he was willing to serve for another year, but some members thought it was time for a change. President Leonard Roellig suggested that the executive committee bring a specific proposal to the next meeting; in the meantime, Thomas Sluberski was asked to "discuss the matter of change in content and editor of the magazine" with Stone. Some at the meeting expressed frustration with *Forum Letter*. Board member Cecile Johnson "objected to criticisms of church officials by Neuhaus." Another member, Keith Wulff, noted that the two most recent issues had not included a "guest editorial"—something the board had requested four years earlier. Others complained that Neuhaus was habitually late in publishing the newsletter. After much discussion, a motion was approved "that the Board continue its present relationship with Neuhaus as editor of Forum Letter with two provisos: 1) Forum Letter is to be written on schedule, and 2) a guest editor is to be included in each issue."[2]

The next meeting took up again the question of who would edit *Lutheran Forum*. Despite Stone's willingness to continue, the board decided to conduct a formal search with the executive committee serving as a search committee. Stone was asked to edit the Lent 1988 issue, and Sluberski was named managing editor for the next two issues. When the board met in January 1988, the executive committee came with something of a surprise. They had interviewed three candidates for the position of editor—Glenn Stone, Charles Lutz, and Paul Hinlicky. Their recommendation was that Paul Hinlicky be named as the new editor of *Lutheran Forum*. Hinlicky was a Christ Seminary—Seminex graduate with a PhD in theology from Union Theological Seminary in New York. He had been ordained by the AELC, transferred to the LCA's Slovak Zion Synod for a few years, then returned to the AELC when he accepted a call to Immanuel Lutheran Church in Delhi, NY. He had also served for three years as a research associate for the LCA's Department for Church in Society. At the age of 36 he already had a long list of journal articles and other publications.

Hinlicky was frank about what he thought should be the direction of *Lutheran Forum*. "A sharper vision is needed of Lutheranism rising to fill the void of vacating liberal Protestantism in American life," he told the executive committee. "Just as all change is not for the good, likewise not every point of view that happens to have been baptized in a Lutheran church merits expression." He was forthright about what his editorship would mean.

> My interests and abilities are in theology and my viewpoint in theology is not uncontroversial. I am, at root, a Niebuhrian; my axe cuts roughly. While I am sure in my own mind that the aforementioned is the right direction for Forum to go, I am

not so sure that I would be the best person to do it. My tone would be more urgent. I have no patience for dilettantism in theology, for cost-free piety or for ecclesiastical self-preoccupation.

This was certainly a different approach from that of the irenic Glenn Stone, but it struck a chord with the board of directors, and they voted unanimously (with one abstention) to offer Hinlicky a two-year contract beginning with the Reformation 1988 issue.[3]

Hinlicky was introduced to *Lutheran Forum*'s readers in the Lent issue with a slightly revised version of a sermon he had preached a few months before. Entitled "A Time of Decision," the sermon manifested the "more urgent" tone he had acknowledged to the board. "I believe," he wrote, "that our Church today is in danger of apostasy, of wholesale secularization, of trading the power of worship for the worship of power." He excoriated the CNLC's report which "commits the new Church to studying 'the root causes of social injustice' and remedial action informed by such study." This objective, he predicted, "promises ... more pastors appointing themselves prophets ... [and] further movement in the direction of the national church acting like a partisan political lobby." Even worse, the stated objective verges on apostasy. Christians already know the "root causes of injustice"—it's "the power of sin." "The last thing our troubled world needs," he concluded, "is for the Church to act as one power bloc alongside others."[4]

Meanwhile, Thomas Sluberski had been anxious to make some physical changes in both *Lutheran Forum* and *Forum Letter*, and the period of transition seemed a good time to do it. The Lent issue of the journal displayed a new cover. Rather than a photograph illustrating the theme of one of the articles—the standard cover for years—this issue's cover was all text. Several boxes served as a kind of table of contents for the issue, each including a quotation from one article. When the board of directors saw it, they were not impressed. "Sleazy," said one. "Looks as if [the cover] has been ripped off," added another. The next issue went in a more traditional direction, featuring an Albrecht Dürer woodcut.[5]

Sluberski also presented to the board a proposed new design for *Forum Letter*, utilizing two columns (rather than the single column that had been the design from the beginning). Neuhaus wasn't enthusiastic about it. He explained the change to readers:

> We hope you think it is an improvement. Improvement or not, it was probably inevitable, what with the 'revolution' in desktop publishing and all that. Then too, Pr Tom Sluberski, ALPB's new director, is incorrigibly devoted to 'progress.' Ten years ago they took away our quill pen, then the old Remington went, and now there's this. If you really don't like the new look, let your editor know and maybe together we can change Pr Sluberski's mind.

The ALPB board rather liked the new design, in spite of Neuhaus; but apparently *Forum Letter* readers agreed with the editor, and after two issues, the newsletter returned to the old format (with a slightly updated typeface).[6]

With Hinlicky not set to come on board until the fall, it fell to Sluberski to edit the Pentecost issue. He made its theme "Essays in Honor of Glenn C. Stone: *A Festschrift*." It seemed an appropriate tribute to the man who had edited the publication since its inception with only a brief hiatus—all but six of 120 issues, Stone had written, "with an important part of those exceptional six." Sluberski led with a gracious tribute to Stone:

> His pastoral way of dealing with people, events, and issues, his editorial skills, his range of knowledge and insight, are proverbial. His is a hard act to follow. We've all heard people say they never met a man they didn't like (and some of us were duly skeptical), but I think those who know Glenn would probably agree that they never met anyone who didn't like Glenn Stone.

The issue contained several laudatory essays by a variety of writers who had known Stone either personally or professionally over the course of his life. Commenting on Stone's departure in *Forum Letter*, Neuhaus called him "a courageous voice of quiet sanity in American Lutheranism."[7]

Ironically, the first issue under the new editor contained the announcement of the death of Adolf Meyer, the long-time editor of the *American Lutheran*. Meyer, 89, had died just hours before a planned worship service honoring the 65th anniversary of his ordination. The service had gone on with a special poignancy as the gathered friends and family celebrated Meyer's entering the Church Triumphant. Meyer had served on the ALPB board of directors for 44 years, most of that time as either managing editor or editor of the *American Lutheran*. He was, Sluberski wrote, "one of the great pastors of Lutheranism in our century. ... Others can point to many areas of service, but the ALPB wants to indicate how much we cherish his memory and want to continue his work."[8]

The church political

"the adjective 'modest' is nothing short of breathtaking"

The ALPB's skepticism toward the "new church" did not abate as the ELCA began operations. In January 1989, Neuhaus began a three-part series in *Forum Letter* which he called "The Church Political." The ELCA, he suggested, is "getting things badly confused" regarding the church and politics. He proposed to consider the ELCA's World Hunger Appeal as a kind of case study. He began by excoriating the claim that the ELCA was engaged in "advocacy" but not "lobbying." They are pretty much the same thing, he insisted, noting that a good slice of the Hunger Appeal's funds had gone to Bread for World—an organization that Neuhaus himself had helped found, but which frankly described itself as "A Christian Citizens Lobby." "It is obvious," Neuhaus argued, "that the ELCA is engaged in political lobbying." Denying it "can only breed further distrust in the church."[9]

Furthermore, lobbying is, by its very nature, a partisan activity, and the ELCA's lobbying "on issue after issue ... supports the Democratic position, usually coming down in favor of the leftward side of the party of liberalism." The church's advocacy programs also offer "constituency education on the issues"—which, Neuhaus wrote, is nothing more than trying to persuade church members to "support the political positions favored" by church leaders.

> [In] the view of many church members, the offense is thus compounded. That their offerings are used to promote public policies that they oppose is the one half of it. The other half is that their offerings are used to 'educate' them into approving this arrangement.[10]

Neuhaus insisted that his objection was not to the specific policies being advocated, but to "the church becoming the servant of _any_ political party or program." He observed that church officials who make these decisions are in fact clueless about the complex issues involved; they are not aware of "the major arguments and literature shaping the current debate about policy alternatives" and they "talk mainly with other activists in other agencies and denominations who share the same assumptions, the same posture, the same jargon."[11]

An exception, Neuhaus noted, was Richard Niebanck, a former church and society staff member in the LCA. Niebanck had been carrying on an extensive correspondence with a current ELCA staff member, trying to understand what was meant by "root causes" of hunger. Niebanck had shared this correspondence with Neuhaus, who quoted the ELCA official:

> 'We are now identifying three ... areas that will receive special attention by staff. They will also receive hunger monies! These three are: the Third World debt crisis, war/arms race/militarism, and environmental degradation/misuse. Together this constitutes a modest attempt for the Hunger Program through [Commission for Church and Society] to highlight three areas involving causes.' [_sic_]

He also quoted Niebanck's response that "the adjective 'modest' is nothing short of breathtaking. The proposal is about as modest as an ant ascending the leg of an elephant with rape on its mind." Allowing that Pr. Niebanck "was getting a little excited there," Neuhaus wondered how a handful of church staff people with "no notable qualifications for the task, and with many other duties to perform" could possibly make a significant contribution to issues on which thousands of actual experts in universities, think tanks, and government agencies were already working.[12]

Why, Neuhaus asked, is it necessary for the ELCA to take positions on these matters? Are the real experts in government and private institutions clamoring for an ELCA policy paper? Of course not. The only people who need such things are church bureaucrats who want justification for the positions they want to take and political activists who want to invoke the church's authority for their positions. "Meanwhile, the alienation of the membership deepens, the churchwide financial crisis becomes more acute, the understanding of the Church's mission in the world is ever more confused, and those who are called to be leaders complain that they are unappreciated."[13]

The article caused great consternation in the office of the Hunger Appeal, which sent a letter to ELCA pastors and leaders complaining that "<u>Lutheran Forum</u> has printed some very misleading statements" (though, as Neuhaus observed, "it cites not one"). ALPB board member Cecile Johnson, who had grown increasingly critical of Neuhaus, rather noisily resigned, complaining about "the current series of tirades against the ELCA World Hunger Fund" in *Forum Letter*. In a letter made public and reported in the *Lutheran*, Johnson said that the Bureau "must face the fact that we could be the principal cause for any break in confidence which may occur" between ELCA members and their national church leaders. The article in the *Lutheran* hinted that "other board members earlier left more quietly, and at least one other member was reportedly considering quitting for similar reasons." Another former board member, William Grentz, told the *Lutheran* that he had resigned "primarily because of 'right-wing' stands of Neuhaus and 'his very critical attitude toward most of what's going on in the church.'" Grentz also cited Neuhaus's "irresponsible" remark about Corinne Chilstrom.[14]

A time of crisis

"the ALPB office is not functioning"

As if this controversy wasn't enough, the board faced still other problems. Sluberski had accomplished the important goal of computerizing operations in the ALPB office. The office itself, however, was suddenly forced to find a new physical home. St. Luke's Lutheran Church, ALPB headquarters since 1980, needed to utilize the space the Bureau had occupied; after investigating some possibilities, the operation relocated to the Wartburg, a Lutheran senior living facility in Mt. Vernon, NY.

But a new facility and a new computer system could not disguise underlying disorganization. In early 1989, the board received letters from both Hinlicky and Neuhaus, from advertising manager Ruth Taylor, and from office assistant Patti Young, complaining that "the ALPB office is not functioning in a satisfactory way." There were bills going unpaid, production problems, a lack of clear procedures. It became so bad that both Taylor and Young resigned—each citing "lack of a 'stable office situation'" as "one of several reasons for their resignations." The *Lutheran* reported Taylor's resignation in the same article in which it had recounted Cecile Johnson's quitting over Neuhaus's criticism of the World Hunger Appeal, commenting that "she would not make public her reasons for leaving"—but the implication was clear that she, too, was unhappy about Neuhaus.[15]

The financial situation was also continuing to deteriorate. In March 1989, president Leonard Roellig told the board they were facing a budget deficit of some $25,000. Subscription renewal notices were far behind schedule; the board would later learn that about a third of the copies of *Lutheran Forum/Forum Letter* were being mailed to people in arrears on their subscriptions. The annual Christmas appeal letter, for decades a significant source of income, had simply not gone out in 1988.[16]

As things seemed to go from bad to worse, Sluberski resigned as executive director, effective June 1, 1989. He reported that he had not been reimbursed for his expenses in 1988, and his salary had not been paid thus far in 1989; the Bureau at that point had only about $4,000 in the bank. The office secretary, Christine Huebsch, also announced her resignation as of July 1. Board minutes of May 1989 noted administrative tasks left undone—subscription renewal notices not up to date, thank you letters for contributions not sent. The Bureau had again been invited to cosponsor the St. Olaf Choir's New York concert in 1990, but given the financial situation, the board declined.[17]

Hoping to bring some order to this chaos, board member Dorothy Zelenko took a leave of absence from her job and volunteered full time in the ALPB office to straighten things out administratively and financially. A mostly new slate of officers was elected in May 1989. Hans Quitmeyer, an attorney, took the reins as president, Pr. James Corgee would be the new vice-president, and Ms. Zelenko agreed to serve as treasurer; Elaine Abrahamson would continue as secretary.[18]

Over the next few months, the situation improved dramatically. There were a few more resignations from the board, but some energetic and supportive new members were welcomed. Ms. Zelenko spent two months in the office, thoroughly reorganizing, catching up on things left undone and establishing new procedures. A new office manager, Donna Kathmann, was hired. Paul Hinlicky was asked to take on some of the tasks of executive director on an interim basis. By September both the financial situation and the morale of the Bureau had improved dramatically, and in November the new president told the board that the financial situation was now stable.[19]

Called to faithfulness

"we fight for that evangelical and catholic future"

It wasn't only the ALPB editors who were concerned about the ELCA's direction. In March 1989, Hinlicky and Neuhaus met in Chicago with Carl Braaten and Robert Jenson, editors of *dialog*, and Oliver Olson and Paul Rorem, editors of *Lutheran Quarterly*. They agreed that their independent journals would sponsor a free conference to discuss what they described as "the crisis in American Lutheranism." It would be known as "A Call to Faithfulness," and it was set for June 1990 at St. Olaf College. The announcement published in *Lutheran Forum* laid out the purpose:

Those who call the Conference are not of one mind in the issues before us—special ministry, ecumenical direction, mission, and social posture—but we are one in concern for the theological and confessional integrity of Lutheranism. To that end, discussion will be informed and led by theological leaders representing opposing positions. ... In the name of Christ and for the sake of His church, this invitation to theological deliberation is issued, in prayer that it will be for us all a call to faithfulness.

Neuhaus promoted the conference each month in *Forum Letter*, suggesting that it had "the potential of being one of the most important gatherings of Lutherans in the last half-century."[20]

"A Call to Faithfulness" was a great success. The planners anticipated 300 participants, but the registrations numbered 895 and perhaps another 100 attended without registering. It was, Neuhaus reported, "overwhelmingly a gathering of parish pastors." The topics included ministry, ecumenism, mission, and church and society—four "areas of major disagreement" among Lutherans. *Forum Letter* summarized the contributions of each of the several speakers: Jenson, Braaten, William Lazareth, George Lindbeck, Gerhard Forde, Joseph Burgess, John Johnson, Paul Sponheim, Larry Rasmussen, and Neuhaus. The most dramatic moment came when Hinlicky, as preacher at the Eucharist, hurled a copy of the *Lutheran* from the pulpit of Boe Chapel, warning against the ELCA's "impending apostasy."[21]

Neuhaus reported that evaluations of the conference "ranged from solid affirmation to wild excitement." It was, he said, "an extraordinary instance of what Luther called the fifth sacrament, 'the mutual consolation of the brethren.' (Meaning, of course, the sisters as well)." Yet there was a weary tone in Neuhaus's account. The St. Olaf conference, he wrote, "was, in equal measure, heartening and sobering. It lucidly portrayed the contending forces in the struggle for the Lutheran soul and for the direction of the ELCA." He then reflected on the meaning of the "evangelical catholic" movement within Lutheranism.

The Lutheran Reformation was a corrective. It was not intended, and it is not possible, to build the fullness of the life of the Church on a corrective. The reality of Roman Catholicism almost five centuries after Augsburg suggests that the separate ecclesial existence of Lutheranism is no longer necessary—and, if no longer necessary, then no longer justified. That, say evangelical catholics, is why working to heal the breach of the 16th century between Rome and the Reformation is a matter of gospel fidelity for confessional Lutherans.[22]

Neuhaus mused that he had been ordained 30 years ago and that the "evangelical catholic understanding of Lutheranism seemed, at times, to be gaining ground over those years." Still, that understanding had always been that of a minority. The ELCA merger, he lamented, has "shifted dramatically the dominant influence to the side of the religion managers, the ideological activists, and the confessional pietists of denominationalism."

The first years of the 'new church' suggest that the shift may be irreversible. In view of the regnant sociological, institutional, and even theological dynamics, the evangelical catholic position becomes increasingly hard to advance within the ELCA. So, as we said, St Olaf was both heartening and sobering. It powerfully clarified the arguments and interests that are contending for the future of Lutheranism.

He then dropped a bombshell: after sixteen years of editing *Forum Letter*, he had decided that "it is time to move on." He thanked his readers for their faithful support through the years, and announced that his successor would be Pr. Russell Saltzman.[23]

Neuhaus had already told the ALPB board much the same thing in April, prior to "A Call to Faithfulness"—it was "time to move on." He cited the heavy responsibility entailed in starting up his new journal, *First Things*, which had debuted in March 1990. Saltzman, then a pastor in South Carolina, had been serving on the board since 1984 (though because of distance, he did not regularly attend meetings). He had written occasionally for *Forum Letter*, and he was also at that time editing *Lutheran Commentator*, a newsletter published by a group called Lutherans for Political and Religious Freedom. When Neuhaus announced his resignation, Saltzman offered to take over the editorship of *Forum Letter*—suggesting as well that perhaps the newsletter might merge with *Lutheran Commentator*. Paul Hinlicky was reticent; in his view, *Lutheran Commentator* was too concerned with political issues—often from a neo-conservative perspective (with which he decidedly did not agree). A bit gun shy after the controversy engendered by Neuhaus through the years, the board decided they were not prepared at that point to name Saltzman editor. They did agree that there should be an editor and "several associate/contributing editors," and they asked the executive committee to develop a specific proposal in consultation with Neuhaus, Saltzman and Hinlicky.[24]

A few days later Hinlicky acquiesced. In a memo to the executive committee, he agreed that Saltzman was "the best qualified candidate available without making an extensive and long search." He was still concerned about Saltzman's *Lutheran Commentator* association, but decided that a quick and smooth transition was essential. "So I think we should appoint him and get on with that." He was willing to consider the proposed merger with *Lutheran Commentator*, but he wanted it "explicitly understood that the ALPB, as an organization promoting confessional Lutheranism, is not committed to any particular political system or ideology ... but to the Two Kingdoms doctrine." As it turned out, others at *Lutheran Commentator* were not as enthusiastic as Saltzman about the proposed merger, and the idea was quietly dropped. Saltzman was appointed editor for a two-year term, with the understanding that Neuhaus would be associate editor for a year, that Saltzman would recruit a team of contributing editors, and that Saltzman would be Hinlicky's subordinate.[25]

Saltzman accepted the position—though not without expressing privately his unhappiness at Hinlicky's characterization of *Lutheran Commentator*. "I don't like the suggestion," he wrote to Hinlicky, "that *LC* has adopted one side of the political spectrum." In fact, "all the *LC* leadership would be appalled at the thought. And if that's the impression I've given as *LC* editor, I should be taken out and shot." He told Hinlicky he had no objection "with you as my, uh, superior (but just remember, I've fathered five children)." He did "expect final editorial control" of *Forum Letter* ("I'm the editor, not a copy boy"), but he assured Hinlicky that he had "a regular habit of advancing copy for critique and refinement." He suggested that he would ask both Hinlicky and Neuhaus (who had already agreed to the post of associate editor) to be his pre-publication critics.[26]

But Neuhaus never served as associate editor. Only weeks after turning the reins over to Saltzman, he dropped another bombshell: on September 8, 1990, he was received into the Roman Catholic Church. This announcement, while not surprising in retrospect, stunned the ALPB for which he had so long been a prominent voice. The new editor of *Forum Letter* was particularly shocked. "When we began negotiations for the editorship of this *Letter*," he wrote, "we asked Richard pointedly if his resignation was prelude to 'pulling a Newman.' He said not." (Saltzman was alluding to John Henry Newman, the Anglo-Catholic leader of the Church of England's 19th century Oxford Movement, who in 1845 converted to Catholicism.) Saltzman's initial reaction to Neuhaus's announcement, he admitted, "was unrestrained anger, accompanied by an unrestrained series of sharp Anglo-Saxon words utterly appropriate to this provocation, as well as a keen sense of, yes, betrayal is not too strong a word." But then he reflected on what Neuhaus's action meant for "the Lutheran evangelical catholic movement in America, a camp in which this *Letter* has pitched its tent." He was convinced that evangelical catholics still had a vital role to play in Lutheranism. "That precisely is why we have signed on for the duration of the trip. We are sorry, more, much more than we can say, that Richard Neuhaus will not be along for the rest of the ride. To our brother in Christ, peace, and God bless."[27]

The Reformation issue of *Lutheran Forum* was already in production when Neuhaus made his announcement, and it contained Neuhaus's lengthy critique of the "church growth movement." The article, entitled "The Lutheran Difference," argued passionately against proposals made by David Luecke and others to "modernize" Lutheran worship and teaching to make it more attractive to newcomers. Neuhaus insisted that this movement was a repudiation of Lutheran teaching on the nature of the church, the sacraments, and justification by grace. His conclusion was ironic, given his recent decision:

> Whatever may be the institutional future of Lutheranism in this culture ... we should face it with banners unfurled. I do believe that, if we choose the course of faithfulness, if we cultivate excellence in preaching, teaching, liturgy and pastoral care, if we lift up the Lutheran difference; if, in sum, we become the evangelical catholics that we claim to be—well, the outgrowth of such a renewal might bring many surprises.

Such outgrowth might even include—not least importantly, but surely not most importantly—church growth.[28]

In the following issue, Paul Hinlicky printed without editorial comment Neuhaus's open letter regarding his decision, followed by an open letter to Neuhaus from George Lindbeck. The Yale ecumenist (and a longtime friend both of Neuhaus and the ALPB) lamented Neuhaus's decision, but tried to cast it in a rather different light. Perhaps, he wrote, Neuhaus would "now be better placed to help Roman Catholics take the ecumenical initiative." He also suggested that Neuhaus's departure might provide a benefit for "evangelical catholic Lutherans."

> You know better than I that many people confuse your politics and your theology. You exemplify for them 'neoconservatism,' on the one hand, and 'evangelical catholicism,' on the other, and they are inclined to mix the two. It is in vain that you insist on the distinction between the Two Kingdoms. ... Will your departure make it easier to fight against this distortion of Lutheran evangelical catholicism? I don't know the answer; but I hope that it does.[29]

Hinlicky did take notice of Neuhaus's departure in an editorial entitled "Our Troubled Ministry." He saw Neuhaus as an extreme example of what he believed too many faithful pastors were experiencing.

> It should go without saying that I bear a decent respect, and urge others to the same, for Richard's plight: how long can anyone endure character assassination at the hands of the intellectually dishonest and incompetent? How often I myself witnessed the spectacle of church politicians who would privately enjoy his advice and counsel only then publicly to disown him! As I see it, Richard endured a very long trial, and when he saw the Lord opening to him a better way to fulfill his vocation, he risked in faith.

Nonetheless, Hinlicky called on others to stay the course. "We at **Lutheran Forum** will persevere. We are undeterred. We fight for that evangelical and catholic future. God will prevail. Jesus is Lord!"[30]

The new *Forum Letter* editor
"the ELCA's top leadership has simply failed to lead"

The ALPB board had asked that the new editor of *Forum Letter* enlist a cadre of contributing editors. They were listed on the masthead of Saltzman's first issue, and nearly every issue featured a piece by one or another of them. The original four included Pr. Richard Niebanck (now serving a parish in New Jersey), Pr. Melinda Heppe (a Pennsylvania parish pastor), Pr. John Pless (LCMS campus pastor at the University of Minnesota), and Dr. Christa Klein (a consultant on theological education to the Lilly Endowment, Inc.). But if the board hoped that *Forum Letter* would change direction with a new editor and a collection of contributing editors, they were quickly disabused of that notion. Under Saltzman, the newsletter continued to be a sharp critic of church leaders and institutions—though he wrote with a kind of whimsy that tempered his barbs and brought a rather different tone to the publication.

His first issue reported on a major controversy at Lutheran School of Theology in Chicago over a faculty appointment to a post in Christian ethics. The two finalists were Reinhard Huetter, a white male, and Elizabeth Bettenhausen, a white female. The latter, however, was "said by critics to be somewhat inarticulate on Christological subjects," while the former was described by one faculty member as "a once in a generation candidate." The faculty agreed, and it was the man who was chosen. Saltzman reported:

> [This situation] rapidly escalated to a grab bag of inclusivity issues, personalities, and *de rigueur* charges of: racism (from black students; Huetter and Bettenhausen are white), sexism (from women students; Huetter is male), racism and sexism (from black women students; Bettenhausen is a woman but not black), and ageism and sexism (leveled by older second-career women students; Huetter is male and younger than Bettenhausen). Doubtless we have left someone out, but, honest, it wasn't intentional.

The "moral of the story," he observed, is the observation of one faculty member that "this is the future of the ELCA. More fights. Count on it."[31]

In subsequent issues, Saltzman blasted an ELCA draft statement on capital punishment ("plunging the ELCA into a partisan fray"). He reported with some bafflement on discrimination lawsuits filed by Robert Preus after his forced retirement from the presidency of Concordia Theological Seminary, Ft. Wayne, IN. He wrote extensively on the draft statement of the ELCA's "Abortion: A Call to Deliberate" (the report is "dismally impaired," he concluded). He analyzed the Gulf War ("a lamentable necessity") and found fault with the *Lutheran*'s editorial opposition to the conflict.[32]

He was particularly critical of the ELCA's leadership. The denomination was experiencing a budget crisis in 1991, and Salzman had a diagnosis: "To put it as delicately as possible, the ELCA has an image problem. Chicago seems to limp along getting itself shot in the foot every couple months or so." But the deeper issue, he said, "and truly we say this with the utmost reluctance and regret—[is] the ELCA's top leadership has simply failed to lead." He offered an example of what he described as "confusion in Chicago":

> Budget cuts two years ago were across the board. The axe fell indiscriminately upon corporate headquarters with no due regard for the relative importance of one division or commission over another. The ELCA's 11th floor offered a crass defense for its slash-and-burn budgeting. What, as one ELCA official reportedly asked, makes the Division for Outreach better than the Commission for Women? Mark this: a leadership unable to distinguish the comparable weight of the Division for Outreach compared to the Commission for Women is indeed a rare and wondrous thing. ... If it has not occurred to anyone, the Division for Outreach and, we shall not forget,

Global Mission are the bureaucratic embodiments of the biblical imperative to 'teach all nations.' And the Commission for Women? That is the bureaucratic consequence of providing a box on the organizational chart for an ideological interest group.[33]

In Saltzman's view, the ELCA's crisis should be laid at the doorstep of Bp. Chilstrom. He surveyed a select group of ELCA executive staff, seminary presidents, bishops, and parish pastors, asking four questions about Chilstrom's leadership. The results astonished him. He first asked "what grade between A and F" they would give Chilstrom. The executives gave him a B+, the seminary presidents a B, the bishops a B-; but among parish pastors (25 selected at random from the *ELCA Yearbook*), the average was a D+, and none rated him higher than C+. Saltzman offered a thoughtful reflection on this disparity; the bottom line, he wrote, is that "attitudes toward the ELCA have undergone a breath-taking transition since its inception. ... Within the space of time it takes most people to pay off a car loan, the ELCA has lost its credit rating."[34]

Saltzman was not entirely negative, however. Reporting on the second ELCA assembly in Orlando, he sensed "a new spirit—even confidence—among delegates, ELCA staff and leadership." There was an "agreeable cheer, patience, sincerity and, well, simple trust" that was "most winsome." All of this "bodes well for the ELCA." He believed that Chilstrom's re-election was largely a matter of not wanting to "sow further seeds of confusion within the ELCA" but acknowledged that Chilstrom had heard and was responding to criticisms. In summary, the ELCA "is not yet a cohesive community, but it may be getting there."[35]

Forum Letter appeared to be "getting there" as well, gaining a solid footing in the post-Neuhaus era. But then readers were startled by an announcement in December that Saltzman had resigned because he was going through a divorce that he called a "personal catastrophe." Paul Hinlicky informed readers of the board's hope that "someday Pastor Saltzman could return to service in the ALPB's ministry of publication."[36]

There were rumors, however, that Hinlicky was not entirely unhappy to see Saltzman go. The interdenominational *Christian Century*'s column "The Underground Ecumenist," a widely-read source of gossip about various American denominations, reported that Saltzman had been "more or less forced out" by Hinlicky.

> The ostensible reason was a marriage in crisis. Sources say the real motive was the desire to get rid of a too-independent voice. The monthly newsletter gained circulation under Saltzman, pastor of a Charleston, South Carolina, congregation. He's as deft as his predecessor at turning a phrase, but his caustic, witty critiques are not spiteful. He's adopted a kinder, gentler tone than either Neuhaus or Hinlicky in skewering the failings of the [ELCA].

Hinlicky adamantly insisted that these charges were unfounded; he personally suspected that the unnamed "sources" were ELCA personnel in Chicago who wanted to discredit both him and the ALPB, though he refrained from making the accusation publicly.[37]

At the time the item appeared, in fact, Saltzman and the board had already agreed that he would resume the editorship in July. Saltzman wrote to the *Christian Century*:

> The Underground Ecumenist has things wrong. While the outward circumstances of my resignation ... unfortunately lent themselves to the interpretation posited ... the fact is I have been reappointed editor with the enthusiastic endorsement of Paul Hinlicky. ... We remain firm colleagues in the fullest sense of the term.
>
> Otherwise, [the] description of me as a 'perceptive writer,' 'deft at turning a phrase,' and 'witty' was uncannily accurate. For an even more accurate portrayal, add the words 'handsome' and 'humble.'

ALPB president Hans Quitmeyer also wrote to the *Century*, telling them they had it wrong. "The 'ostensible reason' [for Saltzman's resignation], as your writer put it, was *the* reason. ... I was there, and I know."[38]

More events and conferences

"Lutheranism is at the center of the storm"

The ALPB board had been planning another Inter-Lutheran Forum dinner for the fall of 1990, but the success of "A Call to Faithfulness" led them instead to sponsor a day-long event that would include worship, a keynote presentation and a luncheon, with various workshops in the morning and afternoon. It was advertised as "St. Olaf—East: Continuing the Call," and the announced theme was "The Future of Lutheranism."

They invited Paul Hinlicky and Richard John Neuhaus to be the speakers. This took a problematic turn when Neuhaus was received into the Roman Catholic Church two months prior to the event; even more awkward, the board had intended to recognize Neuhaus's long service to the ALPB as part of the program. In a decision Hinlicky called "historic," the board proceeded with the plans both to honor Neuhaus and to ask him to provide one of the keynote addresses. In view of the changed situation, the conference theme was changed to "The Future of Reformation." More than 150 participants gathered November 3 at the Wartburg, and the presentations were published in the February 1991 issue of *Lutheran Forum*.[39]

Neuhaus was gracious. He thanked the Bureau and the attendees for their greatness of spirit and reflected on his own decision. He argued that the "living tradition of Catholicism has internalized the authentic concerns of the Reformation"—a truth amply demonstrated by the results of Lutheran/Roman Catholic dialogue over the past decades. "I do not pretend to know what this means for the relationship between our two communions," he admitted.

> A year before his death, the distinguished Orthodox theologian, Alexander Schmemann, told me that Americans will never understand ecumenism. Why is that? I

asked. Because, Schmemann answered, Americans cannot understand anything that does not have a schedule attached to it.

We have neither the schedule nor clear scenario for what, over many years, I have called healing of the breach of the 16ᵗʰ Century between Rome and the Reformation. ...

Ecumenism requires neither schedules nor sure scenarios. Because there is one Christ, the ecumenical imperative is intrinsic to Christian existence. To be Christian is to be ecumenically Christian.

"And this I know," he concluded. "However imperfect our communion, God in Christ has given us to one another, and we must never, we can never, let one another go."[40]

Hinlicky was less sanguine and more acerbic. He argued that contemporary Lutheran leaders have abandoned the doctrine of justification by grace through faith—the article on which the church stands and falls. They prefer "to focus energy on earthly happiness, be it in therapeutic counseling or therapeutic politics, rather than eternal destiny; on human agency rather than human bondage; on our experience and fulfillment rather than the means of grace and discipleship." This dilemma, he argued, is the result of a marriage between the "individualistic religious impulses" of Zwingli and the Lockean liberalism so influential in American cultural life. In truth, it is Christianity itself that is in trouble in North America, and "for good or for ill ... Lutheranism is at the center of the storm."[41]

Hinlicky was convinced that a continuing series of free conferences of one sort or another was the best way to keep these concerns before the church, and work began almost at once on a second "Call to Faithfulness" conference to be held in 1992, again at St. Olaf College. Hinlicky also urged the ALPB board to combine its June 1991 meeting with a consultation to which would be invited a group of "younger pastors and teachers." Planned by Hinlicky and new board member Pr. Sharon Zanter Ross, the invitation went to about three dozen persons. The purpose, Ross told them, was "to begin to concretely construct an agenda which will assist evangelical catholicism to enter the next century with vitality." Some additional ALPB supporters were also invited to join the conversation.[42]

When the consultation convened at St. Matthew's Lutheran Church in White Plains, NY, those gathered (including ALPB board members) heard papers by Pr. Leonard Klein, Pr. Richard Ballard, Pr. Jonathan Jenkins, Dr. Bruce Marshall, and Prof. David Yeago. Marshall's paper was particularly provocative. "In our present situation," he argued, efforts for evangelical catholic reform "are meeting with resistance—theological, bureaucratic, and otherwise."

We should expect that this will continue, and may worsen. Faced with this prospect we will likely find ourselves tempted to anxiety, despair, and perhaps rage. This is in fact temptation, and it is as such to be resisted. If the church is part of the gospel, then the church will be reformed. It's in the bag. We may perform our little labors in utter confidence of this, no matter how meager the immediate results may seem.[43]

Some board members expressed surprise at the direction this consultation had taken. They had expected the invited guests would be advising them about the future direction of the ALPB, and instead there appeared to be a much larger agenda. Dorothy Zelenko would later recall that the theologians "argued enthusiastically among themselves about the church, largely oblivious to the ALPB people who were there." Hinlicky, hearing rumblings about the unhappiness, wrote to Fred Schumacher, ALPB secretary and pastor of St. Matthew's, that it "was not exactly what I had anticipated."

> Yet I think the end result was a solid achievement: schism talk was stopped, the moderates are in charge of drafting the statement of grievances to the ELCA on the basis of commonly accepted Lutheran norms, and the controversial questions of the doctrine of the church are subjected to a study process that I personally will oversee. While I wish the ALPB had more directly benefited and more immediately, let us consider this: that if St. Olaf II and this statement play a catalytic role in changing the ELCA's direction, as sure we must pray God that they do, the ALPB and St. Matthew's will have played a not insignificant role in the history of the Kingdom.

Schumacher replied that he had been expecting "papers on the future direction of ALPB and how best we could ... serve the church," but he insisted that he did "not question ... the value of the conference especially in the light of the results."[44]

Those results, however, turned out to be significantly less than had been hoped. Many years later Hinlicky would reflect on the consultation. "I don't recall," he acknowledged, "that anything ever came of the study project mentioned to Fred [Schumacher]." He did remember that the event ended on a positive note with a "delightful sermon" by ELCA bishop Michael McDaniel, who had recently joined the ALPB board; but McDaniel "saved the day, but not the project." Nothing further appears in the ALPB board minutes about the consultation. The only significant follow-up seems to have been the publication—some 18 months later—of Marshall's paper in *Lutheran Forum*.[45]

That fall the ALPB resumed the older format of an Inter-Lutheran Forum dinner. The 1991 banquet featured Carl Braaten on "Building a Theological Agenda for Lutherans." He outlined what he called "three dilemmas" facing the church. The first, he said, was the question of "whether they are the original Protestants breaking away to start a new and true church or reforming Catholics pushing the cause of evangelical renewal." This has led to "a kind of civil war" between what George Lindbeck calls "denominational confessionalists and evangelical catholics." The second was that Lutherans had "fought for the right and necessity to use the historical critical method [of Biblical study], but it is turning out to be a pyrrhic victory" because the method has "[separated] itself from the paradigm of the church's trinitarian and christological dogmas" and become captive to the *Zeitgeist*. The third was the conflict over the meaning of justification. Braaten argued that "the badge of Lutheran identity has become badly smudged." "One gets the distinct impression,"" he suggested, "that [some] Lutherans feel the necessity to soft pedal justification to commend it to our times," while others are such "resolute champions of justification" that in their thinking it becomes not the chief article but the *only* article.[46]

To address these dilemmas, Braaten insisted that Lutherans must take the Trinity "as the paradigmatic framework for all Christian theology." They must rescue the Bible from its "Babylonian captivity to scholarly specializations" and read the Bible whole again. This will entail learning "to think again in concert with the entire *Una Sancta* in space and time." It will require battling the "theocentric Unitarianism flooding the academy, and just [learning] how to say No!" Lutherans must "find better ways to parse our justification doctrine to set it free from Lutheran jingoism." They must also be willing to grant a "real but limited respect for reason even apart from and prior to faith." This agenda, Braaten concluded, keeps the Lutheran confessions "in continuity with the entire sweep of the catholic tradition," always "for the sake of an evangelical witness within Western Christianity."[47]

These events were all building up to "St. Olaf II" in June 1992. Once again *dialog* and *Lutheran Quarterly* joined *Lutheran Forum/Forum Letter* as sponsors, and once again an impressive array of speakers was announced, representing both "evangelical catholics" and "denominational confessionalists" (now more generally being called "radical Lutherans"). The topics were more focused on specific issues facing the ELCA. Carl Braaten agreed to give the keynote address, which he entitled "The Gospel or What?" Luther Seminary's Walter Sundberg, one of the sharpest critics of the evangelical catholic understanding of Lutheranism, would respond. Several other pairs of speakers (George Lindbeck and Gerhard Forde, David Yeago and Joseph Burgess, Robert Jenson and Meg Madson) were chosen to represent both the "evangelical catholic" and the "radical Lutheran" perspectives—both groups anxious about what they saw as looming apostasy in the ELCA, but with sharply different perspectives on the root of the problem and what to do about it. Finally, Paul Hinlicky, Gracia Grindal, and Robert Benne would critique the ELCA's quota system, each from his or her own point of view.

Braaten's keynote offered the red meat that many attendees expected. "There is a spiritual battle being waged in our church today," he began, calling it the age-old battle between light and darkness, life and death. He asked a profound question: "What did we organize this church to do?" For Braaten, the "one thing needful" is to preach the gospel. But the gospel is proclaimed precisely by the church, and it is in its understanding of the church that the ELCA is deficient.

> Lutheranism should recognize that it cannot solve the problem of the doctrine of the ministry as long as it has a deficient doctrine of the church. The *satis est* clause of

Article VII of the Augsburg Confession is a teaching aimed to defend the purity of Article IV on justification by faith apart from works; it is a soteriological statement and not the blueprint for an ecclesiology. By historical accident Lutherans have suffered the separation of the gospel and the church, and so they have tried desperately to re-invent the church from the doctrine of justification by faith alone. It cannot work. So every ten years or so Lutherans engage in a comprehensive study of the doctrine of the ministry, and wonder why they have made no progress.[48]

But Sundberg had a very different view of what "cannot work." After thanking Braaten for his forthrightness and clarity, he condemned those who elevate the doctrines of the church and the ministry "to all-determining principles."

> There are some in the church who say: 'If we only had a sufficient doctrine of the church with an ecumenically correct doctrine of ministry (this means, of course, the so-called "historic episcopate" and a threefold office of ministry) we will be true to the call to faithfulness.' As a way through the forest of our troubles, I am afraid this will not work.

Sundberg insisted that Luther and his colleagues "did away with what they called 'human traditions,'" including much of what was taught in the 16th century about the church. The Lutheran ecclesiology of *satis est* "was not an 'historical accident'; it was intended."[49]

One interesting aspect of the conference was the appearance of Bp. Herbert Chilstrom, who had accepted an invitation to be present and to speak. He was received warmly, but his message was disappointing to many. He proclaimed his love for "the whole church." He gamely defended what many of those present thought problematic: the quota system, the vesting of ultimate authority in a lay-dominated representational assembly. He admitted that church structures, including even "independent organizations and publications, are imperfect and faulty expressions of what we might hope… yet for all that we are together the church of Christ."[50]

"It took courage [for Chilstrom] just to show up in the midst of 700+ people, the vast majority of whom think he is leading their church down the primrose path," Leonard Klein admitted in *Forum Letter*. Clearly the bishop is a man of "faith, piety, and deep Lutheran commitments." Still, Chilstrom's words did little to reassure those present that their church was on the right track.[51]

But the rest of the presentations, like the Braaten/Sundberg exchange, also evidenced the sharply different perspectives of evangelical catholics and radical Lutherans. This made many despair of the possibility of the two groups making common cause, despite their shared anxiety about the ELCA's direction. It had been, Hinlicky admitted, "a worthy idea, an experiment that had to be tried." But it seems doomed to fail.

> A year ago, **LF** took no little heat for calling a spade a spade when we devoted an issue to the theme of *ecumenical gridlock*. In this edition, readers will discover and verify that gridlock of the ecumenical movement right smack in the middle of our American Lutheranism.[52]

Klein, too, saw as "sobering" the "continuing impasse" between the two views of Lutheran confessionalism. He left little question where he stood—and he was in fact speaking for the ALPB, or at least for its publications. Despite some positive contributions, "radical Lutheranism has not produced what it hoped for."

> The better road forward leads more directly out of older confessionalism and right through—you won't be surprised to hear me say this—the nexus of arguments and concerns loosely collected under the label 'evangelical catholic.' Constructive trinitarian and liturgical theology, ecumenical engagement, reflection on the church as an ethical community, and a fair confrontation with the catholic claims as to order and ministry hold out far more hope for shaping a church life that can meet the challenge of three centuries of assault on Christian faith.

"The conversation needs to continue," Klein wrote, "and it will continue ... in these pages. ... But I trust that both sides see the futility of structuring the debate into any future events like the two gatherings at Northfield."[53]

So there were no more "Call to Faithfulness" events. The Bureau did have a minor role in another theological conference at St. Olaf, "Reclaiming the Bible for the Church," held in conjunction with the Center for Catholic and Evangelical Theology. The June 1994 event was co-sponsored by the ALPB, but it was planned and executed by the CCET. There were announcements of the conference in *Lutheran Forum*, but not much more ALPB involvement even in promotion. A brief editorial note in *Lutheran Forum* put it in context:

> Readers will note that this conference is not a *Call to Faithfulness III*. That effort has run its course and a further public debate between the two major confession-alist factions in the ELCA will do no one any good. We need to move on to constructive theology; that makes this conference as critical a witness as those two earlier events for those who would call the ELCA back to faithfulness. We urge your attendance.

The conference featured an ecumenical group of theologians addressing the crisis of Biblical authority and interpretation; it was heavy with Lutherans, though there were several prominent scholars from other traditions. The papers were later published by William B. Eerdmans Publishing Company. This would be the ALPB's last direct involvement, at least for a while, in such an ambitious theological conference. There were, however, other even more ambitious endeavors on the horizon.[54]

Notes

1. Minutes, ALPB Board of Directors, 22 Sept. 1987.
2. Ibid.
3. Minutes, ALPB Board of Directors, 18 Jan, 1988 (with attachment, Paul Hinlicky, "Statement").
4. Paul R. Hinlicky, "A Time for Decision," *LF* 22, no. 1 (Lent 1988), 17-19.
5. Minutes, ALPB Board of Directors, 24 May 1988.
6. *FL* 16, no. 11 (29 Feb. 1988), 8.
7. Thomas R. Sluberski, "Essays in Honor of Glenn C. Stone: A Festscrift," *LF* 22, no. 2 (Pentecost 1988), 4; *FL* 16, no. 11 (29 Feb. 1988), 8.

8. "In Memoriam: Pastor Adolf F. Meyer, D.D.," *LF* 22, no 3 (Reformation 1988), 7.

9. *FL* 17, no. 12 (8 Jan. 1989), 1-3.

10. Ibid., 5-7.

11. *FL* 18, no. 1 (5 Feb. 1989), 2.

12. Ibid., 4-5.

13. Ibid.

14. *FL* 18, no. 8 (28 Aug. 1989), 4; "Two quit 'Lutheran Forum,'" *Lutheran*, 22 Mar. 1989, 35.

15. Minutes, ALPB Board of Directors, 7 Mar. 1989; "Two quit 'Lutheran Forum.'"

16. Minutes, ALPB Board of Directors, 7 Mar. 1989.

17. Minutes, ALPB Board of Directors, 23 May 1989.

18. Ibid.

19. Minutes, ALPB Board of Directors, 16 Sept. 1989 and 21 Nov. 1989.

20. *LF* 23, no. 4 (Advent 1989), 40; *FL* 18, no. 8 (28 Aug. 1989), 7.

21. *FL* 19, no. 7 (25 July 1990), 1ff.

22. Ibid., 7.

23. Ibid., 8.

24. Minutes, ALPB Board of Directors, 24 Apr. 1990.

25. Paul Hinlicky to Executive Committee, 30 Apr. 1990, ALPB Archives.

26. Russell E. Saltzman to Paul Hinlicky, 3 May 1990, ALPB Archives.

27. *FL*, 19, no. 9 (14 Sept. 1990), 1-4.

28. Richard John Neuhaus, "The Lutheran Difference," *LF* 24, no. 3 (Reformation 1990), 24.

29. George Lindbeck, "To Richard J. Neuhaus," *LF* 24, no. 4 (Advent 1990), 44.

30. Paul R. Hinlicky, "Our Troubled Ministry," *LF* 24, no. 4 (Advent 1990), 4-5.

31. *FL* 19, no. 8 (15 Aug. 1990), 1-2.

32. *FL* 19, no. 11 (23 Nov. 1990), 2; *FL* 19, no. 12 (25 Dec. 1990), 1ff.; *FL* 20, no. 2 (23 Feb. 1991), 3; *FL* 20, no. 3 (24 Mar. 1991), 1ff.

33. *FL* 20, no. 5 (26 May 1991), 2-4.

34. *FL* 20, no. 6 (24 June 1991), 6.

35. *FL* 20, no. 10 (31 Oct. 1991), 1ff.

36. *FL* 20, no. 12 (25 Dec. 1991), 1.

37. Paul R. Hinlicky, telephone conversation with Richard O. Johnson, 20 May 2016.

38. Kate Anders Marlin, "The Underground Ecumenist," *Christian Century* 109, no. 17 (13 May 1992), 509; Letters to the Editor, *Christian Century* 109, no. 21 (1-8 July 1992), 662.

39. "St. Olaf East—Continuing the Call: Editor's Introduction," *LF* 25, no. 1 (Feb. 1991), 4.

40. Richard John Neuhaus, "The Future of the Reformation," *LF* 25, no. 1 (Feb. 1991), 6-7.

41. Paul R. Hinlicky, "The Future of Reformation," *LF* 25, no. 1 (Feb. 1991), 9-10.

42. Sharon Zanter Ross to unspecified recipients, n.d. [ca 1991], ALPB Archives. Paul Hinlicky also signed the letter, but it was written in Zanter's voice.

43. Bruce D. Marshall, "The Church in the Gospel," *LF* 27, no. 1 (Feb. 1993), 24ff.

44. Dorothy Zelenko, e-mail message to Richard O. Johnson, 4 May 2016; Paul Hinlicky to Fred Schumacher, 7 June 1991; Fred Schumacher to Paul Hinlicky, 10 June 1991, ALPB Archives.

45. Paul R. Hinlicky, e-mail message to Richard O. Johnson, 17 Mar. 2016.

46. Carl E. Braaten, "Building a Theological Agenda for Lutherans," *LF* 26, no. 1 (Feb. 1992), 21-22.

47. Ibid., 25.

48. Carl E. Braaten, "The Gospel—Or What?" *LF* 26, no. 4 (Nov. 1992), 4ff.

49. Walter Sundberg, "A Conflict of Creeds," *LF* 26, no. 4 (Nov. 1992), 11ff.

50. Herbert W. Chilstrom, "We Can Love the Church—the Whole Church," *LF* 26, no. 4 (Nov. 1992), 30.

51. *FL* 21, no. 6 (29 June 1992), 1.

52. Paul R. Hinlicky, "In the Forum," *LF* 26, no. 4 (Nov. 1992), 3.

53. *FL* 21, no. 6 (June 29, 1992), 3-4.

54. *LF* 28, no. 1 (Feb. 1994), 7; Carl E. Braaten and Robert W. Jenson, eds. *Reclaiming the Bible for the Church* (Grand Rapids, MI: Wm. B. Eerdmans Publishing Company, 1995).

Chapter 20

A Publishing Ministry

T he ALPB's 1975 statement of purpose had left its mission somewhat open-ended: "the Bureau shall publish appropriate literature and engage in such other activities as it deems useful." By the 1990s, though, the "other activities" had receded into the background and the focus was once again almost entirely on publication—the *Forum* package, but also a new academic journal, a reinvigorated tract ministry, and an increasingly important book publishing program.

Lutheran Forum under Hinlicky
"the forum of that new generation"
When Paul Hinlicky took charge of *Lutheran Forum*, he told the board that his "tone would be more urgent." As the new ELCA developed, *Lutheran Forum* offered an increasingly harsh critique of what Hinlicky called "the crisis in American Lutheranism." In his very first issue, Hinlicky had already sounded the alarm about "the protestantising of Lutheranism into conservative and liberal sects." He saw the magazine's task in stark terms:

> *Lutheran Forum* now becomes the forum of that new generation which is sick of tearing down and wants instead to build up. Barring 'war at the gates,' our ambition for our church is better than to see it dive into the bottomless pit of the hermeneutics

of suspicion in which we were schooled. We have found our way back to Christian faith with the help of Luther, and our aim is to master the crisis, not retreat from it. We see in the demise of Protestantism as a Christian church a microcosm of the crisis of Western civilization, of that godlessness of culture which began, as Luther prophesied, when Zwingli tore asunder what God had joined together. So it is time, we think, to return attention to the Catechism of Luther, to the material questions concerning the essential things of life and salvation.[1]

Hinlicky's approach was to be based firmly in Lutheran confessional theology. That first issue took as its theme "The Small Catechism and the Formation of Piety," while the next four focused on the four *solas* of the Reformation—Christ alone, grace alone, faith alone, Scripture alone. Within those themes, the magazine published essays by many of the foremost teachers and theologians of the church, as well as commentary by parish pastors.

Real life manifestations of the theological crisis were also presented. The first of several "State of the Church Reports," written by Pennsylvania pastor Mark Chapman, described a conference called "Ecumenical Moment '88." It was sponsored by the World and National Councils of Churches and featured the general secretaries of both organizations, as well as other prominent leaders—hardly the "extremist fringe of conciliar ecumenism," he noted. Yet "what they espoused as 'ecumenism' was simply shocking."

> I knew we were in trouble when our first worship 'celebration' found us outdoors at a garden pond offering prayers and water libations to the Seven Spirits of the seven directions of the universe. ... What to any objective observer was sheer paganism, we were told, was simply an exercise in discovering the ecumenical variety of spiritual expression and experience that we must learn to share if we are to be truly one.

"Genuine ecumenism," he concluded, "is not syncretistic religious pluralism ... [but it] is explicitly *Christian*. ... The WCC and NCC have clearly lost grip on this basic and fundamental definition." In the following issue, Amandus Derr told of attending a worship service at ELCA headquarters in which there was not a single mention of God ("neither God nor a person of the Holy Trinity") until the final hymn. "If this was worship," he wrote, "I don't know who was worshiped or why."[2]

Under Hinlicky's editorship, ecumenism was still often front and center, but sunny support of ecumenical dialogue had turned to caution about specific proposals working their way toward consideration in the ELCA. Moreover, writers were skeptical about whether the ELCA was even capable of serious ecumenical work. The developing declaration of full communion between the ELCA and the Episcopal Church, for example, caused Michael Root to ponder a "disturbing question: Can the ELCA carry out a reasoned debate on a major ecumenical proposal? When a seminary professor publicly describes the proposal as 'necrophilia,' one's expectations cannot be high." (His reference was to a widely-repeated comment by Walter Sundberg that "going to bed with Episcopalians is like ecclesiastical necrophilia." Sundberg's remark was, to his embarrassment, published in the *Minneapolis Star-Tribune* and then repeated in *Newsweek* magazine.)[3]

Root was not opposed to full communion with the Episcopalians, though his article was paired with one by Meg Madson sharply criticizing what she called ELCA leaders' attempt to "pressure the ELCA into episcopal succession." But while *Lutheran Forum* writers took different perspectives on the Lutheran/Episcopal proposals, there was almost unanimous opposition to the recommendations of the Lutheran/Reformed dialogues. Guest editorialist Mark Chapman took up *A Common Calling*, which proposed full communion between the ELCA and three Reformed bodies (Presbyterian Church USA, Reformed Church in America, and United Church of Christ). "From the perspective of ecumenical theology," he wrote, 'A Common Calling' is a disaster." It is, however, a "five-star triumph" in "the Realpolitik of denominational mergers."[4]

Lutheran Forum also continued its traditional focus on matters liturgical. The annual *Una Sancta* issue continued, though not quite annually; between 1988 and 1993 it appeared on average every eighteen months. The articles, however, shifted away from the practical liturgical topics of previous years. Now they were often theological treatises or articles about adapting the liturgy in specific ethnic or demographic settings. There was frequent criticism of the "church growth movement" and its "entertainment evangelism" proclivities.

The early years of *Lutheran Forum* had often discussed race relations and civil rights, war and peace, women in church and society, international affairs; under Hinlicky there was a perceptible shift away from social concerns. The editor himself seemed to recognize this. In the Reformation 1989 issue, he suggested that the magazine would now "engage controverted points in our society, beginning with the Advent issue on the theme of 'Abortion and Christian Character.'" It was a good beginning, but the following several issues returned to more internal ecclesiastical matters in preparation for, and following up on, the first "Call to Faithfulness" conference.[5]

He tried again two years later, announcing that "the program of **Lutheran Forum** in 1991 shifts focus from the introspection of the past year on the plight of American Lutheranism to the troubled society in which we live today." The result was still only minimal attention to social issues. The Pentecost 1993 theme was "Quest for a Public Theology," and later that year the magazine took up "The End of Marxism"; but in general, *Lutheran Forum* maintained an introspective stance.[6]

One exception was considerable space given to the topic of sexuality, and especially homosexuality—though this, of course, was a matter that was now convulsing the church itself. When a gay man and two lesbians were illicitly ordained in San Francisco in 1990 ("the latest ELCA disaster," Hinlicky called it), editorial advisor Leonard Klein expressed the magazine's position.

> From Bishop Chilstrom on down, the San Francisco ordinations must be rejected not because the church isn't ready for this yet. They must be rejected, and appropriate

discipline of the involved pastors and congregations must follow, because there is no place in the ELCA for a cadre of clergy who at the most profound and intimate levels of their personal life and at the most clear and public center of their vocation declare that Scripture is not applicable.

In the same issue, Martin Heinecken, professor emeritus of the Lutheran Theological Seminary at Philadelphia, argued that the ordinations themselves were invalid.[7]

The several issues that came before and after the "Call to Faithfulness" conferences cut across all these topics, challenging the ELCA on its social statements, its liturgical and ecumenical initiatives, its theological stances. There were articles dealing with the feminist critique of "God language." The ELCA's quota system came in for regular criticism. *Lutheran Forum* also paid more attention to the Missouri Synod during these years, perhaps because Hinlicky, unlike Glenn Stone, had LCMS roots. But the ELCA and its ills was still the primary topic of discussion.

Sometimes Hinlicky's "more urgent tone" could display an edge of disdain. A promotional offer in 1991 encouraged subscribers to buy bulk copies of *Forum Letter* for congregational leaders as an alternative to the ELCA's *Seeds for the Parish*; the page was headlined, "Tired of *Weeds for the Parish*?" "That's not good," Russ Saltzman wrote to him. "It is simply too provoking and furthers our image, deserved or not, of 'ELCA-bashing.'"

> Ultimately, [we all] want the ELCA to be the theological embodiment of what best represents catholic Lutheranism, a worthy bride with as few blemishes as possible. But I fear we risk turning off potential—you might read 'moderate'—listeners if we get really nasty. And 'weeds' purt'n near does that. I did not take it for satire. It just hit me mean.

Apparently Saltzman's view (several others shared it) prevailed, and the next issue contained the same promo piece but without the provocative headline.[8]

The most prevalent theme in *Lutheran Forum* under Hinlicky was the advocacy of the evangelical catholic vision of Lutheranism. It was laced throughout the papers from and pertaining to the St. Olaf conferences. It was discussed forthrightly in editorials and articles throughout this period (including, it must be said, by writers who profoundly disagreed with the evangelical catholic position; in that respect, the magazine maintained its commitment to being a forum). But clearly Hinlicky believed that the evangelical catholic vision was the mission of *Lutheran Forum*. In a "message to subscribers" in 1991, he marveled that the magazine's renewal rate was a remarkable 90%.

> We don't mind admitting that we were nervous that the loss of Richard John Neuhaus would adversely affect subscriptions. In fact, we have enjoyed something like a 25% net increase in paid subscriptions during the past two years. It is now clear that there has been no change in the growth rate since Neuhaus' departure, let alone a loss! That is evidence ... that the evangelical catholic understanding of Lutheranism is deep as well as broad.

The actual subscriptions records for this period don't substantiate Hinlicky's assertion of a 25% increase in paid subscriptions; there was a slight increase in circulation, perhaps due to increased promotion in 1990 and 1991, but it was not dramatic. For several months during this period no renewal notices were sent; when that was finally rectified, there was a glut of "renewals" which Hinlicky may have interpreted as an "increase in paid subscriptions." In any event, his essential point was correct: the loss of Richard John Neuhaus had not materially impacted the subscription numbers for the *Forum* package. The support for the "evangelical catholic understanding of Lutheranism" seemed to be intact.[9]

Forum Letter in the interim

"Official gobbledegook"

After Russell Saltzman's resignation, Paul Hinlicky temporarily edited *Forum Letter* as well as *Lutheran Forum*. But while Hinlicky held the title of interim editor, in fact Leonard Klein was primarily responsible for the newsletter during this period. Over the next six months, he would write about half the material in *Forum Letter*. Aside from a few contributions from others, Hinlicky would write the rest.

During this interim, *Forum Letter* continued its role of addressing the political side of the Lutheran churches, leaving theology to *Lutheran Forum*. Sometimes this took the form of investigative journalism. In January 1992, Klein told the story of a clumsy attempt by the ELCA's Division for Outreach to start a new "regional mega-church" in the North Fort Worth area. He revealed that they had done so without any consultation with local pastors in the area, and without prior discussion by the synod council. Even worse from Klein's perspective was the plan itself, which was to start a congregation using the techniques of the church growth movement—i.e., a non-liturgical mission with specific racial and economic targeting. Klein reported that the plug had been pulled on the plan, thanks in part to an outcry from local pastors and congregations. He hoped that this experience might result in "a major reassessment of the plans to pilot test some mega-church starts."[10]

The next issue took on the recently released ELCA sexuality study. Hinlicky pulled no punches. "Official gobbledegook," he huffed. "An insult to our intelligence." Klein's longer analysis was hardly more restrained. The report "is another reminder of how bad off the ELCA is." In its "fifty-five tedious pages," the study lists "standard positions on sexual ethics ... alongside other opinions with no hint that one has or should have any priority. Traditional positions are stated in a kind of have-you-stopped-beating-your-wife rhetoric."

> Now, we're sinners and we mess this up right well, just like everything else. The ecstatic power and pleasure of sex are more than most of us can handle well. We sin. The

church must deal pastorally and graciously with those whose struggle with *eros* does not go by the book. ... This is not all that hard, folks. We didn't need a self-important task force to teach us this. In point of fact, we didn't need the task force at all. We had all we needed already, lacking only the guts and brains to use it. The test now will be to see whether the church, particularly its ordained leadership and its bishops, will summon the courage and insight to reject the study and to do the right thing.

The right thing, he concluded, "would be to 'just say thanks' to the committee and send them home. And to fire the prime movers." [11]

The new, old ministry of leaflets

"an added resource for defining Lutheran"

In the 1970s, the Bureau had returned to its ministry of tracts on a limited basis by reissuing several long-time best sellers among the Bureau's inventory. In the 1990s, a decision was made to reinvigorate this ministry with some new releases. The impetus came primarily from lay members of the board, who viewed the tract ministry as one of the most effective ways for the Bureau to communicate with laity. This led to an extended discussion about tracts in May 1993. Ted Wittrock and Glenn Stone provided a history of the Bureau's tract ministry. There was much conversation about what kinds of tracts might be useful in the new situation in which the churches found themselves, and a task force was appointed to develop a specific proposal. [12]

This group, chaired by Connie Seddon, reported at the next meeting that they had agreed on five tracts on the theme of "Lutheran identity." The term "tract" was dropped because it sounded old-fashioned; the series would be marketed as "leaflets." The five were ready for release in mid-1994. The promotional piece in *Lutheran Forum* explained the purpose:

> Need an added resource for defining *Lutheran*? The ALPB would like to help with five new leaflets, planned to focus attention on what is unique about the Lutheran Church. Designed for newcomers to the Lutheran Church, as well as those members who may want a refresher course in subjects central to Lutheranism. Pastors may want to use the brochures as teaching supplements as well as for general distribution. Lay members will value these short, informative pieces about their church. [13]

The leaflets provided very basic introductions to Lutheranism from different perspectives. The first two were written by Christa Klein (though in keeping with longstanding ALPB practice, the authors' names do not appear on any of the tracts). "Lutheran? What's in a Name?" summarized the history of Lutheran Christianity. "Lutherans and Other Christians" provided the foundation for the evangelical catholic view of Lutheranism (without ever using those terms). The intention of the early Lutherans, Klein wrote, "was to be a reforming movement within the Catholic Church, but "Lutherans found themselves caught between two polarizing sets of Christian belief and practice, Roman Catholic and Reformed Protestant, a position that has never been very comfortable and has been the source of internal and external tensions." Lutherans are committed to "protestant principle (justification by grace through faith alone) and catholic substance (that grace is given through Word and Sacrament centered in the church and stewarded by ordained ministers)."[14]

A third leaflet, written by Eric Gritsch, briefly recounted the story of "Martin Luther and the Reformation." The last two dealt with worship. "An Invitation to Lutheran Worship" was a revision of an earlier piece written by Glenn Stone; it explained in simple terms what a visitor to a Lutheran church service might expect. The final leaflet, "Lutheran Faith, Lutheran Worship—Two Sides of One Coin," offered an explanation by Phillip Max Johnson of the connection between the liturgy and the Christian faith. It included a repeated refrain: *As we worship, so we believe; as we believe, so we worship.*"[15]

The new series sold well. In late 1995, Ms. Seddon reported that while the most orders had come from Pennsylvania, New York and California, distribution had reached some 40 states, as well as Canada, the United Kingdom, and the Central African Republic. Some 72% of the orders came from ELCA pastors and congregations, 25% from LCMS, and the rest were unidentified. Oddly, there were no orders from Minneapolis, the "most Lutheran of all cities." By the end of 1996, the ALPB had sold 305 sets of 100 each of the five leaflets, as well as many more in smaller quantities—a total of 206,188 individual pieces. These tracts continued to sell well and were reprinted in the next decade. By the end of 2015, the number of individual tracts sold had surpassed half a million.[16]

Pro Ecclesia

"we are proud of what we were together able to accomplish"

Paul Hinlicky was a man with many ideas, and as executive director of the ALPB, he often got the Bureau involved in projects that stretched and expanded its own sense of its mission. In the fall of 1990, Hinlicky told the board that he was working on "a very exciting development." "I have a verbal commitment from Robert Jenson and Carl Braaten," he wrote, "to serve as editors of a new, prestigious scholarly journal of theology, under the ALPB umbrella. This will be quite a coup for us."[17]

The phrase "under the ALPB umbrella" was perhaps an overstatement. As plans for the new journal developed, Jenson and Braaten established the Center for Catholic and Evangelical theology. This group was primarily responsible for the new journal, which was named *Pro Ecclesia* and made its initial appearance in the fall of 1992. Braaten would describe the relationship between the Center and the Bureau as "a partnership," and the *Pro Ecclesia*'s front matter would say it was published "in cooperation with the American Lutheran Publicity Bureau." In fact, the relationship was primarily a business arrangement. In 1990 Hinlicky had hired Martin A. Christiansen as managing editor of the ALPB publications to free himself of the details of production. Christiansen, a former Lutheran parochial school teacher with a master's degree in English, would initially work part time, with the expectation that he would eventually take over the production management of *Pro Ecclesia* and his position would become full-time. This would not cost the ALPB anything, Hinlicky told the board, because Christiansen would be picking up tasks currently being subcontracted to other companies or persons.[18]

For more than a dozen years, the ALPB acted as the publisher for *Pro Ecclesia*, with ALPB employees and volunteers handling the physical production, managing the subscriptions, and making regular financial and subscription reports to the CCET. There was early conversation about the ALPB having representation on the Center's board, but the CCET was reluctant—though the Bureau's executive director was always invited and frequently attended the annual board meetings as a guest. The relationship between the Center and the Bureau ended in 2005 when the publisher Roman & Littlefield proposed taking over publication of the magazine. The CCET board accepted the offer—primarily, Carl Braaten told the ALPB board, "because this publishing house is believed to have the merchandizing wherewithal to grow the journal." Braaten was effusive in his appreciation for the partnership between the two organizations. It has been "an unmitigated pleasure, marked by unqualified mutual trust and cooperation between the representatives of ALPB and CCET. ... I am extremely grateful." For its part, the ALPB was pleased to have been instrumental in the launching and nurturing of what had become a significant academic theological journal. Fred Schumacher, by then the ALPB's executive director, wrote to Braaten:

> I think I speak for ... the entire ALPB Board ... in saying that we are proud of what we together were able to accomplish in bringing Pro Ecclesia into being and keeping it solvent over the past thirteen years. We continue to pray for your success in bringing it and the vision of the one, holy, catholic and apostolic church that it represents to a larger audience.

Pro Ecclesia had shown a net profit over the years of more than $6,000, which was, in accordance with their original agreement, divided equally between the two organizations.[19]

A book publishing program
"theologically responsible books grounded in the gospel"
Paul Hinlicky's vision for the ALPB also included a robust book publishing program. The Bureau had occasionally published books in the past, either under its own imprint or that of the now defunct Lutheran Press; its books, however, had most often consisted of reprints of articles from one of the ALPB periodicals, and they were (with the exception of *Manual of Practical Church Work* in 1942) quite modest in

size. Hinlicky hoped that the Bureau might begin to publish more substantial books, and to do so more regularly. In 1991 he presented a proposal written by himself and Christian von Dehsen, a young scholar then teaching at Carthage College who was book review editor for *Lutheran Forum*. They noted that contemporary theological publishing generally fell into one of two categories: books were either intended for the academy, often focused on the "latest intellectual trends," or they were intended for a wider, mostly lay, audience looking for their "spiritual needs" to be met. In both cases, they argued, "the theological traditions of the church are frequently abandoned in favor of meeting perceived market trends. Disciplined theological thinking languishes." Thus "the time is rife for the expansion of the ALPB ministry of publication by providing theologically responsible books grounded in the gospel and designed for use in congregations."[20]

Hinlicky and von Dehsen argued that the advent of desktop publishing made it technologically and financially feasible to consider such a program. They outlined what they had in mind:

> Twice a year the ALPB would publish four to six books across the theological fields (e.g., biblical studies, dogmatics, history, liturgics). Authors would be recruited both from the ranks of established scholars ... [as well as] younger scholars. While not overly technical, these books, ranging from 150 to 225 pages in length, would be known as 1) theologically trustworthy, 2) affordable, and 3) oriented to the worshipping and ministering community.

It was an ambitious project, to be sure, one which would require a substantial financial investment. The board had already been discussing a possible capital fund drive, and they decided to incorporate the book publishing proposal into their $100,000 goal. Half of the total, $50,000, was designated for a "revolving fund" to provide start-up capital for the book program (as well as for the proposed *Pro Ecclesia*). Another $15,000 would purchase the new equipment which would be essential if the book program were to go forward. The remaining $35,000 would be an endowment to provide subscriptions to students, retired pastors, and Third World educational institutions.[21]

The capital campaign, however, fizzled. It was approved by the board in November, 1991, and the executive committee was directed to proceed with securing a campaign director. The person they had in mind proved unavailable, and an alternative candidate never emerged. There is no further mention of the campaign in subsequent minutes. A few contributions were received, mostly from board members, but the campaign itself did not progress beyond the proposal stage.

But at least it planted the idea that the ALPB should publish books. If "four to six twice a year" was out of reach, occasional books seemed a reasonable goal, and for the next several years at least one book a year was published—sometimes as many as four. Most of them were not initiated by the ALPB; rather the Bureau increasingly began to receive proposals from authors who thought their manuscripts might be a good match for the ALPB's mission.

The first ALPB book in this new publishing endeavor followed the earlier pattern in the sense that it was a reprint of material first published in an ALPB periodical. Robert Jenson had written what he called "A Large Catechism," published in *Lutheran Forum* in several installments beginning in December 1989. Somewhat revised and expanded, it was released in book form in 1991. It sold well and was reprinted in 1999 and 2013.

The next year, ALPB published *Different Voices/Shared Vision: Male and Female in the Trinitarian Community*. This book contained the papers from a conference sponsored by a group of LCMS women to discuss the Biblical understanding of the relationship between men and women. The papers were edited by Paul Hinlicky, who also wrote an afterword. Publication costs were mostly borne by the group which sponsored the conference. *Lutheran Forum* advertised the book as "the most important publishing event in the recent history of the Lutheran Church—Missouri Synod" and "must reading for every pastor and lay leader" because "it offers a comprehensive alternative to the official theology of the subordination of women held by the synod."[22]

A third book appeared in 1993, this one an anthology of writings by Arthur Carl Piepkorn. The late Concordia Seminary professor and long-time editorial associate for the *American Lutheran* was one of the leading architects of the evangelical catholic movement. Piepkorn's scholarly writings had mostly appeared as journal articles rather than monographs; the ALPB's book, entitled *The Church: Selected Writings of Arthur Carl Piepkorn*, brought together sixteen articles from various publications—writings on the church, but also on the holy ministry, the sacraments, and the Blessed Virgin Mary. This book also sold well, and a second edition was published in 2006.[23]

As the Bureau waded further into book publishing, new manuscripts and proposals continued to be received; a formal book committee was established to review and recommend potential publications. But before any additional proposals were approved, the Bureau produced what would be one of its most important contributions to the life of American Lutheranism.

For All the Saints
"a timely and welcome gift"

At the 1991 consultation between the ALPB board and several (mostly younger) theologians held at St. Matthew's Lutheran Church in White Plains, NY, a casual conversation led to what would become the Bureau's most ambitious and successful book project. The board's secretary, Pr. Fred Schumacher, was also the *pastor loci*, and he offered his study to fellow board member Bp. Michael McDaniel to make phone calls during breaks in the meeting. McDaniel noticed a copy of the four-volume *The Liturgy of the Hours* on

Schumacher's shelf. This work was a popular Roman Catholic breviary, with Biblical and patristic readings together with the daily prayer offices of the church. McDaniel told Schumacher that he also used *The Liturgy of the Hours* in his own devotional practice. "It had all one needed for a disciplined life of Bible reading and prayer," Schumacher later recounted, "and could be taken with one and used in any location."

> We both expressed need for such a breviary in the Lutheran Church that would be of value to pastors and lay people to develop a disciplined prayer-life. Both of us had over the years used books produced by Lutherans but none of them provided in one book all that was needed. ... I said to Bishop McDaniel 'someone in the Lutheran Church should produce a book similar to the Roman breviary' and I asked him if he knew of such a person. He said, 'no,' and then after a pause said, 'Fred, why don't you do it?'

The question kept nagging at Schumacher throughout that day, and he asked Paul Hinlicky what he thought of the idea. Hinlicky encouraged him to raise it with the ALPB board. They responded positively, inviting Schumacher to bring a proposal to the next board meeting.[24]

Schumacher was so excited that he started working on the project immediately—even before the board had seen a proposal. A few days later he asked Dorothy Zelenko, a member of St. Matthew's as well as ALPB treasurer, if she would help. He recruited other volunteers from his congregation, who began entering material into the congregation's computer system. It was, he would later say, a "haphazard" beginning, with little organization or plan. Ms. Zelenko, meanwhile, had taken a couple of books about saints out of the library and was thinking about which ones might be good to include in the proposed book; but one day she happened to stop by the church office and was shocked to find volunteers hard at work, typing quotes Schumacher had already selected into an older word-processing program. She knew she had to find a more sophisticated program quickly if all the pieces of the project were ever to be brought together. It would become an almost overwhelming task, but work on the project now began in earnest.[25]

When the ALPB board met in November 1991, Schumacher brought the proposal before them, projecting a 4-volume set (two volumes for each of the two years of the daily lectionary). The board enthusiastically approved the already underway project, but it became apparent that some basic questions had not been addressed—how many copies should be printed and, more importantly, how would this all be financed? But the board was convinced the project would be a success, and they authorized 2,500 copies of the first volume.[26]

The book was patterned after *The Liturgy of the Hours*. The entry for each day in the two-year daily lectionary cycle included an opening and closing prayer, the three lectionary readings for the day (following the *Lutheran Book of Worship* version of the ecumenical Common Lectionary), and a fourth reading from a non-Biblical source.

Many of the opening prayers were drawn from *The Liturgy of the Hours*. Because that breviary used a single prayer each week during "ordinary time" (i.e., the "green" seasons of the liturgical year), Schumacher added prayers drawn from the *Book of Common Prayer* and some other sources, primarily Paul Scherer's *Love Is a Spendthrift*.

Unlike *The Liturgy of the Hours*, the new breviary drew the fourth reading not just from patristic writers but from the whole history of the church. The only stipulation Schumacher made was that the fourth reading come from a writer no longer living; this was only rarely violated, usually inadvertently. Each volume would also include the complete Psalter (using the *Book of Common Prayer* translation which had been chosen for the *LBW*) and a slightly revised version of the *LBW*'s liturgies for Morning Prayer, Evening Prayer and Compline (without the musical settings). Volumes I and III included the complete text of Luther's Small Catechism. In place of the Catechism in Volume II, Schumacher included Lancelot Andrewes' classic devotional poem "The Dial." He planned to repeat "The Dial" in Volume IV, but ultimately substituted Luther's "A Simple Way to Pray."

It was the fourth reading that was the most complicated, since the potential choices were unlimited. Schumacher was a voracious reader, with a library full of books in which he had marked favorite passages. He also wrote to seminary professors, bishops and pastors he knew, asking for their suggestions. More suggestions came from users of the book as each volume was published. Potential readings were carefully matched with the daily lectionary so that the fourth reading would serve as a kind of commentary on at least one of the Scripture lections for the day.

What complicated this project considerably was the need to obtain copyright permission for many of these fourth readings, as well as for many of the prayers—permission that had to come from several different publishers or individuals, each of them with their own policies, paperwork requirements and time frames for response. "We were naïve ... in thinking that most publishers would simply write back 'permission granted,'" Schumacher explained. "Not so!"

> Augsburg Fortress, our own Lutheran publishing house, charged us for almost every one of the quotes that came from their books and in one situation in which I had made a mistake in asking for a permission in which we were charged we later discovered that the book from Fortress which they had charged us for was quoting the work in another publication that was now in the public domain. A few quotes from Fortress were free, but [for] most we were charged anywhere from $5.00 to $50.00.

The single most expensive quotation was from Martin Luther King Jr.'s *Strength to Love*. The agency representing Dr. King's family asked $400 for the single quote—so much more than any other publisher that Schumacher was inclined to omit it from the book. When he reported this to the board, one member, Ruth Zerner, felt so strongly that at least one quote from King be included that she offered to pay for the quote personally. Ultimately a price of $150 was negotiated, and the quotation was included.[27]

There were other publishers—including Concordia Publishing House and several Roman Catholic companies—who allowed the use of their material without charge. The Roman Catholic Church's International Committee on the Liturgy gave permission to incorporate prayers from *The Liturgy of the Hours*. The Episcopal Church's copyright agent responded that the *Book of Common Prayer* was in the public domain and only its format was under copyright; so along with its translation of the Psalter, many prayers from the *Book of Common Prayer* were used. This generosity allowed the Bureau to keep the cost of the project manageable.

One important decision concerned which Bible translation should be used in the breviary. The National Council of Churches held the copyright for both the Revised Standard Version and the New Revised Standard Version, and there was a significant cost for either. The NRSV was being increasingly used in ELCA congregations, but in the end the decision came down to economics; the National Council of Churches agreed to accept a $300 payment to use the older RSV, with a promise of an additional payment later if the publication was a success. That promise was ultimately fulfilled with a gift of $5,000 from the ALPB to the NCC.[28]

There would not be room in the books for many illustrations, but two varieties were included. Schumacher had long been a fan of Orthodox iconography, and he chose icons for several of the major festivals of the liturgical year and included reproductions—unfortunately, due to cost, in black and white—in each volume, together with a brief explanation of the art. The volumes also included a set of line drawings by Jeffery Neal Larson, a young Lutheran artist whom Schumacher had come to know.

Volume I was ready to go to the printer—Dickenson Press of Grand Rapids, MI, in cooperation with Thomas E. Nelson, the well-known Bible publishers—in mid-1994. Ms. Zelenko loaned the Bureau $10,000 in July for the down payment, and another $10,000 a few weeks later for operating expenses and a publicity mailing to all ELCA and LCMS pastors. The orders began to come in—some 700 pre-publication orders, enough that both loans were repaid by October. *For All the Saints: A Prayer Book for and by the Church* clearly met a need felt by hundreds of Lutheran pastors and laity.

The initial run of Volume I was delivered to St. Matthew's on November 2, 1994, where volunteers sorted and mailed the pre-publication orders. Half of the first printing was sold within two weeks. A series of enthusiastic reviews led to a flood of new orders. Frank Senn's evaluation in *Pro Ecclesia* was typical: "*For All the Saints*," he wrote, "is a timely and welcome gift to the people of God. Its material has been carefully (and one might also say lovingly) collected and crafted into a workable prayer book by the church for the church."[29]

The remaining three volumes were published over the next two years. The first printings of Volumes III and IV were 5,000 copies each, and 2,500 more copies of the first two volumes were reprinted before Advent 1996. Eventually a total of 40,000 copies (10,000 of each volume) were printed. By 2014, when the ALPB celebrated its 100th anniversary as well as the 20th anniversary of *For All the Saints*, total sales had exceeded one million dollars. The breviary became the all-time best seller among ALPB books; it was so successful financially that it has kept the Bureau solvent up to the present day.

Refocusing the mission

"Lutheran tradition as evangelical and catholic"

Paul Hinlicky had brought a new energy to the Bureau, and much had been accomplished since his appointment as executive director in 1989. In addition to the programmatic initiatives, the Bureau's office had in 1991 been moved from the Wartburg Senior Care Center to Immanuel Lutheran Church in Delhi, NY, where Hinlicky was pastor. This change was made in part for his convenience, but also because the Bureau's office manager, Donna Kathmann (soon to become Donna Roche), was living in Delhi; after a year or so the office was moved to her home.

In 1992, however, Hinlicky was feeling worn out; he told the board he would likely resign within the next year and encouraged them to make plans for an orderly transition. Hinlicky had also been wrestling with the future of the *Forum* package. Subscriptions had been declining; perhaps that could be ascribed to the current recession, but it may also be that "it is impossible to fill Richard John Neuhaus's shoes." Without Neuhaus, he suggested, *Forum Letter* "no longer carries its $22,000+/year weight." He suggested three options: (1) an intensive search for a new editor of *Forum Letter* "of equal ability to Neuhaus"; (2) reducing *Forum Letter* to eight issues per year (eliminating the months in which *Lutheran Forum* appeared) and utilizing a "pool of writers" rather than a single editor; or (3) eliminating *Forum Letter* altogether, incorporating the journalistic format into a more frequently issued *Lutheran Forum*.[30]

Just at this time, however, Russ Saltzman asked if he might now resume his editorship, his personal situation having stabilized. The board had heard from readers that they rather liked what *Forum Letter* had become under Saltzman, and several readers urged that he be brought back as editor. Roger Kahle, managing editor of the *Lutheran*, for example, thought Saltzman was "the best editor the *Forum* newsletter has had."

> He combines a lively writing style, a good sense of humor and a care for the facts. I certainly don't agree with all his opinions, but if I only wanted to read those things that I already agree with, I would not be subscribing to *Lutheran Forum* newsletter. I think part of its editorial task is to challenge the reader.

Charles Austin, a pastor and professional journalist, had a similar view. He wrote to the board that he missed Saltzman's "extraordinary intellect, wit, insight and critique," and he urged them to bring Saltzman back. The timing of these letters (they all came shortly before the board's executive committee meeting, the date of which was not widely publicized) suggests that someone—Saltzman or someone on the board sympathetic toward him—did a little pump-priming. In any event, the executive committee got the message, and they invited Saltzman to resume the editorship, effective with the July issue—with the understanding that he would serve the remaining nine months of his original two-year term, and then things would be renegotiated. ALPB president Hans Quitmeyer advised Saltzman that Hinlicky would be proposing a reconfiguration of editorial responsibilities, and while no decision had yet been made, "if we were to accept his proposal, we very likely would no longer have a <u>Forum Letter</u> editor, as such." With that understanding, Saltzman agreed to return as editor.[31]

This decision did not sit well with Hinlicky. While he insisted that he had not pressured Saltzman to resign over his divorce, he also was reluctant to have him return. He simply did not feel that they were on the same wavelength. Hinlicky was hoping to achieve greater editorial consistency between the publications, and he was not sure that was possible with Saltzman. In Hinlicky's view, Saltzman had an unhelpful preoccupation with the sexuality issues facing the church. Even more important, Saltzman was too closely tied to Richard John Neuhaus, and in the wake of Neuhaus's reception into the Roman Catholic Church, it seemed best for the ALPB—and the other proponents of evangelical catholicism—to distance themselves from their provocative and media savvy former editor. If the board insisted on the present two-editor structure, Hinlicky's inclination was to ask Leonard Klein to edit *Forum Letter*.

But Hinlicky's preference was that all Bureau publications be editorially managed by a single team of five, with an "editor-in-chief" and four contributing editors with specific portfolios. He proposed that *Forum Letter* be reduced to eight issues per year under the direction of this team. He asked, however, that the board discuss this direction in the context of a larger conversation about the purpose and direction of the Bureau. At the June 1992 board meeting, he invited Klein, Rebecca Frey and Stephen Bouman to help the board reflect on the Bureau's mission. Klein and Frey each gave presentations; Bouman was unable to attend, but sent a written statement.[32]

Frey compared the current situation in American Lutheranism to that of Henry Melchior Muhlenberg in the 18th century: a wilderness frontier where Christians need to be nurtured. The role of the Bureau's publications, she suggested, is to provide that nurture through an integrative vision that "holds together doctrine, aesthetics, and behavior." She urged the Bureau to continue to publish materials such as the forthcoming Piepkorn volume and suggested consideration of a reinvigorated program of tract publication. Klein emphasized the importance of the ALPB as the vital center of American Lutheranism, with its moderate confessionalism and its ability to "pull together theology, liturgy and ethics." Bouman's paper spoke of the "evangelical catholic tradition" and the importance to the ALPB's ministry of infusing that tradition into the life of the congregation. "The rough beast on which the messianic hope for the world slouches toward Bethlehem," he wrote, "is always the gathering around Word and Sacraments, the parish." The presentations engendered a lively discussion in the board, and Frey and Klein were asked to collaborate on a one-page mission statement incorporating their concerns.[33]

Hinlicky then presented his proposal for reconfiguring the editorial responsibilities. The board went into executive session to discuss it, and it became apparent that they preferred to maintain both the current publication schedule and the existing division of editorial responsibilities, with separate editors for *Lutheran Forum* and *Forum Letter*—though they postponed final action until the November meeting. Furthermore, they proposed that Leonard Klein be asked to succeed Hinlicky as editor of *Lutheran Forum* whenever Hinlicky decided to step down, and they supported the decision the executive committee had already made to invite Russ Saltzman to reassume the editorship of *Forum Letter*.

Hinlicky was disappointed, but he was not one to damage the Bureau because of his own disagreement. In his public comment in the final *Forum Letter* before Saltzman returned, he played the gracious team player. He was "delighted," he said, at the decision, and he put the best construction on the whole episode:

> In a way, the brief interruption in editorial continuity has proven to be something of a blessing. It has shown, foremost, that **Forum Letter** has an institutional life beyond any single personality. The manner in which [Saltzman] assumed the editorship revealed there was a life for **Forum Letter** beyond the 16-year stamp of Richard John Neuhaus. There was at the time, as one can imagine, some considerable doubt about that. ... However, as Russ himself would be the first to say, **Forum Letter** 'survived' not because Saltzman was writing it, but because it was **Forum Letter**, i.e., 'the independent voice for Lutherans.' Leonard Klein, too, in following Saltzman, aided the institutional life of **Forum Letter** not because of who he is, but because of what **Forum Letter** has become through its 21-year history. The pages you hold in your hand from **Lutheran Forum/Forum Letter** are the front line in the struggle for the soul of American Lutheranism.[34]

Hinlicky would later muse that the executive committee's decision about Saltzman was "the beginning of the parting of the ways" between himself and the ALPB. Indeed, shortly after that decision he wrote a letter of resignation which he did not send. But at the board meeting that fall, Hinlicky resigned from both his position as executive director and as editor of *Lutheran Forum*, effective June 30, 1993. "The time in life has come," he wrote, "for me to concentrate my energies on theology. ... I have every confidence that I leave the ALPB in better shape than I found it. ... With vision and vigor, the ALPB is poised for great things." He agreed to continue as a regular columnist for the magazine for the foreseeable future. The board accepted the resignation "reluctantly and with a great deal of regret," but expressed their "joy in knowing Paul would continue to serve the ALPB as a writer." The board then formally approved the executive committee's recommendation that the two publications retain separate editors, that Leonard Klein and Russell Saltzman be appointed to two-year terms as editors of *Lutheran Forum* and *Forum Letter* respectively, and that Fred Schumacher be appointed the new executive director of ALPB, effective July 1.[35]

Hinlicky had no intention of being a lame duck, however, and he worked hard to insure a smooth transition. One priority was the approval of a new ALPB mission statement. The proposal formulated by Klein and Frey had been discussed by the board, but they thought it more appropriate as a statement of editorial policy for *Lutheran Forum* than as a mission statement for the Bureau. One thing was clear: the term "evangelical catholic" had now become an essential part of the Bureau's identity. President Hans Quitmeyer made the point in a letter to the board in June 1992. "Although the ALPB's focus was always confessional and one of fostering Lutheran unity," he wrote, "it is fair say that the ALPB now has become a much more active proponent of evangelical catholicism." Hinlicky agreed, and while admitting that he was "somewhat to credit or to blame for the closer identification of LF with the notion of 'evangelical catholicity,'" he did not believe "that either Richard Neuhaus or Glenn Stone, Richard Koenig or John Tietjen would view that evolution as a departure from the ALPB tradition."[36]

While Hinlicky hesitated to put too much emphasis on what he admitted was mostly "a slogan," it did appear to him and to the board that the term was useful in describing the ALPB's mission. In February 1993, he offered a proposed statement to the board which was then, with a few minor changes, adopted:

> The American Lutheran Publicity Bureau ("ALPB"), established in 1914, is a non-profit organization independent of official church control, linked by faith and confession to the Church it serves. Committed to an understanding of Lutheran tradition as evangelical and catholic the ALPB affirms the Church's scriptural and confessional foundations in order to foster renewal not only with the present Lutheran Church—Missouri Synod, Evangelical Lutheran Church in America, and Evangelical Lutheran Church in Canada, but also other Lutheran churches in North America and abroad and the wider ecumenical community.
>
> The ALPB maintains that all those under Christ who hold fast the Scriptures and Lutheran Confessions have a common life, with a distinctive role to play in conveying the gospel message. In an era in which the Church in North America must address an increasingly dechristianized society, the ALPB makes the theological, liturgical and devotional resources of our confessional heritage accessible and relevant to all Lutherans as well as to friends in other communions.

There are some remarkable things about this new statement—the first being that it was approved less than seven years after the previous mission statement was adopted. There had been a sea change in the American Lutheran scene in those seven years, and yet the change in the ALPB's self-understanding was almost as dramatic.[37]

Here for the first time the ALPB officially stated its understanding of Lutheranism as "evangelical and catholic." Here was the first acknowledgement of an "increasingly dechristianized society." What was lacking is also striking; there was no mention of *Lutheran Forum* and *Forum Letter* as "the major ALPB publications," as they had been dubbed in 1986—perhaps an acknowledgement that with *Pro Ecclesia* and the book publishing program, ALPB had other fish to fry, and so the mission had expanded. There was also no explicit commitment to Lutheran unity or ecumenical relationships, suggesting that the ALPB had come to realize that both can be problematic if they are not based on the Scriptures and the Lutheran confessions. The statement, after approval by the board, was subsequently printed on the title page of *Lutheran Forum* (with a couple of minor editorial changes) in every issue until 1996; it continued to appear elsewhere in each issue through 1998.

Souring on the ELCA

"what compelling reason is there for an ELCA?"

Russell Saltzman was sanguine about the ELCA following the churchwide assembly in Orlando in 1991, but the next two years pushed him back toward a more pessimistic view. The ELCA sexuality study's trajectory, the increasingly loud drumbeat of feminist theology, what he saw as duplicity and/or foolishness on the part of the ELCA's leadership—all these things came to a head at the churchwide assembly in 1993. He could find little positive to say. It was, he said, the "Vengeance of Kansas City."

> Inclusivity and multiculturalism, the twin totalitarianisms that have threatened the [ELCA] since its birth, powerfully manifested themselves at the Kansas City assembly. All things ... bowed before these concepts. Every aspect of the proper life of the denomination that comes into play during an assembly was subjected to an insidious fascism to which even an increasingly hapless leadership paid homage.

It was, he raged, "a *déjà vu,* if you will, of the Weimar Republic in its last days. For a churchly analogy one need only turn to the history of the 'German Christians' of that same period who delivered their church into the totalitarianism of the Third Reich."[38]

In the sharpest language yet from Saltzman's pen, the editor excoriated the assembly's worship (it "did little but trash the central worship tradition of our Lutheran church"), preaching (one preacher "lobbed insults—an accurate phrase—from the pulpit at dissenters from the multicultural myth"), even its deliberations ("the most popular motion at the assembly was to close debate, cut discussion and get on with the agenda"). He lamented the emergence of "The Network," a coalition dedicated to "affirmation of 'committed and faithful same-sex relationships.'" "Our church," Saltzman admitted, "no longer possesses the theological reserves necessary to uphold a lucid ethical tradition." It was so bad that Saltzman was beginning to question the existence of the ELCA itself.

> We think it is becoming increasingly crucial to ask why there should be a Lutheran church in 1993. The conviction that Lutheranism has preserved the catholic faith

without a lot of doubtful additions has been, until recently, a pretty firm tenet. ...
But the reason for a Lutheran church is to confess what Lutherans believe, and one
would think, believe what Lutherans confess. ... But if we no longer believe and teach
anything in particular, and if our worship practices increasingly and so evidently
contradict what we say we believe ... what compelling reason is there for an ELCA?[39]

Saltzman would tone down the rhetoric in subsequent issues, and he would again
see some optimistic signs; he was not ready to give up on the ELCA. His angry account
of the 1993 assembly, however, was gleefully picked up by Herman Otten's *Christian
News*. Otten reprinted the entire article and sent that issue to all ELCA congregations.
This was the last straw for the ALPB board, which had tried for twenty years simply
to ignore Otten. ALPB president Hans Quitmeyer, an attorney, wrote Otten a stern
letter. The reprint, he said, "goes far beyond any fair use."

> Christian News did not request the ALPB's permission to publish any part of
> Forum Letter and the ALPB did not grant such permission. Please be further advised
> that the ALPB does not grant such permission to Christian News. According, we
> hereby demand that Christian News (1) immediately cease any further unauthorized
> publication of exerpts [*sic*] from Forum letter and (2) acknowledge in its next issue
> that the republication of Forum Letter was unauthorized.

The ALPB, he warned, "will take all necessary steps to protect its copyrights, including
referring any additional violations to the United States Attorney's office." Otten simply
printed Quitmeyer's letter (which technically satisfied the second demand), wrote a
defense that amounted to "you wouldn't have given me permission anyway, so why
bother asking," and noted that *Forum Letter* had full permission to reprint anything
from *Christian News*.[40]

Saltzman felt compelled to assure readers (many of whom, since they were ELCA,
knew nothing about Otten and his paper) that there was no connection between *Forum
Letter* and *Christian News*, that Otten had not asked permission to reproduce the issue,
and that if he had asked, it would have been refused. He then took the opportunity
to say that "it is our policy ... to grant one-time reprint rights for congregational use.
Just drop us a note and we'll be happy to oblige. Better yet, contact Donna Roche at
the ALPB office and ask about group subscription rates to *Forum Letter*." Meanwhile,
the board of directors returned to its policy of ignoring Otten.[41]

Notes

1. Paul R. Hinlicky, "The Crisis in American Lutheranism Today," *LF* 22, no. 3 (Aug. 1988), 12.

2. Mark Chapman, "Ecumenical Paganism?" *LF* 22, no. 4 (Nov. 1988); Amandus J. Derr, "Worshipping the Unknown God on Higgins Road," *LF* 23, no. 1 (Feb. 1989), 7.

3. Michael Root, "The Proposal for Lutheran-Episcopal Fellowship: Unity and the Gospel," *LF* 25, no. 2 (May 1991), 22.

4. Meg Madson, "BEM: What Does Sign Signify?" *LF* 25, no. 2 (May 1991), 21; Mark E. Chapman, "Why Can't We Get This Right?" *LF* 27, no. 2 (May 1993), 11.

5. Paul R. Hinlicky, "In the Forum," *LF* 23, no. 3 (Aug. 1989), 3.

6. Paul R. Hinlicky, "In the Forum," *LF* 24, no. 1 (Feb. 1991), 3.

7. Paul R. Hinlicky, "In the Forum," *LF* 24, no. 2 (May 1990), 3; Leonard Klein, "The San Francisco Churchquake," ibid., 7; Martin Heinecken, "Why the Ordinations Were Invalid," ibid., 23-26.

8. *LF* 25, no. 1 (Feb. 1991), 45; Russell E. Saltzman to Paul Hinlicky, 6 Feb. 1991, ALPB Archives.

9. Paul R. Hinlicky, "A Message to Our Subscribers," *LF* 25, no. 2 (May 1991), 44; Dorothy Zelenko, e-mail message to Richard O. Johnson, 4 May 2016.

10. Leonard Klein, "Mega-church Strategy," *FL* 21, no. 1 (25 Jan. 1992), 4.

11. *FL* 21, no. 2 (3 Feb. 1992), 1; Leonard Klein, "Human Sexuality and the Christian Faith?" *FL* 21, no 2 (3 Feb. 1992), 1ff.

12. Minutes, ALPB Board of Directors, 23 May 1993.

13. *LF*, 28, no. 3 (Aug. 1994), 7.

14. "Lutherans and Other Christians," ALPB, 1994, ALPB Archives.

15. "Lutheran Faith, Lutheran Worship: Two Sides of One Coin," ALPB, 1994, ALPB Archives.

16. "Fascinating but Absolutely Unnecessary Information about the New Tract Series," 21 Oct. 1995, ALPB Archives.

17. Paul R. Hinlicky, "Report to the ALPB Board," 26 Nov. 1990, ALPB Archives.

18. Carl E. Braaten, *Because of Christ: Memoirs of a Lutheran Theologian* (Grand Rapids, MI: Eerdmans, 2010), 150; Paul R. Hinlicky, "Report to the ALPB Board," 26 Nov. 1990, ALPB Archives.

19. Carl E. Braaten to Frederick J. Schumacher, 15 Apr. 2005; Frederick J. Schumacher to Carl E. Braaten, 2 June 2005, ALPB Archives.

20. Paul R. Hinlicky and Christian D. von Dehsen, "The ALPB Book Publishing Program: A Proposal," n.d. [1991], ALPB Archives.

21. Ibid.

22. Marie Meyer, et. al., *Different Voices/Shared Vision: Male and Female in the Trinitarian Community* (Delhi, NY: ALPB Books), 1992; *LF* 26, no. 1 (Feb. 1992), 25.

23. Arthur Carl Piepkorn, *The Church: Selected Writings of Arthur Carl Piepkorn*, ed. Michael P. Plekon and William S. Wiecher (Delhi, NY: American Lutheran Publicity Bureau, 1993).

24. Frederick J. Schumacher, "For All the Saints: A Creation of Many Saints, for All the Saints, and by the Saints: A History with Many Anecdotes," 2008, ALPB Archives.

25. Ibid.; Dorothy Zelenko, e-mail message to Richard O. Johnson, 4 May 2016.

26. The record here is a little unclear. Schumacher's "For All the Saints: A Creation of Many Saints" indicates that the board had approved the project at the November 1991 meeting, but there is no reference at all to this in the minutes (though there is some brief reference to it in some pre-meeting correspondence). The first documentation of a proposed initial order of 2500 copies appears to be a cost estimate dated in 1994.

27. Schumacher, "For All the Saints: A Creation of Many Saints."

28. Minutes, ALPB Board of Directors, 22-23 May 1998.

29. Frank Senn, *For All the Saints* book review, *Pro Ecclesia* 5, no. 2 (Spring 1996), 249.

30. Paul R. Hinlicky, "Report to the ALPB Board's Executive Committee," 9 Jan. 1992, ALPB Archives.

31. Roger R. Kahle to Fred Schumacher, 10 Mar. 1992; Charles Austin to ALPB board members, 22 Feb. 1992; Hans Quitmeyer to Russell E. Saltzman, 15 Mar. 1992, ALPB Archives.

32. Paul R. Hinlicky to ALPB Executive Committee, 15 Mar. 1992, ALPB Archives.

33. Minutes, ALPB Board of Directors, 27 June 1992; Stephen Paul Bouman to Paul Hinlicky and the members of the ALPB Board, 23 June 1992, ALPB Archives.

34. *FL* 21, no. 6 (29 June 1992), 8.

35. Paul Hinlicky, e-mail message to Richard O. Johnson, 2 Apr. 2016; Paul Hinlicky to ALPB Board, 31 Oct. 1992, ALPB Archives; Minutes, ALPB Board of Directors, 7 Nov. 1992.

36. Hans Quitmeyer to ALPB Board Members, 15 June 1992; Paul Hinlicky, "Report of the Executive Director," 27 June 1992, ALPB Archives.

37. Minutes, ALPB Board of Directors, 20 Feb. 1993.

38. *FL* 22, no. 10 (7 Oct. 1993), 1.

39. Ibid., 2-6.

40. *Christian News* 32, no. 13 (28 Mar. 1994), 3, 17.

41. *FL* 23, no. 1 (19 Jan. 1994), 2; *FL* 23, no. 4 (29 Apr. 1994), 4.

Chapter 21

A Different Climate

When Leonard Klein took the editor's chair at *Lutheran Forum* in 1993, he was no stranger to the ALPB. A Yale Divinity School graduate, he had been ordained in the LCMS, served briefly in the AELC and then joined the LCA in 1981 when he was called to Christ Lutheran Church in York, PA. Klein had served as one of Paul Hinlicky's editorial advisors through Hinlicky's entire tenure; he had been primarily responsible for *Forum Letter* after Russ Saltzman stepped down and had continued to write for the newsletter after Saltzman's return. He had also edited *Lutheran Forum*'s *Una Sancta* issue since its inception. He would edit *Lutheran Forum* for three tumultuous years. For the first time since the founding of *Lutheran Forum*, the executive secretary of the ALPB was not directly involved in the journal itself, either as editor or managing editor, and as a result the *Forum* package became somewhat more independent of the Bureau's broader ministry. Still, the publications were the primary public voice of the Bureau, and under Klein that voice continued to express a sense of urgency about the direction of American Lutheranism.

Lutheran Forum
"much farther out on a limb"

Klein's first editorial in *Lutheran Forum* reflected on the journal's history and present role. "I inherit an editorial tradition best characterized as 'gadfly,'" he wrote. "Only on occasion 'gonzo.'" He recalled the spirit manifested by the old *American Lutheran* and continued by the *Forum* package, both offering "a lively voice for moderate confessionalism."

> That is a truly unfortunate label, moderation being a virtue mostly in personal habits and politics. But it is the label that best fits a deep, unflinching commitment to the authority of Scripture and the content of the Lutheran Confessions, even as it sees them in ecumenical context and in catholic encounter with the world. The point of view taken by this publication and its sister *Forum Letter* rejects sectarianism and liberalism with equal force.

> In the past that viewpoint meant the freedom to be a cheerful, high-spirited gadfly, tweaking torpid and overly cautious church leaders, arguing for renewal in liturgy, education, stewardship and evangelism, calling attention to encrusted bad habits of pulpit and pew alike. It could be venturesome, at times even a little heady.

Nonetheless, he wrote, it had almost always been possible to maintain a friendly relationship with the various denominations and church institutions.[1]

But times change, he continued, and "I assume the editorship in a different climate. The last generation has been a disaster for anything like moderate confessionalism" because of the conservative rout in the LCMS and the liberal victory in the formation of the ELCA. Now "our little journal has found itself much farther out on a limb and more critical for the Lutheran future than ever before." It is now "at the head of the effort to reclaim any kind of confessionalist center in American Lutheranism." This has led to its editors being viewed as "rabid right-wingers" by the "tenured radicals of the ELCA bureaucracy," but offering "a cup of cold water" to the "beleaguered orthodox Lutherans of the ELCA." Missourians, on the other hand, often think *Lutheran Forum* too focused on the ELCA and its problems; yet thoughtful conservatives "seem grateful for our efforts toward genuine confessionalism and liturgical integrity, while Missouri's moderates identify with our centrist confessionalism." All this is complicated by "our troubled relationship as evangelical catholics to the more radically Lutheran confessionalists who find us, somewhat to our chagrin and somewhat to our amusement, troublingly Roman."[2]

Thus *Lutheran Forum* finds itself "on the ledge and a pretty thin one at that; for in our times centrist confessionalism calls for a higher pitch of rhetoric and a greater vehemence than its name would seem to imply." There is a "great deal at stake" as the Lutheran denominations "separately plunge toward fundamentalism and liberalism."

It is not quite hopeless, for there is still much good among Lutherans—the resources of the liturgy, the catechism, mostly orthodox bishops, thousands of "vigorous and faithful pastors" and parishes. Those pastors "continue to be our primary audience, although we're glad when others listen in." Klein promised that *Lutheran Forum* would "continue ... to enlighten, encourage and sustain the troops in a grueling and wearying struggle to sustain faithfulness, hope and joy."[3]

The new editor followed his predecessor in giving each issue a thematic focus, always with an eye toward the parish pastor. Over the next months the journal took up diaconal ministry, Trinitarian theology, the doctrine of the ministry, questions of gender and sexuality. As promised, there was a regular column from Paul Hinlicky in Slovakia (somewhat pretentiously entitled "Pauline Correspondence") which usually dealt with weightier and more abstract theological matters. There were also substantive book reviews in each issue, continued generous space for an open forum, and often provocative editorials.

Among the latter was a series of essays in which Klein reflected on a question he often heard: "Why are you guys so negative?" He suggested there was "a fault line dividing those who are acutely distressed by the direction of things, and those who think that ... American Lutheranism, even if troubled, could be improved with just some fine tuning." The latter group, Klein admitted, "deserve some answer from those of us who are more apocalyptic." He began by protesting that, as a rule, he and others at *Lutheran Forum* are not, by nature, negative.

> I laugh a lot; the parish office revolves around jokes at my expense; few innocent bystanders suffer because of my existence. Like most of the people who share my opinions about the Church, I enjoy the beauty that is given us in the finer and humbler things of life. Meetings of this journal's editorial board are full of festivity and vitality. Even more to the point, my daily ministry, administration, proclamation and celebration of the liturgy are a source of great joy, hope and satisfaction. I know that to be true also of most of the rest of American Lutheranism's critics.

And that, he continued, is precisely why we are so negative. It is because we see "the dissolution of so much that is good" in the church. He spoke of his "agony ... [over] the inability of the leadership of American Lutheranism to find, lift up and treasure the very things that are the source of my joy and that have been the source of the joy of Christians from the beginning." In such a situation, the "only way to be positive is to be negative." It is the only way to get the attention of a leadership where the prevailing approach is "comfortable mediocrity, fear of rocking the boat and an amazing *naiveté* about the actual conditions of our churches."[4]

He took up the theme again in the next issue, this time with a specific target. Paul Jersild, a professor at Lutheran Theological Southern Seminary, had written an article in *dialog* in which he accused evangelical catholics of "anger, petulance, and superciliousness," and Klein felt obligated to respond. Jersild had identified some evangelical catholic concerns correctly, he wrote, but "he remains baffled. This is largely because he shows no awareness of the pastoral concerns of the movement."

> Whatever else it is, evangelical catholicism is a liturgical movement, its theological emphases primarily pastoral. Most of us are parish pastors and mostly we are worried about good biblical preaching, the weekly eucharist, and a vital sacramental, liturgical life. The 'anger, petulance, and superciliousness' arise from the need to defend the fundamentally Lutheran proposition that the Church is an assembly around Word and Sacrament and from exasperation at pastors who can't remember what they promised in their ordination vows.

Jersild, Klein wrote, offers "another version of Chilstrom's 'love the Church' speech at St. Olaf II. ... It is dependent on a vision of the Church as a voluntary religious society and on a very sanguine appraisal of its problems." But "if ... one is to be a catholic Christian," he concluded, "the only way to be a faithful Lutheran in North America is to be truthful about how bad conditions are and how distorted that vision."[5]

"How bad conditions are" was tackled head-on in the Reformation 1994 issue with the theme "What Is To Be Done?"—illustrated on the cover with a reproduction of a mural depicting Luther throwing the papal bull of excommunication into the fire. Klein invited thirteen authors—eight from the ELCA and five from the LCMS—to respond to this question. Those invited were no slouches; the ELCA authors included James Crumley and David Preus, bishops of the former LCA and ALC respectively, as well as Kenneth Sauer, chair of the ELCA's Conference of Bishops, while one of the LCMS respondents was Samuel Nafzger, executive director of its Commission on Theology and Church Relations.

The diagnoses and prescriptions offered were as varied as the contributors, but there were several common themes. Crumley faulted the ELCA for an almost deliberate failure to develop a sense of identity due to its utter confusion about the respective responsibilities of bishops, pastors, and laity. He urged the elimination of the quota system and an intensive study of the ministry, particularly the role of bishops. Preus pointed to a crisis of confidence in the ELCA, and like Crumley, he identified the root problem as the ELCA's ecclesiological confusion. He, too, advocated an end to quotas, but he was also in favor of ending or sharply curtailing several ELCA offices and commissions.[6]

Parish pastors and laity who contributed used even stronger language. Laywoman Blanche Jenson asserted that "it is time for the ELCA to decide which god is to be worshiped." North Dakota pastor Jack Eichorst wrote of the "deep spiritual sickness" in the ELCA: "this church ... chokes on the central confession of the early church, namely that 'Jesus Christ is Lord.'" Philadelphia pastor Gilbert Doan Jr. suggested that the

ELCA was "sliding toward apostasy" and called the church to acknowledge "the failure which the past ten years constitute."[7]

The Missouri Synod respondents had a little more difficulty addressing the question "what is to be done"—an indication that things were relatively calm in the LCMS at the moment. Still, Nafzger admitted that the Synod was the scene of a recurring battle between "the temptation to accommodate the Gospel to modern politically and socially correct ideas" and "the onslaught of those who in their zeal to defend the truth of God's Word want to add to Scripture, and who ... teach human traditions as the commandments of God." As for "what can be done," the best he could come up with was to "thank God that we belong to a Gospel-centered church committed to upholding the Scriptures as the Word of God" and to ask God's help "to deal with each other with integrity, honesty, and humility." Indiana pastor Joel Brondos suggested that Missourians must stem "the propensity to label others" and seek "a better way of 'doing theology' than is often done at conventions and by commissions."[8]

In introducing this issue, Leonard Klein stated succinctly what *Lutheran Forum* hoped to accomplish. "The identity and direction of Lutheranism," he wrote, "will continue to be a battlefield for us, and **Lutheran Forum** continues to be eager to help interpret where the skirmish lines genuinely are." The skirmish lines as *Lutheran Forum* saw them lay particularly in controversies over ecumenism, worship, doctrine, sexuality and abortion. During the rest of Klein's tenure, each of these areas received significant attention.[9]

Ecumenism

"We are in more of a pickle than we like to think"

The ELCA's churchwide assembly in 1997 was slated to consider three major ecumenical proposals. One was a declaration that the 16th century mutual condemnations between Lutherans and Roman Catholics on the doctrine of justification were no longer applicable to Lutherans and Roman Catholics in the present day. The other two proposed full communion between the ELCA and the Episcopal Church (in what was known as the *Concordat*), and between the ELCA and three Reformed churches (in a proposal called *Formula of Agreement*). *Lutheran Forum* provided consistent and sometimes provocative analysis of these proposals and of the ELCA's ecumenical ventures more generally.

The November 1994 and February 1995 issues, for example, discussed the theme of "Ministry in Ecumenical Dialogue"—a significant matter in the *Concordat* proposal, which called for the ELCA to enter into the historic episcopate. Several issues concerning ordained ministry had not been settled prior to the ELCA merger, and one of the first significant studies in the new church had focused on the topic. The 1993 churchwide assembly had approved the report of the Task Force on Ministry (with significant changes), but many issues were still unresolved.

The papers published in *Lutheran Forum* came from a conference sponsored by the ELCA's Metro DC Synod, and their authors were all significant Lutheran voices in the ecumenical world. William Rusch, director of the ELCA's Department for Ecumenical Affairs, asked "What is One, Holy, Catholic and Apostolic Ministry?" Churches in the "Catholic tradition," he noted, hold that the nature of the ministry "belongs to the constitutive elements of the church and to its continuity and unity in time and space," which means that agreement on ministry is an essential part of closer fellowship between churches. Rusch argued that positive action on the 1997 proposals for full communion would be an important ecumenical witness, demonstrating that the ELCA was willing to "take on" the historic episcopate (but "without condition of validity") while at the same time embracing full communion with Reformed churches without requiring that they also adopt the historical episcopate.[10]

The other articles in the series tackled the role of the ministry in various ecumenical dialogues in which Lutherans had participated (those with Reformed, Episcopal, Methodist, Orthodox, Roman Catholic and African Methodist churches). Leonard Klein's response to this discussion demonstrated the hesitation with which *Lutheran Forum* was approaching the ecumenical proposals. He was concerned that the Lutheran slogan "*satis est*" (from the Augsburg Confession's declaration that the right teaching of the gospel and the right administration of the sacraments "is enough" for unity) tended toward "reduction and negation," making its "usefulness ... as an ecumenical minimum ... very limited." The dialogues have surely accomplished a good deal, but the church must not be hasty.

> My fear is that in hurrying damage will be done. While my greatest concern arises from my opposition to full communion with the Reformed, it is by no means the only concern one might have. Part of the problem is our own internal ecumenical crisis: in the ELCA we are not in full communion with each other. To make an easy case in point, let me say that there is no way that I am in full communion with the Community Church of Joy in Glendale, Arizona [a congregation known for its neglect of traditional Lutheran liturgy in favor of a more "entertainment evangelism" model of church life]. Under no circumstances would I let its pastors near the pulpit or altar of Christ Church, York. Nor would I seek sustenance in Word and Sacrament there.

"We are in more of a pickle than we like to think," he warned. "In hastening to do something, we are in danger of doing the wrong thing."[11]

As the time for decision drew nearer, *Lutheran Forum* staked out a clear position. Leonard Klein spoke for the whole editorial board:

> The withdrawal of Reformation era condemnations of the Roman Church on the locus of justification should be passed. The proposal for full communion with

certain Reformed churches should be turned down. The Concordat with the Episcopal Church is acceptable with major reservations, but its delay or defeat would not distress us.

He then proceeded to spell out in some detail the reasons for each position.[12]

The proposal regarding Rome, he wrote, was clearly appropriate, for the Reformation era condemnations were based on assumptions that simply can no longer be sustained. Full communion with the Reformed, on the other hand, "should be turned down flat" because Lutherans and Reformed have "not reached a level of doctrinal agreement that would warrant full communion with the kind of liberal Protestantism these bodies represent." The biggest issue was the understanding of the Eucharist, just as it had been for Luther at Marburg. The proposal "merely papers over the fundamental differences with an appeal to a generic presence of Christ in the eating and drinking. That this is in fact what many Lutheran pastors believe is regrettable but hardly grounds for full communion."[13]

The editors found the situation with the Episcopalians more complex. "With great hesitation," Klein wrote, "we are prepared to give limited support to the Concordat with the Episcopalians." He admitted that when he was traveling, he often worshiped at an Episcopal congregation, "given the total unpredictability of Lutheran assemblies." Indeed, liturgical integrity was precisely what made the *Concordat* so difficult to oppose. The Episcopal Church, despite its "theological and ethical latitudinarianism," generally "worships as if it meant to be the Catholic Church in the West." Perhaps approval of the *Concordat* would "confront us with our liturgical slovenliness." It might even force us to deal with significant questions about ministry.[14]

Yet even with these advantages, Klein saw many grave concerns—not so much about the *Concordat* itself, but about the politics involved in approving it. He feared that there would be a kind of "horse trade" where "old ALC" Lutherans who had, prior to the ELCA merger, already approved full communion with the Reformed, might now insist on approval of this new agreement as a condition of accepting the *Concordat*. But there was also "an intellectual center of opposition to the Concordat at Luther Seminary," and no comparable organized opposition to the Reformed recommendation. This could well end in the worst possible scenario: acceptance of the Reformed proposal, but rejection of the *Concordat* with the Episcopalians. Far better, Klein wrote, "to have neither than to end up in full communion with the Reformed and not the Anglicans! This would permanently marry the ELCA to liberal Protestantism and spell the end of its prospects as a confessionally Lutheran Church."[15]

In the end, Klein concluded, the most important and natural "dialogue partner of the Augsburg Confession is the Church of Rome," and approval of the *Concordat* as a way of addressing the question of valid ministry is simply a distraction. Indeed, "the consequences of Lutheran-Anglican alliances could even contribute to the prolongation of the Western schism." It may be better to maintain "the current arrangement of interim sharing of the eucharist" with the Episcopal Church rather than pursue a problematic and ultimately unhelpful declaration of full communion.[16]

Forum Letter came out editorially against both the Concordat and the Formula of Agreement. Like Klein, Saltzman felt less strongly about the Episcopal agreement, but he argued that it simply wasn't clear enough exactly what was being proposed. With the Reformed, however, it was much too clear. His opposition was "entirely due to the presence of the United Church of Christ." But it was neither the eucharistic theology (or lack of it) nor the congregational polity that bothered him. "For us it is the issue of gay ministry, or rather the ordination of sexually active gays," a practice which, while it may be de facto among some Episcopalians, is de jure everywhere in the UCC. "Like it or not," he wrote, "sexual behavior and sexuality is a rising topic of divisive interest within and among the churches. Adopting [the proposal] with the UCC in the deal will intensify the widening divisions."[17]

Ecumenism was again the focus of the September 1996 issue of Lutheran Forum—which would also be Leonard Klein's final issue as editor. Taking as its theme "Ecumenical Challenges," the journal offered a broader view, only peripherally mentioning the forthcoming ELCA decisions (which, Klein noted, were being awaited "with trepidation" by many readers). The issue began with another essay by William Rusch, whose service as director of the ELCA's Department of Ecumenical Affairs had ended abruptly with the election of the new presiding bishop. Rusch wrote a personal reflection on the ELCA's "ecumenical task." It had an undertone of sadness. He clearly believed that the ELCA's commitment to ecumenical affairs had diminished in the ten years since its founding, citing its reduced funding of the National and World Councils of Churches. He observed, without elaboration, that "the problem has not been simply financial."[18]

As for the forthcoming decisions on the three proposals, Rusch insisted that he had never favored any kind of "bundling" of the three. Each should be discussed on its own merits; "to do less would be the height of ecumenical irresponsibility." But he lamented the generally low interest in the proposals across the church and noted "a lack of clear signs of support at key places in the life of the ELCA." He realized, he wrote, "that ecumenical reception, the process by which a church makes the results of a dialogue part of its life and faith, is far more difficult than was once thought."[19]

Rusch's article was followed by Carl Braaten's thoughts on "Confessional Integrity in Ecumenical Dialogue." He once again insisted that "Lutherans are evangelical catholics in exile; they are not **émigrés** who have found a new and permanent homeland in something called Protestantism." Indeed, "modern Protestantism is not the legitimate heir of the Reformation. Karl Barth had it right; it is a heresy from the inside out."

That problem can only be addressed "by a profound recovery of the Great Tradition that [Protestants] have betrayed or forgotten."[20]

But a much more serious problem has arisen, Braaten continued, which threatens "to derail the ecumenical movement or nullify its promise altogether."

> The churches are inwardly permeated by the weakening of distinctively Christian beliefs, a disinterest in the Christian truth, the kind of orthodoxy that C. S. Lewis called 'mere Christianity.' All the studies report the same dismal conclusions. This is linked with massive biblical illiteracy among the laity and biblical infidelity among theologians and the clergy, who know what the Bible says on any number of matters, but believe only what they choose to believe. ... The high toleration of heresy and apostasy causes heart failure in the Christian organism.

If Lutherans should continue to gravitate toward "a pan-Protestant front over against Eastern Orthodoxy and Roman Catholicism," he warned, "there will be mass exodus from worldwide Lutheranism into churches that retain continuity with the Great Tradition."[21]

Worship
"there are some things that should be done and some that should not"

Leonard Klein's debut as editor in November 1993 had come in an *Una Sancta* issue—fitting, since he had edited the *Una Sancta* supplements since their inception. Taking as its theme "Growing Pains: LBW & LW at 15 Years," the issue featured several articles evaluating both the successes and the problems of the *Lutheran Book of Worship* and the Missouri Synod's *Lutheran Worship*. One of the problems with *LBW*, wrote Philip Pfatteicher, was that so much of it was "has never been tried" in most parishes. "We ought not discard something that we have not yet learned to use," he urged.[22]

But with so many other matters needing to be addressed, it was nearly two years before the next *Una Sancta* issue was produced. The ELCA had just released a draft of a statement on worship, "The Use of the Means of Grace." In a lengthy editorial, Klein gave it a lukewarm reception. While it was "in some ways disappointing," Klein wrote, "it is important to be grateful for what has been accomplished in this document." It presented Word and Sacrament as "the center of the church's life," and it reasserted "the confessional norm of a full liturgy of Word and Sacrament every Sunday and Holy Day." In many ways, it tried to combat "the Lutheran temptation to nominalist minimalism—doing the least required to get the grace out there."[23]

Still, he noted, "the document repeatedly hesitates at articulating norms even when it assumes them." It states things descriptively ("the church does things this way") rather than prescriptively ("the church should do things this way"). This "may satisfy a certain culture of niceness ... but it is still true that in the Church's liturgical practice there are some things that should be done and some that should not."[24]

The task force attempts to describe good sacramental practice, Klein wrote, but then makes "the practical assumption that we can do whatever we want." He offered an example:

> The simplest and most relevant case in point would be the third paragraph in the preface: 'Our congregations receive and enact the means of grace in richly diverse ways.' Yes, and some of that diversity is splendid, culturally and situationally appropriate. Other versions of course are a scandal and we should not tiptoe around it.

He offered several specific objections: the statement's failure to deal with the issue of lay presidency at the Eucharist, its openness to the use of non-wheat bread and non-alcoholic wine or grape juice, its failure to deal adequately with reverent disposal of the elements after the Eucharistic service. In the end, he wrote, the fact that "it's only a first draft is a reason for encouragement."[25]

That *Una Sancta* issue, however, was mostly devoted to "The Grace-full Use of the Means of Grace: Theses on Worship and Worship Practice," a statement signed by twenty-six Lutheran scholars who were members of the North American Academy of Liturgy. Its framers represented various Lutheran church bodies, and it was addressed to "the Lutheran Churches of North America." The theses were prepared, wrote Frank Senn, "with an eye on influencing the development of statements on sacramental practice in both the ELCIC and the ELCA." The forty theses proposed by the scholars were, Klein wrote, "on the whole superior" to the draft of the ELCA's "The Use of the Means of Grace."[26]

The text of the document was followed by responses from eleven pastors and professors from various Lutheran church bodies. Most were generally appreciative of the document, though not without reservations and criticisms. Klein noted that the disagreements fell into two categories.

> A number of our respondents, particularly those from Missouri, Wisconsin, and the ELS, are deeply troubled by the theses' emphasis on the liturgy as human action. In concert with concerns frequently stated by the ELCA's 'radical Lutherans' centered at Luther Seminary, they protest that Word and Sacrament must be seen as God's action and fear a loss of fundamental Reformation commitments. ...

> Ironically, the second category of disagreements come from several respondents who think the theses not catholic enough. ... They would argue for a more fully eucharistic doctrine of the Church, more explicitly catholic practice, and a greater readiness to reflect liturgically the growing ecumenical consensus on eucharistic sacrifice.

Klein offered the drafters opportunity to respond to the responses, in order that "we might continue a debate on the function and meaning of the liturgy in an American Lutheranism too eager to dispose of it and far too often incompetent in using it."[27]

Two of the signers of the document, Frank Senn and Jay Rochelle, accepted Klein's invitation. Senn tackled some specific points of criticism. He was surprised that many of the responders lamented the focus on liturgical practice, rather than theology; the specific concern of the drafters, he said, had been "how the Word and Sacraments are being *practiced* in parishes. ... We were not writing a full liturgical theology." Rochelle's response also emphasized the importance of liturgical practice as a locus of renewal of Lutheranism as evangelical and catholic.

> Lutheranism, at least where I now live, looks for all the world like another tired version of culture Christianity, with no stress on the magnificence of our heritage as evangelical catholics, or as protestants who cry and, moreover, live *ecclesia semper reformanda*. We are in serious danger of falling prey to the church growth gurus, as have so many in the Missouri Synod. Where there is no vision, the people choose programs. Where there is no Gospel, religion will do.[28]

Doctrine

"a pastorally prophetic meditation"

In 1995, pastors across the ELCA received in the mail a document which invited their reading, discussion, and signature. Entitled "The 9.5 Theses," the statement was drafted by a group of New Jersey pastors after a resolution had been presented at their synod assembly asking the Conference of Bishops to reconsider its statement that baptisms must be done "in the Name of the Father and of the Son and of the Holy Spirit." The resolution was defeated, but several pastors were alarmed by the experience. "The shape of the debate on the synod floor was disturbing," wrote Louis A. Smith in *Lutheran Forum*, for it demonstrated the "widespread support for ... the kind of thinking" the resolution embodied. Smith began to meet with other concerned pastors to discuss what they saw as a doctrinal crisis in the ELCA; they prayed together and considered how that crisis might be addressed. The result was "The 9.5 Theses."[29]

Five of the eight pastors who drafted the document had close ALPB connections. Phillip Max Johnson was serving on the board; he, Richard Niebanck, and Linda Larson were all *Lutheran Forum* editorial advisors, and Ronald Bagnall was a regular columnist. Smith had also occasionally written for the journal. After working individually on proposed language, the group met in retreat to prepare the final statement. An initial mailing was made to several dozen pastors whom the drafters thought might be sympathetic; subsequently a larger distribution utilized a mailing list provided by the ALPB.[30]

It is a "remarkable document," Russell Saltzman wrote in *Forum Letter*, which is neither a "crass appeal to 'take back the church,'" nor "the opening shot for a 'confessing synod,' another phrase for schism." It is simply "a confession of faith."

It calls for and requires no further action. But it will produce consequences. It will divide signatories from non-signatories, however much that may be an unintentional departure from the purpose of the drafters. It will compel all of us to reflect upon things of first importance, the true marks of the true Church. [It] ... is essentially a pastorally prophetic meditation offered to the ELCA. As with all pastoral acts, from preaching a sermon to saying a prayer, [its] ultimate significance is left to the Spirit, with whom rests all our hope for renewal in life and faith.

The statement itself was then printed in full without further comment.[31]

"The 9.5 Theses" began by asserting that the ELCA was facing a crisis of faith. It may appear to be a liberal/conservative struggle, since "many in the ELCA tilt toward the right—the ideologies of enthusiasm, fundamentalism, nationalism and pietism" while others "lean toward the left—the ideologies of activism, feminism, advocacy." But "the real struggle is for faithful adherence to the Scriptures, creeds and confessions over against their subordination to these social or religious ideologies."[32]

There followed nine theses which took strong stands on several doctrinal issues. The first insisted on the name of the Triune God as Father, Son, and Holy Spirit. Subsequent theses affirmed humanity's bondage to sin and the uniqueness of Jesus Christ as Savior, attacked the substitution of "plans and pleas for human betterment" for "the singular and specific promise of the Gospel," insisted on the integrity of Word and Sacrament as means of grace, and rejected those who "would elevate advocacy for self-chosen high-visibility causes above the common [vocation] of Christians in the life of the world." The document also stressed the "God-given unity of the Church in Word and Sacrament" and rejected both liberal and conservative Protestant attempts to generate a unity based elsewhere, reaffirmed the "proper distinction between law and gospel," and upheld a view of the ministry as a specific divine call, not a "helping profession." The ordained, it suggested, must be "subject to an exemplary standard" and "adorn the holy Ministry with holy lives." The document ended with a doxological "Thesis 9.5," quoting the ancient hymn *Te Deum*: "We believe that you will come to be our judge. Come, then, Lord, and help your people, bought with the price of your own blood, and bring us with your saints to glory everlasting."[33]

The entire document was printed again in *Lutheran Forum*, this time with accompanying essays on each thesis written by individual members of the drafting group and an introduction by Louis Smith. Leonard Klein made the publication's position clear, noting first that the document had stirred up quite a bit of resistance.

More important and even more distressing is this: the theses are little more than an innocent restatement of the Augsburg Confession. Those who teach what the theses deny do not have a quarrel with a few pastors. They have a quarrel with Lutheranism. And those who cannot fathom what in contemporary Lutheranism matches what the theses criticize are simply theologically helpless.

"The drafters of the theses" he concluded, "have done a great service for an insufficiently appreciative American Lutheranism, and we are delighted to bring their work to full expression."[34]

ELCA leadership was indeed unappreciative. Bp. Chilstrom sent a memo to those scheduled to be churchwide representatives to synod assemblies, with copies to all executive staff and synod bishops, suggesting they not discuss "The 9.5 Theses." "Our strong advice," Chilstrom wrote, "is that you not raise this issue in synod assembly reports. If questions are asked of you, either in a public or private setting, it would not be wise for you to try to engage in a discussion of any of the details of the document." The memo fell into Russ Saltzman's hands, and he printed excerpts from it in the July *Forum Letter*. "Chicago wants no discussion, period," he commented. How much better if Chilstrom had simply "encouraged everyone to read [the statement], and then sign or not as conscience suggests."[35]

It was all strangely reminiscent of the controversy in the Missouri Synod some fifty years earlier over "A Statement." In each case a group of pastors, many of them connected to the ALPB, met, talked and prayed about a perceived crisis in their church. In each case they issued and distributed a statement expressing their concern and inviting theological discussion, only to meet with a kind of panicked stonewalling by their church's leadership. Ironically, former LCMS president Ralph Bohlmann was the keynote speaker at the ALPB banquet that fall, and he chose to recount the story of "A Statement" in a remarkably irenic and positive way. The address was subsequently published in *Lutheran Forum*, along with the full text of "A Statement" and a response by historian Paul L. Maier. Bohlmann concluded by musing that if the 44 signers were together again in 1995, they likely would once again write and disseminate their statement. "And, who knows," he impishly added, "they might even include 9.5 additional theses that highlight some of current issues! But I believe their concluding word would be the same today as it was then: 'The truth must always be spoken in love. But it must be spoken!' "[36]

In the end, "The 9.5 Theses" caused considerably fewer shockwaves than "A Statement." There was little official reaction and little formal conversation. The drafters of the document were disappointed when H. George Anderson, elected presiding bishop in 1995 to succeed Chilstrom, politely declined to meet with representatives to discuss the theses. Edgar Trexler's history of the ELCA's first ten years didn't even mention the episode.

Yet there was an unexpected result. The pastors who had been rebuffed by Bp. Anderson met in 1996 in Morristown, NJ, with several others who had been invited, and decided to form a "pastoral society" for mutual prayer, consolation, and theological discussion. It would become the Society of the Holy Trinity (or STS, for *Societas Trinitatis Sanctae*), which was officially founded in September 1997. ALPB board member and *Lutheran Forum* editorial advisor Phillip Max Johnson was elected as the first senior of the Society; among the founding members were several others associated with ALPB in one way or another. The new group was discussed at some length at an ALPB board meeting in October 1996, at which time the board agreed "that the relation of the ALPB to the Society would be 'friendly but not official.'"[37]

One aspect of that friendly relationship was the Bureau's agreement to accept contributions earmarked for the Society, and then reimburse the Society for its expenses until the organization was fully operational. The ALPB donated bookkeeping services during this period; when the Society was ready to assume responsibility for its own financial affairs, the Bureau sent them a check for the balance of the donations that had been received. It was a relatively minor matter, but an important factor in enabling the establishment of the Society.[38]

Sexuality

"it is more fashionable ... to repent of homophobia than of fornication"

In 1993 the long simmering controversy about human sexuality erupted in a dramatic way when the task force appointed in 1988 to develop a statement on sexuality released its preliminary report. "The Church and Human Sexuality: A Lutheran Perspective," many believed, upended almost completely traditional Christian teachings about sexuality. It was remarkably unconcerned about sexual activity outside of marriage (though with a caveat about "the importance of a binding commitment"). It didn't condone teenage sexual activity, but if teenagers "choose to be sexually active, we encourage the responsible use of contraceptives." It challenged the traditional Christian view of homosexuality ("to love the sinner but to hate the sin") "because of its harmful effect on gay and lesbian people and their families."[39]

Even more problematic was the bungling of its release. The Conference of Bishops received the report in October 1993; the bishops expressed "appreciation but reservations" about it. Some bishops wanted to stop the distribution, but they were told it was already in the mail (which turned out not to be true). The text was provided to the secular press before it had been distributed to the pastors and congregations of the ELCA, so most Lutherans got their first word about the draft from a sensationalized but essentially accurate account by the Associated Press—an account which began, "Masturbation is healthy, the Bible supports homosexual unions and teaching teens how to use condoms is a moral imperative, says a task force leading the nation's largest Lutheran body into the sex wars."[40]

There was an unprecedented outcry from across the ELCA, with thousands of concerned Lutherans writing or calling the Chicago headquarters or their synod offices in protest. Writing in *Forum Letter*, Russell Saltzman mocked the entire process and scope of the report.

One could not invent a scenario as bad in fiction as happened in fact: The church hires, suppose, a Madison Avenue publicist and asks, 'We want to talk about something likely to cause the greatest possible public damage to the Evangelical Lutheran Church in America; something certain to titillate readers, flabbergast most pastors, and generate 20,000-plus outraged phone calls to headquarters. What would you recommend?' 'Well,' the publicist ruminates. 'Why don't you stack a task force and have them say something about sex. When they do, be certain they imply endorsement of homosexual marriage; make sure they mention masturbation, condoms and teenagers in the same paragraph; and, oh, yes, see to it they license shacking-up while they're at it. Then, afterward, tell everybody, 'Hey, lighten up. It's just a first draft.'"

"The document is dead," Saltzman predicted. "It won't go anywhere except into the trash."[41]

Lutheran Forum offered a theological critique by Bruce Foster. He argued that the task force had badly misunderstood the very nature of the Gospel by turning it into a "general command to love." The statement "has forgotten the confessional concern for distinguishing between law and gospel." Instead they have made the gospel "a general warm fuzzy term used to cover almost any 'good news.'" The document, he concluded, cannot be fixed; it should "simply be withdrawn or defeated in assembly."[42]

Robert Benne of Roanoke College took a similar view in the following issue. The draft, he asserted, is "nearly useless for guiding the life of Lutheran Christians." Benne had often called for pastoral accommodation in matters of sexuality, especially for gays and lesbians.

> But the ELCA statement does not simply call for pastoral accommodation. It wants to redefine or challenge our ethical ideals. It does so by making sexual expression a central Christian calling, by disconnecting the ethic of the Gospel from the Law, and by badly suppressing the debates about the Bible and the nature of homosexuality. We certainly can do better.[43]

In the wake of the response across the church, the draft was effectively withdrawn, the director of the study was reassigned, and an 11-member consulting panel was appointed to work with the task force toward a new study document. The second draft was released in October 1994. Leonard Klein proclaimed it "much better" than the original document, "Lutheran almost to a fault." Still, he saw "one disastrous shortcoming in the draft and that is the treatment of homosexuality." While perhaps not as blatant as the original document in its revisionism, this one still "gently lays out the revisionist version and proposes that the debate be continued!" That, Klein protested, simply "grants ... that the Church may well have been wrong. ... To hold off on restating the classical position in this culture and in the ELCA is to decide for revisionism."[44]

There was otherwise not much direct commentary in *Lutheran Forum* on the second draft, but the journal continued to address sexuality in other ways. In February 1996, for example, Klein published a translation of an article by the German theologian

Wolfhart Pannenberg who opposed any change in the church's teaching on homosexuality. Pannenberg acknowledged "the fact of homosexual inclinations," and argued that the issue is how any "deviations from the [sexual] norm" are to be regarded by the church—certainly "with tolerance and understanding," but in the context of a "call to repentance." A church that teaches that homosexual activity is "no longer a departure from the biblical norm" or recognizes "homosexual partnerships as ... equivalent to marriage" stands in opposition to the witness of Scripture and "has thereby ceased to be an evangelical church in the tradition of the Lutheran Reformation."[45]

The progress toward a social statement on sexuality pretty much ground to a halt after the release of the second draft. Many proponents of change had been angry at what they saw as that document's retreat from the stance of the first draft. This led the ELCA bishops to issue an open letter in March 1996, calling ELCA members "to be sensitive to the gifts and needs of gay and lesbian members, and ... to reach out to all God's people." *Lutheran Forum* editorial advisor Richard Niebanck excoriated the statement, calling it the "bishops' Munich." The bishops, he wrote, "have bought into, wittingly or unwittingly, the homosexual movement's notion of the 'gift of sexuality' which is to be 'lived out' in a variety of ways." The letter "not only appeases, it fairly 'gives away the store'" and "is tantamount to a declaration of bankruptcy, theological, moral, and ecclesial."[46]

Phillip Max Johnson wrote more with puzzlement than anger. He wondered who really drafted the letter. Was it a consensus of the bishops? Did they even talk about it? Whatever the case, it left him with "a deep disquietude about the state of moral discourse and moral leadership in the ELCA." He admitted that the Christian teaching on sexuality is "an arduous ethic grounded in a very specific vision of life lived in covenant faithfulness to God," and one under which "many of us fail and must stumble back to God in humiliation and repentance." But it seems clear enough. The bishops speak of "unresolved issues" regarding homosexuality; what are they?

> Are we unresolved to teach that sexual intercourse belongs to marriage? Are we unresolved as to whether marriage is, by definition in the Christian view of things, heterosexual? Is there some question as to whether or not we ought to ordain persons to the holy ministry who cannot say they will refrain from sexual relations outside of marriage? If our bishops ... are unresolved about a sexual ethic, please let them be specific.

As to homosexuality itself, it is fine that the bishops "wish us all to be civil and respectful of one another." But when they ask us to repent of "words and acts of hatred toward gay and lesbian persons and their families," what exactly are they asking? "Do the bishops think that those who say plainly that homosexual behavior is sinful are thereby hateful or hurtful?" "Admittedly," he concluded, "it is more fashionable these days to repent of homophobia than of fornication."[47]

Abortion

"Real churches don't kill babies"

The contentious question of abortion, a pervasive topic when Richard John Neuhaus was editing *Forum Letter*, had faded into the background after his departure; there was an occasional article in *Lutheran Forum* and a periodic comment in *Forum Letter*, but the topic was not nearly as prevalent as it had been in the early 1980s. In the1990s, however, events brought abortion back to the front. It began with a proposed social statement that was to come to the churchwide assembly in 1991. The first draft was "dismally impaired," Russell Saltzman wrote. But by the time responses had been heard and the final draft was brought to the churchwide assembly, he was less negative, calling the document a finely nuanced statement—"the best that could be expected."[48]

Approved by the assembly overwhelmingly, the statement took what might be called a moderately pro-life stance. "Abortion ought to be an option of last resort," it insisted. The Christian "presumption [is always] to preserve and protect life," though it allowed that there were circumstances in which abortion might be "morally responsible": to save the life of the mother, when the pregnancy resulted from rape or incest, and perhaps in cases of "extreme fetal abnormality, which will result in severe suffering and very early death" of the child. The discussion of abortion law was also rather nuanced; it opposed both criminalization of abortion and complete lack of regulation, but left open just what sorts of restrictions might be appropriate. It stressed that "what is legal is not necessarily moral, and what is moral should not necessarily be enacted into law."[49]

But controversy erupted in 1995 when Minnesota pastor Tom Brock asked the ELCA Board of Pensions whether their health insurance plan paid for abortions. He was told that it did so, in any circumstance with no questions asked. Brock was astonished that this policy was so inconsistent with the social statement. He requested time on the agenda of the ELCA church council to present his concerns, but was refused; he then mailed a letter about the matter to some 11,000 ELCA congregations. In an article in *Lutheran Forum*, he reported on the responses he had received. "It was a sobering experience," he wrote, "to read the responses (some with profanity) and to see how vehemently pro-choice some of our ELCA clergy are."[50]

Brock's concerns, however, struck a chord with many people; at least three synod assemblies approved resolutions asking that the health plan be brought into conformity with the social statement. In response, the Board of Pensions prepared an amendment to the health plan that would restrict payment for abortions to the three circumstances named in the social statement as "morally responsible." Final approval for such a change rested with the church council, however, and Bp. Chilstrom appointed a "working group" to consider the proposal prior to the council meeting. Karen Bloomquist, the

ELCA staff person responsible for the social statement, insisted that the document's "morally responsible circumstances" were descriptive, not prescriptive, and that, in any event, the purpose of the statement was not to mandate policy but simply to offer guidance to the members of the ELCA. That line of reasoning ultimately convinced the council; they rejected the proposal and left intact the health plan's unrestricted payment for abortions.

Leonard Klein was outraged. "The ELCA will continue, consciously and openly," he wrote, "to pay for a most grotesque mortal sin—using offerings gathered at its most sacred assemblies to do so."

> The council looked squarely at an opportunity to honor the fifth commandment and yawned. Faced with a fundamental issue of faith and morals, they addressed it as a question of rules and procedures. This is all bad, and merits as severe judgment as any of the prophets ever called down on Israel and Judah.

"Real churches don't kill babies," he concluded. "The action was schismatic."[51]

In the next issue, Klein elaborated on his position at some length. "Pro-life, that is, traditionally Lutheran, members of the ELCA are being asked to be good soldiers and line up behind the care and thoughtfulness of the church council," he complained. But the issue of abortion is so fundamental, and the catholic consensus throughout history so clear, that "such honoring of disagreements is not possible." He took on, one by one, the arguments being advanced in favor of the church council's action, finding each of them little more than "lame excuses." The council's action demonstrates that "subjective moral deliberation has replaced faithfulness to such a degree that the error of this decision is not even understandable to a large portion of the ELCA." He laid a large part of the blame at the feet of the ELCA's quota system, which had led to a "decision about a fundamental question of faith and morals, a question with grave ecumenical significance, [being] made by a body" two-thirds of whom are laity who "do not bear the Spirit's call to teach and preach." The ELCA, he predicted, will do what it always does in such matters: hunker down and try to wait out the hotheads." But "some of us will remember that when we confess the one, holy, catholic and apostolic Church in the Nicene Creed, we are confronting the likelihood that the ELCA can no longer claim to be fully embraced in that confession." This brings all members of the ELCA to a crisis point: "The communion of saints has been forgotten and the question of continued membership and financial support is laid on every member of the ELCA."[52]

Notes

1. Leonard R. Klein, "The Role of **Lutheran Forum**," *LF* 27, no. 4 (Nov. 1993), 4.
2. Ibid., 4-5.

3. Ibid., 5.

4. Leonard R. Klein, "The Unbearable Lightness of Being," *LF* 28, no. 3 (Aug. 1994), 4-5.

5. Leonard R. Klein, "Evangelical Catholic: 'Why Are You Guys So Negative?' II," *LF* 298, no. 4 (Nov. 1994), 5-7.

6. "What Is To Be Done? ELCA Responses," *LF* 28, no. 3 (Aug. 1994), 16ff.

7. Ibid.

8. "What Is To Be Done? LC-MS Responses," *LF* 28, no. 3 (Aug. 1994), 36ff.

9. Leonard R. Klein, "In the Forum," *LF* 28, no. 3 (Aug. 1994), 3.

10. William G. Rusch, "What is One, Holy, Catholic and Apostolic Ministry?" *LF* 28, no. 4 (Nov. 1994), 18-21.

11. Leonard R. Klein, "Response at the Conference," *LF* 29, no. 1 (Feb. 1995), 45.

12. "Ecumenical Options: A Consensus of the Editorial Board," *LF* 30, no. 1 (Feb. 1996), 4.

13. Ibid., 5-6.

14. Ibid., 6-8.

15. Ibid., 6.

16. Ibid.

17. *FL* 26, no. 6 (June 1997), 3.

18. Leonard R. Klein, "In the Forum," *LF* 30, no. 3 (Sept. 1996), 4; William G. Rusch, "The Ecumenical Task of the Evangelical Lutheran Church in America: Some Personal Observations," *LF* 30, no. 3 (Sept. 1996), 21.

19. Rusch, "The Ecumenical Task," 22.

20. Carl E. Braaten, "Confessional Integrity in Ecumenical Dialogue, *LF* 30, no. 3 (Sept. 1996), 25-26.

21. Ibid., 26-27.

22. Philip H. Pfatteicher, "Still to Be Tried," *LF* 27, no. 4 (Nov. 1993), 22.

23. Leonard R. Klein, "Liturgical Movement in the ELCA," *LF* 29, no. 3 (Aug. 1995), 4.

24. Ibid., 5.

25. Ibid., 5-6.

26. "The Grace-full Use of the Means of Grace: Theses on Worship and Worship Practice," *LF* 29, no. 3 (Aug. 1995), 18; Frank C. Senn, "On 'The Grace-full Use of the Means of Grace': A Response to the Responders," *LF* 29, no. 4 (Nov. 1995), 10; Klein, "Liturgical Movement," 4.

27. Leonard R. Klein, "In the Forum," *LF* 29, no. 3 (Aug. 1995), 4.

28. Senn, "On 'The Grace-full Use of the Means of Grace,'" 10; Jay C. Rochelle, "A Response to the Editor," *LF* 29, no. 4 (Nov. 1995), 5.

29. Louis A. Smith, "9.5 Theses: A Commentary," *LF* 29, no. 4 (Nov. 1995), 18.

30. Ibid.

31. *FL* 24, no. 5 (May 1995), 1.

32. Ibid., 2.

33. Ibid., 2-5.

34. Leonard R. Klein, "In the Forum," *LF* 29, no. 4 (Nov 1995), 4.

35. *FL* 24, no. 7 (July 1995), 1-3.

36. Ralph A. Bohlmann, "Missouri Lutheranism, 1945 and 1995," *LF* 30, no. 1 (Feb. 1996), 17.

37. Minutes, ALPB Board of Directors, 19 Oct. 1996.

38. Dorothy Zelenko, e-mail messsage to Richard O. Johnson, 4 May 2016.

39. Quoted in Edgar R. Trexler, *High Expectations: Understanding the ELCA's Early Years, 1988-2002* (Minneapolis: Augsburg Fortress, 2003), 88-89.

40. Ibid., 91.

41. *FL* 22, no. 12 (28 Dec. 1993), 1-3.

42. Bruce Foster, "You Know Neither the Scriptures Nor the Power of God: An Introductory Analysis of 'The Church and Human Sexuality,'" *LF* 28, no. 1 (Feb. 1994), 45-48.

43. Robert Benne, "Flawed Foundations," *LF* 28, no. 2 (May 1994), 39-41.

44. Leonard R. Klein, "Disaster Averted, Disaster Invited," *LF* 29, no. 1 (Feb. 1995), 6-7.

45. Wolfhart Panneberg, "You Shall Not Lie with a Male: Standards for Churchly Decision-Making on Homosexuality," *LF* 30, no. 1 (Feb. 1996), 29.

46. Richard J. Niebanck, "The Bishops' Munich," *LF* 30, no. 2 (May 1996), 12-13.

47. Phillip Max Johnson, "Fashionable Repentance," *LF* 30, no. 2 (May 1996), 14.

48. *FL* 20, no. 2 (23 Feb. 1991), 3; *FL* 20, no. 10 (31 Oct. 1991), 4-5.

49. Evangelical Lutheran Church in America, "A Social Statement on Abortion," 1991.

50. Tom Brock, "Letters from an Unhealthy Church," *LF* 29, no. 3 (Aug. 1995), 16.

51. Leonard R. Klein, "Why Are You Guys So Negative IV," *LF* 30, no. 1 (Feb. 1996), 9-10.

52. Leonard R. Klein, "The Spirit and the Church," *LF* 30, no. 2 (May 1996), 8-12.

Chapter 22

GROWING PAINS AND CHANGES

There was another editorial change in *Lutheran Forum* in 1996, as Leonard Klein was succeeded by Ronald Bagnall. This was the beginning of a period of stability in ALPB's staffing; for the next decade Bagnall would edit *Lutheran Forum*, Russell Saltzman would continue with *Forum Letter*, and Fred Schumacher would serve as executive director. There was stability within the board leadership as well; Hans Quitmeyer, who had been elected president in 1989, continued in that capacity until 2005. But events in American Lutheranism were not so stable, and the ALPB continued to address the changing times in church and society.

Books

"turned down by the 'mainstream press'"

Largely at Paul Hinlicky's prodding, the ALPB had begun a ministry of book publishing; it hadn't yet found its footing, however, and Hinlicky's dream of "four to six books twice a year" had not come to fruition. By 1994 the Bureau had published *Different Voices/Shared Vision,* Jenson's *A Large Catechism,* the first Piepkorn volume, and the first volume of *For All the Saints.* Word was getting out about the Bureau's publishing venture, and the ALPB was receiving a steady stream of unsolicited manuscripts. Needing a more formal process for review and decision, in 1994 the board established a book committee, chaired by Pr. James Corgee.

The committee's first significant report was made in October 1994. They recommended that the ALPB consider publishing two or three books a year and that the Bureau see itself as a kind of alternative press: "One of the principles for acceptance of manuscripts for publication should be that they have been turned down by the 'mainstream press,' such as Augsburg Fortress and Concordia." By the following May the committee had developed guidelines for manuscript submission and for publication, as well as specific criteria for evaluating manuscripts. They reported plans for two books in 1995 and two more in 1996.[1]

The first 1995 publication was a small book written by Richard Bansemer, *O Lord, Teach Me to Pray*. Bansemer, then bishop of the ELCA's Virginia Synod, based his prayer book on Luther's Small Catechism. For each question and answer in the catechism he provided several prayers which reflected the teaching and piety of Luther's classic. One of the prayers based on Luther's explanation of the fourth commandment, for instance, acknowledged both the difficulty and the joy of honoring one's parents: "Thank you, Lord, for my parents. Though we have had our difficulties with one another, do not let me deprive them of the respect they are due, for in giving them honor, I am thanking you for their love of me." The book, while not specifically intended for young people, was marketed as an appropriate gift for confirmands. It sold well and was reprinted several times over the next fifteen years.[2]

More problematic was Philip Pfatteicher's daily office prayer book. Pfatteicher was well known in Lutheran liturgical circles; he had authored several books for Augsburg Fortress, including the *Commentary on the Lutheran Book of Worship*. His breviary project was dear to his heart, and he expected that Augsburg Fortress would publish it. His book contained liturgies of Morning Prayer and Evening Prayer for Advent, Christmas, Lent and Easter, as well as a four-week rotation during "ordinary time." The liturgies were complete with music (mostly drawn from the *Lutheran Book of Worship,* but with some variations) and a suggested proper hymn for each day (printed with music). It also included the *LBW* liturgy for Compline (somewhat expanded) and other resources for personal devotions.

Augsburg Fortress considered the project, but decided against publishing it. They gave Pfatteicher several reasons for this decision, including the fact that it was not produced with "ecclesial determinations" about its content and it did not attend to "inclusive language and cultural diversity." Pfatteicher angrily replied to the publishing house that their comments "clearly reveal the degree and extent to which the sectarian views of various interest groups, each with a particular agenda, have captured the ELCA."[3]

Pfatteicher had earlier seen an announcement of the planned publication of *For All the Saints*, and he thought the books might complement each other. He sent copies of his correspondence with Augsburg Fortress to Fred Schumacher, who immediately proposed that the ALPB consider publishing the book. The scope of the project was overwhelming, but the ALPB decided to tackle it. The Bureau purchased software that would accommodate the music, and about half the book was keyed into the computer. But progress slowed and finally stopped for several reasons, including Pfatteicher's seemingly unending editorial changes. The book eventually was completed, but not until ten years later, when it was published by Lutheran University Press as *The Daily Prayer of the Church*. In recognition of its longstanding commitment to and investment in the book, the Bureau made a financial contribution toward the publication costs, and the ALPB was listed on the book's title page as co-publisher.[4]

Projected plans for 1996—a book on the diaconate by Stephen Bouman and a second volume of Piepkorn's writings—did not reach fruition, largely because of two untimely deaths. Bouman was working on his book in collaboration with ELCA deacon Tom Dorris, who was tragically killed in an automobile accident in 1994; the planned book died with him. Producing the second Piepkorn volume proved to be more difficult than anticipated. The job of preparing the manuscript had been given to David Gustafson and Russell Graef, but when Gustafson died unexpectedly in 2001, little progress had been made; the project came to a complete halt with his death.

The next book on the docket was completed, but it led to some serious headaches. Robert Tobias was professor of ecumenics at Lutheran School of Theology in Chicago. He had been closely involved in the ecumenical dialogue between Lutherans and Orthodox Christians. He had written a memoir about his experiences with the Orthodox, a sort of anecdotal introduction to Orthodoxy for lay readers, and he was eager for the ALPB to publish it. The book committee agreed to take on the project in 1996 and began to work out the details. The Bureau's conservative estimate of how well the book might sell led to an initial decision to print 1,500 to 2,000 copies, but Tobias had high hopes and asked for 5,000. The board agreed to meet him part way, authorizing a press run of 3,000 copies. The book was published in late 1996 as *Heaven on Earth: A Lutheran—Orthodox Odyssey*, with a forward by former LCA bishop James Crumley.[5]

Almost immediately Tobias began pushing the Bureau to step up its commitment to the volume, which he modestly described as "an extraordinarily important book." He clearly believed the ALPB had been remiss in its marketing (the book had so far sold fewer than 300 copies). His proposal was that some 13,000 additional copies be printed at the expense of the Tobias-Wells Endowments—a family foundation which he had never previously mentioned in his discussions with the Bureau—to be distributed free to all ELCA and Orthodox congregations in the United States. He expected the Bureau to provide an order form to be included with this proposed mailing, encouraging congregations to order additional copies for study groups; the Bureau would then fill those orders. He demanded a response to this proposal within a month.[6]

Fred Schumacher explained to him the public relations problem if those who had bought the book—mostly ELCA pastors—suddenly received a free copy in the mail. "Purchasers might justifiably feel misled," he wrote. "They might even think that this is a new policy that the ALPB would also follow with other publications." He reminded Tobias that marketing takes time. The Bureau had distributed review copies, but it is often several months before reviews are published. Besides, he noted, the proposed 13,000 copies would be insufficient to cover all Lutheran and Orthodox congregations in North America. He commended Tobias's "expanded vision" for the book, but insisted it would "have to wait until our present efforts at making *Heaven on Earth* known have had more time." Until then, he concluded, "we hope that you will honor your agreement with us."[7]

Tobias responded with a plea that two years was too long to wait. The ELCA was expected to approve full communion with the Reformed that summer, and if that happened, further dialogue with the Orthodox "will be dead for two or three generations, probably more." He desperately wanted the book widely distributed before the churchwide assembly's anticipated action. "We are not interested," he huffed, "in a distribution delayed by at least two more years."[8]

This dispute caused the Bureau no little aggravation, but Hans Quitmeyer negotiated directly with Tobias to find a compromise. Their agreement provided that the Tobias-Wells Endowments would purchase 1,000 copies of the book from the ALPB at $6 per copy (about half the cover price), thus reducing ALPB's inventory to approximately the number of copies the Bureau had originally planned. The Bureau would drop any objection to Tobias-Wells printing 13,000 copies for *gratis* distribution to Lutheran congregations, with several provisos as to what could and could not be changed in the new edition, and with specific language indicating the edition was printed with the permission of ALPB. To mitigate the problem of previous purchasers feeling they had been misled into buying the book, it was agreed that the following language would be printed on the copyright page:

> This copy of the special educational edition of *Heaven on Earth: A Lutheran—Orthodox Odyssey* is provided for your congregation compliments of Tobias-Wells Endowments in cooperation with the American Lutheran Publicity Bureau and your own diocese or synod. We hope you will enjoy it and will find it helpful in your ecumenical educational program. Additional copies of the ALPB edition may be ordered at $12.50 per copy; for study groups 5 copies for $40 and 10 copies for $70.

With that understanding, the "special educational edition" was printed and distributed.[9]

After ten years, the ALPB had sold fewer than 1,200 copies of the book. It cannot be known to what extent the poor sales were due either to the free distribution or the action on the Lutheran/Reformed proposal by the churchwide assembly. The fiasco did have at least one positive result, however; it forced the Bureau to establish some clear book publication guidelines to avoid similar problems in the future.

These various difficulties caused some to wonder whether book publishing was in the Bureau's best interest. The book committee pondered whether ALPB really had the resources to continue. "Certainly any expansion of this ministry," they reported to the board, "will require professional assistance and the outlay of financial resources."[10]

Despite the lack of decision on those recommendations, the projects continued. The Bansemer book had sold well, and now he offered another book of prayers, this one based on the Augsburg Confession. It was published in 1999 as *We Believe: A Prayer Book Based on the Augsburg Confession*. It was followed later that year by a second edition of Jenson's *A Large Catechism*, as well as Eugene Lehrke's *Prayers for the Eucharistic Gathering*, which offered collects, offertory and post-communion prayers based on the lectionary readings for each Sunday of the church year.[11]

Next the Bureau published Stephen Bouman's *From the Parish for the Life of the World*, an edited compilation of several of Bouman's *Lutheran Forum* columns with some new material added. It was a charming book, filled with anecdotes and stories about parish life that illuminated important theological themes; Martin Marty's forward to the book compared it to Reinhold Niebuhr's classic *Leaves from the Notebook of a Tamed Cynic*.[12]

It was not, however, an easy book to publish. The initial manuscript was much too long, and it required more editing than anticipated. The board ultimately decided that it could not be done by a volunteer (the usual practice) and agreed to pay for a professional editor. It appeared, Fred Schumacher informed the board in June 1999, that Bouman's book will be "our most costly publication. ... I pray that editing will soon end and we can have this book behind us." The book was finally published in 2000. It sold out in three years, and Bouman approached the board about reprinting it. They decided against it and instead, at his request, released the copyright to the author. He then arranged with Augsburg Fortress to publish a new edition.[13]

With so many complications, it is little wonder that the Bureau's directors questioned whether they really wanted to pursue book publishing. Schumacher told the board in June 1999, "I can't tell you how happy I will be when all these book commitments have been realized. My understanding is that we as a Board have agreed not to take on any additional books until the last of these book projects are behind us." There followed a hiatus of three years before the next ALPB book project came off the press.[14]

Events and commemorations

"we seem to be the sole institutional remnant"

In 1998 board member John Hannah suggested the board sponsor a forum bringing together Lutherans from both the ELCA and the LCMS to discuss the future of Lutheranism in America in the new millennium. "The ALPB holds a unique position," he told the board. "We seem to be the sole institutional remnant of a formerly uniting confessional American Lutheranism." Perhaps, he mused, "the ALPB could serve a useful function in leading a focused discussion for all on the unspoken problem we all worry about—What is the Lutheran destiny?"[15]

At a joint meeting with the editorial staff of *Lutheran Forum,* the board approved an ambitious resolution:

> That ALPB offer its services to [ELCA] Bishop H. George Anderson and [LCMS] President Alvin Berry [*sic*] toward the calling and holding of a 'Millennial Lutheran Forum,' encompassing both clergy and lay participants; and further, that we authorize Bishop Michael McDaniel to send a letter in our behalf making this offer.

Bp. McDaniel drafted the letter, but he thought it inappropriate for it to come from him; after incorporating some minor suggestions from other board members, the letter was sent to Bp. Anderson and President Barry over Fred Schumacher's signature.[16]

The letter noted with pleasure a recent news report that Anderson and Barry would be meeting that August to discuss ways the two church bodies might work together. It suggested that a national conference such as the one they proposed "would not only bring us closer together by a giant step in bridge-building and mutual understanding, but would also greatly strengthen the resolve of men and women all across America who want to be faithful, and need to know that they are not alone."

> We would regard it as a privilege to work with the two of you in the development of a national Lutheran gathering, and we hope that you will want to participate in your official capacity. ...
>
> According to the news release concerning the projected August meeting ... the two of you will be meeting to see if you can arrange for a different group ... to discuss theological issues.
>
> Therefore, the Board of Directors of the ALPB has voted to offer its resources to you, Bishop Anderson and President Barry, in whatever way we may be most useful. Specifically, we look forward to your response to this two-fold offer: to assist in the implementation of some such national gathering as described above, and to assist in the continuing theological discussions that are so desperately needed.

The letter concluded with assurance that the ALPB was "pledging not only our cooperation but our prayers."[17]

The invitation did not meet with the enthusiasm the board had anticipated. Barry's response was tersely courteous. He acknowledged receipt of the letter, and confirmed that he and Anderson would be meeting in August. "I seriously question," he wrote, "whether it would be appropriate to involve the ALPB in discussions of this nature. I believe it would be unwise to involve any unofficial publishing entity in official church relation discussions." He did not say a word about the proposed Millennial Forum.[18]

Bp. Anderson's response was similarly discouraging of ALPB's assistance in formal conversations, though he "would welcome your suggestions for topics that such discussions might involve." He was more positive about the possibility of a forum. Anderson was a historian, and he noted that "free conferences" had been "a useful channel of communication among leaders of several Lutheran bodies" earlier in the century. "I think that it is a good idea," he told Schumacher. He cautioned that it would have to be planned carefully, particularly with respect to worship, but he thought "a group like the ALPB would be a more acceptable sponsor than the two church bodies, given the present state of our church-to-church relations."[19]

Schumacher took Anderson at his word regarding suggestions; he polled the ALPB board and *Lutheran Forum* editorial board and then provided Anderson with a list of five general topics for ELCA/LCMS conversation: "things we and all Lutherans share," "sources of Lutheran doctrine and teaching," "the office of the ministry" (including "consideration of the spiritual and intellectual formation of pastors"), "Lutheran liturgy as an expression of Lutheran belief and a source of Lutheran unity," and "the doctrine of the Church." He also explained that in its offer to be of assistance the ALPB only "meant to suggest our publishing resources" rather than any direct involvement in conversations. He closed by assuring Anderson once again that he and Barry "will both be in our prayers."[20]

Meanwhile, Hannah asked several people what they thought about the proposed forum, and he got a variety of answers. Dean Wenthe at Concordia Theological Seminary in Fort Wayne had been enthusiastic, even offering to help find financial support. Carl Braaten thought it might be a workable idea; like Anderson, he likened it to the earlier "free conferences." He suggested that ALPB seek other organizational sponsors in addition to itself and wondered if a series of conferences in various locations might reach more people.[21]

But response from other organizations and individuals proved discouraging, and in the end the board decided on a much more limited proposal: the ALPB alone would sponsor a one-day "mini-forum" in New York, bringing ELCA and LCMS speakers together to address a variety of topics. The Bureau obtained agreement from the ELCA's Metropolitan New York Synod and the LCMS's Atlantic District that they would encourage pastors and laity to attend. Both Bishop Stephen Bouman and President David Benke, heads respectively of those two judicatories, promised that they themselves would be there.

About 100 people gathered on October 28 at the Wartburg for "Lutheran Forum 2000." They heard presentations by three well-known Lutheran theologians. David Yeago, professor of theology at Lutheran Southern Theological Seminary, spoke about "Sacramental Lutheranism at the End of the Modern Age." Valparaiso University's ethics professor Gilbert Meilaender addressed "The Task of Lutheran Ethics." Liturgical scholar Frank Senn, then pastor of Immanuel Lutheran Church in Evanston, IL, reflected on

"Our Liturgical Present, with Thoughts about Our Liturgical Future." The day also included worship, with ALPB board member Bp. Michael McDaniel as the preacher. It was not quite the national event originally conceived, but as a regional conference it was a success. A wider audience was assured when the three addresses and the sermon were published in the next issue of *Lutheran Forum.*

The Bureau also continued its series of more modest New York area dinners, usually biennially. Typically there was a keynote speaker of some note, as well as an expression of appreciation to one or another ALPB figure. In 1993, George Lindbeck reflected on that year's ELCA churchwide assembly in an address entitled "The Church Faithful and Apostate," and Theodore Wittrock was honored for his years of service to the ALPB, both as executive director and as board member. Two years later Ralph Bohlmann, former president of the LCMS, spoke on "Missouri Lutheranism, 1945 and 1995," while Glenn Stone was the special honoree. ELCA Presiding Bishop Anderson spoke in 1997 on "The Future of Lutheran Unity," and the Bureau honored Dorothy Zelenko. All these addresses were subsequently printed in *Lutheran Forum.* After 1997, there was a sense that the biennial dinner had run its course, and the series was abandoned as a regular event.

During these years the Bureau also returned to an earlier ministry, that of promoting anniversaries of important Reformation events. Fred Schumacher was a collector of commemorative medals, and in 1998 he proposed that the ALPB produce a medal in observance of the 500th birthday of Luther's wife, Katharina von Bora. The board agreed, and the medal was designed by Scott Blazek and struck in both a silver and bronze version. It was not a big seller, but by the end of the anniversary year (1999) the venture had at least broken even financially.

Lutheran Forum under Ronald Bagnall

"to continue the exemplary tradition"

In 1995, Leonard Klein announced he would step down as editor of *Lutheran Forum* after the August 1996 issue. In his final report to the board, he regretted that "the circumstances of Lutheranism in North America right now have required so much sharp critique and 'negativity.'"

> I know that at times some of you have been uncomfortable with this. So have I! But the massive denial and the failure of analysis have created a vacuum. Into that vacuum ... we have arrived. A vocation has been thrust upon ALPB and its publications. We are not alone, but again we are at the head of the pack. I have not always enjoyed that position, but we have not had the luxury of choosing the conditions of our time and place. I hope only that my deep love for the Church and the Lutheran tradition has not been too much obscured by the call I have felt to critical commentary.[22]

The executive committee considered possible successors; they brought two candidates to the January 1996 board meeting, both ELCA pastors serving in New Jersey. Phillip Max Johnson, pastor of St. Paul's Lutheran Church in Jersey City, was currently serving on the board; he had also worked with Klein as an editorial advisor. Ronald Bagnall, pastor of Grace Lutheran Church in Trenton, had a longer association with the ALPB; an associate editor under Glenn Stone in the early days of *Lutheran Forum*, he was one of the group who developed the original proposal for the *Una Sancta* supplement and was currently writing a regular column for the magazine. After interviewing both candidates, the board offered the position to Bagnall—expressing the hope that he would involve both Johnson and Klein's other associate editor, Rebecca Frey, in some editorial capacity.[23]

Bagnall told the board he planned no radical change of direction for *Lutheran Forum*. His intent was "to continue the exemplary tradition of previous editors by being both truly *Lutheran* and truly a *Forum*; that is, that we be open to diverse theological perspectives and opinions as long as the authors uphold and do not undermine the Scriptures, Confessions and Liturgy of the churches of the Augsburg Confession." He would later say that he had two other goals in mind: to improve the design of *Lutheran Forum*, and to solicit more authors from the LCMS and the Evangelical Lutheran Church in Canada, and from among the laity.[24]

Bagnall immediately set to work on these goals. The title page of his initial issue included the names of all those in Klein's editorial group, though with some shuffling of titles. Michael Plekon, for instance, had recently left the Lutheran ministry to be ordained in the Orthodox Church, so Bagnall appointed two "ecumenical advisors"—Plekon and Roman Catholic priest John Gurrieri. The list of editorial advisors also contained some new names (John Larson, Richard Niebanck, Beth Schlegel, Louis Smith)—and all the former editors of *Lutheran Forum* (Koenig, Stone, Hinlicky, and Klein). Bagnall clearly took seriously the "exemplary tradition" in which he was following.

As for the layout and design of the magazine, Bagnall soon began using color pictures on the cover—at first small pictures of renaissance paintings, but then, beginning in 1999, stunning reproductions of more ancient art such as Romanesque murals or Byzantine icons (though occasionally something more contemporary). These pictures, usually closely related to the issue's theme, filled the whole front cover and sometimes the back as well; they gave the journal a very distinctive appearance (though some readers complained that they all looked alike). Bagnall also added lots of white space to the interior of the journal, giving the pages a more graceful appearance.

Over the next few years, Bagnall added new columns. One of the first was "Look and See," written by Louis A. Smith, now retired and living in Virginia. Smith's column was a personal reflection, taking up whatever topic struck his fancy—*adiaphora*, campus ministry, evangelism, the popular "What Would Jesus Do?" campaign among evangelicals. Bagnall's desire to appeal to Canadian readers led to "The True North—Strong and Free," a column by Pr. K. Glen Johnson, a pastor in Calgary, Alberta. "Laity to Laity" by Raymond J. Brown was added in 2000; Brown often wrote about topics that many pastors tended to avoid. A humorous feature, appearing occasionally and entitled "Easter Monday," was written by LCMS pastor Frederick Baue under the pseudonym "Herman Noodix."

Bagnall loved the history and tradition of the church, and he added a feature he called "Credo"—a brief excerpt in the front of each issue from the writings of some significant patristic or Reformation era figure. He soon included a second such excerpt at the back. He occasionally published translations of brief excerpts of works by significant modern theologians. "Documentation" featured excerpts from significant statements by historic and contemporary church bodies or other groups, such as the report of the 1998 Lambeth Conference on Human Sexuality. A feature called "Lutheran Lit" offered excerpts from secular literature that depicted Lutheran characters or themes. The journal frequently published homilies by contemporary Lutheran preachers.

The new editor continued to devote the largest part of each issue to a specific theme. Some focused on praxis and some discussed issues facing Lutheran church bodies; others were on more general theological or historical topics. Under Bagnall, the *Una Sancta* issue appeared without fail each fall, the theme related to liturgy in some way. Often a good portion of an issue printed papers from a theological conference—perhaps one sponsored by the ALPB, or perhaps not. The bulk of the Winter 1999 issue contained presentations from first general retreat of the Society of the Holy Trinity. Over the next dozen issues, no fewer than seven included at least one paper or homily from an STS general or chapter retreat.

Indeed, it sometimes could appear that *Lutheran Forum* was officially connected to the Society—despite the board's earlier decision that their relation to the Society would be "friendly but not official." This led to an interesting kerfuffle in 2004 when Louis Smith, who in addition to being a regular columnist was the vicar of the Society, wrote a controversial piece in which he admitted that his mind had changed about the ordination of women. He had originally supported ordaining women, he wrote, but "as the 80s moved into the 90s, more and more men and women came into the Ministry with minimal catechization and substantial problematic backgrounds." Women often carried "an extra piece of baggage: ... feminist religion." Smith called this a "new pagan religion ... antipathetic to the Christian faith." He asserted that "some of the best and brightest women who had been ordained" were now questioning, not necessarily their own ordination, but the "sufficiency of the theological rationale and exegetical proposals that had been used to support the decision to ordain them." This led Smith to conclude that on ecumenical and Biblical grounds, the decision to ordain women had been a mistake.[25]

There was a firestorm of protest from readers, many of whom were connecting dots in an alarming way. Smith, they reasoned, is an officer of the Society of the Holy Trinity, so his sexist theological pronouncement proves the STS is a reactionary, misogynistic group! *Lutheran Forum* has been publishing a lot of material from the Society, so it, too, must be in that camp! Some ELCA members of the STS were particularly incensed—though one of the STS's purposes was to provide a forum for free theological discussion, and it would probably be fair to say that most ELCA pastors who were members found Smith's column to be provocative and interesting, but not incendiary and certainly not persuasive.

The next issue of *Lutheran Forum* printed several letters responding to Smith. The first was from Frank Senn, the senior of the Society, who first tried to set the record straight. While he was grateful that *Lutheran Forum* had published several addresses and sermons from STS retreats, "it may be useful to point out that LUTHERAN FORUM is not an organ of the Society, and that not all views published in LUTHERAN FORUM reflect the position of the Society." He noted that the STS takes no position on the ordination of women, that its membership from its inception has included ordained women, as well as pastors (mostly, but not exclusively, LCMS) with "misgivings about the practice." "The genius of the Society" he argued, "is that issues on which members disagree (and there are a number of them) are not suppressed in the interest of unanimity." Rather the Society offers a forum for confessionally-based debate, and thus "provides a model for church assemblies and conventions."[26]

Another letter was from Pr. Clint Schnekloth, an STS member, who was outraged by Smith's article. It did not contribute, he complained, to the "pastoral and liturgical renewal" which he thought was the Society's purpose; Schnekloth shortly thereafter resigned from the STS. A third letter was from STS member Pr. Cathy Ammlung, who wondered if Smith was willing to follow his opinions to their logical conclusion—the de-rostering of women currently serving in ordained ministry.[27]

Smith responded to his interlocutors, addressing each of their points, but he insisted that he wrote neither as vicar of the Society of the Holy Trinity nor as a representative of the ALPB. The editorial policy of the magazine is that "this is a forum and those who enter are permitted to hang themselves if they so choose." In an editorial in that same issue, Bagnall reflected on Smith's article at some length—"not the editorial that I would have *chosen* to write," he began, "but it *needs* to be said." The editorial position of *Lutheran Forum* is "not to advocate one way or the other, but serve as a *forum* for civil and charitable discussion on particular issues." The question of who may be ordained is currently being raised again with regard to gays and lesbians, and so "questions need to be asked of opponents and supporters of the ordination of women, and of those who use women's ordination to promote the ordination of persons living in homosexual relationships." The discussion, in other words, needs to be continued. The ALPB board minutes for the May 2004 meeting record rather drolly that "an article by Pr. Louis Smith in the latest Lutheran Forum generated considerable discussion."[28]

While Bagnall did not focus as much on the institutional politics of the churches as had his predecessors, he was not reluctant to take strong editorial positions on issues facing the church—and he did not insist on writing all editorials himself. Under his leadership, editorials might be written by any of the associate editors or editorial advisors; they were always signed, so that the reader knew who was writing.

Former editor Leonard Klein, for example, offered a sober reflection on the continuing debate about the ELCA's ecumenical commitments. The 1997 churchwide assembly had approved the *Formula of Agreement* which declared the ELCA to be in full communion with three Reformed churches, but it had narrowly defeated the *Concordat* that would have done the same with the Episcopal Church—what Klein had earlier described as the worst possible outcome. A few months after the churchwide assembly action, Klein pondered his own opposition to both of the original proposals. He concluded that "the protestant ecumenical proposals lead us away from the true unity of the church" because "they assume pluriform denominationalism as an organizational reality and set out within its confines to reunite the church." Such an assumption is nothing more than "an agreement to get along so long as nobody throws any sand in the gears with hard questions about faith, order and morals." It is simply a cul-de-sac that prevents real ecumenism.

> Ecumenism is a matter of growing toward evangelical and catholic fullness, of repentance for the schismatic blind alleys down which we have gone, and of actually fixing the problems that continue to necessitate the division of the Church. ...
>
> So long as the protestant churches continue in this manner, ignoring the ancient consensus on an array of issues from the Trinity to abortion, any deals between them solidify a witness against that faithfulness represented in Rome, Orthodoxy and in their different way the Evangelicals (to say nothing of the Missouri Synod).

"No amount of marching in the wrong direction is progress," he noted. "And any amount of marching away from Rome and Orthodoxy is a move away from church unity."[29]

Nonetheless, *Lutheran Forum*'s opposition to full communion with the Episcopal Church began to soften. After the *Concordat*'s rejection, ELCA and Episcopal ecumenists hammered out changes they hoped would encourage approval by the ELCA in 1999 and published them as *Called to Common Mission* (*CCM*). The *Concordat*, for example, had called for Episcopal bishops (who claimed to be in the historic episcopate) to participate in the consecration of new ELCA bishops; *CCM* allowed ELCA bishops instead to receive the historic episcopate from bishops of other Lutheran churches (such as the Church of Sweden) which had maintained it.

Lutheran Forum had opposed the *Concordat* in 1997 but now gave a cautious endorsement to *CCM* in an editorial signed not only by Bagnall but by all three of his predecessors. It was hardly an enthusiastic recommendation; the editors acknowledged deep reservations—not about the historic episcopate itself, but about its effectiveness in assuring faithfulness. Neither church, they lamented, had proven itself capable of "[changing] their exercise of their episcopate or pastorate to conform to our common Scriptures and Creeds and our respective confessions of the faith." They were willing to support the proposal simply "because the revised *Concordat* is not contrary to the Scriptures, or Creeds, or our Lutheran Confessions." Furthermore, "there are thousands of faithful Episcopalians—bishops, priests, and parishioners—that have not bowed down to the idols of nature or the ideologies of culture." Along with their cautious endorsement, the editors called for "a renewed episcopacy and ministerium."[30]

But this was followed in the next issue with a guest editorial by ALPB board member Bp. Michael McDaniel, who argued for the defeat of *CCM*. He admitted to being a lifelong Anglophile, who had learned much from and been blessed by his associations with the Episcopal Church. Nevertheless, he was convinced the ELCA must simply call a halt to all its ecumenical initiatives. Approval of the *Formula of Agreement*, he wrote, had "laid bare the shocking incompetence of the ELCA's quota-fashioned assemblies ever to be faithful stewards [of]—let alone bold witnesses to—the *depositum fidei* (an incompetence which should have surprised no one)." McDaniel insisted that "a moratorium must be placed upon all ecumenical activity by the ELCA until it has recovered its fitness for such activity." It can only do so by "rectifying the appalling deterioration of Biblical, confessional, ministerial and liturgical authority which has been undermining our church for some years." We must begin, he asserted, with "rebuilding bridges with the Lutheran Church—Missouri Synod. We need them, and they need us."[31]

The approval of *CCM* in 1999 did not stop the controversy. A group calling itself Word Alone kept up a constant stream of criticism of the agreement, threatening to undermine it by, among other things, arranging for ordinations of pastors by other pastors rather than bishops. In a guest editorial in *Lutheran Forum*, Michael Root, then professor of systematic theology at Trinity Lutheran Seminary in Columbus, OH, accused Word Alone of a "constantly shifting array of misinterpretations" of *CCM*. In his view, the problem was rampant individualism; the opposition to *CCM*, he wrote, has misunderstood freedom as "the freedom of individuals (or, at most, groups of like-minded individuals organized as a congregation) to do as they please, not the freedom of the Church to determine its own life in accord with the Gospel." "What is needed," he concluded, "is a clear commitment to the ordered procedures of the Church and to a catholic and evangelical confessional vision of Lutheranism." This is now urgent as the ELCA "faces a variety of controversial issues."[32]

Those "controversial issues" included particularly the looming battles over sexuality. In that same issue, Bagnall argued that the ELCA had departed from the "catholic consensus" on faith and morals. He saw connections between doctrinal disputes and disciplinary matters. Opponents of *CCM* were now calling for "exceptions" which would allow for those conscientiously opposed to the historic episcopate to be ordained without the involvement of bishops—not so different, Bagnall argued, for those calling for "exceptions" that would allow for the ordination of sexually active gays and lesbians. "The crisis in the ELCA today," he wrote, "is hardly over the historic episcopate. Rather the current crisis stems from the separation of faith and morals, particularly whenever lifestyles and issues of life and death are disconnected from 'the faith that was once for all entrusted to the saints.'"[33]

Forum Letter under Russell Saltzman

"I write for myself"

In 1996, an ALPB board member asked *Forum Letter* editor Russell Saltzman who exactly he was writing for. "I had no ready answer that went beyond mumbling, 'Mostly, I write for myself. If anyone wants to read over my shoulder, they are welcome.'" That perhaps sounded arrogant, he later wrote, but what he meant is that "I write as a parish pastor who encounters the Church at her elemental level, in the parish, and more particularly, a Lutheran parish."

> This is where I meet people summoned to the Word and Sacraments, who struggle with daily faithfulness, and who know—whether they can say it or not in a prescribed 'Lutheran' way—that faith is a gift of the Spirit and not their own work. I write then as a parish pastor who is convicted by the truth of the Gospel, and who finds himself constrained to protest when it appears that the truth of the Gospel has become imperiled. I write, I pray, in service to the Gospel that has saved even me. ...
>
> What appears in *Forum Letter,* then, is not only what I want to write for myself, but what I must write for myself if I am to think of myself as a pastor. It is the parish that feeds *Forum Letter.*[34]

He acknowledged that he—like both his predecessors, Koenig and Neuhaus—was occasionally accused of "being crabby and negative." He did not apologize.

> I do admit, I do not like being known as a negative crab, or 'belly-acher' as a critic said. *Christian Century,* let me note defensively, once called me 'kinder and gentler' than my immediate predecessor. Of course, as my predecessor quickly reminded me, *Christian Century* has been wrong before. ... There are some things of note [in the church] that are quite fine, but they can be read about elsewhere. Sincere and heartfelt crabbiness though, is at a premium. I guess a certain testiness is necessary for the job.

His task, he wrote, is to "challenge the Lutheran church to be Church, to take the Confessions as seriously as the Confessions take themselves. That and parish life, always, lies behind the reporting and commentary I do in *Forum Letter.*" So, he concluded, "I write ... for myself. If there are some few of you who take something away from your reading, I am glad and grateful. It is what *Forum Letter* has tried to do for 25 years, give you something for the trouble of reading."[35]

And indeed, while *Lutheran Forum* debated weighty theological matters, *Forum Letter* focused more on congregational life. Some articles in the newsletter were aimed directly at parish pastors. In 1993, for example, Walter Bouman contributed a six-part series on the use of the *Lutheran Book of Worship*, arguing that many parishes had not yet begun to utilize it effectively. Each article in the series carried a notice explicitly granting permission to reprint for congregational distribution.

More often, however, Saltzman wrote about broader institutional questions from the perspective of a parish pastor. In 1994, for example, after Herbert Chilstrom announced that he would be retiring as bishop of the ELCA, Saltzman proposed a "nominating symposium." He began by suggesting the qualities he thought should be considered when the churchwide assembly met in 1995 to choose a new leader. First of all, it should be someone who has "his orthodox wits about him."

> Should the next bishop sleep with the *Book of Concord* under his pillow? No. The night stand is near enough and a good night's sleep is important to anyone in that office. No one, in short, should seek a self-identified 'evangelical catholic.' We'd settle for a 'Protestant confessionalist.' Still, the next bishop should recognize that the Augsburg Confession is not a declaration of independence, but an ecumenically irenic presentation meant to place the Wittenberg reforms squarely within the norm and practice of the Western Church. He should see the ELCA as part of that larger movement of Gospel reform within and for the Holy Church of Christ.

He suggested several other criteria, but most importantly, the next bishop "must possess a clear and proven capacity for being a bishop"—that is to say, he must have "a bishop's heart for the parish, in the ancient expression of an ancient bishop, 'a servant of the servants of Christ.'" He urged that the decision "be surrounded by fervent prayer for the guidance of the Spirit, that God will name a fit watchman over Israel." Toward that end, he invited ELCA readers to send him five nominations for bishop, ranked in order of preference, together with a few words about why they selected their "top choice."[36]

When all the votes were in, Saltzman was completely surprised. He had prepared copy for all the names he thought might be prominently suggested, and Southwestern Pennsylvania Synod bishop Donald McCoid wasn't even on his radar screen—yet he was the top choice of 35% of the 188 respondents. Other high-ranking names included David Tiede, Dennis Anderson, James Nestingen, William Lazareth and H. George Anderson. Saltzman discounted the last two—Lazareth because he was retired and happily so, Anderson because he had twice before declined to be considered (once for bishop of the LCA, and again at the constituting convention of the ELCA). He then wrote about each of the others, suggesting both the gifts they might bring to the office as well as the "downside"—though with McCoid, he admitted that he could find no downside ("but then, we only had a week to dig").[37]

When the 1995 assembly chose H. George Anderson, Saltzman was only slightly red-faced about having dismissed him the preceding year. "At least he was there in the poll," he pointed out, so *Forum Letter* readers "may claim some credit in bringing his name to the attention of assembly voters a year before anybody else started thinking about him." In any event, Saltzman added, "had we been handing out endorsements, he would have been on our short list."[38]

Often Saltzman poked fun at things in parishes or elsewhere in the church that struck him as ridiculous. He recounted, for instance, the communion instructions included in a bulletin someone had forwarded to him:

> All who believe in Jesus as the Christ may come to the altar for communion. Children may come forward for a blessing. Pastor Ann will come down the center aisle with the bread. After you have received the bread please go up to the altar for your choice of common cup on the left or individual glasses on the right. Grape juice is in the five glasses closest to the server's tummy.

Saltzman excoriated the lack of any reference to Lutheran eucharistic theology (it's nothing but "an average generic 'we-think-Jesus-may-be-in-here-somewhere-or-not' Protestant memorial"). But he just rolled his eyes at "tummy." "'Tummy' (ignoring the grape juice altogether) is just tacky. 'Upper abdominal cavity' sounds more refined, don't you agree?"[39]

There were other topics he tackled that were not so funny. A 1996 disciplinary hearing in the Metropolitan New York Synod of the ELCA came to his attention. A married male pastor had been involved, more than 15 years earlier, in a consensual affair with a female intern, who was subsequently consecrated as a deaconess. They had mutually ended the affair, after which the male pastor (and presumably the female) had sought a confessor, made confession, received absolution. Now, all these years later, unrelated and unsubstantiated charges were made against the male pastor, and in the process of investigation, the affair came to light. The male pastor (though not the female deaconess) was brought up on charges. Synod bishop James Sudbrock insisted the offense merited removal from the roster; the synod's disciplinary committee unanimously disagreed. They recommended that the appropriate penalty was suspension "until such time as ... satisfactory evidence has been provided ... [showing] repentance and amendment of life." "Informally," Saltzman wrote, "committee members tell us, the panel found that the lack of evidence showing any other incidents of sexual misconduct constitute the sought after repentance and amendment of life"—which is to say, they expected the bishop would "take a hint, declare 'time served' adequate suspension ... and restore [the pastor] to his ... parish" (which had supported the pastor and was eager to have him back). But Sudbrock refused to lift the suspension, turning it into a *de facto* defrocking. This action was, Saltzman wrote, one reason the bishop was not re-elected at the subsequent synod assembly.[40]

Why was the bishop so adamant? Saltzman reported the answer given him by one Metro New York clergywoman: "Because he was in thrall to dim-witted feminists who hated [the pastor]." An alternative view, he suggested, is that the bishop and the ELCA's attorney, Phillip Harris, genuinely believe that "ELCA policy requires removal of the pastor in any and all cases of sexual misconduct." Harris pointed out that every misconduct case brought before a disciplinary committee prior to this one had resulted in removal from the clergy roster; but Saltzman responded that dozens of other cases never reached a disciplinary committee because they had been handled in other, more pastoral, ways.[41]

Saltzman then drew a larger lesson from the incident. "It is hard to know what to do with all this," he admitted.

> There are, of course, compelling reasons why the Evangelical Lutheran Church in America must be alert to cases of sexual misconduct. Foremost is the ordination pledge made by pastors to adorn their office with 'faithful service and holy living.' Scandal that brings the office into disrepute is a serious failure of a pastor's vows of ordination. [The pastor's] sin was real and required confrontation. ... But so, even after the passage of 16 years, was evidence of his repentance and regret. After sifting through as much as we can, we conclude he became a target of convenience by [the bishop] and his staff, a conjunction of misguided conviction and ideology. It was that and the legalism now infusing the whole question of sexual conduct that brought this case to trial. This does not excuse [the pastor's] sin. Still less does it settle the question of discipline. But it needs to be asked—in a theological rather than an ideological context—if 'forgiveness' may never entail 'restoration' to a position of trust?

"The church," he concluded, is "a place where the Old Adam still contends for dominance [and where] fools and knaves will abound. The real challenge for the church trying to live her theology—one that includes admonition, confession, absolution—is to distinguish between the two."[42]

Knowing that this article could cause some controversy, Saltzman sent copies to the ALPB executive committee for their review prior to its publication, and at their suggestion, he had removed language that made clear the specific person referred to in the "dim-witted feminists" comment. Even with that change, however, the issue infuriated the synod's newly elected bishop, Stephen Bouman, a longtime friend of the ALPB. "I can't tell you how angry I am about your article," he wrote to Saltzman—specifically about the "dim-witted feminists" line, which "does nothing to build up the Body of Christ [but] is just mean and petty."[43]

Bouman sent a copy of the letter to executive director Fred Schumacher, who agreed that the comment about "dim-witted feminists" was unfortunate. He stressed, however, that Saltzman "is given complete editorial freedom as was the case with Richard Neuhaus. He does not express the views of anyone but himself." On the other hand, he recalled a recent situation where Saltzman had written an article about a controversy at Augsburg Fortress. Schumacher had called a "highly regarded" churchman about it and was told much of it was untrue; the executive committee had then advised Saltzman to pull the article, and he had done so. A few months later virtually everything in the article had proven to be true and was reported in the *Lutheran*. "In the issue before us," he told Bouman, "I believe that he reported fairly on what is at stake with [the pastor] and the future of the ELCA and Synod in this matter."[44]

The matter was discussed in detail at the next board meeting, and it was agreed that the president would write to Saltzman reporting on the substance of the conversation. The board, Hans Quitmeyer wrote, was critical of the "dim-witted feminists" comment, which "unnecessarily alienated many of our readers. ... We wish your otherwise excellent treatment had not been undermined by off-putting, uninsightful name calling." He also reported that "some members of the Board sense that you seem to relish taking every opportunity to snipe at women and 'feminists.'" "Happily," he concluded, "you have never been less than welcoming and respectful of our views and I hope you read this letter in that spirit."[45]

One regular feature of *Forum Letter* was significant—and often acerbic—coverage of the national meetings of both the ELCA and the LCMS. Saltzman didn't always attend himself, but he asked various correspondents to report their impressions to him, and then he typically wrote the report. Two years after his strident critique of the worship and preaching at the 1993 ELCA churchwide assembly, he was again more hopeful. At the 1995 assembly in Minneapolis, worship was "'green book' orthodoxy." He even had kind things to say about Bp. Chilstrom's opening sermon. There was a lot of talk about sexuality, but the assembly kicked the can down the road. The full communion agreements were presented, but the vote was still two years off. About the only thing of consequence was the election of H. George Anderson to succeed Chilstrom. "As ELCA assemblies go, this one was positive."[46]

Leonard Klein's report in 1997 ended on a similar note, but with a more discouraging spin. Worship had been good, he admitted, but the passage of the ecumenical proposals—to which he devoted almost his entire article—was a disaster. "This was perhaps as good an assembly as the ELCA could have," he concluded, "but unless one thinks that the future toward which it tends is where the catholic faith should be moving, one would have to conclude that the best of assemblies can also be the worst."[47]

Missouri Synod conventions were also covered in some detail. Since a majority of *Forum Letter* readers were now ELCA, these reports tended to use a lot of space interpreting events to readers who might find them mystifying. The 1995 account, for example, suggested that despite the lack of clear controversy, there were several places where "the convention's 'conservatives' turned the screws another notch on 'moderates.'" It also noted "the strength that younger pastors are beginning to have in the synod."

> For the most part, pastors who have graduated from the seminary in the last fifteen years are less pragmatic than their older colleagues. The theological thinking of many of these younger pastors has been shaped by the heritage of Hermann Sasse (a virtual unknown outside the LC-MS theological stream), transmitted by Norman Nagel and Ronald Feuerhahn at St. Louis and Kurt Marquart at Fort Wayne. Young enough to have escaped conscription into the Missouri Wars, they nonetheless have heard the war stories but carry none of the scars the veterans proudly bear and regularly bare. ... Their concerns tend to concentrate on ministry and liturgics, marked by a confessional consciousness often missing from their elders. ... On several key resolutions, their votes counted.

"There is," Saltzman concluded, "much to admire about the Missouri Synod, a Lutheran body possessing great gifts." He quoted August Mennicke, who had been ousted at the convention from his office of first vice-president. Mennicke spoke, Saltzman wrote, of the danger in "confusing eternal gifts with those that are less than eternal. How well Missouri distinguishes between the two remains an untold story."[48]

When Saltzman was first appointed editor, one stipulation had been that he recruit a cadre of contributing editors so that his would not be the only voice represented in *Forum Letter*; he had duly appointed John Pless, Melinda Heppe, Richard Niebanck and Christa Klein, and they had contributed regularly. In 1993, Saltzman thanked them warmly, saying that "they often have been a source of support and encouragement, and they have provided [me] with necessary critique and challenge." But it was time, he went on, "to bring up a new set of contributing editors"—a group more "representative of Lutheran diversity." He announced that Pless, a Missouri Synod pastor, would continue; new appointees included a Wisconsin Synod pastor, Michael Albrecht, and three ELCA pastors: Charles Austin, Karen Kepner, and Ruth Ballard. Over the next months, most of them contributed at least one article to *Forum Letter*.[49]

But two years later, Saltzman wrote a piece on the "trouble with contributing editors." They are, he complained, "supposed to be quiet sorts." They may occasionally contribute, but "a wise editor knows the names are there to lend credibility to the publication, if that's possible, and is otherwise content." But now, he reported, "two of ours ... have done something else." Michael Albrecht, it turned out, had "gotten himself and his congregation bounced" from the Wisconsin Evangelical Lutheran Synod. Albrecht and the other pastors at his parish had expressed the opinion that Scripture does not forbid women being given the right to vote in the congregation; this was contrary to WELS teaching. The pastors had not advocated "woman suffrage" (as the WELS called it)—indeed, their own parish didn't allow women to vote. But they insisted that while Wisconsin had the right to ban woman suffrage, "it should not represent that choice as a scripturally-mandated doctrine." "Daring stuff in WELS circles," Saltzman noted wryly. Albrecht would continue as a contributing editor, but of course no longer represented the Wisconsin Synod.[50]

The issue with Charles Austin was quite different. Austin had been a friend of the ALPB, but he was also a writer for the ELCA's *Lutheran Partners* and a strong supporter of the ELCA. He had become increasingly unhappy with the editorial positions of *Lutheran Forum* under Leonard Klein. When *Forum Letter* published "The 9.5 Theses," he reached his limit and promptly resigned as contributing editor. He posted news of his resignation on an internet forum, which is how Saltzman found out about it; a letter of resignation had been sent by mail, but "touchingly, he trusted it would reach us before he posted his remarks on the Internet." Saltzman expressed regret for Austin's resignation, but assumed his "integrity of conscience [and] good motive." "We all contend and argue, as we rightly should," he wrote, "knowing a better Judge to judge it all at the end."[51]

A few months later, John Pless also resigned. He had contributed to *Forum Letter*'s report on the 1995 Missouri Synod convention, but was dissatisfied with how his remarks were integrated with others in the final article. This led Saltzman to ask the board if he might simply discontinue the contributing editors. Recognizing that Saltzman had in fact regularly sought and published articles from many other writers, they agreed; the January 1996 issue appeared with Saltzman's name only on *Forum Letter*'s flag.[52]

Saltzman saw himself as a reporter and commentator, and he didn't often venture into considering large philosophical questions. Shortly after cutting loose his contributing editors, however, he took up a question Leonard Klein had raised after resigning from *Lutheran Forum*: Is the ELCA still Church? The question, Saltzman admitted, "doesn't seem to go up our natural alley."

> Our interests are simpler. Give this editor a scandal or two to expose; let him skewer a few fools; let him quote 'five glasses of grape juice nearest the server's tummy.' ... But ask whether the ELCA is still Church, ah, gosh. That hurts. To ask the question—Is the ELCA still 'holy, catholic, apostolic'?—is to suggest the strong possibility that it is not. That is a fearsome question.

But it is also, he suggested, the wrong question. "The real question is whether it was ever confessionally meant to be Church." The Reformers did not mean to establish a new church, but saw themselves as still part of the Church—one, holy, catholic, apostolic. Their institutions were intended to be temporary. But Lutherans "have made virtues of our necessities, and now in some cases our virtues have become vices we cannot escape." The root of the problem, he suggested, is that our "temporary" institution lacks a teaching office, and that makes us "subject to all the shattering temptations that have always tempted the Church, and which seem to afflict big-time Protestantism with especially devastating effect."

> Nonetheless, over and against all that stands the Confessions and the Tradition, calling us all to greater faithfulness. We may yet heed that call. ... The challenge of evangelical catholicism, if indeed it is a movement rooted to the Confessions and not some kind of party slogan, is to actively engage the continuing crisis that is the ELCA; to do it not only for the sake of the Church which is catholic, but also for the sake of the institutional ELCA which is not.[53]

Notes

1. Minutes, ALPB Board of Directors, 16 Oct. 1994 and 13 May 1995.
2. Richard F. Bansemer, *Lord, Teach Me to Pray: A Catechetical Prayer Book for Personal Use* (Delhi, NY: ALPB, 1995), 16.
3. Frank Stoldt to Philip Pfatteicher, 15 Aug. 1993; Philip Pfatteicher to Frank Stoldt, 23 Aug. 1993, ALPB archives.
4. Philip H. Pfatteicher, *The Daily Prayer of the Church* (Minneapolis, MN: Lutheran University Press, 2005).
5. Robert Tobias, *Heaven on Earth: A Lutheran—Orthodox Odyssey* (Delhi, NY: ALPB, 1997).
6. Robert Tobias to Frederick J. Schumacher, 24 Jan. 1997, ALPB Archives.
7. Frederick J. Schumacher to Robert Tobias, 12 Feb. 1997, ALPB Archives.
8. Robert Tobias to Frederick J. Schumacher, 19 Feb. 1997, ALPB Archives.
9. John M. Quitmeyer to Robert Tobias, 6 Mar. 1997, ALPB Archives.
10. Minutes, ALPB Book Committee, 7 May 1997.
11. Richard F. Bansemer, *We Believe: A Prayer Book Based on the Augsburg Confession* (Delhi, NY: ALPB, 1999); Robert W. Jenson, *A Large Catechism*, 2nd edition (Delhi, NY: ALPB, 1999); Eugene A. Lehrke, *Prayers for the Eucharistic Gathering* (Delhi, NY: ALPB, 1999).
12. Martin E. Marty, "Forward," in Stephen P. Bouman, *From the Parish for the Life of the World* (Delhi, NY: ALBP Books, 2000), 8.
13. Executive Director's Report, 26 June 1999, ALPB Archives.
14. Ibid.
15. "A 'Super Lutheran Forum,'" attached to Minutes, ALPB Board of Directors, 31 Jan. 1998.
16. Minutes, ALPB Board of Directors, 22-23 May 1998.
17. Frederick J. Schumacher to H. George Anderson and Alvin L. Barry, 3 June 1998, ALPB Archives.
18. Alvin L. Barry to Frederick J. Schumacher, 18 June 1998, ALPB Archives.
19. H. George Anderson to Frederick J. Schumacher, 1 July 1998, ALPB Archives.
20. Frederick J. Schumacher to H. George Anderson, 11 Aug. 1998, ALPB Archives.
21. Minutes, ALPB Board of Directors, 24 Oct. 1998.
22. Leonard R. Klein to ALPB Board, 31 May 1996, ALPB Archives.
23. Minutes, ALPB Board of Directors, 27 Jan. 1996.
24. Ronald Bagnall to Hans Quitmeyer and Frederick Schumacher, 11 May 1996; Ronald Bagnall, "Report to ALPB Board," 23 Oct. 1999, ALPB Archives.
25. Louis A. Smith, "How My Mind Has Changed," *LF* 38, no. 1 (Spring 2004), 49-50.
26. "Letters to the Editor," *LF* 38, no. 2 (Summer 2004), 4-6.
27. Ibid.
28. Ibid.; Ronald B. Bagnall, "Whose Call?" *LF* 38, no. 2 (Summer 2004), 7-8; Minutes, ALPB Board, May 8, 2004, ALPB Archives.
29. Leonard R. Klein, "Steps Away from True Unity," *LF* 32, no. 1 (Spring 1998), 6-7.

30. Ronald B. Bagnall, Leonard R. Klein, Paul R. Hinlicky, and Glenn C. Stone, "*Ubi est verbum, ibi est ecclesia*—Churchmanship and the *Concordat*," *LF* 33, no. 1 (Spring 1999), 7-8.

31. Michael C. D. McDaniel, "Why the *Concordat* Must Be Defeated," *LF* 33, no. 2 (Summer 1999), 5-6.

32. Michael J. Root, "Opposition to *Called to Common Mission*," *LF* 34, no. 1 (Spring 2000), 9-10.

33. Ronald B. Bagnall, "'Faith and Morals': Catholic Consensus and *Called to Common Mission*," *LF* 34, no. 1 (Spring 2000), 8.

34. Ibid.

35. Ibid.

36. *FL* 23, no. 3 (25 Mar. 1994), 1-2, 5.

37. *FL*, 23, no. 9 (29 Sept. 1994), 1-3.

38. *FL* 24, no. 9 (Sept. 1995), 7-8.

39. *FL* 26, no. 2 (Feb. 1997), 4-5.

40. *FL* 26, no. 1 (Jan. 1997), 3-5.

41. Ibid., 5.

42. Ibid., 6.

43. Stephen Bouman to Russell Saltzman, 19 Dec. 1996, ALPB Archives.

44. Frederick J. Schumacher to Stephen Bouman, 23 Dec. 1996, ALPB Archives.

45. Hans Quitmeyer to Russell Saltzman, 29 Jan. 1997, ALPB Archives.

46. *FL* 24, no. 10 (Oct. 1995), 1ff.

47. *FL* 24, no. 10 (Oct 1997), 7.

48. *FL* 22, no. 9 (Sept. 1995), 1ff.

49. *FL* 22, no. 4 (Apr. 9, 1993), 4.

50. *FL* 24, no. 8 (Aug. 1995), 1.

51. Ibid., 2-3.

52. Minutes, ALPB Board of Directors, 21 Oct. 1995.

53. *FL* 26, no. 2 (Feb. 1997), 2-4.

Chapter 23

A NEW MILLENNIUM

[A]s the new millennium approached, the issues facing American Lutheranism became more and more complex. The LCMS was conflicted again by disputes between conservatives and the shrinking number of moderates. The ELCA continued to be roiled by disagreements over its ecumenical relations. Both church bodies battled over worship and liturgy, and both experienced controversial changes in leadership. The ALPB publications offered ongoing commentary on all these issues. At the same time, the Bureau continued to evolve in its own understanding of ministry beyond just the *Forum* package. It resumed its book publishing ministry after a brief hiatus, experienced staff changes with both *Forum Letter* and *Lutheran Forum*, and said farewell to several persons who had been key members of the ALPB family.

Staff changes and new projects

"It sounds bonkers"

Martin Christiansen had been managing editor of *Lutheran Forum* since 1990; he had worked also on *Pro Ecclesia* and the ALPB's book publishing projects. In 1999, however, *Lutheran Forum* editor Ronald Bagnall recommended a change in the light of new technology which was altering the way magazines did layout and design. Bagnall was willing to learn this technology and to assume much of the work formerly done by the managing editor. He recommended that the board eliminate that position and hire someone who could solicit advertising and do promotional work for all the ALPB publications. The executive committee agreed, and the position of managing editor was eliminated. "We owe Martin a great deal of thanks," Schumacher told the board. "I will always remember him trying to fit in a few minutes of sleep at 6 AM in St. Matthew's Library after having worked on Volume I of *For All the Saints* for some 15 or 16 hours straight. I will ever be grateful for his dedication to the cause of the ALPB." Christiansen would continue to work on specific ALPB projects on a contract basis; the proposed promotional position was never filled.[1]

Russell Saltzman had, with the board's permission, dropped his contributing editors, but in 2001 he proposed that an associate editor for *Forum Letter* be authorized. The board agreed, and Saltzman recommended the appointment of Richard O. Johnson, an ELCA pastor in Grass Valley, CA, who had occasionally contributed to the newsletter. Saltzman introduced Johnson in the January 2002 issue:

> [He] holds an M.Div. from Yale Divinity School, a Ph.D. in church history from the Graduate Theological Union and, once upon a time, he was a pastor of the United Methodist Church. For several years he was a contributing editor of *engage/social action*, a, well, liberal Methodist magazine engaging in social action. I know, I know. It sounds bonkers, picking an ex-Methodist from Yale living in California. But of that, he himself will tell you more another day.[2]

Several new initiatives were begun about this time. The Bureau entered the internet age and established a website, alpb.org. The site offered information about the ALPB and promoted its various publications. Soon was added "Forum Online," an interactive forum; *Forum Letter*'s new associate editor was given primary responsibility to moderate the online conversations. At the recommendation of Theodore Wittrock, the board agreed to reissue the 1961 recording "The Best in Lutheran Hymns" as a compact disc. This "40th anniversary edition" was produced in 2001 and was well-received; by the end of 2003, more than 1500 copies had been sold.[3]

The Lutheran Identity leaflet series had done well, and requests came for a Spanish language version of the tracts. The board approved the translation project in 1997, but progress was slow and it became necessary to find a new translator. The tracts were finally printed in December 1999, thanks in part to a generous grant from Aid Association for Lutherans. An amusing report was given at the January 2000 board meeting by Connie Seddon, who had overseen the tract ministry since its resumption in 1993. Seddon had advocated abandoning the word "tract" in favor of "leaflet," but now she expressed a change of heart:

Much light ribbing has been directed at the Tract Committee because we began in 1993 without a clear idea of whether our products should be known as old-fashioned 'tracts,' trendy 'leaflets,' or something else. *In light of the ALPB's distinguished history of tract production, we have finally decided to unabashedly call our products 'tracts,'* although, as our new letterhead shows, we have added the description 'and educational brochures.' It is hoped that this will adequately explain to folks that our tracts are not 'inspirational' pieces, but serve an educational purpose and thus tend to require a longer format than most tracts.

But the Spanish translation of the Lutheran Identity series, along with the human sexuality and family life tracts published about the same time, proved to be the last gasp of ALPB's venerable tract ministry. In the internet age, the medium had simply outlived its usefulness.[4]

Uproar in Missouri

"Theology is the best indoor sport they know"

Since the upheaval of the 1970s, the Missouri Synod had been relatively calm. In 1992, conservative president Ralph Bohlmann had been ousted by an even more conservative Alvin L. Barry, demonstrating that Missouri's right wing was firmly in control. But in 2001, the LCMS was thrown a curve ball. President Barry, widely thought to be a shoo-in for re-election, died unexpectedly a few months prior to the 2001 convention. Moderates had already been organizing to defeat the incumbent president, though they were thought to have little chance of success. Barry's death left everything wide open. Nominations for president, which in Missouri came from congregations in the months prior to the convention, had already closed. "The presumed 'moderate' candidates were already in place," reported John Hannah, "but the far right [who had supported Barry] had to re-group and ended up divided on their choice of a candidate." After a contentious and dramatic voting process, Gerald Kieschnick, president of the Texas District and one of the preferred candidates of the moderates, was elected by 18 votes over the emerging conservative favorite, Dean Wenthe. Though he is "a conservative's conservative," Hannah wrote, Kieschnick "recognizes that he must conduct his office for the sake of all members of the synod. It is in that sense that this reporter predicts the purity cult will fade in influence." In other respects, however, conservatives were still firmly in charge. The day after ELCA presiding bishop H. George Anderson brought gracious greetings to the convention and appealed "for reconciliation and a recognition of a common Lutheran heritage," the delegates "solemnly declared that the ELCA could no longer be regarded as an 'orthodox Lutheran body.'"[5]

Only weeks after the convention, the terrorist attack on the World Trade Center and other sites rocked the nation, and it led to an extended and ugly battle in the Missouri Synod. David Benke, president of the Atlantic District (and a former member of the ALPB's board of directors), took part in an interfaith prayer service at Yankee Stadium a few days after the attack. "Conservative LCMS reaction," Russell Saltzman wrote, "was immediate, sharp and sustained. Some of the conservative reaction—by any standard you care to apply—was simply and unutterably vile."[6]

It was not Benke's first time in the crosshairs. In 1999, he had taken part in a New York City service of prayer for the poor. He had, Saltzman recounted, been "summarily summoned to [President] Barry's office and—this is not too strong a word—forced to sign a confession and an apology or face immediate removal from the district presidency." Despite his apology, Benke had written a lengthy explanation of why he had chosen to participate—more *apologia* than apology—and it was published in *Lutheran Forum,* to the irritation of Barry and other LCMS leaders.[7]

After the 9/11 attack, however, Benke sought the advice and counsel of the new LCMS president ahead of time, and Kieschnick encouraged him to participate in the service. This did not stop Benke's detractors. The issue was whether the Yankee Stadium event was a "worship service" (clearly forbidden, since it was not only ecumenical but interreligious) or a "civic event" (allowable under LCMS rules). "Conservatives produce the program for the event, saying it was worship," Saltzman reported. "Moderates point to the presence of [media personality] Oprah [Winfrey] and say 'get real.'" In any event, the extraordinary nature of the situation, as well as Kieschnick's prior approval, meant that "conservative ire at Benke and Kieschnick runs the risk of discrediting LCMS rightists as merely, if not always, mean-spirited."[8]

Whether they were mean-spirited rightists or heroic defenders of orthodoxy, the conservatives forged ahead; eighteen pastors and three congregations filed formal charges against both Benke and Kieschnick. Charges against Kieschnick were dropped due to a constitutional technicality, but the case against Benke went forward. Under LCMS rules, responsibility for judging him would normally have fallen to Kieschnick; but having approved Benke's participation before the fact, he recused himself, and the LCMS board of directors referred the matter to the five vice presidents. First vice president Daniel Preus had already publicly rebuked Benke, so he recused himself as well. That left the case in the hands of second vice president Wallace Schulz, who, after considering the matter for a few months, suspended Benke from office. Saltzman suspected that "outraged lay reaction"—inflamed by widespread media coverage—would lead to a reversal.[9]

Schulz had recently been appointed the speaker on the *Lutheran Hour,* the radio program sponsored by the International Lutheran Laymen's League. Within days of his judgment of Benke, the ILLL's board of directors, not wanting to be dragged into the

Benke controversy, suspended Schulz. "The entire conflict," Saltzman wrote, "demands some deeper reflection, but that is unlikely to happen."

> This is the Missouri Synod's *That 70's Show*, reprising bell bottoms, sideburns, a polyester leisure-suited quest for doctrinal purity. Or maybe this is *Groundhog Day*, the main character dumbly doomed to stupidly frustrating repetitions of the previous day. Benke's prayer, concluded in 'Jesus' precious name,' set off only the latest painful battle in a never-settled war between 'moderates' and conservatives.

Saltzman was clearly sympathetic toward the moderates, and yet he admitted that conservatives did have a point. He was concerned about "the whole picture of patriotic ecumenism that has exploded in the wake of the World Trade Center." Do "civic concerns somehow trump important theological questions"? In truth, "Benke's prayer, like it or not, especially in the presence of non-Christians praying their own prayers, raises some real and some very genuine conceptual and theological puzzles for all of us." Nonetheless, he concluded, "what the Missouri Synod decidedly lacks is any degree of institutional grace and good humor, any willingness to cut the other guy just a little slack." It's all a "tragic reflection of how seared Missouri still is by the battle of the early 1970's. Benke and Schulz are but the latest victims. ... Like we said, *Groundhog Day*."[10]

Benke appealed the suspension, which was then referred to a dispute resolution panel. As that panel deliberated in secret, another strange twist took place. Missouri's Commission on Constitutional Matters (essentially the LCMS's "Supreme Court") issued several rulings that bore on the case against Benke. As John Hannah reported in *Forum Letter*, the commission ruled:

> 1) An action taken with the approval of one's immediate ecclesiastical supervisor is not liable to disciplinary action. 2) No person, member or board of the Missouri Synod may disrupt, hamper, or harass the president of the LCMS. 3) Members who abuse bylaws by bringing clearly unsupportable charges or complaints, give offense, and should be dealt with accordingly. 4) There is no constitutional provision for the LCMS president to be recused from—nor for anyone to assume—duties that are his alone.

These decisions were after the fact, and thus did not pre-empt the appeal already under consideration, so "in grand tragic style, it must play out to the appointed end." Ultimately Benke's appeal was successful, and in May 2003 he was reinstated. The Atlantic District proceeded to enthusiastically re-elect him to the position from which he had been suspended.[11]

As the episode came to an end, Saltzman opened the forum to a very different point of view in an essay by former contributing editor John Pless. The defenses offered for Benke's action, he wrote, "ring hollow with an empty sophistry that seeks a loophole where there are none. ... Emotive arguments have been used that subordinate faith to love. Any critical, theological engagement of unionism and syncretism are dismissed as 'unloving.'"[12]

Saltzman admitted that he found the Missouri Synod somewhat mystifying. "I look at the LCMS as an outsider trying to understand what's happening—not always with any success."

> Should anybody wonder, I would wish for a more moderate Missouri. The LCMS frequently *seems* much too heated, much too unloving, much too ready to jump on some poor guy. ... That's how it *seems*. But chatting with pastors on the ground, there's a different and far more cheerful picture that emerges, and it is one of genuine pride in their church even as they greet the day's troubles with a resigned, if not fond, sigh. Theology is the best indoor sport they know, and they play it with true relish and not a little dash. There's something to be said for that.[13]

Unrest in the ELCA

"This is our church too"

As events continued to unfold in the Evangelical Lutheran Church in America, many in the more traditionalist camp began to wonder if there was a future for them in the ELCA. This became a matter of regular discussion in the pages of *Forum Letter*. It began with an e-mail from one of Saltzman's seminary classmates. "Bob" had recently had a difficult conversation with a parishioner angry about the denomination's direction, and he now was wondering "how much longer I can stay in ... a church [the ELCA] which seems to have lost its moorings both theologically and ethically." "Is it now time," he asked, "to organize a confessing synod?"[14]

Saltzman recalled the question Leonard Klein had posed a year earlier as to whether the ELCA was "still church," and his own retort that it was never meant to be "church." He still thought that was correct, but now he was entertaining the question of whether the ELCA was indeed "confessional." "That question," he observed, "is open to increasing scrutiny." Clearly the LCMS doesn't think so, and "there is a lot of Missouri chat these days, some of it idle, some not, about safety nets for ELCA pastors who might want to bail out."

> On bad days I ... start checking the lines on my parachute. On good days I get so submerged in parish life I just don't have time to worry about any of it. On so-so days, I wonder if the LCMS is really prepared to engage the ecumenical implications of the Confessions. Some Missouri hardliners think confessional unity is getting the pope's signature on the *Augsburg Confession*. For others, even that wouldn't be sufficient.

But a confessing synod? "Sheer romance (though I'd probably join)." Similar movements in other denominations have been ineffective, and there is "no reason to suppose that an ELCA confessing synod would do any better." He couldn't recommend Missouri, at least not at present, nor any of the smaller Lutheran bodies, and "neither Rome nor Orthodoxy is a real choice for Lutherans, particularly for Lutheran pastors." So even though "I've toyed on and off over the years about leaving the ELCA," he admitted, "I think in the final resort I'll probably remain here."[15]

The exchange generated "more response in less time than we ever anticipated," Saltzman reported the next month. Some of the responses were from ELCA pastors "who felt Bob's pain" (though one "thought Bob was a crybaby and your editor verging to disloyalty"). But many were from people in the LCMS and other smaller Lutheran bodies, explaining why their group was the logical place for disgruntled ELCA pastors to land. Saltzman's response was thoughtful and pointed:

> Our subscribers include readers in all the U. S. Lutheran bodies so we're not really in a position to seek enlistees for a round of Lutheran wars, assuming for one moment we had any inclination in that direction. But we will wring our hands over anything that seems to be a departure from the confessional, catholic and ecumenical endeavors to which *Lutheran Forum* and *Forum Letter* have always been committed. If the majority of our complaints in this newsletter focus on the ELCA, it is possibly because ELCA subscribers comprise our largest audience and because it is the body to which the editor belongs. But there are ample targets among all the Lutheran church bodies.

Saltzman gave the last word to "a prominent Chicago pastor":

> The answer to Bob and others is that there is such a thing as a loyal opposition. ... Pastor Bob and his faithful member should have the attitude, 'This is our church too.' We're not going to leave the field just because some bullies came along and changed the rules. We will fight for our church until we are forcibly evicted.[16]

Two months later Saltzman reported that Pastors David Gustafson, Jennifer Ferrara, and Patricia Ireland—three "sometime contributors to *Lutheran Forum* and *Forum Letter*"—had recently "left for Rome." In truth, Saltzman acknowledged, evangelical catholicism *does* lead to Rome. "Properly speaking, Lutherans are Catholics in exile, an exile that must someday end and for which one must offer ardent prayers." But for now, he concluded, "there is still a need for the Lutheran movement" because there are still "theological questions that should not go begging. The greatest gift Roman Catholics and Lutherans can give each other is their careful theological constructions."[17]

Saltzman's reflections elicited substantive responses from former *Lutheran Forum* editor Leonard Klein, ALPB board member John Hannah, and LCMS theologian David Scaer. Scaer argued that the LCMS was a good alternative for disaffected ELCA pastors, noting that most of the objections often raised against Missouri (failure to ordain women, close[d] communion) were even bigger issues with both Rome and Orthodoxy. Hannah admitted that he had considered becoming Roman Catholic at a couple of times in his life, most recently when his wife made the decision to do so; he was committed to remaining Lutheran (in his case, in the LCMS) precisely because of his ecumenical commitment. Clergy who leave, he suggested, "end up in no position to advance Christian unity."[18]

But Klein was not convinced by Saltzman's arguments for staying. "What would be the point of being a loyal opposition in something that is not Church?" he asked. "The ELCA does not know whether it believes, teaches or confesses with the *una sancta*, and its constitutional teaching authority is not really the church." Klein saw only three viable options: Missouri, Rome, or Orthodoxy. The problem, he mused, "is not that a few bullies have pulled off a *Putsch* but that intrinsic weaknesses in our tradition have made this cultural captivity possible, perhaps inevitable. ... As far as I can see," he concluded, "there is only one legitimate reason for staying, and that is the pastoral care of these valid Christian assemblies of separated brethren."[19]

Ecumenical controversies

"a miserable failure"

The continued resistance from the Word Alone Network to *Called to Common Mission* was discussed extensively in the ALPB publications. In February 2000, a group of dissidents met in Milwaukee and drafted the "Common Ground Resolution." "We believe voting members of the 1999 Churchwide Assembly did not anticipate the depth and extent of opposition [to *CCM*'s provisions] that appears to exist," they said. In response, the ELCA bishops affirmed the churchwide assembly's adoption of the agreement but expressed a willingness to explore ways in which a synod bishop, "in unusual circumstances and with appropriate consultation," might authorize a candidate to be ordained by an ELCA pastor who was not a bishop. The ELCA church council that summer asked for proposed legislation that would do precisely that.[20]

The ALPB publications firmly opposed this approach. Michael Root, writing in *Forum Letter*, called it "a bad idea" which would serve only to do what *CCM* opponents want: "it keeps the pot boiling, it preserves the feeling that matters are still open for negotiation and decision." He urged the church council to reject the approach and demonstrate that "the ELCA is a church that is true to its word, a church that does not unilaterally alter ecumenical agreements, a church that can make a theological decision and stick to it."[21]

Russell Saltzman was still being criticized by some readers for having supported *CCM*. "Who got to Saltzman?" was the way one reader phrased it. Saltzman explained once again why he had opposed the original *Concordat*, and why he had come to support the revised *CCM*. He was still, he admitted, "frankly cautious about the linkage between the ELCA and the Episcopal Church. There is no one associated with the *Forum* publications who is not." Besides, readers should not expect "unbiased evaluations" from him. "This is a newsletter of opinion—mostly mine, but I hope not uninformed opinion—and, I guess you'd call it, interpretative news." Still, he noted that he had given generous space in *Forum Letter* for writers who did not agree with him.[22]

The provision for exceptions was indeed adopted by the 2001 churchwide assembly. Saltzman, however, now came to regret his endorsement of the agreement in the first place. In an essay entitled "Repenting of a good deed," he first reminded readers of the relationship between the ALPB and its publications:

> The ALPB did not endorse *CCM*. The ALPB board of directors is composed of both Evangelical Lutheran Church in America and Lutheran Church Missouri Synod members. For itself, the board has generally, if not obsessively, stayed away from decisions internal to the major Lutheran bodies. ... Those things are left to mouthy editors, like myself. The remarkable thing about working for the ALPB as a writer is the absolute freedom of expression the board has always granted to its editors. *Lutheran Forum*'s and *Forum Letter*'s endorsement of *CCM*, for the record, was not greeted with universal approval by all the individual board members, but they said so as individuals, not as board members.

So Saltzman took full responsibility for his earlier decision to endorse the ecumenical pact. But, he went on, "That was then. This is now." *CCM* was, as an ecumenical model for global Lutheranism and Anglicanism, "a miserable failure" which "must be laid at the feet of" the Episcopalians. The problem, he wrote, was the chaos left in the wake of the consecration of V. Gene Robinson, the openly gay and partnered bishop of New Hampshire. The internal controversy about this within the Episcopal Church and the outraged reaction within world Anglicanism has left the Episcopal Church "increasingly marginalized." The ELCA is now in communion with "an Episcopal province that is no longer in communion with half the Anglican community. It was a nice idea, but *CCM* should be rescinded."[23]

Lutheran Forum and *Forum Letter* also reacted to other ecumenical agreements. ALPB writers were generally enthusiastic about the Joint Declaration on the Doctrine of Justification, a significant statement of Lutherans and Roman Catholics globally. *Forum Letter* discussed the implications of the 2003 papal encyclical *Ecclesia de Eucharistia* and the 2005 Lutheran/Roman Catholic Dialogue statement, *The Church as Koinonia of Salvation: Its Structures and Ministries*. When Pope John Paul II died in 2005, *Forum Letter* devoted much of the next issue to that event, with appreciations of the late pontiff by Paul Hinlicky and Richard Johnson, as well as Saltzman's "A Lutheran to-do list for the next Pope." There were occasional comments about other ELCA ecumenical dialogues during this period, particularly with the United Methodist Church; on that one, ALPB writers were more cautious.[24]

ELCA politics

"the worst one we could have elected"

Forum Letter continued its lively coverage of the churchwide politics of the ELCA. When H. George Anderson announced that he did not wish to serve a second term as presiding bishop, Saltzman discussed the names he had been hearing. He divided them into three categories. First were the "symbolists," those who represented a certain highly-profiled politically symbolic position, such as gay/lesbian advocates and feminists. Then there were "congregationalists," most of them former ALC pastors from the upper Midwest, sympathetic to the concerns of Word Alone. Finally there were "confessionalists"—evangelical catholics, many of them former LCA. The terms, he admitted, "are very, very broadly employed."[25]

He then listed eight names. Two of them were "congregationalists"—Bp. Stanley N. Olson and *Lutheran Partners* columnist Pr. Steven McKinley. Only one was a straight "confessionalist," Bp. Donald McCoid (who had surprised Saltzman in 1995 by topping his poll when Saltzman hardly knew who he was). The "symbolists" were several: Bp. Andrea DeGroot-Nesdahl (a woman, but she also had a foot in the congregationalist camp), Bp. Mark Hanson and Bp. Peter Rogness (both strong supporters of "gay/lesbian inclusion"), and Dr. Kenneth Echols, president of Lutheran School of Theology at Chicago (an African American, but well-regarded by many in all three camps). The eighth person whose name Saltzman had heard, Pacific Lutheran Theological Seminary president Timothy Lull, Saltzman counted out because he would pass the "Sherman test" ("If nominated, I will not run; if elected, I will not serve").[26]

A few months later he added another "congregationalist" to the list: Luther Seminary professor James Nestingen. Saltzman had not included Nestingen because, while he had been a favorite of some six years previously when Anderson was elected, he had rather firmly put the kibosh on his own candidacy. Saltzman had learned, though, that Nestingen had been accepting some speaking engagements where he was being openly described as "a serious candidate being considered for election as the next presiding bishop."[27]

At the assembly in August, the first few ballots narrowed the contenders to three: Hanson, Nestingen, and McCoid, one representative of each of Saltzman's three groupings. Nestingen was eliminated after the fourth ballot—and what happened next was a surprise.

> In a pinch congregationalist votes will always shift to a confessionalist, at least that was the pattern six years ago. Though the ecclesiological differences are often profound, congregationalists and confessionalists both share a cultural affinity at odds with the easy liberalism of the symbolists. That's what happened in this election too. But not enough. Of Nestingen's 224 votes from the fourth ballot, 85 went to [fellow Minnesotan] Hanson on the final ballot, but only 137 went to McCoid. Regionalism trumped culture—the upper Midwest (Nestingen) vs. the East (McCoid), if you like—and probably contributed to McCoid's loss and Hanson's victory.

Saltzman suggested another factor as well, "probably a larger factor than many are willing to admit. The Big Screen." With proceedings projected on large screens in the massive assembly hall, most voting members could only see the images. "The Big Screen liked Hanson. He looked good and sounded good. He was easily articulate, frequently eloquent." McCoid, "unfortunately, looked like Arlen Specter, the Pennsylvania senator," and "the Big Screen treated his face with, shall we say, less than fulsome kindness." Hanson defeated McCoid on the final ballot by 34 votes.[28]

Saltzman wrote that there were "decidedly divided reviews about [Hanson's] future leadership and the direction in which he is likely to lead."

> Positively, said one bishop who knows Hanson well, 'We'll see something actually change because of Mark. When he talks about making mission a priority, he means it. We'll actually see some real evangelistic effort. He has very good "public presence," the best I've ever seen.' ... Or not. 'Of the three candidates,' according to a detractor, 'he was the worst one we could have elected. He talks a smooth piety, but it's really nothing more than his social agenda, and that's all to the left.'

With that mixed assessment, Saltzman wished Hanson well.[29]

Two years later, *Forum Letter* correspondent W. Stevens Shipman proclaimed that year's churchwide assembly "the Mark Hanson Show"—a comment more on Hanson's domination of the schedule than his admitted skills as a presider. Hanson had proposed a strategic plan for the ELCA, and he took significant time each morning as he "unpacked the components" of the plan.

> Rumor—well, more than rumor—has it that by Friday several bishops strongly advised him to get on with the business of the assembly. That got stuffed into Friday and Saturday, and by Saturday voting members were compelled to severely limit debate so things could get finished on time. ... Would the Council of Nicea have resolved the Trinitarian crisis if debate had been restricted to three two-minute speeches from each side?[30]

At the 2005 assembly, the ALPB added a new dimension: live blogging from the scene by *Forum Letter* associate editor Richard Johnson. Johnson posted in real time, also answering questions and responding to comments by those following on alpb.org. Similar coverage was provided for the next LCMS convention, and it became a significant and much appreciated source of information for those who could not be present at the actual event.

Liturgy and sacraments

"God's faithfulness trumps our faithfulness (or unfaithfulness)"

The ALPB's longstanding interest in sacramental theology and practice continued to be expressed in its publications. There was, for instance, extensive discussion about who should be admitted to the Eucharist. Both the LCMS and the ELCA debated this question, though from quite different perspectives.

ALPB writers continued to question the LCMS policy of close[d] communion. Writing in *Forum Letter*, Pr. William Mugnolo cited a recent study indicating that "the majority of Lutherans, contrary to their church's most important article of faith, believe that salvation can be earned by a person's good works." Their survey showed that members of the Assemblies of God were much more likely to affirm "justification by faith through grace." For Mugnolo, this raised a difficult problem. Missouri admits only confirmed members of LCMS congregations to the Sacrament, but "who in fact would prove the most worthy communicant?"—a member of the Assemblies of God who "may not believe in the Real Presence but understands justification by grace," or a Missourian who affirms the Real Presence but denies justification? The LCMS, he wrote, "seems intent upon picking out the doctrinal specks from others' eyes while ignoring the logs in its own."[31]

In *Lutheran Forum*, David L. Pearcy reviewed the LCMS's Commission on Theology and Church Relations document "Admission to the Lord's Supper" and found it wanting. Analyzing 1 Corinthians 11.28-29, a text often used to justify close[d] communion, he argued that Paul's primary concern was to exclude from the Eucharist those whose lives did not reflect their Christian faith. This is quite different from denying the Eucharist to someone from a different church body. "We need to be terribly and fearfully careful in our efforts to be the Church of God," he counseled, "when in the name of love, we refuse the feeding of God's children."[32]

In the same issue, John Hannah's guest editorial drew a connection between Missouri's "zeal for 'close[d] communion'" and her reluctance to embrace the weekly Eucharist, that longstanding ALPB concern. Enforcing the practice is so cumbersome (the "prominent announcements declaring non-invitation," the "dutifully somber ushers, reminiscent of nightclub bouncers") that "any proposal to multiply the number of occasions for such a painful ordeal is met with opposition." He also argued that the concept of closing the Sacrament is more a Reformed than a Lutheran concept, one which does violence to Lutheran theology because it emphasizes our faithfulness rather than God's. "God's faithfulness trumps our faithfulness (or unfaithfulness) every time," he insisted. "That truth is vital to Lutheran integrity."[33]

In the ELCA, an early straw in the wind for what would become a decade later an increasingly insistent demand for a completely open invitation to the Eucharist (extended even to the unbaptized) was an article in the *Lutheran* by Pr. Olin K. Sletto. "If God's love is truly inclusive," Sletto wrote, "why would we exclude someone [not baptized] who wants to come and taste and smell God's love in the bread and wine?" Russ Saltzman was indignant. "Under the lash of Pr. Sletto's rapier-like logic," he responded, "those pastors who still give priority to baptism are committing exclusivism and un-niceness, which are grave, grave sins and for which all should swiftly repent." "Theological acuity of this sort wouldn't fill a paper sandwich bag," he huffed, "nor fight its way out of a wet one if it had to combat 'sin, death and the devil.'" "What is not tragic, but comic," he added, "is *The Lutheran* thinking, first, that Pr. Sletto's piece was worth publishing and, second, that folks are agreeable to continuing a yearly subscription at $15.95 so they can read more like it."[34]

Resuming the book ministry

"truly a landmark publication"

After the challenges presented by the Tobias, Pfatteicher and Bouman books, the ALPB board was understandably shy about taking on new book projects. In the early years of the new millennium, there was little discussion in the board meetings about book publishing. The book committee apparently dissolved, though Fred Schumacher reported that manuscripts were being received and reviewed. Finally a proposal came that caught the fancy of the board: a new edition of Berthold von Schenk's *The Presence: An Approach to the Holy Communion.* Von Schenk had served for many years as pastor of Our Saviour Lutheran Church & School in the Bronx, and he had been a leader in the liturgical movement in the LCMS. He had served on the ALPB board back in the 1930s, and he had been instrumental in the resurrection of the journal *Una Sancta* in the 1950s. *The Presence* was a profound reflection on the Eucharist, long popular with Lutherans who hoped to recover the centrality of the Sacrament in Lutheran worship; it had been first published in 1945, but had been out of print for some time, and there was enthusiasm about the possibility of making the book available again. Glenn Stone agreed to edit the text and write an introduction for the new edition, but by the time of his death in 2009, the project had not been completed.

Meanwhile, von Schenk's autobiography, *Lively Stone,* also came to the board for possible publication. Von Schenk wrote the manuscript during the last years of his life, years in which he was struggling increasingly with dementia. The book had an autobiographical structure, though it often departed from a chronological account to offer von Schenk's opinions and philosophy about the concerns that had enlivened his life and ministry. The manuscript had been given some "smoothing out" by Pr. Charles Evanson, and was then sent to Concordia Historical Institute shortly before von Schenk's death in 1974. There it sat until C. George Fry and Joel R. Kurz discovered it and decided to edit it for publication. They approached the ALPB about the possibility of publishing the work.[35]

The board discussed the proposal at length in January 2005. Schumacher suggested the book would be a good companion piece to *The Presence,* which was still in the editing process. Some believed, however, that the manuscript needed more work, both in its annotations and in toning down some of von Schenk's harshly candid comments about his contemporaries. The board voted to publish the book on the condition that

Fry and Kurz allow additional editing. This was accepted, and Paul Sauer, a new ALPB board member and the current pastor of von Schenk's former congregation in the Bronx, took on the task. Sauer gave a tantalizing preview in June when he was the keynote speaker at the ALPB Board of Directors Dinner (a new incarnation of the former Inter-Lutheran Forum events). His presentation, "Berthold von Schenk: Pioneer and Paradox," was published in *Lutheran Forum* that fall, and *Lively Stone* was released a few months later. *The Presence*, on the other hand, continued to languish. After Stone's death, the board asked Sauer to complete Stone's work and to write an introduction. The new edition was finally published in 2010—some nine years after the project had been approved by the ALPB board.[36]

A rather different manuscript proposal was presented to the board by Glenn Stone in February 2003. That year marked the tercentenary of the ordination of Justus Falckner—the first Lutheran ordination in North America. Falckner, a German, was ordained in 1703 at Gloria Dei Church, the Swedish Lutheran congregation in Philadelphia, under the auspices of the Church of Sweden. Despite his historical significance, Falckner was not well known. Stone contacted George Handley, president of the Lutheran Archives Center at Philadelphia, and Kim-Eric Williams, a Lutheran clergyman who directed the Swedish program at the University of Pennsylvania, wondering if there were plans for a biography of Falckner—either a new work, or a republication of Delbar Clark's 1946 *The World of Justus Falckner*. Williams believed that there had been considerable new research since Clark's book was written which made its reissuing problematic. He was planning to study that summer in Sweden where he would have access to Swedish archives, and he volunteered to write a new biography of Falckner.

Stone proposed that the Bureau publish the biography, which he would edit, in cooperation with the Lutheran Archives Center. The ALPB would market the book for one year; if at the end of that time the sales had not fully covered the publication cost, the Archives Center would reimburse the Bureau for the balance. Any remaining copies of the book after that year would be turned over to the Archives Center, which would handle future sales. The ALPB board agreed to this plan, and the book was published later that year as *The Journey of Justus Falckner*. H. George Anderson, who had a distinguished career as a church historian prior to his election as presiding bishop of the ELCA, wrote the forward for the book—truly, he wrote, "a landmark publication." Anderson's judgment was confirmed when Kim-Eric Williams was awarded the Lutheran Historical Society of the Mid-Atlantic's Biglerville Prize for 2004, an honor given for a work of mature scholarship in the field of American Lutheran history.[37]

An additional Falckner volume was also published that year, a translation of the catechism he had written in 1708. Written in Dutch, it was the first Lutheran theological book of any kind published in the New World. The Bureau agreed to publish the translation by Martin Kessler as a companion volume to the biography;

Fundamental Instruction: Justus Falckner's Catechism was released a few months after Williams's biography.[38]

Still another offering during this period was Eric Gritsch's *A Handbook for Christian Life in the 21ˢᵗ Century*. Gritsch was the distinguished emeritus professor of church history at Gettysburg Lutheran Seminary, but this book was written for lay Christians. Advertised as an appropriate text for an adult study group, it was intended as a modern catechism, with chapters on evil, justice, Baptism, church, Lord's Supper, prayer and music—each with accompanying questions for discussion. Gritsch was widely known in Lutheran circles, and he himself very actively promoted the book. The board was informed just months after publication that "the Gritsch book has become more quickly profitable than any other book we have published." It would be one of the Bureau's best sellers.[39]

Personal journalism

"... and even, please God, cranky journalists"

Russell Saltzman often described the genre of *Forum Letter* as "personal journalism," and in addition to commentary on major issues in American Lutheranism, he occasionally wrote very personal essays. Sometimes he poked fun at himself as a pastor. A classic example was "Bowser's Wedding," where Saltzman told of a marriage liturgy in his church that featured a dog as ring bearer, complete with a doggie tuxedo. He used the incident to reflect on the cultural captivity of weddings, and the failure, even by active church members, to understand that the marriage rite is the church's liturgy. But he was clearly embarrassed. "As for ordained simpering wimps like me," he concluded, "well, if there isn't a purgatory where Lutheran pastors may expiate their sins, there ought to be."[40]

He took a good bit of ribbing, and for months—even years—afterward, readers sent him stories of dogs and weddings, dogs and funerals, dogs and church. When Martin Marty made a comment in his *Christian Century* column about dogs as ring bearers, Saltzman figured he was being targeted.

> He's talking to me, right? He read my story about Bowser and couldn't resist a little dig, huh? He's probably still upset I called him a liberal with a bow tie. I meant it affectionately; I like bow ties. But he puts 'dog' and 'wedding' and 'ring-bearer' in the same sentence, what am I supposed to think? ... Maybe he didn't have me explicitly in mind. But you can understand why I am understandably sensitive about this.

At least, he conceded, it proved that Marty read *Forum Letter*.[41]

Sometimes Saltzman offered tales from his own life that were deeply moving. In an essay entitled "Fear of Abandonment," he told the story of his adoption. While expressing deep devotion to his adoptive parents, he wrote of his gradually growing need to know more about his birth parents. He had constructed in his own mind a romantic fantasy based on little bits of information he had heard: "pretty girl, lonely soldier, failed romance, doomed love." But then he learned something unexpected and unwelcome: his birth mother's pregnancy was the result of step-sibling incest. He admitted that he found some strange comfort in this knowledge, for now he understood "why my mother could not keep me, would not keep me. ... I was not abandoned to adoption. I was rescued by it." But there was also a starker realization: "Today, not even my own church, the Evangelical Lutheran Church in America, is able to flatly say that unborn babies like me should live."

> No woman has an absolute right to abortion, so my church says in its social statement on abortion. But it goes on, conversely, to say that no fetus has an absolute right to birth. The woman decides—after of course appropriate moral reflection with sympathetic listeners, but she decides. Pregnancies created in circumstances such as those of [my birth parents] in 1947 are in 1998 now fair targets for 'morally responsible' abortions, according to my church. ... When it comes to my birth the church that values my baptism is ambivalent at best about my right to life in the womb.
>
> Abortion is personal to me, as personal as my adoption. It is personal not only to the woman who aborts, but to me; to me, to the unborn children like me, it is personal. It is our person that is in jeopardy.[42]

Another time he wrote about the baptism of his son, a refugee from Vietnam whom he and his wife adopted as a teenager, and he used that as a context to give an account of his own coming to faith. He told about the death of his best friend when they were teenagers, and his resultant anger—"not at God, for he did not exist. Yet, somehow still at God because he was not." He explained how his wife had "nagged me to church," which he insisted must be Lutheran. "It seemed to me that if I were going to deny the presence of the Lord in the Eucharist, I should attend a church where there was a doctrine of the Real Presence to deny." He admitted that a primary reason he had for going to church was that he wanted to run for the state legislature, and he thought it would look good on his résumé. He wrote about his reluctant and convoluted journey to the moment when he was "surprised to find myself a believer," and then the even more surprising call to pastoral ministry. It was all, he confessed, "an absurd mercy."[43]

Still another personal piece that touched many hearts was Saltzman's reflection on his youngest daughter Hattie turning four. It bothered him. He had lived with a whole succession of three-year-olds, and now that seemed about to end. He figured that, based on the government cost of raising a child, he was spending $24.37 a day on her. Yet three "is the year you get to finger-paint, carve pumpkins, color Easter eggs, play hide-and-seek, and maybe catch some lightning bugs." Or you'll "hear her theological speculations about the Holy Trinity, which are considerably more convoluted than anything taught at seminary and, by several orders of magnitude, definitely more inventive."

When she's three you possess encyclopedic knowledge and can answer all questions that begin with 'Why?' You will ponder the mysteriously magnetic effect of puddles when she's three, and discover anew the wonder of rocks, the rising of the moon, the remarkable curve and angle of an ordinary stick. When she's three and the tab is running at $24.37 a day, love her without limit, charge it to Visa, and never once count the cost.[44]

Saltzman's personal reflections were thoughtful and winsome, but there continued to be some who thought that *Forum Letter* was a tad negative. As volume thirty-one came to a close, the editor asked Martin Marty (who did indeed read the newsletter) "to say anything he might like" about *Forum Letter*. Marty suggested that Saltzman's view, at least of the ELCA, was too often "glass half empty" instead of "glass half full." "I wish *Forum Letter* would now and then turn its attention to the thousands of earnest, sincere, struggling, hopeful, frail congregations and their leaders, and tell their stories, and give them encouragement."

> [Prophecy] comes with good grace only if the prophet is above the fray and has no investment in elements of the status quo—and criticism is most effective and listened to when it is born of love-hate relations that have more love than hate. ... We do not need puff pieces, glossings over. We simply would welcome a bit more sympathy for the front line people who have very difficult jobs, and who never get strokes. (This includes most local pastors.)

In short, Marty said, "be who you are and keep doing what you do, but with a bit more evidence of love for the church in its weakness and frailty."[45]

Glenn Stone responded to Marty, agreeing "with much of his analysis" and yet insisting that often "the empirical Church falls short of its God-given nature and task," and someone needs to call it back.

> [We] need prophets (and reformers, and even, please God, cranky journalists), who themselves fall short of their calling, to call us to renewal. Issues of 'half full/half empty' or whether you attract more flies with honey or vinegar are certainly subject to debate. Overall the Church needs to hear from both perspectives. After all, God sent both an Amos and a Hosea to ancient Israel.

> The ELCA has access to many publications, official and unofficial. Some of them, mainly the official ones with substantial subsidies and sizable circulations, seem to specialize in encouragement, maybe at times 'puff pieces, glossings over.' That leaves the other side to venues like the *Forum Letter*.

He added that "one of the great strengths of *Lutheran Forum/Forum Letter* and its predecessor *The American Lutheran* over the past 86 years is that for most of that period the editors have been parish pastors, as they are today." They are in fact on the front lines, and it is "out of the manifest life of the Body of Christ that our 'critical solidarity' with the Church arises."[46]

Farewells

"I am proud of having been associated with ALPB"

In any organization that lasts for many decades, there is a lot of turnover in personnel. People die, they move away, they retire, they lose interest or simply cut back their involvement. During the first half of the decade of the 2000s, the ALPB seemed to suffer too many losses for all those reasons and more. The first blow came in the summer of 2002, when Theodore Wittrock died. Wittrock had been closely involved with the Bureau for over fifty years—more than half of its existence. He had become executive secretary in 1948; when he left that position in 1969 for parish ministry, he immediately agreed to serve on the Bureau's board of directors and was still serving at the time of his death. Glenn Stone wrote a tribute to Wittrock for *Lutheran Forum*:

> Surely it was the warmth of his personality, his enthusiasm, his ability to come up with new ideas and his dedication to carrying them out that caught the attention of the American Lutheran Publicity Bureau and became in turn the source of his many contributions to its development. On this page, we may perhaps be pardoned for believing that his most enduring contribution was the dream (and its realization) of an inter-Lutheran publication of ideas and their interchange, begun in 1967 and called LUTHERAN FORUM.

Stone recalled the words he had spoken when the ALPB had honored Wittrock at one of the Inter-Lutheran Forum dinners: "When we think of the American Lutheran Publicity Bureau and LUTHERAN FORUM, we know that Ted Wittrock is part of the 'rock' from which we were hewn."[47]

ALPB leaders were taken by surprise in 2003 when Leonard Klein, who had edited *Lutheran Forum* for several years, written often for *Forum Letter*, and then served on the board of directors, announced that he was resigning—not just from the board, but from the ministry of the ELCA. Klein's disenchantment with Lutheranism had been growing for many years. He and his wife, historian Christa Ressmeyer Klein, were received into the Roman Catholic Church shortly thereafter; three years later he was ordained a Roman Catholic priest. A similar step was taken in 2006 by Phillip Max Johnson, a board member since 1993 and editorial associate of *Lutheran Forum* since 1996. In his letter of resignation, he told the board, "I am proud of having been associated with ALPB. I continue to regard it as a vital work, not only for Lutherans, but also within the ecumenical struggle for faithfulness to Christ." These departures led executive director Schumacher to ask that the board spend some time discussing "how the continuing exodus to the Roman Catholic Church by Pastors affiliated with the ALPB might affect our readership."[48]

Another significant farewell came in 2005 when Hans Quitmeyer, who had served on the board since 1985 and had been president since 1989, was transferred by his company to Minneapolis. Quitmeyer had brought much needed continuity to the board after a series of short-term presidents. John Hannah, who would succeed Quitmeyer as president, expressed the feelings of many on the board: "You presided with great distinction and have left an exemplary institution molded by your leadership. I always admired your gentleness and your determination in meeting all the ALPB challenges." The board named him "President Emeritus"—the first former president to be so honored. They did so, Hannah told Quitmeyer, because of their "overwhelming sense of your long term contribution in stabilizing the ALPB and setting us on a course that allows us to contribute to the Church for a long time to come."[49]

Notes

1. Executive Director's Report, 26 June 1999, ALPB Archives.
2. *FL*, 31, no. 1 (Jan. 2002), 8.
3. Minutes, ALPB Board of Directors, 20 Jan. 2002; Report of Sales, 25 Jan. 2004, ALPB Archives.
4. Report of the Tract Committee to ALPB Board of Directors, 3 June 2000, ALPB Archives.
5. John Hannah, "Missouri's Millennium: The LCMS in Convention," *FL* 30, no. 9 (Sept. 2001), 2-4.
6. *FL* 30, no. 12 (Dec. 2001), 2.
7. David H. Benke, "The Scandal Is in the Specifics," *LF* 33, no. 2 (Summer 1999), 39-43.
8. *FL* 30, no. 12 (Dec. 2001), 3.
9. *FL* 31, no. 8 (Aug. 2002), 2.
10. *FL* 31, no. 9 (Sept. 2002), 2-3.
11. John Hannah, "The Never-ending Story: The LCMS and Benke," *FL* 32, no. 4 (Apr. 2003), 6-7.
12. John T. Pless, "The LCMS after Yankee Stadium: An Assessment," *FL* 32, no. 5 (May 2003), 7-8.
13. *FL* 32, no. 10 (Oct. 2003), 8.
14. *FL* 27, no. 2 (Feb. 1998), 2.
15. Ibid., 3.
16. *FL* 27, no. 3 (Mar. 1998), 4-6.
17. *FL* 27, no. 5 (May 1998), 4-6.
18. *FL* 27, no. 7 (July 1998), 3-4.
19. Ibid., 2-3.
20. Edgar R. Trexler, *High Expectations: Understanding the ELCA's Early Years, 1988-2002* (Minneapolis: Augsburg Fortress, 2003), 145; ELCA News Service, "ELCA Bishops Adopt Pastoral letter on 'Called to Common Mission,'" 9 Mar. 2000, elca.org <www.elca.org/News-and-Events/3806> (accessed 13 July 2016).
21. Michael Root, "A Bad Idea: Planned Exceptions to *CCM*," *FL* 29, no. 10 (Oct. 2000), 4-5.
22. *FL* 30, no. 2 (Feb. 2001), 5.
23. *FL* 33, no. 3 (Mar. 2004), 2-3.
24. *FL* 33, no. 3 (Mar. 2004), 1-3; *FL* 34, no. 1 (Jan. 2005), 1-3; *FL* 34, no. 5 (May 2005), 1-5; *FL* 32, no. 7 (Jul. 2003), 4-6.
25. *FL* 29, no. 12 (Dec. 2000), 4.
26. Ibid., 4-5.
27. *FL* 30, no. 4 (Apr. 2001), 2.
28. *FL* 30, no. 10 (Oct. 2001), 2-3.
29. Ibid., 5.
30. *FL* 32, no. 10 (Oct. 2003), 1.
31. William F. Mugnolo, "How Do We Get to the Lord's Supper?" *FL* 29, no. 11 (Nov. 2000), 8.
32. David L. Pearcy, "CTCR's *Admission to the Lord's Supper* and Paul's First Letter to the Corinthians," *LF* 25, no. 1 (Spring 2001), 25.
33. John R. Hannah, "The LCMS Unionism Scare and the Restoration of the Weekly Eucharist," *LF* 25, no. 1 (Spring 2001), 8.

34. *FL* 34, no. 4 (Apr. 2005), 1-3.

35. C. George Fry and Joel R. Kurz, "Acknowledgements" and "Editorial Notes on Text" in Berthold von Schenk, *Lively Stone: The Autobiography of Berthold von Schenk* (Delhi, NY: ALPB Books, 2006), 7, 11.

36. Paul Sauer, "Berthold von Schenk: Pioneer and Paradox," *LF* 39:3 (Fall 2005), 25-30; Berthold von Schenk, *Lively Stone: The Autobiography of Berthold von Schenk* (Delhi, NY: ALPB Books), 2006; Berthold von Schenk, *The Presence: An Approach to the Holy Communion* (Delhi, NY: ALPB Books, 2010).

37. Minutes, ALPB Board of Directors, 3 Feb. 2003; H. George Anderson, "Forward," in Kim-Eric Williams, *The Journey of Justus Falckner* (Delhi, NY: ALPB Books and Lutheran Archives Center at Philadelphia, 2003), 5.

38. Justus Falckner, *Fundamental Instruction: Justus Falckner's Catechism: The First Lutheran Catechism Written and Published in North America A. D. 1708* (Delhi, NY: ALPB Books, 2003).

39. Eric W. Gritsch, *A Handbook for Christian Life in the 21st Century* (Delhi, NY: ALPB Books, 2005).

40. *FL* 29, no. 10 (Oct. 2000), 3.

41. *FL* 30, no. 5 (May 2001), 8.

42. *FL* 27, no. 5 (May 1998), 1-4.

43. *FL* 30, no. 3 (Mar. 2001), 1-5.

44. *FL* 30, no. 7 (July 2001), 6-7.

45. Martin E. Marty, "*Forum Letter* and the Half-Empty Vision of the ELCA," *FL* 31, no 11 (Nov. 2002), 4-5.

46. Glenn C. Stone, "Response to Marty," *FL* 31, no. 11 (Nov. 2002), 5-7.

47. Glenn C. Stone, "In Memoriam: Theodore Wittrock (1920-2002)," *LF* 36, no. 3 (Fall 2002), 8-9.

48. Phillip Max Johnson to John R. Hannah and Frederick J. Schumacher, 25 July 2006, ALPB Archives; Minutes, ALPB Board of Directors, 23 Sept. 2006.

49. John Hannah, e-mail message to Hans Quitmeyer, 24 Oct. 2005, ALPB Archives.

Chapter 24

_____

DEBATING SEXUALITY

O f the many conflicts confronting Lutheranism at the turn of the millennium, none was as contentious and volatile as the debate over human sexuality. The controversy primarily affected the Evangelical Lutheran Church in America; the doctrinal conservatism of the Missouri Synod largely insulated it from attempts to change traditional Christian doctrine in this area. The ALPB sought to offer resources that addressed the deeper theological issues beyond simply the ELCA political fight, but the Bureau's publications also commented frequently on the specific battles in the ELCA—so much so that some Missouri Synod readers "expressed weariness with the apparent ALPB emphasis on the issues related to human sexuality."[1]

The church and sexuality
"Purity of heart, chastity of mind and body"

Controversy about human sexuality—particularly homosexuality—had swirled around the ELCA from its inception. In 1996, the ALPB decided to use a well-tested medium to address the issue in a positive way by producing a series of tracts on human sexuality and family life. This was not the first time the Bureau had addressed this topic in a tract. Early in the "sexual revolution," about 1965, it had published "A Christian View of Sex." "The subject of sex is often considered too hot to handle," the tract had begun. "It makes us all feel a little uneasy and, therefore, most people are unable to speak about it." It had outlined a decidedly traditional and theologically conservative view. Sex is a good gift of God, the writer suggested, and yet "the devil and sin have touched sex and, therefore, it may become unclean." The gift must be used as God intended. "If a person eats like a pig by leaning all over the table and slopping his foods he may hurt the appetites of people around him." In the same way, sex must be "used according to God's rules of decency, lest the misuse of it offend God ... and vulgarize something that is good." The proper context for sex is marriage, the writer concluded, and "we are to enter married life as virgins and in married life to remain faithful and loyal. ...We must set our brakes according to God's laws and ask Him for help to do so and for forgiveness when we don't."[2]

While that may have been a daring approach in 1965, it clearly would not do thirty years later. The new series continued to uphold traditional Christian teachings, but in language that might gain a hearing at the end of the century. The first five tracts were published in May 1998, all of them written by ALPB board member Phillip Max Johnson. These tracts laid a foundation for understanding sexuality from a Christian perspective. "You, Your Body, Your God" was addressed to "Christian young people and other Christians who face hard decisions about sex." It took its cue from 1 Corinthians 6.19: "Do you not know that your body is a temple of the Holy Spirit within you, which you have from God, and that you are not your own?" It is, Johnson wrote, "a remarkable claim." The Christian's body "is not simply a chemical collection of appetites and need" nor a "physical shell for your inner spiritual self." "Your body is also you!"[3]

The tract then summarized the traditional Christian doctrine of sexuality and marriage: "In the Christian vision of life *sexual intercourse is a gift of God to be received only by those who are married.* Ideally, all explicitly sexual activity is meant to lead to and flow from marriage." Johnson admitted that this ethic "is demanding. It involves self-discipline and even self-sacrifice. We must not be afraid to say this clearly and face this in our own lives."

> There are many men and women who suffer under this sexual ethic: those who are single by choice or circumstance, those who long to marry or have given up on marriage, those whose drives are predominantly homosexual, a married woman separated from her husband, a man whose wife is seriously ill for years and cannot share sexually. In every generation there are thousands of such persons in the Church. In humility and courage, they offer their loneliness to God and seek his strength to remain obedient. Their suffering is only increased when other Christians give way to the culture of permissiveness—offering the excuses and self-justifications that are not hard to come by.

Every Christian, he concluded, fails "in the struggle to trust and obey God." But "believing in God's forgiveness, we can have the humility to confess our sins rather than try to redefine morals to conform to our failures."

> Purity of heart, chastity of mind and body: these are expressions you may not have heard very much. Yet these quiet and heroic virtues are embodied in hidden saints all around you. It will not be hard for you to find excuses for abandoning the Christian struggle for purity. But by the strength of the Holy Spirit in you, renewed every day by God's forgiveness, you may find the happiness hidden in a Christian's free obedience to God.[4]

These themes were elaborated in the next tract, "Spiritually Safe Sex." The ethic "toward which the Bible points us," Johnson wrote, is an "either/or": "*Either* you marry, striving to live faithfully with your partner for the rest of your life, *or* you refrain from sexual intimacy with others." Adultery, fornication, homosexual acts, lust, pornography, sexual violence—these are "spiritually and morally unsafe" for the Christian.[5]

The remaining three tracts in this first series focused on marriage and parenthood. "What Does Your Marriage Mean?" was addressed to couples, inviting them to reflect on Paul's use of marriage as an image of Christ and the church. "The Love That Can Be Promised" was more explicitly intended for couples preparing for marriage; it discussed the nature of marital love—a love defined and shaped by the vows exchanged in the wedding service. "Both Parents and Priests" spoke of the vocation of parenthood, and offered some practical advice as to how parents might fulfill the promises made when a child is baptized.[6]

The second half of the series was published two years later; these tracts tackled more controversial topics. Rebecca Frey wrote two of the new tracts. "When Home Is Where the Hurt Is" spoke to "those who are living in violent households, or concerned about someone who is living with violence." "When 'Love' Hurts" focused on sexual abuse. The tract explained that such abuse can take many forms—some which "may seem less serious than others, but none of them ... harmless." It reminded readers that "no act of violence can rob you of your new life in Jesus Christ. ... Remember *who* you are and *whose* you are: *Child of God, sealed by the Holy Spirit and marked with the cross of Christ forever.*"[7]

The other three tracts, written by Phillip Max Johnson, addressed abortion and homosexuality. "When New Life Is an Unwelcome Gift" began by citing Psalm 139: "It was you who formed my inward parts; you knit me together in my mother's womb." After acknowledging some of the reasons women may seek abortions, the tract stated forthrightly that "the Christian Church through history has taught that the taking of human life, even in its very early form," is a violation of the fifth commandment. Johnson acknowledged that in some rare circumstances, "Christians may consider an abortion a tragic necessity in order to preserve the mother's life." Such cases, however, are rare; generally, "faithful living means protecting and honoring the unborn life." He also reassured women who might be struggling with guilt from a past abortion that "God does not abandon or refuse to forgive those who seek him."[8]

The final two tracts in the series discussed homosexuality. In "Is This the Way God Made Me?" Johnson admitted that we simply do not know much about whether sexual attraction is genetic or environmental. But even if a genetic basis for same-sex attraction could be established, *"what would this mean for moral decisions about behavior?"* He rejected the argument that one should simply follow one's "natural sexual desires," some of which are "considered by Christians to be morally dangerous or sinful." Christians, the tract insisted, will "struggle to obey," even when it seems impossible. "Then we begin to find that the Word bears within it hidden joys and new freedoms." It promises that "anything given up for God, even the most cherished 'pieces' of our selves, will get mysteriously returned, healed, and purified for life eternal."[9]

The final tract posed a fundamental question: "Can Homosexual Love Be Blessed?" Johnson outlined the Biblical and theological reasons that Christian churches have traditionally "taught that homosexual love is a violation of the will of God" and listed factors that brought about "a drastic rethinking of sexual morality." "Is resistance to these winds of change an example of a reactionary, self-serving Christian majority digging in its heels against the spread of greater justice and freedom?" he asked. He considered several of these factors, arguing that each is faulty from the Christian perspective and that *"these* winds of change are not the breath of God's Holy Spirit." "A Christian cannot think it compassionate," he mused, "to encourage others in ways of life that violate the law of God." God offers all Christians, including homosexuals, the grace of his forgiveness—"the blessing of freedom in the struggle to deny ourselves, take up our cross, and follow Jesus in the way of life-changing obedience."[10]

The tracts were an admirable attempt to provide a pastoral and theologically serious resource for Christians struggling with issues of sexuality and family life, but they were not as successful as the Bureau had hoped. By mid-2011, some 243 packets of the first series were sold (each packet containing 100 of each of the five tracts), and about 167 packets of the second series. Thousands more individual tracts were distributed. The best seller was the uncontroversial tract on preparing for a child's baptism; nearly 8,000 had been ordered, in addition to the 24,300 distributed in the series packets. These numbers should not be discounted; after all, the tracts potentially got into the hands of thousands of readers. Still, sales were far below those of the Lutheran Identity series being marketed during the same period (orders for which reached some 688 packets, with the top seller in that series, "Invitation to Lutheran Worship," generating orders for an additional 52,390 individual tracts).[11]

Four years after the second series had been published, Connie Seddon, chair of the Bureau's Tract Committee, reflected on the disparity of sales between the two series. "It is difficult to gauge ahead of time what the popularity of a particular series of tracts might be," she observed. Though the Christian Sexual Morality series had not sold as well as hoped, responses from both pastors and laity suggested "there is great appreciation for the quality of the work the ALPB has been providing."

> The tracts themselves might be considered educational brochures rather than typical tracts, and for this reason are more likely to be used in small group settings than placed in tract racks of local congregations. Perhaps this means that any tracts printed in the future should be printed in smaller quantities.

The sexuality essays had indeed been considerably meatier than one might expect in a tract. But there may have been other reasons for the disappointing sales. Perhaps some ALPB patrons simply did not agree with the traditional sexual morality articulated in the series; perhaps some pastors were unwilling to display tracts with such controversial content. The bigger issue was likely that in a period when rapid changes were occurring in media and communications, the utility of written tracts was quickly declining.[12]

Conference on Christian Sexuality

"a vigorous apologetic for the Christian sexual ethic"

Another ALPB venue for addressing these issues was a conference on sexuality held in October 2002. The conference was the idea of *Forum Letter* editor Russell Saltzman, who organized the event and hosted it at his parish, Ruskin Heights Lutheran Church in Kansas City, MO. Ever since the 2001 churchwide assembly, Saltzman had been thinking about a free theological conference upholding the traditional Christian view of sexuality as a constructive contribution to the conversation that the ELCA seemed determined to continue.[13]

He presented his idea to the ALPB board in January 2002, and they agreed to underwrite the expenses of the conference. In the March 2002 *Forum Letter*, Saltzman outlined a long list of questions he hoped the "ALPB Conference on Christian Sexuality" would tackle—theological, political, ethical, ecclesiological, disciplinary. He made it clear that he had no intention of providing a "'balanced' series of presentations." The conference would rather "serve as a platform for the theological critique of gay theology." Gay advocates, he noted, "have had ample opportunity and doubtless will have many future occasions to make their case."[14]

Saltzman announced a preliminary list of speakers which included several prominent pastors and laity (mostly in the ELCA), as well as some less familiar names. He later added Robert Gagnon, a Presbyterian New Testament professor at Pittsburgh Theological Seminary. Abingdon Press had recently published his *The Bible and Homosexual Practice: Texts and Hermeneutics*, a staunch defense of the traditional Biblical interpretations; Saltzman had read it and was impressed, so he promptly asked Gagnon to be the keynote speaker.

Meanwhile, planning for the event took an interesting turn when a brouhaha at Trinity Lutheran Seminary came to Saltzman's attention. The seminary had sponsored a "Day of Prayer and Reflection" about homosexuality, primarily organized by Walter Bouman—longtime friend of ALPB and a former contributing editor of *Lutheran Forum*. Bouman had enlisted Robert Gagnon as one of the speakers, but his presentations at Trinity had outraged pro-gay sympathizers; two days after the event Bouman wrote a nine-page reflection on how he had decided to invite Gagnon and how much he regretted his "complicity in bringing [Gagnon]" to the event. Gagnon, Bouman fumed, turned out to be a "fanatical man," a "manipulator" with "desparate [*sic*] psychological needs." This reflection was widely distributed, and it fell into Saltzman's hands; he promptly forwarded a copy to Gagnon.[15]

Gagnon then wrote an extensive reply to Bouman, responding to each of the points in what he described as Bouman's "hateful and intolerant analysis of the day's proceedings and a slanderous personal attack on me." The report in *Forum Letter* on the Trinity Seminary event, published over the names of both Russ Saltzman and Richard Johnson, admitted that the editors "were not present at the event, so we cannot judge what may have been said there. From the tone and content of these two accounts, however, we have to say that Gagnon comes off looking considerably better than Bouman." The article resulted in Bouman writing both to Saltzman and to executive director Fred Schumacher, acknowledging the "public rebuke," admitting that some of his evaluation of the event had contained "inappropriate material," and reporting that he had apologized both to the seminary president and to his bishop (though apparently not to Gagnon) for "any embarrassment or damage that may have been done." He insisted, however, that he had been seriously misinterpreted, and argued that much of the *Forum Letter* article was simply incorrect.[16]

Saltzman and Johnson responded to Bouman in the October issue, right on the eve of the ALPB conference. Bouman's reference to the original article as a "public rebuke," they wrote, was "a characterization considerably stronger than we would use (we might go as far as 'chiding')." They passed along Bouman's apology and noted that "it takes humility and generosity of spirit to publicly admit that one was out of line. Dr. Bouman's apology is a good example to us all." Nonetheless, after "[reviewing] each of [Bouman's] comments carefully and [comparing] them to the document we were quoting," the editors declared that they "did not find much that needs correction" in the original article. Other than a couple of very minor points, "we stand by the story as it was published."[17]

With all this in the background, Gagnon's keynote address at the October conference was anticipated eagerly by the nearly 300 in attendance at the conference in Kansas City. He did not disappoint; many attendees thought his passionate defense of "Scripture's unequivocal witness against homosexual practice" was by itself worth the price of admission. The other speakers were also well received, each addressing the topic from a different perspective—ethics, theology, ecumenical relations, pastoral care, psychology.

All things considered, the conference was regarded as a success. There had been moments of doubt for Saltzman as October approached. In the September issue of *Forum Letter*, he reflected on his experience as the chief organizer.

> I have never in my editorship experienced such, well, hostile mail as the sponsorship of this conference has produced. A 'sex-obsessed homophobe' is among the more generous epithets flung my way. If I thought the dispute over *Called to Common Mission* was intense, and I thought it was, that business pales in comparison. At the same time, I hope we may keep in mind that the question of gay sexuality is not The Big Thing. Pretty big, but not the biggest.[18]

Saltzman had said all along that he had no intention of sponsoring an "anti-gay rally"; rather he had hoped for "a vigorous apologetic for the Christian sexual ethic, theologically grounded and biblically faithful." He felt vindicated by a letter he received after the conference from a psychotherapist who worked for Lutheran Social Services, a woman who was a convinced advocate for "the full inclusion of gays in the life of the church."

> 'I wonder,' she writes, 'if I was the only person at the conference who disagreed with most of what I heard.' ... In spite of that, 'I want you to know that I was very glad I attended. It was clear to me that this group [the conference lecturers] treated this issue and the people involved in it with respect and compassion. I could see the deep love of the gospel and of Christ present in this group. It was clear to me that this was anything but a gay-bashing, homophobic band of fanatics. That is not what I found. ... I will now do what I can to present a voice of reason and understanding in the circles in which I move. ... Your conference was a real service to me. Even though my views have not changed, my knowledge and perspective on this topic is different now in a good way that I hope will be helpful for both sides.[19]

The nine papers from the conference were subsequently published jointly by ALPB Books and Kirk House Publishers as *Christian Sexuality: Normative and Pastoral Principles.* Included in the book was "A Pastoral Statement of Conviction and Concern," which had been presented and discussed in Kansas City. Drafted prior to the event by Robert Benne, Leonard Klein, retired bishop Paull Spring, and Richard Johnson, the statement was read to the attendees and revised twice in the light of discussion. It repudiated "all forms of prejudice and hatred" but insisted that "Christian love requires the clear proclamation of God's truth which alone can free and reconcile us." It concluded with a statement of what exactly was at stake:

> Because we love the whole church, many of us are facing a potential crisis of conscience regarding the Evangelical Lutheran Church in America. We earnestly desire to remain actively engaged in the life and mission of our church, but we observe that

the ELCA is becoming schismatic and sectarian. We therefore pray that our church's reflection on human sexuality be determined by an obedient listening to the Word of God and by a faithful witness to that Word.

The statement was signed by many of those present and by hundreds more during the coming months. The ALPB board, in accordance with their traditional reticence to get involved in specifically denominational controversies, decided against formally endorsing the statement. Still, the board was enthusiastic about the conference's success, and they willingly sponsored a second, more regional, event the following October in Runnemede, NJ, featuring several of the speakers from the Kansas City conference; their addresses were subsequently published in *Lutheran Forum*.[20]

Sexuality in *Forum Letter*
"the ELCA does not know what to teach about homosexuality"

The gathering storm over sexuality was extensively discussed in the ALPB publications. *Forum Letter* regularly commented on events and occurrences that reflected the controversy. In January 1998, the newsletter expressed astonishment that the ELCA's Lutheran Youth Organization [LYO] had proposed what an ELCA news release called a "year-long prayer emphasis for homosexual, bisexual and transgender youth" and an LYO "pre-event" for such youth at the next national youth gathering. Saltzman was skeptical.

> With somewhat more optimism than possibly warranted, the release announces that 'approximately 500,000 [LYO] members will ... pray and fast for the [quoting the LYO board] "personal and faith issues facing gay, lesbian, bixsexual, and transgendered youth."' ...
>
> We find ourselves harboring a suspicion that the youth of the church are again being manipulated. It happens. The natural and laudable impulses of youthful tolerance of and for nearly everything and everyone are being twisted to conform to a generally secular sexual ethic that is distinguished mostly by its denial of any sexual ethic at all, save that of license.

He cited instances of gay activists influencing Lutheran youth, such as the inclusion at a recent national ELCA youth gathering of a speaker who argued that the "ELCA message to gays and lesbians ... should be 'Come in and come out.'" The church's message for youth, Saltzman insisted, should be the "classical Christian message on sexuality":

> [V]irginity is not deviancy, desires are not needs, wants are not necessities, license is not freedom, impulses can be checked, lust is not love, not all appetites should be fed, and life lived only for sexual satisfaction is life dissipated. But that is not what our youth will hear, not from ELCA youth ministries at any rate.

A few months later, Saltzman reported that the plans for a "pre-gathering" had been dropped—not, according to the LYO board, because of the widespread publicity of the plan in the secular media, but because the youth organization believed it could not "create a safe environment for gay, lesbian and bisexual young people who decided to attend." Saltzman scoffed that "Lutherans Concerned, the ELCA's gay lobby, has held its several gatherings for years with nary a moment of discomfort. ... [It] is easier to intimate others' violent prejudice than to admit any possible lapse in one's own good sense."[21]

As the sexuality study task force proceeded with its work, Saltzman kept close tabs on the process. When *Lutheran Commentator* published a rather hysterical article about the built-in bias of the study task force, Saltzman was unconvinced. He rolled his eyes at the *Commentator*'s assumption that certain task force members would vote in favor of gay ordination because they had supported the full communion agreement with the Episcopal Church. "To which," Saltzman wrote, "we judiciously say 'oh, pish.'"[22]

Nevertheless, he agreed with the *Commentator* that the task force would recommend liberalization of the church's view of homosexuality. "Frankly, though, so what?" The task force's recommendation is not going to settle the matter. Besides, "what ELCA officials want in the moment isn't 'full acceptance'—something that would surely agitate restless parishes—so much as 'slow acceptance.'" The gay and lesbian advocates will keep pushing until that becomes "total churchwide acceptance. Period."[23]

In 2004, *Forum Letter* published an article which exhibited Saltzman's skills as an investigative reporter. Several months earlier a Texas pastor, Gerald Patrick Thomas, had been convicted on multiple counts of sexual abuse of minors and sentenced to 397 years in prison. In the wake of his conviction, a lawsuit was filed by the families of the teenaged boys molested by Thomas—a lawsuit that named several officials of the ELCA, the Northern Texas/Northern Louisiana Synod, and Trinity Lutheran Seminary (where Thomas had been educated, and from where he had served his internship). Saltzman obtained copies of several of the depositions in the case; he carefully laid out the accusations that had been made and the responses of those accused. It was alleged that officials at Trinity Seminary had known of Thomas's "problem," and that his file at the seminary included a report of his serving alcohol to teenaged boys and allowing them to view gay pornography while he was on internship. Among those named in the lawsuit was James Childs, who had been academic dean at the seminary when all this happened but who was now directing the ELCA sexuality study.

Saltzman criticized the seminary for allowing Thomas to proceed to ordination and first call, though he admitted that they were probably correct in claiming that their authority in the matter was limited. More significantly, he wrote, the case demonstrates the ELCA's inconsistency in enforcing its rules.

> What is evident is that some synod bishops construe an absence of formal allegations—never mind how well-known the problem may be—to mean it does not exist. ... The crisis of the Roman Catholic scandal, we point out, isn't just that some pastors acted badly, but that so many bishops failed in their responsibilities to enforce policies in existence. ...
>
> Meanwhile, though, since the ELCA does not know what to teach about homosexuality, the 'paternal,' 'pastoral' approach, disgraced as a way of dealing with heterosexual predator offenses, seems to be alive and well when the context is homosexuality.

Saltzman thought Childs wasn't really to blame for any of it; nonetheless, he urged Childs to resign as director of the sexuality study. That would be "a forthright effort on his part to restore to the task force's leadership, and to the ELCA, some of the credibility that has been considerably damaged by the ... lawsuit." If Childs won't resign, Saltzman concluded, perhaps "the task force should resign for the sake of the ELCA." Childs did not resign, nor did the task force; the defendants in the suit (or rather, their insurance carriers) ultimately paid the victims some $69 million either in pre-trial settlements or damages awarded by the jury.[24]

The Thomas story illustrates the way that the debate over sexuality impacted the church in many different contexts, with the questions it raised about how a seminary dealt with a potentially problematic intern in the charged atmosphere of the sexuality study. Another example came to light in a story, published in *Forum Letter* later that year, which revealed that Luther Seminary in St. Paul, MN, had placed a seminarian on internship who identified herself as transgendered (i.e., she was in the process of transitioning from female to male). The seminary's director of contextual education told *Forum Letter* that the student was "in a process of 'discernment'" both vocationally and sexually. "Let us ... express our honest sympathy for the student," the editors wrote, "who obviously, as we said, has some real issues to resolve, and is apparently struggling with them honestly and openly."

> But after saying that, then we must strenuously question whether an internship in an ELCA congregation really is the right place to work these things out. Can you visualize the student, oh, teaching seventh-grade catechism classes? What does her (let's just settle on that pronoun, for simplicity's sake) gender confusion teach, exactly, about creation, about vocation, about identity?[25]

Furthermore, the article revealed that the pastor who was supervising this intern was herself a lesbian, ordained only five years, who had publicly acknowledged that she was not in compliance with the ELCA's policy proscribing pastoral service by a person in an active homosexual relationship. The congregation involved had only 67 members, and the internship was being funded jointly by the seminary and by the Extraordinary Candidacy Committee, a group seeking to change ELCA policies about sexuality and ministry. To cap it off, few faculty members at Luther were aware that the internship assignment had been made ("No way she should be placed in a congregation at this point," one told *Forum Letter*); nor had the bishop and staff in the synod where the student was placed been told anything about the potential controversy. "Based on this one instance," the editors wrote, "we would judge that Luther's placement process is flawed at best, dysfunctional at worst."

> In this area, as in so many other areas of the church these days, we confess to a deep
> despair about the policies and practices of the ELCA. What is said on paper—the
> ELCA confessional statements and governing documents—turns out to be worthless
> whenever enforcement might impinge upon a favored agenda. And when this affects
> the training and formation of future pastors, well, we are not very optimistic about
> things getting better any time soon.[26]

In the aftermath of the *Forum Letter* article, the seminarian's endorsement was revoked by her synod's candidacy committee. While there was appropriately no public statement about why that action was taken, the student herself and the congregation where she had been assigned complained, Saltzman wrote, that the committee acted "because, thanks to *Forum Letter*, the 'political climate' was not right."

> If that is really the case, then shame on them. If they honestly think they made an
> appropriate decision in the original endorsement, they ought to have defended it,
> no matter what we or anyone else said about it.
>
> But if the whole thing was really just about 'politics'—well, then, it only confirms
> what we originally suggested, which is this student seems to have been used as a
> pawn by those advancing a certain agenda for the ELCA.[27]

Forum Letter also published several articles during these years treating sexuality questions more philosophically. In June 1998 Saltzman pondered the question of gay marriage—an "ineffably poignant" concept that "seeks to imitate the straight world." The editor saw it as "only another manifestation of the rampant sexual irregularity that plagues heterosexual arrangements." "From serial divorce to live-ins in the Unending Quest for Great Sex portrayed as the single's life on network comedies," he wrote, "the straight world is not in a very good position to be pointing fingers at any one."[28]

Saltzman occasionally expressed his own ambivalence about homosexuality. "I would like—for several personal reasons—to find a biblical hermeneutic and a doctrinal theology of creation that admits homosexuality," he wrote in February 2002. He spoke of gay friends and colleagues, and acknowledged that the issue "touches my own family." "There's a part of me," he admitted, "that genuinely says, okay, let's just do it. But finally I get stuck with what I regard as a theological impossibility." The problem for him "begins with Scripture," for he could not easily dismiss the Scriptural passages traditionally understood to condemn homosexual practice. He was left with the conviction that homosexual acts are sinful—just as myriad heterosexual "sexual irregularities" are sinful. God is a gracious God—but it is "only a presumptive pride to believe that God's grace finds us only to confirm us as we are."[29]

Homosexuality was not the only sexuality issue on the ELCA's agenda during these years. In 2001, the ELCA's church council issued a "Message on Commercial Sexual Exploitation." The document, associate editor Richard Johnson wrote, "underscores the difficulty contemporary Lutherans have in speaking coherently about sex." It dealt with pornography, phone sex, escort services, prostitution and strip clubs—all things, he wrote, to which "we are certainly opposed." The statement, however, placed much of the blame on the "system of sexual exploitation." The church, it said, must "repent of our complicity in this tangled web," including both those actively involved in it ("a small subset of ELCA members, one would hope," Johnson mused, "but then who knows?"), as well as "those of us who deny the existence of such a system, who fail to act against it, or even who just show 'lack of love for young people.'" The statement then urged "the usual range of social activism." What was lacking, Johnson wrote, was "a word or two about the darkness in the human soul—in every human soul, as far as we can tell—which wants to distort God's gift of sexual love." Despite a "brief nod to traditional Christian teaching in a paragraph which begins, 'Lust plays its role,'" the message seems to see lust as just "the initial stage of 'compulsive, addictive behavior.'"

> [Lust's] traditional place among the seven deadly sins suggests that in the Christian view, lust is sinful in and of itself, and most of us are guilty. The penitent doesn't generally come to the confessor and say, 'I've sinned by looking at pornography, and thereby I've exploited women and children and magnified social injustice.' No, the penitent has the good sense to know there is sin here, much deeper than exploitation. It is the sin of lust, 'the desire of the flesh.' It stands on its own two feet, thank you, and doesn't really need a train of social and economic consequences to make it evil. ...

> What if the church council's message had been something like this: 'We are to fear and love God so that in matters of sex our words and conduct are pure and honorable, and husband and wife love and respect each other' (*Small Catechism*). It would have left out a lot of psycho-social rhetoric, to be sure, and perhaps it would be too simple in a complex world. But it would have saved a lot of paper, it would have been read by a lot more people, and it would have had, one thinks, a lot more staying power.[30]

Lutheran Forum and sexuality

"No wonder there is such confusion!"

While *Forum Letter* kept abreast of the ELCA's discussion of human sexuality, *Lutheran Forum* offered a meatier theological approach. The Summer 2001 issue took as its theme "In the Image of God: Male and Female." The editors made no secret of their purpose; the introductory page told readers that the traditional Biblical teaching about sexuality "is under assault within the Church itself by those whose propaganda would lead believers to think that homosexual behavior is acceptable in the sight of God," while *Lutheran Forum* "is unashamedly dedicated to the promulgation of the Church's traditional teaching on human sexuality, marriage, and family."[31]

The issue began with an editorial by Ronald Bagnall criticizing the proliferation of "exceptions" being made by synods and bishops who refuse to enforce the church's policy on homosexuality in the clergy. "The question," he wrote, "is one of integrity: Does the ELCA mean what it says? Or has the ELCA simply become a weather vane, checking out which way the wind is blowing?" This was followed by articles defending traditional Christian sexual morality by several different writers, among them Leonard Klein, who warned that "the ELCA has neither the authority nor the liberty" to change Christian teaching, "and surely not unilaterally." It may try to do so by "a sheer act of parliamentary power ... but such actions would still be heretical and schismatic."[32]

A year later Bagnall published a paper by a Princeton Theological Seminary student, Sarah Hinlicky. Entitled "Sex, the Law, and Faith," the essay was originally written as a presentation before an independent conference on sexuality in the Upstate New York Synod. In the published version, Hinlicky offered an afterthought:

> After the conference was over, I saw with the irritating clarity of hindsight that I had made a critical miscalculation in my presentation of the material. I was operating on the assumption that we have been, in fact, teaching the Christian sexual ethic in our churches, or even that we were teaching any sexual ethic at all; and that regardless of what it was, it was falling on deaf ears and needed some reworking. But the overwhelming testimony of both the clergy and [laity] present at the conference was ... that we were not teaching any ethic at all. There is a complete and deadly silence in our churches about sexuality. No wonder there is such confusion![33]

The Winter 2003 issue of *Lutheran Forum* had as its theme "Our First Parents ... the Holy Family." It consisted largely of papers from the October 2003 ALPB-sponsored conference on sexuality in Runnemede, NJ. The lead article was by Richard Niebanck, who reflected an increasing urgency about the crisis. "No question about it," he averred. "The time of reasoned conversation is long gone. The revisionist steamroller is advancing with accelerating speed. ... The Church of our children and grandchildren is at stake." Niebanck traced the history of the push for a revised view of marriage over the past several decades, dating back to a controversial debate about divorce in the Lutheran Church in America in the 1960s; he quoted one theologian from that era as remarking, "The LCA was about to position itself right smack in the middle of the *Zeitgeist*."[34]

Niebanck's conclusion was somber. "I fear that the picture I've presented is not a hopeful one. In fact, the more I wrote the more I came to conclude that the battle for the soul of our institutional church body is all but lost." He suggested how faithful Christians might proceed. "Above all," he wrote, "we must repent of our sins. Of *our* sins, not those of others, for it as much through our inattention to sacred doctrine, our desire to be liked, our own failure to model the godly life ... that the present state of affairs has come to pass."[35]

The issue also included two papers not presented in Runnemede. Ethicist Robert Benne urged the ELCA to uphold traditional Christian sexual ethics. To do otherwise, he argued, would be "a sign of further accommodation to a culture that has few moral restraints, and that is very close to license." Churches that make this accommodation "are in decline because they offer little that people can't get from the culture." His concern was not simply for homosexuality, but for "the general laxity of teaching and practice concerning *heterosexual* morality in our own church." He called for "a renewed commitment to the grand teachings of Christianity on these matters, beginning with a retrieval of our doctrine of marriage, around which all Christian sexual ethics revolves."[36]

Finally, the issue offered something of a counterview by Marc Kolden, systematic theology professor at Luther Seminary in St. Paul. Kolden argued against making any decision at the churchwide assembly in 2005, when the report of the sexuality task force would be presented. Rather he suggested that ELCA members simply "agree to disagree." It might be possible, he suggested, for those who uphold traditional Christian teachings about sexuality (he included himself in this group) to tolerate certain things—such as lifelong sexual unions between two people of the same sex—recognizing that "those who approve of same-sex unions *may* be correct," and that this is a penultimate matter that need not destroy the unity of faith. Even so, he saw the church's actual blessing of such unions to be a different matter. "It is one thing," he wrote, "to allow something to go on or even to accept it in some ways, but it is something quite different to give it public endorsement: to say that this is what the Church believes, teaches and confesses."[37]

A time of decision

"a compromised compromise"

As the 2005 churchwide assembly approached, there was great anxiety among many in the ELCA as to what might be decided. The sexuality task force was coming with three recommendations: (1) that the ELCA resolve to live together faithfully while disagreeing about sexuality; (2) that the ELCA, while not endorsing same-sex marriage, encourage "faithful pastoral care" of same-sex couples; (3) that while the ELCA should maintain its formal sexual standards for clergy (i.e., that homosexual relationships be forbidden), bishops should be free to refrain from disciplining either pastors who are in fact in such relationships or congregations that call them. The recommendation, the *Forum Letter* editors wrote, is masked as "no change" when in fact it is "a sea change in policy and practice" that amounts to "local option." It is "a compromised compromise."[38]

Lutheran Forum had quite a bit more to say about the recommendations. In the Spring 2005 issue, Bagnall published "A Statement of Pastoral and Theological Concern," signed by seventeen prominent Lutheran scholars—most of them professors (active or retired) at ELCA seminaries or colleges, but also former LCA bishop James Crumley. The statement urged the defeat of the recommendations which, they believed, "would alter fundamentally the ecclesiology" of the ELCA and would in turn "threaten not only the unity and stability of the church but ... its ability to proclaim the truth of the Gospel."[39]

The following issue—published on the eve of the churchwide assembly—offered a stinging critique of the task force proposal by Karl Donfried, an ELCA pastor and religion professor at Smith College. The recommendations, he insisted, "have no demonstrated Lutheran theological foundations, and are based on questionable assumptions and a series of false presuppositions." The result will be "a heterodox ELCA" marked by "enormous tensions at the local level"; it will be a church that will "operate on the basis of deception."[40]

In the end, the churchwide assembly accepted the first two recommendations of the task force, but rejected the third. *Forum Letter* provided a lengthy analysis, concluding that the bottom line was no change:

> So what does it mean? ... [It] means *status quo*—persons in same-sex relationships (committed or otherwise) are precluded from serving as pastors in the ELCA. Whether synod bishops will accept this judgment remains to be seen. ...
>
> There will be continued ambiguity over same-sex blessings. The church council prior to the assembly was asked to clarify just what was meant by Recommendation 2 [on pastoral care for same-sex couples]. Specifically, would its approval indicate that the ELCA authorizes same-sex blessings, or not? The council wouldn't answer, suggesting that anything they said on the matter would only confuse things further rather than clarify them—a fascinating response when fully considered, something along the lines of, 'We don't know what we mean; that's our story and we're sticking to it.'

This, of course, was not the end of controversy over sexuality. The ALPB publications would continue to report and offer commentary on the issue as it ultimately sparked a schism within the ELCA, leading to the establishment of a new Lutheran church body.[41]

Notes

1. Minutes, ALPB Board of Directors, 22 Oct. 2005.
2. "A Christian View of Sex," ALPB, ca. 1965, ALPB Archives.
3. [Phillip Max Johnson], "You, Your Body, Your God," ALPB, 1998, ALPB Archives.
4. Ibid.
5. [Phillip Max Johnson], "Spiritually Safe Sex," ALPB, 1998, ALPB Archives.
6. [Phillip Max Johnson], "What Does Your Marriage Mean?", "The Love That Can Be Promised," and "Both Parents and Priests," ALPB, 1998, ALPB Archives.
7. [Rebecca Frey], "When Home Is Where the Hurt Is" and "When 'Love' Hurts," ALPB, 2000, ALPB Archives.
8. [Phillip Max Johnson], "When New Life Is an Unwelcome Gift," ALPB, 2000, ALPB Archives.
9. [Phillip Max Johnson], "Is This the Way God Made Me?", ALPB, 2000, ALPB Archives.

10. [Phillip Max Johnson], "Can Homosexual Love Be Blessed?" ALPB, 2000, ALPB Archives.

11. Sales from October 15, 2010 through May 18, 2011, Agenda attachment, ALPB Board of Directors Meeting, 21 May 2001, ALPB Archives.

12. Connie Seddon, Report of the ALPB Tract Committee, 8 May 2004, ALPB Archives.

13. *FL* 30, no. 10 (Oct. 2001), 6.

14. *FL* 31, no. 3 (Mar. 2002), 1-2.

15. *FL*, 31, no. 8 (Aug. 2002), 4.

16. Walter Bouman to Frederick Schumacher, 10 Aug. 2002, ALPB Archives.

17. *FL* 31, no. 10 (Oct. 2002), 3-4.

18. *FL* 31, no. 9 (Sept. 2002), 4.

19. Ibid.; *FL* 31, no. 12 (Dec. 2002), 1-2.

20. Russell E. Saltzman, ed., *Christian Sexuality: Normative & Pastoral Principles* (Minneapolis, MN: Kirk House Publishers, 2003); ibid., 7-8; Minutes, ALPB Board of Directors, 11 Nov. 2002.

21. *FL* 27, no. 1 (Jan. 1998), 1-3; *FL* 27, no. 4 (Apr. 1998), 4.

22. *FL* 31, no. 7 (July 2002), 5.

23. Ibid.

24. *FL* 33, no. 6 (June 2004), 3-4; Carol Marin, "Protestant sex abuse: A $69 million jury award," *Chicago Tribune*, 28 Apr. 2004. <articles.chicagotribune.com/2004-04-28/news/0404280117_1_ sexual-abuse-roman-catholic-molestation-crisis-sex-abuse> (accessed 8 July 2016).

25. *FL* 33, no. 11 (Nov. 2004), 2.

26. Ibid., 4-5.

27. *FL* 34, no. 4 (Apr. 2005), 7.

28. *FL* 27, no. 6 (June 1998), 5-6.

29. *FL* 31, no. 2 (Feb. 2002), 1-4.

30. *FL* 31, no. 7 (July 2002), 5-6.

31. "In the Forum," *LF* 35:2 (Summer 2001), 1.

32. Ronald B. Bagnall, "When Exceptions Become the Rule," *LF* 35, no. 2 (Summer 2001), 7; Leonard R. Klein, "The Traditional Response to the Question of Homosexuality," *LF* 35, no. 2 (Summer 2001), 27.

33. Sarah E. Hinlicky, "Sex, the Law, and Faith," *LF* 36, no. 2 (Summer 2002), 24.

34. Richard J. Niebanck, "What's at Stake," *LF* 37, no. 4 (Winter 2003), 12-13.

35. Ibid., 15-16.

36. Robert Benne, "Why the ELCA Should Uphold Traditional Christian Sexual Ethics," *LF* 37, no. 4 (Winter 2003), 28.

37. Marc Kolden, "Another Viewpoint: Can We Agree to Disagree?" *LF* 37, no. 4 (Winter 2003), 34-38.

38. *FL* 34, no. 2 (Feb. 2005), 2.

39. "A Statement of Pastoral and Theological Concern: A Response to the Report and Recommendations from the Task Force for ELCA Studies on Sexuality," *LF* 39, no. 1 (Spring 2005), 40-41.

40. Karl P. Donfried, "False Presuppositions and Questionable Assumptions: A Critical Analysis of the Recommendations from the ELCA Church Council to the ELCA Churchwide Assembly on Sexuality Studies Dated April 11, 2005," *LF* 39, no. 2 (Summer 2005), 16.

41. *FL* 34, no. 10 (Oct. 2005), 4.

Chapter 25

TRANSITIONS

T he first decade of the new millennium was tumultuous for American Lutheranism. There were renewed moderate/conservative battles in the LCMS, while the ELCA seemed inexorably headed for a major explosion over human sexuality. Through this turmoil, the ALPB faced its own challenges. Newly elected president John Hannah had only been in office a few months when the editors of both *Lutheran Forum* and *Forum Letter* announced they would be leaving. While the editorial vacancies demanded immediate attention, the board also continued to develop its book publishing ministry and to think about its mission and its future in the rapidly changing American Lutheran landscape.

Forum Letter and ecclesiastical politics
"the dumbest thing since unsliced bread"
Following the ELCA's 2005 compromise on sexuality, there were those—including the editor of *Forum Letter*—who began to think more seriously about how to continue to serve in a church body that seemed to be moving toward a radical change in its understanding of sexual ethics, marriage and ordination. Russell Saltzman had been

unenthusiastic about a "dissenting synod," a concept that had been raised over the past several years, but he was beginning to reconsider. Even before the ELCA's "compromised compromise," he reflected on "issues for a dissenting Lutheran synod." He found it ironic that the matter of homosexuality should throw those whom he now called "Lutheran protestants" together with "evangelical catholics." Both claim to be dedicated to the Lutheran confessions, he mused, and both are opposed to the ELCA's direction on sexuality. Yet there were other issues over which they continued to argue with one another—issues, he argued, which must be resolved before any "dissenting synod" comprising both parties could be considered.[1]

He identified five specific matters of contention and then offered his own point of view about how they should be handled. The first was the propriety of including a Eucharistic prayer in Holy Communion. While he personally preferred to do so and disagreed with those who believed it did violence to Lutheran theology, he thought it was ultimately a matter of little consequence. He offered a similar view on the question of lay presidency, arguing that the practice could coexist with "a 'high view' of the pastoral office."[2]

Next came two ecumenical disputes: the historic episcopate and the Lutheran/Roman Catholic Joint Declaration on the Doctrine of Justification. Both, he believed, should be non-issues. *Called to Common Mission* had given Lutherans the historic episcopate, but it had proven to have little value and was not worth further argument. The agreement with the Roman Catholics on justification "has gone into the dead letter box." Continued dialogue is important, but the specifics could easily be put off for the present.[3]

The final issue was the question of Lutheran identity. He strongly insisted on the priority of the Lutheran confessions in defining what it means to be Lutheran and criticized those who would "quote Luther *against* the Confessions." Lutherans, he reiterated, are "reluctant exiles from the Church of Rome."

> How we get 'back to Rome,' though, is pretty much up to Rome. I've always thought if the Pope was more serious, he'd start making some inactive calls. In any case, I do not accept the view that we are Protestants—not in the generic North American sense—or that from the very beginning we intended to found a 'new' church. ... We are Catholic regarding the Real Presence, 'eating orally,' as the Confessions put it. We are Catholic by the confessional standard of offering the sacrament weekly. We are Catholic in teaching baptismal regeneration, ... in the preference for continuing private absolution, ... in a host of other ways—and in none of these ways are we intentionally aping anything Roman. We come by our catholicity honestly and we have our own way of being Lutheran Catholics—Lutheran on the doctrine of grace, Catholic in an understanding of the universal Church.

The fault lines between "Lutheran protestants" and "evangelical catholics," he concluded, are nothing new in Lutheranism, and the two sides "lived rather happily within the ELCA's predecessors." But in the current crisis, they must find new ways to work together. "Time to call a truce."[4]

The essay elicited responses from both sides of the divide. The sharpest came from Mark E. Chapman, a former ELCA pastor and frequent defender of the evangelical catholic vision of Lutheranism. He sent the ALPB board a strident critique of Saltzman's essay, arguing that the whole notion of a "dissenting synod" was wrongheaded and "achieves nothing except the isolation of the dissenting voice." But he was particularly appalled at Saltzman's list of issues and how he treated them. All five, he wrote, are "dogmatic topics central to the life of the Church." They must not be "set aside ... over the issue of the ELCA Sexuality Study proposals."[5]

The critique provoked a lengthy conversation at the next ALPB board meeting. "After considerable discussion," the minutes reported, "the consensus of the Board was that the ALPB continue to discuss issues, but that it not be aligned with any party in the ELCA or the LCMS." Chapman's critique was reworked substantially and published in *Lutheran Forum* as a more positive proposal entitled "Fundamental Unity: Evangelical-Catholic Non-Negotiables."[6]

Given the Bureau's insistence "that it not be aligned with any party," it was ironic (and perhaps somewhat inconsistent) that at that same meeting the board approved a motion to "prepare a plaque expressing appreciation to the Rev. Dr. Roy [Harrisville] III for his leadership of Solid Rock Lutherans." This group was a coalition which had organized in opposition to the proposals of the sexuality study task force at the 2005 churchwide assembly. ALPB had not joined the coalition, though ALPB board member Robert Benne had served on Solid Rock's board of directors, and both Saltzman and Fred Schumacher had been individual members of the organization. Of course this was not the first time the ALPB, while officially remaining neutral, had been identified with one or another group in the church through the activities and commitments of its personnel.[7]

Solid Rock had intended to dissolve after the 2005 assembly, but it called a meeting in late September 2005, held at Saltzman's congregation in Kansas City, where there was discussion about forming a continuing group to work for reform in the ELCA. Saltzman reported on the event in *Forum Letter*:

> The gathering included the top leadership of the Word Alone Network (call them Lutheran evangelicals) and evangelical catholic Lutherans (call them, well, call them that.)
>
> Word Alone has jumped ahead on formation of a confessing association, somewhat to the discomfort of some evangelical catholics. Much of our discussion was spent trying to understand just what Word Alone was up to, and would it include any room for evangelical catholics. Given some of the virulence in the debate over the historic episcopate ... a good deal of mutual suspicion marks any gathering that includes evangelical catholics and Lutheran evangelicals.

> Here's the short of it, in my opinion. The only ELCA Lutheran reform organization capable of providing the logistical support necessary in forming a confessing association is Word Alone. To make it as simple as possible, Word Alone has the photocopiers.

Saltzman was convinced the Word Alone leadership truly desired a broadly-based coalition. "There are of course many wrinkles to smooth out," he concluded, "not least are the different theological emphases [between the groups]. ... But the effort, I believe, is worth it."[8]

While the ELCA battled over sexuality, the LCMS's crisis over David Benke's participation in the post-9/11 interfaith event in New York City continued to have fallout in the Synod, and *Forum Letter* followed the rather strange story. At Missouri's 2004 convention, conservatives made a concerted effort to oust LCMS president Gerald Kieschnick. They had many complaints about him, but the most neuralgic was his role in the Benke case. Delegates that year, however, did not follow the usual pattern of voting conservative. Not only was Kieschnick reelected (albeit by a thin margin), four of the five vice presidents who had supported Benke's suspension were unseated. As Saltzman put it, "the moderates pretty much got the whole store."[9]

But the conservatives did not go gently. A lawsuit was filed by more than a hundred plaintiffs (mostly pastors, but also some LCMS teachers and deaconesses and a few congregations) against Kieschnick and first vice president William Diekelman. The defendants had, the suit alleged, monkeyed with the electoral circuits prior to the 2004 convention in order to elect more convention delegates likely to vote for them. The suit also asked that the court acknowledge the LCMS board of directors (which was still in conservative hands) as the supreme authority in the Synod—supreme, specifically, over the Commission on Constitutional Matters, which had ruled against those who had tried to include Kieschnick in the disciplinary charges brought against Benke in 2001. The 2004 convention had decisively defeated a proposal to give the board that authority, but now the lawsuit attempted to undo that action.

This very complicated case was outlined for *Forum Letter* readers by John Hannah. He admitted that his assessment may seem "unusually Machiavellian," but then "there have been Machiavellian forces at work in the Missouri Synod for years."

> LCMS rank and file are only beginning to learn about this latest development They are not pleased. First, the plaintiffs ignore St. Paul's strong advice that Christians not sue Christians (1 Cor. 6.1-11). ...
>
> Even if the law suit was filed as a class action, most members are saying, 'You are not suing on my behalf.' Frankly, unless there is some unforeseen change of circumstances, the [conservatives] will lose by even more votes come the 2007 convention.

And if that happens, Hannah concluded, "few mainstream members will lament the better prospects for calm and the absence of disruption."[10]

Forum Letter kept readers up to date on the lawsuit (which was not being widely publicized through official synodical publications). In 2006, it appeared that a settlement was at hand until four members of the LCMS board of directors asked the court to rule on the part of the suit related to that board's authority. Saltzman again expressed his mystification at Missouri.

> As far as we're concerned, the whole thing is the dumbest thing since unsliced bread. God does work mysteriously, so it's said, and I guess God even works through the Lutheran Church Missouri Synod. But we must say, some days, 'tis a true mystery how.

But the very next month, he reported that the motion by the board members had been withdrawn, and the case had been dismissed. "Apologies were made broadly to the LCMS and more particularly to President Gerald Kieschnick, and good feelings of mutual joy were expressed by all."[11]

The lawsuit provoked an interesting incident behind the scenes at the ALPB. When the Bureau applied for a display table at the 2007 LCMS convention, the request was turned down. At first Missouri officials said it was because ALPB publications might be in competition with Concordia Publishing House. ALPB president Hannah protested that ALPB's books were aimed at a very small market and they were highly unlikely to be anything CPH would publish, but he was told that the committee allocating convention space had decided that they had "the right balance and mix of exhibitors" and they were sticking with their original decision.[12]

This all seemed suspicious to Saltzman, who spoke to one of his sources in the LCMS leadership. He learned that the real reason for the denial was the presence of Frederic Baue on the masthead of *Lutheran Forum* as an editorial advisor. Baue was one of the plaintiffs in the lawsuit; he had, in fact, been dropped as editorial associate more than a year before, but there was a backstory. When Ronald Bagnall was named editor, he recruited a large group of editorial associates. The editorial associates had a couple of meetings during the early years, but after about 2002 the group had essentially ceased to function. They continued to appear on the masthead of the magazine, though the number of names on the list gradually decreased—usually through death or departure from Lutheranism, but sometimes for other reasons. Stephen Bouman's name was dropped at the request of some board members as his public position on the ELCA's sexuality issues became increasingly at odds with the commitments of the Bureau.

When Baue's name appeared as one of the plaintiffs in the lawsuit, Hannah urged Bagnall to remove his name from the masthead. The editor was reluctant to do so; he wanted to talk with Baue before making "a determination for myself about his advisory role with *Lutheran Forum*." Apparently after that conversation Bagnall was convinced, and Baue's name was quietly dropped in the Summer 2006 issue—which, as it turned out, was Bagnall's final issue as editor.[13]

New editors

"I prefer simply to step aside and go off into the sunset"

In May 2006, the board was taken by surprise by Bagnall's abrupt announcement that he planned to retire effective July 31, and that the summer issue of *Lutheran Forum* would be his last. Bagnall was also retiring from some forty years of parish ministry. His letter to executive director Fred Schumacher came just two weeks before the spring board meeting, so this became the major item of business when the board met on May 20. Bagnall's son David had been doing the layout for the journal, and he, too, resigned. Realizing that it would be impossible to find a new editor on such short notice, board member Paul Sauer agreed to edit the fall issue (and the winter issue, if necessary), with the assistance of John Hannah; Martin Christiansen had already agreed to do the layout for the next two issues. A search committee was appointed. The board, wishing to clear the deck for whomever the new editor might be, also asked associate editors Rebecca Frey and Phillip Max Johnson to resign.

At the same meeting, Schumacher announced that Russell Saltzman had decided to retire as *Forum Letter* editor effective July 31, 2007. Saltzman was anxious to give the board plenty of time to select the next editor; he recalled only too well the panic in the board when Neuhaus had abruptly resigned without even a word of copy ready for the next issue. The board added the responsibility for recommending Saltzman's successor to the search committee's task. They also spent some time discussing their hopes for the future direction of both publications. *Lutheran Forum* had, in the opinion of some, become somewhat esoteric. Several wished that it might be more "lay friendly" and offer "more good news." The primary concern expressed about *Forum Letter* was that it should strike a better balance between ELCA and LCMS issues; there was a sense that too much space was being given to the ongoing struggles in the ELCA (ironic, since two decades earlier there had been complaints about "too much attention to LCMS issues").[14]

Another concern about *Forum Letter* was expressed by board member Ray Kibler—briefly at the meeting, but more expansively in an email to other board members some weeks later. He urged that "the identity and role of the Forum Letter as a cranky critic of the church" be abandoned. *Forum Letter* has spent too much time "[airing] ELCA dirty linen"; the ALPB "run[s] the risk of becoming ... a community of grumps who only talk to ourselves."[15]

Kibler intended his criticism to go only to board members, but he inadvertently included Saltzman in the distribution. Saltzman's response was gracious, though understandably somewhat defensive.

> Actually, I've always thought of 'cranky critic' as one of my better qualities, given the range of personal and public characterizations available. It is always a disappointment to find it is not a universally lauded attribute. ...

As to the question of dirty linen, well. Let me ask, would the ELCA be better off without Forum's coverage of the transgendered seminarian at Luther? ... How would things be better in the LCMS if we had not provided extensive commentary on the lawsuit against Kieschnick? If that is airing dirty linen, then good, I'm frankly all for it. On these and other subjects, much needs to be aired.

Kibler apologized to Saltzman personally—he did not mean to call Saltzman himself a "cranky critic," but the newsletter "as a whole." His real point was that the board ought to have a discussion about *Forum Letter*'s purpose before engaging a new editor.[16]

A few board members agreed with Kibler's concerns, but others came to Saltzman's defense. "Please note," wrote Ray Brown, that "the biggest sarcasm in FL is directed by the editor toward himself." "Provocative writing always has its dangers," he concluded, "but it does keep more worthwhile readers than it loses." Gregory Fryer had a different view. An occasionally negative tone, he suggested, "is inevitable given that the editor is dealing continually with a *heartbreak*. Where else can we look except to *Forum Letter* for the concrete reports on the myriad manifestations of an unworthy construal of Lutheranism at play in our generation?" Robert Benne agreed. "I find so much awry in the ELCA that if we were silent about that we would miss one of our great opportunities and obligations."[17]

All this electronic communication took place a few weeks before the board's fall meeting, when the search committee would bring recommendations regarding both publications. The board had intended to host a dinner honoring Ronald Bagnall for his years of service with *Lutheran Forum*, but Bagnall demurred. Fred Schumacher quoted his words to the board: "My work on *Lutheran Forum* is over and I prefer simply to step aside and go off into the sunset. I've worked in the background all of my life and plan to continue in this fashion. Thanks for the invitation but I must decline your kind offer." Still wanting to thank Bagnall for his service, and recognizing his emphasis in *Lutheran Forum* on the visual arts, the board commissioned iconographer Dimitri Andreyev to write an icon of "Christ Pantocrator," which they then presented to Bagnall in appreciation for his many contributions to the ministry of the ALPB.

The search committee initially approached James Nuechterlein, a former Valparaiso University professor who had been working with Richard John Neuhaus at *First Things*, the journal Neuhaus founded after his departure from *Forum Letter*. Nuechterlein declined, but he urged the committee to consider Sarah Hinlicky Wilson, a doctoral student at Princeton who had worked as an editorial assistant at *First Things*. She was an ELCA pastor, a graduate of Lenoir-Rhyne College and Princeton Theological Seminary; she was also the daughter of former *Lutheran Forum* editor and ALPB executive director Paul Hinlicky. The committee contacted Wilson, and they were impressed; she quickly rose to the top of a list of potential candidates.

The committee felt strongly, however, that the journal needed to give more attention to the LCMS, and they weren't sure a female ELCA pastor would be the best choice
to accomplish that goal. They decided that an ELCA/LCMS editorial team would be an
interesting way to address the concern. After debating various possible combinations,
they recommended the appointment of Sarah Hinlicky Wilson as editor of *Lutheran
Forum* and Paul Sauer as associate editor.

This was a bold recommendation. Wilson was a particularly young choice, not well
known to the board (though of course many of them knew her father). Several board
members were familiar with her writing, however; she had published several pieces in
First Things, Christianity Today and *Books and Culture.* She seemed eager to take on the
Lutheran Forum editorial task.

The recommendation of Paul Sauer was also a break from ALPB tradition. In the
past, the choice of associate editors had been made by the editor rather than the board.
But Sauer, though not much older than Wilson, had been involved with ALPB for some
time and provided both experience and continuity. A graduate of Valparaiso University
with a degree in classical civilizations, he had earned MDiv and STM degrees from
Concordia Seminary in St. Louis. He had never met Wilson, but had no hesitation in
serving with her on the *Lutheran Forum* editorial team.

Wilson attended the October 2006 board meeting and presented some lively ideas
about the future direction of *Lutheran Forum*—eight pages of them. She began with
her sense of the "overall mission" of the journal:

- To produce a magazine that pastors and educated laypeople will want to read
  cover to cover because it edifies and interests them.

- To articulate an attractive, evangelical, and compelling vision for Lutherans in
  North America and the wide world

- To discuss fairly and rationally the hard issues that face the Lutheran community,
  speaking the truth in love.

- To give particular attention to negotiating the multiple histories of Lutherans
  in America and how they have helped or hindered our unity, in the interest
  of peacemaking.

- To discern the role of the Lutheran leaven in the American lump.

She outlined plans to increase readership, expand the number of authors, develop a
website, and improve the design and style of the magazine. She provided a long list
of topics she would like the journal to address. She promised that *Lutheran Forum*
would not contain "pot-shots, thinly veiled contempt, messy thinking, *reductio ad
absurdum* attacks, *ad hominem* attacks, knock-down arguments" or other examples
of "poor thinking and greater delight in the defeat of one's enemies than in the triumph of the truth."[18]

The board was impressed with her energy and enthusiasm. The one drawback was that Wilson was currently teaching on a fellowship whose terms limited her ability to do other outside work, and so she could not start until the following May. Sauer and Hannah agreed to continue to edit the journal in the interim, and the board approved the appointment of the team of Wilson and Sauer. They also agreed to hire Andrew Wilson, the new editor's husband, to take over the important job of layout for the journal.

Russ Saltzman had recommended that Richard Johnson be appointed to succeed him. The search committee agreed, but they suggested that action be postponed until the board (most of whose members had never met Johnson) could invite him to attend a meeting for face-to-face conversation. That meeting took place in May, and after interviewing Johnson, they appointed him *Forum Letter*'s next editor.[19]

The board raised with Johnson their desire to be more attentive to Missouri Synod issues, and he indicated that his intent was to appoint an LCMS associate editor. His choice was Peter Speckhard, a Missouri Synod pastor then serving Faith Lutheran Church in Green Bay, WI. Speckhard had contributed a couple of articles to *Forum Letter* in the past, and he had been an active participant in Forum Online. He also happened to be the nephew of former *Forum Letter* editor Richard John Neuhaus. In introducing him to readers, editor Johnson noted that he was chosen in part to address the need for more coverage of the Missouri Synod, "but even more because we think he's articulate and interesting." Speckhard offered a Missouri perspective that was rather different from the more moderate East coast Lutheranism that had dominated the ALPB for most of its history. He was, theologically and culturally, clearly more in the Midwestern mainstream of the Synod; occasionally he would ruffle the feathers of the traditional ALPB Missouri constituency (although, interestingly enough, ELCA readers were often more appreciative of his contributions). He was no isolationist, however; he was willing to engage in serious debate of controversial issues. Johnson viewed his appointment as one which might keep the ALPB's ministry connected to an increasingly conservative younger generation of Missouri Synod pastors.[20]

Lutheran Forum in the interim

"our work of renewal is clearly laid out"

Paul Sauer was responsible (assisted by John Hannah) for four issues of the journal; during this interim, he kept the basic format that had been developed under Bagnall. The first issue (Fall 2006) took as its theme a long-time concern of the ALPB: "The Catholicity of the Lutheran Church." Two articles were reprints of much earlier essays from the former *Una Sancta* by now deceased writers, both of whom had ALPB connections: Arthur Carl Piepkorn's 1952 "The Catholicity of the Lutheran Church" and Berthold von Schenk's 1958 "A Blueprint for Your Catholic Parish." There were also articles by several contemporary writers, each offering a different perspective on Lutheran catholicity.

The next two issues contained critiques of the new hymnals recently published by both the LCMS and the ELCA, as well as interviews with persons closely involved with each project. Sauer's final issue circled back to the question of Lutheran identity. Its first feature article was from the pen of ALPB board member Robert Benne. In "Sunset or Dawn? The Lutheran Calling to Public Life in America," Benne offered a sharp critique of both the ELCA and the LCMS in their public engagement. Missouri's underlying conviction that the LCMS itself is "the one and only true church in Christendom" has led to a "fear that engagement with other Christians—even other Lutherans—will in some sense contaminate Missourians." This insularity has led many of the brightest Missouri Synod theologians to leave the Synod, "especially those who wanted to engage the public world." ELCA intellectuals, on the other hand, have often become "uninterested in classical Lutheran themes" and have instead "been symptomatic of a move toward liberal Protestantism that is all too evident at the elite levels of the ELCA." What is needed, Benne pleaded, "is a Missouri with a freer spirit and an ELCA that is more seriously centered on its confessional heritage." But he was not sanguine about either possibility; he granted that the Holy Spirit might well "send flames of renewal among us, but we can put obstacles in its way that will insure continued decline."[21]

There were also two articles addressing the concern about Lutheran pastors and theologians "swimming the Tiber or the Bosphorus"—leaving Lutheranism for Roman Catholicism or Orthodoxy. One was a sermon by LCMS pastor Albert Collver entitled "For Those Who Didn't Swim," preached to a congregation whose pastor had resigned to join the Antiochan Orthodox Church. The other was a paper by Frank Senn, presented at the general retreat of the Society of the Holy Trinity, entitled "Staying Put"—a poignant presentation, since Phillip Max Johnson, Senn's predecessor as senior of the Society, had recently been received into the Roman Catholic Church. Senn noted Luther's patient acknowledgement that the Roman Catholic Church was not lacking the marks of the church, and urged that Lutherans show the same patience toward their own church bodies.

> For all their theological waywardness, sometimes downright error, and slippery slide toward unintended apostasy, our churches are still places where the external marks of the church are here and there visible—just as they were in the papal Church before, during, and after Luther's time. If the word of God is not rightly divided into law and gospel, if there is some lack in our use of the means of grace, if the office of the public ministry is not always occupied by reliable incumbents, if our public worship is not quite the 'right praise' (*orthodoxia*) it is meant to be, if the costs of discipleship are not being paid, then our work of renewal is clearly laid out.[22]

Book publishing continues
"we will return to a simple letter of agreement"

Meanwhile, the ALPB's book publishing ministry proceeded—though it often seemed as if the Bureau was still rather tentatively feeling its way. Some titles continued to sell reasonably well, particularly *For All the Saints* and the books by Robert Jenson and Eric Gritsch. Others were much less successful. The Bureau regularly received unsolicited manuscripts, most of which were judged not suitable for publication. The biggest problem with the endeavor, however, seemed to be the limited financial resources dedicated to this ministry, as well as the lack of a coherent and consistent process by which manuscripts could be evaluated and decisions made.

Back in the 1990s a book committee had been established, but it had not worked well and within a short time had essentially disappeared. For years the evaluation of manuscripts fell primarily to executive director Schumacher. He would report his recommendations to the board, and they generally would agree. The publication process would then meander along, steered by Schumacher. There was neither a standard publication agreement nor well-defined guidelines for what sorts of books the ALPB would publish. A 1998 task force on "processes of production" had urged that a part-time book editorial director be sought, but nothing ultimately came of the recommendation.

Another attempt at a more deliberate system was made in 2005 when board member Phillip Max Johnson proposed that a new committee be formed to review potential publications. He suggested that the board establish "(1) a firm process of decision-making about what ALPB publishes and (2) about the way in which we confer with authors about the content of their work." He envisioned an editorial group that would "receive and consider all unsolicited *or solicited* manuscripts, make an initial evaluation, and provide their recommendations to the board of directors." The current process, he complained, is "haphazard, unproductive, and potentially confusing to authors." Once a decision to publish is made, he went on, there should be a single editor who would work with the author through the editing process. "ALPB has plenty of talent available to it (on and off the board) to establish this more deliberate process," he insisted. "Surely this would also make things easier for our executive director."[23]

The board agreed, at least in principle, and Johnson and another board member were asked to develop a more detailed plan. Meanwhile, Schumacher asked several board members to serve on the new committee; while most were willing, no one wanted to chair the committee. When Johnson resigned from the board and was received into the Roman Catholic Church, the plan for a book editorial committee died.[24]

Ultimately the board settled on what it called a "champion system" for evaluating manuscripts and shepherding them toward publication. If the executive director thought a manuscript worth considering, it would be circulated to see if an individual board member would agree to act as champion and advocate for its publication. If so, the champion would present the case to the board, which would then decide whether to publish. The weakness of the system was that different board members brought different skills and levels of interest to the process. In some cases, the champion continued to work with the author and the executive director on design details, distribution of complimentary copies and promotional efforts; in other cases, the champion did no more work on the book after the board's agreement to publish it and all these details were left to the executive director.

About this time, there was renewed interest in publishing a second volume of the writings of Arthur Carl Piepkorn. The volume on the church, published in 1993, was nearly sold out, and several board members wanted the Bureau to do a second edition. The first edition, completed just as Paul Hinlicky was leaving as executive director, had been something of a "rush job," and it contained many typographical and other errors. As this project was being contemplated, Schumacher contacted Philip Secker, who had been a doctoral student of Piepkorn. Secker had long wanted to make Piepkorn's work more widely available; after Piepkorn's death in 1973, he had obtained permission from the professor's widow to produce a collection of her husband's writings. He had hoped that Augsburg Fortress would agree to publish it, but when they declined, the project languished. Now Secker, recently retired, had returned to the Piepkorn venture. He had established what he called the Arthur Carl Piepkorn Center for Evangelical Catholicity as a first step in bringing his dream to fruition. Schumacher suggested that the ALPB might be interested in publishing an additional volume and invited Secker to meet with the board in June 2005.

Secker believed there was enough material for three additional volumes. His vision was that they would be organized thematically around the topics of the Scriptures and confessions, ministry and the unity of the church, and worship and the Christian life. The board agreed to publish the three volumes; they also agreed to a second edition of their 1993 book, which would, in this iteration, be revised and corrected and would now carry the designation "Volume 1 of the *Selected Writings of Arthur Carl Piepkorn.*"

The project ran into difficulties almost from the beginning. The original volume had been edited by William Wiecher and Michael Plekon. While they were enthusiastic about the proposal, they understandably wanted to be involved in any revisions. Negotiations on a new contract led to a frustrating delay in publishing the volume, but it finally was completed in November 2006. The subsequent volumes, however, proved more problematic. Secker and the board could not come to an agreement about several matters, including who would hold the copyright, how many free copies would be given to Secker for distribution, and what restrictions there might be on future dissemination of the material through electronic means. Secker wanted to make Piepkorn's work available as widely and economically as possible; he therefore hoped to explore producing electronic versions in addition to the printed material. The Bureau had a sense of *déjà vu*, remembering their concerns with the Tobias book about free distribution cutting into the sales of the books. Furthermore, Secker's enthusiasm for the project led him to continued research which he wanted to incorporate into the books. In September 2006 Schumacher reported to the board that the project "keeps getting delayed as [Secker] finds new information and sources. This has been very frustrating."[25]

When it became apparent that agreement was not going to be possible, Secker decided to publish the volumes himself. Volume 2 was released that year under the imprint "CEC Press"; the third and fourth volumes have not been published. One result of this frustrating experience was a resolution by the board that in the future "we will return to a simple letter of agreement with all authors or they will be asked to publish elsewhere."[26]

Two additional books were published in 2007. One was a third book by Richard Bansemer. This time it was not a book of prayers, but a book about prayer—specifically prayer when one finds oneself in a difficult situation. Entitled *Forced to Pray: God's Chosen Under Pressure*, the book examined the lives and prayers of Biblical characters Jonah, Job, Mary, Jesus and Paul.[27]

The other was a book quite different from anything previously published by ALPB. Kathryn Ann Hill's *Rich in Grace: The Bible of the Poor for 21st Century Christians* was a modern edition of the 15th century *Biblia Pauperum* ("pauper's Bible"), a book of woodblocks which depicted Biblical stories artistically, aimed primarily at people who could not read. Each block was a triptych whose center panel depicted an incident in the life of Christ, while the right and left panels illustrated Old Testament stories prefiguring that incident. Hill's book utilized 38 of these woodcut images and accompanied them with brief poetic meditations. Three of these were published in the Winter 2006 issue of *Lutheran Forum*.[28]

It was an unusual choice for ALPB; previous manuscripts of poetry had been received over the years and had been rejected because the Bureau had agreed not to publish poetry (an easier reply to a poet than "we don't like your work"!). The *Biblia Pauperum* woodcuts were not easily accessible, however, and Schumacher was convinced the book might be attractive to certain academics who incorporated the medieval work in their teaching. Furthermore, Mrs. Hill was proactive in encouraging the board to publish the book. She presented the board with a three-page marketing plan, listing bookstores that might want to carry it (together with reasons why), magazines that might review it or in which ads might effectively be placed, and internet sites that might take notice of it. Given the board's past struggles with book promotion, this was a welcome approach. The board agreed to publish *Rich in Grace*.

In 2006 both the ELCA and the LCMS produced new service books/hymnals which, while containing some laudable features, were viewed as unsatisfactory by those of the evangelical catholic perspective. This led to a discussion among board members about the possibility of publishing an independent liturgical book that might appeal to many Lutherans in both church bodies who were disappointed with *Lutheran Service Book* (LCMS) or *Evangelical Lutheran Worship* (ELCA). The idea was suggested by John Hannah. He ran it by a couple of prominent liturgical scholars, one ELCA and one LCMS, who both responded positively. He then invited board members to respond via email prior to the May 2006 board meeting. Reaction was decidedly mixed. "If the ALPB can put out something as fine as *For All the Saints*," Robert Benne wrote, "it can also put out the best hymnal in Lutheranism." But others wondered if the Bureau had the resources for such a massive undertaking, and some thought that by the time such a project could be completed, most congregations would have already purchased their new denominational hymnals. Connie Seddon raised a more profound question:

> I don't know that such an undertaking is the proper role of the ALPB. Have we thought about how we ourselves would contribute to the further fragmentation of the church with such a product, designed to suit a small minority group? Currently, we are witnessing a proliferation of hymnals and worship supplements being self-published by individuals and small groups (some with liturgical or musical 'expertise,' and some with none), as well as church bodies. Do we want to add to the proliferation?

That May board meeting, as it turned out, was preoccupied with the unexpected need to find new editors for both *Forum* publications, and discussion of an ALPB service book/hymnal was tabled. But the hesitations had overwhelmed the initial enthusiasm, and the matter never came up again.[29]

Transition at *Forum Letter*
"significantly different philosophies about punctuation"

Russell Saltzman retired as *Forum Letter* editor in August 2007. His penultimate issue included a retrospective appreciation by Robert Benne. Benne summarized the shape the newsletter had taken under Saltzman, particularly commending his inclusion of a wide variety of voices as writers in *Forum Letter*. "This practice imbued the *Letter* with rich diversity of opinion," he noted. "I attribute this wholesome practice to generosity on Russ's part, not to any likely dearth of things to say himself." But taking a long view, Benne noted "how important the *Letter*, and its companion, *Lutheran Forum*, have been and are to the Lutheran churches in America."

> Both publications serve as loyal critics of Lutheran churches in which many other critics either sullenly fall silent or angrily leave, while most pastors and laity simply 'go with the flow.' They stand for a capacious Lutheran orthodoxy when there are ever fewer voices to do that. The ELCA wants to speak the language of liberal Protes-

tantism and the Missouri Synod is tempted toward sectarian isolation. *Forum Letter* and *Lutheran Forum* serve as indispensable rallying points for the many Lutherans who currently identify with 'evangelical catholicism,' as well as for the increasing number who will be attracted to that strand of Lutheran self-understanding as it is articulated by a new generation of editors.[30]

Saltzman offered his own valedictory in his final issue. He recalled his comment many years earlier, when asked for whom he wrote, that "I write for myself. If anybody wants to read over my shoulder, I'm glad to let them and grateful when they do." He expanded on that assertion by adding that he had always written "not only what I want to write for myself, but what I must write for myself if I am to think of myself as a pastor. It is the parish that first feeds *Forum Letter*." But something else was important to say.

> Over the course of 17 years, I have argued as my predecessors did for the Lutheran confessions as an evangelically catholic standard for the Lutheran churches. The *Forum* publications challenge the Lutheran churches to take the confessions as seriously as the confessions take themselves. I've tried to do that with some verve and punch. Sometimes I've used polemic (not that there is anything wrong with a well-packaged bit of polemic judiciously applied), sarcasm (same deal), and satire (think of it as puncturing the balloons of pretentiousness). And when I covered news, I hope it was fairly done, even factual, while never balanced. The balance at *Forum Letter*, remember, always tips to the confessions.

"That's what I did," he concluded. "I wrote for myself with those points in mind. ... I have sought always to advance understanding of the Lutheran confessions, to stimulate parish renewal, and provide encouragement to the laity and pastors alike."[31]

Saltzman had edited the newsletter for some seventeen years, and the board recognized his service at what was now being called the ALPB Board Dinner in October. Richard John Neuhaus agreed to be the speaker for the evening, with Saltzman giving a response. When he learned that Neuhaus would be speaking, Saltzman decided he must address "the question all Lutherans must answer, and which Richard's very presence tonight provokes: Why not Rome?" The answer, as Saltzman articulated it, was that "every serious Lutheran saying 'not Rome' must say in some way, 'Because after every consideration, here is where God has placed me, and here I shall serve Him (not as I ought, but only as I am able).'" It is, he said, "as simple as that, and as complicated." In his own case, his commitment to parish ministry was the bottom line. God had called him to this ministry, and "who am I to tell Him I can no longer be Lutheran? I must instead be the best Catholic a Lutheran can be, and there I rest content, trusting all else to the Lord."[32]

When Richard Johnson took the *Forum Letter* reins in September 2007, he assured readers that in the "new regime" they "shouldn't anticipate any radical changes; we follow the rule of thumb 'if it ain't broke, don't fix it.'"

Of course there are differences between the former and the current editor. He came to Lutheranism from agnosticism, I came from Methodism (how big that difference is, we will not discuss). He's a Republican, I'm a Democrat (though certainly not always a happy one). He's lived in the heartland most of his life, I'm a fourth-generation Californian. We do have significantly different philosophies about punctuation, about which, truth be told, I'm happy I no longer have to dispute.[33]

With that introduction, *Forum Letter* continued to do what it had been doing for many years. That same issue included a report on that summer's LCMS convention by newly-appointed associate editor Peter Speckhard. The narrow reelection of Gerald Kieschnick as president, he reported, may mask "genuine areas of relevant unity, areas in which a church body speaks unambiguously and nearly unanimously as a unified voice to the culture." The convention had evidenced such near unanimity in addressing social issues, particularly abortion and homosexuality. There continue to be areas of disagreement—fellowship and worship issues above all—but these are now more practical than doctrinal disputes, at least in the way they are discussed. All things considered, though, "the LCMS has a better set of problems facing it than just about any other church body I can think of. These days, that's no small matter."[34]

The next month, Johnson followed with a report on the ELCA's recent churchwide assembly—quite a different gathering than that of Missouri. Mark Hanson, the presiding bishop, had indicated he was willing to serve a second term—"not quite the same as 'openly campaigning,'" Johnson wrote, "but the precise difference eludes me." Hanson narrowly missed being elected on the first ballot by falling just short of the 75% required, and was then easily chosen on the second ballot. But on social issues, and specifically on human sexuality, there was little sign of unanimity. Though the proposed social statement on sexuality was still in process, the advocates of change were pushing hard for some incremental step in 2007. They got it with the narrow approval of a motion by Paul Landahl, bishop of the Metro Chicago Synod, urging and encouraging ELCA synods and bishops to "refrain from or demonstrate restraint in" disciplining pastors who are in a "mutual, chaste and faithful committed same-gender relationship," as well as the congregations that may call them. Johnson summarized the result:

> And so the ELCA is now in the interesting position of having a policy that 'precludes' sexually active gays and lesbians from service as pastors, and also having an official recommendation from its highest legislative body that bishops ignore that policy. ... We do live in a time of ambiguity.

The ELCA, he concluded, was headed for a "bumpy ride in the two years until the next assembly."[35]

Facing the future

"an increasingly post-Christian and secular culture"

In just a couple of years, the ALPB had passed through a major transition—not only a new president for the first time in more than a decade, but new editors and associate editors at both ALPB publications. It was a natural time to review the ALPB's mission statement. The most recent version had been adopted fifteen years earlier; now the new president appointed a task force to review that statement and bring recommendations to the May 2008 board meeting.

The task force didn't see the need for any substantial change to the mission statement, though they did suggest some tweaking of the language in two areas. Where the earlier statement had specifically mentioned renewal of the LCMS, the ELCA, and the ELCIC, the task force suggested a less specific formulation: "the Lutheran bodies of North America." This may have reflected a growing sense that the conflicts in the ELCA might ultimately result in the formation of a new church body (or perhaps more than one). The other suggested change was to alter language speaking about North America's "increasingly dechristianized society" to read instead "increasingly post-Christian and secular culture," a change which simply brought the statement into conformity with current sociological language. The mission statement as adopted read:

> The American Lutheran Publicity Bureau ("ALPB"), established in 1914, is a non-profit organization independent of official church control, linked by faith and confession to the Church it serves. Committed to an understanding of Lutheran tradition as evangelical and catholic, the ALPB affirms the Church's scriptural and confessional foundations in order to foster renewal within the Lutheran bodies of North America, Lutheran churches abroad, and the wider ecumenical community. The ALPB holds that all those under Christ who hold fast the Scriptures and Lutheran Confessions have a common life, with a distinctive role to play in conveying the gospel message. In an era in which the Church in North America must address an increasingly post-Christian and secular culture, the ALPB makes the theological, liturgical and devotional resources of our confessional heritage accessible and relevant to all Lutherans as well as to friends in other communions.[36]

The May 2008 meeting also included a wide-ranging brainstorming session. There was discussion (yet again) about whether to change the Bureau's name and about how to celebrate the ALPB centennial in 2014 and the Reformation quincentennial in 2017. Most interesting was a conversation about "the possible future of ELCA dissent and the ALPB." Board members mused about different scenarios that might emerge from the sexuality conflict in the ELCA, and how the ALPB might be called to serve whatever institutional groups might be formed in its wake. It would not be long before that became a more urgent discussion.[37]

Notes

1. *FL* 34, no. 7 (July 2005), 1.
2. Ibid., 2-3.
3. Ibid.
4. Ibid., 4.
5. Mark E. Chapman, Clarifying Restatement Regarding Pastor Saltzman and a Dissenting Synod, 5 July 2005, ALPB Archives.
6. Minutes, ALPB Board, 22 Oct. 2005, ALPB Archives; Mark E. Chapman, "Fundamental Unity: Evangelical-Catholic Non-Negotiables," *LF* 39, no. 4 (Winter 2005), 12-19.
7. Minutes, ALPB Board of Directors, 22 Oct. 2005.
8. *FL* 34, no. 11 (Nov. 2005), 7-8.
9. *FL* 33, no. 9 (Sept. 2004), 2.
10. John R. Hannah, "Missouri vs. Missouri—making the case," *FL* 34, no. 11 (Nov. 2005), 3-4.
11. *FL* 35, no. 9 (Sept. 2006), 7; *FL* 35, no. 10 (Oct. 2006), 8.
12. David Fiedler, e-mail message to John Hannah, 24 Apr. 2007, ALPB Archives.
13. Ronald Bagnall, e-mail message to John Hannah, 15 Jan. 2006, ALPB Archives.
14. Minutes, ALPB Board of Directors, 20 May 2006.
15. Ray Kibler, e-mail message to ALPB Board of Directors, 21 Sept. 2006, ALPB Archives.
16. Russell Saltzman, e-mail message to Ray Kibler, 22 Sept. 2006; Ray Kibler, e-mail message to ALPB Board of Directors, 23 Sept. 2006, ALPB Archives.
17. Raymond Brown, e-mail message to ALPB Board of Directors, 22 Sept. 2006; Gregory Fryer, e-mail message to ALPB Board of Directors, 22 Sept. 2006; Robert Benne, e-mail message to ALPB Board of Directors, 22 Sept. 2006, ALPB Archives.
18. Sarah Hinlicky Wilson, Lutheran Forum: Proposals, [Oct. 2006], ALPB Archives.
19. Minutes, ALPB Board of Directors, 19 May 2007.
20. *FL* 36, no. 9 (Sept. 2007), 6.
21. Robert Benne, "Sunset or Dawn? The Lutheran Calling to Public Life in America," *LF* 41, no. 2 (Summer 2007), 10ff.
22. Frank C. Senn, "Staying Put," *LF* 41, no. 2 (Summer 2007), 31.
23. Phillip Max Johnson, e-mail message to Glenn Stone, Gregory Fryer, Rodney Eberhart, Robert Hartwell, and Fred Schumacher, 11 July 2005, ALPB Archives.
24. Minutes, ALPB Board of Directors, 22 Oct. 2005.
25. Meeting Agenda and Notes, ALPB Board of Directors, 23 Sept. 2006, ALPB Archives.
26. Minutes, ALPB Board of Directors, 21 Jan. 2007.
27. Richard Bansemer, *Forced to Pray: God's Chosen Under Pressure* (Delhi, NY: ALPB Books, 2008), 6.
28. "*Biblia Pauperum:* Poetry by Kathryn Ann Hill," *LF* 40, no. 4 (Winter 2006), 57-59.
29. Robert Benne, e-mail message to ALPB Board of Directors, 26 Apr. 2006; Connie Seddon, e-mail message to ALPB Board of Directors, 27 Apr. 2006, ALPB Archives; Minutes, ALPB Board of Directors, 20 May 2006.
30. Robert Benne, "Fume and fuss: on the departing editor," *FL* 36, no. 7 (July 2007), 5-7.
31. *FL* 36, no. 8 (Aug. 2007), 5-7.
32. *FL* 37, no. 1 (Jan. 2008), 4-5.
33. *FL* 36, no. 9 (Sept. 2007), 6.
34. Ibid., 4-5.
35. *FL* 36, no. 10 (Oct. 2007), 2, 6.
36. ALPB Mission Statement (as agreed, 31 May, for immediate approval on 25 Oct. 08), ALPB Archives.
37. Brainstorming Session of Board, 31 May 2008, ALPB Archives.

Chapter 26

American Lutheranism Unraveling

N ew editorial teams took charge at both ALPB publications just as controversies in the ELCA and the LCMS were coming to a head. Under the new editors, one thing did not change: *Lutheran Forum* only rarely commented on church political issues, while *Forum Letter* tackled them head on. The ALPB also contributed to the discussion by publishing several books that directly addressed the crisis in American Lutheranism.

Lutheran Forum under Wilson and Sauer
"our agendas are going to be in plain sight"

Lutheran Forum had a new look beginning with the Fall 2007 issue, signaling new directions planned by Sarah Hinlicky Wilson and Paul Sauer. Gone was the colorful classic iconography that had graced the cover during Ronald Bagnall's tenure. In its place came the work of a series of contemporary artists. The first was a set of sketches of Martin Luther, Katie Luther, Phillip Melanchthon and Martin Chemnitz, in a Mosaic-like pattern originally intended as a T-shirt design. A new column entitled "On the Cover" featured the artist, in this case Kelly Klages, discussing her or his work as an expression of Christian faith. This became a standard in the new design, presenting a wide array of artistic genres—from the accessible sculpture of Sarah Hempel Irani to the surrealism of Finnish painter Palu Hemminki. The observation some had made that the covers "all looked alike" certainly no longer applied.[1]

Under Wilson and Sauer, individual issues of *Lutheran Forum* no longer had a stated theme; instead, there was a series of consistent features, most written by different authors each time. Some of these columns appeared in every issue. "Old Testament" and "New Testament" presented discussions of selected passages by a variety of Biblical scholars. "Studies in Luther" offered reflections on many diverse aspects of the Reformer's life and teaching, such as Jared Wicks' analysis of Luther's vocation as an Augustinian friar or Micah Kiel's explanation of "Why Luther Liked Tobit."[2]

Regular features also included "American Lutheran History," "Lex Orandi, Lex Credendi" (on liturgical issues), and "Hymn"—usually a newly composed text and/or hymn tune, with permission granted to duplicate for congregational use. Other columns occurred less regularly. "Global Lutheranism" told stories of Lutherans in various countries of the world. "Public Witness" discussed the church and socio-political issues. "Beyond Augsburg" gave readers a glimpse into non-Lutheran theological movements. "Seminarians" provided an opportunity for Lutheran seminary students to write on topics of interest to them. "Hagiography" introduced readers to lesser known but fascinating figures in church history (usually from the modern era). Occasionally the journal included book reviews and poetry.

Every issue began with two editorial pieces, one each by Wilson and Sauer. They wrote about whatever was on their mind. Their inaugural number introduced them to their readers. Wilson was forthright:

> It has been said that the one great contribution of post-modernism to scholarship will be the autobiographical clause in the introduction. This is it. My associate Paul Sauer and I don't believe in hidden agendas: our agendas are going to be in plain sight.

She proceeded to reflect on her own life as a "pastor's kid," a student at Lutheran institutions, a pastor. She admitted that "church breaks your heart" because it never quite fulfills what Christ has called it to be.

> We have one Lutheran church body in this country that looks quite a lot like Galatia, tending toward the legalistic and unforgiving, at the expense of the gospel. And we have another Lutheran church body that looks quite a lot like Corinth, tending toward the antinomian and unrepentant, at the expense of the law. The cold but real comfort for us is that these maladies have such a fine pedigree. They are the very things that the church on earth is always tempted by—has always been tempted by, even under the guidance of no less a preacher than the apostle Paul himself.

She longed for a church more like Philippi—"a church that provoked Paul to joyful, not tearful, prayers ... a church that produced a harvest of righteousness to the glory of God." Such a church is "on balance more faithful than faithless," and *Lutheran Forum* intended to "map out, in some small way, the path of Philippi."[3]

Paul Sauer was similarly autobiographical. He wrote of growing up in an LCMS congregation, his education at Valparaiso University, his passionate involvement in the pro-life movement. He recalled meeting Richard John Neuhaus, who advised him to "read Jaroslav Pelikan's *History of Christian Doctrine*, and then read anything written by Arthur Carl Piepkorn." It was because of that advice, Sauer wrote, that "I am a Lutheran today." In Piepkorn's work, he discovered Lutheranism's claim "to the heritage of the one, holy, catholic and apostolic church." He found himself captivated by "the evangelical catholic soul of Lutheranism."[4]

And so the new editors forged what was in many respects a new magazine. There was none of the apocalyptic fury often expressed by Paul Hinlicky or Leonard Klein; there was little of the dour angst reflected by Ronald Bagnall. Indeed, under Wilson and Sauer, *Lutheran Forum* seldom commented directly on ecclesiastical politics, leaving that task even more than before to *Forum Letter*. Rather they offered readers challenging material across the theological disciplines, and they introduced a wide range of new writers.

Church politics did find space in a new *Lutheran Forum* website, which featured brief commentary on a variety of topics by the editors and several other regular columnists, as well as an opportunity for readers to respond. Wilson told the ALPB board in 2009 that her purpose in developing the website was to allow the print journal to be "the 'positive vision for Lutheranism' ... with relatively little in the way of hot-button issues. The web was to be the place for them—and it certainly has been!" This was particularly true as the controversy about sexuality heated up in the ELCA. Wilson noted that in the year leading up to the ELCA's churchwide assembly in 2009, visitors to the web site "more than septupled from the previous year, from an average of 1000 unique visitors to over 7200." The web page allowed "a good number of opinions to get aired, while still maintaining high editorial and 'vision' standards for the print journal."[5]

Dissension in the ELCA

"Pseudo-Isaiah, I think"

In 2005, ELCA members who were concerned about what they viewed as the ELCA's "confessional drift" formed an organization called Lutheran Coalition for Reform ("Lutheran CORE"). The ALPB chose not to join the coalition since it was almost exclusively concerned with ELCA issues, but Lutheran CORE was frequently discussed in *Forum Letter*, beginning with a report on its first major conference in 2007.

Lutheran CORE raised many concerns, but certainly sexuality was now the hottest issue on the ELCA agenda. Work on a social statement continued, and it was anticipated that the document would go to the churchwide assembly for discussion in 2009. *Forum Letter* editor Richard Johnson described the anticipation as "hopes and fears"—"Just about everyone who cares at all about this either 'hopes' the statement will say one thing or 'fears' it may say another." He wondered whether the ELCA really needed a social statement on sexuality. Most of the ELCA's social statements, he mused, addressed public policy issues—peace, race, the environment. But while there are certainly areas where this issue touches public policy (the definition of marriage, the regulation of pornography, sexual abuse), the church's primary responsibility is "to teach the Biblical and confessional view of the gift of sexuality, and the parameters of sexual morality." In this, the ELCA has been sadly deficient.

> The ELCA has no effective way to say, 'This is what we understand a Christian approach to sexuality to be.' We seem able only to address the subject as public policy, or as disciplinary requirements for 'rostered leaders.' There's not much there to help a junior high Sunday School teacher instruct his or her students on what the church teaches about appropriate and moral sexual behavior.

He noted that the church council had approved a "message" back in 1996, which "isn't a bad statement" and deals only with matters on which there was then widespread agreement. Johnson advocated simply stopping the social statement process.

> Perhaps the best thing the task force could do would be to admit, 'We have no consensus—not just about homosexuality, but also several other aspects of sexual morality.' Perhaps we could just have the churchwide assembly affirm the 1996 message (if indeed it still represents 'consensus') and leave it at that. It's generally wiser, if you don't have anything useful to say, to keep quiet.[6]

That advice, of course, would not be taken. The first draft of the new statement was released just before Holy Week 2008. This time ELCA pastors got a 24-hour advance warning so they would not be caught unawares. Johnson's review in *Forum Letter* was critical. He noted that the document itself often used some variation of the phrase "humble and bold" to describe its proposals, and he suggested the statement was neither. The substance of the report was in fact a generally boring commentary on much of traditional Christian teaching, one "offering a little bit to both sides" on the issue of homosexuality. It recognized that "on this key issue we have no consensus"—which, Johnson suggested, "leaves wide open the possibility of offering some kind of implementing resolution that allows for ordination of persons in same-sex relationships, at least on a 'synod option' basis." He had nothing but scorn, however, for the tone of the document.

> I must admit that I always read statements like this with a good bit of eye-rolling. So often they sound like something produced by the Communist Party Central Committee—not in content ... but in writing style. Pedestrian prose, often more like a social science textbook than a theological treatise, yet enlivened every so often by the drafters' attempt to wax poetic. My favorite sentence is this one at line 837: 'Our endocrine systems bathe the inner world of our bodies in cascades of gendered hormones.' But that only narrowly beat out line 1370: 'The work of healing is unending and the cry of the neighbor for sustaining love, justice, and protection

from harm tears at the heart of the Church.' Sounds almost Biblical, doesn't it? Pseudo-Isaiah, I think.

Then in June, *Forum Letter* offered additional critiques of the draft by Kenneth Sauer and Paull Spring, both retired ELCA bishops. Much of it they found "worrisome"—the report's apparent undermining of the view of marriage as "a covenant of fidelity between one man and one woman," its weak understanding of what "pastoral care" might mean. They argued that the document needed to be "significantly re-framed and re-structured."[7]

Of course, it wasn't just the church that was grappling with questions of sexuality; American society itself was going through a sea change in its attitudes. When same-sex marriage was legalized in California in 2008, the bishops of the ELCA synods in that state all issued pastoral letters offering advice to pastors and congregations about how to respond. The bishops, editor Johnson wrote, seemed much more concerned about the legal and constitutional issues involved. "Whatever happened to a bishop's obligation to be a guardian of the faith of the church? Well, that might get controversial, of course. It is better to take refuge in constitutions than to put any trust in Scripture." He compared the bishops' statements with a pastoral letter from one of California's Roman Catholic bishops—one which reiterated Catholic teaching on marriage ("note: *teaching*, not *policy*").[8]

When the final draft of the proposed sexuality statement was released months later, Johnson asked associate editor Speckhard to analyze it. The LCMS pastor found himself traveling in a strange land—it was "less like visiting Canada than it was like visiting India. For all we have in common, the LCMS and ELCA have grown apart so fast and furiously that my expedition into this study did not cover the familiar-with-a-twist ground I expected; I found it almost entirely foreign territory." He was astounded by the statement's assertion that there are different views of homosexuality within the ELCA held by people who feel equally "conscience-bound." "An LCMS paper," Speckhard observed, "would simply dismiss as nonsense the idea that two mutually-exclusive positions could both be conscience-bound by the Word." When the statement advocated producing a liturgy for divorce, Speckhard could hardly believe it. "Toto, I don't think we're in Missouri anymore."[9]

He echoed many of the same critiques Johnson had offered of the first draft. The 33-page statement was, he wrote, "an aesthetic abomination." A college freshman at Valparaiso University who handed in a paper like this "would receive it back the next day with a polite but firm, 'Whatever this is, it will not do.' (Trust me on this. I know.)" But "the bloated prose serves the obvious revisionist agenda of the writers." Rather than providing genuine moral guidance, "the task force only offers the general rule that trust is good and hurting people is bad." He admitted that he was an outsider, but suggested that the churchwide assembly just vote it down and dissolve the task force.[10]

The editor came to the same conclusion. One purpose of such statements, he wrote, is to "inform the conscience of [the church's] members in the spirit of Christian liberty," which is "precisely why this social statement should not be approved." He suggested (tongue in cheek, he admitted) that the assembly simply adopt the Missouri Synod's 1981 "Human Sexuality: A Theological Perspective" (though he allowed that the section on "headship in marriage" would need to be excised).[11]

Along with the social statement, the task force proposed a series of policy recommendations regarding committed same-sex relationships and the possibility of gays and lesbians serving in ordained ministry. The first would allow congregations and synods to "recognize, support, and hold publicly accountable life-long, monogamous, same gender relationships." If the assembly approved this, the second proposal committed the ELCA to "finding a way for people in [such] relationships to serve as rostered leaders." Johnson found the proposals and the rationale offered for them to be contradictory and likely to result in a *de facto* splitting of the ELCA into 65 separate synodical entities. "Would we then even be a church?" Besides, "it is hard to maintain enthusiasm for a denomination which cannot agree on something as basic as the standards required of its pastors."[12]

At the churchwide assembly, all the proposals were approved more or less intact—the sexuality social statement and the recommendations that permitted pastors to be in same-sex relationships. One exception was a phrase added to the social statement which recognized that referring to these relationships as "marriage" is a "conclusion [that] differs from the historic Christian tradition and the Lutheran Confessions." In the *Forum Letter* report that filled most of the October 2009 issue, the editor found this astonishing. It was, he wrote, "a flash of—what can we call it? honesty? arrogance? *hubris*?" in which the assembly "simply admitted that what they were advocating stands against the Christian tradition and the confessions."[13]

Schism

"And so, here I stay"

In the wake of these decisions, there was talk of schism. Lutheran CORE changed its name to "Lutheran Coalition for *Renewal*" (rather than "Reform"), indicating thereby that it was no longer focusing on reform of the ELCA but on providing some alternative medium of fellowship for Lutherans irrespective of church body association. There was again discussion by the ALPB board about formally affiliating with Lutheran CORE, but they decided that "for the present the ALPB will be supportive, but will not commit to direct affiliation with CORE."[14]

Lutheran CORE convened a convocation in September 2009 in Fishers, IN, just weeks after the ELCA's churchwide assembly. There were, *Forum Letter* reported, "lots of speeches, and lots of emotion." The proposal of the Lutheran CORE leadership was that a "free-standing synod" be established, one which would be open to congregations and individuals who wanted to leave the ELCA, but also to those who wanted to stay but find some alternative source for many of the services provided by the ELCA.[15]

Within a short time, however, this proposal had morphed into the establishment of a new church body. Another Lutheran CORE convocation the following summer at Upper Arlington Lutheran Church, near Columbus, OH, began with a theological conference on the theme "Seeking New Directions for Lutheranism." ELCA officials were becoming increasingly anxious about just what those "new directions" might be, and when Lutheran CORE attempted to buy an advertisement in the *Lutheran* promoting the conference, they were rebuffed on the grounds that Lutheran CORE was "schismatic." *Forum Letter* was disdainful: "*The Lutheran* advertises all kinds of things having no official relationship to the ELCA—travel agencies, retirement communities, commercial groups—and yet they can't accept an ad for a conference led by ELCA theologians?" Noting that *Forum Letter* doesn't normally run advertisements, the newsletter printed the refused ad copy "as a public service." "We'll go further," editor Johnson noted, "and recommend that you attend."[16]

Lutheran CORE came under attack from another direction when the ELCA's *Journal of Lutheran Ethics* published a polemical piece by Jon Pahl, a professor at Lutheran School of Theology at Philadelphia, accusing Lutheran CORE of "white male backlash" and a string of ancient heresies. "Serious analysis is one thing," editor Johnson responded in *Forum Letter*. "Hysterical accusations are quite another." Pahl's article is "hardly the objective evaluation of a scholar."

> Pahl gives himself away even more dramatically with this zinger: 'So, while I hope to remain in dialogue and fellowship with individuals who oppose full inclusion of faithful LGBT people in the church or society, I can no longer tolerate the violent policies and practices, and the heretical leanings, which justify homophobia.' (He left out the requisite apology for having actually tolerated these things for so many years.)

"Yeah," Johnson added, "that's conducive to dialogue all right."[17]

The theological conference met as planned, then adjourned and moved to a larger venue for what would be the constituting convention of the North American Lutheran Church (NALC). *Forum Letter* covered the event sympathetically, though not with full-throated support. "The biggest question," wrote Johnson, "is: will it fly?"

> It was announced with great delight that 18 congregations had already joined the new church, even before it was established. But in a year's time, how many congregations will join? The estimates I heard range from 100 to 1,000. If it hit the high end of that range, it would be the fourth largest Lutheran church body in the United States—but it would still be slightly more than a tenth the size of the ELCA, at least in terms of congregations.

Over the next months, *Forum Letter* tracked the progress of the new church body and the reactions of ELCA officials (which were generally uncharitable). "Nasty things, church fights," Johnson wrote. "And as in bitter divorces, absolutely nobody wins."[18]

The ALPB board had promised to be supportive of Lutheran CORE, and one manifestation of support was the Bureau's publication of the lectures from the 2010 theological conference as *Seeking New Directions for Lutheranism: Biblical, Theological, and Churchly Perspectives,* edited by Carl Braaten. Many of the presentations were made by people who had been associated with the ALPB in one way or another through the years, including Paul Hinlicky and Robert Benne. The blurb on the back of the book was pointed:

> While the conference speakers are critical of many current policies of the ELCA, their purpose is to envision a future for Lutheranism with integrity in an ecumenical age whose bedrock is faithfulness to Holy Scripture, the Ancient Creeds of the Church and the Lutheran Confessions.

The NALC and Lutheran CORE continued the pattern over the next few years of combining a theological conference with the annual meeting of the new church body. Every year through 2014, the conference papers were published by the ALPB.[19]

While *Lutheran Forum* had generally eschewed commentary on current church political disputes, the events of 2009 and 2010 almost demanded some notice in the journal. Just prior to the churchwide assembly in 2009, Sarah Wilson argued that faithful ELCA members must "speak the truth in love." The proposed sexuality statement and accompanying recommendations are "outright recipes for internal ecclesiastical catastrophe" as well as "ecumenical catastrophe." She advised readers on how to approach the forthcoming assembly ("take the risk of making your convictions public," "pray for our church to exercise 'right judgment'") and what to do afterward if the assembly approves the recommendations ("increase your benevolences—and reroute them," "recognize the dire situation as a renewed call to evangelism"). She advocated sticking with the ELCA:

> I plead with all of you who adhere to traditional Lutheran teaching shared by the church catholic on this issue: *do not abandon your brothers and sisters who are in error.* Do not abandon your sin-, death-, and devil-ridden church. Love them, stick by them, and do not cease to witness to them until love and truth come back together again.[20]

Following the assembly, Wilson elaborated on her reasons for believing that people should stay in the ELCA. "This is a messy argument about the church and the sinners who populate it," she admitted. Her argument was not addressed primarily to those considering leaving Lutheranism altogether ("my gripe with the ELCA is not Lutheran theology but the lack thereof") or joining some existing Lutheran body ("such arguments can only reinforce this mutually destructive competition between us"). Rather she wanted to address "those who are drawn to ... staying Lutheran but cutting out and starting afresh." In America, the "tendency to split at the slightest friction has made an embarrassing mess of the religious landscape."

> The instinct to purity has done little to promote the truth ... and there is little evidence of love in it. ... If there is to be any integrity to our being as church, it's

time to stop playing the game that actually plays us, jump off the hamster wheel of denominational splintering, and renounce schism once and for all as a solution to ecclesiastical trouble.

A new denomination, she predicted, will "be known as the church that shuns gay people. The fact that this is not technically true will be of little consequence. It will be a real and persisting identity for this new body." Staying with the ELCA does not mean "quiescent acceptance of the new status quo"; rather it is "to stay and resist, for the sake of the many souls who are subject to this jurisdiction and for the repentance of those who have taught and acted badly." Ultimately, Wilson argued, "you don't want to face the Lord on judgment day and say, 'I broke fellowship with the unrighteous because I was sick of dealing with them,' lest He say the same thing back to you!"[21]

Lutheran Forum offered other arguments for staying in the ELCA. Frank Senn wistfully acknowledged that the "churchly tradition" of Lutheranism cannot "translate into institutional loyalty" since institutions pass away.

> The congregation in which I was baptized no longer exists. The congregation in which I was confirmed no longer exists. The congregation in which I was ordained no longer exists. The college I attended as an undergraduate (Hartwick) is no longer Lutheran. ... The seminary in which I matriculated no longer exists. ... The denomination in which I grew up, the ULCA, no longer exists. Neither does the LCA in which I was ordained. I am not overly sad about this; I realize we have here 'no abiding city.'

> The more heartwrenching loss is that of a solid confessional basis in my current denomination, the ELCA, that has become increasingly sectarian. ... We are focused now on the issue of homosexuality. But in truth there are other matters that also contribute to the crisis of faith: the doctrine of the Trinity as it effects orthodox worship, the saving work of Christ as it impacts Christian mission, the doctrine of the ministry as it affects teaching authority in the church, the confusion of law and gospel as relates to political correctness and cheap grace.

Nonetheless, Senn continued, there is little reason to think that some new body will be much of an improvement, and so "we have nowhere better to go. ... While we await our resurrection, we bear the cross of Christ by living in his divided body."[22]

Still another perspective was offered by Erma Seaton Wolf, an ELCA pastor who had served on the steering committee of Lutheran CORE. She wrote eloquently of her own decision to stay in the ELCA—"torn but ultimately believing that creating a new Lutheran denomination was a mistake and the loss of an opportunity to write a different outcome for this chapter in American Lutheran history."

> I will never know if that was indeed the case; the time has passed, and the opportunity, if indeed it truly existed, will not come again. The NALC is now a reality, experiencing growth numerically and in other ways. I will and do pray for it to become a strong witness to the gospel of salvation in Jesus Christ. ...

But I am also praying and working for the renewal and strengthening of the Evangelical Lutheran Church in America. ... The ELCA is not unique in being a cracked earthen pot. ...

None of this promises to be easy. Many friends have questioned me as to why I insist on remaining in the ELCA. ... What is the point? Such inconvenience, discomfort, even risk of opprobrium and public rejection is seen as being for no good purpose and a waste of one's potential. ...

But I am reminded over and over from Scripture that success in God's economy looks and feels more like failure. In fact, it *is* failure: rejection, loss of authority and status, sorrow, and finally death. ... But blessing and new life is exactly what we are promised, though hidden from plain view.

"And so," she concluded, "here I stay. May God help us all."[23]

Critiquing the NALC

"at best uninterested in NALC and at worst hostile"

There were some in the NALC who seemed to expect the ALPB publications would be uncritical of the new church body; after all, the board had promised to be "supportive" of Lutheran CORE, which had served as midwife for the NALC. *Forum Letter* continued to offer generally positive coverage of the annual theological conferences and NALC convocations and to chastise ELCA officials who treated harshly congregations and pastors who wished to leave the ELCA for the NALC. But the ALPB's editors did not view the NALC as above criticism. A serious kerfuffle erupted at the 2013 ELCA churchwide assembly when NALC bishop John Bradosky took offense at some words of Presiding Bishop Mark Hanson. Bradosky, along with his assistant, David Wendel, had been invited to the assembly as ecumenical guests. With all the representatives from various churches standing on the stage, Hanson made the comment that upset Bradosky:

> When a church first defines itself over against another, the road to reconciliation is much more arduous. This church at its founding said 'that's not what it means to be Lutheran. To be Lutheran is to first define ourselves on the basis of our relatedness.' [When we do that,] then we are called immediately into deeper conversation to attend to those things that keep us more fully together.

Wendel later wrote in the NALC's newsletter that Hanson had shown "open disrespect for our bishop and the NALC." The NALC officials left the assembly in anger; Bradosky wrote a note to the ELCA's ecumenical staff person, Donald McCoid, raging about Hanson's "passive-aggressive display of anger couched in the language of reconciliation."[24]

Forum Letter's editor had been covering the assembly, and he viewed the incident quite differently. He believed that Hanson had not been referring to the NALC at all, but to the 16th century Reformers defining themselves "over against another." "Please understand," Johnson wrote, "I am not at all a fan of Mark Hanson. ... But this appears to me to be a rather unfortunate overreaction" on the part of Bradosky.

I was present in the assembly hall and had no sense that Bp. Hanson was offering anything other than the usual ecumenical/interreligious platitudes. I have watched the video of the session several times and have seen nothing that has changed my opinion. ...

For the NALC bishop to accuse Hanson of 'passive-aggressive anger' is hardly a response that will move the two churches beyond hard feelings, and to report this publicly in the NALC newsletter seems unfathomable to me. In the Christian community, the first effort should always be to interpret the neighbor's actions in the kindest way. If one still feels one has been insulted, one speaks privately to the offender; one does not post one's hurt feelings on the internet, at least not right out of the box.[25]

Johnson also refuted Wendel's assertion that the newly elected presiding bishop, Elizabeth Eaton, "when asked how she would relate to the NALC ... recalled that Jesus tells us to love our enemies, even though our enemies are sometimes Lutheran." The remark, Johnson noted, came in a press conference in response to a question that he himself had asked. He quoted the full context of what Bp. Eaton had said (referring not just to the NALC but also Lutheran Congregations in Mission for Christ, another group composed largely of former ELCA congregations):

In baptism we are brothers and sisters in Christ and we do claim the same Lutheran heritage. ... The manner in which those denominations were formed has been extremely painful to our church, and it's not going to be something that can be quickly forgotten. ... But we're supposed to love our enemies and pray for those who persecute us, *and since these are actually brothers and sisters*—well you know, families may be tougher than enemies, but we'll do what we can through God's grace.

"So no," he concluded, "Bishop Eaton did not call the NALC (and LCMC) 'enemies'— quite the reverse. She called them 'brothers and sisters in Christ.'"[26]

The issue provoked a lengthy discussion at the next ALPB board meeting. The minutes noted that "people in the hierarchy of NALC, whom we count as friends and partners in the Great Commission, did take offense ... and they were displeased with Pastor Johnson's commentary and thus ... displeased with ALPB." The board recognized that Johnson had reported his observations "as fairly and honestly as he could," and that the ALPB publications are, after all, a forum—a "free exchange of ideas, bounded only by faithfulness to the Holy Scriptures and the Confessions." They also noted that this was hardly the first time in the ALPB's history where "people have taken issue with something printed" in the publications. But this led to a wider concern that "rightly or wrongly, the NALC hierarchy considers [our publications] at best uninterested in NALC and at worst hostile," and they perceive "a sense of divide caused by ALPB." This, the minutes recorded, "has never been an intention of the ALPB Board."[27]

A few months later, former editor Russell Saltzman weighed in on the controversy in his *Forum Letter* report on that year's NALC convocation in Charleston, SC (Saltzman had joined the NALC, and was in fact serving as dean of one of the new church's mission districts). He cited the churchwide assembly issue as one of the "creaks" of the NALC—missteps that might be expected in any new organization. The accusation that Hanson had deliberately insulted Bradosky, he wrote, "is open to disagreement. Clearly NALC staff thought [so] (as well as some ELCA folks), but numerous others, both ELCA and NALC, dismissed Hanson's remarks as merely one of his awkward ecumenical moments and thought his intention was misinterpreted." The incident, however, "was not a fit issue to air" in the NALC newsletter and simply "made everyone except Hanson look churlish."[28]

The challenge of being a pan-Lutheran ministry became more complicated with the founding of the NALC. Within a few years of its birth, there was significant NALC representation on the ALPB board—both because of previously ELCA board members who left to join the new church and because of newly elected members who were already members of the NALC. Many subscribers to the *Forum* publications were among those who left the ELCA. Still, the board continued to insist on both the ALPB's independence from any Lutheran church body and on the freedom given the editors to address issues—sometimes critically—in all the Lutheran structures.

Meanwhile, in Missouri
"nothing is ever easily parsed"

As the ELCA appeared to be coming apart at the seams, there was new turmoil brewing in the LCMS. Two major items seemed destined to provoke some controversy at the 2010 convention. One was a series of constitutional amendments proposed by a "blue ribbon task force" which would make several structural changes in LCMS governance. Associate editor Speckhard described the issue succinctly for non-Missourians:

> In broad terms, President Kieschnick leads those who say this is not (or shouldn't be at any rate) your grandfather's church. What worked in the past doesn't work anymore and needs changing. The anti-incumbent side says it not only is your grandfather's church but would be a far cry better off if it acted like it more often.

Speckhard saw both sides as expressing "the same anguish over the condition of the church in the modern world," but he doubted whether "a task force, no matter how blue the ribbon, can recommend anything beyond faithfulness and prayer that will make any difference."[29]

In the end, most of the proposals were approved, but they paled in importance next to the unexpected results of the presidential election. Gerald Kieschnick had served for nine years and was willing to continue in the office. He had twice been re-elected on the first ballot, though with modest majorities. Kieschnick was considered a relative moderate by Missouri standards, and as the 2010 convention approached it became apparent that conservatives were coalescing behind Matthew Harrison, the executive director of LCMS World Relief and Human Care. "Nothing is ever easily parsed in Missouri," editor Johnson wrote in *Forum Letter*, "and we know self-identified evangelical catholics who line up behind each of these men, and with some enthusiasm." He invited a proponent of each candidate to make the case for their man.[30]

The convention that year was covered for *Forum Letter* by Scott Yakimow. "Conventional wisdom," he wrote, "was that President Gerald Kieschnick would win a fourth term by a nose." When the results of the first ballot were announced, however, Harrison had defeated Kieschnick with some 54% of the votes. It was the beginning of a new era in the Missouri Synod.[31]

A very public controversy broke out in late 2012 in an incident reminiscent of district president David Benke's participation in an interfaith event (or worship service, depending on who was telling the story) following the September 11, 2001, attack on New York. This time the setting was a school shooting in Newtown, CT. The local LCMS pastor, Rob Morris, gave the benediction at an interfaith vigil. Unfortunately for him, there was extensive media coverage, "and there," Johnson wrote in *Forum Letter*, "before God and everybody (and perhaps before all those gods of other religions) was a Missouri Synod pastor praying in the presence of the heterodox."[32]

Conservatives in Missouri, seemingly in the ascendency following the election of Harrison, began an internet campaign against Morris's action. One far right Missouri website, "Steadfast Lutherans," included a comment that "the gunman killed the body which lasts for 70 or 80 years. ... False teaching and practice kills the soul which lives for eternity in heaven or hell." *Forum Letter* noted that Harrison "took an admirable first step" by asking the website to take the comments down. Harrison also indirectly asked the ALPB's Forum Online moderators to remove a thread where there had been a lively discussion about the incident; the moderators (Speckhard and Johnson) decided to leave the thread but close it to further comment.[33]

Forum Letter reported that Harrison was talking behind the scenes with Morris and his district president, and the result was a statement from Morris that "I believed my participation to be, not an act of joint worship, but an act of ... mercy and care to a community shocked and grieving." He recognized, however, that others had a different view and apologized "where I have caused offense by pushing Christian freedom too far." Harrison then wrote a letter to the Synod expressing his judgment that this was in fact "joint worship," but since Pr. Morris had apologized, he urged anyone contemplating filing charges to refrain from doing so. But when the story of the apology hit the press, there was outrage among some LCMS members, to say nothing of the public at large, that Morris had been pressured to apologize. Harrison then issued what editor Johnson called "an extraordinary statement from a denominational head," admitting his own "responsibility for the debacle" and apologizing for "[increasing] the pain of a hurting community." He also apologized to Morris, his congregation, the Newtown community, and to the Synod "for embarrassment due to the media coverage." It was, Johnson wrote, "an admirable statement ... and yet [Harrison] is now taking it from all sides."[34]

Forum Letter under Johnson and Speckhard
"thoughtful observation of the church"

Forum Letter hardly restricted itself to church politics and institutional concerns. The editors often wrote very personal reflections on life and faith, much as Russell Saltzman had done during his editorship. In 2008, Johnson wrote about an "unexpected journey" with a friend who had murdered his wife. He puzzled about how such a thing could happen.

> How could this happen? I don't need to look far to find the answer. It is in my own heart, where that voice of rebellion also whispers. I'd like to think that a person who kills another is a monster, but more often he is just an ordinary person who does a monstrous thing. Indeed, if there is a monster, it lives in me, too. ...
>
> 'Sin is couching at the door.' That line from Genesis 4 has always been one of the most terrifying in Scripture for me, because I know it to be true. And so a vicious murder is shocking; but it is not really surprising. Very little about human beings is, in the end, surprising. It is, after all, why we need a redeemer. It is why God sent his Son.

He told of how he began to visit the killer in jail, and how he was asked to testify at his trial as a character witness. The man was ultimately convicted and sentenced to prison. "When I am praying the litany now," he wrote, "the line that asks God 'to be merciful to all who are imprisoned' takes on a new meaning, even a kind of passion." The piece received the top award from the Associated Church Press in 2008 for feature article in a newsletter.[35]

Another article told the difficult story of an ELCA bishop who had abandoned his faith. Soon after his retirement, he had publicly questioned the resurrection. Then, after a cancer diagnosis, he announced that he no longer believed in God. "He certainly didn't believe in an afterlife," Johnson wrote. "He was convinced that when he died, that would be it. And he wasn't shy about sharing this unfaith with any who would listen." His memorial service was "one of the emptiest and most depressing experiences I have ever had."

> There was virtually no mention of God. There was no prayer. There was no Scripture. There was a lot of talk about what a fine man he was, a man of integrity. There was music. The assembly was invited to sing John Lennon's 'Imagine'—'Imagine there's no heaven, it's easy if you try, no hell below us, above us only sky.'

The editor wondered what the church should do when a pastor loses his or her faith. "I have no answers. I have questions, to be sure, but even more, I have grief and sadness. And I have a confession: 'Lord, to whom can we go? You have the words of eternal life.'"[36]

Other pieces were in a lighter vein. Associate editor Speckhard wrote a satirical essay entitled "Temple prostitution: a modest proposal." He suggested that temple prostitution has a long history in the Bible—mostly negative, but then that's because of its association with idolatry. "The Biblical writers never foresaw or contemplated sanctified, faithful, God-pleasing prostitution in the churches and thus never wrote about it." Besides, Jesus himself seemed to "have a soft spot for prostitutes."

> Now think of the benefits. This program would attract the very demographic we have had such trouble reaching (young men). It would end our fiscal woes. Think of the money we could raise to feed the hungry! ... It would also provide a teaching opportunity against the age-old heresy that the body is evil. God made us with perfectly natural sexual urges. Why are you so hung up on sex? ...
>
> I certainly don't insist that anyone become a temple prostitute or worship God with the help of one. But I do say that there have always been willing prostitutes and willing clients who have been marginalized by traditional sexual mores, and the time has come to change that. And the way to change it is to stop the marginalizing. We'll all benefit from being a healthier, more inclusive, more faithful, more forgiving, and more satisfied church body if only we'll be open to the idea of God doing something new.

The spoof, with its not so subtle pillorying of the arguments being made for changing the church's teaching on sexuality, cost *Forum Letter* a handful of subscribers; others read it with great glee. "In all the years I have been reading the *Forum Letter*," one reader wrote, "I have never laughed so hard. ... What a hoot!!! ... Thanks for giving this little old life long Lutheran a fun read." The Associated Church Press agreed, giving the piece an honorable mention in the category of humor in that year's "Best of the Christian Press" awards.[37]

Speckhard also ruffled some feathers with an article about taking some of his parishioners on a pilgrimage to the Holy Land, sharing the tour with other groups and individuals from various denominations. He wrote of his decision that his group would not participate in the last day's communion service with the other pilgrims but have their own service. While this was perfectly in keeping with LCMS policy, it was regarded with some amusement and befuddlement by the non-Lutherans on the trip. Speckhard explained his decision. "In the tragedy-soaked history of the people of God," he reflected, "it remains an offense that we couldn't commune together that day. But it wasn't the greatest potential offense."

> True, it would have been easy just to go along and get along—nobody would have put me up on charges or anything—but I think more blessing came from the opportunity to explain our practice and actually practice it than would have come from ignoring it and just communing together for the sake of the friendships we had formed with the other groups by touring together. Somehow closed communion, though awkward, keeps the focus where it needs to be, preserves what genuine spiritual unity there is to be had and prevents doctrinal scattering and dissolution.

"In the Holy Land," he concluded, "I was glad to be a part of a denomination that takes such things seriously."[38]

The piece got lots of reaction, both appreciative and angry. To some readers, Speckhard's perspective represented the harsh LCMS conservatism the ALPB had always opposed. Two responses from LCMS pastors, both critical of Speckhard, were printed in a subsequent issue of *Forum Letter*, one accusing him of "ecumenical aloofness." Speckhard responded graciously but firmly.

> Surely everyone can recognize divisions as tragic. Nobody delights that there is a brick wall dividing the Cave of the Nativity. But it is ecumenical aloofness to breezily dismiss the reasons for that wall and those who built it, to act as though most Christians through the centuries and across the globe were making much ado about nothing by insisting upon separate altars for separate confessions, to pretend as though our willingness to commune together somehow shows or creates any genuine unity. ... [Those] who take their own and everyone else's confession of faith seriously and whose practice is right in line with historic Christian practice get called ecumenically aloof, while those who really are aloof, who really do introduce new and alien practices and who really do fail to take seriously what Christians have always taken seriously claim to be ecumenically engaged.[39]

To many non-LCMS readers, on the other hand, Speckhard had provided a coherent and even rather winsome explanation of Missouri's official communion practice, and while they might not agree, they at least understood and respected it in a new way. The diverse responses led to some discussion in the next ALPB board meeting. "Interestingly," the minutes reported, "the most vocal supporters of Pastor Speckhard on the board were ELCA."[40]

Awards from the Associated Church Press were regularly received during these years. ALPB publications had received occasional recognition from ACP in the past in its "Best of the Christian Press" competition, but between 2009 and 2015 *Forum Letter* took at least one award every year. The newsletter received the highest (twice) or second highest award (four times) in the category "Best in Class—Newsletters" every year but 2013 (though that year *Lutheran Forum* was similarly recognized in the competition for magazines). In 2015, one of the judges commented on "*Omnium gatherum*," a *Forum Letter* feature begun originally by Richard John Neuhaus in 1978 and continued by subsequent editors, which included brief notes and comments about a wide variety of things:

> There is a wonderfully engaging writing style here, one with a lot of personality and a sharp wit grounded in thoughtful observation of the church. The breadth of topics and issues touched on is impressive. The editorializing (and I don't mean to use the term pejoratively) that comes forth from this approach can border on the snarky, but the substance underneath makes you think, and to that end, any reader who has a different view and comes away perhaps turned off by the style ought still to respect the conclusions and opinions here (if they're being honest and fair-minded).

"That's our aim," Johnson mused, "and if they're not being honest and fair-minded, I guess they let their subscription lapse."[41]

Book publishing
"the evangelical catholic understanding"

The Bureau continued to publish three or four books each year. In addition to the Lutheran CORE theological conference lectures, there were three volumes of essays from theological discussions held under the auspices of Ascension Lutheran Church in Calgary, AB, and its pastor, K. Glen Johnson. These papers were written for specially constituted commissions of international ecumenical representatives (pastors, theologians and others). The first was published as *The Banff Commission* in 2008. The purpose, wrote Glen Johnson, was to "address the malaise that has overtaken our Lutheran churches, identify the real nature of the problem, and give advice to pastors and congregations about how we shall remain faithful in the midst of the storm clouds that gather around us." Subsequent volumes dealt with congregational ministry to persons of varying sexual orientations and the Lutheran teaching on marriage and the family.[42]

There were other books as well. Several were published with parish pastors in mind, such as two volumes written by longtime *Forum Letter* editor Russell Saltzman. *The Pastor's Page and Other Small Essays* consisted of articles Saltzman had written for his congregational newsletters. *Speaking of the Dead: When We All Fall Down* was a collection of funeral sermons written for diverse situations, together with Saltzman's reflections on "what a funeral sermon must say and what it must not." It was, wrote David Mills, former editor of *Touchstone* and former executive editor of *First Things*, "a moving book, but one that kept me off balance as I read. Russ tells us, and his people, the Gospel, but it is the Gospel ... which doesn't magically solve all the problems we suffer living in the world we live in."[43]

The Bureau also published additional liturgical books. Rod Ronneberg's *A Little Book of Canons* was issued in 2011. It offered a series of Eucharistic prayers, keyed to church times and seasons. Some pastors had expressed frustration with the suggested "prayers of the people" offered by Augsburg Fortress Publishing House; often these were deemed by some too "politically correct" or just plain silly. (*Forum Letter* occasionally skewered these prayers, one of which asked God to "restore the homes of manatees and sea turtles.") As an alternative, the ALPB offered another book by Richard Bansemer, *Prayers of the People: Petitionary Prayers Guided by the Texts for the Day.* Bansemer provided intercessions for each Sunday of the three-year cycle of the Revised Common Lectionary, as well as some additional holy days and special services. With both the Ronneberg and Bansemer books, purchasers could request the texts in digital form, at no additional charge, to facilitate use in local congregational bulletins.[44]

Finally, the Bureau published some shorter works by Lutheran theologians. Former ALPB executive director Paul Hinlicky's *Preaching God's Word according to Luther's Doctrine in America Today* was primarily a book of sermons. In the introduction, Hinlicky recounted how a stint as pastor of two Virginia congregations had led him to realize "how little or how poorly my people had been catechized in the recent past." The result was a series of sermons on basic Christian doctrines, which then became this book.[45]

Two small books by Robert Jenson were among the ALPB's offerings. *Lutheran Slogans: Use and Abuse* considered several of the watchwords of the Reformation ("justification by faith," "priesthood of all believers," "real presence," etc.). Every movement needs slogans, he wrote, but "the problem is that as over time they become increasingly necessary, they just so tend to acquire lives of their own, and then can become untethered from the complex of ideas and practices which they once evoked." In a brief chapter on each of several of these Lutheran slogans, Jenson explained how they had become "untethered" and how we might re-appropriate them in a more useful way.[46]

The ALPB also published Jenson's *On the Inspiration of Scripture*, a slim book that Valparaiso University's Gilbert Meilaender called "brief but deceptively weighty." Jenson began with a confession: "my concern with the inspiration of Scripture is a recent and indeed—considering how long I have been writing and teaching theology—embarrassingly late development." The extended essay, however, expounded the insights of a lifetime of theological study.[47]

Carl Braaten had edited several of the books published by the ALPB, but in 2012 he contributed a manuscript of his own, *Essential Lutheranism: Theological Perspectives on Christian Faith and Doctrine*. His aim, he wrote, was "to present the essentials of confessional Lutheran theology in an ecumenical and pluralistic age." But he was very clear on what "confessional Lutheran theology" means:

> I do not believe that any old kind of Lutheranism will do. There are heretical and apostate forms of Lutheranism evident for all eyes to see. Many of the German Christians in Hitler's Nazi regime were Lutherans. Bearing the name 'Lutheran' is no guarantee of being faithful to the gospel of Jesus Christ.

"The red thread that runs throughout this book," he wrote, "is the conviction that the evangelical catholic understanding of the biblical Christian faith is the most faithful interpretation of the Lutheran theological heritage in an ecumenical age." That understanding had really come to characterize the ALPB's publishing ministry itself.[48]

Transitions

"he really didn't leave us"

In January 2009, Richard John Neuhaus died. Neuhaus had been an early columnist for *Lutheran Forum* and then editor of *Forum Letter* from 1974 to 1990. He was, during much of that period, the most prominent "public voice" of the American Lutheran Publicity Bureau. *Forum Letter* produced a special double issue commemorating its former editor. "What *Forum Letter* is today is probably due to Richard John Neuhaus as much as to anyone else," editor Johnson wrote. The issue contained tributes by Russell Saltzman, Gilbert Meilaender, James Nuechterlein, Charles Austin, Richard Koenig, Larry Bailey, and David Benke, as well as several pages of quotations from Neuhaus's writings in *Forum Letter.* The spring issue of *Lutheran Forum* also included tributes by John Hannah and Robert Benne. Commenting on Neuhaus's reception into the Roman Catholic Church, Benne observed that "he really didn't leave us if we think of ourselves as Christians first and only then as Lutherans. We can all claim him as a unique and irreplaceable Christian who made his mark on American public and religious life."[49]

There were other persons very important in the ALPB's history who died around this time. Glenn Stone, founding editor of *Lutheran Forum,* longtime executive director and later board member of ALPB, died in June 2009. *Lutheran Forum* printed Ronald Bagnall's sermon at Stone's funeral, as well as a lengthy tribute by Dorothy Zelenko, who had worked with Stone for many years as an ALPB board member. She recalled words written to Stone by a previous ALPB president, John Leonard, when he retired from the board in 1985:

> My service bridged the ancient and the modern ALPB. There were giants in the first phase but I doubt that any one has been as vital to the organization for as long a period as you have been. Without you there would not have been a Board to serve on. I don't doubt it—no one should.[50]

Richard Koenig, founding editor of *Forum Letter,* died on Reformation Day 2011, and Martin E. Marty, who was Koenig's brother-in-law, wrote a remembrance for the newsletter, describing Koenig as "intense." "It was said of him that he never under-reacted to events or stimuli." If one could poll all the pastors, students and parishioners Koenig had influenced, Marty mused, "we'd find them remembering Richard with many stories, recalling how he could inspire them, nudge them, entertain them, and cheer them. Intensely."[51]

Notes

1. Kelly Klages, "The Uncomfortable Aesthetic of Truth," *LF* 41, no. 3 (Fall 2007), 64ff.; Sarah Hempel Irani, "A Lutheran Sculptor of Mary," *LF* 41, no. 4 (Winter 2007), 64ff.; Panu Hemminki, "Surrealistic Faith and Faithful Surrealism," *LF* 42, no. 2 (Summer 2008), 64ff.
2. Jared Wicks, "Brother Martin, Augustinian Friar," *LF* 42, no. 1 (Spring 2008), 33-36; Micah D. Keil, "Why Luther Liked Tobit," *LF* 43, no. 4 (Winter 2009), 29-31.
3. Sarah Hinlicky Wilson, "Church Breaks Your Heart," *LF* 41, no. 3 (Fall 2007), 5.
4. Paul Robert Sauer, "The Certain Ambiguity of Catholicity," *LF* 41, no. 3 (Fall 2007), 7.
5. Sarah Hinlicky Wilson, Editor's Report [to ALPB Board of Directors], Nov. 2009, ALPB Archives.
6. *FL* 37, no. 1 (Jan. 2008), 1-3.
7. *FL* 37, no. 4 (Apr. 2008), 2-3; *FL* 37, no. 6 (June 2008), 4-6.
8. *FL* 37, no. 8 (Aug. 2008), 3-4.

9. *FL* 38, no. 4 (Apr. 2009), 2.

10. Ibid., 2-5.

11. *FL* 38, no. 5 (May 2009), 1-3.

12. *FL* 38, no. 6 (June 2009), 1-3.

13. *FL* 38, no. 10 (Oct. 2009), 2.

14. Minutes, ALPB Board of Directors, 7 Nov. 2009.

15. *FL* 38, no. 11 (Nov. 2009), 1-2.

16. *FL* 39, no. 6 (May 2010), 8

17. *FL* 39, no. 7 (July 2010), 1-2.

18. *FL* 39, no. 10 (Oct. 2010), 5; *FL* 40, no. 1 (Jan. 2011), 2.

19. Carl E. Braaten, ed., *Seeking New Directions for Lutheranism: Biblical, Theological, and Churchly Perspectives* (Delhi, NY: ALPB Books, 2010); *No Other Name: Salvation through Christ Alone* (Delhi, NY: ALBP Books, 2011); *Preaching and Teaching the Law and Gospel of God* (Delhi, NY: ALBP Books, 2012); *On Being the Church in These Precarious Times* (Delhi, NY: ALPB Books, 2013); *Rightly Handling the Word of Truth: Scripture, Canon, and Creed* (ALPB Books, 2014).

20. Sarah Hinlicky Wilson, "Speak the Truth in Love," *LF* 43, no. 2 (Summer 2009), 2, 5.

21. Sarah Hinlicky Wilson, "Why Stay?" *LF* 43, no. 4 (Winter 2009), 3-8.

22. Frank C. Senn, "Lutheran Identity and Denominational Loyalty," *LF* 44, no. 4 (Winter 2010), 55-56.

23. Erma Seaton Wolf, "Here I Stay," *LF* 45, no. 1 (Spring 2011), 55-58.

24. Quoted in *FL* 42, no. 10 (Oct. 2013), 5-6.

25. Ibid., 6.

26. Ibid., 7.

27. Minutes, ALPB Board of Directors, 11 Jan. 2014.

28. Russell E. Saltzman, "Doing the Charleston," *FL* 43, no. 9 (Sept. 2014), 6.

29. *FL* 39, no. 3 (Mar. 2010), 2, 4.

30. Ibid., 4ff.

31. Scott Yakimow, "The times, they are a changin'," FL 39, no. 9 (Sept. 2010), 3.

32. *FL* 42, no. 3 (Mar. 2013), 2.

33. Ibid.

34. Ibid., 3.

35. *FL* 37, no 2 (Feb. 2008), 2, 4.

36. *FL* 38, no. 9 (Sept. 2009), 2, 4.

37. *FL* 38, no. 11 (Nov. 2009), 5-6; *FL* 39, no. 1 (Jan. 2010), 8.

38. *FL* 41, no. 5 (May 2012), 4.

39. *FL* 41, no. 6 (June 2012), 7.

40. Minutes, ALPB Board of Directors, 12 May 2010.

41. *FL* 45, no. 6 (June 2016), 8.

42. *The Banff Commission* (Delhi, NY: ALPB Books, 2008), 19; *The Jasper Commission* (Delhi, NY: ALPB Books, 2009); *The Lake Louise Commission: The Sacred Family* (Delhi, NY: ALPB Books, 2011).

43. Russell E. Saltzman, *Speaking of the Dead: When We All Fall Down* (Delhi, NY: ALPB Books, 2014).

44. Rod L. Ronneberg, *A Little Book of Canons* (Delhi, NY: ALPB Books, 2011); *FL* 45, no. 4 (Apr. 2016), 8; Richard F. Bansemer, *Prayers of the People: Petitionary Prayers Guided by the Texts for the Day* (Delhi, NY: ALPB Books, 2014).

45. Paul R. Hinlicky, *Preaching God's Word according to Luther's Doctrine in America Today* (Delhi, NY: ALPB Books, 2010), 7.

46. Robert W. Jenson, *Lutheran Slogans: Use and Abuse* (Delhi, NY: ALPB Books, 2011), 6.

47. Robert W. Jenson, *On the Inspiration of Scripture* (Delhi, NY: ALPB Books, 2012), 1.

48. Carl E. Braaten, *Essential Lutheranism: Theological Perspectives on Christian Faith and Doctrine* (Delhi, NY: ALPB Books, 2012), 11-13.

49. *FL* 38, no. 3 (Mar. 2009); Robert Benne, "Richard John Neuhaus, the Mover and Shaker," *LF* 43, no. 1 (Spring 2009), 17.

50. John Leonard to Glenn Stone, 3 July 1985, quoted in Dorothy Zelenko, "A Legacy of Steady Faithfulness and Hope," *LF* 43, no. 3 (Fall 2009), 15.

51. Martin E. Marty, "Richard E. Koenig: a remembrance," *FL* 40, no. 12 (Dec. 2011), 6-7.

Chapter 27

Toward the Future

T he ALPB's programs had often focused on anniversaries—from the quadricentennial observance of the Reformation in 1917 to the anniversaries of the Bureau itself or of its publications. *Forum Letter* celebrated its 40th year of publication in 2011 by including each month an excerpt from some earlier issue. But there were other anniversaries ahead. The Reformation quincentennial was just a few years away, while the Bureau would celebrate its own centennial in 2014. The decade of the 2010s thus became a time for reflection on the ALPB's mission and future.

ALPB's future

"to cultivate a new generation of Lutheran evangelical catholics"

The question of whether the name "American Lutheran Publicity Bureau" still expressed the group's mission had come up occasionally in the past. It described well the original purposes of the organization—to publicize the Lutheran church in a nation where it was still often unknown, and to help congregations utilize "modern methods" of publicity. In the 21st century, the Lutheran church was no longer unknown or viewed as "foreign" among Americans, and congregations had long ago become familiar with "modern methods" (though those methods were now changing at a dizzying pace, with the internet, social media, and the collapse of print journalism's exclusive monopoly as an information source). In May 2010, the board took up the name question again. There was a strong feeling that any new name should try to maintain the historic and well-known "ALPB" initials. Could the organization be re-branded as something like "American Lutheran Publications Board" or "American Lutheran Publishing Board"? After considerable discussion, the board unanimously agreed not to make any change. The "American Lutheran Publicity Bureau" it would remain.[1]

But if the name would stay the same, there was a general feeling that some other aspects of the Bureau would need to change if its ministry was to continue. There were several concerns. The tract ministry, for most of a century a constant in the ALPB's offerings, was given up in 2012 with the realization that tracts "seem to increasingly be a device of yesterday." The most recent tracts on human sexuality, it was agreed, had been excellent, but there just seemed to be little market for them.[2]

The ALPB still had not made much progress in promoting its books and other products. Typically, little was done beyond announcing new books on the ALPB website and in the publications. Review copies were sent to various journals, but the nature of the ALPB books often meant that few journals were interested in reviewing them. The most successful books tended to be those where the authors themselves took on personal responsibility for promotion.

For many years, the Bureau had utilized a cadre of "ALPB liaisons" across the country who would receive complimentary copies of ALPB resources in return for their agreement to promote them in their ELCA synod or LCMS district, with tables at conventions or other kinds of personal promotion. This system had been suggested by Fred Schumacher in 1990, shortly after he joined the board, and it was formally established in 1993, but it had never proven to be as successful as had been hoped. Geographical coverage had been spotty; by 2012, there were liaisons in only 24 ELCA synods (out of 65) and five LCMS districts (out of 35), as well as six from different geographical areas of the NALC. In many judicatories, it was increasingly difficult for unofficial agencies like the ALPB to be granted display space at conventions. The various liaisons, volunteers all, had significantly different levels of commitment and ability in marketing ALPB products. In 2012 Schumacher told the board he had recently asked for volunteers to serve as liaisons at a Society of the Holy Trinity retreat; a dozen pastors had expressed interest, but more than half of them were not even subscribers to the *Forum* publications.[3]

Another promotional method begun in the 1990s was an offer of a free year's subscription to *Lutheran Forum/Forum Letter* to all graduates of Lutheran seminaries in North America, with the expectation that at least some of them would purchase a subscription after that free year. For a while this was successful. From 2001 to 2004, for example, some 242 students had accepted the offer, and about a quarter of them later went on to become paid subscribers. But the program was always problematic. The invitations were distributed to the seminaries with the request that they be passed on to the graduates, and while some seminary personnel were conscientious about doing so, in other cases the invitations were simply placed on a table for students to pick up. As seminary enrollments declined, the offer yielded fewer and fewer results; in 2012 only 14 graduates took advantage of it, and only two of them maintained the subscription after the free year. Still, in 2010 executive director Schumacher could report that 106 current paid subscribers (about 4% of the total) had originally begun with the free seminary graduate subscription offer.[4]

Another longtime program, the annual Christmas appeal, continued to yield good results. A remarkably high percentage of ALPB subscribers made an annual contribution to the Bureau—some 14% in 2012, for example; this had been an important source of ALPB funding for many decades. And ALPB subscribers were a loyal group. In 2013, it was reported that some 24% of current subscribers had been subscribing since 1986 or before. The board recognized, however, that subscribers were an aging group, and that such support might not go on forever.[5]

Subscribers were also a dwindling group. In 2013 for the first time the number of paid subscriptions to *Lutheran Forum/Forum Letter* dropped below 2,000. For many years subscription levels had remained steady at around 5,000, then had begun to decline slowly. The drop between 2000 and 2013 was about 30%. Declining subscriptions were coupled with declining advertising revenue. These problems were not unique to the Bureau's publications; it was an era when print journalism generally was facing tremendous challenges, one of which was the movement of advertisers away from print media in favor of electronic media. But it forced the board to think once again about the future of its ministry.

It was clear that a presence on the internet would be increasingly important. There had been several attempts to address this need. The Bureau had a home page where visitors could learn about its ministry and order subscriptions, books or other products. The page contained a link to Forum Online, the discussion site established in 2004, which offered enthusiastic and sometimes heated discussion by a very diverse group of Lutherans and others about current issues facing church and society. On the other hand, *Lutheran Forum*'s website had proven to be something of a disappointment; it was discontinued in 2016, with the intention of folding some of its features into the main ALPB site. A *Lutheran Forum* page on Facebook continued, but did not attract much traffic. The ALPB established a presence on YouTube in 2011, with videos of the 2002 ALPB Christian Sexuality Conference (a bit after the fact, to be sure, but most of the addresses were still relevant). The print-oriented nature of the ALPB's existing ministry, however, did not lend itself very easily to a video format.

Discerning new ways to promote the ministry wasn't easy. An *ad hoc* committee on marketing was appointed in 2010 and brought several recommendations. These were discussed over the next several meetings; a few minor ones were instituted, but no major changes resulted. Sometimes this was because the ideas, after full consideration, did not seem feasible; more often it was because an organization run entirely by volunteers and with only part-time staff simply didn't have anyone who could invest the time in pursuing more complicated proposals. The board also suffered from an ailment not unknown in church and other voluntary organization governing bodies: a tendency to talk about matters at length without ever reaching a conclusion. A classic example of this could be seen in the minutes of the November 2, 2013, board meeting: "Pastor Hannah stated that we had spent too much time ineffectually discussing book publications, without resolution. Pastor Eberhardt recommended an action committee for that purpose. No action taken."[6]

At the next meeting, president John Hannah cited that note and appointed a "Task Force Fresh Look." The group was chaired by board member Robert Benne, and it included members who were both newer to ALPB and younger than most others on the board. They began their work with some reflections from Benne. He understood their task to be primarily to discuss the book publishing ministry, given that that decisions about what goes into *Lutheran Forum* and *Forum Letter* are made by the editors, "with some nudges now and then from the Board." He outlined his understanding of the board's current informal process of receiving and evaluating proposed book manuscripts, editing and publishing the books, and promotion, and then briefly summarized the kinds of materials ALPB had published in the past.[7]

Then he turned to "what we might do in the future." He acknowledged that electronic publishing formats seem to be the wave of the future, though he argued that ALPB ought not abandon hard copy. "Probably everything we do," he suggested, "should be available in both hardcopy and electronic versions." He acknowledged that this might necessitate "mov[ing] beyond volunteer labor."[8]

Most of Benne's reflection had to do with the kind of material ALPB should publish in the future. He noted that the background assumption that the Bureau publishes "orthodox Lutheran theology of an evangelical catholic sort" had not really been carefully articulated by the board, so he gave it a shot:

> Let's say it is a centrist interpretation of the Lutheran confessional tradition that sees itself as part of the Great Tradition. It avoids the accommodations of liberal Lutheranism (caving in on the uniqueness and decisiveness of Jesus Christ and on sexuality issues, the two places where the modern world is most vigorous in its attack on Christian teaching) on the one hand and a sclerotic rigid confessionalism and biblicism on the other. We ... cannot simply repeat the formulations of the past. But we also must respect the boundaries delineated by the settled teaching of the church catholic. ...

[Evangelical catholic] means first the classic European meaning of 'evangelical'—an emphasis on the free gift of God's grace in Christ as the central meaning of the Gospel. ... The phrase also means a continuing focus on sacramental practice as central to Christian worship and a high respect for the whole sweep of historical Christianity, classical liturgy and vestments of the church, the church year, classic Lutheran hymns, and the commemoration of great Christian figures. It also means an understanding that the Lutheran movement ... is a yet needed reforming movement within the church catholic.

Benne argued that ALPB should promote this vision of Lutheranism "in all that it does"—both by making available the work of "the older generation that has been so important in bearing our tradition," but also by seeking "to find and cultivate a new generation of Lutheran evangelical catholics who can carry on this mission."[9]

The task force generally agreed with Benne's description of what the mission of ALPB had been and should continue to be. They acknowledged the need to "be very intentional about what we produce in the future" so as not to "spread ourselves too thinly." The group also suggested the importance of moving "into academic level publishing of materials that will further the cause of ALPB." With all this in mind, the task force recommended the appointment of three committees. The first would focus on seeking out "promising younger authors who can possibly become the orthodox evangelical catholic writers of the future." The second would focus on developing an academic publishing initiative. The third would work on "more vigorous and effective marketing of ALPB materials," including an evaluation of the ALPB's internet presence and possible strategies for expanding it. What might become of these recommendations is not yet evident, and in any case, that belongs to the history of the Bureau's second century. But clearly the board was taking seriously the need to think differently about its mission in the coming decades.[10]

Continuing to provide a forum

"Ours is an age of shallow reading"

Meanwhile, the *Forum* publications continued to do what they had been doing. *Forum Letter* offered news and commentary on the increasingly splintered American Lutheran scene. There was coverage of the national assemblies, conventions and convocations of the ELCA, LCMS and NALC, as well as the ELCIC. In December 2013, correspondent W. Stevens Shipman reported on the 2013 "annual gathering" of Lutheran Congregations in Mission for Christ, a fellowship that had been established years before by dissenters from the ELCA's ecumenical agreement with the Episcopal Church. It was hardly a group that embodied ALPB's evangelical catholic sensibilities; the opening worship, Shipman reported, "betrayed no connection with the classic structures of

Lutheran liturgies." But he noted that the group was now "probably the fourth-largest Lutheran group in North America" and thus "increasingly a force to be reckoned with in North American Lutheranism." They are also, he admitted, "a nice bunch of people when they come together."[11]

Forum Letter continued to discuss ALPB's traditional concern for liturgical integrity—often by highlighting practices that the editor found disconcerting. In a piece entitled "Liturgical chaos," Johnson reflected on his experiences doing pulpit supply for ELCA congregations. He expressed astonishment that pastors and congregations could so easily "pretty much junk [the liturgy], while still loudly claiming that they are being faithful to it."

> It reminds me just a bit of an online recipe site to which I subscribe. People post recipes, and then there are reviews. Very often the comments are along the lines of 'This was a really great recipe, and I changed it by ...' and then the reviewer lists all the substitutions, omissions, additions that he or she made, effectively rendering it an entirely different recipe; but still, the original one was 'really great,' except I never actually made it.

He told of congregations that had badly scrambled the usual liturgy, putting various parts of it in unaccustomed places, or that had omitted large sections of the liturgy altogether. Johnson suggested three reasons that congregations and pastors do this: first, the "tyranny of time" that demands the service last no more than an hour; second, the "do it my way" American culture wedded to a distorted Lutheran view of *adiaphora* which honestly believes that we just don't have to, and probably shouldn't, follow any prescribed pattern; and third, the aversion to discomfort and challenge that makes people resist things like confessing their sins or reciting "meaningless dogma." But "the liturgy is not the personal property of individual pastors or congregations," he observed. "Nobody can stop a congregation or pastor from slicing and dicing it in whatever way they might want, but when they do that, it's no longer the church's liturgy. It is a sectarian aberration, and that's not what Lutherans really should be about."[12]

Forum Letter also excoriated the practice in some ELCA parishes of utilizing contemporary "creeds" or "affirmations of faith" (homemade or borrowed from someone else) as a substitute for the ecumenical creeds. "How can you ask a worshiper to confess assertions which may or may not reflect 'the faith of the church,'" the editor wondered, "but which in any event take him/her utterly by surprise, so there is no opportunity to reflect on whether in fact it *does* articulate the faith which we confess?"

> The ecumenical creeds are *our* creeds; they are what define who we are as Christians. Modern 'affirmations,' recast for the sake of an illusive 'relevance,' are by definition not *our* creeds, and pastors or liturgists have no business foisting them on a congregation. ...
>
> So spare me your 'modern affirmations.' They do not belong in the liturgy of the church, if in fact they belong anyplace at all. If there are Lutheran pastors who don't

get this, one would hope that someone—lay people in their congregation, their bishop, maybe even their confirmation students—might teach them what the creeds are and why we confess them.[13]

Both *Forum* publications took on the growing tendency in ELCA congregations to welcome everyone to receive the Eucharist—even the unbaptized. A resolution approved at the churchwide assembly in 2013 asked for a study of whether the official ELCA teaching that the Eucharist is intended for the baptized should be changed. *Forum Letter* mentioned the issue frequently, and editor Johnson expressed concern about it.

> It raises pretty serious theological and ecclesiological issues when a congregation decides they can just abandon the teaching that the Eucharist is for the baptized. I'm no 'closed communion' Lutheran confessionalist type of guy, but I'm just sayin'— I'd almost rather go that direction than 'y'all come.' There's more integrity to it.[14]

Lutheran Forum published a critique of this "radical hospitality" movement in the ELCA by former editor Paul Hinlicky. This direction, he argued, "indicates how empty the theology and practice of *baptism* has become." It is baptism that is "the true radical hospitality," but it is "an abuse of the Supper—not to mention an abuse of the unbaptized—to make the sacrament into a tool of proselytism, taking advantage of visitors with no understanding of these holy things." For the church to approve this "would take the ELCA another huge and fatal step in the wrong direction."[15]

Lutheran Forum's commitment to serious theological engagement led to a 2013 "reading challenge" to readers. The journal offered a suggested list of readings for the year, drawn from Scripture, patristic and medieval writers, Reformers, contemporary theologians and ecumenical documents. Later that year the editors offered a more explicit challenge to engage in what the editors called "deep reading." Editors Wilson and Sauer explained what they had in mind.

> Ours is an age of shallow reading. Blog posts, 140-character Tweets, internet memes, and infographics fill up the tiny spaces of our frenetic days: pithy, unnuanced, and unchallenging. Like a diet of sweets, they fill us up but leave us malnourished. Longer works, if read at all, are likely as not to be crass fiction or self-help manuals for surviving an increasingly cutthroat, market-driven society that cannot value anything without a price tag. Not surprisingly, these broader cultural trends have infected the church as well.

The result, they went on, is "pastors who excuse the atrophying of their minds on the grounds of their ministerial duties," who "read the Scriptures only professionally for sermon-writing," and who "abandon their explorations in all the theological disciplines ... after seminary has ended." Parishioners, on the other hand, often "resent the time their pastors spend reading" and "ignore their own mandate to be students and readers of the Scriptures." Wilson and Sauer urged pastors to block out "uninterrupted time for reading" on a weekly basis because it is "central, not peripheral, to the Christian life."[16]

Looking back and ahead

"The Lutheran version of evangelical catholicism will not die"

As the 500th anniversary of the Reformation approached, the Bureau began to plan ways of observing that event. One project, spearheaded by executive director Schumacher, was a series of "Reformation Countdown Medals." The Bureau commissioned nine medals, designed by LCMS pastor and artist Scott Blazek, depicting various incidents during the "pre-Reformation" period (primarily events in Luther's life). An inexpensive version was issued in gold anodized aluminum for widespread distribution to Sunday school children and adult parishioners, with a limited number of bronze and silver medals struck for purchase by collectors. The accompanying material gave a brief explanation of each medal, as well as children's sermon ideas that might be used in when the medals were distributed.

The first medal was issued in 2011; nearly six thousand were sold—about two hundred in the collector's edition, the rest in the gold anodized aluminum. One or two additional medals came out each year, and while sales gradually declined for each successive medal, orders still numbered in the thousands. The final piece, depicting Luther's posting of the 95 Theses, was scheduled for release in 2017, the quincentennial year. Missouri Synod and various independent Lutheran publications gave the project good publicity; to Schumacher's frustration, ELCA publications refused to do so.

The Reformation quincentennial also led to another incarnation of the Martin Luther comic book, *God's Man of Faith*. Originally published in 1959 with a text by John Tietjen, the book had been revised by Glenn Stone (to tone down pre-Vatican II polemics) and reissued in 1983. In 2012, ALPB board member Dr. Jeffrey Gaab made additional minor revisions. The plan was to produce a new version that could be put on the ALPB website in 2017 for free download.

Before the Reformation anniversary, however, the ALPB made plans to celebrate its own centennial. There were many ideas. One project, again spearheaded by Fred Schumacher, was yet another commemorative medal in honor of the anniversary. This one, also designed by Scott Blazek, was intended to be a collector's item rather than something for mass distribution. The front depicted Luther, with the caption, "What Would Luther Do? Today!" He was looking at a computer screen, on which appeared the captions "Lutheran Forum" and "Forum Letter." The reverse said, "American Lutheran Publicity Bureau 1914-2014: Independent Voice of Lutheranism," with a Luther rose and several other traditional Lutheran symbols.

There had been occasional discussion through the years of publishing a history of the ALPB, but not much had come of it. When the Bureau celebrated its golden anniversary in 1964, a five-part historical sketch had been published in the *American Lutheran*, written by Alan Graebner and Alfred Klausler; as the centennial approached, the board believed it was time for a more complete treatment. They asked Martin Conkling, a professor at Concordia College in Bronxville, NY, to take on the task. Fred Schumacher reported to the board in October 2007 that he had met with Conkling and given him early ALPB minutes and other archival material; the professor met with the full board in May 2009 to outline the proposed book. Conkling worked on this project for several years, but was not ultimately able to complete it; in 2014 the board would turn responsibility for the history over to the present writer.

The Bureau's longtime critic Herman Otten beat the board to the punch by publishing his own polemical "history" of the ALPB, spread over several issues of *Christian News* and entitled "A Century Toward Apostasy and Victory: A History of the ALPB 1914-2014." Otten promised that his work would be published in book form "when funds permit," and it would "include documentary evidence showing that the ALPB at times has supported evolution, women pastors, higher criticism of the Bible, and homosexuality." Over the next months, Otten published chapters that were largely re-hashes of his hysterical criticism of the ALPB over the years. He offered to provide free copies for distribution at the ALPB centennial banquet—an offer which was politely declined. Otten, always the conspiracy theorist, wondered why the ALPB's centennial history had not yet appeared. "Did [the author] uncover some facts the ALPB would like suppressed? Any honest historian who researches the evidence would find what CN reveals in its history of the ALPB. The ALPB wants the facts suppressed."[17]

The culmination of the anniversary year was a banquet, held October 12, 2014, at JC Fogarty's restaurant in Bronxville, NY. The event brought together more than a hundred supporters and friends of the ALPB, many of whom had played key roles in the Bureau over the past decades. The program that evening featured addresses by Richard Johnson and Robert Benne—both of which were subsequently uploaded to YouTube and published in *Lutheran Forum*.[18]

Johnson spoke about the history of the Bureau. He recalled the vision of the founders of the Bureau as "a 'Lutheran Forward Movement'—putting the Lutheran church 'forward' into the American consciousness and pushing the church itself 'forward' into a greater engagement with American culture." He told of the decision to publish the *American Lutheran* and recounted how, under the editorship of Paul Lindemann, it became the most important ministry of the Bureau—and how then, under Adolf Meyer, it played an increasingly vital role in the life of the Missouri Synod. He explained how the Bureau had become a consciously inter-Lutheran ministry in the 1960s, and he recalled the transition from the *American Lutheran* to *Lutheran Forum* and *Forum Letter*. He highlighted other major contributions of the ALPB to the life of the Lutheran church in America, particularly the highly successful *For All the Saints*.[19]

He then read some phrases from the ALPB's 1993 mission statement:

Committed to an understanding of Lutheran tradition as evangelical and catholic, the ALPB affirms the Church's scriptural and confessional foundations in order to foster renewal ... with the ... Lutheran churches in North America. ... In an era in which the Church in North America must address an increasingly dechristianized society, the ALPB makes the theological, liturgical and devotional resources of our confessional heritage accessible and relevant to all Lutherans as well as to friends in other communions.

"That's certainly not how they would have said it in 1914," Johnson observed, "or 1944, or even 1964. But it's really just a restatement of what the ALPB's commitment has been all along: we serve and we proclaim a changeless Christ in a changing world."[20]

Johnson concluded by quoting Paul Lindeman in 1919, as the Bureau observed its fifth anniversary:

We were hopeful, but not optimistic. But the blessing of the Lord and the hearty support of our friends have long since put us to shame and it is with grateful hearts that we gaze back upon the traversed way. We can say with all humility that by the grace of God the American Lutheran Publicity Bureau has been an agency for good in our Lutheran Church.

"May it always be so!" Johnson added.[21]

Robert Benne's task was to look at the future of the ALPB, but he also took a few minutes to speak about the past. He acknowledged his own growing up in a very low church Lutheran tradition, and recounted how he had come to embrace the evangelical catholic understanding of Lutheranism that the ALPB had long championed. He spoke briefly of the challenges facing the ALPB at its founding in 1914 and at its 50th anniversary in 1964. But "what a different situation we confront!"

One wing of Lutheranism is constantly bothered by those who wield the Brief Statement as a weapon to keep Missouri quarrelsome and narrow-minded. The other wing, like the Protestant mainline it emulates, has accommodated so dramatically to American elite secular culture that little Lutheran fiber is left. Liturgical practice is all over the map, more varied perhaps than at any time since 1918.

In this new context, Benne admitted, "things look pretty grim."[22]

Yet Benne saw hope for the future for the evangelical catholic view, which "I believe has perennial allure and salience."

[The ALPB] will press forward a churchly catholic Lutheranism that emphasizes sacramental practice, liturgical integrity, respect for the whole sweep of Christian history, strong oversight and theological accountability, and high-quality art, music, devotional materials, and hymnody in the church. We will emphasize our desire for Christian unity—for one, holy, catholic, and apostolic church—and insist that Lutheranism is indeed a reforming movement within that church catholic. And we will seek out and invite those of many traditions who are attracted to our version of evangelical catholicism.

He cautioned that no Lutheran denomination would fully embrace this vision of Lutheranism, though there would be important strands of it within the NALC and the LCMS, as well as "a diminishing strand within the ELCA as it bends increasingly toward liberal Protestantism." He acknowledged that the ALPB would need to find a way to move beyond print media to more modern means of communication.[23]

"But about the vision we bear," Benne asserted, "I also have little doubt. The Lutheran version of evangelical catholicism will not die." He expressed confidence that in fifty years there would be a sesquicentennial celebration which will "look back to see how in the years following 2014 the ALPB played an indispensable role in guiding the Lutheran movement at its best through perilous times." And with those hopeful words, the centennial banquet of the ALPB came to its close.[24]

Epilogue

"continuity and change"

As the Bureau was poised to begin its second century, another significant transition took place. Fred Schumacher, who had served as executive director since 1993, announced that he would retire at the end of 2014. He was succeeded by Paul Sauer, pastor of Our Saviour Lutheran Church and School in the Bronx, NY. Sauer had been associated with the Bureau for several years, first as a board member and then as associate editor of *Lutheran Forum.*

Sauer himself wrote about the change in the Winter 2014 issue of *Lutheran Forum* under the heading "Continuity and Change in the ALPB." He traced briefly the history of the Bureau, recalling some of the theological stars in the constellation of ALPB writers and editors through the years. But then he noted that "the greatest impact of the ALPB ... has always been on the daily lives of parish pastors and parishioners through American Lutheranism. It is not surprising, then, that parish pastors played such a formative role in providing leadership throughout its history." He paid tribute to Schumacher's twenty-one years as executive director—years in which he, too, remained a parish pastor. "I look forward to continuing Fred's legacy of pastoral leadership," he wrote, "as the Lutheran community navigates its way through what appear to be increasingly tumultuous waters."[25]

Sauer's use of the phrase "continuity and change" aptly described the ALPB's hundred-year history. The Bureau had always been blessed with great stability in its leadership at every level. Schumacher's twenty-one years was a long tenure, yet it was matched by Theodore Wittrock's twenty-one years, and Glenn Stone had served for thirteen years. Schumacher would follow both Wittrock and Stone in serving as a board member after leaving the staff position. Most of the periodical editors—always the most public voice of the Bureau—had likewise served long tenures. The *American Lutheran* was edited by its founder, Paul Lindemann, for twenty years, and then by Adolf Meyer for twenty-four (though he technically held the title for only eight). Several on the team that assisted Meyer also served during much of his tenure. The magazine's successor, *Lutheran Forum* was edited by Glenn Stone for twenty-two years (with a brief break in between two terms), and by Ronald Bagnall for ten years. Richard John Neuhaus edited *Forum Letter* for sixteen years; he was surpassed by his successor, Russell Saltzman, who served for seventeen years.

There was also notable continuity in the less visible administrative positions. Here the most remarkable service was that of Julius F. E. Nickelsburg, who joined the board in 1918 and was almost immediately hired as business manager—a position he held until his retirement in 1953, some thirty-five years later. He, too, served on the board after his retirement and continued to edit his column in the *American Lutheran* until his death. From 1971 to 1988, Elly (Pfeifer) Spangenberg served as office manager for the Bureau and circulation manager for the periodicals. That position was filled in 1989 by Donna (Kathmann) Roche, who is still serving at the time of this writing in 2017.

Board leadership, too, reflected long continuity and stability. While the tenure of board presidents was often not more than two or three years, there were important exceptions. August Bobzin had served for twenty years (1931-1951), John Kavasch for ten (1951-1961), Hans Quitmeyer for sixteen (1989-2005); John Hannah, elected in 2005, is still serving in 2017. Several others, though their presidential service was shorter, were active board members for many years before and after their terms. Paul H. Scaer, pastor of Trinity Lutheran Church in Flatbush, Brooklyn, was elected secretary of the board in 1928 and served for twenty-five years. Arthur A. Rauf began serving as treasurer in 1920, and he served until his death in 1948—some twenty-eight years. When Chester Edelmann retired as ALPB treasurer in 1982, he had served more than thirty years; he continued as assistant treasurer when Theodore Wittrock took over the responsibility. Dorothy Zelenko was elected treasurer in 1989 and is still serving in 2017. These are only a few of the dedicated ALPB board members through the years, many of whom have had remarkably long tenures with the Bureau.

But continuity without change is a recipe for the death of any organization, and as the ALPB began its second century, special efforts were being made to recruit a new generation of leaders. When Paul Sauer became executive director, he took a leave of absence from his position as associate editor. Two young Missouri Synod pastors, Matthew Staneck and Matt Gonzales, served in the interim as "guest editors." Ultimately Sauer resigned as associate editor, and his place was taken by Staneck and Piotr Malysz, another young LCMS pastor. The editors of both *Lutheran Forum* and *Forum Letter* consciously sought out and published young writers. There were also deliberate attempts to recruit younger board members who might help the ALPB take the steps necessary to move its mission forward in a rapidly changing culture. Where this will lead, only God knows. However the specifics of the ALPB's ministry might change over the next decades, its joyful task will be, as Robert Benne put it at the centennial banquet, to press forward the case for "evangelical catholicism, Lutheranism at its best." The American Lutheran Publicity Bureau will continue (to reprise a much older slogan) to preach "a changeless Christ for a changing world."

Notes

1. Minutes, ALPB Board of Directors, 15 May 2010.
2. Minutes, ALPB Board of Directors, 3 Nov. 2012.
3. Executive Director's Report, Minutes, ALPB Board of Directors, 3 Nov. 2012.
4. Executive Director's Report, Minutes, ALPB Board of Directors, 15 May 2010.
5. Minutes, ALPB Board of Directors, 11 May 2013.
6. Minutes, ALPB Board of Directors, 2 Nov. 2013.
7. Report of the Future Publications Committee of The American Lutheran Publicity Bureau, 2014, ALPB Archives.
8. Ibid.
9. Ibid.
10. Ibid.
11. W. Stevens Shipman, "Among the LCMC," *FL* 42, no. 12 (Dec. 2013), 5.
12. *FL* 43, no. 4 (Apr. 2014), 2-4.
13. *FL* 43, no. 8 (Aug. 2014), 4.
14. *FL* 41, no. 1 (Jan. 2012), 4.
15. Paul R. Hinlicky, "The Truth About 'Radical Hospitality,'" *LF* 48, no. 3 (Fall 2014), 38-39.
16. "An Exhortation to Deep Reading in the Church," *LF* 47, no. 4 (Winter 2013), inside front cover.
17. *Christian News* 52, no. 1 (Jan. 6, 2014), 6; 52, no. 40 (Oct. 20, 2014), 16.
18. *LF* 49, no. 1 (Spring 2015), 49-59.
19. Richard O. Johnson, "The ALPB's First Century," *LF* 49, no. 1 (Spring 2015), 49f.
20. Ibid., 54.
21. Ibid.
22. Robert Benne, "The ALPB and the Lutheran Future," *LF* 49, no. 1 (Spring 2015), 58.
23. Ibid., 58-59.
24. Ibid., 59.
25. Paul Robert Sauer, "Continuity and Change in the ALPB," *LF* 48, no. 4 (Winter 2014), 9-10.

APPENDICES

Appendix A: Original members of the ALPB Board of Directors

[Those marked with an asterisk were members of the original "preliminary" executive committee; the others were elected to the board at the 1914 organizational meeting.]

*The Rev. Henry P. Eckhardt (1866-1949), the organizing force behind the Bureau and its first president, was born in Baltimore. He was a graduate of Concordia Seminary in St. Louis, and served as a chaplain in World War I. He served as pastor of Grace, Cleveland, OH, Grace, Jersey City, NJ, and St. Andrew's, Pittsburgh, PA. He was the first president of the English District, and was a vice-president of the LCMS from 1917 to 1926. He died in Pittsburgh in 1949.

*The Rev. John H. C. Fritz (1875-1953) served briefly on the preliminary executive committee, but resigned because he took a call in St. Louis. He was born in Ohio in 1875. He served Our Saviour in Brooklyn (1901-1914); a strong advocate of the use of English, he founded and edited the *New York Lutheran*, an English language church paper. He taught at Concordia Seminary, St. Louis for many years, serving as dean from 1920 to 1940. He was devoted to the cause of publicity in the church and was a co-founder of KFUO radio in St. Louis. He died in St. Louis in 1953.

*The Rev. Paul Lindemann (1881-1938) was born in Pittsburgh in 1881. His pastorates included Bethlehem in Bayridge, Trinity in Brooklyn, Grace in Jersey City, NJ, and Church of the Redeemer in St. Paul, MN. At the time of his death in 1938 in St. Paul, he was president of the English District. He edited ALPB's *American Lutheran* from its inception in 1918 until his death.

*The Rev C. Ferdinand G. Schumm (1864-1926) was born in 1864 in Ohio. Ordained in 1889, he served First Evangelical Lutheran Church in Worcester, MA, a congregation in Webster, MA, St. John's Evangelical Lutheran Church, Bayonne, NJ (1900-1925), and Church of the Redeemer in Pittsburgh, PA, from 1925 until his death in 1926.

*The Rev. Martin F. Walker (1877-1967) was born and raised in York, PA, graduating from Concordia Seminary in 1899. He received an MA degree from Columbia University in 1902, pastored churches in New York City and Buffalo, and was a professor at Concordia Collegiate Institute, Hawthorne, NY (now Concordia College, Bronxville, NY) 1902-1906. He was president of the Lutheran Church—Missouri Synod's English District 1938-1945.

*The Rev. John Henry Volk (1876-1941) was a native of Boston. Ordained in 1899, he served pastorates in New York City (Immanuel), Kenosha, WI, Auburn, IA, and then St. John's in Bayonne, NJ (where he was serving while on the ALPB board). He later served parishes in Boston and in Brooklyn, where he died.

The Rev. Karl Kretzmann (1877-1949) was born in Indiana, and served pastorates in Stamford, CT, Baltimore, MD, New York City, and Orange, NJ. He was a founder of Concordia Historical Institute in St. Louis, and was appointed the first full-time curator there in 1943. He died in St. Louis in 1949.

The Rev. Walter Koenig (1873-1949) was born in New York, graduated from Concordia Seminary in St. Louis and was ordained in 1894. He served parishes in Pitcairn, PA, and Whitestone, Queens, NY, and then was pastor of St. Paul's, Paterson, NJ, from 1909 to 1925. He died in Paterson in 1949.

*Frederick C. Lang (1851-1933), ALPB's first treasurer, was born in Mecklenburg and came to America as a 10-year-old boy. He was the co-owner of Tietjen & Lang Dry Dock Co. in Hoboken, NJ, and a bank director for Hoboken Trust. An active member of Grace Lutheran Church in Jersey City, NJ, he died in 1933.

*Henry F. Ressmeyer (1854-1921) was born in Hanover and emigrated to the United States in 1871. He was an executive with Aitken & Son, one of New York's major retail clothing stores, and a member of St. Matthew's Lutheran Church. In addition to ALPB, he was heavily involved in Lutheran educational enterprises, especially Concordia College in Bronxville, where the first women's dormitory bears his name. He died in New York in 1921.

*Charles Schmidling (1876-1936) was a native of New York; he served for several years as the financial secretary of ALPB. He was an insurance executive, working for 45 years for the New York office of the Phoenix Assurance Company of London. He was a charter member of Lutheran Church of Our Saviour in Brooklyn, and a board member of many Lutheran ministries and institutions in the New York area. He died in 1936.

H. J. Thunhorst was probably the Henry Thunhorst, born in Germany in 1868, who owned a Manhattan saloon. He immigrated in 1886. A member of an English District congregation, he was associated with other ALPB personnel, serving, for example, on a district Committee on the Four-hundredth Anniversary of the Reformation with Pr. Henry Eckhardt, Pr. Marcellus Walker and F. C. Lang. He was still living in New York as late as 1930.

Gustav Zimmermann (1874-1958) was an active lay member and longtime president of Trinity Lutheran, Brooklyn (where Paul Lindemann was pastor from 1904 to 1913). He was born in Brooklyn in 1874, and spent most of his career as a top aide to Eugene Higgins, a wealthy New York socialite. He was involved in several Lutheran agencies, including the Lutheran Education Society, Bethlehem Children's Home, and Lutherland in Pocono Pines, PA. He died in 1958 at his summer home in the Poconos.

Appendix B: Presidents of ALPB

The Rev. Henry P. Eckhardt (1866-1949); see biographical information in Appendix A. *ALPB President 1914-1920*

Theodore Lamprecht (1858-1928) was born in Brooklyn and confirmed at Trinity Lutheran Church in New York. He attended Concordia College in Ft. Wayne and Concordia Seminary in St. Louis, but decided against the ministry and instead went into the woolen business. He was extremely successful, and became a well-respected philanthropist within Lutheran circles. He was one of the founders of the Lutheran Laymen's League and its first president; he also served for several years as president of the Bethlehem Orphans' Home. He was a leading force in the American Lutheran Board for Relief in Europe after World War I. He died in Cannes, France, while on a round-the-world trip. *ALPB President 1920-1928*

Henry A. Dahlen (1890-1971) was born in Minnesota to Norwegian immigrants; he lived much of his life in New Jersey and was the president and majority owner of the Deslaurier Column Mould Company. In addition to his work with ALPB, he was a major donor to Valparaiso University and one of the founders and a board president of Lutherland in Pocono Pines, PA. *ALPB President 1928-1931*

The Rev. August F. Bobzin (1893-1983) was a native of Chicago and a graduate Concordia Lutheran Seminary in Springfield, IL. He served mission congregations in Connecticut, then Our Savior Lutheran Church, North Bergen, NJ (1921-1931), Bethlehem Lutheran Church in Brooklyn (1931-1941), and then served many years at Resurrection Lutheran Church, Flushing, NY. He came on the ALPB board in 1928 and was president from 1931 to 1951. He was also for several years the chair of the LCMS board of European Affairs and was active in various capacities in the Atlantic District. He died in West Hempstead, NY. *ALPB President 1931-1951*

The Rev. John A. Kavasch (1909-1990) came from a family of pastors; his father, an uncle, and a brother were all ordained. He was born and raised in Hartford, CT, where his father was pastor for more than 50 year. Kavasch graduated from Concordia Seminary in St. Louis was called to Calvary Lutheran Church, Verona, NJ, where he served for many years; he later accepted a call to St. Peter's Lutheran Church in Huntington Station, NY, and was there until his retirement. He came on the board of ALPB in 1941, and continued as a board member following his presidency. *ALPB President 1951-1961*

The Rev. Rudolph P. F. Ressmeyer (1924-2017), the grandson of one of the founders of the ALPB (Henry Ressmeyer) and the son of one of its first staff members (Rudolph S. Ressmeyer), was born in Baltimore, and graduated from Concordia Collegiate Institute, Bronxville, NY, and Concordia Seminary, St. Louis. He served Holy Cross Lutheran Church in Spokane, WA, Emmanuel Lutheran Church, Baltimore, MD, and Our Redeemer Lutheran Church, Seaford, NY. He was executive director of Long Island Lutheran High School, and was elected president of the Atlantic District of the LCMS in 1967; in the wake of the Seminex controversy, he was removed from the presidency by LCMS president Jacob Preus in 1976, but the district convention refused to accept his removal. He thereupon resigned from the presidency and became bishop of the East Coast Synod of the Association of Evangelical Lutheran Congregations. He came on the ALPB board in 1955. *ALPB President 1961-1964*

Fred Engelman (1919-2014) was born in New York, but spent much of his life in New Jersey. He was a retailer, the founder the Fred Engelman Co. which manufactured women's sportswear. He was for many years a member and an elder at Calvary Lutheran Church in Verona, NJ, and then a charter member of Somerset Hills Lutheran Church in Basking Ridge, NJ. He first came on the board in 1953 and served for more than 30 years. Along with John Kavasch, at that time his pastor, Engelman developed the "Sharing Christ Program" which was later adopted and published by the Bureau. After retirement, he lived in Maryland and Colorado Spring, CO, where he died in 2014. *ALPB President 1964-1969*

The Rev. Theodore Wittrock (1920-2002) was born in Kansas, son of a pastor. He graduated from Concordia College in Ft. Wayne and Concordia Seminary in St. Louis. After ordination, he was an LCMS missionary-at-large in Southern California, then was pastor of Trinity Lutheran in Trona, CA, and Our Savior Lutheran in Ridgecrest, CA. In 1948, he became executive secretary of the ALPB, holding that position for the next twenty-one years. During that time he also served as pulpit assistant at Resurrection Lutheran Church in Flushing, NY. In 1969, he was installed as pastor of Redeemer Evangelical Lutheran Church in Bronx, NY, and he served there until 2000. He continued with the ALPB as a board member, was president from 1969 to 1972, and later served as treasurer. He also served on the boards of directors of the Atlantic District and Concordia College, Bronxville. *ALPB President 1969-1972*

John H. Leonard (1922-2009) was a native of New York City. He had a long career in the advertising business, retiring as a vice president of the firm Dayle Dane Bernbach in 1987. He taught at New York University's Stern School of Business, and served on the NYU board of trustees. He was on the ALPB board for decades, serving as president from 1972 to 1976. He also chaired the board of directors of the Wartburg Home in Mt. Vernon, NY, and was a board member of the American Bible Society. He was an active lay leader for many years at St. Mark's Evangelical Lutheran Church in Yonkers, NY. He died in Ridgefield, CT, in 2009. *ALPB President 1972-1976*

Harold Midtbo (1911-2002) was a native New Yorker with a degree in finance and accounting from NYU, as well as a master's degree in education. He spent 36 years in the international oil industry, retiring as vice president and director of Esso Eastern. An active member at different times of Trinity Lutheran Church in Brooklyn and Grace Lutheran Church in Scarsdale, NY, he was also a member of the board of trustees of New York Theological Seminary and Luther College in Teaneck, NJ. He served on the executive committee of the Lutheran World Federation for many years. In his later years, he moved Grapevine, TX, where he died in 2002. *ALPB President 1977-1979*

The Rev. George R. Matzat (b. 1940) was born in Brooklyn. He completed his seminary training at Concordia Seminary, St. Louis, and earned a master's degree in sociology from St. Louis University. He was pastor of St. Stephen's Lutheran Church in St. Louis 1966-71, and then served with Lutheran World Relief for five years. He was then called to St. Peter's Evangelical Lutheran Church in Huntington Station, NY (1976-1990). He was later Director of Capital Development for Wartburg Lutheran Services in New York and a financial planner for Thrivent Financial in Long Island. *ALPB President 1979-1983*

The Rev. Richard Pankow (1932-2010) was a native of Buffalo, NY. Ordained in the ULCA, he served St. John Lutheran Church in Syracuse, NY, St. Paul Lutheran Church in Valley Stream, NY, and Lutheran Church of the Good Shepherd, Brooklyn, NY. He served on the ALPB Board from 1977 to 1989. *ALPB President 1983-1985*

Leonard O. Roellig (1927-2010) was born in Detroit, MI. He was a physicist, teaching first at Wayne State University and then the City University of New York, where he served as vice chancellor. He was active in many different Lutheran congregations and organizations in addition to the ALPB. *ALPB President 1986-1989*

John M. "Hans" Quitmeyer (b. 1950) was a native of Detroit who came to New York to practice law. After some years in private practice, he joined the Honeywell law department, and then served as General Counsel of AdvanSix. His career prompted several moves and gave him the opportunity to be an active lay leader at Holy Trinity and Immanuel Lutheran Churches in Manhattan, St. Michael's in New Canaan, CT, St. John in Summit, NJ, and Normandale Lutheran in Edina MN. *ALPB President 1989-2005*

The Rev. John Hannah (b. 1939) was born in Hampton, IA, and graduated from Concordia Senior College in Ft. Wayne, IN, and Concordia Seminary, St. Louis. He was ordained in 1965 and served St. John's Lutheran Church, Bethany, and St. Paul's Lutheran Church, Royalton, MN. He then went on active duty as an army chaplain, serving 1970-1993. He served Trinity Lutheran Church in Bronx, NY, 1993-2009. In addition to his ALPB involvement, he served as ecumenical officer of the Atlantic District, LCMS, as well as on the boards of several other Lutheran agencies. *ALPB President 2005-*

Appendix C: Executive Committee Chairmen

[During the first several years of the ALPB, the president was something of a figurehead who did not necessarily regularly attend meetings and participate in the ongoing work of the board. During this period, there was a chair of the executive committee who really functioned as the executive officer of the Bureau. While the minutes are not always clear (and not always extant), at least five men filled this role during the first decade and a half. It appears that the offices of president and executive committee chair essentially merged around 1930 during the presidency of Henry Dahlen, who was already serving as an active board member.]

The Rev. Karl Kretzmann (1877-1949) was the first executive committee chairman, serving in 1914-15; see Appendix A.

The Rev. C. Ferdinand G Schumm (1864-1926) served from 1915 to 1917; see Appendix A.

The Rev. Arthur John Conrad Brunn (1880-1949) was a native of Chicago. Ordained in 1903, he was the organizing pastor of Emmaus Lutheran Church in Brooklyn, and then the organizing pastor of St. Peter Lutheran Church in Brooklyn, where he served until his death. He was president of the Atlantic District 1930-1941 and second vice president of the LCMS from 1941 until his death. In addition to many synodical responsibilities, he served on the ALPB board for many years and was chair of the executive committee from 1917 until sometime in the mid-1920s. He was also an associate editor of the *American Lutheran*.

The Rev. George Schmidt (1883-1948), a native of New Jersey, was founding pastor of Trinity Lutheran Church, Brooklyn. He then served Immanuel Lutheran Church in Manhattan 1919-28, Immanuel Lutheran in Southey, Saskatchewan, during the 1930s, and then Hope Lutheran Church in Seattle, WA, 1939 until his death. He chaired the executive committee for a time during the late 1920s.

The Rev. Frederick H. Lindemann (1891-1958) was born in 1891 in Indiana, the younger brother Paul Lindemann, one of the founders of ALPB and longtime editor of the *American*

Lutheran. He was ordained in 1914 and served St. John's Lutheran Church in Waterbury, CT, Trinity Lutheran Church in the Bronx, Trinity Lutheran Church in Long Island City, Redeemer Lutheran in St. Paul, MN, North Park Lutheran Church in Buffalo, NY, and finally Lutheran Church of Our Redeemer in Chappaqua, NY. He came on the ALPB board in 1918 and chaired the executive committee in 1929-30; he was also on the editorial board of the *American Lutheran* for many years.

Appendix D: Executive Staff

Julius Fritz Ernst Nickelsburg (1874-1967) was a mainstay of the ALPB through the first half of its life. An active lay member of Immanuel Lutheran Church in New York City (where the ALPB was organized), he was later a founding member of St. Mark's Lutheran Church in Yonkers. He was a businessman and a journalist, and with those skills he came on the ALPB board of directors in 1915 and served until 1953. In 1917, he went to work full time for the Bureau. Over the years his job title changed several times, but he was essentially the executive director for most of the years until the hiring of Ted Wittrock in 1948. He retired in 1953 but continued to write the "News Briefly Told" column for the *American Lutheran.*

The Rev. Theodore Wittrock served as executive secretary 1948-1969; see Appendix B.

The Rev. Glenn C. Stone (1928-2009) was born in Chicago, educated at Augustana Theological Seminary and ordained in the Augustana Synod; he served several parishes in the New York area, and did graduate work in theology at Union Theological Seminary. He was secretary of publications for the National Lutheran Council's Division of Public Relations (1962-1966), and editor of the NLC's magazine *National Lutheran.* He was the founding editor of *Lutheran Forum* in 1967 and served until 1988 (with a brief hiatus in 1971-72). From 1973 to 1986 he was also executive director of the ALPB. He later served on the ALPB's board of directors.

The Rev. Thomas Sluberski (b. 1939) was born in New Jersey. Ordained in the LCMS in 1969, he had several pastoral and educational ministries in the U. S. and abroad, including years as a professor at Concordia College, Bronxville, NY. He served as executive director of ALPB 1986-1989.

The Rev. Paul R. Hinlicky (b. 1952), a native of New York, was ordained in the AELC in 1978 and served parishes in New York State, including Immanuel in Delhi. He earned a PhD from Union Theological Seminary. He edited *Lutheran Forum* 1988-1993, was interim editor of *Forum Letter* in 1991-92, and served as executive director of ALPB 1989-1993. He subsequently became Tice Professor of Lutheran Studies at Roanoke College in Virginia.

The Rev. Frederick J. H. Schumacher (b. 1939) was born in Brooklyn and ordained in the LCA in 1964. He spent his entire pastoral career at St. Matthew Lutheran Church in White Plains, NY. He was serving on the ALPB board of directors when he agreed to take the job of executive director in 1993, a position from which he retired in 2014.

The Rev. Paul R. Sauer (b. 1973) was born in Connecticut and educated at Valparaiso University and Concordia Seminary. He has served at Our Saviour Lutheran Church and School in Bronx, NY since 2001; he has also been an officer of the Atlantic District (LCMS), an assistant professor at Concordia—New York, and is a chaplain in the U. S. Army Reserves. After several years serving on the ALPB board of directors, he became executive director in 2015.

Appendix E: Editors

[Through a century of ALPB publications, there have been numerous editors with a variety of different titles and job responsibilities, as well as dozens of associate editors and contributing editors. The following list includes only those who were primarily responsible for one or another of the publications. It is roughly chronological.]

The Rev. Paul Lindemann was editor of the *American Lutheran*, 1918-1938; see Appendix A.

The Rev. Adolf F. Meyer (1899-1988) was a native of Kansas. He was ordained in 1923 by the Missouri Synod and served for nearly 50 years as pastor of St. Mark's Lutheran Church in Yonkers, NY. During most of that time, he was associated with the ALPB and the *American Lutheran*, beginning as associate editor 1925, then managing editor from 1926 to 1954 and editor from 1954 to 1962. He also served on the ALPB board of directors 1923-1967, and on the LCMS Press Committee 1926-1948.

The Rev. John Tietjen (1928-2004) was managing editor of the *American Lutheran* 1959-1962, and then editor 1962-1967. A New York native, Tietjen was named president of Concordia Seminary in St. Louis in 1969. He led the exodus from that school which resulted in the establishment of Christ Seminary—Seminex and later served briefly as bishop of the ELCA's Metropolitan Chicago Synod.

The Rev. Glenn C. Stone (1928-2009) was the founding editor of *Lutheran Forum* in 1967; see Appendix D.

The Rev. Richard E. Koenig (1927-2011) was a native of St. Louis. Ordained in the LCMS in 1952, he served parishes in New York and Massachusetts before accepting a call to edit the LCA's magazine for clergy, *Partners*, in 1978; he continued to edit the ELCA successor, *Lutheran Partners*, until 1986, when he returned to parish ministry. He was an editorial associate for both the *American Lutheran* and *Lutheran Forum*; he edited *Lutheran Forum* in 1971-72 and was the founding editor of *Forum Letter*, 1972-74

The Rev. Richard John Neuhaus (1936-2009) was born in Canada, but later moved to the United States and became a naturalized citizen. After serving as one of the original columnists in *Lutheran Forum,* he edited *Forum Letter* 1974-1990. He was ordained in the LCMS, but later joined the AELC and then the LCA and the ELCA. While he served a parish in Brooklyn for several years, his more significant vocation was in religious journalism, and he edited a number of different publications over the years. In 1990 he was received into the Roman Catholic Church and subsequently ordained to the priesthood.

The Rev. Paul R. Hinlicky (b. 1952) was editor of *Lutheran Forum* 1988-1993; see Appendix D.

The Rev. Russell E. Saltzman (b. 1947) edited *Forum Letter* 1990-2009 (with a brief hiatus in 1991-92). A native of Kansas, he was ordained in 1980 in the ALC after a brief career in journalism and politics. He served parishes in Nebraska, Illinois, South Carolina and Missouri. He joined the NALC shortly after its founding, but later left the ministry and was received into the Roman Catholic Church.

The Rev. Leonard R. Klein (b. 1945) edited *Lutheran Forum* 1993-1996, but had a much longer association with ALPB as writer and board member. A Pennsylvania native, he was ordained in the LCMS in 1972, later serving in the AELC, LCA and ELCA. His longest pastorate was at Christ Lutheran, York, PA. He later resigned from the ELCA ministry and was received into the Roman Catholic Church; he was subsequently ordained to the priesthood.

The Rev. Ronald B. Bagnall (b. 1940) edited *Lutheran Forum* 1996-2006; he had earlier been an associate editor both of *Lutheran Forum* and *Forum Letter*. A native of Jamestown, NY, he was ordained in the LCA in 1965 and served several parishes in New York and New Jersey.

The Rev. Richard O. Johnson (b. 1949) became editor of *Forum Letter* in 2007. A native Californian, he was originally ordained in the United Methodist Church. After serving two UMC parishes, he was received into the ALC in 1984 and pastored Peace Lutheran Church in Grass Valley, CA, for 29 years. He earned a PhD in church history from the Graduate Theological Union, and has been an affiliate associate professor of church history for Fuller Theological Seminary.

The Rev. Paul R. Sauer was interim editor of *Lutheran Forum* 2006-2007; see Appendix D.

The Rev. Sarah Hinlicky Wilson (b. 1976) has edited *Lutheran Forum* since 2007. A native of St. Louis, she was ordained as an ELCA pastor in 2003 and served a parish in Trenton, NJ, before spending several years working for the Institute for Ecumenical Research in Strasburg, France. She holds a PhD in systematic theology from Princeton Theological Seminary, and is widely published in both scholarly and popular religious journals.

Appendix F: ALPB Office Locations
1914-1918: Grace Lutheran Church, Jersey City, NJ
1918-1919: 234 East 62nd St., NYC
1919-1922: Hartford Bldg, 22-26 East 17th St., NYC
1922: 105 East 22nd St. NYC
1922-1924: 105 East 22nd St. NYC
1924-1932: 69 Fifth Ave., NYC
1932-1954: 1819 Broadway, NYC
1954-1967: 2112 Broadway, NYC
1967-1971: 315 Park Ave. South, NYC
1971-1980: Gustavus Adolphus Church, E. 22nd St., NYC
1980-1988: St. Luke's Lutheran Church, W. 46th St., NYC
1988-1991: The Wartburg, Mt. Vernon, NY
1991-   : Delhi, NY

INDEX OF NAMES

Hemmeter, Pauline C., 166
Hemminki, Palu, 466
Heppe, Melinda, 339, 407
Herbert, Arthur, 32, 34, 171
Herzel, Catherine W., 235
Herzfeld, Will, 32, 34, 171
Heuer, H., 172
Higgins, Eugene, 500
Hill, Kathryn Ann, 459
Hillmer, William, 219
Hinlicky, Paul R., xi, 322-323, 330-332, 334-339, 341-346, 349-353, 355-359, 362-365, 369, 371, 389, 397, 419, 453, 458, 467, 472, 482, 491, 504-505
Hitler, Adolf, 129-130, 133, 162, 482
Hoffman, Oswald C. J., 124, 142, 150, 153, 156, 160, 171, 173, 175-177, 183, 192, 200, 211
Hohenstein, W. E., 93
Homrighausen, Edgar W., 230-231
Hoover, Herbert C., 51
Hoover, J. Edgar, 128, 164
Horgan, Thaddeus, 300
Hotchkin, John, 287, 301
Hoyer, George W., 218-219
Huebsch, Christine, 335
Huetter, Reinhard, 340
Hughes, Langston, 165
Huldschiner, Robert E., 235

Irani, Sarah Hempel, 465
Ireland, Patricia, 417

Jacobs, Paul E, 236
Jahn, J. N. H., 82
Jenkins, Jonathan, 343
Jensen, Franklin, 289
Jenson, Blanche, 372
Jenson, Robert W., 283, 335-336, 345, 355, 358, 389, 393, 457, 482
Jersild, Paul T., 371-372
Jessup, David, 303
John XXIII, 204
John Paul I, 299
John Paul II, 286, 299-300, 419
Johnson, Cecile, 296, 330, 334
Johnson, John, 336
Johnson, K. Glen, 398, 481
Johnson, Lois Solberg, xii
Johnson, Lyndon B., 233-234
Johnson, Philip A., 250
Johnson, Phillip Max, 355, 379, 381, 384, 397, 428, 432-434, 452, 456-457
Johnson, Richard O., 412, 419, 421, 436-437, 442, 455, 461-462, 467-471, 475, 477-478, 481, 483, 490-491, 493-494, 506

Jordahl, Leigh D., 318

Kahle, Roger R., 362
Kavasch, John A., 163, 172, 175, 179-183, 193, 210, 242, 496, 501
Kefauver, Estes, 163
Kennedy, John F., 58, 203-205
Kepner, Karen, 407
Kessler, Martin, 424
Kibler, Ray F., III, 452-453
Kieffer, G. L., 49
Kiel, Micah, 466
Kieschnick, Gerald B., 413-414, 450-451, 453, 462, 476-477
Kieschnick, Melvin, 238-239
King, Martin Luther, Jr., 230, 281, 360
Klages, Kelly, 465
Klausler, Alfred P., 204, 210, 492
Klein, Christa Ressmeyer, 339, 354, 407, 428
Klein, Leonard R., xi, 285, 290-291, 322, 343, 346-347, 351, 353-354, 363-365, 369-380, 383, 386, 389, 396-397, 400, 406, 408, 416-418, 428, 437, 443, 467, 506
Klopf, Richard, 185-186
Knutson, Kent S., 267-269
Koenig, George K. A., 32, 34, 48, 90, 173
Koenig, Richard E., 205-206, 210, 219-20, 223, 242, 249-250, 256-258, 265-269, 271-272, 274, 277-282, 288, 365, 397, 402, 483, 505
Koenig, Walter, 4, 23, 500
Kohn, W. C., 21
Kohn, William, 311
Kolden, Marc, 444
Kraft, Detlaf A., 244
Kraft, William, 129
Kretzmann, A. B., 93
Kretzmann, A. T., 147
Kretzmann, Julius, 69
Kretzmann, Karl, 4, 7, 9, 23, 499, 503
Kretzmann, Otto P., 43, 65, 67, 69, 87, 89-93, 109-113, 115, 127, 130, 140-147, 150, 153-155, 160, 173-177, 244, 256
Kronmann, Roger Bates, 318
Kuenning, Paul P., 315
Kurth, Erwin, 60
Kurz, Joel R., 423

La Guardia, Fiorello, 130-131
LaFontaine, Charles, 298
Lamprecht, Theodore H., 14, 25-28, 31, 51-53, 93, 500
Landahl, Paul R., 462
Lang, Frederick C., 3-4, 11, 14, 93, 500
Lankenau, F. J., 65-68

Olson, Oliver K., 335
Olson, Stanley N., 420
Ott, Mel, 128
Otten, Herman, 276-277, 312, 367, 493
Overhage, Paul, 14

Pahl, Jon, 471
Pankow, Richard, 295, 305, 312, 320, 502
Pannenberg, Wolfhart, 383-384
Pannkoke, Otto H., 2-4, 11, 26-27, 70, 125
Paul VI, 299
Pearcy, David L., 422
Pelikan, Jaroslav, 204-205, 221, 242, 467
Pfatteicher, Philip H., 377, 390-391, 423
Pfotenhauer, Friedrich, 7, 18, 28, 61, 65-67,
    74-75, 116
Pieper, F., 19
Pieper, Franz A. O., 18-19, 82, 106, 208, 257
Piepkorn, Arthur Carl, 171, 173, 175-177, 203,
    218, 231-232, 242, 244, 249, 290, 358, 363,
    389, 391, 455, 458, 467
Pius X, 161
Plekon, Michael, 397, 458
Pless, John T., 339, 407-408, 415
Polack, W. G., 113, 126-127, 156, 167
Preus, Daniel, 414
Preus, David W., 256, 267, 287, 289, 298, 303-
    304, 315, 321-323, 372
Preus, Jacob A. O., 256-264, 267, 277-278, 283,
    299, 313, 501
Preus, Robert D., 340

Quitmeyer, John "Hans," 335, 342, 363, 365, 367,
    389, 392, 406, 428-429, 496, 503

Rasmussen, Larry, 336
Rauf, Arthur A., 496
Rechlin, Edward, 40, 42, 94
Reed, Luther D., 38
Reim, Edward, 192
Ressel, Delvin, 133
Ressmeyer, Henry F., 3, 11, 14, 242, 500-501
Ressmeyer, Rudolph P. F., 242, 260-262, 277, 296,
    327 n16, 501
Ressmeyer, Rudolph S., 31, 39, 65, 242, 501
Restin, Lena, 23
Restin, Otto H., 23
Reu, J. Michael, 88, 93
Richman, Ralph, 196
Robb, Ed, 303
Robinson, Jack Treon, 87-88, 140-141, 144,
    147-148
Robinson, V. Gene, 419
Roche, Donna Kathmann, 335, 362, 367, 496

Rochelle, Jay, 379
Roellig, Leonard, 295, 297, 324, 330, 335, 502
Rogness, Peter, 420
Romoser, Carl, 37
Romoser, George, 8, 22, 40
Rongstad, James, 230
Ronneberg, Rod L., 481
Roosevelt, Franklin D., 128, 130, 163
Root, Michael, 350-351, 401, 418
Rorem, Paul, 335
Ross, Sharon Zanter, 343
Rosso, Dante, 162
Rudnick, Milton, 242
Rusch, William G., 374, 376

Sabourin, Clemonce, 134
Safer, Morley, 303
Saltzman, Hattie, 426
Saltzman, Russell E., ix, xi, 321-322, 337-342,
    352-353, 362-367, 369, 376, 379, 381-383,
    385, 389, 402-408, 412, 414-422, 425-427,
    435-441, 447-453, 455, 460-461, 476, 478,
    481, 483, 496, 506
Sasse, Hermann, 407
Sauer, Kenneth H., 372, 469
Sauer, Paul R., 424, 452, 454-456, 465-467, 491,
    495-496, 504-506
Scaer, David P., 417
Scaer, Paul H., 496
Scharlemann, Martin H., 259
Schenk, Berthold von, 79-80, 167-168, 423-424,
    455
Scherer, Paul, 360
Schick, George V., 113
Schlegel, Beth, 397
Schlesinger, Arthur M., Sr., 159
Schliepsick, Theodore, 134
Schmemann, Alexander, 342-343
Schmid, Byron, 288
Schmidling, Charles H., 3, 14, 500
Schmidt, Gail Ramshaw, 290, 297
Schmidt, George, 34, 503
Schmidt, Pamela, 254
Schnekloth, Clint, 399
Schoenfeld, William, 2
Schreier, Peter, 302
Schuller, Robert, 316
Schuller, David S., 233, 245 n 10
Schulz, Paul, 65-67, 146
Schulz, Wallace, 414-415
Schulze, Andrew, 133-134, 231
Schulze, Raymond, 290
Schumacher, Frederick J. H., 344, 356, 358-361,
    365, 389, 391-396, 406, 412, 423, 428, 436,